The Axial Age and Its Consequences

The Axial Age and Its Consequences

EDITED BY

Robert N. Bellah and
Hans Joas

THE BELKNAP PRESS OF HARVARD UNIVERSITY PRESS

Cambridge, Massachusetts, and London, England • 2012

Copyright © 2012 by the President and Fellows of Harvard College
All rights reserved
Printed in the United States of America

Library of Congress Cataloging-in-Publication Data

The Axial Age and its consequences / edited by Robert N. Bellah and Hans Joas.
    p. cm.
   Rev. papers delivered at a conference held July 3–5, 2008 at the University of Erfurt.
   Includes bibliographical references (p.   ) and index.
   ISBN 978-0-674-06649-6 (alk. paper)
   1. Civilization, Ancient—Congresses. 2. Comparative civilization—Congresses.
3. Philosophy, Comparative—Congresses. 4. Religions—Congresses. I. Bellah,
Robert Neelly, 1927– II. Joas, Hans, 1948–
  CB311.A885   2012
  930—dc23   2012008329

To the memory of Karl Jaspers

Contents

Introduction   1
    ROBERT N. BELLAH AND HANS JOAS

Fundamental Questions

1. The Axial Age Debate as Religious Discourse   9
    HANS JOAS

2. What Was the Axial Revolution?   30
    CHARLES TAYLOR

3. An Evolutionary Approach to Culture:
Implications for the Study of the Axial Age   47
    MERLIN DONALD

4. Embodiment, Transcendence, and Contingency:
Anthropological Features of the Axial Age   77
    MATTHIAS JUNG

5. The Axial Age in Global History:
Cultural Crystallizations and Societal Transformations   102
    BJÖRN WITTROCK

6. The Buddha's Meditative Trance:
Visionary Knowledge, Aphoristic Thinking, and
Axial Age Rationality in Early Buddhism   126
    GANANATH OBEYESEKERE

7. The Idea of Transcendence   146
    INGOLF U. DALFERTH

A Comparative Perspective

8. Religion, the Axial Age, and Secular Modernity in
   Bellah's Theory of Religious Evolution   191
   JOSÉ CASANOVA

9. Where Do Axial Commitments Reside?
   Problems in Thinking about the African Case   222
   ANN SWIDLER

10. The Axial Age Theory: A Challenge to Historism or
    an Explanatory Device of Civilization Analysis?
    With a Look at the Normative Discourse
    in Axial Age China   248
    HEINER ROETZ

Destructive Possibilities?

11. The Axial Conundrum between Transcendental
    Visions and Vicissitudes of Their Institutionalizations:
    Constructive and Destructive Possibilities   277
    SHMUEL N. EISENSTADT

12. Axial Religions and the Problem of Violence   294
    DAVID MARTIN

13. Righteous Rebels: When, Where, and Why?   317
    W. G. RUNCIMAN

Reevaluations

14. Rehistoricizing the Axial Age   337
    JOHANN P. ARNASON

15. Cultural Memory and the Myth of the Axial Age   366
    JAN ASSMANN

Perspectives on the Future

16. The Axial Invention of Education and Today's
    Global Knowledge Culture   411
    WILLIAM M. SULLIVAN

17. The Future of Transcendence: A Sociological Agenda   430
    RICHARD MADSEN

18. The Heritage of the Axial Age: Resource or Burden?   447
    ROBERT N. BELLAH

Bibliography: Works on the Axial Age   *469*
Contributors   *539*
Index   *543*

The Axial Age and Its Consequences

Introduction

ROBERT N. BELLAH AND HANS JOAS

The notion that in significant parts of Eurasia the middle centuries of the first millennium BCE mark a significant transition in human cultural history, and that this period can be referred to as the Axial Age, has become widely, but not universally, accepted. Since the very term "Axial Age" is unfamiliar to many, we may begin with a brief explication of it. It has become common to refer to certain texts in literature, philosophy, and even theology as "classics," that is, as enduring subjects of interpretation, commentary, and argument that make them, whenever they were first composed, contemporary and part of the common heritage of educated people in our now cosmopolitan world. But if we ask when do the first classics appear, the answer is in the middle centuries of the first millennium BCE. The canonical Hebrew prophets, Amos, Isaiah, and Jeremiah, among others; the central texts of Greek philosophy, Plato and Aristotle in particular; the early texts of Chinese thought, the *Analects* of Confucius and the *Daodejing* (perhaps the most frequently translated text in the world); and early Indian texts such as the *Bhagavadgita,* and the teachings of the Buddha in the Pali Canon: these and others from the same period can be cited. We refer to these as texts, for that is how we know them, but many of them were composed orally and were not written down for some time. This fact, together with the fact that writing was in use in several areas in the third and second millennia BCE, indicates that it was not writing as such that led to the creation of "classics," though writing was essential for their later dissemination. It was Karl Jaspers who thought that the appearance of these classics at the beginning of several major living traditions in the world justified the term "Axial Age" to describe the period in which they appeared. Hans Joas in his chapter describes the reasons Jaspers gave for this choice of terminology and the history of earlier attempts to understand the contemporaneous emergence of these traditions.

By seeing the Axial Age as the period of the emergence of formative traditions of religious and philosophical thought, traditions that have been greatly elaborated subsequently without the original formulations being left behind, the contributors to this volume are not implying that culture began in the Axial Age and that what went before it can be ignored. It is true that there are no classics in the sense defined above that precede the first millennium BCE. The tale of Gilgamesh might be cited as an exception, though it has only marginally entered the canon of world literature, but if so, it is the exception that proves the rule. Nevertheless, the Axial Age is only intelligible in terms of what went before it: a very long and very significant history in which human culture did emerge as a way of relating to the world shared by no other animal.

The chapters in this volume are revised versions of papers presented at a conference on "The Axial Age and Its Consequences for Subsequent History and the Present" held at the Max Weber Center of the University of Erfurt in Germany on July 3 to 5, 2008. The chapters on the Axial Age in Robert Bellah's then work in progress *Religion in Human Evolution*[1] were distributed to the participants in the Erfurt Conference not as the focus of the conference itself, but only as a stimulus to which the participants could react or which they could ignore as they chose. It is, however, worth noting that these are the last four of eight substantive chapters in Bellah's book, and that they are preceded by chapters on the deep biological evolution of capacities that would make religion possible once our species had evolved; on religion among largely egalitarian tribal peoples; religion among chiefdoms, that is, early hierarchical societies; and religion in the great Bronze Age monarchies of the third and second millennia BCE: Mesopotamia, Egypt, and China. Bellah's book ends with the Axial Age and is much more concerned with its background than its consequences. So, while our conference from the beginning contemplated including papers dealing with consequences of the Axial Age right up to the present, Bellah, though he alludes briefly to some of those consequences in the final chapter of his book, is there mainly concerned with the Axial Age itself in relation to what preceded it. The editors left the matter of whether contributors would write about the Axial Age, its background, or its consequences entirely up to the contributors.

The evolutionary psychologist Merlin Donald has profoundly influenced Bellah's work on religion in human evolution, and it is Donald's chapter in this book that goes most deeply into the background without which the Axial Age is unintelligible. Donald has traced the evolution of human culture through four stages, with the first, episodic culture, being shared with other higher mammals. Distinctly human culture begins with mimetic culture in which meanings were expressed through bodily actions and gestures and language was absent or only incipient, and then goes on to mythical culture where full human language allowed narratives to arise and myth to form the focus of cultural organization. The fourth cultural capacity arose with the emergence of theoretic culture in the Axial Age, giving the possibility of universalizable discourse, but not replacing any earlier cultural form. In Donald's scheme each form of culture is reorganized with the emergence of successive capacities, but not abandoned. The details of Donald's position can be found in his chapter, but it is worth quoting from it in summary as to the relation between the various capacities:

> This notion, that every stage of human cognitive evolution found a permanent home in the evolving collective system, is somewhat similar to the evolutionary principle of conservation of previous gains. Previous successful adaptations remained in the system where they proved themselves effective, and the system slowly became more robust and capable of surviving almost any major blow. This occurred without changing the basic facts of human biology, or the existential dilemma facing every human being.
>
> The modern mind reflects this fact. It is a complex mix of mimetic, mythic, and theoretic elements. Art, ritual, and music reflect the continuation of the mimetic dimension of culture in modern life. The narratives of the great religious books reflect the mythic dimension, as do the many secular myths of modern society. These two great domains—the mimetic and the mythic—are mandatory, hard-wired, and extremely subtle and powerful ways of thinking. They cannot be matched by analytic thought for intuitive speed, complexity, and shrewdness. They will continue to be crucially important in the future, because they reside in innate capacities without which human beings could not function.

In close relationship to Donald's work, the German philosopher Matthias Jung focuses on another aspect of the Axial Age: semiotic transcendence. For him—and one could say that this idea had already been adumbrated by Ernst Cassirer in his philosophy of symbolic forms, particularly in his way of distinguishing between myth and religion—the characteristic feature of the Axial Age is the recognition of symbolicity as symbolicity, the understanding of symbolic signs as pointing to a meaning that can never be fully exhausted by these signs. Jung connects this point with the debates in contemporary philosophy of language and hints at the complex consequences this insight has for our understanding of cultural evolution.

Although several chapters in this book refer to periods earlier than the Axial Age, it is Jan Assmann's chapter that deals most extensively with a pre-Axial culture, that of ancient Egypt. His chapter usefully reminds us of the richness of thought and reflection in ancient Egypt, the degree to which it anticipated elements of Axial culture, and its significant contribution to Axial developments in ancient Israel and Greece.[2] Similar arguments could be made about ancient Mesopotamian contributions to Israel and Greece and second-millennium BCE Chinese contributions to developments in China in the second half of the first millennium BCE. A deeper understanding of the roots of the Axial revolution in the immediate past of the Axial societies as well as in the deep past of human culture is a problem that is in need of continuous research and rethinking, a problem that this book can only raise in hopes of stimulating further work.

A number of chapters in the book help us to better understand the Axial Age itself, or to raise questions about it. Charles Taylor provides a useful overview of the Axial cultures and focuses on the emergence of the idea of an unqualified good around which the other aspects of Axial culture can be understood. Johann Arnason and Björn Wittrock in different ways suggest the importance of close historical understanding of each case and an awareness of profound differences as well as similarities among them, each suggesting a "pluralist" rather than a homogenizing approach to the cultures denoted as axial. Two essays provide deep and novel insight into particular Axial cultures, that of Heiner Roetz on Axial Age China and that of Gananath Obeyesekere on early Buddhism.

Roetz gives a close reading of tendencies toward universal ethics in Axial Age China, but he insists on holding a high standard in terms of which various tendencies can be so evaluated. This leads him to the conclusion that in the case of China, and by implication the other Axial cases as well, the universalization of ethics was incomplete, with the possibility of regression to more particularistic ethics left open. For Roetz the Axial Age, rather than being celebrated for its particular achievements, should be a challenge to us to overcome its failures in the long-term quest of a truly universal human ethic.

Obeyesekere, with respect to early Buddhism, takes almost an opposite approach. He suggests that our modern notion of the theoretic, what he calls "conceptualism," though found in Axial India, is inadequate as an exclusive way of understanding what was happening. He emphasizes the presence of visionary experience and aphoristic thinking as moving beyond purely rational thought, though with universalizing consequences.

Ingolf Dalferth's essay is the only one that was commissioned after the conference. Reviewers suggested that, since "transcendence" is such a central term in Jaspers' conception of the Axial Age, a chapter on this idea would be helpful. Dalferth begins by explicating Jaspers' conception and gives the philosophical background upon which Jaspers drew. He then offers a contrasting theological conception of transcendence that is helpful in understanding the Abrahamic, particularly Christian, use of the term, but which would have less applicability to other Axial traditions.

Quite a few chapters in this book take a perspective from the Axial Age and then follow out implications for later ages, in some cases even for the present. W. G. Runciman asks why, if universal ethics has implications for politics, what he calls "righteous rebels" arise in so few and so particular situations. José Casanova asks whether our present preoccupation with the "religious-secular binary" has roots in the Axial Age and what we can learn from such an inquiry. David Martin raises the question of religious violence and the degree to which Axial religions have contributed to it. Shmuel N. Eisenstadt suggests the profound ambivalence of the Axial heritage, from which both constructive and destructive consequences have emerged. William Sullivan contrasts the Axial invention of education as a kind of ethical/spiritual formation with current ideas of education in advanced modern societies and suggests that we still have much to learn from earlier understandings. Ann Swidler uses her work in contemporary Africa to suggest that pre-Axial and Axial cultures are still in tension in many parts of the world and that the problems raised in the Axial traditions are live issues in much of the world.

Richard Madsen has tackled one of Jaspers' most unsettling questions: Is it possible that we have entered a new Axial Age? Is the world of globalized culture where no single tradition can be sealed off against all the others the possible seedbed of new forms of cultural and religious innovation? He uses his extensive knowledge of recent developments in Asian religions to illustrate the questions he asks.

We have decided that detailed outlines of the chapters contained in this book would be redundant in this introduction. We have merely tried to suggest the riches that these chapters provide, including some of the tensions between them. Using our brief comments and the chapter titles, the reader can decide how to navigate the volume and discover what a diverse and distinguished group of scholars has to offer. The bibliography provides the reader with the opportunity to delve deeper into the large body of literature on the Axial Age. It does not simply comprise the references cited in the book, but lists as primary sources those formulations of the "Axial Age" concept that precede Jaspers' famous 1949 book *Vom Ursprung und Ziel der Geschichte*, as well as the extensive secondary literature that Jaspers inspired.

Joas and Bellah in the opening and concluding chapters of the book suggest that the question of the Axial Age is not just academic: the deep self-understanding of educated people of all the world's cultures is at stake. The Axial Age was a moment of great religious creativity; no one can seriously think about it without some response to the issues raised in that fertile period. How we think about the Axial Age is to some extent how we think about ourselves and the human project at this perilous moment in history.

Notes

We would like to express our sincere gratitude to Christian Scherer, who has not only compiled the bibliography to this volume, but also been of invaluable assistance in the whole process of preparing this volume for publication.

1. Robert N. Bellah, *Religion in Human Evolution: From the Paleolithic to the Axial Age* (Cambridge, MA: The Belknap Press of Harvard University Press, 2011).

2. For more detail the reader is referred to Assmann's comprehensive book *The Mind of Egypt: History and Meaning in the Time of the Pharaohs* (New York: Metropolitan Books, 2002), which is a translation of *Ägypten: Eine Sinngeschichte* (Munich: Hanser, 1996).

Fundamental Questions

1

The Axial Age Debate as Religious Discourse

HANS JOAS

It is an undisputed fact that Karl Jaspers invented the term "Axial Age" in his 1949 book *Vom Ursprung und Ziel der Geschichte,* but it is also uncontested that the basic idea behind the new term is much older and was not first developed by Jaspers himself. While these facts seem to be clear, the same cannot be said about the exact meaning of the concept of an Axial Age, the origins of the term, and the origins of the idea behind it. In the following, I will offer some material that could help to clarify these three matters, but the main purpose of this chapter is not a contribution to conceptual history. These reflections are only necessary as a presupposition for my main argument. I will argue that the Axial Age debate of the last decades is not only one of the most important developments in the area of the comparative-historical social sciences, but also a religious discourse—a series of highly complex attempts of intellectuals to position themselves with regard to the problem of "transcendence," its role in history, and viable forms of its articulation in the present.

But let me first briefly return to the question of the origin of Jaspers' idea and concept. For all readers familiar with Georg Simmel's last book *Lebensanschauung,* the term "axis" would seem to have been inspired by him, because in Simmel we find the idea of an "axial rotation" as the crucial step in the genesis of ideal validities.[1] Love, according to Simmel, may have been induced by corporeal impulses, but when the original desire has led to the formation of intense personal relationships, then these relationships take on their own independent existence and become the source of demands and norms. What Simmel means by "axial rotation" is the genesis of autonomous forms of culture that, although being a product of life-processes, now have a retroactive effect on these processes of life themselves. Religion for Simmel is the most perfect rotation around the forms which life produces in itself. The leading American expert on Simmel, Donald Levine, has speculatively claimed that Simmel's idea is the origin of Jaspers' expression.[2] But this seems to me to be not really plausible since Jaspers does not have the autonomy of cultural products in mind when he speaks of an axial turn, but the "axis" of world history—the one point in history that allows a dichotomous distinction between everything that came before or after it.

Moreover, Jaspers himself does not refer to Simmel in the relevant passage, but to Hegel. He saw Hegel as the last great representative of a long tradition of Occidental thinking about history for which since Augustine there was no doubt that the self-revelatory acts of God constitute the decisive turning points in world history. He indirectly quotes Hegel,[3] for whom the birth of Christ was the crucial dividing line, the axis of world history. For Jaspers, writing after World War II, such a Christo-centric claim was no longer acceptable and had to be replaced by an empirically tenable and universally acceptable alternative. The problem with his reference to Hegel is, however, that no such passage has so far been detected in Hegel's entire work. What comes closest to it is a passage in his lectures on the philosophy of history in which Hegel calls the idea of the trinity of God the decisive principle—"the axis on which the History of the World turns. This is the goal and starting point of History."[4] While these sentences may sound like the source of Jaspers' book title, the problem with the whole quotation is that Hegel in the German original does not use the word "axis," but "Angel"—a word that is normally translated as "hinge" or "pivot." Could it be that Jaspers' confusion of "Achse" and "Angel" is the origin of the term we all use today?

More interesting than this whole philological question, however, is the problem of the intellectual origin of the idea itself. Here Jaspers was indubitably influenced by the writings of Max Weber, his brother Alfred Weber, and through them by Weber's close colleague and longtime friend Ernst Troeltsch and Troeltsch's friend Wilhelm Bousset. They all wrote about similarities between the ancient Hebrew prophets and comparable phenomena in other civilizations and used terms like "prophetic age" or "synchronistic age" to designate these similarities as the common features of a specific phase in world history. They were in turn influenced by important scholars from the field of religious studies (Hermann Siebeck) and Indology (Rhys Davids) so that one could already speak of an "Axial Age debate" around 1900.[5] But all these authors were not the first debaters either. Jaspers himself mentioned two forerunners: the Sinologist Victor von Strauss and the classicist and philosopher Ernst von Lasaulx. While von Strauss had only a few words to say on this topic in his commentary on Lao Tse,[6] Lasaulx truly developed at length the idea taken up by Jaspers in a remarkable and almost completely forgotten book of 1856, *Neuer Versuch einer alten, auf die Wahrheit der Tatsachen gegründeten Philosophie der Geschichte.*[7] But Lasaulx himself also mentioned some forerunners,[8] and at the moment it looks as if the earliest formulation of the Axial Age thesis is from Abraham-Hyacinthe Anquetil-Duperron (1731–1805). He was a deeply Catholic and royalist French scholar who spent almost six years in India, wrote an empirically founded work on "oriental" forms of political rule, criticizing Montesquieu's distorted ideas about oriental despotism, and studied the ancient Iranian religious traditions. He has long been considered one of the founders of Iranian studies. In the year 1771 he claimed that the ideas articulated by Zoroaster probably in the sixth century BCE were part of a more general "revolution" in different parts of the world.[9] I take it to be an empirical question whether even earlier formulations of this thesis will be found in the future. In any case, one must not assume that later authors were always influenced by earlier writers in this regard.

But what exactly does the Axial Age thesis refer to—beyond an observation of a certain parallelism in the cultural transformation of four or five major civilizations between 800 and 200 BCE? The best shorthand characterization is from the American Sinologist Benjamin Schwartz, who called the Axial Age "the age of transcendence";[10] it would perhaps be even more precise, although maybe a bit pedantic, to speak of the *age of the emergence of the idea of transcendence*. A cosmological chasm between a transcendental sphere and a mundane one is then seen as the defining characteristic of axiality. Others, for example Arnaldo Momigliano, speak of an "age of criticism"[11] and emphasize the relativization of all mundane realities as the crucial feature of the age—an aspect that also plays the greatest role in Shmuel Eisenstadt's sociological elaboration of the Axial Age thesis. The main emphasis in Eisenstadt's work is on the desacralization of political domination that is a result of the emergence of transcendence, on the Axial Age as the origin of new forms of criticism, controversial claims about the true meaning of divine commandments, a growing separation between ethnic and religious collectivities, and a new historical dynamic.

There is no serious contradiction between the two characterizations, but only a difference in emphasis. The emphasis is either on a profound transformation of religious presuppositions or on the social and political consequences of this religious transformation. But this image changes when the focus on "transcendence" itself is questioned. Björn Wittrock has explicitly denied the view that the Axial Age can be characterized by its reference to transcendence. He proposes to consider "an increasing reflexivity of human beings and their ability to overcome the bounds of a perceived inevitability of given conditions in temporal and social orderings" as its defining characteristic instead.[12] For him it is a matter of context and contingency whether this transformation leads to a cosmology in terms of transcendence or immanence. Empirically, the most contentious case in this connection is ancient China.[13] A similar view is expressed by Johann Arnason, Eisenstadt, and Wittrock in their introduction to a jointly edited volume when they call the "epoch-making innovation that gave rise to enduring civilizational identities as well as to religious visions of universal community" in the Axial Age the most striking manifestation of social creativity in human history.[14] Creativity here, it seems to me, replaces the assumption of a divine revelation of truth without any further discussion. When Wittrock speaks of cases without a cosmology of transcendence, one could, of course, exclude them from the set of relevant cases and restrict the investigation to those in which the idea of transcendence did indeed play a role. What I am aiming at is the fact that all contributions to the Axial Age debate are permeated by assumptions about and attitudes toward religion. It is difficult to find a language for the transformations of the Axial Age that is neither bound to a specific religious faith nor to unreflected secularist premises. When I spoke of the "emergence" of the idea of transcendence, I chose this expression in order to avoid speaking either of its "discovery" or its "invention"—because "discovery" refers to an understanding of religious evolution that considers the Axial breakthrough as progress, whereas "invention" is a term that can only be plausible from a secularist perspective for the creative achievements of mankind in that period. Furthermore, if "transcendence" is not the defining characteristic of the Axial Age, a possible loss of transcendence in our age is much less dramatic, much less of a threat to moral universalism than if it is. A return to the original claims of the Axial Age can be seen as a prophetic plea for a forceful liberation from later attenuated versions of the fundamental impulses of post-Axial religion and of philosophy—or as a dangerous regression to obsolete fanaticisms. Not only can the different versions of the Axial Age be played out against one another: Athens or Jerusalem?—there can also be a nostalgia for pre-Axial myths and cosmologies or a radical modernism that sees the heritage of the Axial Age as a mere preparation for a modernity that is in its core independent from it. This affects the implicit views on our relationship to the Axial turn—whether we think of it in terms of replacement and supersession or in terms of addition and integration.[15]

We can use, therefore, the contributions to the Axial Age debate on the one hand as a probe to find out the tacit religious (or antireligious) assumptions in important theories of history and social change, and on the other as a means to provide contemporary debates about religion with additional material from history and sociology. This chapter restricts itself to three main contributors: Ernst von Lasaulx, Max Weber, and Karl Jaspers. It leaves out the oldest predecessors as well as Alfred Weber and Eric Voegelin (who had studied with Jaspers and Alfred Weber) and all contemporary figures.

I. Lasaulx's Organicist Defense of Revelation

Lasaulx's name and work, once admired by great historians like Lord Acton and Jacob Burckhardt, are so completely forgotten today that it is probably appropriate to offer some biographical information about him first.[16] Born in 1805 into an aristocratic German-speaking family of Luxemburgian origin, he had strong connections with several major figures of the conservative-Catholic milieu in nineteenth-century Bavaria. He was a student of Joseph Görres, the former Jacobin revolutionary, who had turned into the leading figure among Catholic intellectuals. Lasaulx was married to a daughter of Franz von Baader, another leading Catholic thinker of the time. As a young classicist he was invited to join the entourage of the Bavarian prince Otto when he became the first king of Greece after its independence from the Ottoman Empire in 1832. This brought him to Greece, and from there he traveled through the Middle East, returning with the deep conviction that Christianity can only be understood as the fusion of components from ancient

Greece and ancient Judaism. For him Greek thinking appeared to be a kind of second, apocryphal Old Testament. When he returned to Germany, his academic career led to a professorial position at the University of Munich, where, among others, Lord Acton was one of his students. Interestingly, he also became involved in political matters, protesting against the Bavarian king when he tried to provide his lover—the dancer Lola Montez—with an aristocratic title; he was suspended from his academic position and became a member of the national assembly in Frankfurt during the revolution of 1848.

His main scholarly ambition was to reconstitute a Christian perspective in the writing of universal history, and this in an age of an increasing nationalization of historiography. Until the seventeenth century such a Christian perspective had dominated historiography in Europe, but since then it had gradually lost out to a strict separation of empirically grounded historiography and a theological discourse about the history of salvation. Lasaulx and other romantic thinkers assumed that a new "organicist" understanding of history would enable them to revitalize the older unity of theology and historiography—not by a return, though, to dogmatic or biblically founded statements about history, but in an empirically defensible manner. The title of his main work of 1856, literally translated, is "A new attempt at an old philosophy of history, based on the truth of facts." I interpret this title as referring to a new attempt indeed in an area that had been given up—an attempt "at an old philosophy of history," and this in an empirically grounded manner. Lasaulx distinguished himself from other conservative Catholic thinkers of his time by going beyond an understanding of the teachings of the Catholic Church as revealed truth in opposition to all other versions of Christianity and all other religions. Instead, he defended an "inclusivist" understanding of religion in which all religions belong to one process of the religious development of mankind.[17] Such an inclusivist understanding was the logical presupposition of an application of "organicist" metaphors or theorems to the history of religion. Lasaulx draws a strict parallel between the development of the individual and the development of whole peoples. For him religious faith is always the point of departure. A kind of adolescent doubt is a necessary but transitory phase, after which there are two possible outcomes: desperation or a reconciliation with faith. He extends the analogy to the point where a weakening of vitality, a process of aging, is considered to be as relevant for peoples as it is for individuals. This is also the reason why some have misleadingly called Lasaulx a kind of forerunner to Oswald Spengler's speculations on history. This analogy also allows Lasaulx to interpret phenomena of secularization as indicators of a general "organismic" decline. For him religious indifference, a lack of respect with regard to the existing religious tradition, the reception of other forms of faith, the formation of sects, skepticism, or complete loss of faith are all called characteristic symptoms of degeneration, and he claims they can mostly be found among the higher and better educated strata, although he calls their representatives "Halbwisser."[18] According to Lasaulx, the immortality of the soul and the existence of divine entities become the object of intellectual speculations only when the original vitality, for which doubt in them is absurd, is being lost. Whereas the vital forces of a people believe in such a situation that the Gods have become angry at them or that humans have betrayed the Gods of their fathers, among the educated nothing but superstition survives.

But this analogy of biological and religious evolution has a clear limitation in Lasaulx.[19] Religion itself does not develop in accordance with the laws of organismic development. Religious institutions do not grow older and decay—on the contrary: while the Catholic Church had witnessed the emergence of the European dynasties, it will also—he speculates—be present at their demise and survive them. The main difference here between older theological views of history and Lasaulx's new version is that he seems to exclude a religious revitalization of an aging people. In his framework, other peoples take over the role of major proponents of a particular faith, instilling it with new vitality. While these speculations may sound quite plausible today with regard to the globalization of Christianity (and, incidentally, the low fertility rates of secularized countries),[20] their intellectual foundation is obviously very shaky. But the "inclusivist" and "developmentalist" understanding of religion and its relationship to philosophy predisposes Lasaulx to go beyond a culturalist understanding of the emergence of Greek philosophy. It is in immediate connection with the passages that describe the parallels between the adolescence of individuals and that of peoples that he clearly spells out the Axial Age thesis *avant la lettre:* "It can by no means be coincidental that at about the same time, 600 before Christ, there appear in Persia Zoroaster, in India Gautama Buddha, in China Confucius, among the Jews the prophets, in Rome the king Numa and in Hellas the first philosophers ... as reformers of popular religion; this remarkable coincidence can have its foundation only in the inner substantial unity of mankind and the life of peoples ..., not in the particular effervescence of one national spirit."[21] It would seem as if Jaspers had directly taken it up from here.

Jesus Christ is, for Lasaulx, the most important of the heroes of human history; but for him not only Moses participates in the history of revelation and salvation, but also Socrates, Buddha, Zoroaster, and others. There is a subterranean move in Lasaulx from the observation of parallels between the Judeo-Christian history of salvation and other religious breakthroughs to a merely hero-centered view of history. In his book he gives a long list of such heroes, which includes almost contemporary figures like Hamann, Kant, Goethe, Gluck, Mozart, and, unsurprisingly, Görres. This intellectual move did not remain unnoticed by the Catholic Church. A few years after its publication, his book was put on the index of prohibited writings. Lasaulx died in 1861 and did not live to see his writings classified as heretic. He seems to have been willing to submit to such a verdict. But whatever his personal reaction would have been, the decision of the Congregation of the Index was a fatal blow for his work because it led to its complete neglect in Catholic circles, while it was perceived as overly Catholic and reactionary among liberal historians and philosophers.[22] Even liberal Catholics, however, like the great Church historian Ignaz von Döllinger, distanced themselves from Lasaulx because of his leveling of the difference between Christ's role in salvation and a mere secular understanding of religious history. Characteristically, resurrection and the expectation of Christ's coming again did not play a role in Lasaulx's philosophy of history.

But one could also turn this judgment around. Whereas the pope and the Catholic theologians of the time perceived the difference between the official doctrine of the Church and Lasaulx's speculations—and they were undoubtedly correct in this regard—one could also see Lasaulx's book as an attempt to reintegrate the history of religion with religious discourse in a way that is similar to the intellectual path Troeltsch was to take later. The parallels between different "world religions" have been and must continue to be a challenge for all religious believers, but also for secular minds. The question of "revelation" cannot simply be put to rest. It is the problem of one or several revelations, and the problem of revelation in the perspective of philosophy that Lasaulx had touched upon. This is the point where Jaspers, coming from a totally different background and pursuing his own philosophical project, would take up the thread from Lasaulx almost a century later.

II. Max Weber's Reductionist View of Sacramental Experience

Although he never used the expression "Axial Age," Max Weber has to figure prominently in any serious reconstruction of this debate. There is a brief passage in the subchapter on prophets of the "sociology of religion" chapter in *Economy and Society* where Weber refers to Greek and Indian parallels to the Hebrew prophets—probably under the influence of Bousset, but without mentioning him at this point;[23] there is also a famous footnote in Weber's study on Hinduism with an additional reference to China and a refutation of Eduard Meyer's "strange" (as Weber says) attempt to find a biological explanation of this coincidence.[24] But much more relevant than these brief passages is the fact that Weber's whole analysis of the role of the prophets plays such an important role in his understanding of the history of religion. It is not an exaggeration to say that for Weber the prophets or the prophetic age constitute *the* crucial event in the history of religion—the turning point between tens of thousands of years of "magical" religion and the new age of postmagical "salvation religions." In the last few decades we have witnessed an enormous output of research on the sources of Weber's analyses, on his specific achievements, and on the empirical adequacy of his views.[25] It obviously does not make sense to even try to characterize this literature here; in our context, I will restrict myself to one single point that is, however, at least in my eyes, of enormous strategic importance for the reevaluation of Weber's contribution. The point I have in mind is Weber's understanding of what "sacraments" are, what their relationship to magic is, and what their role in the modern age could be. Are sacraments the mere post-Axial equivalents of magic or are they radically different from everything pre-Axial?

In large parts of the secondary literature on Weber[26] one can find a sharp contrast between the writings on the history of religion that formed the backdrop to Weber's work and his own writings. Whereas the writings of other late-nineteenth-century German scholars are often characterized— and rightly so—as biased in favor of Protestant Christianity according to which Protestant Christianity is the highest and final point of religious evolution, Weber's own work is seen as free from such inclinations, as a sober and historically extremely well-informed sociologically oriented systematization and conceptual clarification of a huge amount of material from the global history of religion. Against this widespread view, my claim is that even the so-called chapter on "sociology of religion"—that is, the text on "Religious Communities"—and the famous "Zwischenbetrachtung" ("Intermediate Reflections") in Weber's comparative studies have a latent *narrative* structure. For the story that is contained in this text a certain view of Calvinist Protestantism, its past and its future, is absolutely constitutive. And, of course, a certain view of the given superiority of the "West." Others have argued before that Weber's purpose in his comparative research was not so much "a broad comparative analysis *per se,* but rather to discover, in the study of non-European contexts, points of comparison to 'our occidental cultural religions.' Weber had a certain view of the uniqueness of the West that has to be called extremely problematical, if not untenable according to our current knowledge, for example, about China,"[27] and that has become less and less plausible even for the superficial observer because of the economic transformation of Asia in our time. I am mentioning this argument because it bolsters my claim of a narrative structure in Weber that should be made visible so that it can be critically evaluated.

This narrative structure is of enormous importance for Weber's assumptions about nonascetic Protestantism and about China, but above all about Catholicism. Perhaps the shortest way to make clear what I have in mind is to draw attention to the hyphen between magic and sacramental that one finds so frequently in Weber's work: "magical-sacramental." On the analytical level, the distinction between magic and sacramental, between human attempts to use superhuman forces for their own purposes ("magic") and a willingness to serve God and to open oneself up to the mundane presence of the transcendent ("sacramental"), is absolutely crucial—and Weber is very well aware of that. Weber also points out that—sociologically—the contrast is often blurred.[28] And there is no doubt that this is to some extent empirically correct. The "demagicization" of religion is a long process that started in the Axial Age, but certainly did not end then.[29] It had and has to be achieved again and again whenever a post-Axial religion was or is transferred to a pre-Axial culture as, for example, in the Christianization of Europe. But if we pay attention not just to the explicit definitions in Weber's work but also—in a "deconstructive" way—to his examples and asides, we realize that his text is shot through with remarks about Catholicism that reduce Catholic practices, if not doctrines, to pure magic. Right at the beginning of the text on "Religious Communities" he mentions southern Europeans spitting at the image of a saint if the expected result does not come about; no church doctrine, no declaration of a church council that distinguishes between the adoration of God and the mere veneration of a saint, does help here, Weber claims.[30] While this certainly is a realistic description of features in the world of popular Catholicism, there are many other passages where Weber—and not the theologically uneducated religious practitioner—is responsible for blurring the relevant distinction. For Weber, the Catholic priest during the Mass and in absolving from sins seems to be a magician.[31] Weber observes that in the Catholic Mass the sermon plays a smaller role than in Protestant services and sees in this fact the inverse proportionality of magic and ethical teaching.[32] The sacrament of the Eucharist, the physical fusion with the divine body of Christ, is explicitly called "essentially magical" by Weber.[33]

Most readers of Weber's texts today are probably not even aware of the fact that these statements sound like insults to Catholic ears. They may have internalized a Protestant image of Catholicism, or as secularists they may consider these denominational differences to be mere hairsplitting. They therefore don't realize that Weber's seemingly value-neutral characterizations are in direct continuity with Protestant anti-Catholic polemics from the time of the Reformation on. In other contexts, Weber even goes so far as to describe Catholicism as a form of polytheism. Weber's understanding of monotheism was neither based on an appropriate view of trinitarian doctrine nor of the cult of canonized saints, who certainly cannot be seen as "independent deities who have undergone a semi-involution."[34] It is not necessary to go into greater detail here. My point is not that Weber had an overly positive image of Protestantism—he detested Lutheranism and was deeply ambivalent about Calvinism—but that his analysis has a narrative structure and is couched in temporal categories like "disenchantment" and "rationalization" that are only seemingly neutral. While the notion of "rationalization" had not been a driving force for Weber's analyses from the beginning but had only gradually emerged in his thinking as a conceptual roof under which he could store his various diverging investigations and therefore had to cover so many different phenomena that I often have difficulties seeing what their common denominator allegedly is, the meaning of "disenchantment" seems to me to be clear: it is certainly not—as has frequently been assumed—secularization (whatever that exactly means), but "demagicization," a process that occurs when processes in the world lose their "magical meaning"; they happen but do not "mean" anything.[35] By construing the sacraments and the human experience connected with them as quasi-magical, as remnants of or relapses into the world of magic, Weber treats Catholicism, and to a certain extent even Lutheranism, as pre-Axial and excludes it from any claim to being a serious contemporary option. For him all religions demand at some point a sacrifice of the intellect,[36] and Catholicism to a particular degree. We should not forget that this was written at a time when Catholic modernism played an important role in international intellectual debates and when the so-called liturgical movement was about to emerge.

Even in the "Zwischenbetrachtung," which can be read as a mere typology of conflicts between value spheres and religious orientations, Weber makes claims about the inner consistency of religious orientations that should not be taken at face value. For him it is either Puritanism with its belief in the predestination of salvation or an "acosmistic" ethos of fraternity as in India that is fully consistent; everything else for him is mere compromise or lack of clarity and self-reflection. But this view, which is presented as the result of a purely rational schematization of options, is based on a problematic understanding of the relationship between religious experience and intellectual treatments of the problems of theodicy;[37] it thus misses the inner consistency of an understanding of religion based on "sacramental experience"[38] and the radical transformation of religious experience in the framework of post-Axial religion, and therefore distorts the range of options under contemporary conditions.

An interpretation of Weber's sociology of religion as it is proposed here helps to reembed Weber in his intellectual milieu; many of his pronouncements lose their canonical character. They can be seen again as depending on the specific views of his sources of information and as contributing to a scholarly, but also to a quasi-religious discourse. It fits with attempts, for example, to show how much Weber's overly sharp distinction between Lutheranism and Calvinism with regard to their political implications is a result of interconfessional Protestant polemics within Protestantism in German nineteenth-century theology.[39] Eckart Otto in his turn has compared the understanding of the Hebrew prophets in Weber's and Troeltsch's thinking and demonstrated that—despite certain similarities—their deep-seated motivations were different and not without influence on their conclusions. "When E. Troeltsch characterizes theodicy as 'practical' which means that explanation is not in the centre of prophetic interest because the prophets do not want 'to explain destiny, but to bring about a practical decision and attitude' (Troeltsch), then this dialectic of inner experience and post factum reflection in E. Troeltsch is directed against rationalist misinterpretations of the role of the prophets. In Max Weber, however, the goal is to demonstrate the 'purely religious' motivation and political and economic independence of the prophets and to mark the point where charisma is transformed in the process of rationalization and 'Veralltäglichung.'"[40] Troeltsch's analysis of the role of the Hebrew prophets was an attempt to learn from a historical case how a religious tradition can be renewed in a time of crisis, whereas Weber looked at the formative influences a religion could have on economic, social, and political processes and the effect these processes can have on religion. Both research programs are, of course, legitimate. But the differences between them are connected with crucial differences in their diagnoses of contemporary religion. Whereas both Troeltsch and Weber came to the conclusion that Puritanism was exhausted, this meant for Weber that the most consistent form of Christianity had reached its end, while for Troeltsch (and myself) this meant that other forms of Christianity—both doctrinally and institutionally—would be important in the future. A powerful role of the post-Axial religions in the contemporary world can probably not be articulated in Weber's theoretical framework. This, however, is not an empirical finding of Weber, but an inherent consequence of the narrative structure of his presentation of religious history.[41]

III. Karl Jaspers: Communication about Transcendence

In the philosophical literature on Karl Jaspers, his Axial Age thesis plays only a surprisingly modest role. Philosophers apparently tend to leave the empirical merits of this thesis to historians, sociologists, and others. The nonphilosophers, in their turn, mostly simply take up the thesis, ignoring its ramifications in Jaspers' oeuvre.[42] Contextualization here often means only an emphasis on the fact that the relevant book came out shortly after World War II, and there is indeed no doubt that it is a reaction to the shattering experiences of Nazism and the war. But it would be terribly simplistic to interpret the book as just one more contribution to the booming literature on the specificities of the "Abendland" at that time. Jaspers' book was not as self-congratulatory as most of this literature was, and it tried to deal with Europe in a non-Eurocentric way. Moreover, it did not criticize Eurocentrism, as later academic radicals have done, out of a self-hatred of the West, but attempted to offer a new defense of universalism. Such a new defense was directed against the ideologies of the time: communist tyranny and the secularization enforced by it, the Nazi attempts to return to Germanic, pre-Christian, pre-Axial religion and other political and philosophical moves of a "detranscendentalist" kind, an ideology of scientism, a mere continuation of European religious traditions as if nothing had happened, all teleological philosophies of history, a complete split between philosophy and religious questions. Against all these ideologies Jaspers' plea was to recognize the plurality of existing universalisms and to develop a philosophical conception of the possibilities of their mutual understanding.[43] Jaspers himself came from a Protestant background, but made it very clear in his writings and interviews that he was not a believer.[44] He said, for example, that not only did he not believe in revelation or in Christ as an incarnation of God, but that he did not even understand what exactly was meant when Christ was called the son of God, an incarnation of God. He had, however, the greatest respect for the post-Axial religious traditions. He called his discovery of the coincidence of religious innovations in the Axial Age an "incredibly exciting facticity"—not just one empirical phenomenon among innumerable others, but an empirical fact and not an article of faith so that all peoples and religions could accept it. His way out of the seemingly aporetic situation of a plurality of and the threats to universalism was not the claim that philosophers could reconstruct everything that is reasonable in the faith of believers, but that philosophy could serve as the mediator in the communication of believers. That is why I see in his work an important inspiration not only for the comparative-historical sociology of religion, but also for a theory of the specificities of our communication about our fundamental values and our experiences of transcendence. Such a communication, according to Jaspers, presupposes seeing other faiths, and not only our own, as attempts to articulate the never-fully expressible experiences of the divine, but it also modifies our relationship to our own religious tradition because we learn to see our own religious traditions not as dogmatically fixed doctrines, but as never-completed attempts at articulation. In this view, we are not expected to break with our formative religious experiences and traditions, but to rearticulate them in authentic ways. Interreligious dialogue, but also the dialogue between philosophy and religion(s), thus can lead to a better self-understanding on all sides.[45]

When Jürgen Habermas was awarded the Karl Jaspers Prize in 1995, he pointed out in his speech that Jaspers' whole philosophy has to be seen as an attempt to find a third way between a relativist historicism and an abstract universalism.[46] This philosophy can in a certain sense also be seen as a continuation of Weber's and Troeltsch's work. Jaspers was not only influenced by Weber's writings on the "world religions" when he developed the Axial Age thesis, but also wanted to get out of what he perceived as an impasse in Weber's thinking.[47] The strong emphasis on ultimate value commitments in Weber and on the inevitability of an Either-Or, of existential decisions among competing values, should not be read in a decisionist and arbitrary sense as if such a choice is ultimately arbitrary and as if no reasonable communication between the proponents of different values were possible. In order to reach that goal, we need a theory of the communication about such values and of the experiences in which our commitment to them is founded. This communication cannot be mere empathy, but it cannot be mere rational-argumentative discourse either. Jaspers' reconstruction of the fundamental innovations of the Axial Age is intended as a basis for such a dialogue between philosophy and the post-Axial religions and also among these religions. In that sense, Jaspers' constitutive contribution to the Axial Age debate does not simply have an explicit religious dimension (as in Lasaulx) or an implicit one (as in Weber); it is itself an attempt to provide the foundation for a contemporary discourse that is open to all religious articulations of the transcendent and to nonreligious forms of moral universalism.

Jaspers' thinking, if this interpretation is correct, is close to other attempts to get beyond historical relativism without breaking with the insight that even universalistic validity claims are not founded in "reason" as such, but have a contingent history of emergence that is not irrelevant for their evaluation. As one can interpret Georg Jellinek's book on human rights as an attempt to reconstruct the inviolability of human rights in a historicist framework,[48] and as one can see Troeltsch's whole life-work as arising out of this tension,[49] one can interpret Jaspers' Axial Age thesis as a reconstruction of the ideas of transcendence and revelation in a framework that could be called an existentially transformed historicism. This claim makes sense only, of course, if we do not fall prey to the assumption that there was a complete rupture between pre-World War I historicism and post-World War I philosophies of existence; there were more elements of "existential reasoning" before the war and there was more historicism after the war than this conventional view admits. I do not think, however, that Jaspers' own philosophy is the last word in this debate. On the contrary, as the writings of Eisenstadt and Robert Bellah demonstrate so convincingly, they are more a point of departure than a final statement, both with regard to historico-sociological questions and with regard to a theory of the communication about values.

Bellah writes in his masterful essay "What Is Axial about the Axial Age?" that "transcendental realms are not subject to disproof the way scientific theories are," but "inevitably require a new form of narrative, that is, a new form of myth"[50] and we can derive from that statement that not only did the structure of myths change in the Axial Age, but that our debate on the Axial Age also goes beyond empirical questions and addresses the mythical structure of our contemporary self-understanding. My emphasis on the religious dimensions of the Axial Age debate has therefore not been intended as a debunking effort, nor as a critique of ideology, but as an encouragement to consciously connect empirical research on the history of religion with the most fundamental questions of our orientation in the contemporary world.

Notes

1. Georg Simmel, *Lebensanschauung* (Munich and Leipzig, 1918). An English translation of this important work has now been published, more than ninety years after the original: *The View of Life* (Chicago, 2010). On the concept of "Achsendrehung" ("axial rotation") in Simmel, see Hans Joas, *The Genesis of Values* (Chicago, 2000), 78ff. Simmel's book influenced the early Heidegger and his understanding of death: Michael Großheim, *Von Georg Simmel zu Martin Heidegger: Philosophie zwischen Leben und Existenz* (Bonn, 1991). See also John E. Jalbert,

"Time, Death, and History in Simmel and Heidegger," *Human Studies* 26 (2003): 259-283, and the instructive introduction to the English translation of Simmel's book by Donald Levine and Daniel Silver, ix–xxxii.

2. Donald N. Levine, "Note on the Concept of an Axial Turning in Human History," in Said Amir Arjomand and Edward A. Tiryakian, eds., *Rethinking Civilizational Analysis* (London, 2004), 67–70. One could argue indeed that Simmel, in his essay on Michelangelo, interprets the "detranscendentalization" of Renaissance art as an axial turn and in that sense applies his terminology to the rise and decline of "transcendence," but he does not speak of that change as a turning point in world history. See Georg Simmel, *Philosophische Kultur* (Potsdam, 1923), 168.

3. Karl Jaspers, *Vom Ursprung und Ziel der Geschichte* (Munich, 1949), 19. English: *The Origin and Goal of History* (New Haven, 1953), 1.

4. The English quotation is from Georg Wilhelm Friedrich Hegel, *The Philosophy of History* (New York, 1956), 319. See Austin Harrington, "Europa in Weimar: German Intellectuals and the Idea of the West, 1914–1933" (manuscript "Habilitationsschrift," University of Erfurt, 2009, 215, n. 60).

5. Martin Riesebrodt, "Ethische und exemplarische Prophetie," in Hans Gerhard Kippenberg and Martin Riesebrodt, eds., *Max Webers Religionssystematik* (Tübingen, 2001), 193–208.

6. Victor von Strauss writes in his commentary on Lao Tse (Leipzig, 1870) about these similarities, calls them very mysterious, and explains them by the unitary origin of mankind, on the one hand, and the effects of a higher spiritual power, on the other. On Lasaulx see below.

7. Subsequent page references to Lasaulx refer to the new edition of this book, ed. Eugen Thurnher (Munich, 1952).

8. Lasaulx mentions August Friedrich Gfrörer, *Urgeschichte des menschlichen Geschlechts* (Schaffhausen, 1855), 206–207, and Eduard Röth, *Die ägyptische und die zoroastrische Glaubenslehre als die ältesten Quellen unserer spekulativen Ideen* (Mannheim, 1846), 348, who refers to Anquetil-Duperron as his source.

9. Dietrich Metzler, "A. H. Anquetil-Duperron (1731–1805) und das Konzept der Achsenzeit," *Achaemenid History* 7 (1991): 123–133. He refers to Anquetil-Duperron's translation and edition of the Zend Avesta of Zoroaster (Paris, 1771). For a characterization of Anquetil-Duperron's achievement, see Jürgen Osterhammel, *Die Entzauberung Asiens: Europa und die asiatischen Reiche im 18. Jahrhundert* (Munich, 1998), 293–296. He calls Anquetil-Duperron's work "the foundational document of a truly polyphonic world historiography" (293).

10. Benjamin I. Schwartz, "The Age of Transcendence," *Daedalus* 104, no. 2 (1975): 1–7.

11. Arnaldo Momigliano, *Alien Wisdom: The Limits of Hellenization* (Cambridge, 1975), 8–9. For Eisenstadt, see his chapter "The Axial Age in World History" in Hans Joas and Klaus Wiegandt, eds., *The Cultural Values of Europe* (Liverpool, 2008), 22–42.

12. Björn Wittrock, "Cultural Crystallization and Civilization Change: Axiality and Modernity," in Eliezer Ben-Rafael and Yitzhak Sternberg, eds., *Comparing Modernities: Pluralism versus Homogenity [sic]; Essays in Homage to Shmuel N. Eisenstadt* (Leiden, 2005), 83–123, here 112.

13. Both Benjamin Schwartz, in "The Age of Transcendence," and Robert Bellah strongly make the claim that there are terms for transcendence in several of the Chinese traditions and that Confucianism should definitely be considered a religion with post-Axial traits.

14. Johann Arnason et al., "General Introduction," in Arnason et al., eds., *Axial Civilizations and World History* (Leiden, 2005), 1–12, here 7. This volume also contains an article by Arnason on the history of the Axial Age thesis—an article, however, that is more programmatic than historical: "The Axial Age and Its Interpreters: Reopening a Debate," 19–49.

15. I find it remarkable that Jürgen Habermas referred to Jaspers' Axial Age thesis in his contribution to the reconstruction of historical materialism. See Jürgen Habermas, "Geschichte und Evolution," in Habermas, *Zur Rekonstruktion des Historischen Materialismus* (Frankfurt am Main, 1976), 200–259, here 241. But it is also remarkable that he prefers the idea of "replacement" over the idea of "integration" without even discussing the alternative—for example with regard to the relationship between "narrative" and "argumentative" explanations. This is a major difference between his views (at that time, at least) and those of Robert Bellah.

16. The main sources for this biographical information are Axel Schwaiger, *Christliche Geschichtsdeutung in der Moderne: Eine Untersuchung zum Geschichtsdenken von Juan Donoso Cortés, Ernst von Lasaulx und Vladimir Solov'ev in der Zusammenschau christlicher Historiographieentwicklung* (Berlin, 2001), 236ff., and the introduction by Eugen Thurnher to the reprint of Lasaulx's book *Neuer Versuch einer alten, auf die Wahrheit der Tatsachen gegründeten Philosophie der Geschichte*, 7–60. See also Friedrich Engel-Janosi, "The Historical Thought of Ernst von Lasaulx," *Theological Studies* 14 (1953): 377–401. For a general characterization of this intellectual milieu, see the unsurpassed chapter "Die Auseinandersetzung mit dem Zeitgeist" in Franz Schnabel's 1937 history of the nineteenth century: *Deutsche Geschichte im neunzehnten Jahrhundert*, vol. 4: *Die religiösen Kräfte* (Munich, 1937), 164–202. He calls Lasaulx a nephew of Görres, which is not correct (ibid., 168). Görres was in fact married to Catherine von Lasaulx, a cousin of Ernst von Lasaulx.

17. See Schwaiger, *Christliche Geschichtsdeutung*, 267.

18. Lasaulx, *Neuer Versuch*, 159.

19. In this regard my interpretation is different from that of Schwaiger, *Christliche Geschichtsdeutung*, 267.

20. Pippa Norris and Ronald Inglehart, *Sacred and Secular: Religion and Politics Worldwide* (Cambridge, 2004). For a brilliant critique of this influential book,

see Daniel Silver, "Religion without Instrumentalization," *Archives Européennes de Sociologie* 47 (2006): 421–434.

21. Lasaulx, *Neuer Versuch,* 137 (my translation).

22. Schwaiger, *Christliche Geschichtsdeutung,* 244.

23. Max Weber, "Religiöse Gemeinschaften," in *Max-Weber-Gesamtausgabe* [Collected works of Max Weber] I/22-2, 183–184. He does mention Bousset later in the text (276).

24. Max Weber, "Hinduismus und Buddhismus," in *Gesammelte Aufsätze zur Religionssoziologie* II (Tübingen, 1921, 7th ed., 1988), 155.

25. Wolfgang Schluchter's work is particularly worth mentioning here: *Religion und Lebensführung,* 2 vols. (Frankfurt am Main, 1988).

26. An exemplary case: Edith Hanke, "Erlösungsreligionen," in Kippenberg and Riesebrodt, eds., *Max Webers Religionssystematik,* 209–226, particularly 214.

27. Björn Wittrock, "Cultural Crystallizations and World History: The Age of Ecumenical Renaissance," in Johann Arnason and Björn Wittrock, eds., *Eurasian Transformations, Tenth to Thirteenth Centuries* (Leiden, 2004), 41–73, here 42–43.

28. Max Weber, "Religiöse Gemeinschaften," 157–158.

29. On the complexities of the developments in postmedieval European Christianity in this regard, see Keith Thomas, *Religion and the Decline of Magic* (New York, 1991), and now Charles Taylor, *A Secular Age* (Cambridge, 2007), and my review essay on this book: Hans Joas, "Die säkulare Option. Ihr Aufstieg und ihre Folgen," *Deutsche Zeitschrift für Philosophie* 57 (2009): 293–300. The present study is not the right place to delve into the theological attempts to formulate a consistent theory of the sacrament, from Augustine through the medieval scholastics to contemporary thinking. For an overview, see the excellent entry "sacrament" in *Lexikon für Theologie und Kirche* (Freiburg, 1999), vol. 8, 1437–1455.

30. Weber, "Religiöse Gemeinschaften," 123.

31. Ibid., 154.

32. Ibid., 124.

33. Ibid., 343.

34. The best study on this specific point still is Werner Stark, "The Place of Catholicism in Max Weber's Sociology of Religion," *Sociological Analysis* 29 (1968): 202–210, here 203. A rather polemical attempt to criticize Weber's sociology as part of the "liberal Protestant metanarrative" can also be found in John Milbank, *Theology and Social Theory: Beyond Secular Reason* (Oxford, 1990), 92–98. On Milbank, see my critical response: "Sophisticated Fundamentalism from the Left?" in Hans Joas, *Do We Need Religion? On the Experience of Self-Transcendence* (Boulder, 2008), 65–80. The British Jesuit Anthony Carroll has published the most extensive study on this topic: *Protestant Modernity: Weber, Secularization, and Protestantism* (Scranton, 2007). See also my review of this book in *The Journal of Religion* 90 (2010): 445–447, and Manuel Borutta, *Antikatholizismus: Deutschland und Italien im Zeitalter der europäischen Kulturkämpfe* (Göttingen, 2010), 116–120 (on Weber).

It is a remarkable fact that Ernst Troeltsch, the Lutheran theologian, explicitly defended the Catholic understanding of the sacraments against a "magical" interpretation by emphasizing the ethical character of the preparation for them and of their effects. See Ernst Troeltsch, "Protestantisches Christentum und Kirche in der Neuzeit" (1909), in *Kritische Gesamtausgabe*, vol. 7 (Berlin, 2004), 114ff.

35. Weber, "Religiöse Gemeinschaften," 273.

36. Max Weber, "Zwischenbetrachtung," in *Gesammelte Aufsätze zur Religionssoziologie*, vol. 1, 566.

37. See Joas, *Do We Need Religion?*, 16.

38. Robert Bellah, "Flaws in the Protestant Code: Some Religious Sources of America's Troubles," *Ethical Perspectives* 7 (2000): 288–299.

39. Friedrich Wilhelm Graf, "The German Theological Sources and Protestant Church Politics," in Hartmut Lehmann and Guenter Roth, eds., *Weber's Protestant Ethic: Origin, Evidence, Contexts* (Cambridge, 1987), 27–50.

40. Eckart Otto, *Max Webers Studien des Antiken Judentums* (Tübingen, 2002), 246–275, here 270 (my translation).

41. In his polemical critique of *A Secular Age*, the book of the (Catholic) Canadian philosopher Charles Taylor, Charles Larmore uses Weber's views on religion as if they were the last word of an empirically founded sociology of religion (see "How Much Can We Stand?" *The New Republic*, April 9, 2008, 39–44). This shows how important a contextualization of Weber's views is.

42. Among the few exceptions are two articles by Aleida Assmann, "Jaspers' Achsenzeit, oder Schwierigkeiten mit der Zentralperspektive in der Geschichte," in Dietrich Harth, ed., *Karl Jaspers: Denken zwischen Wissenschaft, Politik und Philosophie* (Stuttgart, 1989), 187–205, and "Einheit und Vielfalt in der Geschichte. Jaspers' Begriff der Achsenzeit neu betrachtet," in Shmuel N. Eisenstadt, ed., *Kulturen der Achsenzeit*, vol. 2 (Frankfurt am Main, 1992), 330–340. See also the following publications: Norbert J. Rigali, "A New Axis: Karl Jaspers' Philosophy of History," *International Philosophical Quarterly* 10 (1970): 441–457; Georges Goedert, "Die universalgeschichtliche Einheitsidee bei Karl Jaspers," *Jahrbuch der Österreichischen Karl-Jaspers-Gesellschaft* 11 (1998): 9–27.

43. Karl Jaspers, *Der philosophische Glaube angesichts der Offenbarung* (Munich, 1962).

44. For example: "Philosophie und Offenbarungsglaube. Ein Gespräch mit Heinz Zahrnt," in Hans Saner, ed., *Karl Jaspers: Provokationen; Gespräche und Interviews* (Munich, 1969), 63–92, here 89 and 85.

45. On Jaspers' importance in this regard, see Jörg Dittmer, "Jaspers' 'Achsenzeit' und das interkulturelle Gespräch," in Dieter Becker, ed., *Globaler Kampf der Kulturen? Analysen und Orientierungen* (Stuttgart, 1999), 191–214.

46. Jürgen Habermas, "Vom Kampf der Glaubensmächte. Karl Jaspers zum Konflikt der Kulturen," in Habermas, *Vom sinnlichen Eindruck zum symbolischen Ausdruck* (Frankfurt am Main, 1997), 41–58.

47. On the relevance of Weber for Jaspers, see Dieter Henrich, "Karl Jaspers: Denken im Blick auf Max Weber," in Wolfgang Mommsen and Wolfgang Schwentker, eds., *Max Weber und seine Zeitgenossen* (Göttingen, 1988), 722–739. Henrich does not comment on the Axial Age topic at all!

48. Hans Joas, "Max Weber and the Origin of Human Rights," in Charles Camic et al., eds., *Max Weber's "Economy and Society": A Critical Companion* (Stanford, 2005), 366–382.

49. See my "Ernst Cassirer Lecture": "A German Idea of Freedom? Cassirer and Troeltsch between Germany and the West," *Occasional Paper of the Swedish Ernst Cassirer Society* 2 (2005).

50. Robert Bellah, "What Is Axial about the Axial Age?" *Archives Européennes de Sociologie* 46 (2005): 69–89, here 81.

2

What Was the Axial Revolution?

CHARLES TAYLOR

Any view about the long-term history of religion turns on an interpretation of the Axial Age. What was the nature of the Axial revolution? This is sometimes spoken of the coming to be of a new tension "between the transcendental and mundane orders," involving a new conception of the "transcendental."[1] But "transcendental" has more than one meaning. It can designate something like a "going beyond" the human world or the cosmos (1). But it also can mean the discovery or invention of a new standpoint from which the existing order in the cosmos or society can be criticized or denounced (2). Moreover, these two meanings can be linked. The place or being beyond the cosmos may yield the new locus from which critique becomes possible. The Hebrew prophets condemning the practices of Israel in the name of God come to mind.

Again, potentially linked to these two is another change: the introduction of second-order thinking (3), in which the formulae we use to describe or operate in the world themselves come under critical examination.

Possibly linked with these three is another change: what Jan Assmann calls "implied globality" (4).[2] The notion here is that the transcendent being, or the principles of criticism, may be seen as of relevance not just to our society, but to the whole of humanity. But the link with our own society may be weakened in another way. Any of the above changes may bring with them a new notion of the philosophical or religious vocation of individuals. Indeed, the changes may themselves be introduced by such individuals who invent or discover new forms of religious or philosophical life. The Buddha or Socrates come to mind. This can be the origin point of a process of "disembedding" (5), a process I would like to deal with in the following discussion.

These five may be seen as rival accounts of what axiality consists in, but it might be better to see them as potentially linked changes, in which case the issue between them would be more like this: Which of these changes provides the best starting point from which to understand the linkages in the whole set?

Without wanting to challenge any of these readings, I would like to suggest a sixth way of conceiving the change. It was a shift from a mode of religious life which involved "feeding the gods"—where the understanding of human good was that of prospering or flourishing (as this was understood), and where the "gods" or spirits were not necessarily unambiguously on the side of human good—to a mode in which (a) there is notion of a higher, more complete human good, a notion of complete virtue, or even of a salvation beyond human flourishing (Buddha) while at the same time (b) the higher powers according to this view are unambiguously on the side of human good. What may survive is a notion of Satan or Mara, spirits which are not ambivalent, but rather totally against human good. I make some of the links clear from the outset, because I would like to present this change in our understanding of the good (6) as a facet of the change I call disembedding (5).

The full scale of this far-reaching change becomes clearer if we focus on some features of the religious life of earlier, smaller-scale societies, insofar as we can trace this. There must have been a phase in which all humans lived in such small-scale societies, even though much of the life of this epoch can only be guessed at. If we examine (what we know of) these earlier forms of religion (which coincide partly with what Robert Bellah called "archaic religion"),[3] we note how profoundly these forms of life "embed" the agent. And that happens in three crucial ways.

First, socially: in Paleolithic and even certain Neolithic tribal societies, religious life is inseparably linked with social life. This meant first of all that the primary agency of important religious action—invoking, praying to, sacrificing to, or propitiating Gods or spirits, coming close to these powers, getting healing, protection from them, divining under their guidance, and so forth—was the social group as a whole, or some more specialized agency recognized as acting for the group. In early religion, we primarily relate to God as a society.

This kind of collective ritual action, where the principal agents are acting on behalf of a community, which also in its own way becomes involved in the action, seems to figure virtually everywhere in early religion, and continues in some ways up till our day. Certainly it goes on occupying an important place as long as people live in an enchanted world. The ceremony of "beating the bounds" of the agricultural village, for instance, involved the whole parish, and could only be effective as a collective act of this whole.[4]

This embedding in social ritual usually carries with it another feature. Just because the most important religious action was that of the collective, and because it often required that certain functionaries—priests, shamans, medicine men, diviners, chiefs, and so on—fill crucial roles in the action, the social order in which these roles were defined tended to be sacrosanct. This is, of course, the aspect of religious life which was most centrally identified and pilloried by the radical Enlightenment. The crime laid bare here was the entrenchment of forms of inequality, domination, and exploitation through their identification with the untouchable, sacred structure of things. Hence the longing to see the day "when the last king had been strangled in the entrails of the last priest." But this identification is in fact very old, and goes back to a time when many of the later, more egregious and vicious forms of inequality had not yet been developed, before there were kings and hierarchies of priests.

Behind the issue of inequality and justice lies something deeper, which touches what we would call today the "identity" of the human beings in those earlier societies. Just because their most important actions were the doings of whole groups (tribe, clan, subtribe, lineage), articulated in a certain way (the actions were led by chiefs, shamans, masters of the fishing spear), they couldn't conceive of themselves as potentially disconnected from this social matrix. It would probably never even occur to them to try.

In this way people are embedded in society. But this also brings with it an embedding in the cosmos. For in early religion, the spirits and forces with whom we are dealing are in numerous ways intricated in the world. We can see this if we look at the enchanted world of our medieval ancestors: for all that the God they worshipped transcended the world, they nevertheless also had to do with intracosmic spirits, and they dealt with causal powers which were embedded in things: relics, sacred places, and the like. In early religion, even the high gods are often identified with certain features of the world;

and where the phenomenon which has come to be called "totemism" exists, we can even say that some feature of the world, an animal or plant species, for instance, is central to the identity of a group.⁵ It may even be that a particular geographical terrain is essential to our religious life. Certain places are sacred. Or the layout of the land speaks to us of the original disposition of things in sacred time. We relate to the ancestors and to this higher time through this landscape.⁶

Besides this relation to society and the cosmos, there is a third form of embedding in existing reality which we can see in early religion. This is what makes the most striking contrast with what we tend to think of as the "higher" religions. What the people ask for when they invoke or placate divinities and powers is prosperity, health, long life, fertility; what they ask to be preserved from is disease, dearth, sterility, premature death. There is a certain understanding of human flourishing here which we can immediately understand, and which, however much we might want to add to it, seems to us quite "natural." What there isn't, and what seems central to the later "higher" religions, is the idea that we have to question radically this ordinary understanding, that we are called in some way to go beyond it.

This is not to say that human flourishing is the end sought by all things. The divine may also have other purposes, some of which impact harmfully on us. There is a sense in which, for early religions, the divine is always more than just well disposed toward us; it may also be in some ways indifferent; or there may also be hostility, or jealousy, or anger, which we have to deflect. Although benevolence, in principle, may have the upper hand, this process may have to be helped along, by propitiation, or even by the action of "trickster" figures. But through all this, what remains true is that divinity's benign purposes are defined in terms of ordinary human flourishing. Again, there may be capacities which some people can attain, which go way beyond the ordinary human ones, which, say, prophets or shamans have. But these in the end subserve well-being as ordinarily understood.

By contrast, with Christianity or Buddhism, for instance, there is a notion of our good which goes beyond human flourishing, which we may gain even while failing utterly on the scales of human flourishing, even *through* such a failing (like dying young on a cross); or which involves leaving the field of flourishing altogether (ending the cycle of rebirth). The paradox of Christianity, in relation to early religion, is that, on one hand, it seems to assert the unconditional benevolence of God toward humans; there is none of the ambivalence of early divinity in this respect; yet, on the other hand, it redefines our ends so as to take us beyond flourishing.

In this respect, early religion has something in common with modern exclusive humanism, and this has been felt and expressed in the sympathy of many modern post-Enlightenment people for "paganism"; "pagan self-assertion," thought John Stuart Mill, was much superior to "Christian self-denial."[7] (This is related to, but not quite the same as, the sympathy felt for "polytheism," which I want to discuss later.) What makes modern humanism unprecedented, of course, is the idea that this flourishing involves no relation to anything higher.

The portrait of the early triple embeddedness is well drawn by Francis Oakley, in his discussion of the history of monarchy:

> Kingship ... emerged from an "archaic" mentality that appears to have been thoroughly monistic, to have perceived no impermeable barrier between the human and divine, to have intuited the divine as immanent in the cyclic rhythms of the natural world and civil society as somehow enmeshed in these natural processes, and to have viewed its primary function, therefore, as a fundamentally religious one, involving the preservation of the cosmic order and the "harmonious integration" of human beings with the natural world.[8]

Human agents are embedded in society, society in the cosmos, and the cosmos incorporates the divine.

Now as earlier mentions suggest, I have been speaking of "early religion" to contrast with what many people have called "post-Axial" religions.[9] The reference is to what Karl Jaspers called the "Axial Age,"[10] the extraordinary period in the last millennium BCE when various "higher" forms of religion appeared seemingly independently in different civilizations, marked by such founding figures as Confucius, Gautama, Socrates, and the Hebrew prophets.

The surprising feature of the Axial religions, compared with what went before, what would in other words have made them hard to predict beforehand, is that they initiate a break in all three dimensions of embeddedness: social order, cosmos, human good. Not in all cases and all at once: perhaps in some ways Buddhism is the most far-reaching, because it radically undercuts the second dimension: the order of the world itself is called into question, because the wheel of rebirth means suffering. In Christianity there is something analogous: our world is disordered and must be made anew. But some post-Axial outlooks keep the sense of relation to an ordered cosmos, as we see in very different ways with Confucius and Plato; however, they mark a distinction between this and the actual, highly imperfect social order, so that the close link to the cosmos through collective religious life is made problematic.

But perhaps the most fundamental novelty of all is the revisionary stance toward the human good in Axial religions. More or less radically, they all call into question the received, seemingly unquestionable understandings of human flourishing and hence inevitably also the structures of society and the features of the cosmos through which this flourishing was supposedly achieved. The change was double, as I mentioned above. On one hand, the "transcendent" realm, the world of God, or gods, of spirits, or Heaven, however defined, which previously contained elements which were both favorable and unfavorable to the human good, becomes unambiguously affirmative of this good. But on the other hand, both the crucial terms here, both the transcendent and the human good, are reconceived in the process.

We have already noted the changes in the first term. The transcendent may now be quite beyond or outside of the cosmos, as with the Creator God of Genesis, or the Nirvana of Buddhism. Or if it remains cosmic, it loses its original ambivalent character, and exhibits an order of unalloyed goodness, as with the "Heaven," guarantor of just rule in Chinese thought,[11] or the order of Ideas of Plato, whose key is the Good.

But the second term must perforce also change. The highest human goal can no longer just be to flourish, as it was before. Either a new goal is posited, of a salvation which takes us beyond what we usually understand as human flourishing, or else Heaven or the Good lays the demand on us to imitate or embody its unambiguous goodness, and hence to alter the mundane order of things down here. This may, indeed usually does, involve flourishing on a wider scale, but our own flourishing (as individual, family, clan, or tribe) can no longer be our highest goal. And of course, this may be expressed by a redefinition of what "flourishing" consists in.

Seen from another angle, this means a change in our attitude to evil as the destructive, harm-inflicting side of reality. This is no longer just part of the order of things, to be accepted as such. Something has to be done about it. This may be conceived as an escape through self-transformation, or it may be seen as a struggle to contain or eliminate the bad, but in either case evil is not something just to be lived with as part of the inevitable balance of things. Of course, the very sense of the term "evil" also changes here, once it is no longer just the negative side of the cosmos, and comes to be branded as an imperfection.[12]

We might try to put the contrast in this way: unlike post-Axial religion, early religion involved an acceptance of the order of things, in the three dimensions I have been discussing. In a remarkable series of articles on Australian Aboriginal religion, W. E. H. Stanner speaks of "the mood of assent" which is central to this spirituality. Aboriginals had not set up the "kind of quarrel with life" which springs from the various post-Axial religious initiatives.[13] The contrast is in some ways easy to miss, because Aboriginal mythology, in relating the way in which the order of things came to be in the Dream Time—the original time out of time, which is also "everywhen"—contains a number of stories of catastrophe, brought on by trickery, deceit, and violence, from which human life recouped and reemerged, but in an impaired and divided fashion, so that there remains the intrinsic connection between life and suffering, and unity is inseparable from division. Now this may seem reminiscent of other stories of a Fall, including that related in Genesis. But in contrast with what Christianity has made of this last, for the Aboriginals the imperative to "follow up" the Dreaming, to recover through ritual and insight their contact with the order of the original time, relates to this riven and impaired dispensation, in which good and evil are interwoven. There is no question of reparation of the original rift, or of a compensation, or of making good of the original loss. What is more, ritual and the wisdom that goes with it can even bring them to accept the inexorable, and "celebrate joyously what could not be changed."[14] The original catastrophe doesn't separate or alienate us from the sacred or Higher, as in the Genesis story; it rather contributes to shaping the sacred order we are trying to "follow up."

I can perhaps sum up this post-Axial notion of higher good, in terms of four features. (a) It is defined as going beyond (whatever is locally understood as) ordinary human flourishing: long life, prosperity, freedom from disease, drought, natural catastrophe, and so on. (b) There were vocations with special higher powers before, like shamans, for instance; but now the higher good doesn't just consist of special powers; it is in some sense a goal for all human beings. This is so even if this aspect is downplayed or countervailed by notions of hierarchy. Thus for Plato, the philosophical life is not for everyone; but at the same time it amounts to the fullest realization of the nature which all human beings share. (c) This good is our goal as human beings in virtue of the way things are—whether the demands of God, or the nature of things, or the Fourfold Noble Truth, or whatever. In consequence, the goal is endorsed by whatever higher beings, gods, spirits, or the cosmos are recognized by the culture concerned. This contrasts with the pre-Axial ambivalence of many of these beings to human flourishing. (d) Grounded in the way things are, endorsed by higher powers, this goal is unitary, harmonious, and inwardly consistent.

The resulting religious life in the post-Axial age combines elements of the pre-Axial in some kind of amalgam, one that is often unstable. The post-Axial pushes toward individual spiritual "virtuosi," to use Max Weber's word (which includes monks, Bhikkus, Platonist sages, and so on). The great "higher" religions, which become entrenched within and help to shape civilizations, have this hybrid character and the resultant tensions.

Axial religion didn't in fact do away with early religious life. It doesn't at once totally change the religious life of whole societies. But it does open new possibilities of disembedded religion: seeking a relation to the divine or the higher, which severely revises the going notions of flourishing, or even goes beyond them, and can be carried through by individuals on their own, and/or in new kinds of sociality, unlinked to the established sacred order. So, monks, Bhikkus, sanyassi, devotees of some avatar or God strike out on their own; and from this springs unprecedented modes of sociality: initiation groups, sects of devotees, the sangha, monastic orders, and so on.

In all these cases, there is some kind of hiatus, difference, or even break in relation to the religious life of the whole larger society. This may itself be to some extent differentiated, with different strata, castes, or classes, and a new religious outlook may lodge in one of them. But very often a new devotion may cut across all of these, particularly where there is a break in the third dimension, with a "higher" idea of the human good.

There is inevitably a tension here, but there often is also an attempt to secure the unity of the whole, to recover some sense of complementarity between the different religious forms. So that those who are fully dedicated to the "higher" forms can, on one hand, be seen as a standing reproach to those who remain in the earlier forms, supplicating the powers for human flourishing, and, on the other hand, nevertheless can also be seen as in a relationship of mutual help with them. The laity feed the monks, and by this they earn "merit," which can be understood as taking them a little farther along the "higher" road, but also serves to protect them against the dangers of life, and increases their health, prosperity, fertility.

So strong is the pull toward complementarity that even in those cases where a "higher" religion took over the whole society, as we see with Buddhism, Christianity, and Islam, and there is nothing supposedly left to contrast with, the difference between dedicated minorities of religious "virtuosi" (to use Max Weber's term again) and the mass religion of the social sacred, still largely oriented to flourishing, survived or reconstituted itself, with the same combination of strain, on one hand, and hierarchical complementarity, on the other.

From our modern perspective, with 20/20 hindsight, it appears as though the Axial spiritualities were prevented from producing their full disembedding effect because they were, so to speak, hemmed in by the force of the majority religious life, which remained firmly in the old mold. They did bring about a certain form of religious individualism, but this was what Louis Dumont called the charter for "l'individu hors du monde":[15] that is, it was the way of life of elite minorities, and it was in some ways marginal to, or in some tension with, the "world," where this means not just the cosmos which is ordered in relation to the Higher or the Sacred but also the society which is ordered in relation to both the cosmos and the sacred. This "world" was still a matrix of embeddedness, and it still provided the inescapable framework for social life, including that of the individuals who tried to turn their backs on it, insofar as they remained in some sense within its reach.[16]

I have described these as "unstable" amalgams, but this feature is perhaps a potentiality, which isn't always actualized. Let's look at some of the possible sites of tension in these religious forms.

First, (i) to return to the reference to polytheism above, the new understanding of our higher good, which is itself endorsed by God or the Cosmos,

Heaven, or some other higher reality, is itself unitary and coherent. The good human being for Plato was harmonious; to attain Nirvana is to come to perfect peace; the sage is in ideal equilibrium. This contrasts very sharply with a potentiality of pre-Axial religions, realized in certain forms of polytheism. The demands of higher beings on us may be in tension with each other. Insofar as our good (flourishing) is bound up with our meeting these demands, the human good itself can be seen as combining elements which are at best in tension, in more dire straits even contradictory.

Take the story of Hippolytos, dragged into a disastrous love triangle with his father and Phaedra, in which he loses his life. Hippolytos is portrayed as devoted to Artemis, so devoted that he is celibate. But this too great attachment is bound to rouse the jealousy of Aphrodite, the goddess of marriage and sexual love. Her hand is visible in the love entanglement into which he is unwittingly and unwillingly drawn, and which costs him his life.

There is an ambivalence in the story. There is something heroic and admirable in Hippolytos' single-mindedness. In a sense it aspires to go above the human condition. For mortals the prudent thing is to "pay one's dues" to all the immortals, and to navigate at our own level between the rocks they lay out for us. Perhaps a similar moral can be drawn from the story of Oedipus, whose ability to see overt reality with exceptional acuity is paid for by a blindness to the inarticulate depths (which Tiresias for his part is aware of).

We might recognize a "disenchanted" analogue of this insight in, for instance, the philosophy of Isaiah Berlin, with his insistence on the potential conflict between the goods we subscribe to.

Another potential site of instability is (ii) what I described above as the second level of embedding, that of social order in cosmic order. Axial revolutions, which relate to a new, unitary higher good, transform this cosmic embedding. The surrounding order now perhaps really merits the attribute "cosmic" with the full resonance of harmonious unity which attaches to this Greek term. Previously, the various gods, spirits, or higher beings could make incompatible demands on humans, as we have just seen, and were not all unambiguously favorable to human welfare. Now the proper cosmic order is frequently unified and aligned with the higher human good; indeed the cosmic frame can set the standard by which human social orders are to be judged and criticized. In some cases, as with Buddhism or the Hebrew Bible, the potentiality is opened for a standpoint of critique that can judge the condition of the cosmos itself. But this didn't inhibit the development of a normative understanding of cosmic order even in the civilizations animated by Buddhism, or by postbiblical revelations.[17]

These post-Axial "higher" religions can still have a place for spirits who are ill-disposed toward the human good, such as Satan or Mara. But now they are classed as radical enemies of the normative order, and are destined in the end to be defeated. Or else a god can retain his or her Janus-faced ambivalence, as with Pattini or the Isvara form of Shiva in Sri Lankan Buddhism; but the destructive side is clearly marked as against and the restorative side as for the normative order.[18] Or else, taking purchase in a higher good from which the cosmos itself can be judged, a god who wreaks destruction of worldly things can be seen as working for the good, as doing a work of purification, as with certain understandings of Shiva or Kali.

But the cosmic battle itself is not the site of potential instability. This lies rather in the fact that the two-tiered normative order, that of society in cosmos, can itself be seen as not fully self-sufficient, as needing to draw on its opposite, its negation, to sustain itself.

I want to mention two types, which deserve much fuller discussion, but which I can only briefly indicate here.

(1) The equilibrium in tension of Latin Christendom emerged and became evident in Carnival and similar festivities, such as the feasts of misrule, or boy bishops, and the like. These were periods in which the ordinary order of things was inverted, or "the world was turned upside down." For a while, there was a ludic interval, in which people played out a condition of reversal of the usual order. Boys wore the miter, or fools were made kings for a day; what was ordinarily revered was mocked, and people permitted themselves various forms of license, not just sexually but also in close-to-violent acts and the like.

(2) The example of the second type is drawn from Sri Lankan Buddhism. I draw here on Bruce Kapferer's fascinating study of sorcery and exorcism.[19] A sorcerer's spell binds me, impedes, even paralyzes my life. It cuts me off from the sources of health and goodness. In this way, it contravenes the normative order. The origin stories, which are called on to understand sorcery and to underpin the ceremonies of exorcism, make this relation clear. They relate ur-events in which the ideal normative order was attacked and deeply

damaged. These provide the paradigm for the sorcerer's aggression. And the myths also relate how the damage was undone. But in these it becomes clear that the healing could only be effected and the order restored by drawing on the same power of sorcery which disrupted the order in the first place. This ambivalent stance toward the sorcerer's power is reenacted in the various rites of exorcism.

Thus on one level it is clear that there is an ideal, Buddha-inspired normative order, that established by King Mahasammata in the beginning. This is utterly opposed to the forces of disruption which various demon-figures attempt to inflict. But on another level, the act of restoration has to draw on these same forces. Restorer figures are ambivalently placed toward this order, as their myths of origin indicate.[20]

We get a result which is similar and yet different from the previous type. As with Carnival, we reveal the normative order to be not really self-sufficient. It must somehow draw on its opposite. But where with Carnival (at least as read by Victor Turner) the opposite of order is simply its dissolution, a chaos which contains restorative powers, here we are dealing with its active negation. Order must draw on the forces of its enemy. In both cases, the tension, which can easily be seen as a contradiction, is a source of potential instability.

In Latin Christendom, we get an upsetting of this shaky equilibrium, in the long movement of reform (beginning with Hildebrand, but carrying through the Reformation, Counter-Reformation, and so on). Here the site of the previous instability, the two-tiered order of society-in-cosmos, is what is undermined and then destroyed.

What had yet to happen in the first post-Axial millennium was for the two-tiered matrix to be itself transformed, to be made over according to some of the principles of Axial spirituality, so that the "world" itself would come to be seen as constituted by individuals. This would be the charter for "l'individu dans le monde," in Dumont's terms: the agent who in his ordinary "worldly" life sees himself as primordially an individual, that is, the human agent of modernity.

And something like this did come about in the long movement of reform in Latin Christendom from the eleventh century. This involved the development among important elites of a buffered identity, impervious to the enchanted cosmos. This both animated and was rendered firmer by disciplines of thought and conduct. These disciplines in turn aimed not only at the reform of personal conduct, but at reforming and remaking societies so as to render them more peaceful, more ordered, more industrious.

The newly remade society was to embody unequivocally the demands of the Gospel in a stable and, as it was increasingly understood, a rational order. This had no place for the ambivalent complementarities of the older enchanted world: between worldly life and monastic renunciation, between proper order and its periodic suspension in Carnival, between the acknowledged power of spirits and forces and their relegation by divine power. The new order was coherent, uncompromising, all of a piece. Disenchantment brought a new uniformity of purpose and principle.

The progressive imposition of this order meant the end of the unstable post-Axial equilibrium. The compromise between the individuated religion of devotion, obedience, or rationally understood virtue on one hand, and the collective often cosmos-related rituals of whole societies on the other, was broken, and in favor of the former. Disenchantment, reform, and personal religion went together. Just as the Church was at its most perfect when each of its members adhered to it on their own individual responsibility—and in certain places, like Congregational Connecticut, this became an explicit requirement of membership—so society itself comes to be reconceived as made up of individuals. The great disembedding, as I propose to call it, implicit in the Axial revolution, reaches its logical conclusion.

This involved the growth and entrenchment of a new self-understanding of our social existence, one which gave an unprecedented primacy to the individual.

This project of transformation was an attempt to make over society in a thoroughgoing way according to the demands of a Christian order, while purging it of its connection to an enchanted cosmos, and removing all vestiges of the old complementarities, between spiritual and temporal, between life devoted to God and life in the "world," between order and the chaos on which it draws.

This project was thoroughly disembedding just by virtue of its form or mode of operation: the disciplined remaking of behavior and social forms through objectification and an instrumental stance. But its ends were also intrinsically concerned with disembedding. This is clear with the drive to disenchantment, which destroys the second dimension of embeddedness; but we can also see it in the Christian context. In one way, Christianity here operates like any Axial spirituality; indeed, it operates in conjunction with another such, namely, Stoicism. But there also were specifically Christian modes. The New Testament is full of calls to leave or relativize solidarities of family, clan, society, to be part of the Kingdom. We see this seriously reflected in the way certain Protestant churches operated, where one was not simply a member by virtue of birth, but had to join by answering a personal call. This in turn helped to give force to a conception of society as founded on covenant, and hence as ultimately constituted by the decision of free individuals.

This is a relatively obvious filiation. But my thesis is that the effect of the Christian, or Christian-Stoic, attempt to remake society in bringing about the modern "individual in the world" was much more pervasive, and multi-tracked. It helped to nudge first the moral, then the social imaginary in the direction of modern individualism. This becomes evident in the new conception of moral order which we see emerging in modern natural law theory. This was heavily indebted to Stoicism, and its originators were arguably the Netherlands neo-Stoics Justus Lipsius and Hugo Grotius. But this was a Christianized Stoicism, and a modern one, in the sense that it gave a crucial place to a willed remaking of human society.

So the great disembedding occurs as a revolution in our understanding of moral order. And it goes on being accompanied by ideas of moral order. This revolution disembeds us from the cosmic sacred—altogether, and not just partially and for certain people as in earlier post-Axial moves. It disembeds us from the social sacred and posits a new relation to God, as designer. This new relation will in fact turn out to be dispensable, because the design underlying the moral order can be seen as directed to ordinary human flourishing. This, the transcendent aspect of the Axial revolution, is partly rolled back, or can be, given a neat separation of this-worldly from other-worldly good. But only partly, because notions of flourishing remain under surveillance in our modern moral view: they have to fit with the demands of the moral order itself, of justice, equality, nondomination, if they are to escape condemnation. Our notions of flourishing can thus always be revised. This belongs to our post-Axial condition.

The developments I have described in the last section not only show up certain instabilities of post-Axial religion, they also liquidated the whole unstable amalgam which was their locus. And along with this, they also eliminated instabilities (i) and (ii). We now live within the primacy of moral codes which are meant to define the entirety of our moral obligation, and to have ironed out all contradictions and tensions. The big question which is posed by this entire evolution is whether we have gained or lost crucial insights into the human condition through the transformations they have wrought.

This raises a crucial question about the place of the Axial transformation in human history. Granted that these introduced changes were of immense importance in human history (which is why we think it worthwhile to define just what those changes were), what are we to think of the pre-Axial life which they transformed?

Is this merely superseded, relegated to an unrecoverable past? Or is it in various ways still present, and inescapably so, in post-Axial life? Bellah's crucial insight, formulated in the phrase that "nothing is ever lost," points us toward some version of the second answer. Following him, I would find it incredible that our history has been one of unadulterated gain, for this would mean that the features I have outlined in the pre-Axial past have been indeed well lost.

Notes

This chapter was originally published in a collection of my articles, *Dilemmas and Connections: Selected Essays* (Cambridge, MA: The Belknap Press of Harvard University Press, 2011), 367–379. Copyright © 2011 by Charles Taylor; reprinted by permission of the publisher.

1. S. N. Eisenstadt, ed., *The Origins and Diversity of Axial Age Civilizations* (Albany: State University of New York Press, 1986), 1.
2. See his contribution in this volume.
3. See his "Religious Evolution," chap. 2 of *Beyond Belief* (New York: Harper & Row, 1970).
4. Robert Bellah, in his article "What Is Axial about the Axial Age?" *Archives Européennes de Sociologie* 46, no. 1 (2005): 69–89, makes a similar point about what he calls "tribal religion": "Ritual in tribal societies involves the participation of all or most members of the group" (69). He contrasts these with "archaic societies," which term designates the large-scale states that arose in the ancient world, and subjugated

many of the smaller face-to-face societies. These were hierarchical, and their crucial rituals focused on crucial figures, kings or priests. But the face-to-face rituals continued, down at the base, and in Bellah's mind, do so right up to our time. I have been greatly helped here by the much richer account of religious development in Bellah's work: first in his "Religious Evolution" in *Beyond Belief,* and more recently in the article quoted above. The contrast I want to make in this chapter is much simpler than the series of stages which Bellah identifies; the "tribal" and the "archaic" are fused in my category of "early" or "pre-Axial" religion. My point is to bring into sharp relief the disembedding thrust of the Axial formulations.

5. See, e.g., Godfrey Lienhardt, *Divinity and Experience* (Oxford University Press, 1961), chap. 3; Roger Caillois, *L'Homme et le Sacré* (Paris: Gallimard, 1963), chap. 3.

6. This is a much commented upon feature of Aboriginal religion in Australia; see Lucien Lévy-Bruhl, *L'Expérience mystique et les symboles chez les primitifs* (Paris: Alcan, 1937), 180ff.; Caillois, *L'Homme et le Sacré,* 143–145; W. E. H. Stanner, "On Aboriginal Religion," a series of six articles in *Oceania* 30–33, (1959–1963). The same connection to the land has been noted with the Okanagan in British Columbia; see J. Mander and E. Goldsmith, *The Case against the Global Economy* (San Francisco: Sierra Club Books, 1996), chap. 39.

7. John Stuart Mill, *On Liberty,* in *Three Essays* (Oxford: Oxford University Press, 1975), 77.

8. Francis Oakley, *Kingship* (Oxford: Blackwell, 2006), 7. Bellah makes a fundamentally similar point, I believe, in "What Is Axial": "Both tribal and archaic religions are 'cosmological,' in that supernature, nature and society were all fused in a single cosmos" (70).

9. See, for instance, Eisenstadt, ed., *The Origins and Diversity of Axial Age Civilizations;* see also Bellah, "What Is Axial."

10. Karl Jaspers, *Vom Ursprung und Ziel der Geschichte* (Zurich: Artemis, 1949). In using these terms, "Axial" and "post-Axial," I am groping for an expression to distinguish two quite different forms of religious life, one of which goes back much further than the other. But I am not necessarily accepting much of what Jaspers associated with this term. For instance, I have no final view on whether we can identify a particular "Axial Age" *(Achsenzeit)* when these important changes occurred in civilizations far removed from each other more or less simultaneously. The issue of what these important changes consist in has recently come back to the center of scholarly attention, along with the renewed concern with defining different civilizational traditions, after a long infertile period in which Western thinkers remained spellbound by the extraordinary idea that there was a single path, from "tradition" to "modernity," which all societies were bound to travel, some much earlier than others. See, for instance, Johann Arnason, S. N. Eisenstadt, and Björn Wittrock, *Axial Civilizations and World History*

(Leiden: Brill, 2005). I don't want to take a stand in their very interesting debates, for instance that between Eisenstadt and Wittrock about which changes were crucial to the transitions. For my purposes here, the contrast between pre- and post-Axial is defined by the features I enumerate in my text.

11. See Cho-Yun Hsu, "Historical Conditions of the Emergence and Crystallization of the Confucian System," in *Axial Age Civilizations,* ed. S. N. Eisenstadt, 306–324.

12. In this sense, I agree with Eisenstadt's formulation of one of the key changes of the Axial period, "the emergence, conceptualization and institutionalization of a basic tension between the transcendental and mundane orders"; with, of course, the understanding that the "transcendental" order itself changes when the tension arises. Eisenstadt, *Axial Age Civilizations,* 1.

13. Stanner, "On Aboriginal Religion"; the expression quoted figures in article 2, *Oceania* 30, no. 4 (June 1960): 276. See also by the same author "The Dreaming," in *Reader in Comparative Religion,* ed. W. Lessa and E. Z. Vogt (Evanston: Row, Peterson, 1958), 158–167.

14. Stanner, "On Aboriginal Religion," article 6, *Oceania* 33, no. 4 (June 1963): 269.

15. Louis Dumont, "De l'individu-hors-du-monde à l'individu-dans-le-monde," in *Essais sur l'individualisme* (Paris: Seuil, 1983).

16. I want to take account of Stanley Tambiah's reservations about Dumont's formula "individual outside the world" in relation to the Buddhist renouncer; see S. J. Tambiah, "The Reflexive and Institutional Achievements of Early Buddhism," in *Axial Age Civilizations,* ed. S. N. Eisenstadt, 466. The Bhikku is outside the "world," in the sense of the life of the society relating to the cosmos and gods. But this doesn't prevent, even perhaps renders inevitable, (a) a new kind of sociability in which renouncers come together (the Sangha), and (b) relations of complementarity between renouncers and those in the world, whereby the latter can have some part in what the renouncers are directly seeking ("merit"), or even (although this may appear a deviation) whereby the spiritual power of monks can be directed to the ordinary life-goals of the laity.

17. I have discussed this at greater length in *A Secular Age* (Cambridge, MA: Harvard University Press, 2007), 45–54.

18. Bruce Kapferer, *The Feast of the Sorcerer: Practices of Consciousness and Power* (Chicago: University of Chicago Press, 1997).

19. Kapferer, *The Feast of the Sorcerer.*

20. Ibid., chap. 3.

3

An Evolutionary Approach to Culture

Implications for the Study of the Axial Age

MERLIN DONALD

One of my early heroes was the great literary theorist Northrop Frye. His book *Anatomy of Criticism* took my young undergraduate imagination by storm. Frye was a system builder, and I saw in his approach the possibility of exploring the deepest interactions between the flow of cultural change, and the reactions of creative minds to their situated historical contexts. Great writers obviously held a high place in the governance of ideas and beliefs in the cultures he examined. Yet their minds were also, unavoidably, creatures of the cultural moment. The deep structure of their minds—the shifts in cultural contexts that Frye was tracking—could not be understood outside their specific time and place.

A little later, in graduate school, the neuropsychological theories of D. O. Hebb revealed to me another possibility: that it might be possible to discover the deep structure of the mind by focusing on the workings of the brain. Some years later, acknowledging this, I wrote: "Hebb was also a system-builder, but he worked down in the dark mechanistic depths of the mind. Where Frye had been on the bridge, surveying the passing landscape of human culture, Hebb was in the engine room, tinkering with the mental machinery below. For the past twenty years I have worked down in the engine room, and this is my attempt to connect what is happening at the cultural surface with what little we know about what is happening below" (Donald 1991, 403). The last sentence still applies.

Most of the contributors to this book fall more into the Frye tradition than I do and survey the landscape of culture with far more expertise than I can muster. But they at least doff their caps to those of us who work down in the engine room, and I hope this will lead to more interdisciplinary exchanges between the biological and cultural spheres of academe.

Robert Bellah's (2011) ideas about a theoretic revolution during the Axial Age address some of the earliest events in the long, painful, bloody (and still unfinished) transition from the governance of Mythic culture to that of Theoretic culture. In the cognitive domain, this translates into a changed relationship between two powerful ways of representing reality, and two uniquely human cognitive systems, each derived from both biology and culture. However, on reading his chapters, I find myself challenged to clarify exactly what I meant by proposing the Mythic and Theoretic categories in the first place. Their origins lie in the most elemental cognitive components of the systems needed to generate such cultures: memory mechanisms, representational tools, and the new possibilities these create in the public arena. Obviously (and unsurprisingly), these broad categories carry different baggage for different disciplines, and leave plenty of room for differences of opinion over the definition of the Theoretic mode and the appropriate methodology for its investigation in historical, as opposed to experimental, contexts.

It should be understood that the transition from the Mythic to the Theoretic mode, although a radical step in human cognitive evolution, was cultural in its origins. Biologically, we are the same creatures as the people who lived during the Axial Age; and, in the cognitive domain, they were probably similar to their ancestors of a few thousand years earlier. There is no good evidence suggesting otherwise. Theoretic culture emerged largely from a series of cumulative cultural innovations on the part of creative individuals. However, these innovations changed the nature of the cognitive games people played, and eventually altered how we perceive, think, remember, and conceive of reality; they even changed our sense of selfhood. These were radical changes. However, we should not assume that there was any serious evolution of basic mental capacity, in the biological sense, during the Axial Age.

The transition to Theoretic culture involved much more than a shift in the direction of intellectual reflection or abstraction. It also entailed a major change in the way human beings constructed reality and remembered what they knew. This was also true of earlier transition periods in human evolution, with the difference that this transition was less dependent on changes in biological memory, and more on the invention of efficient artificial memory media—that is, on various symbolic technologies that could store representations outside the brain. However, there was much more to it than external memory storage: new media also enabled human beings to restructure their cognitive system, especially on the collective level. The new organizational and institutional structures that emerged from this process were truly revolutionary in their effect. Before reviewing the principles underlying the notion of Theoretic culture, it might be useful to review the underlying rationale for developing a cognitive classification of human culture in the first place (Donald 1991, 1993, 1998a, 2008).

Basic Principles Underlying the Cognitive Classification of Hominid Culture

Human cultures are by nature cognizing entities; that is, cognitive activity is an integral part of their definition. Thus human cultures can perceive, remember, decide, construct worldviews, and represent reality. The field of cognitive science is typically identified with the study of single individuals, as if the mind were locked in a brain box (which, to a large degree, it is). However, human beings have a shared knowledge base, anchored in culture, which is not restricted to the experience of individuals and is substantially wider and deeper than any single person's comprehension of it. The cognitive activities of a culture are organized, governed, and distributed across an entire population group. No individual mind can encompass the knowledge of an entire culture. Rather, a cultural knowledge base is stored "in culture," that is, displayed and refined in the public domain and remembered by the group. Moreover, a shared knowledge base can be highly idiosyncratic, which explains the tremendous variety found in human cultures.

The gradual process of coevolving of the hominid brain and culture, so that individuals increasingly fall under the sway of their cultures, might be called "emergent enculturation." This is the reverse side of the evolution of representational skill at the species level. Once representations become public, the public domain soon outstrips the capacities of individuals, and they become heavily dependent on the state of the group knowledge. Brain evolution ceased at one point to be the dominant partner in this interaction. As a consequence of this shift, the human brain has been adapting to the presence of cognizing culture for a very long time.

This scenario of human cognitive evolution revolves around a radical shift from the "isolated minds" of other mammals toward the "collective" mental work that characterizes symbol-using cultures. The collective knowledge bank of culture is not, strictly speaking, a mind. Cognitive activity depends ultimately on individual capacity; however, the latter constitutes a major part of a distributed cognitive system. Enculturation has been a crucial factor in establishing the parameters of capacity in individuals. Rapid hominid enculturation has undoubtedly interacted with galloping brain evolution. The ability of individuals to cope with a rapidly evolving representational culture had immediate, and at times drastic, fitness implications. Humans work and think together; isolated humans have always had a very poor chance of survival and reproduction.

Our genetic proximity to primates emphasizes the uniqueness of human cognitive evolution. Much larger genetic distances between species can exist without correspondingly massive cognitive differences. Chimpanzees are genetically closer to humans than they are to most other primates, and yet their cognitive profile is far closer to that of other primates than it is to that of humans. This suggests that, to account for the enormous cognitive gap between chimpanzees and humans, genetics is not enough, we need to invoke an additional factor: brain-culture coevolution.

This entails a series of changes progressing in parallel. Culture establishes the environment within which ontogenesis will take place, but the developing individual also contributes to the cultural environment. The representational environment can change, to a degree, during a person's lifetime, and it changes dramatically across generations. However, the primary creative source of that change is the individual mind and brain. The level of intellectual capacity of the group, visible at the cultural surface, is thus a product of both factors, enculturation and raw brain capacity.

Nothing quite like this takes place in other species. There may be shared patterns of learning (even mollusks have "local traditions" for feeding), and there are parent–child interactions in many complex animals, but these can be accounted for in terms of basic conditioning and learning theory and should not be confused with the shared representational cultures of humans, whereby ideas, memories, and world models are shared.

Other species start at the same point in each generation; not so humans. We do it from a new cultural base. The cognitive environment created by culture deeply affects the way individual brains deploy their resources. Based on archaeological data, the process of deep enculturation must have started slowly in the Lower Paleolithic, or perhaps even earlier, with gradual increments to a primate-like knowledge base. It has accelerated exponentially in anatomically modern sapient humans. Throughout this coevolutionary process, one aspect of selection pressure has never been diluted: the more rapid and substantial the change at the level of culture, the more crucial for survival is the individual's capacity to assimilate the current state of that culture.

Hominid cultures are classifiable in terms of their underlying cognitive support systems and their governing styles of representation. Various features of hominid society may be used as a basis for classifying them. A classification by stone-tool technology gives us Paleolithic, Mesolithic, and Neolithic cultures; metal technology yields Copper, Bronze, and Iron Age cultures; diet-based classifications give us preagricultural and agricultural societies; writing technology yields preliterate and literate cultures; kinship systems lead to patriarchal and matriarchal societies, and so on. These kinds of classifications typically do not address cognition directly, although they might single out aspects of behavior that are directly influenced by cognition.

However, the cognitive dimension is one of the most fundamental in setting the parameters of a culture. Most other classifications of culture simply assume certain levels of cognitive development in the members of the culture, without making this explicit. While the surface of cultural evolution is marked by various concurrent changes, such as the presence of better tools, different dwellings, complex social organization, elaborate decoration, and the presence of symbols, the source of the changes observable at the cultural surface often lies deeper, in the cognitive system.

This leaves us with many candidates to define the dimensions of human cognition, and it is not immediately evident which of them are most important. At first glance, language might appear to be the most obvious cognitive dimension to single out. The emergence of language is often presented as the major cause of cognitive evolution in hominids. But what is language, reduced to its fundamentals? In the Behaviorist and Connectionist traditions, one might single out generally improved learning capacity as a more basic variable; or one might choose the capacity to form new associations (see Jerison 1973). There are many other traditional semiotic and cognitive classifications, usually based on theories of symbolic communication. However, none of these seems to do justice to the collective dimension of cognition, or deal adequately with the apparent qualitative changes in the brain that marked the succession of hominid cultures as they progressed from one stage to the next; hence the need for a more comprehensive theory.

Many cognitive functions underwent radical change in hominids. These include a wide range of voluntary nonverbal expression, iconic and metaphoric gesture, mutual sharing and management of attention, self-cued rehearsal, refinement and imitation of skills, generative (self-cued and innovative) imagery, improved pedagogy, and other means of diffusing skill and knowledge (such as social ritual). In addition, there was also faster communication, increased memory storage, a capacity for voluntary (explicit) retrieval from memory, new forms of representation (including words and larger narrative structures), autobiographical memory, shared representational control of emotions and instinctual reactions, more complex overall structure (architecture) of representation and memory, and, finally, the integration of material culture into a distributed cognitive-cultural process. The list could easily be extended to include many other features and traits.

The features special to human culture and cognition are extraordinarily complex, general in their applications, and interrelated; and it appears unlikely that they evolved in parallel, each for a separate reason. There must be simplicity in any underlying Darwinian process, even one that supports the emergence of very complex features. The tentative list of evolving primate functions may be reduced to a much shorter list: (1) evidence for qualitatively new governing representations, (2) which are inherently public in their manner of expressing knowledge, (3) and a novel, semiautonomous layer of culture that follows from the emergence of the first two factors.

My criterion for establishing three major evolutionary "transitions" in cognition (as opposed to minor changes) was that all of these fundamentals had to converge in any proposed cognitive-cultural transition period. In this case, archaeological and genetic evidence can establish a rough chronology, and cognitive neuroscience can provide a reference model for a logical sequence of change.

Memory retrievability was one of the first requirements. Human beings can search their memory banks; other species cannot. Language is one of the major benefits of this ability, but, paradoxically, language also vastly amplifies this ability to recall. The most basic benefit of voluntary access to memory is skill; the refinement of skill demands that previous performances become available to voluntary recall. This ability is more basic than language, because the retrievability of morphemes (a skill) is a logical precondition of language, and therefore recall cannot be attributed exclusively to language itself. On the contrary, no morphophonology could have evolved without a prior capacity for voluntarily retrieving the procedural memories that encode morphemes. Language must have emerged long after our ability to rehearse and refine skill (Donald 1991).

There are two possible routes to evolving improved procedural memory retrieval. The first would be a brain-based feature, such as a precise addressable system for locating specific memories in the brain, perhaps something resembling a file allocation table. However, since this does not exist in nonhuman mammals, an address system would have to have evolved in such a way as to impose something resembling a file allocation table on preexisting primate cognitive architectures. This seems highly unlikely, to say the least, given the complex design of the nervous system. The second possibility is to evolve a system based partly in culture, which could yield accessible representations by hanging a cultural coding system on a more primitive brain-based recall feature, without invoking any radical changes in the design of the primate neural address system.

In the light of current research, the second route is the only feasible approach to language evolution. A new representational process with this feature of self-retrievability would provide a new memory storage strategy for the hominid brain. Public systems are necessarily based on output (knowledge that cannot be "expressed" would stay locked inside the individual brain). Therefore, this adaptation must have engaged the production systems of the brain, especially the voluntary movement systems.

A rule thus emerges as a basis for a valid cultural-cognitive classification system: at each new stage of cognitive evolution, there should be evidence of an expanded range of voluntary expressive outputs, resulting in an increase in the variability of behavior and thought, and a change in public culture. This holds equally for each stage in human cognitive evolution, although the degree of change might be quite different at each stage. Thus, to establish an evidential foundation for each stage or transition, there should be proof of a major change in each of the three parameters listed above: (1) a new category of memory representation (2) that is inherently public and (3) supports a distinct cognitive-cultural "layer," which has its own mechanism and rationale.

Establishing a Rough Chronology of Hominid Cognitive Evolution

Using these criteria, the first two major transition periods in hominid cognitive evolution seem to correspond roughly to two important speciation events in the prehistory of our species: first, the emergence of species *Homo* over two million years ago, and then the emergence of sapient *Homo* from archaic forms, over the past half million years. These two extended evolutionary events coincide approximately with the first two major cognitive-cultural periods of change in human evolution, with the first leading to advanced motor skills, and Mimetic culture; and the second to language, storytelling, and Mythic culture. Of course, specialists may want to propose finer distinctions within these wide time periods, and such distinctions may be justified. Moreover, it is possible that stone toolmaking was achieved first by late australopithecines, several hundred thousand years before the speciation of *Homo*. But toolmaking advanced further only after the appearance of *Homo*, with the appearance of Acheulean industries, and there seems to be no doubt that these two speciation events coincide with major anatomical changes in *Homo*, as well as changes in the survival strategy of the species.

Table 3.1 summarizes some of the main features of the model (Donald 1991, 1993, 1998a, 2001). Cultures are classified here primarily in terms of their *dominant or governing representations*. The labels given to each stage—Episodic, Mimetic, Mythic, and Theoretic—correspond to the nature of the "top" representational structures that control thought, memory, and perception in the corresponding stages of human cognitive and cultural evolution. As hominids evolved better mimetic and linguistic abilities, first mimetic and then narrative thought dominated the hominid cognitive agenda. This is a cascade, or cumulative, model: previous adaptations are preserved, following the principle of conservation of gains. Top or governing representations were thus not the only cognitive-cultural representations circulating in the human matrix as evolution moved forward; they were the ones with the most influence at that stage. For example, in Mythic cultures, the governing ideas tend to be narrative constructs, which dominate whatever mimetic and episodic representations are present in those societies.

The starting point for this scenario is Miocene primate culture. This was approximated by comparing the two ape species closest to humans, gorillas

Table 3.1. Proposed successive stages, or "layers," in the evolution of primate/hominid culture, using a cognitive criterion for classification

Stage	Species/period	Novel forms of representation	Manifest change	Cognitive governance
Episodic	Primate	Complex episodic event-perceptions	Improved self-awareness and event-sensitivity	Episodic and reactive; limited voluntary expressive morphology
Mimetic (1st transition)	Early hominids, peaking in *H. erectus*; 4M–0.4 mya	Nonverbal action-modeling	Revolution in skill, gesture (including vocal), nonverbal communication, shared attention	Mimetic; increased variability of custom, cultural "archetypes"
Mythic (2nd transition)	Sapient humans, peaking in *H. sapiens sapiens*; 0.5 mya–present	Linguistic modeling	High-speed phonology, oral language; oral social record	Lexical invention, narrative thought, mythic framework of governance
Theoretic (3rd transition)	Recent sapient cultures	Extensive external symbolization, both verbal and nonverbal	Formalisms, large-scale theoretic artifacts, and massive external memory storage	Institutionalized paradigmatic thought and invention

Note: mya = million years ago. Each stage persists into the next and continues to occupy its cultural niche; thus fully modern human societies incorporate aspects of all four stages of hominid culture. The upper Paleolithic seems to be situated pretty clearly in the oral/mythic cultural tradition, but it set the stage for the expansion.

and chimpanzees, and drawing out common cognitive traits. Following standard evolutionary logic, a trait common to both of these modern species must have been present in the primate ancestor we share with them. On this basis, it is fair to label the representational style of apes as "episodic," that is, concrete and reactive, and bound to their sophisticated mastery of social and environmental events.

A key contrast between these apes and humans is their remarkably limited and stereotyped range of expressive outputs. This applies even to Savage-Rumbaugh et al.'s (1993) demonstration of symbolic skills in bonobos. They can comprehend a surprising amount of gesture and speech in an episodic context, but cannot invent such representations de novo, or transcend a specific context. Their gesturing is very limited, and they cannot generate even the simplest kinds of pantomime or metaphoric gesture. It may appear ironic that modern apes find it much easier to learn a human symbolic system, such as an electronic keyboard of symbols, than a simple set of gestures. But this is because the keyboard is a means of bypassing mimesis and the need to self-generate a set of expressions. In sum, though their powers of understanding are formidable, modern apes evidently find it impossibly difficult to construct meaningful expressive actions that encapsulate and reflect their own understanding of events. By extension, their Miocene common ancestor with humans must have also lacked that expressive capacity.

During the evolution of the hominid line, this expressive limitation was obviously overcome, inasmuch as hominids have evolved both mimesis and language. I have proposed that mimesis came first, because it is a logical precondition for the evolution of language (Donald 1998b). Moreover, mimetic expression would have been sufficient to sustain the type of culture that characterized hominids for millions of years. Mimesis is the conceptual "missing link" between the episodic cultures of apes and the classic preliterate oral cultures of most documented human societies.

Mimesis is an embodied, analog, gestural mode of expression that is inherently reduplicative and collective in nature. It turns the public arena of action into theater. Hence, in a sense, the primal form of distinctly human culture is theatrical, embodied, and performance-oriented. Humans are actors, and initially, in its archaic form, the public face of Mimetic culture was a theater of embodied action, manifest especially in the well-documented proliferation of refined skills among archaic hominids. It was also evident in their ability to coordinate their hunting behavior (suggesting at least some limited conventionalized gesturing) and in the emergence of ritualized patterns of cultural practice, such as coordinated seasonal migrations, shared campsites, and some division of labor.

Mimesis is easy to misunderstand (and even to miss altogether) if one subscribes to a logic-based account of thought and language. For example, C. S. Peirce's system of classifying symbols steps from the indexical to the symbolic in a single saltation, and leaves out mimetic expression completely. This is the heart of my objection to Deacon's (1997) theory of language evolution. The same applies to many other attempts to reduce thought to some form of formal logic or Language of Thought (as in Fodor 1975). Mimesis does not easily fit this mold, because it is an analog form of expression, without explicit symbols or grammars. Mimetic pantomimes are closer to the logic of neural nets: holistic, impression-forming reduplications of prior events that amount to vague, impressionistic, and imprecise performances.

Mimesis is pure embodied action. It entails a revolution in primate motor skill at the highest level of control. In mimetic performances, action is connected directly to event-perception. Why would such a capacity have evolved? The answer is *skill*. The primary selection advantage of mimetic capacity is being able to refine and disseminate skills. Early hominids were highly skilled—much more so than apes. This is evident in the archaeological record from finished stone tools that are 2.6 to 3.4 million years old. Conceivably, mimesis might have started to evolve much earlier. Based on stone tools alone, we know that late australopithecines, *Homo habilis,* and certainly *Homo erectus,* had the ability to rehearse and evaluate, and thus refine, their own actions. This is direct evidence for mimetic capacity. Rehearsal is essentially a mimetic action: the individual must reenact a previous performance in order to practice and improve it.

Human mimetic performances are supramodal; that is, they can engage any voluntary action system. The implications of evolving a supramodal capacity to review and rehearse action were tremendous: the entire skeletomotor repertoire of hominids became voluntarily modifiable, and the refinement of skill became possible. Moreover, given the close relation of action to emotion, there was a major emotional dimension to mimetic skill. Mimesis would have changed the primate repertoire for expressing emotion, which was inherited by hominids.

One corollary of this development was increased variability in the morphology of action in hominids. The body became a plaything, something with which to experiment. As a result, mimesis greatly increased the variability of behavior and emotional expression in society, while simultaneously increasing the pressure to conform, which is also inherently mimetic. The result was the rapid emergence of largely nonsymbolic forms of human culture; the public surface of such a culture can be seen as "reflective" of coordinated group action patterns, while individuals "reflect" the group.

Mimetic culture still forms the underpinning of human culture. It persists in numerous cultural variations in expression, body language, and expressive custom (most of which people are unaware of and cannot describe verbally), as well as in elementary craft and tool use, pantomime, dance, athletic skill, and prosodic vocalization, including group displays. The mimetic dimension of modern culture is recognizable by its primarily analog mode of imagining, which is sometimes (inappropriately) called "simulation." This type of imagination—mimetic imagination—recreates an experience in real time. It survives in the performing arts and in the essentially theatrical nature of human relationships and living patterns. It also survives in music and visual art. Most visibly, it is the basis of role-playing, fantasy, and self-identification with various roles.

Although its evolution was originally driven by selection pressure favoring the obvious utilitarian advantages of skills such as toolmaking, mimesis inadvertently presented a revolutionary opportunity for the human species. It provided the basis for a shared collective memory system for the group. By this I mean a system of remembrance that is able to "store" the customs and styles of a group in distributed social-cognitive networks of practice. Such networks are distributed across many brains, and they are held together by social and emotional bonds that cause the interacting members of a culture to cohere into working groups. These networks efficiently consolidate and transmit the mimetic "knowledge base" for any given culture, passing it on to the next generation. Although mimetic actions are always played out in individuals, the mimetic knowledge base of any culture is larger than any individual, and in its complete form resides only in the cultural plexus, which thus serves as a collective memory record, even in cultures that lack language. It records and transmits the customs, styles of emotional expression, skills, and rituals of the group in and to the networked minds that make up the culture. Although such networks may exist in rudimentary form in other species, they had to expand to sustain the kind of cultures that were characteristic of early *Homo*.

In its early form, this collective social-cognitive process had to rely entirely on the brain's innate procedural and emotional memory systems, distributed across many brains, rather than in those of any single individual. This knowledge base contained an enormous amount of information about skill and the conventional expression and control of emotion. Emotional expression is for the most part culturally idiosyncratic in its details, and its specific forms are learned in the context of mimetic scenarios. Children must learn how to react emotionally in a way that is compatible with their culture, and they achieve this by reduplicating observed cultural parameters in action and feeling. This can lead to wide disparities between cultures. For example, where one culture might prohibit ambition and rebelliousness, another might promote them. One consequence of this is that the surface of social life can vary significantly between human cultures, much more so than between other primate cultures. Learning was thus central to hominid social life very early in human evolution, and was critical not just for the improvement of skills but also for emotional expression.

Mimetic communication, independently of language, can support limited public storage and transmission of knowledge by nonverbal means, such as gaze, gesture, and mimetically coordinated group behavior. Mimetic capacities generated a new class of hominid representations that accumulated over generations, shaping the forms and standards of behavior in emerging hominid cultures, and preserving both motor and social skills in the context of consensual body language, accepted convention, and group gesture. This became a defining feature of hominid life and remained as the prototype of later human cultures, even after we evolved language. Mimesis was a successful adaptation that endured for well over two million years without language. This does not rule out the presence of the mimetic equivalent of words—simple conventionalized gestures—long before language emerged at the level of narrative, much later in hominid evolution.

The second major hominid cognitive transition mediated the shift from a purely mimetic form of culture to speech, storytelling, and fully developed oral-mythic culture. This revolutionary development precipitated a representational shift away from slow-moving mimetic customs, toward group storytelling, which can convey huge amounts of knowledge at speeds that are inconceivable in a mimetic context. With language, the collective knowledge base would thus have accelerated its development to the point where narrative became the dominant, or governing, cognitive mode of hominids, replacing mimetic governance with an allegorical form of thinking that I have labeled "Mythic." This radical new capacity was scaffolded on the preexisting mimetic competence, and would have been impossible to evolve without it (see Donald 1998b).

Judging from archaeological and paleontological evidence, this radical change emerged only recently, over the past three or four hundred thousand years, and culminated in the speciation of modern *Homo sapiens*. Oral culture is the signature of our species. It is a specialized adaptation that supplements, but does not replace, the cognitive functions served by Mimetic culture. This adaptation introduced a new layer of culture, so that both human cognition and its associated cultural domains became more complex and multilayered.

Mythic culture is so named because its governing representations cohere, in any given culture, in a shared narrative tradition: an oral, public, standardized version of reality, full of mythic archetypes and allegories, can exert direct influence over the form of individual thought. The central structures of oral-mythic culture emerged as the hominid capacity for language became universal. It was a direct product of language, and it introduced both a level of culture that remains firmly at the center of human social existence, and a powerful means of recall from memory that proved faster and more precise than the imagery-driven retrieval enabled by mimetic representation. Language also revolutionized thought. The essence of language lies in its power to address, define, and organize knowledge and to make it accessible to further reflection.

The advent of language also provided a novel means of collective remembrance, a shared narrative. This shared record affected the developmental process, providing the grounding for autobiographical memory, that is, for a personal narrative of the self. This process emerged from the same semantic foundation as mimetic expression itself: the event-representation. Narrative acts, like mimetic acts, are constructed from event-representations, and the whole elaborate cognitive system of *Homo,* including mimesis and language, is effectively an increasingly abstract and powerful hierarchy of event-representations (Donald 1991; Nelson 1996). This has had many ramifications on human brain design. The power of language to parse and reduce very large and complex events into compact coded messages required significant changes to the executive and metacognitive systems of the brain, and to memory capacity (Donald 2001).

The public expressive offspring of this budding new narrative ability was a liberated imagination that enabled human beings to rearrange complex events in imagination or even to invent fictitious ones, as in storytelling and fantasy, allowing limitless variations in how the shared reality of the group might be construed. This powerful ability is exclusive to our species, and is one of our signature cognitive traits, but it complicated social life immensely. The search for coherence and trust dictated a set of social controls, and cognitive governance became a survival-related necessity. The ruling myths of human society, including stories of origin, rationalizations of power, legends of tribal identity, allegories of correct behavior, and many other ruling ideas, have provided top governance for all the classic forms of society and have had an enormous impact on how human life is lived.

The depth of enculturation that a human infant typically experiences has no equivalent elsewhere in the biosphere, when examined in terms of the intimate cognitive embrace of the society into which it is born. Exposure to this kind of deep enculturation can result, quite literally, in an alteration of one's mental structure, or cognitive architecture. This can occur because culture not only influences mental development but sets up the actual apparatus with which one conceives reality. This shaping influence continues throughout life, on every level, and various scholars (perhaps most notably Charles Taylor in *Sources of the Self*) have tried to find a way to reconcile this all-encompassing cultural embrace with our Western notions of individuality and autonomy.

In the context of what we know about the brain and its relationship to the cognitive system, the effect of culture on the human mind amounts to a virtual symbiosis. The human brain has coevolved alongside its cognizing cultures for two million years and has reached a point where *it cannot realize its design potential outside of culture.* The apparatus of mind itself, and the operational configuration of the brain, which regulates it, are, in significant part, a result of enculturation. This is due to the extreme plasticity inherent in the expansion of the cerebral cortex that occurred during human evolution. We are a species that, above all, adapts and learns, and does this in groups. Our personal experiences can translate into group knowledge and thus give a human society the potential to function as a cognitive network. We share mind. Our cultures are vast mindsharing networks that enable us to think, remember, decide, and plan in the context of what the group knows, intends, tolerates, or condemns. This property, found only in humans, gives human culture a cognitive dimension that structures the individual brain.

Cognizing cultures are highly unpredictable; they generate an unprecedented amount of continually changing knowledge—as in common gossip, for example—and tracking the state of that social knowledge bank is a survival-related cognitive skill. One of the primary drivers for the evolution of language may have been the need to track the fast-changing state of social knowledge in groups. A human mind that has never developed language is nevertheless distinctly human in many ways; but it is tremendously impaired in the domain of social knowledge. Even the episodic memory system, the most personal and vivid of our memory systems, is deeply impaired in those who lack language. Deaf people who have acquired sign language as adults have great difficulty remembering anything about their prelanguage lives or selves. Language is thus a vital component of human autobiographical memory.

However, language does not self-install in an infant who is isolated from society. It is acquired only after the individual joins a social group (even a group of two) and assimilates the codes, rules, and associated meanings of whatever communication system the group may have. This is usually a gradual, guided process, involving the acquisition of attention skills that make it possible for the child to know where to look in order to narrow the range of possible meanings that could be affixed to the chaos of sound emitted by adults speaking. Culturally embedded human infants can pick up language in a seemingly effortless manner, yet the isolated human infant cannot even conceive of the possibility of language when left on its own. Such a child, even if instructed later as an adolescent or adult, will never be able to master language or symbolic thinking. Here, as the work of Trevarthen (1980), Tomasello (1999), and Nelson (1996), among others, has shown, early socialization is the key factor. Moreover, an understanding of reciprocal attention and an awareness of knowledge in others are crucial for language learning. Schaller (1991) has shown that deaf people raised without sign, but who are otherwise normally socialized, can acquire language as adults, provided their emotional and attentional connections with society were established early enough.

In summary, the organizational structures of two critical cognitive subsystems, mimesis and language, are dependent on growing up in a specific kind of social-cognitive ecology. This insight has moved experimental literature away from the idea of innate, self-organizing language modules toward the investigation of such basic cognitive skills as joint attention, play and mimetic games, imitation, triadic gaze, and the child's awareness of others, a complex epistemological domain sometimes known as intersubjectivity, or theory of mind. This work is nicely summarized in Nelson's book *Young Minds in Social Worlds* (2008).

An important corollary to this idea is that, as hominid culture has evolved, so has the human mind. While the early emergence of mimetic capacity must have been entirely dependent on the biological evolution of the brain, the evolution of language was interwoven with social and cultural evolution. This was a coevolutionary scenario: as one of the two factors (culture and biology) changed, so, inevitably, did the other. The direction of hominid cognitive evolution was increasingly dependent on hominid cultural evolution. Hominids were becoming the ultimate social species, whereby the mind was merging with culture.

These two changes, mimesis and language, set the stage for the later explosion of material culture in modern humans. In the human evolutionary succession, the two early adaptations that gave humans, first, distinctive *nonverbal* intellectual skills, and then *verbal* intellectual capacities, were biologically driven. Moreover, they were interrelated, inasmuch as the second transition undoubtedly triggered a further expansion of nonverbal mimetic capacities. Oral-mythic culture, as documented in anthropology, encompasses both the mimetic and mythic capacities of humans. Typically, in such cultures, despite the strong presence of mimetic representations, the oral realm dominates. This complex cultural structure, grafted onto an underlying cognitive architecture that remained basically primate, defined the cognitive inheritance of all humans in the Upper Paleolithic.

The Third Transition: The Rise of Theoretic Culture

The third transition, a cultural explosion that has gradually led humanity from preliterate cultures to symbolically literate societies and theoretic governance, has been marked by a long, sporadic but nevertheless culturally cumulative history.

The invention of new memory media was an event of prime importance in this transition, because it readjusted the parameters of communication and memory in the collective social-cognitive structures of society. This culminated in advanced systems of writing and the subsequent externalization of memory storage, which gradually changed the governance hierarchy so that ideas and images, and especially the historical record, were brought under centralized control.

This shift was facilitated by the technology of writing and other crafted symbolic devices, including built structures such as temples and monuments. The revolutionary nature of these developments is not immediately obvious, but reflection leads to the conclusion that the cognitive properties of external memory (as opposed to internal or "biological" memory) are fundamentally different from those of the memory systems of the brain. Table 3.2 illustrates some of these special properties.

Using a computational analogy, it is evident that a distributed system of computers with the memory features listed in the right column of Table 3.2 (external memory media) would have radically different capabilities from a system limited to those features found in the left column (internal or biological memory media). The same applies to a distributed memory system consisting of brains in culture. Under the right circumstances, the addition of external memory devices will afford an increase in the cognitive potential of the system, in direct proportion to the sophistication of those devices. The differences between the two columns imply that, in some historical circumstances, symbolic media could give human beings a technologically driven increase in the capability of the distributed social-cognitive system that governs society. The changes in this system also would have affected individuals born into the network, by changing the course of cognitive development.

Artificial memory media are crucial because they can remove some of the memory load imposed by a task and turn many difficult mental operations into simple automatic rituals: for example, addition and subtraction can

An Evolutionary Approach to Culture

Table 3.2. Comparison of the properties of internal and external memory

Internal memory	External memory
Internal memory record (engram).	External memory record (exogram).
Fixed physiological media.	Virtually unlimited physical media.
Constrained format, depending on type of record, and cannot be reformatted.	Unconstrained format, and may be reformatted.
Impermanent and easily distorted.	May be made much more permanent.
Large but limited capacity.	Overall capacity unlimited.
Limited size of single entries (e.g., names, words, images, narratives).	Single entries may be very large (e.g., novels, encyclopedic reports; legal systems).
Retrieval paths constrained; main cues for recall are proximity, similarity, meaning.	Retrieval paths unconstrained; any feature or attribute of the items can be used for recall.
Limited perceptual access in audition, virtually none in vision.	Unlimited perceptual access, especially in vision.
Organization is determined by the modality and manner of initial experience.	Spatial structure, temporal juxtaposition may be used as an organizational device.
The "working" area of memory is restricted to a few innate systems, such as speaking or subvocalizing to oneself, or visual imagination.	The "working" area of memory is an external display which can be organized in a rich 3-D spatial environment.
Literal retrieval from internal memory achieved with weak activation of perceptual brain areas; precise and literal recall is very rare, often misleading.	Retrieval from external memory produces full activation of perceptual brain areas; external activation of memory can actually appear to be clearer and more intense than "reality."

become trivial tasks, whereas they are next to impossible without appropriate written notations. Symbolic devices can influence the representational process itself, by changing the constraints on imagination. External symbolic technologies can also create stable displays that allow iterative cycles of refinement and permit completely new types of representations. Examples of revolutionary symbolic systems might include currencies, monetary systems, paintings and sculptures, symbolic buildings such as churches, maps, mathematical equations, scientific diagrams, novels, architectural schemes, economic reports, archives, and records of trade. The availability of such things can greatly improve the ability of a society to think clearly.

Another revolutionary development following the invention of symbolic technology was cognitive engineering, that is, the deliberate design of devices designed to serve a purely cognitive end: the creation of a mind-state in a specific audience. Books, plays, musical performances, and public spectacles assumed great importance because they could set up states of mind in individuals that simply cannot be brought into existence any other way. This empowered a new class of creative individuals and changed the political demands placed on governments. This demonstrates the wide influence of a changed cognitive ecology.

External symbols have supported the growth of a novel, semiautonomous realm of human culture, including an institutionalized literate elite. It has also generated a new layer of culture, not yet universal, but already placed in a governing position globally: Theoretic culture. The emergence of Theoretic culture depends upon an entrenched change in how humans think and solve problems. The thought process itself can be changed by means of cultural algorithms driven by interactions with external symbols, which gradually develop into mental habits that support paradigmatic thought; these are epitomized in bureaucracies. These habits of mind, after thousands of years of experience with symbolically literate cultures, remain difficult to transmit to cultures that lack them. Theoretic skills include a variety of thought-algorithms that are by no means innate and whose genesis is inconceivable outside the context of a highly symbol-dependent society.

I have called the outcome of this third cognitive stage Theoretic culture because, where the superstructure of external symbolic control has become established to a sufficiently high degree, it has become the governing mode of representation. Paradigmatic or logico-scientific thought, a style of group thinking that is quite different from the narrative thought skills that govern traditional culture, is not innate to the human brain or even to the larger collective structures of culture. It consists of certain habits of thought—algorithms that function in a close iterative symbiosis with external symbols and that are governed by institutional structures in society.

Theoretic culture is dominated by a relatively small elite with highly developed literacy-dependent cognitive skills, and its principal instruments of control, such as codified laws, economic and bureaucratic management, and reflective scientific and cultural institutions, are external to the individual memory system. This type of representation has gradually emerged as the governing level of representation in some modern societies. Although it dominates science, engineering, education, government, and the management of the economy, it includes only a minority of humanity, and even in that minority, its influence remains somewhat tenuous.

Theoretic culture is thus still in the formative stage, and the third transition is incomplete. Human beings have retained—and indeed have little choice in this—the major elements of the first two transitions, because they are, in effect, hardwired, whereas the algorithms of Theoretic culture are not. Even the most recent, cutting-edge postindustrial cultures encompass all these collective cognitive mechanisms and cultural levels at once, and certain aspects of the culture of the developed world remain totally dominated by the mimetic and mythic domains. Recent research on child development supports this notion; the cognitive enculturation of modern children is highly complex, as they are led through a tangled web of representational modes and intricate institutionalized algorithms. In effect, we have become complex, multilayered, hybrid minds, carrying within ourselves, both as individuals and as societies, the entire evolutionary heritage of the past few million years.

Sophisticated external memory technology (writing included) is too recent an innovation for the human brain to have adapted, in the Darwinian sense, to its presence. Perhaps the most convincing evidence of this is the simple fact that most children, from any culture, can acquire full literacy in virtually any system of writing. This argues strongly against a built-in brain adaptation for reading and in favor of a universal human property of exceptional neural plasticity. The "literacy brain," those circuits that have been identified as the neural foundation of reading and writing, is evidence of that plasticity. Entirely cultural in origin, the literacy brain is superimposed on the brain's innate wiring. There is now a growing experimental literature on this topic (see Dehaene 2007; Donald 2010).

Minds that have acquired full literacy in some domain are made at once more powerful, because they gain access to a shared external resource of ideas and operations, and more vulnerable, because their deeply conditioned interface in the brain of a literate person constitutes a direct path into the deepest semantic systems of the brain. The interface architecture, normally acquired in childhood, continues to change throughout life. Its acquisition requires considerable resources and probably involves trade-offs against the brain's capacities in other areas.

The Axial Age and the Initial Shift toward Theoretic Culture

During the first millennium BCE, certain cultures were sufficiently developed that they built cities of some size, could rely on efficient food supply systems that produced a surplus in most years, and had governments whose tentacles extended far beyond the boundaries of the city. At the same time, these cultures had to absorb the harsh realities of the new order: absolute authority at the top and a very clear signal that the individual was reduced in stature, relative to the power of the social hierarchy as a whole. In their distinctive ways, each of the cultures discussed by Bellah (2011) adapted to new conditions of life. These new conditions included a variety of major cultural changes, including centralized state control over wealth and property, a state monopoly on violence, and the adoption of literacy and record-keeping. These conditions had already emerged in some earlier civilizations, notably Egypt and Sumer, but by the time of the Axial Age, humanity had accumulated much longer experience with a densely populated, hierarchical, and city-ruled lifestyle.

The technology of thinking and recording data also changed in important ways. With the wide use of visual symbolism and ritual, along with more sophisticated systems of writing, there were new opportunities, inherent in the radical display and retrieval properties afforded by the improved media of external symbolization to review and refine ideas, and to list and record the reflections of individual thinkers for later public examination. There was also an extensive division of cognitive labor (in all four Axial societies covered in Bellah's book) introduced by the new order, with a rigid class structure and enormous discrepancies in access to knowledge and education.

This produced a class of people who had a more focused and intellectually oriented way of life, as well as a literate audience, and created a demand for what one might call performers in the "public metacognitive" domain, that is, a domain whose principal concern was the oversight and analysis of human life itself, its origin, purpose, and subtleties. This generated a rich thematic narrative tradition, mostly in the form of selected stories, anecdotes, and archetypes. The last were often portrayed in visual art and epitomized certain strata of society, or areas of cultish interest.

This constituted a more formal kind of public reflection on every aspect of life, from astronomy to zoology, including, of course, morality and the social order. This systematization of inquiry was a relatively new phenomenon, and the relative stability of society enabled this activity to be carried out at a sufficiently safe distance from bare survival needs that it afforded the extraction of abstract principles and practices. The latter went far beyond the compilation of simple folk aphorisms and generated a tradition of learned specialists to whom most people, including the ruling class, looked for guidance. Those traditions transcended space and time, even in India, because they were supported by a rich variety of artificial memory devices, ranging from monuments and sacred buildings to various forms of visual art. This enabled the continuation of those traditions over long periods of time, even after major disruptions due to wars, famines, and other disasters. Then, as now, the scholars paid very close attention to the surviving work of their forebears. Whether the reference points were written documents or built environments did not matter, provided there was some sort of permanent record against which to measure present action. Buddhism, Confucianism, and monotheistic Judaism are highly distinctive traditions, and one is hesitant to generalize across such diversity, but it seems reasonably safe to conclude that they shared at least this enduring structural property.

In Greece, this trend became even more pronounced. The people in charge of the tradition were, for the most part, professionals or semiprofessionals: scribes and scholars, philosophers, poets, playwrights, artists, and literate aristocrats. The Greek process was more public, more diverse, more specialized, and less arcane. For a brief period in Greece, this public intellectual reflective activity developed into an evidence-based, analytic approach that bore a significant resemblance to the modern methodology of analytic thought. This was less true of other Axial Age civilizations, with the possible exception of China in some limited domains. However, it is important to note that Theoretic culture, as a governing force, did not spring fully armed from this situation, even in Greece.

The Axial Age might be considered the first period that germinated the seeds of later full-blown Theoretic cultures, such as those currently governing the developed world. The evolutionary trend in the direction of institutionalized analytic thinking grew very slowly, and one valuable lesson we can draw from the diversity of views summarized in Bellah's (2011) survey is that there were many possible responses to civilized life in the first millennium. For example, whereas the Greek experiment depended heavily on the habits of written scholarly reflection, India did not. It is debatable whether the germs of true Theoretic culture existed anywhere but Greece at that time. But the habit of analysis, reflection, careful definition of terms, and the recording of debates carried over generations, and often at a great distance, slowly grew, spread, and sowed the methodological seeds of a future revolution.

That revolution can be viewed as a long historical shift from mythic to theoretic cognitive governance, a shift that has taken over two thousand years, and is still not complete. The dominance of the theoretic mode has been consolidated only in the past two centuries, and it is far from being universal or permanent. There are residual tensions that emerge from deep structural incompatibilities between mythic and theoretic cultural-cognitive governance. These are outlined briefly in Table 3.3.

The tendency of mythic traditions to be deep and slow to change stems from their highly emotional roots in the mimetic domain: ritual, custom, and rigid networks of practice, as well as stories that strongly support group solidarity at the expense of inclusion and tolerance. Mythic cultures are by nature authoritarian, and Theoretic cultures are able to become less authoritarian (although they too can fall back into rigid authoritarianism). It is clear that these two cultural domains are difficult to reconcile. Yet they collide daily in a globalized economy. There is no alternative to this, and their reconciliation poses an urgent challenge in the modern world.

The evolutionary context leads to at least one major insight: cognitive-cultural adaptations occurred in cascade, with each previous stage remaining in certain domains where it served its purpose well. Thus the mimetic still dominates in certain areas of cultural activity, and the mythic in others. The cognitive system available to human beings has become wider, richer, and much more flexible over time. This has happened despite the uneven historical trajectory produced by the combination of sudden spurts of ad-

Table 3.3. Some apparent incompatibilities between mythic and theoretic styles of cognitive governance

Mythic	Theoretic
Narrative	Analytic/paradigmatic
Authority-based	Evidence-based
Slow, deep	Fast, shallow
Inner focus	Outer focus
Implicit analog logic	Explicit symbolic logic
Highly emotive	Much less emotive
Closed beliefs	Open-ended beliefs
Allegorically grounded	Analytically grounded
Largely oral mediation	Largely technological mediation
Fixed, stable	Change-oriented, unstable

vancement, long periods of stagnation, and many periods where this trend toward increased complexity was severely reversed.

The trend widened to incorporate the institutional arena, with the emergence of formal religious organizations, often identified with government, and later, the educational system. The collective memory record also expanded in a deeper cognitive sense, in that the accumulated wisdom was written down, reviewed critically, edited, and often reformulated for future generations. Above all, writing enabled scholars to build an apparatus of thought that stepped outside the normal restrictions of time and space and enabled conversations and debates to endure much longer than the life spans of any of the participants. This was also possible without an extensive written tradition, through rigidly preserved oral customs embedded in a physical environment that preserved memory by consolidating practice. In both cases, artificial memory supplements were crucial to the preservation of the tradition. However, there is no doubting the advantages of having a written tradition. Writing added precision, and lent itself to wider variations in opinion.

This notion, that every stage of human cognitive evolution found a permanent home in the evolving collective system, is somewhat similar to the evolutionary principle of conservation of previous gains. Previous successful adaptations remained in the system where they proved themselves effective, and the system slowly became more robust and capable of surviving almost any major blow. This occurred without changing the basic facts of human biology, or the existential dilemma facing every human being.

The modern mind reflects this fact. It is a complex mix of mimetic, mythic, and theoretic elements. Art, ritual, and music reflect the continuation of the mimetic dimension of culture in modern life. The narratives of the great religious books reflect the mythic dimension, as do the many secular myths of modern society. These two great domains—the mimetic and the mythic—are mandatory, hardwired, and extremely subtle and powerful ways of thinking. They cannot be matched by analytic thought for intuitive speed, complexity, and shrewdness. They will continue to be crucially important in the future, because they reside in innate capacities without which human beings could not function.

All of this must be placed in perspective. The Axial Age was not all things to all men, so to speak. It did not see the invention of writing or literacy, which were crucial cognitive innovations. These had emerged much earlier, in Egypt and Sumer. The same was true of numeracy, central governments, currencies, trade, bureaucracies, archival data, and libraries, all of which came before. The Axial Age profited from these developments, but it did not invent them. However, taken together, these prior developments set the stage for the Axial Age and led to the creation of a new kind of social organization that was better able to deal with much larger population densities, and the ensuing complications of daily life, than societies of any previous era. They led eventually to a more specialized division of cognitive labor, which allowed the cognitive activities of a society to be governed in a managed corporate hierarchy, that is, a bureaucracy.

Viewed as cognitive networks, bureaucracies were revolutionary in their function. Despite the fact that they are universally reviled, their emergence was a major innovation. Bureaucracies are distributed cognitive networks whose main functions are usually cognitive in nature: classification, decision-making, planning, oversight, review, prioritizing, and control. They have undoubtedly had a major effect on the ability of human beings to carry out their cognitive business in the public domain, including such activities as remembering, deciding, planning, and representing reality in large groups.

However, bureaucracies also preceded the Axial Age in some degree, and once again, it cannot take the credit for their invention. Thus we must conclude that the unique genius of the Axial Age did not reside in this particular contribution either.

The Axial Age reaped the benefits of these earlier innovations. The stage had been set for a different kind of cognitive innovation, on a more abstract conceptual level. The central feature of the Axial Age, if there was a common feature in these four highly diverse societies, was a representational, or worldview, revolution. These societies had each achieved a significant degree of literacy (with the possible exception of India, but Bellah [2011] made a good case for regarding their unique oral tradition as an effective substitute), an existing bureaucracy, and a basic framework of social institutions. However, they did not yet have the conceptual coherence that large societies need to function smoothly. A new vision of human destiny was needed, one that could harness the potential inherent in these powerful new societies. In each case, a vision emerged, and each was revolutionary in its effect. Axial societies provided their citizens with a means of connecting with a shared conceptual framework to cope with the intellectual and spiritual challenges of living in a new kind of social context.

As indicated at the beginning of this section, the Axial Age might be regarded as the time when humanity went through a major evolutionary step in self-monitoring and supervision that can be described as metacognition. This capacity is really an abstract form of self-awareness, a feature of mind that is essential for planning action and for conscious self-regulation in general. Metacognitive oversight also occurs at the group level, and even at the population level, especially in the various arms of government. Social-cognitive networks are able to develop perceptions, plans, and memories, and to make decisions; and all of this requires metacognitive oversight, that is, constant evaluative feedback on the effectiveness of these activities. This is characteristic of governments and corporations, as well as smaller organizations, and the successful functioning of such groups is contingent on essentially the same mechanism of oversight—a collective equivalent of metacognition—implemented for the benefit of the whole society.

Axial Age religions provided metacognitive oversight at the group level, enforced by theocratic bureaucracies. This took different specific forms in each society, but there was a common pattern: these cognitive-regulatory agencies became prominent somewhere in the power structure. This oversight function also played out on the level of the individual life, in the form of ritualized procedures for self-examination, self-correction, and self-directed improvement toward the attainment of a personal ideal. The details were different, but the underlying trend was the same.

The Axial Age was, above all, a period when human society began to reflect consciously on how to construct an institutional process of collective self-regulation. It saw the establishment of several traditions whereby a public process could institutionalize the metacognitive supervision of both individual and collective behavior. Although the process was always monopolized by an elite (perhaps less so in Greece), it nevertheless provided a vital feedback loop from individual to society, and returned a degree of responsibility back to the individual. Reflection on the process of thought and action became an essential part of public and private life.

Humanity, or rather, that part of humanity confronted with the need to solve the problems of an increasingly urban and literate society, was experimenting with novel ways to view the human world. For some time, these societies had been trying to cope with a new way of life that was different from anything that had come before. The old visions and worldviews were apparently not adequate to the task of carrying people through these new times. Perhaps old ideas had failed to make societies cohere as they had in the past, in simpler tribal structures. Perhaps they had failed in the important task of keeping the peace or establishing an enduring social order. These stresses all present cognitive challenges to the basic assumptions that people make when they live in a community and share resources. The answer to the challenge was a formal process of metacognitive oversight.

This is admittedly a speculative thesis. Careful historical analyses will be needed to expand, disprove, or verify many of these assertions. The Axial Age is often associated with the birth of the modern world's most successful and enduring religions and philosophies, and with the beginnings of systematic science and philosophy. But I argue that it was much more than this, because those developments are not what they might seem on a superficial examination. In the evolutionary scenario described above, one must view religious thinking, and especially the religious innovations of the Axial Age, as the absolute cutting edge of human experience at that time. It is revealing that the focus of this effort was not so much the analysis of the physical universe, but rather of the challenges presented by the new conditions of life in a civilized environment.

References

Bellah, R. N. 2011. *Religion in Human Evolution: From the Paleolithic to the Axial Age.* Cambridge, MA: The Belknap Press of Harvard University Press.
Deacon, T. W. 1997. *The Symbolic Species: The Co-evolution of Language and the Brain.* New York: W. W. Norton.
Dehaene, S. 2007. "Cultural Recycling of Cortical Maps." *Neuron* 56: 384–398.
Donald, Merlin. 1991. *Origins of the Modern Mind: Three Stages in the Evolution of Culture and Cognition.* Cambridge, MA: Harvard University Press.
———. 1993. Précis of *Origins of the Modern Mind* with multiple reviews and author's response. *Behavioral and Brain Sciences* 16: 737–791.
———. 1998a. "Hominid Enculturation and Cognitive Evolution." In *Cognition and Material Culture: The Archaeology of Symbolic Storage,* ed. C. Renfrew and C. Scarre, 7–17. University of Cambridge: Monographs of the McDonald Institute for Archaeological Research.
———. 1998b. "Preconditions for the Evolution of Protolanguages." In *The Descent of Mind,* ed. M. C. Corballis and I. Lea, 120–136. Oxford: Oxford University Press.
———. 2001. *A Mind So Rare: The Evolution of Human Consciousness.* New York: W. W. Norton.
———. 2008. "The Sapient Paradox: Can Cognitive Neuroscience Solve It?" *Brain,* December 2, doi: 10.1093/brain/awn290.
———. 2010. "The Exographic Revolution: Neuropsychological Sequelae." In *Becoming Human: Innovation in Material and Spiritual Cultures,* ed. C. Renfrew and L. Malafouris, 71–79. University of Cambridge: Monographs of the McDonald Institute for Archaeological Research.
Fodor, J. 1975. *The Language of Thought.* New York: Thomas A. Crowell.
Frye, N. 1957. *Anatomy of Criticism: Four Essays.* Princeton: Princeton University Press.
Hebb, D. O. 1949. *The Organization of Behavior.* New York: Wiley.
Jerison, H. 1973. *Evolution of the Brain and Intelligence.* New York: Academic Press.
Nelson, K. 1996. *Language in Cognitive Development: The Emergence of the Mediated Mind.* New York: Cambridge University Press.
———. 2007. *Young Minds in Social Worlds.* Cambridge, MA: Harvard University Press.
Peirce, C. S. 1897. "Logic as Semiotic: The Theory of Signs." In *The Philosophical Writings of Peirce,* ed. J. Buchler, 98–119. New York: Dover Books, 1955.

Savage-Rumbaugh, E. S., J. Murphy, R. A. Sevcik, K. E. Brakke, S. L. Williams, and D. M. Rumbaugh. 1993. *Language Comprehension in Ape and Child*. Chicago: University of Chicago Press.

Schaller, S. 1991. *A Man without Words*. New York: Summit Books.

Tomasello, M. 1999. *The Cultural Origins of Human Cognition*. Cambridge, MA: Harvard University Press.

Trevarthen, C. 1980. "The Foundations of Intersubjectivity: Development of Interpersonal and Cooperative Understanding in Infants." In *Human Ethology: Claims and Limits of a New Discipline*, ed. M. von Cranach, K. Foppa, W. Lepenies, and D. Ploog, 530–571. Cambridge: Cambridge University Press.

4

Embodiment, Transcendence, and Contingency

Anthropological Features of the Axial Age

MATTHIAS JUNG

The process most often invoked in describing the hallmark of the Axial Age—or, to circumvent tricky problems of timing and synchronicity, of the Axial cultures—is the "discovery of transcendence." "Transcendence," however, covers a wide range of meanings. When applied to the distinction between our cognitive grasp of the world and its internal structure, for example, it denotes an epistemological conviction that is entirely neutral with regard to religious truth claims. The Axial Age debate emphasizes another aspect: it takes the religions and philosophical worldviews developed in the Axial cultures to be focused on a transcendent realm, a divine higher reality conceived of as a normative criterion for the mundane order of society. This development obviously has many facets and is embedded within a wide range of related changes spanning from technology to means of transportation, to political organization. But one way or another, the sharp distinction between this world and the transcendent realm of truth and normativity seems to be at the center of the decisive developments. Yet it is far from clear what that means in terms of its anthropological preconditions and possible consequences. If we follow Karl Jaspers' reading of the Axial Age, the main anthropological point was *Vergeistigung* ("intellectualization" or "spiritualization"). But *Vergeistigung* is a tricky and precarious achievement for organisms whose relation to the world is shaped by their corporeality. Consequently, my essay tries to tackle these problems from the perspective of a philosophical anthropology rooted in a conception of the human being as an embodied symbol-user.

From this vantage point, it seems helpful to start by distinguishing between two facets of the concept of transcendence: one placing the emphasis on *content,* the other on *semiotic structure.* Both aspects are interdependent and rooted in characteristic properties of human, that is, symbolic language and the corresponding modes of consciousness. Most symbols relate to their referents indirectly, by relating to other symbols (among them iconic and indexical signs, which refer directly) and thus enable speakers to refer to "objects" which transcend the here and now: the world in its entirety, possible worlds, etc. In terms of the *content* of articulation, this symbolic reference to a realm of meaning that transcends the local settings is the dominant aspect. In comprehensive worldviews as they emerged in the Axial Age, it leads to new forms of symbolization in which the contrast between universal aspirations and particular contexts generates a previously unknown dynamics of change. A prominent case is the emergence of the Confucian concept of *ren* (humaneness), in which an egalitarian anthropology is put up against all traditional forms of group morality.[1] Parallel developments can, for example, be found in ancient Israel (the prophets shunning the established practices of sacrifice) or Greece (philosophers like Xenophanes criticizing anthropomorphic conceptions of the gods).

These fascinating developments, however, have a structural, semiotic side as well, and a full understanding of the Axial Age's impact requires the integration of both: if symbols refer indirectly, their content inevitably transcends the immediate experience of the symbol-users. The discovery or construction of transcendent realms of meaning is one side of the coin, the awareness of their remoteness from the conceptual abilities of human beings the other. An example of the dominance of the latter can be found in classic Chinese Daoism with its emphasis on the semiotic gap between the deeper reality and its linguistic representations. If we follow the hints of evolutionary anthropology, this double-sided achievement appears to be the conscious historic appropriation of something already implicit in the earlier phylogeny of symbolic competences, namely their power to release communication from the constraints of physical contact with the environment. As I would like to show later on, we need this distinction between the primordial acquisition of symbolic means and their reflexive, higher-order use in order to connect anthropological and historical discourse. Without it, it would be very difficult to employ Merlin Donald's stages of human evolution for the understanding of the Axial Age, as Robert Bellah does for example.

In the picture I would like to draw, it is essential that the Axial civilizations encountered transcendence in a twofold manner: on the level of religious and philosophical worldviews *and* on the level of the process of symbolizing itself. Naturally, both levels are intimately connected, and this is where historical anthropology, concerned with reconstructing contingent paths of human culture, meets philosophical and evolutionary anthropology—both are concerned, in different ways, with reconstructing the overarching structural conditions of this cultural diversity. This aspect of the concept "Axial Age" is crucial because it points to conceptual alternatives to the clear-cut dichotomy between universal features of mankind on the one hand and cultural variables on the other. Some properties of *homo sapiens*' cognitive development in general may open up historical possibilities that are only realized in some cultures but, once realized, produce universal possibilities for all. I find this insight captured succinctly in Paul Ricoeur's term "inchoate universals."[2]

But even if the Axial Age's discovery of transcendence can be interpreted in this manner, as a contingent event of universal importance, the transcendence of the signified over signification is still only one side of a semiotic coin whose other side remains physiological and physical embodiment. This is what Jaspers completely ignores in his original account of the Axial Age. For him, the decisive point is the *displacement* of the mythical by the rational, and in his existentialist, tragic account, the Axial Age's upheaval of thought failed, and did so—among other reasons—because the chasm between the intellectual avant-garde and ordinary people became too deep. But this leaves out another possibility, for which I will argue here: that the discovery of transcendence is misconceived as the move to freestanding, second-order thought alone and, for reasons connected with the internal logic of symbol-usage, that it had to find a new place for embodiment and interactive, contextualized forms of meaning as well. This necessity created a hitherto unknown tension, which to me seems among the worthiest candidates for Ricoeur's inchoate universals in anthropology. Symbolic meaning, in establishing reference by creating inferential patterns between symbols horizontally, introduces the possibility of transcending local and historical limitations, but it can never rid itself of corporeal relations to the world in the form of qualitative situations and local interactions. Thus ever since the Axial Age, human beings have been confronted with the challenge to acknowledge both the contingency and universality introduced by the transcendence of meaning over symbols and the equally inescapable embodiedness of meaning. If we consider the range of problems in which this challenge can be seen, spanning from philosophy of religion to the cognitive sciences, it is close to impossible to overestimate the significance of the Axial Age.

My essay starts with an examination of the Bellah/Donald scheme of evolution, placing it in the context of anthropological considerations centered on the concept of "making it explicit." This necessitates a closer look at the models of sequentiality that are implied in the use of evolutionary schemes. The main challenge will be to conceptualize the relation between the earlier and the later stages of anthropological evolution in such a manner that neither embodiment nor symbolic universality are lost in the process. Two examples from the Axial Age will historically flesh out these rather abstract deliberations, and finally I will suggest an anthropology of embedded transcendence as the appropriate conceptual framework for dealing with the Axial Age and its contemporary importance.

Four Rungs on the Ladder of Explication

Bellah relies on Donald's *Origins of the Modern Mind* to integrate his own account of religious evolution and his interpretation of the Axial Age into the larger framework of mankind's phylogeny. In this book, the anthropogenetic development has three phases: a mimetic period is followed by a mythical and finally a theoretic one, each transition constituting a new level of consciousness, relegating the evolutionarily older ways of relating to the world to some cultural niche—yet always preserving, never replacing them, so that all stages are simultaneously present in modern societies. In a later book, *A Mind So Rare,* Donald tackled the problem of consciousness and argued forcefully against reductionists like Daniel Dennett, the "capo di tutti capi of the Hardliner School,"[3] that it is not the subpersonal functioning of cognitive modules that dominates the human stage, as Dennett and large parts of contemporary cognitive psychology would have it, but rather consciousness itself as a "multilayered, multifocal capacity."[4] Donald's approach emphasizes the conscious mind and its achievements to such a degree that it sees "culture itself, as well as its two principal by-products, languages and symbols" as "consequences of a radical change in the nature of consciousness."[5]

Donald's critique of Dennett's epiphenomenalistic view of consciousness is entirely convincing and supported by impressive empirical findings. But do the causal relations between consciousness and symbolic forms really only flow from the former to the latter, as Donald's talk about culture and language as "by-products" seems to imply? This is obviously a crucial point when it comes to the relation between the humanities and the life sciences, but, less obviously, it is crucial for an understanding of the anthropological importance of the Axial Age as well. This is clear upon further consideration of the significance of Bellah's first principle of inquiry, "nothing is ever lost,"[6] in light of the relationship between pre-Axial stages of sign-usage and the Axial breakthroughs. My suggestion is therefore to supplement the Donald/Bellah scheme of human evolution in two ways: first, by systematically integrating mutually reinforcing feedback loops between levels of consciousness and different modes of sign-usage. For this I will rely on Terrence Deacon's account of the coevolution of brain and language in his book *The Symbolic Species*.[7] Second, I will situate it within the anthropological framework of "making it explicit," to borrow a phrase from Robert Brandom. For Brandom, this phrase is meant to capture the distinctly human capability of using symbols to create a "space of reasons" (Wilfrid Sellars), in which the implicit meaning of practices is made explicit in propositions exchanged and criticized in conversation—the "great good for discursive creatures" like us.[8] Here I will use the phrase somewhat liberally to stand for the anthropological insight that we are expressive beings all the way down, constantly engaged in symbolic interpretation of what we are feeling and doing. In this way, I place myself in a tradition of thought leading from Wilhelm von Humboldt to Ernst Cassirer and Helmuth Plessner, while giving it a pragmatic twist that borrows some elements of Brandom's thought.

Thus we arrive at an anthropological ladder of explication with four distinct but functionally connected rungs, each of which relates a mode of consciousness (Donald/Bellah) to a step on the way from the implicit to the explicit (Brandom) and a specific form of sign-usage (Deacon). This prepares the ground for the question I take to be crucial for understanding the Axial Age in its relationship to Modernity, namely: How is the sequentiality of this explication process related to the holistic and integrative nature of symbolic communication and hence of religious and otherwise comprehensive worldviews?

The ladder of explication, following Donald and Bellah, is erected on the ground of the "episodic culture" we share with other primates, in which reality is structured and individuated by feelings and habits which respond to situations. The first transition then leads to "mimetic culture," in Donald's words "the murky realm of eye contact, facial expressions, poses, attitude, body-language, self-decoration and tones of voice."[9] Mimetic consciousness marks the presymbolic starting point of symbolic meaning, the first rung on the ladder of explication. It transforms events that simply happen and conduct that simply occurs into structured, meaningful sequences, in which meaning is shared via mutual embodiment. As recent research in cognitive science, for example by Shaun Gallagher,[10] has established beyond doubt, mimetic meanings are operative not only in the phylogeny of humanity but in ontogeny and in the everyday experience of competent adults as well. Long before cognitive capabilities like theories of other minds are established, we are related to our conspecifics via the direct coupling of our sensory-motor systems, in which empathy is acted out mimetically. In the terms of Brandom's pragmatic linguistics, one could talk about meaning implicit in practices and in the norms established when things are done in a specific manner.

Donald's second transition, leading to the second rung of my ladder, results in mythic, narratively structured consciousness and can be identified with the use of ordinary language—yet without the employment of its built-in logical features of reflexivity, which is the hallmark of theoretical culture. In Donald's evolutionary scheme, which provides the framework for Bellah's account of the Axial Age, mythical culture is oral symbolic culture. The third transition, starting about forty thousand years ago and finally leading to rung number three, theoretical culture, is brought about not by the acquisition of a new type of signing and reference, but rather by a new internal sophistication of language, a revolution in the technology of symbols, namely the development of external symbolic devices, first of all of inscription systems. It is here that I want to introduce Deacon's story of symbolic evolution. Deacon and Donald both highlight the continuity of the human brain structure with the "old primate brain" *and* the qualitative novelty of human consciousness, and Donald even underlines the "spiraling coevolution of thought and symbol,"[11] but for him the emphasis is on the phylogeny of consciousness and cognitive evolution, whereas Deacon focuses on the reciprocity of brain and sign-usage development. His understanding of the latter is inspired by the semiotics of Charles Peirce, which he takes as a guideline to structure phylogeny. The basic distinction is between three types of signs, Peirce's famous trichotomy of icon, index, and symbol, and the main transitions occur between three forms of reference and meaning corresponding to iconicity, indexality, and symbolicity. If we try to map Deacon's threefold distinctions onto the Donald/Bellah scheme, some interesting difficulties arise that are highly instructive for our understanding of the Axial Age.

Starting with mimetic consciousness, it seems plausible to identify it semiotically with the stage of iconicity. Mimesis dwells on likenesses and corresponds to the phenomenal aspect of cognition, to Dewey's "underlying and pervasive quality"[12] and to Peirce's firstness. Likewise, it comes quite naturally to connect mythical consciousness, the second transition, to indexality: causal or pseudocausal one-to-one relations between entities. When Cassirer talks about mythical *concrescence* and its universalized physiognomic view, he seems to imply that mythical worldviews expand the iconicity of face-to-face situations into a system of indexical correspondences. The same line of thought is pursued by Lévi-Strauss in his reflections on the binary nature of the mythical. But this does not fit into Donald's schema, in which the mythical period is already characterized by the use of symbolic representation. And symbolicity, in Peirce's semiotics, clearly marks a higher and decisive level of sign-usage, one which incorporates the early stages but creates something qualitatively new, namely indirect reference, reference via the horizontal connection of symbols through inferences. Now I think it is possible and helpful to reconcile and synthesize Deacon's and Donald's accounts by paying attention to the temporal lag between the emergence of a new means of signification and its conscious appropriation. In that way, the mythical period might be reconstructed as the time when symbolic competences evolved, but as far as worldviews are concerned were still used primarily for indexical purposes, for communicating systems of binary relations between persons and social groups on the one hand and, roughly, the world on the other. The introduction of Deacon's model and its construction along the lines of the icon/index/symbol-distinction sensitizes us to the functional relatedness of Donald's layers or stages—I will come back to this later—and to the possibility of asynchronicities. The emergence of semiotic means and their full-fledged, reflective usage do not necessarily coincide; on the contrary, a long time may elapse until the possibilities implicit in semiotic performances are realized. This is another implication of the anthropology of "making it explicit": the dynamics leading from meanings implicitly embedded in practices to their explicit formulation is not restricted to the transition from extralinguistic practices to language. It might be operative within language as well, as becomes apparent on the two higher rungs of my Brandomian ladder.

The third rung, as I have already hinted at, is characterized by modern, theoretic culture, supported by an "external symbolic universe."[13] In Brandomian terms, this amounts to explicit reasoning. The symbolic structure of language with its indirect reference and its logical operators, which allow for the explication of inferential networks, are explicitly put to use. Donald connects this stage primarily with memory and storage technology, with written language, which undoubtedly plays an important part. Nevertheless, I want to emphasize that the possibility of higher-order thought is already implicit in the emergence of symbolicity. Relating symbolically to the word, be it in face-to-face communication or in reading and writing, implies the use of indirect reference, and thus a gap between the sign and the signified is introduced that is not found in sign-systems based on iconicity and indexicality alone. Of course, to stress the importance of symbolicity is not to exclude the possibility that some of its specific properties are only expressed once additional devices are invented and the necessary "external scaffoldings"[14] are in place. But these scaffoldings, if my interpretation is correct, were only able to trigger the development of theoretic culture because the emergence and use of symbolic language made it possible to loosen the representational tie between the sign and the signified. This must have happened in a twofold manner: the introduction of indirect reference, inferential reference between signs, had the effect of relegating direct reference in iconic and indexical relations to the second place in the functioning of language—thus enabling seemingly "freestanding" symbolizations, in which indirect reference is used to articulate beliefs with universal validity claims. But in doing so, in a process that fully deserves to be characterized as "dialectic," inferential reference also produced the possibility of semiotic transcendence, the experience of the arbitrariness of signs and hence the underdetermination of reference. Ever since, the Axial tension between the transcendence of content and its semiotic counterpart has prompted attempts to reconcile both.

If we relate these considerations to the evolutionary ladder of explication, it seems clear that Donald's transition between mythic and theoretic culture should be seen as an internal development of symbolic culture. From the perspective of content, theoretical culture is, as Bellah also emphasizes, the attempt to reflectively come to terms with the narrative ordering of the world on the mythical level, and on the structural side it elaborates the anthropological consequences of symbol-usage with its twofold transcendence. Once again it seems helpful to use the notion of asynchronicity, of a time-lag between plain usage and reflective usage, in this case of the kind of second-order thought that is only possible within a system of indirect reference that allows for the embedding of clauses in higher-order clauses. Connecting the changes brought about in the theoretic stage of culture with the perfecting of external scaffoldings and in particular with the internal development of symbolicity helps to solve two problems that arise when one tries to situate the Axial Age within Donald's scheme. The first problem is that theoretic culture is conceived as an anthropological universal, but the Axial breakthrough happened only in some, not in all civilizations. Did the others never reach the level of theoretic culture? The second problem relates to questions of timing: the transition to theoretic culture started about forty thousand years ago, and if we connect its emergence primarily with the externalization of memory, it is hard to see how this might be taken as a convincing explanation for the discovery of transcendence and why it took so long to occur. But if we emphasize the importance of the discovery of symbolic as opposed to directly referential communication, the two problems disappear: we can establish an internal but contingent relationship between the properties of symbolicity and the discovery of transcendence, and furthermore we can employ the notion of a time-lag between possibilities as performatively enacted and possibilities as explicitly appropriated in order to understand the Axial cultures as different attempts to make explicit what happens when living beings acquire a symbolic relationship to the world. Theoretic culture can thus be seen as a universal step in the development of humanity that is not restricted to the Axial cultures, while these cultures nevertheless take on a special importance since it was only there that the anthropological possibilities emerging with the invention of symbols were actually made explicit.

So far, my Brandomian ladder comprises only three rungs, and in the Donald/Bellah scheme there is no fourth. Donald himself has suggested that the invention of mass media and computational cognitive tools might be interpreted as a new phase in the erecting of external scaffoldings and thereby as a cognitive revolution. But even independently of how much influence we are willing to grant technologies in the development of Modernity, I would like to emphasize that the dynamics of reflective symbolic usage are not exhausted with the establishment of theoretic culture. I have so far distinguished three stages in the process of making it explicit: (1) meaning embodied in mimetic practices, (2) the prereflective use of symbolic language in narrative-mythological culture, and (3) its reflective turn in theoretic culture. When theoretic culture emerges, the logical powers of symbolic languages are put to use to make explicit the inferential relations between the discursive commitments implicit in what we have said or are willing to say. This is what Brandom calls "rational"[15] expressivity. When rational expressivity is used to make explicit what is implicit in its own performances, "logical"[16] expressivity emerges, the use of reason for reasoning about reason (4). I am tempted to point out the parallels between this fourth rung of the ladder of explication and the condition of Modernity. Such an interpretation would underline the continuity between the Axial Age, in which the intertwined character of transcendence and contingency came to be experienced for the first time, and the consciousness of both universality and pluralism that has manifested itself in Modernity. But the main line of my argument does not depend on the plausibility of these tempting parallels; rather, it rests on an interpretation of the Axial Age as an important move in the self-explication of embodied symbol-users. This raises another question that I regard as being of the utmost anthropological importance: How are the rungs of the ladder related?

Three Models of Sequentiality

The ladder metaphor I have chosen suggests an ordered sequence and some sort of cognitive gain involved in mounting the higher rungs. But aside from this, it is open to various interpretations: Does having mounted the ladder make its lower rungs obsolete, as implied in Wittgenstein's famous picture at the end of his *Tractatus* about finally throwing away the ladder? Or is it rather the case that even reflective propositional language embodies and presupposes earlier versions of sign-usage? The answer to this question is closely connected to our judgments about the impact of the Axial Age. If, as I have argued, the Axial breakthrough consisted in the reflective explication of possibilities already implicit in the mastery of symbolic language, its relevance lies precisely in the combination of historical contingency, pertaining to path-dependent developments, and anthropological universality, pertaining to the evolution of cognition describable as climbing the ladder of explication. About the evolutionary processes that finally brought about the unlikely feat of symbolic reference we can only guess. Deacon speculates, interestingly enough, about the advantages "the regulation of reproductive relationships by symbolic means"[17] might have offered for solving the socio-ecological dilemma of hunting as a strategy for subsistence. But given the availability of semiotic means for indirect reference, it was a question of contingent historic development, not of anthropological necessity, that those means, tens of thousands of years later, were used to make explicit the transcendence of the symbolized over the symbol itself more or less simultaneously and in at least four different regions of the world. Thus part of the fascination of the Axial Age stems from the fact that it marks the point of convergence where historical and evolutionary anthropology meet. My thesis is that when comprehensive worldviews were formed in the Axial cultures, the problem of the relation of symbols to other signs, of language to meaning embodied in the iconicity of feelings and the indexicality of direct interaction, gained a new urgency. (Obviously this way of describing it is a retrospective and hopefully a helpful framework from the standpoint of philosophical anthropology, not the operative language of the Axial Age. The problem I am hinting at can be seen on the level of content in new opinions about the relation between king and state, in a new assessment of the importance of rituals, in the formation and codification of Holy Scriptures, etc., but it is also prominent in the prohibition on images in Exodus and Deuteronomy, which in my view relates to semiotic transcendence.)

On Bellah's principle "nothing is ever lost," it seems evident that the theoretic culture of the Axial breakthrough proceeded in dialogue with mythic culture, which is already symbolic in terms of linguistic capabilities, but less so in terms of its generalized worldview. Mythic culture was itself largely based on the sensory-motor mimetic culture, which in turn relied upon the qualitative immediacy of episodic culture. To further clarify the interdependencies at work here, I suggest distinguishing three different explanations of this sequence, *the supplemented Enlightenment scheme,* the *hybrid-mind scheme,* and the *holistic-difference-plus-continuity scheme.*

The first scheme highlights the gain in rationality and the aspect of liberation implied in the transition from direct to indirect reference, and I find its best expression in Jürgen Habermas's commentaries on the Axial Age. For him, the first commandment signifies, above all, *emancipation:* "Philosophically, the momentous cognitive spurt of the Axial Age is captured in the First Commandment—the emancipation from the chain of lineages and the arbitrariness of mythical powers. Back then, the great world religions . . . reached straight through the uniformly even plain of narratively linked contingent appearances and tore open the rift between the deep and the surface structure, between essence and appearance, that first gave humanity the freedom of reflection, the power to distance themselves from the swaying immediacy."[18] Once again the important question is: How exactly should the liberating transition from the contingencies of qualitative immediacy and narrative structure to reflective thought be conceptualized? The literal meaning of Habermas's formulation leaves it open whether the transition lies in reflective rearticulation and thus reappropriation of particular identities or in their abolishment in favor of freestanding discourse, while the negative connotations of Habermas's metaphors suggest that "swaying immediacy" and the "even plain of narratively linked contingent appearances" are somehow left behind when the cognitive ladder of explication has been climbed. But Habermas realizes—and that seems to distinguish him from Brandom's expressive rationalism—that the gains of propositional and logical clarity on the higher rungs of the ladder entail a loss in expressive powers as well. Thus he supplements the classic Enlightenment perspective insofar as he constantly stresses the importance and indispensability of cultural traditions as "semantic resources" that await "translation" or that can never be translated into propositional discourse. This picture concedes the embodiment of semantic practices, but the philosophical emphasis is almost entirely on the indirect reference of symbolic discourse, which is also seen as the normative foundation of ethics.

The Enlightenment scheme with its emphasis on rationality accentuates the categorical difference of human cognition from the earlier rungs of my ladder. In Donald's books—and in Bellah's work on religious evolution, as far as he follows Donald—we find a different picture. On the one hand, Donald's evolutionary account of human cognition constantly underlines the continuity with other life-forms and the shared ancestry with other mammals; on the other hand, he depicts the evolution of collective conscious abilities as "the great hominid escape from the nervous system."[19] Qualitative immediacy is seen as something shared across species ("the raw feeling of being human is probably not qualitatively different from the raw feeling of being any kind of primate"),[20] but we also vastly transcend the biological realm through our cultural devices, shared cognitions, and external scaffoldings. Thus the unity of human consciousness is conceptualized as a functional unity comprised of several layers or concentric rings, and the dominant metaphor is "hybridity." "We are hybrids, half analogizers, with direct experience of the world, and half symbolizers, embedded in a cultural web."[21] From the vantage point of the *hybrid-mind scheme* adopted by Bellah, the evolutionary sequence is seen as the acquisition of new layers that functionally integrate the previous capabilities on the level of the organism without essentially changing it. The bonds between embodied and symbolic components of experience are stronger than in the classical or the supplemented Enlightenment scheme, but still the layers are seen as independent. Hybridity connects logically and factually independent entities, like in a hybrid car, where the combustion engine and the electrical one are functionally integrated in order to produce ecofriendly locomotion without being essentially related to one another. I am convinced that the hybrid-mind scheme still underrates the holistic nature of our embedded semiotic relation to the world. And since, as I have argued, the Axial development of second-order thought should, on the semiotic level, be understood as the conscious appropriation of symbolicity, this is potentially misleading when the impact of the Axial cultures is at stake.

What we need, then, is an anthropological scheme that does justice both to the fact that symbol-usage transforms a being's relation to its environment holistically, in *all* its aspects, and to the evolutionary continuity implied in the transitions that Donald describes. Such an account, which I have somewhat clumsily called the *holistic-difference-plus-continuity scheme*, helps us to understand how the discovery of transcendence simultaneously gave rise to a new awareness of embodiment, thus generating a dynamic tension between transcendence and embodiment that has characterized cultural developments since then and that has gained new momentum in Modernity. On this view, the climb up the ladder of explication in phylogeny and ontogeny not only entails the mastery of higher semiotic competences on each rung, which presupposes the earlier ones, but also the qualitative alteration of episodic, mimetic, and mythic culture as they become functional elements within a holistic structure. To my knowledge, it was the tradition of expressivism from Johann Gottfried Herder and Wilhelm von Humboldt to Wilhelm Dilthey, later given an evolutionary turn by the American pragmatists, that first developed such an account. In his book *The Symbolic Species*, Deacon refers to an important part of this tradition, the semiotics of Peirce. For Deacon, the "unbroken continuity between human and nonhuman brains" coexists with a "singular discontinuity between human and nonhuman minds,"[22] since we are the symbolic species. Symbolicity constitutes something genuinely new, namely indirect reference, but it is based on the direct reference embedded in the signs for communication that other mammals and especially primates use as well. And being "based on" for Deacon does not just mean presupposing it, but functionally integrating and thus altering it. Taking up Peirce's trichotomy of icon, index, and symbol, Deacon recognizes that there exist simple forms of communication based on similarities of which organisms are qualitatively aware, and I associate that with Donald's episodic culture. Mimetic culture is based on the sensory-motor coupling of the communicating organisms and on established indexical reference, correspondences between *types* of events. According to Deacon, in the functional hierarchy of semiotics it presupposes iconic reference in the same way as the symbolic reference of mythic and then theoretical culture presupposes both icons and indices. And that means that meaning is always embodied. Icons are rooted in qualitative awareness and indices in the regularities of motor-exchange with the environment. The indirect reference of symbols enables its users to transcend the local limitations of embodiment and thus allows for the discovery of the transcendent and universal. But this type of reference is never freestanding; it always relies on embodied relationships to the world in order to establish itself and to distinguish transcendent meaning, however problematic, from the mere flight of fancy. "Language," as Gallagher has aptly put it, "transcends embodiment at the same time that it depends on it."[23] The point of the holistic-difference scheme is that the genuinely new character of symbol-usage as transcending the local environment—the "difference" part—comes not from the abandonment but the functional reintegration of embodied relationships to the world—the "holistic" part. Accordingly, if we see the Axial cultures embedded in the framework of cultural evolution suggested here, we arrive not just at a multilayered cognitive architecture but an intricate entanglement between the three types of signs and the corresponding cultures. It is my conviction that we need this holistic notion of entanglement if we are to understand the dynamics of the Axial cultures. The following two examples should demonstrate why I consider the framework sketched above helpful for this enterprise.

Two Examples from Israel and the Christian Tradition

My first example is taken from Bellah's discussion of the Axial breakthrough in Israel, which he connects with the books of Exodus and above all Deuteronomy. The historical background, as Bellah points out, is one of "unparalleled violence":[24] the northern kingdom already destroyed, Judah in a vassal relation to Assyria. It was against this background that the idea of a covenant between Yahweh and his people developed, modeled on the vassal covenants widespread in the Near East, but transcending it by rejecting sacral kingship. Two aspects of Bellah's interpretation are of special importance: the invention of a "portable religion" and the ambivalent figure of Moses. When in Deuteronomy 4 the occupation of the promised land is made dependent upon the observance of the divine law and the latter identified with the text itself, the indexical relations between a people and a promised homeland are made contingent upon the symbolic, inferential relations established horizontally in the text itself. The prohibition on images found in the same chapter fits perfectly into this framework of inverting the bottom-up order of reference. Pictures are icons which, when used in the service of representation, gain an indexical structure: the present picture stands for the absent entity. Accordingly, one plausible way to understand the prohibition on images is to see it as the prohibition of iconic and indexical reference insofar as they are not imbedded in the framework of indirect, symbolic reference, which allows for an articulation of the difference between sign and signified. The decisive lines seem to be Deuteronomy 4:15: "... for ye saw no manner of similitude on the day that the LORD spake unto you in Horeb out of the midst of the fire." Thus it is not permitted to reiconify symbolic meaning.[25] In the overall structure of Deuteronomy, it seems that the truth contained in the inferential network of the text and its normative performance through living by the law are the necessary preconditions of the "lower" indexical truth, namely possession of the promised land.

This creates a portable religion, in which the umbilical cord to a particular form of physical existence is not cut but stretched and made contingent upon a normatively structured way of living. This produces an inevitable tension: for the inversion of the order of justification, so to speak, from direct experience to norms explicit in symbols, can only be accomplished in the name of direct experience. Local experiences, embodied in feelings and in physical interaction, concisely summarized in unifying narrations, form the motivational backdrop to the development of the idea of a covenant signified not indexically but only symbolically. But even this move to transcendence cannot rid itself of the impact of embodiment; it only virtualizes the promised land. In the Hebrew Bible, this tension between the portability of religion and the local context of its emergence and its hopes for the future is made explicit in the intermediate setting of Deuteronomy's narrative: the exodus has already taken place, the promised land not yet been reached. In the interim, which is the temporal structure of religious experience, the indexical relations relate to a formative past which had to be left behind—Egypt—but as it concerns the future, they are replaced by merely symbolic relationships to the promised land.

The same structure can be found in the figure of Moses, whose leadership in embodied religion is confined to the way out of Egypt and who himself only points (indexically) to the promised land, the direct reference of religious experience, but never qualitatively experiences it, receiving instead the revelation of the Word. This revelation is strongly connected with violence, which permeates the experiential background of the Mosaic narration, and he acts violently himself. In Exodus 32, immediately after having received the two tablets, Moses proceeds to order the sons of Levi to kill three thousand men after the prohibition on images was broken. But this is not the whole story: Bellah refers to Michael Walzer's discussion of the two faces of Moses as a leader: the Leninist and the social-democrat, the first seen in acts like that mentioned above, the second in his reform work as a teacher and a prophet. My thesis is that this deep and disturbing ambiguity reflects the semiotic ambiguity of the discovery of transcendence: the internal relation between transcendence and contingence, which has been a source of violence ever since.

Transcendence on the level of content is inevitably coupled with the experience of contingency, because the move from local indexicality to universal symbolicity can never be a substitution, as I have tried to show above, but only a functional reframing of the earlier forms of reference based on physical interchange and direct experience. As Hans Joas and Bellah put it in the proposal for the conference this essay was originally written for, in each of the Axial cases an "appreciation of the particular history and cultural tradition had to be reconciled, however uneasily, with the aspiration for religious and ethical understandings that would be universally human."[26] The contingency of local beliefs and cults, as long as these were articulated in a language that, albeit already symbolic in structure, focused on narrative summaries of embodied feelings and practices only, remained hidden for the people engaged in them and can only be seen from the third-person perspective. But in the course of the Axial breakthroughs the quest for universal content could reveal not only the *contingent contingency*, so to speak, of the older, polytheistic worldviews which were to be overcome, but also the *necessary contingency* of the new, monotheistic articulations of meaning.

I am convinced that the proclivity to violence, which Jan Assmann sees as the hallmark of the "Mosaic distinction" between pairs of predicates like universally true and *toto coelo* false etc. is closely connected to this uncertainty that inevitably accompanies universal aspirations. The Bible offers ample proof of the resulting violent quest for certainty, even if most of it took place on the narrative rather than the factual level. Assmann definitely has an important point to make here, but there is another side to the coin as well, which we can see symbolized in Moses the reformer.

In his account, Bellah emphasizes that Moses was a teacher and prophet, not a king, and that at the heart of the stories surrounding him is the search for a new kind of political community in which kingship is stripped of its religious connotations and the covenant between a people and God provides the rules of living. This is a decisive move beyond the traditional identification of God and king, and it can be understood as a forceful expression of the consciousness of transcendence. And if I am right in insisting that the price to be paid for the elevation of local deities to universal transcendence consisted in a corresponding and unsettling rise of the consciousness of contingency, the other side of monotheistic intolerance becomes visible: an ability to acknowledge the limited nature of the symbols in which the experience of transcendence is articulated. Over the course of time, this led to ambitious theories of analogic expression, most prominently at the Fourth Council of the Lateran, where the relation between creator and created is determined as follows: "inter creatorem et creaturam non potest tanta similitudo notari quin inter eos maior sit dissimilitudo notanda."[27] All articulations of the transcendent thus inevitably produce inarticulacy—albeit a reflective one. In this manner, the grasp on universality is combined with the concession that all attempts to do so are in vain. The Fourth Council of the Lateran distorts this fascinating insight by not putting it to use self-reflectively and instead placing it within the rigid context of the damnation of heretics. Nevertheless, it is plausible to see the doctrine of analogy as a late result of a process that was triggered when the Axial cultures first experienced the entanglement of content transcendence with its semiotic counterpart.

A second example of this semiotic consciousness of embedded transcendence, the possibility of which is the result of Axial Age developments, can be found in the Gospel according to Matthew, in the parable of the weeds (Matt. 13:24–30). Wheat and weeds are planted together, and the field's owner refuses to let his servants pull the weeds out, "lest in gathering the weeds you root up the wheat along with them." This can be given a semiotic interpretation: since the transcendent good is only accessible through symbolic meanings permeated with contingency, and since there is no way to tell the similar and the dissimilar parts of the analogy apart, it is wise to be tolerant and refrain from constructing dualisms.

Rainer Forst has argued[28] that this is one of the main passages in the Bible that support Christian tolerance, but that the parable nonetheless remains embedded within a violent picture of the Judgment Day, and thus shows the ambivalence of the Christian arguments for tolerance. Forst's interpretation is convincing to a great extent and makes it very clear how closely the quest for certainty and the acknowledgment of its opposite can be intertwined, and how often they are. However, it should be amended in two important points: first, the eschatological framing of the parable with its violent language ("fiery furnace," "weeping and gnashing of teeth," etc.) is at least partly due to the well-known rhetorical figure of depicting the worst in a drastic manner to keep it from happening. The images of doomsday violence are something more than and different from sadistic dreams of revenge projected into the future; they describe an outcome to be avoided by living righteously, which includes tolerance. Second, Forst argues: "All the reasons provided for horizontal tolerance presuppose that there is just as little doubt concerning the knowledge of the truth of God as there is about His authority and the coming of His final judgment. Tolerance is indebted to this knowledge of a higher truth and justice."[29] While I do not deny that tolerance was in point of fact often counteracted by such eschatological visions of divine intolerance, I still want to emphasize that the Axial discovery of semiotic transcendence also enabled a mode of thought in which, strictly speaking, there was no such thing as true knowledge of God, not even in revelation, because every sign had to be seen as revealing more dissimilarity from the signified than similarity. In the parable of the weeds, the tension between the demand for tolerance on the one hand and the revenge motifs on the other reflects the Axial tension between the universality of transcendent validity claims and the semiotic contingency of reflective symbol-usage.

In this respect, it is important to realize that the consciousness of semiotic contingency, even if it can only be made explicit in theoretical, second-order language as used for the first time in classical Greece (and also in the Fourth Council of the Lateran's doctrine of analogy cited above), may well be operative in narrative speech as well—long before and alongside its entry into propositional, discursive language. This is exactly what we should expect considering the time lag and the gap of historic contingency between developmental possibilities and their reflective appropriation. A closer examination of this point would require a semiotic account of the possibilities that narrative structures offer for a reflective stance that considers alternatives and frames reality within the context of possibilities. The use of parables—such as that of the weeds—to highlight similarities against a background of obvious differences and the accompanying analogical mode of thought would have to play an important role in such considerations, though that exceeds the scope of my essay. What my two examples were supposed to show was that both the story of Moses, carefully set in a context of transition, and the use of parables as a means of expression should be interpreted as instances of embedded transcendence—a form of symbol-usage which combines the experience of transcendent meanings with an implicit acknowledgment of both the inevitable difference between sign and signified and of the embodied setting in which it arose.

The Elementary Unit of Symbolic Explication: Anthropological Consequences

On the Brandomian ladder of "making it explicit" described above, the Axial breakthrough involves the internally connected discoveries of second-order thought and transcendence and thus belongs to its third rung. But "belonging" seems too weak a term, since it was only after and by means of this factual, contingent discovery that the possibility for metareflective thought on the fourth rung eventually emerged and thus enabled Modernity to construct ladders of explication at all. From this point of view, the anthropological impact of the Axial Age can be understood as the emergence of inchoate universals for the reflective self-appropriation of embodied symbol-users. The plural "universals" is fully justified here, because in each of the paradigm cases China, India, Israel, and Greece the relation between embodiment and transcendence was framed in a particular manner—but so is the talk about universality, for in each case the local starting point is transformed into comprehensive worldviews with universal aspirations. And the perennial tension between transcendent and mundane orders, between symbolic reference and corporeal experience, which emerged as the heritage of the Axial breakthroughs, reveals the semiotic structure of experience that is the hallmark of our "symbolic species." For this reason, the *holistic-difference-plus-continuity scheme* of anthropological development sketched above proves useful. It enables us to capture both the historical and logical sequentiality implied in the three moves from episodic to mythic to theoretical culture as well as the fact that "nothing is ever lost," as Bellah puts it. From an anthropological standpoint inspired by truth-conditional concepts of meaning focused on propositional content, Bellah's principle is far from evident, but in the evolutionary perspective opened up by Donald, it is. As Charles Taylor has convincingly argued in his well-known articles on theories of meaning and on the question of human action,[30] we need an expressivist anthropology to do justice to this embodied character of our relation to the world. Otherwise we are in danger of distorting the meaning of "making it explicit," by overestimating the expressive—not the reflective— powers of rational discourse, into "leaving us implicit." But feelings and embodied interactions are constitutive dimensions of meaning, not merely as vestiges of the evolutionary past, but as functionally indispensable components of symbolic communication.

In this regard the expressivist tradition increasingly fits with evidence taken from the cognitive sciences and neuroscience. Donald's books offer powerful support for this antireductionist stance, and Deacon has recently shown in great detail how the evolutionary formation and everyday operation of symbolic competences depend upon indexical relationships that are in turn dependent upon iconic relationships. The shift in mnemonic strategy that leads from learning sets of indices to grasping logical relationships between symbolic tokens enables indirect reference and in the long run makes the discovery of transcendence possible. But this indirect type of reference is a relation between tokens indexically related to instances of their use, and this use refers to instances of qualitative immediacy, direct experience. The outcome of all this is that nothing ever gets lost, but everything is changed forever when experience becomes mediated by symbolic competencies. What emerges in a theoretical culture is a holistic unity of behavior and semantic explication, in which the indirect reference of symbolic language is both enabled and restricted by embodied forms of signification working via direct reference. This functional holism and unity, however, is only one side of the coin; the other is the inevitable tension between the local and the universal aspects of meaning. And that implies that climbing the ladder of explication is both a loss and a gain. Greater reflexivity entails less qualitative immediacy and sensory-motor interaction, and iconic and indexical meanings cannot be translated into propositional discourse without loss.

For the remainder of this essay, I want to explore the consequences this anthropological framework has for our understanding of the Axial Age. I take as my starting point the relation between the embodiedness of symbol-usage and the cultural embeddedness of symbol-users. In his recent book,

A Secular Age, Taylor included a chapter titled "The Great Disembedding,"[31] which deals with the disturbing effects of the Axial revolutions on the triple pre-Axial dimensions of embeddedness: human good, social order, cosmos. As he points out, in early religion human flourishing was conceived of in terms of "prosperity, health, long life, fertility,"[32] which is to say as an abundance of natural goods and the fulfillment of natural desires. This "naturalistic" embeddedness of the human good into the corporeal well-being of the organism in its environment was itself embedded in a social order for which the "primary agency was the social group as a whole,"[33] not the individual. And finally, both dimensions were related to the ordered cosmos, because "in early religion, the spirits and forces with whom we are dealing are in numerous ways intricated in the world."[34] In this way, "human agents are embedded in society, society in the cosmos, and the cosmos incorporates the divine."[35]

To me it seems evident that the three dimensions of pre-Axial embeddedness correspond to different rungs on the ladder of explication and accordingly to different types of sign-usage. The naturalistic conception of the good emphasizes the importance of immediate, qualitative experience. As far as well-being on the physical level is concerned, what you feel is what you get, and semiotically we are on the level of iconic presentation. The primacy of the social group as an actor is reflected by the incorporation of the individuals in the quite literal sense of mutual integration of sensory-motor schemes, and this is what happens in collective ritual. Emerging from collective experience, rituals—here I follow the interpretation developed by Deacon—establish enacted, highly redundant sets of indexical relationships between the individual actors, the group, and the respective focus of the ritual and in that way play an important role in preparing the move from direct to indirect reference, which can only take place when a sufficient number of indexical relationships have already been established. When we finally reach the symbolic stage, indirect reference to everything, to the world as such, can be and actually is added. But as long as symbols are used within the range of immediate and group experiences only—and Deacon suggests that the evolutionary driving force for their development actually was the need to stabilize social relations connected with reproductive needs—their ability to transcend the local context of iconic and indexical meaning could not endanger the triple embeddedness which Taylor sees as the hallmark of "early" religion.

Mapping the features of this triple embeddedness onto the anthropological ladder of explications thus has two consequences. First, it shows that Taylor's triple embeddedness reflects the triadic structure of embodied sign-use and its development and functional integration from icons over indices to symbols. Second, and more important, it enriches our understanding of what Taylor calls "the Great Disembedding." This process plays a crucial role in his account of Modernity, and it is reconstructed in terms of the Axial revolution and its consequences in subsequent history. In Taylor's account, the triple move, at least in Latin Christendom, toward personal religion, social reform, and cosmological disenchantment is the "logical conclusion"[36] of the decontextualization that was implicit in the Axial revolution: the human good is no longer framed in terms of naturalistic well-being, society is no longer seen as a well-functioning social body, and the world is conceived of as different from its creator, in the same way as the transcendent referent of the sign differs from it. My thesis is that these undeniable processes of disembedding, since they all presuppose the reflective use of symbols, are not only still functionally related to the qualitative immediacy of feeling and the indexical structure of bodily interaction but inevitably produce *new modes* of direct reference, either internally or in accompanying countermovements. Symbol-users can escape embodiment only by reasserting it.

Lutheran Pietism is a good example.[37] It began with Luther's *sola scriptura*, a new affirmation of symbolic truth that represented a new thrust of post-Axial disembedding. This Lutheran move, seen, for example, in Johann Arndt's famous *Four Books on True Christianity*, becomes radicalized into the negation of the world achieved through the "Bußkampf" ("inner struggle of penitence") indispensable for salvation. And the negation of the world especially includes the pre-Axial, naturalistic conception of qualitative well-being. But the necessity to ground indirect reference in its direct forms reasserts itself and finally leads to an unprecedented emphasis on lived experience in its immediacy, to a craving for certain qualities of feeling alleged to authenticate the meaning of the scripture. In this way, the disembedding that can be seen in the emphasis on the individual, in doing away with mediating rites and institutions, etc., produces new and, so to speak, artificial forms of embodiment in lived experience. And the story does not end there, because the impossibility of recognizing the correct and thus salvational form of relationship between personal lived experience and symbolic meaning even reintroduced social mediation. When in 1670 Philipp Jakob Spener initiated the *collegium pietatis* in Frankfurt am Main, the piety of inwardness was supplemented with social interaction, and necessarily so, because there is no way to correlate symbolic and qualitative meaning without the mediation of intersubjectivity. As the example of Pietism shows, even the "Great Disembedding" can only rearrange the conditions of embodiment—it can never abandon them.

Notes

Wolfgang Knöbl read an earlier version of this essay. I am very grateful for his helpful comments.

1. See Heiner Roetz, *Confucian Ethics of the Axial Age: A Reconstruction under the Aspect of the Breakthrough towards Postconventional Thinking* (Albany: State University of New York Press, 1993), chap. 10.
2. Paul Ricoeur, *Das Selbst als ein Anderer* [*Soi-même comme un autre*] (Munich: Fink, 1996), 350 (my translation).
3. Merlin Donald, *A Mind So Rare: The Evolution of Human Consciousness* (New York and London: W. W. Norton and Company, 2002), 39.
4. Ibid., 10.
5. Ibid., xiv.
6. Robert N. Bellah, *Religion in Human Evolution: From the Paleolithic to the Axial Age* (Cambridge, MA: The Belknap Press of Harvard University Press, 2011), 13.
7. See Terrence W. Deacon, *The Symbolic Species: The Co-evolution of Language and the Brain* (New York and London: W.W. Norton and Company, 1998).
8. Robert Brandom, *Making It Explicit: Reasoning, Representing and Discursive Commitment* (Cambridge, MA: Harvard University Press, 1998), 644.
9. Donald, *A Mind So Rare*, 265.
10. See Shaun Gallagher, *How the Body Shapes the Mind* (Oxford: Oxford University Press, 2006).
11. Donald, *A Mind So Rare*, 274.
12. John Dewey, "Qualitative Thought" [1930], in Larry A. Hickman and Thomas M. Alexander, eds., *The Essential Dewey*, vol. 1: *Pragmatism, Education, Democracy* (Bloomington and Indianapolis: Indiana University Press, 1998), 195–205, here 197.
13. Donald, *A Mind So Rare*, 260.

14. See Andy Clark, *Being There: Putting Brain, Body and World Together Again* (Cambridge, MA: MIT Press, 1997), 45–47.

15. Brandom, *Making It Explicit,* 650.

16. Ibid.

17. Deacon, *The Symbolic Species,* 400.

18. Jürgen Habermas, *Zeit der Übergänge* (Frankfurt am Main: Suhrkamp, 2001), 185–186 (my translation).

19. Donald, *A Mind So Rare,* 305.

20. Ibid., 320.

21. Ibid., 157.

22. Deacon, *The Symbolic Species,* 13.

23. Gallagher, *How the Body Shapes the Mind,* 127.

24. Bellah, *Religion in Human Evolution*, p. 308.

25. I find this semiotic line of interpretation supported by recent research in biblical exegesis. See Christian Frevel, "Du sollst Dir kein Bildnis machen!—und wenn doch? Überlegungen zur Kultbildlosigkeit der Religion Israels" in Bernd Janowski and Nino Zchomelidse, eds., *Die Sichtbarkeit des Unsichtbaren: Zur Korrelation von Text und Bild im Wirkungskreis der Bibel* (Stuttgart: Deutsche Bibelgesellschaft, 2003), 23–48, here 45.

26. Robert N. Bellah and Hans Joas, *Proposal for a Conference to Be Held at the Max Weber Center of the University of Erfurt, July 3–4, 2008.*

27. Denzinger-Schönmetzer, *Enchiridion Symbolorum Definitionum et Declarationum de rebus fidei et morum,* 36th ed. (Freiburg: Herder, 1976), 806 (p. 262).

28. Rainer Forst, *Toleranz im Konflikt: Geschichte, Gehalt und Gegenwart eines umstrittenen Begriffs* (Frankfurt am Main: Suhrkamp, 2003), 65–66.

29. Ibid., 66.

30. See Charles Taylor, *Philosophical Papers 1: Human Agency and Language* (Cambridge: Cambridge University Press, 1985).

31. Charles Taylor, *A Secular Age* (Cambridge, MA, and London: Harvard University Press, 2007), 146–158.

32. Ibid., 150.

33. Ibid., 148.

34. Ibid., 150.

35. Ibid., 152.

36. Ibid., 146.

37. My interpretation is indebted to Magnus Schlette's philosophical reading of Pietism. See Magnus Schlette, *Die Selbst(er)findung des Neuen Menschen: Zur Entstehung narrativer Identitätsmuster im Pietismus* (Göttingen: Vandenhoeck & Ruprecht, 2005).

5

The Axial Age in Global History

Cultural Crystallizations and Societal Transformations

BJÖRN WITTROCK

The Axial Age denotes a series of profound cultural transformations that occurred in some of the major civilizations of the Eastern Mediterranean, the Near East, and South and East Asia in the centuries around the middle of the first millennium BCE. The term was coined by Karl Jaspers in a small book, *Vom Ursprung und Ziel der Geschichte*, which appeared in 1949.[1]

Jaspers, who at the time had played an important role, together with Alfred Weber and others, in trying to reconstitute the University of Heidelberg after the end of Nazi rule, erroneously believed he was using a term from Hegel's lectures on the philosophy of history. His objective, however, was not to reenact a version of Hegelian historicism. Instead the book, like Friedrich Meinecke's *Die deutsche Katastrophe* (1946), was an effort to rethink the intellectual legacy of Europe against the background of the complete human and cultural catastrophe of totalitarian rule, war, and the Holocaust. It was not an effort to abandon historical reasoning but rather to search for an understanding of history that did not take the European experience as the self-evident vantage point or the Christian idea of the birth of Jesus Christ as the only important turning point in history.

Perhaps one might read Jaspers' book as one of the first efforts by a leading European philosopher and intellectual to decenter our understanding of history and to prepare the stage for a view of history as a set of analogous quests within different civilizations that had hitherto been regarded in isolation from each other or as involved in conflict-ridden contestation. When historians today write about cultural encounters and entangled histories, they seem to owe a debt of gratitude to Jaspers' early contribution.

However, there were also a series of precursors to Jaspers, including Hegel, but also several thinkers in the eighteenth and nineteenth centuries, as well as Max and Alfred Weber and others in the early twentieth century. Jaspers himself was aware of this and paid homage not least to Alfred Weber. However, compared to most of his precursors and contemporaries, Jaspers' formulations were more explicitly aimed at overcoming a sense of European self-sufficiency. In this respect, his approach differed from Max Weber's sociology of the great world religions, first published in 1920 and 1921 in three massive volumes—undoubtedly one of the most fascinating comparative studies in the history of the social sciences.[2]

These volumes are full of empirical synthesis and comparative reflections, yet Weber's declared purpose is not to engage in a broad comparative analysis per se but rather to discover, in the study of non-European contexts, points of comparison to "our occidental cultural religions."[3] In fact, the whole introduction, *Vorbemerkung,* starts with a passage highlighting the specificity and unique character of Western science and then asserts the unique nature of the major societal institutions in the Occident that are ultimately constituted by a specifically Western notion of rationality. The very first question formulated by Weber in the introduction is: "which chain of conditions has entailed that precisely on the terrain of the Occident, and only here, cultural manifestations appeared, which, however,—as we like to imagine—were placed in a direction of development of *universal* importance and validity?"[4] The immediately following sentence then reads: "Only in the Occident is there *'science'* at the stage of development that we today recognize as 'valid.'"

The words "as we like to imagine" signal a skeptical stance toward such claims. However, it is probably not coincidental that Weber begins the collection with his famous analysis of the Protestant ethic and the spirit of capitalism. The achievements of the West implicitly serve as the point of departure for comparative reflection. This entails that comparative interpretations tend to be cast "in terms of the *absence* of certain preconditions."[5]

In the introduction Weber also ventures a number of statements about the unique nature of Western cultural, economic, political, and administrative institutions, as in the assertion that "the legally trained civil servant as carrier of the most important functions of everyday life has not been known in any country as in the modern Occident."[6] Against the background of our current knowledge of the history of, for example, China, a statement of this type may look untenable. More importantly, however, the key question is by which categories a comparative study of institutional and conceptual transformation across civilizations might be conducted. In this context, studies inspired by Jaspers' notion of the Axial Age have provided a number of categories that may be fruitfully applied in comparative and historical research beyond the Axial Age proper, and also in the study of deep-seated cultural and institutional transformations more generally.

One element in this type of analysis is the effort to link conceptual change to processes of sociopolitical transformations and upheavals. Another element is to explore different varieties of social formations both in ancient times and in the contemporary period. In this context, it has been argued that it is more fruitful and reasonable to discern different varieties of both modernity and axiality, "multiple modernities" and "multiple axialities," than to subsume significant variations under all-embracing categories.[7]

In the following, I shall propose a way of conceptualizing the nature of major societal transformations. I shall firstly outline some of the characteristics that Jaspers attributed to the Axial Age.

Secondly, I shall give a more systematic conceptualization of the changes in human reflexivity that occurred in the Axial Age.

Thirdly, I shall take up the problem of the societal and cultural background of the Axial Age transformations. In particular, I shall discuss the extent to which the cultural transformations entailed ruptures or continuities relative to earlier patterns of development.

Fourthly, the focus will shift to an analysis of the Axial Age per se. In particular, I shall indicate what I consider the main paths of development that emerged during this period in different parts of the Old World.[8]

An important question, which I can only indicate in this contribution, is whether it is possible to outline a comparative framework that may account for the cultural and societal transformations of the Axial Age across the different civilizations in which it emerged. I shall argue that this is indeed the case. There seem to be three key conditions for the emergence not only of the Axial Age but, more generally, for periods of deep-seated transformations that may be labeled periods of cultural crystallization. Essentially, these conditions refer to the destabilizing but also enabling conditions inherent in new economic opportunities and in the introduction of new technologies. In the Axial Age, such changes were often related to the introduction of tools and weapons based on iron production that eventually resulted in economic, agricultural, urban, and population growth—but also in warfare of a more violent nature with more pervasive consequences. Changes of these types have historically tended to exert a powerful pressure in the direction of new forms of social organization, including forms of inheritance, ownership, and production. A second class of conditions refers to the existence or at least widespread perception of political crisis or even crisis of civilized life itself. This may to some extent have to do with civil strife and conflict but also with imminent external threats. However, the possibility that a conjunction of economic-technological opportunities and of acute political and societal crisis will give rise to a profound rethinking that may open up fundamentally new institutional pathways crucially depends on the existence of fora, of some arenas where interpreters of new ideas may elaborate and articulate these ideas; in other words, on both the existence of a stratum of literati and of some degree of autonomy from central political power for a significant segment of this stratum of literati.

In the concluding section, I shall point to one major problem inherent in all comparative-historical research, and indicate how it might be addressed in the comparative study of conceptual and societal change that I defend.[9] In passing, I shall indicate some of the consequences of the research on the Axial Age for our conceptualization of later periods of cultural crystallizations and societal transformations, for example, the changes occurring in high cultures across Eurasia in the early second millennium CE or the formation of different varieties of modernity.[10]

The Idea of the Axial Age

In *Vom Ursprung und Ziel der Geschichte,* Jaspers argued that our understanding of history is related to the emergence and institutionalization of forms of critical reflexivity. Needless to say, this emergence is dependent on a range of human capacities, most fundamentally perhaps the emergence of language itself, but also that of external systems for the storage of human memory, notably the existence of systems of inscribing events in a form that allows for preservation and for retrieval at later points in time. Jaspers also recognized the complexity and sophistication of the long history of narrative accounts in the form of myths and of rituals associated with such myths.

However, the distinctive feature of the Axial Age was, Jaspers argued, the emergence of not only forms of thought that involved transpositions and variations of mythical narratives, but also new forms of thinking that clearly transcended the limits of existing practices of human society. The Axial Age entailed the possibility of humans giving expression to visions and ideas of the world beyond the constraints of existence at a specific time and place. For Jaspers, this marked the transition from *mythos* to *logos,* a breakthrough in critical reflection and indeed the emergence of history in the sense of the epoch in human existence characterized by a reflexive, historical consciousness.[11] Others, including Yehuda Elkana, have described this transition as the emergence of second-order reflexivity, that is, reflection on the forms and substance of thought itself. In other words, it had to be possible to reflect not only upon the course of day-to-day activities but upon the conditions of thinking itself.

In earlier tribal societies, the invocation and articulation of mythical beliefs in ritualistic practices would normally serve the social and cultural coherence of a collective. They would, of course, involve practices outside of the bounds of day-to-day practices of production and reproduction. They might also involve or usher in changes in the collective life of a community. In this way, myths could be reinterpreted and supplanted or even replaced by additional myths, as could imaginations about the primacy of different forces or divinities associated with the different forms of myths. However, this is only a question of continuation or partial adaption, not yet of a critical reflection and rejection of some myth by way of questioning its premises or engaging in a comparative exposition of its merits and shortcomings in a, say, Aristotelian, dialogical form. This started only in some societies in the Old World around the middle of the first millennium BCE.

In some, but not all, cases, this capacity for transcending the bounds of given reality and given beliefs was closely tied to the emergence of cosmologies that made an explicit and sharp distinction between a mundane and a transcendental sphere. In such cases, practices existing in a mundane sphere could be reflected upon and criticized as failing and deficient or even fundamentally flawed from the vantage point of requirements and demands imposed by a transcendental sphere. In this sense, Axial Age thinking had deep implications for the practices of the early states of archaic societies of Bronze and Iron civilizations. These early states involved rule over extensive territories and often a hierarchical order where new rituals emerged and supplanted those of earlier tribal societies.

These new rituals tended to be performed within relatively small elite circles and involved an articulation of the role of the supreme political ruler as embodying divine features. Inevitable societal misfortunes and catastrophic events could lead to cracks in the cosmology and practice of these early states as well as to elaborate processes of reinterpretation of myths, what some observers have termed mytho-speculation. However, the forms of thought that emerged in the Axial Age allowed for a principled critique of rulership; they prevented rulers, "kings," from being gods and subjected them to potential critique for not ruling properly according to the callings of divine grace or to the Mandate of Heaven.[12]

The idea of the Axial Age as outlined by Jaspers had the character of a bold idea briefly sketched. The same is true of earlier analogous statements by Alfred Weber and his brother Max, who in certain formulations came to venture very similar notions without using the term itself. Later, Eric Voegelin, with his own elaborate conceptual schemes, followed a similar line of reasoning in his magnum opus *Order and History*. In the 1970s, the Harvard sinologist Benjamin Schwartz and a group of prominent scholars, including Peter Brown, Louis Dumont, Eric Weil, and Robert Darnton, took up the notion of the Axial Age in a path-breaking special issue of the journal *Daedalus*, devoted to the theme "Wisdom, Revelation, and Doubt: Perspectives on the First Millennium BCE."[13]

However, the scholar who "has done more than anyone to make the Axial Age significant for comparative historical sociology"[14] is Shmuel Noah Eisenstadt. Together with the leading Weberian scholar Wolfgang Schluchter, Eisenstadt made it the focus of a sustained research program. In collaboration with a large number of historians and linguists, Eisenstadt extended the analysis considerably. In fact, it is largely due to him and to Robert Bellah that humanistic scholars in fields such as Egyptology, Assyriology, Sanskrit studies, history of religion, Sinology, and many others have come to gain respect for and interest in historical social science. It is also due to Eisenstadt and Bellah that the idea of the Axial Age has in later years come to be center stage in social science debates and theorizing with theoretically orientated scholars such as Jürgen Habermas, Hans Joas, José Casanova, and Charles Taylor now deeply engaged in the dialogue about the Axial Age.

Bellah and Eisenstadt represent different intellectual styles, but both of them have been crucial in transmitting to the scholarly community at large a strong sense of the intellectual urgency of the debates around the idea of the Axial Age. This idea has been the subject of an increasingly intense but also increasingly well-informed debate, involving ancient historians, historians of religion and philosophy, and linguists.[15] As a result, the Axial Age debate emerged as one of the great scholarly discussions of the last century.[16]

A Systematic Conceptualization of the Axial Age

The concept of the Axial Age in Jaspers' original formulations encompasses deep-seated intellectual and cosmological shifts that occurred in different forms but with striking, if relative, simultaneity in some societies across the Eurasian hemisphere, specifically in ancient Israel, Greece, India, and China. These shifts were manifested in such different forms as the thought of Confucius and, two centuries later, Mencius in China, Buddha in India, the Hebrew prophetical movement, and the classical age in Greek philosophy. Neither in Jaspers' early formulations nor in the more recent ones by scholars collaborating with Shmuel Eisenstadt has there been an entirely successful effort to relate these cosmological shifts to other types of human activities. Maybe the most important direction in future research will be to spell out the links between the set of intellectual and cosmological breakthroughs and the sea-changing institutional transformations that a limited sense of the concept of the Axial Age denotes.

Jaspers' position rests on the assumption that in the centuries around the middle of the first millennium BCE a major shift occurred in the way reflectively articulate human beings in some of the high cultures in the Eurasian hemisphere reconceptualized their existential position. The breakthrough was manifested in different ways in the different civilizations. However, in all forms it involved the textual articulation of an increasing human reflexivity and *reflexive consciousness,* the ability to use reason to transcend the immediately given. This reflexivity was manifested in dramatic shifts in four major dimensions:

- Firstly, an elaboration of more reflective cosmologies, often in terms of positing a more or less fundamental and discursively argued separa-

tion between a *mundane* and a *transcendental sphere*. This also involved an *articulation* and *interpretation* of such cosmologies in terms of their oral mediation as well as their textual *inscription,* and the emergence of a set of rules for the authoritative interpretation of such texts. Such processes of codification and standardization inevitably entailed breaches with some previously coexisting set of beliefs and practices. They also entailed the potentials for new interpretative contestations. This set the stage not only for the articulation and diffusion of orthodoxy but also for heterodox challenges.
- Secondly, the articulation and inscription of an increasing *historical consciousness,* an awareness of the temporal location and the limitations of human existence and thereby a sense of relative contingency.
- Thirdly, new conceptualizations of social bonds and connectedness, that is, imaginations of what might be called sociality.
- Fourthly, an increasing awareness of the *malleability* of human existence, of the potentials of *human action* and human agentiality within the bounds of human mundane temporality or, as in the case of Iranian culture, with respect to the relationship between actions in a mundane and a transcendental sphere. Conceptualizations of agentiality became increasingly premised on more individualistic assumptions than had previously been the case.

This, I maintain, is a valid description even if this core of the meaning of the Axial Age in its original formulation has subsequently been elaborated in various ways. It is important to see that any particular articulation of a position on any of these existential dimensions will inevitably involve some assumptions that are contextually bound and culturally specific. It would, for instance, be illegitimate to tie the meaning of the Axial Age to an insistence on the occurrence of some specific cosmology, say, premised on notions of transcendence as opposed to immanence, or on some specific account of the dramatic increase in historical consciousness that we associate with the Axial Age. What is not culturally specific is the idea that the Axial Age is a period of deep change in fundamental dimensions of human existence, namely radical shifts, as textually manifested, in reflexive consciousness concerning *cosmology, historical consciousness, and conceptions of sociality and of human agency.*

This change is broadly contemporaneous across vast regions of the Old World. It entails the consolidation or the emergence of a set of different cosmologies and makes possible a set of different institutional paths of development of lasting importance.

For all contestations about historical accounts, such a delimitation of the notion of the Axial Age provides not only a fruitful starting point for the study of global history and for an understanding of its relevance to the social and human sciences at large. Such a conceptualization has the additional advantage that it is not based on an unjustifiable teleology or some form of cultural imposition.

Some interpretations, most notably those of Merlin Donald and Bellah, highlight the Axial Age as the beginning of a fourth evolutionary stage in the development of human culture, coming after the earliest forms of human interaction in so-called episodic culture, mimetic culture, and, with the development of language and the possibility of constructing "a unified, collectively held system of explanatory and regulatory metaphors," a "comprehensive modeling of the entire human universe" in so-called mythic culture.[17] The Axial Age in this type of evolutionary scheme represents a fourth fundamental stage marking the so-called theoretic age that allows for a new type of critically reflexive activities complementing those of bodily reactions and mimetic imitation and gesturing, and those of mythical narratives.

The Cultural and Societal Contexts of Axial Transformations

One problematic question is that of the relationship of societal and cultural formations before and after the so-called Axial breakthrough. Jaspers argued that the Axial Age constitutes the origin of history, in the sense of the history of human beings who have consciously reflected on their own location in temporal and cosmological terms and tried to form their own existence from the vantage point of such reflections. This is an argument that might easily be read so as to deny the historicity of previous civilizations in a way that cannot be made compatible with available historical and archaeological research. However, there is no need to draw such a drastic conclusion. In fact, virtually all scholars after—and before—Jaspers have taken great care to elaborate on the nature of the societal predecessors of Axial Age civilizations. Most of these scholars have tended to highlight the degree to which the transformations of this age have to be seen as continuations and intensifications of features inherent in earlier cultures and societies.

Several of the contributors to the volume on *Axial Civilizations and World History,* for example, have highlighted the fact that in China, Greece, and the Near East a key factor behind the dramatic increase in reflexivity and critical discussion may have been precisely the breakdown of the established practices and assumptions prevailing in earlier civilizations. Whether we look at Egypt, Greece, Mesopotamia, or China during the Shang and Zhou empires, these civilizations clearly do not fall "outside of history." On the contrary, the Axial transformations involved significant continuities relative to these earlier civilizations.

Maybe the most fruitful way to approach this *problematique* is to focus on the relationship between two types of components: the interpretation and redefinition by key Axial Age writers of an imagined legacy of their own societies and civilizations, and their own linguistic strategies and conceptual innovations that often involve the generalization, or rather universalization, of key characteristics in their interpretations of these traditions. Thus the Confucian ethic is not a completely new conceptualization, but rather an articulation of a tradition, synthetic in its own ways, and the universalization of some of the most important virtues that had traditionally been seen as limited to the aristocratic strata. In this case, as in several others, axiality is a reaction to a new type of human condition where neither the structures of kinship and physical proximity nor those of a self-legitimizing empire suffice any longer to embed the individual in a context of meaning and familiarity.

Some preliminary observations can be put forward concerning the background of the Axial Age transformations:

Firstly, these transformations had as their background not tribal societies but the early states of archaic societies, that is, forms of political and cultural order with considerable spatial extension and with highly regulated forms of elite ritual linked to the center of political power.

Secondly, because of the extensiveness and centralization of political power and of cults and rituals linked to the center, there were inevitable and recurring strains and tensions that in themselves tended to engender conditions that were propitious for the kind of deep-seated transformations that the Axial transformations involved. Furthermore, some of the most powerful early states came to impinge upon and pose a threat to a range of neighboring societies. The Assyrian and Neo-Babylonian states are obvious examples, and the Achaemenid Empire in the Iranian, Near Eastern, Eastern Mediterranean, and Western Indic worlds, the most extensive political entity up till then, is perhaps the archetypical case in point. (In the Chinese case, the threat to life as it was known was to some extent, but much less than at many other points in time, related to nomadic incursions. Nevertheless, it had to do with the breakdown of political order and with upheavals and civil wars in the wake of the downfall of the Zhou dynasty and the threat this posed for orderly, civilized life.)

Thirdly, the Axial transformations were initiated and had their intellectual source of inspiration and articulation in sites outside the direct political center, where there was awareness of activities in the political center and where the consequences of these activities were tangibly perceived. These sites, however, were also peripheral enough to allow for a stratum of interpreters that could elaborate on alternative cosmologies in some degree of autonomy from the center. This crucial role of the interpreters, the "Träger," of a new worldview has been particularly emphasized by Eisenstadt.[18] The emergence of the world religions is also part of this *problematique.*

Fourthly, the relationship between the Axial Age and the emergence and diffusion of the great world religions has been extensively examined. The idea of such a relationship has been at the core of much reasoning concerning the Axial Age hypothesis. It seems undeniable that the intellectual and ontological shift, described in terms of a breakthrough, has important links to deep-seated shifts in religious practices. It is, however, also clear that the exact nature of such links is in many cases open to different interpretations. In the simplest and perhaps most succinct formulation, it could be stated that the great world religions had their origins in the Axial Age and that subsequent religious revelations and visions and their textual inscription, codification, and the religious movements they gave rise to, had the Axial breakthroughs as a necessary background.

It is also true that many previous forms of ritualistic practice were, in a different guise, continued in religious practice after the Axial breakthroughs. Furthermore, in the core epoch of transformation, the fact that the most important proponents of the transformations had a peripheral and heterodox position vis-à-vis mainstream cultural and political order led to an opening of horizons and the emergence of a variety of critical voices. Eventually, however, the Axial ruptures were either marginalized or else given a standardized form and became more or less closely tied to new political centers and to new cultural-religious orthodoxies. But there still remained the potential for the emergence of new heterodox interpretations that could easily and rapidly take the form of a serious threat to central political power, no matter how closely linked the clerical and religious interpreters had become to that center.

Five Paths of Axial Transformations

In most interpretations of the Axial Age, a relationship is discerned between the Axial Age as a shift in cosmology and ontology, on the one hand, and the emergence of imperial-like political orders, on the other. This raises three questions that concern, firstly, the imagined nature of Axial- and pre-Axial Age political orders; secondly, the continuities of such orders; and thirdly, the consequences of the Axial breakthrough for political orders.

As to the first question, Jaspers' characterization of pre-Axial political orders in terms of "small states and cities" is not tenable.[19] On the contrary, as we have seen in the previous section, it was precisely the extensiveness and power of some of the early imperial-like states that constitute the background for the emergence of the Axial Age. In this section, I shall briefly and in schematic form touch upon the second and third questions.

As we have seen, it is possible to delineate a meaningful conceptualization of the Axial Age as an epoch in global history that involved profound shifts in at least four fundamental and inescapable dimensions of human existence, namely cosmology, historical consciousness, and the emergence of new conceptions of sociality and human agency. The Axial Age is not the only period where deep-seated shifts of this type occurred. It is, however, the most consequential cultural crystallization before the Common Era.

The redefinitions that characterize a period of cultural crystallization always occur in a given historical context. The practical and institutional implications of these shifts open up a range, though not an unlimited range, of new horizons of human practice. Thus while there is no one-to-one relation between a given shift in culture and cosmology and a particular institutional path of development, it is still possible to argue that in a given context some institutional paths are made conceivable, in a literal sense of the word, and others are not.

There are five distinctly different paths of Axial transformations linking cultural and cosmological shifts to institutional transformations, none of which should be given either empirical or normative preferred status. In the present context, I shall briefly outline their differences.

Firstly, there is the development in the Near East whereby, in a complex process of influence and juxtaposition, the Mosaic distinction (to use Jan Assmann's terminology) between true and false in religion and, as a consequence, a distinction between religion and politics is drawn in ancient Israel (but not, despite several preparatory steps, in ancient Egypt). Eventually, this distinction, in the prophetic age and in Second Temple Judaism, gave rise to a path of development that may be termed transcendental-interpretative.

Significant elements include processes of textual inscription and standardization as well as interpretative contestation and the interplay between carriers of orthodoxy and heterodoxy. The participants in these contestations exhibit a remarkable independence relative to political power. Sometimes this leads to a withdrawal from political power. However, more often their activities impinge upon the world of rulership, sometimes explicitly, sometimes inadvertently, sometimes as heterodox dissent or even rebellion, and sometimes as support for established power.

Secondly, there is a related path, fundamentally influenced by Near Eastern developments, but in key respects distinctly different. It is a tradition that gradually emerges in the Greek world and that may be termed a philosophical-political path of development. It involves contestation and deliberation that exhibit intense concern about human potentials and action, about the location of human beings in history, and constant reflection on the human condition. In this case, a clear distinction between a transcendental and a mundane sphere, absolutely central to the transcendental-interpretative tradition, is relatively insignificant. There is no standardized religious cosmology inscribed in codified texts. Instead, contestation is dialogical, if often textually transmitted, and has a philosophical and largely pragmatic character with regard to the political and moral life of a given community, a *polis*, as an inevitable reference point. The key protagonists in these contestations act in a context that is characterized by a previously unknown combination of intellectual independence, institutional autonomy, and political engagement.

Thirdly, there is the particular Chinese path that involves, at least from a period a millennium earlier than the Axial Age proper, the gradual merging and synthesis of different regional ritualistic practices and political orders in a broad cultural tradition that may be termed universal-inclusive. Key features of the cultural and political orders are clearly articulated hundreds of years before the Axial Age; in some respects, Confucius, Mozi, and later Mencius and the legalists write against the background of a perceived loss of cohesion, and indeed the demise of this earlier order, and seek a renewed articulation of it. Cultural and scientific developments can be and have been described as stepwise shifts, nevertheless they exhibit important ruptures and advances in the period of the Axial Age, as do certain aspects of political and social thought that show a renewed emphasis on tradition, history, and human agency.[20]

A fundamental feature of this path of axiality is that it is universal-inclusive but at the same time characterized by a high degree of contingency, even in the political sphere. Thus already in pre-Axial Zhou political thought the Mandate of Heaven transfers the ultimate legitimacy to political order. However, it is a revocable mandate and improper conduct is incompatible with the maintenance of this mandate. Therefore, heavenly sanctioned imperial rule is nonetheless contingent and open to doubt, critique, and potentially revolt. Similarly, there is a synthetic cultural order composed of highly different original traditions, some of which may perhaps best be understood as forms of moral philosophy, and two of which, Confucianism and Daoism, have little if any concern for a distinction between transcendental and mundane spheres. Precisely for this reason the universal-inclusive path of the Sinic world allows for and involves constant philosophical contestation between different traditions. In a sense, a Mosaic distinction need not be drawn in a context where the relationship between political and religious order has always been much more open-ended than in the early Near East polities of Egypt and Mesopotamia.

Fourthly, in India early Buddhism constitutes an Axial challenge to Vedic religion.[21] This challenge involves, through a process of semantic appropriation, transvaluation, and contestation, a focus on history and agentiality, and thereby brings out the potentials of a critical stance toward what are no longer seminaturalistic practices but rather conventions that may be transgressed.

It is precisely in reaction to this challenge that an articulation of Vedic religion occurs. The Indic world of Vedic religion may have been distinctly non-Axial, but Vedic religion could not avoid an engagement with the cultural systems that grew out of the early Axial transformations. Whereas the philosophical-political axiality of Greece and the universal-inclusive axiality of the Sinic world had political order as its explicit or implicit center of attention, the political implications of the Indic path—let us call it pluralistic-semantic—largely remained potential or entirely contingent (with the possible exception of the Maurya Empire under Ashoka).

Fifthly, the geographical and political space where all of the major traditions of Eurasia actually interacted is the area of the Achaemenid Empire and its Hellenistic and Iranian successors. In many ways, cultural traditions in the Iranian lands came to serve as direct or indirect sources of inspiration for several of the world religions and imperial orders. However, knowledge of key aspects of religious and even political practices not only in the Achaemenid Empire but also the Sassanian Empire is lacking. Nevertheless, the path of development in the Iranian lands may be termed one of a dualistic-agential tradition, where the relationship between political and religious order is seen as one of mutual dependence and close interaction, where there is a distinction between a transcendental and a mundane sphere, but where the battles within these spheres have direct implications for all actions in the mundane sphere.

It is a tradition with an articulated cosmology, but in its dualistic conceptualization of this cosmology it differs fundamentally from the cosmology of the mainstream of Judaism, Christendom, and Islam. This also means that the cosmological distinction between a transcendental and a mundane sphere is consistent with a strong this-worldly orientation of practical engagement and action in the realm of political order. The relationship of the main intellectual-religious carriers of this cosmology to political power is characterized by proximity and reciprocal dependence. As in other forms of axiality, there are also forms of heterodoxy and dissent. However, on the whole, there is a more explicit and direct link to imperial power here than is found along the other paths of axiality.

The Achaemenid Empire came to exert a far-reaching influence on later types of imperial orders in the region of the Mediterranean and the Near

East. In the first millennium CE, the Sassanian Empire saw itself as the legitimate heir of the Achaemenid Empire.

The Byzantine Empire—for half a millennium the main competitor of the Sassanian Empire in the Eastern Mediterranean and Near Eastern region—with its Hellenistic and urban legacy was structurally different from the Sassanian Empire. However, from the seventh century onward and as a result of the loss of rich urban centers in Syria and Egypt in the wake of the original Islamic onslaught, it increasingly came to exhibit many features reminiscent of the Iranian imperial model. This was so in terms of changes in military-territorial organization in a direction that in medieval Western Europe came to be called feudal. It was also the case in terms of a gradual change in relationships between political and religious orders.

The Achaemenid Empire was the first imperial political order that was premised on an Axial cosmology and that involved a close reciprocal, but not symmetric, relationship between the leading representatives of political and cosmological-religious orders. The same is true for the Sassanian Empire and for the successor of that empire, namely the new Islamic political order, at least as it emerged with the establishment of the Abbasid Caliphate.

As was the case with the Roman Empire, the Achaemenid Empire was characterized by a tolerance toward minority cultures and languages. Unlike the Roman Empire, however, it did not engage in efforts to promote the language of the rulers, that is, Old Persian, relative to the language of other peoples of the empire. However, the Iranian empires, as well as the classical Roman Empire, involved elements of, to use Sheldon Pollock's term, ethno-transcendence, that is, the assignment of a crucial place in the imperial project to an ethnically defined people that is linked both to the temporal extension of empire and to its divine protection.

Both the Roman and Iranian imperial patterns are distinctly different from that of India, but also from the cultural-political order of ancient Israel and ancient Greece during the early Axial transformations—and of course also from that of non-Roman and non-Axial Europe. In both ancient Greece and ancient Israel, the position of the intellectual carriers of interpretative elaborations was characterized by greater independence relative to the holders of political power. This is one reason why it would be erroneous to assume a necessary relationship between axiality and imperial order. One

Table 5.1. Carriers of Axial thought and their role in different civilizations

Region of emergence	Cultural-cosmological focus	Relation to political power	Ethnolinguistic force
Ancient Israel	Transcendental-interpretative	Strong independence	Autonomous
Greece	Philosophical-political	Strong independence	Weakly ecumenical
China	Universal-inclusive	Weak dependence	Strongly ecumenical
India	Pluralistic-semantic	Strong independence	Weakly ecumenical
Iran	Dualistic-agential	Strong dependence	Ethnotranscendence cum linguistic pluralism

may indeed argue that the post-Axial imperial orders, while often embracing a cosmology of Axial origins, often involved severe institutional constraints and a reduction in intellectual autonomy for the carriers of Axial thought. Some of these points are summarized in Table 5.1.

The table highlights the three conclusions indicated above. Firstly, a qualitative increase in reflexivity, historical consciousness, sociality, and agentiality is characteristic of the Axial Age and is the very premise for the distinction between political order and religious-cultural order and hence for the possibility of a challenge to the legitimacy of political order. "Kings can no longer claim to be gods." Once this possibility has been conceptually permitted, it is a potential that can never be "unthought," that is, the potential of a fundamental challenge of established order can never again be permanently removed. However, the cultural-cosmological construct that allows for such a distinction may, but does not need to, rest on a crucial distinction between the transcendental and mundane spheres. In fact, in four of the five paths of axiality this is not the case.

Secondly, the institutional position of the interpreters of a given cultural-religious cosmology determines whether the potentials of the increased reflexivity are being realized or not. Within each of the five paths of axiality, there was always interplay between orthodoxy and heterodoxy, and there were always contending articulations of a given cultural-cosmological order. Often, as in the cases of India and China, there was also contention between deeply different cosmologies. Even in the case of Sassanian Iran, Zoroastrian orthodoxy had always to contend with heterodox interpretations (Zurvanism, Mazdakism).

Thirdly, there is a complex interplay between three broad sets of factors that determine and release the potentials of a cultural crystallization, namely the confluence of a deep-seated political and cultural crisis; an imminent threat to the survival of a culture and its political manifestation; a surge of economic opportunities and potentials of growth; and the creation of arenas of articulation and interpretation with a relative distance and independence of immediate subjugation and subservience to political power.

There are also fundamental differences in terms of the ethnolinguistic force of the different paths of axiality. From the perspective of our own age, it is difficult not to reflect upon the fact that virtually all modern imperial orders exhibit a form of Roman, Eastern Mediterranean path rather than the less impositional path of other Axial civilizations, or the more ecumenical path of China. From the point of view of modern social thought and with the newly awakened interest in imperial orders, it seems that the study of the Axial Age, if nothing else, might serve an urgent need to broaden the range of imagination of modern social and political thought.

Meaning and Action in Historical Context

A perennial problem in historically orientated research is that of formulating criteria of adequacy for the assignment of meaning to historical phenomena. One broad category of such efforts is constituted by what is sometimes labeled historicism. As an encompassing term for a wide range of different historical research programs in the nineteenth and early twentieth centuries, it refers to a general tendency to see meaning as a category that is immanent in the historical process itself. The task of the historian is then to explicate or articulate this meaning by way of a historical reflection and reasoning that is able to grasp in its categories the essential nature of the historical process itself. Studies with a focus on the Axial Age have often been accused of engaging in a form of historicism whereby value is assigned to the outcome of historical processes to the extent that they are seen as teleologically defined achievements of human development. In this contribution, I have tried to demonstrate that such an assessment is not accurate. While it is true that a notion of the self-reflexivity of humanity is crucial to thinkers as different as Hegel and Jaspers, it is also clear that the study of global history in terms of cultural crystallizations cannot legitimately be characterized as a form of historicism.

Neither Jaspers nor Eisenstadt can be characterized as engaging in historicist reasoning. It is simply a non sequitur to draw the conclusion that the rejection of a teleological imposition of meaning onto historical processes also entails the rejection of any notion of meaning in historical processes. Why would meaning have to be a property that could only be ascribed to broad historical trends and their explications in abstract reason by a privileged group of interpreters, be they state philosophers or the political vanguard of historical progress? In some contemporary forms of reasoning it is asserted that there can be no assignment of meaning outside of the actual range of subjective perceptions of events. If so, historical research will not only begin but also end with a given multiplicity of subjective impressions and their linguistic expressions.[22]

Is there a way of avoiding both a teleological imposition of meaning and the reproductive fallacy of extreme subjectivism? One obvious alternative is the historical research inspired by speech act theory. This type of theory provides a method for reformulating questions of meaning in history as questions of language use in particular contexts. Texts and utterances will then be analyzed against the background of conventions of language use and canons of discourse that obtained in a given context. The problem is, however, to what extent such an analysis permits statements that go beyond the analysis of a range of particular speech acts.[23]

Most speech act theorists would probably say that this is a question that should be tackled pragmatically and as well as possible given our knowledge of conventions in given contexts. What cannot be handled in this way falls outside the realm of questions that can be posed from a scholarly point of view. This is reasonable enough, but it may not be sufficient for us to give a focus to such wider questions. In the field of social theory, Habermas solves the problem by elaborating a form of universal pragmatics that takes the most general preconditions of dialogical speech as its starting point. That is an obvious advantage for normative analysis but less so for empirical research, particularly of a historical nature.

It is here that scholars such as Jaspers and Eisenstadt raise important questions beyond those that most speech act theorists find interesting or indeed legitimate. Thus beyond the speech acts proper and beyond the given conventions, there are certain unavoidable dilemmas posed by our very existence as reflecting human beings. These existential dimensions pertain to the finitude of our own existence, to universal anthropological necessities of drawing boundaries between the inside and outside of a community, and of recognizing the temporal and social location of our own existence relative to that of others. This stance reflects basic properties inherent in reflexive human existence.

Our capacity to reflect upon our own situation entails the inevitability of a boundary between the world and ourselves; the world is no longer a seamless web from which we cannot even reflectively distance ourselves. This, of course, is what Jaspers saw as the origin of history, in the sense not of biological reproduction but of the self-reflexivity of humankind. Reflexivity entails the unavoidability of some boundary between inside and outside, no matter where this boundary is drawn and how it is constructed. Our realization of the finitude of our own existence entails a reflection on our temporal and historical location. These types of reflexivity and our realization of the existence of orderings in relations between oneself and other human beings entail the potential of concepts of changing states of the world, of what social scientists today would call agentiality. The idea of the Axial Age as a form of cultural crystallization involves precisely an analysis of shifts in the interpretation of such notions of human reflexivity and of their institutional implications.

Here, two statements of caution are necessary. Firstly, the recognition of these inevitable dimensions of reflexive human life does not entail any specific theory of meaning. It is compatible both with an analysis—as that of the Cambridge contextualists—that emphasizes the role of conventions and rejects that of hermeneutic interpretation, as well as a hermeneutic or historical intentionalist analysis. Secondly, the particular positions adopted along these phenomenological dimensions may of course vary dramatically across historical epochs and civilizations. A critic might then say that these dimensions are so general that they are of little interest or importance. Such a comment would, however, be mistaken. On the contrary, an analysis of this type has two invaluable characteristics. Firstly, it provides an analytical focus for the study of individual speech acts and contestations. I have suggested the term cultural crystallization to denote periods of fundamental reconceptualizations of positions on these phenomenological dimensions, leading to basic reconfigurations or reassertions of macroinstitutional practices. Secondly, an analysis in this vein opens up the possibility of reintroducing civilizational analysis into empirical historical research.

Ultimately, the cultural crystallizations that constitute formative moments in global history involve an institutional articulation and interpretation of the human condition, of what it means to conceptualize the finitude of our own existence in a world premised on assumptions of the potentially infinite malleability of the world upon which and into which our actions impinge, and of what historical existence may mean in such a world. As already argued, such a methodological stance does not presuppose an idealistic theory of history. On the contrary, the comparative materials at hand suggest that transformations and reformulations tend to be cast against the background of a profound crisis of established political order and of new possibilities in the realm of economic practices, including trends toward increasing productivity and growth in key sectors of the economy. However, they do presuppose, in order to become historically efficacious, arenas that grant at least a minimal degree of autonomy to intellectual practices, a certain protection from the powers-that-be to groups of literati who try to articulate conceptions of new societal arrangements or rather arrangements that are seen to safeguard key components of a cultural legacy or cultures of a threatened life-world.

This seems to be the case whether we focus on events during the so-called Axial Age or on the period in the tenth to thirteenth centuries when new macroinstitutional patterns emerged on the far Western and far Eastern edges of the Old World, that is, in Western Europe and in China during the Song-Yuan-Ming transition, or in Japan in the crucial period of the emergence of Japanese "feudalism."[24] It is also true for the period of the transition from early modern more or less absolutistic polities to other forms of order during the emergence of multiple modernities in the course of the eighteenth and nineteenth centuries. However, the institutional practices that emerged out of these formative periods were proposed on the basis of reinterpretations of social practices in terms of key dimensions of sociality, historical consciousness, agentiality, and cosmology by means of which human beings interpret their conditions of existence.

Finally, however, the ways in which various institutional projects were realized—or, to use another terminology, the ways in which promissory notes became institutional realities[25]—are protracted contestations and confrontations. The outcome of these contestations rests on the ability of different actors to draw on and mobilize available resources. However, resources themselves do not articulate institutional choices, only human beings do, and they do so in terms of what it means to be a human being with a finite existence and endowed with capacities to act in the world and to change it.

Notes

1. Karl Jaspers, *Vom Ursprung und Ziel der Geschichte* (Zurich: Artemis/Munich: Piper). English translation: *The Origin and Goal of History,* trans. Michael Bullock (London: Routledge & Kegan Paul / New Haven: Yale University Press, 1953).

2. Max Weber, *Gesammelte Aufsätze zur Religionssoziologie,* vol. 1: *Die protestantische Ethik und der Geist des Kapitalismus; Die protestantischen Sekten und der Geist des Kapitalismus; Die Wirtschaftsethik der Weltreligionen*—part I: *Konfuzianismus und Taoismus;* vol. 2: *Die Wirtschaftsethik der Weltreligionen*—part II: *Hinduismus und Buddhismus;* vol. 3: *Die Wirtschaftsethik der Weltreligionen*—part III: *Das antike Judentum* (Tübingen: J. C. B. Mohr, 1920–1921).

3. Weber, *Gesammelte Aufsätze,* vol. 1, 15.

4. Ibid., 3. The translations of these quotations from Weber's work are mine.

5. Said Amir Arjomand, "Transformation of the Islamicate Civilization: A Turning-Point in the Thirteenth Century?" *Medieval Encounters* 10, no. 1 (2004): 213–245, here 213 (italics in the original). The quotation refers to a broad tradition in the analysis of civilizations. The whole issue is also published in book form with the same editors as that of the triple issue, namely Johann P. Arnason and Björn Wittrock, *Eurasian Transformations, Tenth to Thirteenth Centuries: Crystallizations, Divergences, Renaissances* (Leiden: Brill, 2004); paperback edition, 2011.

6. Weber, *Gesammelte Aufsätze,* vol. 1, 15.

7. See, for example, the issue of *Daedalus* 129, no. 1 (2000), reprinted as Shmuel N. Eisenstadt, ed., *Multiple Modernities* (New Brunswick, NJ: Transaction, 2002).

8. The first four parts of the present contribution constitute a revised and extended version of my chapter "The Meaning of the Axial Age" in Johann P. Arnason, Shmuel N. Eisenstadt, and Björn Wittrock, eds., *Axial Civilizations and World History* (Leiden: Brill, 2005), 51–85.

9. This section draws on my contribution "Cultural Crystallization and Conceptual Change: Modernity, Axiality, and Meaning in History" to the Festschrift dedicated to Reinhart Koselleck, *Zeit, Geschichte und Politik / Time, History and Politics*, ed. Kari Palonen and Jussi Kurunmäki (Jyväskylä: Jyväskylä University, 2003), 105-134.

10. For a more detailed account, see Wittrock, "The Age of Ecumenical Renaissances," in Arnason and Wittrock, *Eurasian Transformations*, 41-73.

11. Jaspers' notion may be said to have some distant affinity with what Hegel proposed in his lectures on the philosophy of history, although both their styles of reasoning and their conclusions are quite different. Hegel's ascription of such a capacity, as in the case of Iran, has, perhaps unsurprisingly, caused much less attention and controversy than his denial of it in the case of India. As to these precise cases, both Jaspers and Bellah tend to take the opposite stance, whereas Max Weber in his discussion of the "prophetic age" includes both India and Iran in the analysis.

12. The Egyptologist Jan Assmann has, perhaps more consistently than anybody else, insisted on this point. He has highlighted the way in which Pharaonic Egypt was on the verge of an Axial breakthrough without ever fully achieving it. For a succinct statement of Assmann's position, see for example his "Axial 'Breakthroughs' and Semantic 'Relocations' in Ancient Egypt and Israel," in Arnason, Eisenstadt, and Wittrock, *Axial Civilizations*, 133-156.

13. *Daedalus* 104, no. 2 (Spring 1975).

14. Robert N. Bellah, "What Is Axial about the Axial Age?" *European Journal of Sociology* 46 (2005): 69-89, here 76. This article gives an excellent and succinct statement of Bellah's basic position and attests to his lasting contribution to the Axial Age debate.

15. This fact is most evident in the following publications edited by Eisenstadt: *The Origins and Diversity of Axial Age Civilizations* (Albany: State University of New York Press, 1986); *Kulturen der Achsenzeit I: Ihre Ursprünge und ihre Vielfalt*, part 1: *Griechenland, Israel, Mesopotamien*, part 2: *Spätantike, Indien, China, Islam* (Frankfurt am Main: Suhrkamp, 1987); *Kulturen der Achsenzeit II: Ihre institutionelle und kulturelle Dynamik*, part 1: *China, Japan*, part 2: *Indien*, part 3: *Buddhismus, Islam, Altägypten, westliche Kultur* (Frankfurt am Main: Suhrkamp, 1992).

16. In the recent past, efforts have been made to take stock of this debate and to indicate the long-term consequences and relevance of this debate to key problems in present-day historically oriented scholarship on major transformations of societies and civilizations. See especially Arnason, Eisenstadt, and Wittrock, *Axial Civilizations*. This effort is continued in the present volume.

17. Merlin Donald, *Origins of the Modern Mind: Three Stages in the Evolution of Culture and Cognition* (Cambridge, MA: Harvard University Press, 1991), 214.

18. See, for example, Shmuel N. Eisenstadt, "Cultural Traditions and Political Dynamics: The Origins and Modes of Ideological Politics," *British Journal of Soci-*

ology 32 (1981): 155–181; reprinted in Eisenstadt, *Comparative Civilizations and Multiple Modernities I* (Leiden: Brill, 2003), 219–247.

19. See Johann P. Arnason, "The Axial Age and Its Interpreters: Reopening a Debate," in Arnason, Eisenstadt, and Wittrock, *Axial Civilizations,* 19–48.

20. Christoph Harbsmeier, "The Axial Millennium in China: A Brief Survey," in Arnason, Eisenstadt, and Wittrock, *Axial Civilizations,* 469–507; Hsu Cho-yun, "Rethinking the Axial Age—The Case of Chinese Culture," in Arnason, Eisenstadt, and Wittrock, *Axial Civilizations,* 451–467.

21. See Sheldon Pollock, "Axialism and Empire," in Arnason, Eisenstadt, and Wittrock, *Axial Civilizations,* 397–450.

22. See Reinhart Koselleck, "Vom Sinn und Unsinn der Geschichte," *Merkur* 51 (1997): 319–334, here 324f.

23. I have taken up these issues extensively in my contribution to a Festschrift dedicated to Hans Joas: "Menschliches Handeln, Geschichte und sozialer Wandel: Rekonstruktion der Sozialtheorie in drei Kontexten" in Bettina Hollstein, Matthias Jung, and Wolfgang Knöbl, eds., *Handlung und Erfahrung: Das Erbe von Historismus und Pragmatismus und die Zukunft der Sozialtheorie* (Frankfurt and New York: Campus, 2011), 343–375.

24. See Paul Yakov Smith and Richard von Glahn, eds., *The Song-Yuan-Ming Transition in Chinese History* (Cambridge, MA: Harvard University Asia Center, 2003), and Arnason and Wittrock, *Eurasian Transformations*.

25. See my "Modernity: One, None, or Many?" *Daedalus* 129, no. 1 (Winter 2000): 31–60.

6

The Buddha's Meditative Trance

Visionary Knowledge, Aphoristic Thinking, and Axial Age Rationality in Early Buddhism

GANANATH OBEYESEKERE

Meditative Trance

Discussions of the great historical religions that developed during the Axial Age centered on their preoccupation with universal transcendental religious soteriologies and ethics that spilled over the confines of earlier small-scale societies. They also entailed a preoccupation with theoretical or conceptual thinking, an attempt to understand the world through the mediation of abstract concepts. I do not know how far these issues are relevant for all Axial Age religions, but they are perhaps true of most of them. However, it is also the case that *our* theoretical discussions could ill afford to neglect what I think is true of most of these religions, namely, an antecedent or consequent preoccupation with visionary experience and the derivation of knowledge outside of reason. Perhaps the neglect of visionary knowledge is due to our formulating Axial Age thinking on the model of Enlightenment rationality, particularly as it developed during the eighteenth and nineteenth centuries. While Axial Age visionary experiences have strong family resemblances to such phenomena as shamanism, spirit possession, and mediumship found in small-scale societies, the former tend to transcend the values of the local community and are articulated with transcendental salvific goals and ethics. These are some of the themes that I want to explore in relation to early Buddhism, using as my model the Buddha's own deep meditative trance, and focusing on the derivation of visionary knowledge during his so-called Enlightenment, a term that has European rationalistic resonances. For me the Pali term *bodhi* is best translated as "Awakening."

I begin with the well-known Buddha mythobiography where the Buddha-to-be (Bodhisattva) lives in luxury as a prisoner of hedonism confined to his father's palace, undistracted by the world's ills. He decides to leave the imprisoning palace with his charioteer, and during four consecutive visits he sees the "four signs": that of a feeble old man, a sick man, a dead man with relatives weeping over the bier, and finally the detached figure of a yellow-robed renouncer. Disillusioned with hedonism, the Bodhisattva comes to the royal palace, and there he sees the sleeping women of the harem in postures of disgust, snoring, with spittle forming around their mouths—the skull beneath the skin, as it were. He then finds that a son has been born to him. He steels his heart and, bidding his wife and infant silent farewell, leaves the palace for the "homeless" life because, it should be remembered, from the Buddhist viewpoint, the life of domesticity is also a kind of prison. Cutting off his hair and shedding his royal clothes for the vestment of the renouncer, he studies under ascetic gurus of his time, practicing extreme asceticism and body mortification. He has now become a prisoner of asceticism. Buddhist texts and sculptures vividly portray the emaciated and suffering Buddha who, the myth affirms, experienced a kind of death. Abandoning asceticism and adopting the "middle path," the Buddha moves from the banyan tree to the *bodhi* tree *(Ficus religiosa)* nearby, the tree under which he would achieve his spiritual "Awakening." Facing the East, again symbolizing a rising, he decides not to move until he finds out the truth of existence. The next mythic episode occurs when, meditating under the *bodhi* tree, he is assailed by Mara, Death himself (who is also Eros of the Buddhist imagination) waging war against the Buddha. This grand episode is described in graphic detail in the popular traditions, and I shall not deal with it here except to say that Mara attacked the Buddha with multiple weapons, but the sage remained untouched, such being the power of the perfections *(pāramitā)*, the moral heroisms practiced in past births.

According to the *Bhayabherava Sutta* ("The discourse on fear and dread") the Buddha, during the first watch of the night, entered into the four states of meditative trance (*jhāna* [Pali], or *dhyāna* [Sanskrit]) leading to complete equanimity which permitted him to recollect in all details his former existences. Thus: "I recollected all my manifold past lives, that is, one birth, two births, three births, forty births, fifty births, a hundred births, a thousand births, a hundred thousand births, many eons of world-contraction and expansion: 'There I was so named, of such a clan, with such an appearance, such was my nutriment, such my experience of pleasure and pain, such my life-term; and passing from there, I reappeared elsewhere; and there too I was so named, of such a clan, with such an appearance, such was my nutriment, such my experience of pleasure and pain, such my life-term; and passing away from there, I reappeared here.'" Immediately follows the Buddha's assessment of truth-realization through vision: "This was the first true knowledge attained by me in the first watch of the night. Ignorance was banished and true knowledge arose, darkness was banished and light arose, as happens in one who abides diligent, ardent, and resolute."

During the second watch, "true knowledge" continued to appear to the Buddha when, with his "divine eye," he redirected his mind to the long panorama of the passing and rising of human beings such that he could see them "passing away and reappearing, inferior and superior, fair and ugly, fortunate and unfortunate" through the operation of the universal action of karma and rebirth.[1] And in the last watch, which must surely be close to dawn and to a literal awakening, he discovered the nature of error and the Four Noble Truths of Buddhism and, according to some accounts, the critical theory of causal interconnectedness of things known as *paticcasamuppāda* (Sanskrit: *pratītya samutpāda*), translated as "dependent origination" or "conditioned genesis," the fundamental idea being that things have no reality on their own but are relative and dependent on one another and consequently lack inherent existence. No form of essence underlies the changing world of existence.

After this first Awakening when he becomes Buddha or the Awakened One, popular accounts tell us that he spent another seven weeks (or seven days) in meditation, in which he met with further spiritual adventures in an entirely vivid imagistic medium. The most famous of these is where Mara's daughters entice him with erotic pleasures. They tell their father that some men desire virgins, others women in the prime of life, while yet others prefer middle-aged or old women and that they would take all these guises to seduce the Bodhisattva. But the Buddha, still meditating on his moral perfections or heroisms *(pāramitā)*, remained unmoved. One can say that the daughters of Mara constitute the return of the women of the harem, but without their masks and marks of disgust. It is also the return of the repressed threatening to break through the controls imposed by asceticism. Yet eroticism cannot tempt the sage because his deep trances (*jhānas*) have taken him beyond desire and therefore he cannot succumb to temptation. After the seven weeks (or days) are over, the hero is reborn again, or in Buddhist terminology, he is the "*Fully* Awakened One" *(sammā sambuddha),* a term that European scholars influenced, I think, by their own Enlightenment have generously sanctified as "the Enlightenment." The double entendre of "awakened" is very significant: first, the Buddha has passed the liminal stage and emerged into a new life-form and the founding of a new order; second, his is a spiritual Awakening, a discovery of a way of salvific knowledge. The term "awakened" therefore can be employed as a designation for those who have achieved this state through the initiatory spiritual model based on a symbolic death and rebirth, once again aligning the Buddha's experience with those virtuosos in small-scale societies without of course subsuming the former into the latter. I think one can even say that the Buddha's experience under the *bodhi* tree is the *mysterium tremendum* of Buddhism.

Time and Space in Visionary Experience

My preceding discussion is a reminder that the Buddha's experience under the tree of Awakening is uniquely Buddhist, but from a purely formal or structural viewpoint it can be related to similar experiences outside of the Buddhist tradition. Consider the Buddha's meditative experience during the second watch where, employing his "divine eye," he *sees* human beings passing through endless existences *(samsāra),* from their human lives to their fate in heavens and hells, dependent on their karma. The "divine eye" that unfolds his visionary experiences is not part of his ordinary sensory apparatus but an inner "eye" that other visionaries also possessed. Note that during the first watch the Buddha recollected or remembered his past existences, including eons of world expansion and contraction, but whether this is "remembering" in our conventional usage is open to doubt. In the second watch also the past lives of others *appear* before him in visual form, each watch being a period of four hours. In this kind of experience, empirical time, or time as we normally understand it in our waking lives, gets stretched in incredible ways. There is a disparity between normal time and dream time (or empirical and mythic time) such that we can dream of long episodes in a few short time-bound moments. Yet these "timeless" experiences are, according to our texts, framed within four-hour time-bound periods ("watches").

I would like to make the case that in many ways the Buddha's experience of vast episodes appearing in a brief span of time has its parallel in the dream experience so brilliantly examined by Freud, who noted a similar compression-expansion of time as a feature of dreams. Freud mentions the case of a "dramatic author" named Casimir Bonjour, who wanted to sit with the audience during the first performance of his play. But being fatigued, "he dozed off just at the moment the curtain went up. During his sleep he went through the whole five acts of the play, and observed the various signs of emotion shown by the audience during the different scenes. At the end of the performance he was delighted to hear his name being shouted with the liveliest demonstrations of applause. Suddenly he woke up. He could not believe either his eyes or his ears for the performance had not gone beyond the first few lines of the first scene; he could not have been asleep for more than two minutes."[2] Although Freud himself did not think of the contrast between empirical and mythic time as a function of the dream work, every dreamer has surely experienced it. And so have the mad in their hallucinations.

What about space and how are visions related to space? This is a complicated question because Buddhist visionaries fill space in incredible ways and engage in space adventures of a fantastic nature, surpassing shamanic virtuosos in their cosmic travels. For now, following the preceding argument, I will deal with the visionary expansion of limited empirical space, that is, a distinction between empirical space and mythic space that, once again, I believe has its parallel in the dream life. I shall give two illustrative examples of the telescoping of space from both within and outside the Indian tradition.

1. The first is a well-known story from the *Bhagavata Purāna*, the great text of devotional Hinduism: "One day, when Krishna was still a little baby, some boys saw him eating mud. When his foster mother, Yasoda, learned of it, she asked the baby to open his mouth. Krishna opened his tiny mouth, and, wonder of wonders! Yasoda saw the whole universe—the earth, the stars, the planets, the sun, and the moon and innumerable beings—within

the mouth of Baby Krishna. For a moment Yasoda was bewildered thinking, 'Is this a dream or a hallucination? Or is it a real vision, the vision of my little baby as God himself?' "[3]

2. The following appears in *Revelations of Divine Love* by Julian of Norwich (c. 1342–1416): "And I was still awake, and then our Lord opened my spiritual eyes and showed me my soul in the middle of my heart. I saw my soul as large as it were a kingdom; and from the properties that I saw in it, it seemed to me to be a glorious city. In the centre of that city sits our Lord Jesus, true God and true man, glorious, highest Lord: and I saw him dressed imposingly in glory."[4]

In both the *Bhagavata Purāna* and *Revelations of Divine Love,* the vision of expanded space could be simultaneously literal and symbolic, at the very least a visualization of the idea that the Kingdom of God is within oneself. As Julian says: "He sits in the soul, in the very centre, in peace and rest, and he rules and protects heaven and earth and all that is."[5]

The reverse process, wherein a large space is contracted into a small one, also occurs, but not as commonly. Here is the Tibetan space-traveler and "treasure-seeker" Pemalingpa (1450–1519) writing of this kind of experience: "I had a bamboo hut erected on the hill called Sershong.... While I was staying in retreat there for three months I had sight of the whole world like a myrobalan flower placed in the palm of one's hand, entirely clear and pure."[6] Reverse telescoping of space is also beautifully expressed in the Tibetan theory of meditation wherein the virtuoso might be able to visualize the entire *maṇḍala* (the imagined circle of deities with the guru or personal deity at the center) reduced to "a drop the size of a mustard seed at the tip of one's nose, with such clarity that one can see the whites of the eyes of all 722 deities—and can maintain this visualization with uninterrupted one-pointed concentration for four hours."[7]

Visionary Knowledge

The kind of visionary knowledge that I have discussed thus far entails, I think, the abdication of the Cartesian *cogito,* at least when knowledge *appears* before the "eye" of the seer, irrespective of the religious tradition involved. Thus Julian's characterization of her visions as "showings."[8] The Buddha's showings during the first and second watches of the night occur when discursive thought is in abeyance, as is clearly recognized in early Buddhist texts. This means that the thinking-I is suspended during trance, dreaming, and psychotic fantasies and also in fleeting moments when pictures as well as thoughts of a nondiscursive nature float into our ken. One must not assume that cerebral activity is suspended during this state. I am inclined to postulate the idea of *passive cerebration* as against the active I-dependent cerebral activity involved in our rational discursive thinking processes. Going back to Christianity's past, John of the Cross tells us that one hears God with the hearing of the soul and one sees God "with the eye of the passive intellect," a kind of passive thinking that arises from the soul and not to be identified with *ratio* or reason.[9] And speaking of locutions, John perceptively adds that the "soul receives God's communication passively" and that the "reception of the light infused supernaturally into the soul is passive knowing."[10] Meister Eckhart posits the idea of man's *active* intellect, "but when the action at hand is undertaken by God, the mind must remain passive."[11] As with the Buddha, when thoughts are received by the passive intellect, they can be and often are re-cognized through the work of the active ego. Nietzsche had a similar idea: "A thought comes when 'it' wishes and not when 'I' wish, so that it is a falsification of the facts of the case to say that the subject 'I' is the condition of the predicate 'think.' *It thinks*: but that this 'it' is precisely the famous old 'ego' is, to put it mildly, only a supposition, an assertion, and assuredly not an immediate certainty." For Nietzsche, even "It-thinking" is tainted with agency, compelling one to think "according to grammatical habit."[12] For convenience I shall occasionally use Nietzsche's trope, reformulated as "I-thinking" and "It-thinking."

Given the preceding discussion, the conventional view of Buddhism as an exclusively rational religion has to be seriously reconsidered. It was the theosophist-cum-rationalist Colonel H. S. Olcott who asserted that "Buddhism was, in a word, a philosophy, and not a creed," and this credo has become the standard view of native intellectuals in contemporary Buddhist societies.[13] Yet contrary to modern Buddhist intellectuals, the Buddhist *ratio* is radically different from both the Greek and the European Enlightenments.[14] The European Enlightenment with its reification of rationality ignored or condemned visionary experiences; not so the Greek, it seems to me. Plato employed reason for discovering true knowledge, but neither he nor Socrates condemned or ignored such things as the work of visionaries and prophets and personally believed in the oracle at Delphi. By contrast, the Buddha condemned all sorts of popular "superstitions" as base or beastly arts in a famed discourse known as the *Brahmajāla Sutta* ("The net of Brahma") but never visions and knowledge emerging through meditative trance (*jhāna*).[15] During the first and second watches the Buddha sees his own life histories that then are extended to include those of human beings in general, their births and rebirths in various realms of existence. Through the "pictorialization" of births and rebirths, the Buddha can grasp the doctrine of karma and rebirth, can *see* it operating. During the third watch he discovered the existential foundation of Buddhism, these being the Four Noble Truths of Buddhism: *dukkha,* suffering, the unsatisfactory nature of existence owing to the fact of impermanency; *samudaya,* how *dukkha* arises owing to *taṇhā,* thirst, attachment, greed, desire, or craving; *nirodha,* cessation of craving that might ultimately lead to nirvana; and *magga,* or the path that can help us realize nirvana, also known as the "noble eightfold path" including right understanding, right thought, right speech, right action, right livelihood, right effort, right mindfulness, and right concentration. Right concentration is *samādhi* or the meditative disciplines leading to complexly graded states of trance (*jhāna, dhyāna*) that permitted the Buddha to intuit the very truths mentioned above.

We do not know *how* the Four Noble Truths appeared to the sage in the dawn watch. An early text, however, gives us a clue regarding the manner in which intuitively derived knowledge is given rational reworking. It says that when an Awakened Being has arisen in the world, there is a great light and radiance (associated with direct visionary knowledge), and then "there is the explaining, teaching, proclaiming, establishing, disclosing, analyzing, and elucidating of the Four Noble Truths."[16] The Buddha adds: "This, bhikkhus [monks], is the middle way *awakened* by the Tathagata [Buddha], which *gives rise to vision, which gives rise to knowledge,* which leads to peace, to direct knowledge, to enlightenment, to Nibbana [nirvana]."[17]

We have noted that some texts say that while in trance the Buddha discovered the doctrine of conditioned genesis or dependent origination, the central doctrine highlighting the interdependence of all actions and giving philosophical justification for the world of becoming, change, and instability. Conditioned genesis provides the epistemological or theoretical justification for the Four Noble Truths. Yet in contrast to the first two watches, in the third, or dawn watch, thoughts are no longer represented in picture form but rather as *ideas* that enter into the passive consciousness of the thinker when deep trance is thinning out into daybreak. Unlike the discovery of the Four Noble Truths, we can make an informed guess as to how conditioned genesis entered the mind of the Buddha. There are detailed discussions of this doctrine in Buddhist texts, but one enigmatic formula repeats itself in many with only minor variations. For example, in one discourse the Buddha tells an inquirer named Sakuludayin: "I shall teach you the Dhamma: when this exists, that comes to be; with the arising of this, that arises. When this does not exist, that does not come to be; with the cessation of this, that ceases."[18] In this discourse the Buddha equates conditioned genesis with the Buddhist doctrine itself, anticipating similar formulations by later Mahayana thinkers. Moreover, this formula exists by itself, whereas in the very next discourse it is incorporated in a larger context and then given a conceptual label: *paticcasamuppāda*. Here one of his disciples asks: "In what way can a bhikkhu [monk] be called skilled in dependent origination?" The Buddha responds:

When this is, that comes to be;
With the arising of this, that arises.
When this does not arise, that does not come to be;
With the cessation of this, that ceases.

He then briefly *explains* the enigmatic formula thus: "That is, with ignorance as condition, formations [come to be]; with formations as condition, consciousness; with consciousness as condition, mentality-materiality; with mentality-materiality as condition, the six-fold base; with the six-fold base as condition, contact; with contact as condition, feeling; with feeling as condition, craving; with craving as condition, clinging; with clinging as condition, being; with being as condition, birth; with birth as condition, ageing and death, sorrow, lamentation, pain, grief, and despair come to be. Such is the origin of this whole mass of suffering."[19] The discursive strategy is reasonably clear. The formulaic statement is elaborated in various degrees of complexity and length in Buddhist texts.[20]

In my current research I am examining that manner in which whole or partial texts are received by the passive consciousness of the visionary, whether it be a Mahayana or Vajrayana Buddhist; or a Christian penitent in the Middle Ages; or a later dreamer like William Blake or Madame Blavatsky; or for that matter someone like Joseph Smith. Unfortunately, many of us ordinary intellectuals do not have the gift of vision and even if we had there is no way that our astral, visionary, or dream manuscripts would be taken seriously by our respective professions! Hence my suggesting that the Buddha's formula of conditioned genesis not only fits the third watch or dawn/daybreak, it is also a mode of thought that is not at all alien to us. *It is expressed as an aphorism.* While the Buddha is not given to aphoristic thinking in general, Mahayana thinkers such as Nagarjuna were masters of the aphorism, as were some Western thinkers, such as Nietzsche and Wittgenstein. I have no space to deal with Wittgenstein's aphoristic thinking at length and therefore shall confine myself primarily to Nietzsche.

"The gestation of all really great creation," Nietzsche mused sentimentally, "lies in loneliness."[21] Loneliness did not mean an aversion to human company but rather the cultivation of solitude that permits thoughts to enter Nietzsche's field of "awareness." He, like the Buddha, was a wanderer but one living under the shadow of chronic disease and dread of madness, never in one place for long, and rarely in his German homeland. Victor Helling dubbed him the "great hermit of Sils-Maria" (CN, 21). According to Sebastian Hausmann, a stranger with whom Nietzsche once walked, "He spouted his thoughts forth, more in the form of aphorisms, always leaping one to the other" (CN, 139). Paul Lanzky thought that Nietzsche really valued human company; yet he also mentioned his "longing for stillness, indeed this temporary reveling in the idyllic" (CN, 174, 178). Nietzsche's ambivalence toward his solitariness was intrinsic to his character, and although he complained of his isolation and loneliness, he also seemed to enjoy it and could not do without it. That longing was probably best realized in Sils-Maria with its secluded forest paths tempting the wanderer to be alone with himself (CN, 182–183). It was in this kind of solitude that the aphorisms of *Daybreak, The Joyful Science,* and *Beyond Good and Evil* were written.

I suggest that it is in such silent meditative contexts that aphoristic thinking emerges into consciousness without an intrusive "I"; no wonder that Nietzsche, like other wanderers, could speak to his shadow on the importance of "It-thinking." Visions are not Nietzsche's forte. Not so with the nondiscursive silent thoughts he reexpressed through the literary genre of aphorisms. For Nietzsche, as for Wittgenstein, aphorisms became the vehicle for the expression of thoughts that occurred outside of the *cogito*. What I call "aphoristic thinking" is not necessarily congruent with the literary genre of aphorism; they can be expressed in other genres also, as in Blake's "proverbs of hell" and in his *Laocoön*. Similar "fragments" appear in the well-known enigmatic sayings of Zen masters.

The aphoristic mentality—the mentality that converts nonreflexive thought into aphorisms and similar literary forms—does not necessarily arise from trance or similar conditions of suspended consciousness. It only requires moments when active egoistic thinking is in abeyance. As in the case of dreams, one cannot capture such thoughts as they emerge into consciousness, but, as with dreams, one has to be satisfied with the remembered text. It is difficult to fully recollect aphoristic thoughts, although, as with Nietzsche, one can be trained to do so. Reinhardt von Seydlitz reports that in 1877, a year before Nietzsche left the University of Basel to become a wandering ascetic, he "kept next to his bed a slate tablet on which, in the dark, he jotted down the thoughts that came to him on sleepless nights" (CN, 91). Much later, in 1884, in his favorite Sils-Maria, Resa von Schirnhofer recounts a marvelous piece of advice given by Nietzsche himself: "keep paper and pencil on hand at night, as he himself did, since at night we are often visited by rare thoughts, which we should record immediately on awakening in the night, for by morning we can usually not find them again, they have fluttered away with the nocturnal darkness" (CN, 149). For Nietzsche, the aphoristic mode of work had practical purpose, as he noted in 1882: "I felt close to death and therefore pressed to say some things which I had been carrying around with me for years. Illness compelled me to use the briefest mode of expression; the individual sentences were dictated directly to a friend; systematic realization was out of the question. That is how the book *Human, All Too Human* was written. Thus the choice of the aphorism will be understandable only from the accompanying circumstances" (CN, 129).

Let me now get back to the Buddha's discovery of dependent origination during the dawn watch. It is immaterial to me whether the empirical Buddha actually had this experience; often enough mythos represents in symbolic form the reality of the truth-seeker. The Buddha's dawn watch or Nietzsche's "daybreak" opens one's dimmed consciousness to aphoristic thinking wherein one can observe again the "passive intellect" at work. To my mind the formula of conditioned genesis is fully consonant with the third and final watch opening into daybreak. Aphoristic thinking condenses It-thoughts, just as dreams might be condensations of images. Even with Nietzsche or Wittgenstein, the written aphorism can be interspersed with I-thinking. Yet when written aphorisms are close to their original thought processes, they possess the kind of enigmatic quality we noted in the Buddha's formula on conditioned genesis. Not only are they thick with meaning, but they also frequently require exegeses, either by the author or by others, for them to be fully comprehended. The enigmatic, thick, often poetic nature of aphorisms defies translation and is amply demonstrated in Nietzsche's work and in the work of another wandering ascetic and "mystic," Wittgenstein, another man with no fixed abode.

I have affirmed that solitude is something *cultivated* like the meditative space in Andrew Marvell's poem "The Garden," and the poet's garden tempts me to speculate on the role of gardens in the meditative askeses of different places and times. Prior to his Awakening, the Buddha was in the town of Uruvela, where he saw "an agreeable piece of ground, a delightful grove with a clear-flowing river with pleasant, smooth banks and a nearby village for alms resort."[22] Monasteries in the Buddha's own time contained spaces for meditative solitude. Indeed donors gifted their orchards and gardens to monks in the earliest period of Buddhism. When Buddhism was introduced to Sri Lanka in the third century BCE, the evidence is clearer: monasteries were associated with forest groves, gardens, or orchards. In some myths the forest is tamed or enclosed and converted into a space for solitude.

It is in gardens or in similar spaces of solitude that the enigmatic or aphoristic utterances of Zen monks occurred. Solitude is not the search for loneliness: the Buddha, Nietzsche, Wittgenstein, Zen monks, and others like them enjoyed congenial human company whenever it was available; and some of us know that such company is hard to find. Meditating monks were "hermits," but they rarely lived in total isolation from the world. They enjoyed the company of fellow meditators and lay folk without losing the capacity to be absorbed unto themselves, living alone like the single horn of the rhinoceros [or unicorn], as one Buddhist text puts it.[23] Wittgenstein once spoke of his sojourn at Red Cross in Ireland, where mental solitude was conjoined with physical isolation: "Sometimes my ideas come so quickly that I feel as if my pen was being guided"—something impossible to realize in the stuffy academic world of Cambridge with its overwhelming preoccupation with Enlightenment rationality.[24] I am not sure whether Wittgenstein was aware of his spiritual affinity in this regard with some of the visionaries in his European tradition such as Catherine of Siena, Teresa of Avila, William Blake, and Madame Blavatsky, all of whom claimed that large chunks of texts simply came to them through some divine or astral source, thoughts without a thinker, as it were.

Unlike Nietzsche, Wittgenstein was not exclusively an aphoristic thinker. His *Tractatus Logico-Philosophicus* was written in aphoristic form, but not all of his work was. Yet aphorisms sparkle everywhere in his writing. Bertrand Russell pointed out the significance of this mode of work in the *Tractatus* when in an admirable understatement he described some of its propositions as "obscure through brevity."[25] Wittgenstein's aphoristic density of expression eluded the brilliance of his two mentors, Russell and Gottlob Frege. When he was given a copy, Frege could barely begin to read it; and Wittgenstein thought that Russell did not understand a word of it. Neither could most philosophers until painful exegeses by Wittgenstein's disciples made his thoughts accessible to a larger audience of philosophers. Those enigmatic statements are evident in the opening propositions of the *Tractatus,* perhaps the very ones that baffled Frege and put him off:

1. The world is all that is the case.
1.1 The world is the totality of facts, not of things.
1.11 The world is determined by the facts, and by their being *all* the facts.
1.12 For the totality of facts determines what is the case, and also whatever is not the case.
1.13 The facts in logical space are the world.
1.2 The world divides into facts.
1.21 Each item can be the case or not the case while everything else remains the same.[26]

And so on and so on. In fairness to Wittgenstein it must be said that the aphoristic statements in the *Tractatus,* we now know, were less haphazard than Nietzsche's but ordered into a systemic totality through I-thinking without, however, losing their aphoristic quality. Nevertheless, whether it is Nietzsche or Wittgenstein, aphoristic thought is hostile to footnotes or bibliographical references. One could even say that it is meaningless to have such things in aphorisms. They would distract from, and dilute, the power of the aphoristic message.

Rationality

I am sympathetic to Karl Jaspers' idea of the Axial Age transformation of the religious life, but I resist any strict periodization. In Jaspers' work and in Shmuel Eisenstadt's and Robert Bellah's recent reformulations, this transformation entailed a preoccupation with soteriology and an ethics that transcended the world of everyday reality and the preexisting forms of the religious life localized in the small community.[27] The Axial religions of India, as elsewhere, tended to be "universal" in the sense that their soteriology was meant for all. Following the creative thought of the mathematician turned Indologist, D. D. Kosambi, one could relate that expansion of thought to the changes taking place in India's "second urbanization."[28] This period saw profound changes in political and economic life in India that I shall now briefly describe.

First, two new emerging empires, Kosala and Magadha, violently swallowed the many small independent Kṣatriya "republics" like the Buddha's own place of birth that had collective decision-making assemblies known as *sangha*s or *gana*s. To deal with this threat, some small republics banded together in a loose political alliance known as the Vajjian confederacy; but this too was short-lived. Other republics lasted much longer. The "full and frequent assemblies" of these *sangha*s and *gana*s were so much idealized by the Buddha that he not only named the Buddhist order after them but also borrowed their organizational principles and transferred them to the monastic assembly, as did his rival Mahavira, the spiritual leader of the Jainas.

Second, there was the emergence of new cities and the development of trade and commerce and concomitantly a new class of wealthy traders, bankers, and entrepreneurs, generally known as *seṭṭhi*s. Many of these supported the new salvation religions. Kosambi argues that the development of trade and the movement of caravans transcended local groups and traditional political boundaries. Two caravan routes were especially significant: the *uttarāpatha,* the northern route into the Indus region of Brahmanic culture, and the *dakshināpatha* that went south into the modern Deccan, both routes providing access for Buddhist monks and other teachers to spread their faiths.[29] These trade routes needed policing, which the new empires provided. Thus, says Kosambi, an alliance was forged between the merchant classes and the kings. He adds that the time was right for the emergence of universalizing and transcendent religions that paralleled the obsolescence of older political communities and the creation of wider ones.[30] These changes in turn paralleled the outward looking and universalizing orientations of the new religions, the one probably influencing the other. Nevertheless, an "orientation" cannot account for the content of a doctrine; therefore a direct tie-in between economic and political change and the *thought* of the new religions of the Ganges Valley is difficult to substantiate. Some scholars have suggested that the sense of pessimism and the emphasis on suffering that these religions formulated can be related to the social disruptions and dislocations of traditional life-forms of the sort that Durkheim conceptualized as "anomie." But one can as easily argue that such conditions could lead to a preoccupation with hedonism instead of postulating a world of impermanence and hopelessness. Indeed, the Buddha myth recognizes that hedonism is no solution to the ills of the world.

What seems to be occurring at this time is the emergence of thinkers questioning preexisting values and proposing a variety of salvific and nonsalvific solutions to the problems of existence. The Buddhist texts describe nonreligious thinkers such as various kinds of materialists, sophists, and nihilists. The social changes of the time provoked thinkers to deal with a variety of existential issues, almost all geared to general and universalized knowledge that transcended, though not necessarily replaced, the values and ideals of the local community. For example, the Buddha borrowed the model of the *sangha* from the republican organization of the time; but his *sangha* was no longer tied to a specific political unit; it was the universal church, "the *sangha* of the four quarters." So with the religious doctrine or *dhamma/dharma*: it was not localized in any specific community or groups but contained a salvific message for all. The figure of the founder is also not exempt from this process. Once the Buddha decides to become a renouncer, he ceases to be a member of the local community; furthermore, as the Buddha he is one of a long line of redeemers, previous Buddhas. Thus the three main axes of the religion—the Buddha, the Dhamma, and the Sangha—are all universalizing conceptions.

Is there any concept that one can employ to designate the multiple strands of the Indic reform that I have highlighted thus far? These ideas, namely, "ethicization," or the conversion of local moral values into those geared toward salvation; the universalizing (and transcendental) thrusts in soteriology; and "axiologization," where every aspect of species existence is given ethical and soteriological significance, are part of the systematization of thought and life-forms that one might, following Max Weber, label as "rationalization." Although Weber used the term "rationalization" in bewildering ways, it is fair to say that one important sense of rationalization is "systematization of thought." However, this meaning of rationalization is useful only for identifying the general or totalizing sweep of thought, not for specifying its components. Weber did have a restricted and more useful definition of rationalization as the kind of intellectual action that "the systematic thinker performs on the image of the world: an increasing theoretical mastery of reality by means of increasingly precise and abstract concepts."[31] I borrow the term "conceptualism" from European scholasticism for describing an intermediate position between realism and nominalism, but I give it a different twist to designate the invention and use of abstract terms and formulations. Thus my use of conceptualism is not synonymous with rationalization but is one component of it and close to what Bellah perhaps meant by theoretic thinking.

While conceptualism is intrinsically associated with the systematization of thought or rationalization, one can have the systematization of thought without conceptualism. The unifying worldview of the ethical prophet might entail a systematization of thought; and I suspect that there are many specialists in small-scale societies given to rationalization in this sense.[32] Yet, while the biblical prophet had abstract ideals, he hardly used abstract *concepts* to understand the world; and indeed he shunned concepts or found them irrelevant to his passionate and intense soteriological vision. Conceptualism, as I am using it, is rarely found in the Bible. It is only in the Platonic heritage of later Christian, Judaic, and Islamic thinkers that one encounters careful and deliberate conceptualism. To conclude: what is unique to Axial Age religions is a form of "rationalization" that includes the development of transcendental and universalizing soteriologies; and ethicization is a basic feature of that universal and transcendental vision. These soteriologies do require systematic probing into the nature of existence, but I am not sure whether they necessarily involve "conceptualism." The latter entails the supervening of abstract concepts for grasping the nature of the world, and it is religions like Buddhism that exemplify it. In the Buddhist doctrinal tradition, the conceptual imperative is so strong that one could reasonably speak of a "Buddhist Enlightenment" that parallels the Greek and the European, provided we do not confuse the Buddha's "Awakening" with his later "Enlightenment," wherein ideas that emerged through vision are retrospectively given conceptual and systemic formulation. Hence such things as the Four Noble Truths and the theory of dependent origination that I have already discussed; the doctrine of the impermanence of things *(anicca)*; the five atomic principles or *skandha*s that constitute the ever-changing body; the doctrine of "no soul" *(anatta)*; the idea of rebirth linking consciousness; complex theories of perception and consciousness; the classification and analysis of states of concentration or absorption *(jhāna, dhyāna)*; and so on. These ideas are rarely presented as purely abstract discourse until we come to the later philosophical and psychological analyses known as the *Abhidhamma* (Sanskrit: *Abhidharma*).[33] Rather, concepts are woven into the dialogues of the Buddha that deal for the most part with the nature of existence and the transcendence of the everyday world. Yet although Buddhist conceptualism is necessary for an intellectual understanding of the religion, it has to be abandoned at a certain point in the salvation quest, along with discursive thought in general.

One can have a feel for the kind of speculative thought characteristic of the period by dealing with those thinkers whom the Buddha labeled "eel-wrigglers" and "hair-splitters." The reference to these dialecticians comes from the *Brahmajāla Sutta*, the fascinating text mentioned earlier. In it the Buddha discusses eleven false theories (*vāda*, lit. "arguments") about the soul.[34] Among the dialecticians of these theories are the eel-wrigglers. When a question is put to one of them, "he resorts to eel-wriggling, to equivocation, and says: 'I don't take it thus. I don't take it the other way. But I advance no different opinion. And I don't deny your position. And I don't say it is neither the one, nor the other.'"[35] Or he might say: "There is not another-world. There both is, and is not, another-world. There neither is, nor is not, another-world.... There is fruit, result, of good and bad actions. There is not. There both is, and is not. There neither is, nor is not."[36]

Eel-wrigglers are familiar to us in academia; so are the hairsplitters, a subclass of the eel-wrigglers who, like the author of this essay, engage in "breaking to pieces by their wisdom the speculations of others."[37] These kinds of dialectics are used by the Buddha himself when dealing with ideas that cannot be expressed in ordinary discursive language. Paradox and equivocation are part of the language the religious virtuoso uses to describe ineffable states, or the unity of self with god, or of all existence as refractions of the deity. It is "neither this nor that," in the language of Eckhart; or the "not this—not this" of the Upanishadic formula; it is the language of T. S. Eliot's "Ash Wednesday." And it is the language of Parmenides in Plato's *Parmenides*.[38] Though parodied by the Buddha because of the extremes to which it is carried, the dialectics of the eel-wrigglers and hairsplitters indicate a powerful rationalizing impulse in any society.

Notes

Portions of this essay are reprinted, with permission of the publishers, from my recent book, *The Awakened Ones: Phenomenology of Visionary Experience* (New York: Columbia University Press, 2012, © 2012 Columbia University Press), and my earlier book, *Imagining Karma: Ethical Transformation in Amerindian, Buddhist, and Greek Rebirth* (Berkeley: University of California Press, 2007).

1. This and the preceding quotation from *Bhayabherava Sutta* are from the translation of the *Majjhima Nikāya* or "The Middle Length Sayings of the Buddha" by Bhikkhu Nanamoli and Bhikkhu Bodhi (Boston: Wisdom Publications, 1995), 105–106.

2. Sigmund Freud, *The Interpretation of Dreams,* 2 vols. (London: The Hogarth Press, 1981), 498.

3. *Srimad Bhagavatam, The Wisdom of God,* trans. Swami Prabhavananda (Hollywood: Vedanta Press, 1943), 190.

4. Julian of Norwich, *Revelations of Divine Love,* trans. Elizabeth Spearing (London: Penguin Books, 1998), 33.

5. Ibid.

6. Michael Aris, *Hidden Treasures and Secret Lives: A Study of Pemalingpa (1450–1521) and the Sixth Dalai Lama (1683–1706)* (London: Kegan Paul, 1989), 43.

7. Geoffrey Samuel, *Civilized Shamans: Buddhism in Tibetan Societies* (Washington, DC: The Smithsonian Institution, 1993), 236.

8. Julian of Norwich, *Revelations of Divine Love,* 41.

9. John of the Cross, "Spiritual Canticle," in Kieran Kavanaugh, ed., *John of the Cross: Selected Writings* (New York: Paulist Press, 1987), 211–283, here 249.

10. Ibid., 119.

11. Raymond B. Blakney, trans., *Meister Eckhart: A Modern Translation* (New York: Harper and Row, 1941), 110.

12. Friedrich Nietzsche, *Beyond Good and Evil: Prelude to a Philosophy of the Future,* trans. Walter Kaufmann (New York: Vintage Books, 1966), 24. To resolve this issue let me consider in more detail Nietzsche's notion of It-thinking formulated in *Beyond Good and Evil* (1886). In it he lampoons those "harmless self-observers who believe there are 'immediate certainties,' for example, 'I think,' or as the superstition of Schopenhauer put it, 'I will'; as though knowledge here got hold of its object purely and nakedly as 'the thing in itself,' without any falsification on the part of either the subject or the object." These ideas are further hammered out in his late work *Twilight of the Idols* (1888) before his own reason was finally blotted out. Nietzsche's terrible wrath is focused on Descartes and Kant, who represent for him the folly of Western metaphysics. "It is *this* [reason] which sees everywhere deed and doer; this which believes in will as cause in general; this which believes in the 'ego,' in the ego as being, in the ego as substance, and which *projects* its belief in the ego-substance on to all things.... Being is everywhere thought in, *foisted on,* as cause; it is only from the conception 'ego' that there follows, derivatively, the concept of 'being.'" These references are from *Beyond Good and Evil,* 20–24, from B. J. Hollingdale, trans., *Twilight of the Angels/The Anti-Christ* (London: Penguin, 1990), 61 (italics in the original).

13. Henry Steele Olcott, *Old Diary Leaves: The History of the Theosophical Society,* vol. 2: Adyar (Madras: Theosophical Publishing House, 1974), 169.

14. See *Imagining Karma,* especially 283–287, for a discussion of the three Enlightenments.

15. "The Brahmajala Sutta: The Supreme Net," in Maurice Walsh, trans. and ed., *The Long Discourses of the Buddha: A Translation of the Dīgha Nikāya* (Boston: Wisdom Publications, 1995), 67–90.

16. Bhikkhu Bodhi, *The Connected Discourses of the Buddha: A New Translation of the Saṃyutta Nikāya,* 2 vols. (Boston: Wisdom Publications, 2000), vol. 1, 1862.

17. Ibid., 1844 (my italics).

18. "The Shorter Discourse to Sakuladayin," in Bhikkhu Nanamoli and Bhikkhu Bodhi, trans., *The Middle Length Discourses of the Buddha,* 654–662, here 655.

19. "The Many Kinds of Elements," in Nanamoli and Bodhi, trans., *The Middle Length Discourses,* 925–930, here 927.

20. See, for example, "Dependant Origination," in *Nidāna Saṃyutta* ("Connected Discourses on Causation"), in Bhikkhu Bodhi, *The Connected Discourses,* vol. 1, 533–554.

21. Sander L. Gilman, ed., *Conversations with Nietzsche: A Life in the Words of His Contemporaries,* trans. David J. Parent (New York: Oxford University Press, 1991), 128. Hereafter this work is abbreviated as "CN."

22. *Ariyapariyesana Sutta* ("The Noble Search") in Nanamoli and Bodhi, trans., *The Middle Length Discourses,* 253–277, here 259.

23. See "The Unicorn's Horn," in *Sutta Nipāta,* trans. H. Saddhatissa (London: Curzon Press, 1987), 4–8, here 4.

24. Ray Monk, *Ludwig Wittgenstein: The Duty of Genius* (London: Vintage Books, 1991), 521.

25. Ibid., 166.

26. Ludwig Wittgenstein, *Tractatus Logico-Philosophicus,* trans. D. F. Pears and B. F. McGuinness (London and New York: Routledge, 1974), 5 (emphasis in original).

27. Karl Jaspers, *Vom Ursprung und Ziel der Geschichte* (Zurich: Artemis, 1949); Shmuel N. Eisenstadt, "The Axial Age: The Emergence of Transcendental Visions and the Rise of Clerics," *European Journal of Sociology* 23 (1982): 294–314; and of course Robert Bellah's chapter in this volume.

28. In D. D. Kosambi, *An Introduction to the Study of Indian History* (Bombay: Popular Book Depot, 1956), and *The Culture and Civilization of Ancient India in Historical Outline* (New Delhi: Vikas Publishing, 1976). The first urbanization refers to the Indus Valley civilizations of India.

29. Kosambi, *The Culture and Civilization,* 111–120, 124–126.

30. D. D. Kosambi, *Ancient India* (New York: Pantheon Books, 1965), 101–103.

31. Max Weber, "Social Psychology of the World Religions," in *From Max Weber,* ed. Hans Gerth and C. Wright Mills (New York: Oxford University Press, 1976), 293–294.

32. Weber, *The Sociology of Religion,* trans. Hans Gerth and Don Martindale (Glencoe: Free Press, 58–59).

33. *Abhidhamma* is the third and, historically, the last part of the canon dealing with obsessively classificatory philosophical and psychological commentaries by monks.

34. In this instance I shall use the older edition, see Rhys Davids, trans., *Brahmajāla Sutta* ("The Perfect Net"), *Dialogues of the Buddha,* part 1 (*Sacred Books of the Buddhists,* vol. 2) (London: Pali Text Society, 1995 [1899]), 1–55.

35. Ibid., 37–38.

36. Ibid., 40–41.

37. Ibid., 38–39.

38. See especially statements by Parmenides in *Parmenides* 147b and 166c, in Albert Keith Whitaker, trans., *Plato's Parmenides* (Newburyport: Focus Publishing, 1966), 55 and 89.

7

The Idea of Transcendence

INGOLF U. DALFERTH

The idea of an Axial Age has many facets. However, in Karl Jaspers' thought its decisive feature "is man's reaching out beyond himself by growing aware of himself within the whole of Being."[1] "In some way or other man becomes certain of transcendence," and thereby becomes human in a new and decisive sense: "It is impossible for man to lose transcendence, without ceasing to be man."[2] Reference to transcendence is the defining characteristic of Axial man.[3] Its correlate in human life is "faith"—not the faith of a particular religious tradition but what Jaspers calls "philosophic faith,"[4] a faith that can be spelled out as a "[f]aith in God, faith in man, faith in possibilities in the world."[5] Transcendence is "the infinitude of the Comprehensive,"[6] the ultimate encompassing reality that exists beyond the world of time and space. It cannot be objectified in our immanent terms of subjectivity and objectivity but is the ultimate nonobjective One that grounds them. Faith, on the other hand, is the immanent mode of existence that is aware of and directed to transcendence. "Faith alone sets in motion the forces that master man's basic animal instincts, deprive them of overlordship, and transform them into motors of upsurging humanity."[7] Since humanity is defined by reference to a transcendence that by its very nature will never be fully present in this life, being oriented by transcendence manifests itself in permanent human *transcending*. Thus human search for unity in a common history will be an unending task. "Unity as the goal . . . cannot become real. . . . The One is rather the infinitely remote point of reference, which is origin and goal at one and the same time; it is the One of transcendence. . . . If universal history as a whole proceeds from the One to the One, it does so in such a way that everything accessible to us lies between these ultimate poles."[8]

The quest for transcendence, then, is the humanizing force of human history. It is that which sets history in motion and directs it toward its end. But it is a quest for a reality that can never become fully present in history but overcomes history. Jaspers echoes a long Western tradition when he writes: "To the transcendent consciousness of existence, history vanishes in the everlasting present."[9] It is the eternal beyond of history, the true world of Being beyond this world of unending change and becoming. But what is the point of referring to such a transcendent world? What is its ontological character, force, and status? Is there such a beyond? Or is longing for it "a moral-optical illusion,"[10] as Nietzsche decried it, because the "'apparent world' is the only world: the 'true world' is just a *lie added to it*"?[11]

I. Paradigms of Transcendence

Jaspers' view of transcendence grows out of a long tradition of mystic experience and thought in the West (Meister Eckhart, Nicholas of Cusa) and the East (Buddhism). It reworks in its own existential way (as philosophic faith) the (neo-)Platonic contrast between a changing temporal world of immanence and an unchanging eternal world of transcendence. But this vision of a true world beyond the phenomenal world of experience and history is only one strand of understanding transcendence. The term has a long and complex history with many different meanings that cannot be merged into a single coherent concept. To indicate its range of meaning, let me briefly recall five major paradigms of (understanding) transcendence in the Western tradition.

1. True World

One of the most influential paradigms in Western thought is exemplified by Plato's allegory of the cave.[12] What the people in the cave take to be the real world is in fact only an illusion. They do not see the things as they are but only the shadows of the things projected on the wall of the cave of the things that pass in front of the fire behind them. The philosopher who has left the cave and acclimatized to the brightness of the sun knows better. He has seen the real world beyond the cave, and he can and should tell the others in the cave that what they take to be real is in fact an illusion even though they won't believe him and ridicule him. The contrast on which Plato's allegory draws is the difference between the apparent and the real world, the *ontological transcendence* of the true or real world, and our confusion about the true world: inside the cave we take the apparent world to be the true one, but as soon as we leave the cave we can see that we were mistaken.

The allegory draws on a spatial—and, in a metaphorical sense, epistemic and ontological—difference between *inside* and *outside* that suggests not only that there are two "spaces"[13] (immanent world/transcendent world) but that we can move from the immanent world inside the cave to the transcendent world outside the cave. This requires someone (the philosopher) who can see both the immanent world and the transcendent world and compare them critically. It is precisely this position of a "third" who is tied neither to the immanent nor to the transcendent world but who can freely move between them that has become radically questioned in modernity. If, as Nietzsche points out, there is no other place than the world in which we live, then the philosopher cannot move to and fro but will always stay inside the cave, and the idea of a transcendent world will not be the idea of a true world beyond the apparent one but just an illusion. However, in its secularized modern version Plato's view is not simply reversed and the true world identified with the illusionary world of Plato's cave, but rather the whole distinction between immanence and transcendence suggested by the allegory is rejected: we do not live in an immanent world in which we have lost the feeling for transcendence, but we live in the only world there is and have no need any more to describe our situation in terms of the distinction between immanence and transcendence. The idea of an ontological transcendence has lost its point where this world is no longer experienced as an immanent world.

2. Eternal Truth

Another major paradigm of transcendence is the Christian reworking of the Platonic tradition of ontological transcendence in the idea of *divine transcendence*. In light of the radical distinction between creator and creation and, at the same time, utter dependence of the creature's nature and existence on the creator, the transcending movement of the creature was seen as being confined in principle to the realm of creation and not able to transcend its limits and scrutinize the mind of the creator. The decisive line dividing immanence and transcendence is drawn not between temporal phenomena and permanent structures of the created world, between the potentiality of matter and the actuality of form, or between the changing realities of the physical world and the unchanging truths of mathematics and metaphysics, but rather between all this on the one side and the creator on the other. The ideas in the divine mind are the paradigms of everything that is possible, actual, or necessary in creation. Since from an Aristotelian perspective everything is possible that was, is, or will be actual, and everything is necessary that is not impossible nor merely possible or contingent, the divine ideas are in principle different from everything that is actual, possible, and necessary in creation. They are the source and standard of all truth, but they are not one of the truths in creation or as such accessible to us. Our mind can grasp truths insofar as what we know *(intellectus)* corresponds *(adequatio)* to what is the case *(res)* in creation, but the criterion of this correspondence is to be found neither in the world nor in our mind but solely in the eternal ideas of the divine mind, which are the paradigms both of what there is in creation and of our knowledge of it.

Thus the Christian paradigm of eternal truths is not merely built on the difference between the actual, the possible, and the necessary but on the more fundamental difference between *creator* and *creation,* the eternal truths in the divine mind and their partial and incomplete actualization in the analogous counterparts that are embedded in the created order and accessible to our created minds. We can only infer the eternal truths from their incomplete analogs in creation, but we can never penetrate the divine mind and grasp the paradigms immediately and as such. Divine transcendence is more radical than ontological transcendence and hence accessible only in a purely negative way: we know that we can know anything true only because of it, but we also know that we can never know this truth as such. At best we can know that we cannot know the truth but only some inkling of it according to the principle that the differences are greater than the similarities. We are tied to the ignorance of our immanence and can never penetrate into the transcendence of divine truth.

The idea of divine transcendence became secularized when in early modernity the relation of truth was no longer conceived in terms of an essential reference to the paradigms in the divine mind but as a relation between human mind and the world. The criteria of the true are no longer the paradigm ideas in the divine mind, nor the clear and distinct ideas of the human mind as Descartes suggested, but the facts; and the facts are not merely what we come to know by observation, as Descartes thought, but through creation and invention, as Vico argued: *verum et ipsum factum convertunter*.[14] In a full sense we can only know what we know how to make, and in order to find this out we must explore our human capacities, not divine transcendence.

3. True Knowledge

A third major paradigm of transcendence is the *epistemic transcendence* that takes center stage when divine transcendence is abandoned as the ultimate criterion of truth, unity, and completeness of knowledge.[15] Since knowledge always involves a distinction between knower (subject) and what is known (object), the paradigm takes on two forms: the infinity and inexhaustibility of what can be known (epistemic transcendence) and the inscrutability of the knower (subjective transcendence). Epistemic transcendence is a corollary of the insight that there is always more to be known than we in fact know; that the world is more complex than the most complex account we can give of it; and since the totality of what can be known is no longer defined by the paradigmatic ideas in the divine mind, true and comprehensive knowledge is only possible as an open-ended epistemic process in time. There is always more to be known, and everything known can be known better: any given state of knowledge can be transcended extensively (more knowledge) and intensively (better knowledge). Epistemic transcendence is the hallmark of human knowledge after the demise of divine transcendence.

4. True Self

However, since the totality of knowledge is no longer determined by the totality of paradigmatic truths but by an open-ended process of research and discovery in time, the totality of knowledge at any given time can only be defined by reference to the knowing subject that synthesizes it into a temporal unity and whole. There is no epistemic unity that is not the result of an epistemic unifying; and there is no epistemic whole that is not the result of an epistemic synthesizing. However, precisely here we hit upon the fourth paradigm of transcendence: *subjective transcendence* or *the transcendence of the ego*.[16] In post-Cartesian philosophy "transcendence" refers not merely to that which lies outside the subject, for example the outside world or the other. Rather, there is no unity of knowledge without the I (subject) as the unifying principle. But when the I seeks to know itself (self-knowledge) it discovers that whatever it knows (the "I known") is not the same as the "I that knows" (the "knowing I"). There is an abyss between the knowing subject and the very same subject known as an object by this subject. We may say with Kant: "The *I think* must be *able* to accompany all my representations: for otherwise something would be represented in me that could not be thought at all, which is as much as to say that the representation would either be impossible or else at least would be nothing to me."[17] But when the *I think* accompanies a representation of myself, there is an irreducible difference between *what* is thought (the representation of me) and the fact *that* it is thought (my *I think*). Therefore, Kant rejects Descartes' view that we have a more direct knowledge of our existence as a mind than of the existence of bodies outside us, including our own.[18] What we do know is the difference between the knower and the known even in cases of self-knowledge. We are different from the one whom we know when we know ourselves.

This is the subjective transcendence that soon becomes elaborated in other respects as well. In Kant it becomes the starting point for a transcendental account of the free and autonomous self that cannot be reduced to the empirical self that acts in time and space. Yet it can also be described in psychological terms by reference to *Bovarysme,* for example, which Jules de Gaultier understands as a special manifestation of the general human "faculty of believing one is different from what one is."[19] The difference between me and I that is experienced in subjective transcendence cannot be overcome from a third-person perspective because the difference becomes manifest only to the experiencing and thinking self but not to others. Whatever answers are given to the question "Who am I?," whether by myself or by others, I can always, and with reasons, insist on being different. Subjective transcendence seems to be a corollary of the irreducible difference between third-person and first-person descriptions: I cannot describe myself from an objectifying perspective without at the same time distinguishing myself from it. The act of the description and the content of the description never coincide.

5. *True Other*

A fifth paradigm of transcendence, which has been of particular relevance in recent years, is the *ethical transcendence* of the other.[20] "Transcendence as such," as Emmanuel Levinas put it, "is 'moral consciousness.' Moral consciousness accomplishes metaphysics, if metaphysics consists in transcendence.... The being as being is only produced in morality."[21] Real transcendence is not experienced in the epistemic self-transcendence of the ego that cannot know itself without thereby distinguishing itself from itself, for this remains completely within the bounds and the horizon of the ego. It is rather a relational human affair that is experienced "as a pressure, a 'call' that is recognized only in the response that one is compelled to make to it."[22] Only when the presence of the irreducibly other person in a face-to-face situation compels me to respond to it am I forced to leave the horizon of my own intentionality and step beyond myself. "The Other—absolutely other—paralyzes possession, which it contests by its epiphany in the face."[23] While it is true that I see the other from my point of view and hence construe him to some extent in my terms, it is also true that "the relation with the other is a relation with a Mystery."[24] For the "Other, insofar as Other, is not only an *alter ego;* the Other is that which I myself am not."[25] This puts my subjectivity into crisis.[26] As a knowing subject I can return "to myself through the detour of the object" without being fundamentally changed. But from the encounter with the Other I return not to me as I was before but as "*put into question* or *awakened* by the Other.... To be in question—this is to be unto God.... Uprooted from the concept of an Ego by the question of the Infinite, I am responsible for the Other [*autrui*], my neighbor. Someone starts to speak in the first person. There is no more Ego in his being put into question—neither as substance nor as concept."[27] Ethical transcendence is not merely a challenge to move beyond the bounds of my ego but rather the experience of becoming another in the experience of the Other. Who I become is not of my own making. In being put into question by the other I become passively what I could never have become actively: the neighbor of my neighbor.

Some have described the shifts in the meaning of "transcendence" marked by the sequence of the paradigms of *ontological, divine, epistemic, subjective,* and *ethical transcendence* as a change from "vertical"[28] to a "lateral"[29] or "horizontal transcendence." Whereas a "'vertical transcendence' suggests

The Idea of Transcendence   153

leaving the immanent world, leaving the phenomenal, for another world, either in a transcendence to the heights or a transcendence to the depths," "horizontal transcendence" "is the project of self-transcendence, the understanding that we are incomplete, thrusting ourselves into an incomplete future," but it "also includes the rethinking of transcendence in the context of ethics."[30] But the problem is more complex, as not only Levinas's account of transcendence shows.[31] The "categories—vertical and horizontal—are heuristic distinctions that ultimately break down, for the vertical inflects the horizontal, and vice versa."[32] But how exactly? And how does this affect the use of the idea of transcendence in a philosophical project like that of Jaspers?

II. The Logic of Transcendence

1. Drawing a Distinction

In order to address these issues, we have to discuss the problem from a larger and more differentiated perspective. I start with the obvious: "transcendence" is one term of a pair that always has to be considered together: *transcendence/immanence*. Just as transcendence is the reverse of immanence, so immanence is the reverse of transcendence: you cannot use the one without implying the other.

This has far-reaching consequences. According to Niklas Luhmann, for example, religions are not concerned solely with transcendence nor merely with immanence but rather "with the distinction as such,"[33] that is, the unity of the difference between immanence and transcendence.[34] Thus the code of all religious communication is the distinction between immanence and transcendence, the observable and the unobservable.[35] Religions try to observe not merely one side of this distinction but rather the paradoxical unity of the difference between the observable and the unobservable, and they do so "in the realm of the observable,"[36] that is, in the sphere of immanence. "Immanence is everything that the world as it is offers to innerworldly observation.... Transcendence is the same—but viewed otherwise. The immanent representation [communication] operates with a point of reference outside the world. It treats the world as if it could be viewed from outside."[37]

This, of course, is impossible, not for metaphysical but for methodological reasons. On the one hand, one cannot observe from where one observes while one does so (the blind spot of every observation); on the other hand, an observer can never observe both sides of the distinction that makes the observation possible, at least not at the same time. I may be here or there, but if I use the distinction "here/there," I use it *here* and not there. Similarly, religions use the distinction "immanence (observable) / transcendence (unobservable)" in the realm of immanence, not transcendence, but since they can never operate in the realm of the unobservable but only of the observable, the unity of the difference between immanence and transcendence becomes a paradoxical unity in a twofold sense: religions cannot observe the transcendent side but only the immanent side of the distinction, and they cannot observe the unity of the distinction because of the blind spot of every observation.[38]

2. *The Reentry of the Distinction*

Thus, the distinction between immanence and transcendence *(immanence/transcendence)* is always a distinction drawn in the realm of immanence and thereby recurs or reenters on the side of immanence. In terms of Spencer Brown's *Laws of Form*,[39] it is a distinction between a marked space (immanence) and an unmarked space (transcendence) that is repeated ("reentry") in the marked space: *immanence (immanence/transcendence)*.[40]

This distinction is drawn in order to avoid a problematic closure of immanence, a cutoff of the world as it is from what it may, will, should, ought to, or might be. The reason for doing this need not primarily be—as Nietzsche thought—an illusory interest in a world beyond but an interest in the world in which we live: only by placing our world as it is against the backdrop of a different world can we see what might or ought to be different, how it could or should be changed to become the world we wish it to be, or why we cannot change it in such a way. Of course, if we do not speak of transcendence, then there is no point in speaking of immanence either: to ignore the one side of the distinction dissolves not merely that side but the whole distinction. As Nietzsche clearly saw in "How the 'true world' finally became a fable," when the "true world" has become "an obsolete, superfluous idea," when the "true world is gone: which world is left? The illusory one, perhaps? . . . But no! *We got rid of the illusory world along with the true one!*"[41] We do not live in a merely immanent world when we stop contrasting it to a

The Idea of Transcendence 155

transcendent world. The world becomes flat but not an immanent world when it is no longer seen against the backdrop of transcendence. This is true whether we regard this as a loss or a gain. The loss of the idea of transcendence is not merely the loss of a "lie added to" the real world in which we live but a radical transformation of the meaning of this world, and so, too, is the inverse process, the discovery of the idea of transcendence.

3. Absolute and Relative Transcendence

Understood in this sense, the meaning of the idea of transcendence is determined by the difference between immanence/transcendence construed from the side of immanence. This introduces a fundamental ambiguity into the understanding of transcendence that has been part of its history from the very beginning. On the one hand, "transcendence" points to something *beyond* all immanence, something—it cannot even be called a "something" in any meaningful sense—that is *different in principle* from anything immanent and at the same time necessary for it: without it, there would be no immanence. I call this "Transcendence" (with a capital "T") or "Absolute Transcendence." On the other hand, it is one side of a distinction made *in the realm* of immanence and as such marks a *dimension within immanence,* a dimension that is *possible* within immanence without going beyond immanence. I call this "transcendence" (with a lowercase "t") or "relative transcendence." Relative transcendence can only occur in the marked space of immanence that is contrasted to the unmarked space of Absolute Transcendence. And just as the contrast to Absolute Transcendence marks immanence as Immanence (with a capital "I"), so the reentry of the distinction on the side of Immanence establishes the contrast between transcendence and immanence (with a lowercase "i") within Immanence. Only within the marked space of Immanence can we distinguish between transcendence and immanence, so that the difference between *immanent immanence* and *transcending immanence* (or relative transcendence) is a dependent or secondary contrast between marked and unmarked spaces *within* the marked space of Immanence.[42]

Now the *positing* of the difference, or the *drawing* of the distinction, between Immanence and Absolute Transcendence is an act that takes place in the marked space of Immanence and is therefore a move of relative transcending or *transcending immanence*. However, according to its own self-understanding, this move would be impossible as a move *within Immanence* without presupposing the difference between Immanence and Absolute Transcendence.[43] Absolute Transcendence is the absolute presupposition of making this move, whether one is aware of this or not, not only in Collingwood's semantic sense[44] (because *what* one states cannot be true or false without presupposing Absolute Transcendence) but also in the pragmatic sense that *making* this move or *drawing* this distinction would be impossible without Absolute Transcendence. But then, just as Absolute Transcendence is necessary for Immanence (and for the distinction between immanent immanence and transcending immanence to be possible), so Immanence (and hence also the possibility of distinguishing between immanent immanence and transcending immanence) is necessary for Absolute Transcendence: it is impossible that there is Immanence without Absolute Transcendence, and vice versa. However, whereas the distinction between Immanence and Absolute Transcendence is the condition of the possibility of distinguishing between immanent immanence and transcending immanence, it is not necessary to construe the goal of transcending immanence as Absolute Transcendence when distinguishing it from immanent immanence. Therefore there is an asymmetry between the first and the second distinction: the difference between *Immanence/Absolute Transcendence* as such does not require the difference between *immanent immanence/transcending immanence* to be made (the meaning of the former does not depend on the reentry of the distinction on the marked side of Immanence). But you cannot *distinguish* between *Immanence* and *Absolute Transcendence* without thereby also distinguishing between *immanent immanence* and *transcending immanence*, and making the latter presupposes the former even where relative transcendence is not construed as implementing Absolute Transcendence.

It follows that the very making of a distinction between immanence and transcendence makes it possible to distinguish between two kinds of transcendence and immanence in the horizon of immanence: Absolute Transcendence, which is the absolute other of the horizon of Immanence (and thereby defines it as a horizon of *Immanence*), and relative transcendence or transcending immanence, which is a relative other within the horizon of Immanence (and never more than a case of what Taylor calls "immanent transcendence").⁴⁵ Both distinctions help to orient human life in this world by placing it against a backdrop conceived as an absolute contrast between Immanence and Absolute Transcendence or as a relative contrast between immanence and transcendence within Immanence.

4. Multiple Meanings of the Distinction

This orienting distinction between immanence and transcendence can be implemented in different ways and thus takes on very different meanings in different contexts. Luhmann interprets it in terms of the binary code *observable/unobservable* in the context of his functional analysis of religious communication in modern society. This interpretation can be applied to the absolute difference between Immanence / Absolute Transcendence as well as to the relative distinction between immanent immanence and transcending immanence. But this is not always the case. Sometimes a reading can only be applied to the dependent distinction: *matter/form* or *old/new*, for example, can be used in the horizon of Immanence in a recursive way so that whatever state is distinguished from "form" (or "new") as "matter" (or "old") can, when the "form" or the "new" have been reached, become the "matter" (or the "old") of a new transcending toward a new "form" (or the "new") that has not yet been actualized. In this sense Nietzsche expects human beings today to be just the "matter" of their future form as supermen, and Luther can describe human beings in this life to be the mere matter of what God will make of them in the future life: "homo huius vitae est pura materia Dei ad futurae formae suae vitam."⁴⁶ But at other times the interpretations offered apply only, or primarily, to the distinction between Immanence and Absolute Transcendence. Thus it can be interpreted from different perspectives not only as the difference between *observable/unobservable* but also as *being/Being* (ontological perspective), *conditioned/unconditioned* (cosmological perspective), *apparent/true* (cognitive perspective), *knowable/unknowable* (epistemological perspective), *intelligible/unintelligible* (semiotic perspective).

The point to be noted is that whenever these interpretations are applied to the Immanence / Absolute Transcendence distinction, they are construed as mutually exclusive and complete: there is only a marked and an unmarked space but not a neutral space (neither marked nor unmarked). But when applied to the reentry of the distinction on the side of Immanence (which does not always make sense), the interpretations are transformed from dual into trial markers[47] which allow for a marked (*observable, conditioned, apparent, knowable, intelligible,* and so on), an unmarked (*unobservable, unconditioned, true, unknowable, unintelligible,* and so on), and a neutral space (*neither observable nor unobservable, neither conditioned nor unconditioned, neither apparent nor true, neither knowable nor unknowable, neither intelligible nor unintelligible,* and so on). This unmarked space is important if there is to be a *movement* from the marked to the unmarked space that does not lead beyond Immanence to Absolute Transcendence but rather to a new marked space within Immanence that was before an unmarked space within Immanence. Thus if "we 'transcend' this world for another world and then reach it, it becomes immanent, hence transcendence is not beyond the world; rather, it is a passage from one world to another."[48] But such a passage is only possible if there is also a neutral space that is neither marked nor unmarked. And it is in this betwixt and between that the important rituals and *rites de passage* are situated that allow a culture to perform in ordered (and not chaotic and interruptive) way the move from the marked to the unmarked side, from the old to the new, from the immanent immanence to the transcending immanence.

5. *"Transcendence" as a Descriptive and a Limit Term*

What Jaspers calls the discovery of transcendence can thus be understood as the conscious reentry of the distinction between immanence and transcendence on the side of immanence, which establishes (the possibility of) two distinctions: the difference between *Immanence* and *Absolute Transcendence,* and the difference between *immanent immanence* and *transcending immanence* (or relative transcendence). Both allow for different interpretations. But, as we have seen, the sense of the distinction between *Immanence/Absolute Transcendence* cannot be construed in a completely parallel fashion to the sense of the distinction between *immanent immanence/transcending immanence* (relative transcendence). The latter marks a *boundary* that can be transcended; the former a *limit* that cannot be transcended.

It was a central insight of Kant's critical philosophy that we must distinguish between *boundaries* or *bounds (Grenzen)* and *limits (Schranken).* The former can be transgressed and point, in a positive sense, to a beyond, whereas the latter do not. "Bounds (in extended beings) always presuppose a space existing outside of a certain definite place, and enclosing it; limits do not require this, but are mere negations, which affect a quantity, so far as it is not absolutely complete."[49] Limits are horizons that can neither be reached nor transcended, only pushed back. Boundaries, on the other hand, can only be identified if we have a mechanism that allows us to look at them from the other side. "In mathematics and natural philosophy human reason admits of limits but not of bounds, viz., that something indeed lies without it, at which it can never arrive, but not that it will at any point find completion in its internal progress. The enlarging of our views in mathematics, and the possibility of new discoveries, are infinite; and the same is the case with the discovery of new properties of nature, of new powers and laws, by continued experience and its rational combination."[50] Thus mathematics and the sciences have both limits and boundaries: they have limits insofar as no given state of mathematical or scientific knowledge exhausts the infinite possibility of progress in mathematical and scientific insight. But they also have boundaries. To claim that all knowledge is mathematical or scientific is a dogmatism that cannot be critically justified. However, that there is a beyond of mathematical and scientific knowledge cannot be spelled out or stated in mathematical or scientific terms but only from a perspective that allows us to see *both* the realm of mathematics and science *and* the realm beyond mathematics and science in a certain way. There is no way of showing, in purely mathematical or scientific terms, that mathematical and scientific knowledge is all the knowledge there is, that is, it is an account of knowledge that is both epistemically consistent and complete in that it comprises not only all possible *mathematical and scientific knowledge* but all *knowledge* that is possible.

If we apply Kant's distinction to the problem before us, we can see the important difference between understanding "transcendence" as a *descriptive term* or a *limiting term.* In the first sense the distinction between immanence and transcendence is construed as a distinction between two realms or "spaces," a marked space where we are (immanence) and an unmarked space beyond the space where we are (transcendence). This is relatively unproblematic in the case of relative transcendence because by a change of place (here/there), by the passage of time (today/tomorrow), by improving our self-knowledge (my self-knowledge now / my self-knowledge then), or by learning from others (our culture/foreign culture) we arrive at a new and different state that was "transcendent" when we started but has now become "immanent." Whatever boundary or borderline we transcend in this way makes what was transcendent at the start become something immanent at the end: we do not reach for a world beyond but merely move from one world to another.

However, in the case of Absolute Transcendence this becomes highly problematic, in whatever way we construe it. There is no way of moving from our position on the marked side of Immanence to the unmarked side of Absolute Transcendence, whether we construe the difference in a cosmological sense (natural world/supernatural world), metaphysical sense (temporal/eternal), theological sense (creation/creator), ethical sense (self/other), or eschatological sense (old life/new life). In doing so, we are always on the Immanence side of the difference and not on the side of Absolute Transcendence. Therefore, the distinction between *Immanence/Absolute Transcendence* marks not a boundary but a limit, and the term "Transcendence" does function here not as a descriptive but as a limit term: it marks the decisive difference in terms of which we understand our situation as *immanence* independent of, and presupposed by, any particular move we make in it.[51]

III. Interpreting Transcendence

The importance of the difference between descriptive and limit terms has not always been understood. This shows in the three major ways of reading or interpreting the distinction between immanence and transcendence (or Transcendence) in the course of history, each resulting in a type with many different implementations. Thus we can understand the distinction from the perspective of immanence as *immanent transcending*, or from the perspective of transcendence as *transcendence becoming immanent*, or from the perspective of the positing the difference between immanence and transcendence as either an *immanent* or a *transcendent positing* of the distinction or difference.

1. Immanent Transcending

From the side of Immanence the distinction can be construed in spatial, temporal, anthropological, or historical (cultural) terms as *transcending* one's place, time, or self-understanding, or cultural tradition. This can be described in a positive and a negative respect. In a negative respect (moving away from) it involves departing from or abandoning one's situation so far (discontinuation of one's earlier orientation). In a positive respect (moving to) it is a move either to another "marked state," that is, another place, time, self-understanding, or historical culture (new orientation), or to an "unmarked state" that is no longer that from which one departs in transcending but has not yet been determined in a new way (lack of orientation). In the former sense life has changed in fact, but not in principle: it is still a life of immanence lived in a particular way even though we describe it in new and different terms (we live no longer in medieval but modern times). In the latter sense one has not arrived anywhere but is "on the move." This seems to be a characteristic feature of the self-understanding of human life in modernity, which has broken with its traditions but has not (yet?) arrived at a clearly defined new place, time, self-understanding, or culture. We characterize our contemporary situation retrospectively in contrastive terms as postmodern, post-Christian, postsecular, postcolonial, and so on by marking it off from something taken to be past; but we have no clear vision of how to describe or call it in positive terms. Or we restrict what we mean by "transcending" to the moves described by Alfred Schütz, Thomas Luckmann, and others[52] in the many "small" ways of "transcending the everyday world" or the "great" transcendences that "occur in sleep and dream, in daydreaming and ecstasies, in crises and death and finally in theoretical orientations."[53] However, whatever these transcending moves lead to, they will never lead us beyond the determining horizon of immanence but stay within immanence. So whether we transcend in these "small" or "great" ways, whether we arrive at a new orientation or not (yet), we orient ourselves within immanence, not by reference to a transcendent beyond, and *a fortiori* not by transcending *per impossibile* into Transcendence.

Where human beings attempt to do this, or where the transcendence in terms of which they seek to understand and orient themselves in their immanence is construed as Absolute Transcendence, they frequently develop *radically negative conceptions of Transcendence*. The point is not that there is nothing of which one could speak but, on the contrary, that there is something of which one cannot speak. Transcendence is not construed as "Failed Immanence"[54] but as a *positive beyond* of immanence. This is obvious in the Platonic, or rather Philonic, traditions of negative theology, which speak of the Transcendent (ἕν) not in terms of what it is but what it is not (ἐπέκεινα τῆς οὐσίας) because it is not one of the many, but that which is beyond the many but presupposed by it because it is constituting the difference *between* one and many (ontological transcendence). But it is also the case in those recent traditions that, like Levinas, construe the Transcendent as the other (person) whom we can never fully and adequately understand in our own terms, but who remains radically and irreducibly different from us (ethical transcendence). And it is the case with those radically subject-centered epistemic accounts of Transcendence—from Augustine to Descartes or Kant—that construe the fundamental beyond of all human striving not in terms of the limits of knowledge (what we can know) but of the paradox of self-knowledge (what we discover when we seek to know ourselves): whatever we come to know about ourselves is not identical to we who know it. The I who knows in "I know myself" is different from the I that is known, because the performance of the act of knowing cannot be reduced to another determination added to what is known. There is an abyss in the very center of the self, as Augustine thought, even though this can be explained in terms of the irreducible difference between a self-representation (a representation of myself by me) and the act of self-representing (my representing my self-representation to me), as Kant saw. Just as in the first case the One remains a mystery, so in the second case the Other and in the third case, the Self. Whether we call the first a case of *vertical transcending* and the others cases of *horizontal* or *lateral transcending*[55] does not make a difference to the fact that they are all types of immanent transcending—types of human transcending toward (what is taken to be) the Transcendent (whether conceived in ontological, theological, epistemological, ethical, or whatever terms) that take place, and remain, in Immanence and never cross the decisive line to the Absolute Transcendence.

2. Transcendent Transcending

In the light of this the other option of reading the difference between immanence and Transcendence has always been to start not from Immanence, nor from the difference between immanent immanence and transcending immanence on the side of Immanence, but rather from the side of Absolute

Transcendence. This involves a change of what is taken to be the marked and the unmarked space of the distinction. Whereas in all cases of *immanent transcending* the side of Immanence is marked and the side of Absolute Transcendence is unmarked, this is just the other way around in all cases of *transcendent transcending*: now the side of Absolute Transcendence is the marked side, and the side of Immanence the unmarked one. Thus the Immanent or conditioned is seen as a consequence of the self-differentiation of the Absolute Transcendent or Unconditioned. By distinguishing itself from itself the Transcendent becomes the Unconditioned that, without ceasing to be the Transcendent, constitutes the difference between Immanence and Absolute Transcendence not merely by distinguishing itself from Immanence *(Immanence/Absolute Transcendence)* but rather by breaking into the Immanent in such a way that its reentry makes it impossible not to distinguish between immanence and transcendence within Immanence *(immanent immanence/transcending immanence)*. Absolute Transcendence is thus at the same time, but in different respects, the other side of Immanence or immanence as such *(Immanence/Absolute Transcendence),* and that which posits the difference between immanence and transcendence within immanence *(immanent immanence/transcending immanence)*.

The Platonic tradition has interpreted this as the difference between, on the one hand, the completely transcendent and inaccessible ἕν and, on the other, the νοῦς in which the ἕν differentiates itself into knower and known and as such takes the first step from the utterly unknown and unknowable One to the many. Christian theology has reinterpreted this in the light of its radical distinction between creator and creation as the difference between *God* (Absolute Transcendence), *Creator* (Absolute Transcendence as the condition of the possibility of the reality of the difference between immanence and transcendence), and *Revealer* (Absolute Transcendence that discloses itself as Creator by presenting itself as Revealer to his creatures). Moreover, Christian theology made clear, first, that God was free but not forced to create: God could have been God but not creator, and precisely this shows that the contingent fact of creation is not an accident or a mistake but something that God willed and hence something good for which it is appropriate to be grateful. And Christian theology also made clear, second, that the knowledge of God as Creator can, in the last resort, not be read off from creation as such but becomes clear only in the light of God's self-revelation in creation: only those who know themselves to be God's creatures because God reveals himself to them as their God can experience and see the world as God's creation and God as its Creator. Thus, for us to know God is to know God as Creator, to know God as Creator is to know oneself as God's creature, and to know oneself as God's creature is possible only if, and insofar as, God discloses himself to his creatures as their God and creator, helper and savior, redeemer and final consummator of the goal of their lives.

The whole complicated train of thought bears witness to the difficulty of this approach: since we have no access to Absolute Transcendence as the beyond of our Immanence but only to the various transcendences within our Immanence, the whole dynamic and point of establishing the difference between Immanence and Absolute Transcendence as well as between immanent immanence and transcending immanence must be situated in Absolute Transcendence itself. But this requires us to construe the difference between Immanence and Absolute Transcendence not as a limit (i.e., in terms of a negative theology) but as a boundary (i.e., in terms of a positive theology); and this in turn is only possible if Absolute Transcendence itself can be understood to create a perspective for us from which we can meaningfully interpret that which is a limit from our perspective as a boundary. We cannot see it this way from our perspective; we can only come to see it as a boundary if we have reason to speak of both Immanence and Absolute Transcendence in descriptive terms; and this is only possible if Absolute Transcendence discloses itself to us in our Immanence as that which constitutes the difference between Immanence and Absolute Transcendence by making us posit the difference between immanence and transcendence in such a way that we construe "transcendence" as "Absolute Transcendence," and "Absolute Transcendence" not as a limit concept but as a descriptive term—a term that designates an activity in its own right and not merely a limit of the immanent activities that we can describe from our own perspective. Thus only by enlarging our possibilities in such a way that we see the difference between Immanence and Absolute Transcendence not merely from our immanent perspective in negative terms as a limit, but also from the perspective of Absolute Transcendence as a boundary, we can meaningfully speak of Absolute Transcendence in positive terms. This, however, is only possible if we distinguish between our transcending (which always transcends from our immanent immanence toward Absolute Transcendence without ever being able to pass this line) and the transcending of Absolute Transcendence (which transcends from Absolute Transcendence into our immanence by, first, establishing Immanence and, then, by breaking into it and presenting itself as Absolute Transcendence under the conditions of Immanence). But this shows that the difference between Immanence (conditioned) and Absolute Transcendence (unconditioned) cannot be construed from the side of the unconditioned without thinking a movement of self-differentiation on the side of Absolute Transcendence (absolute activity) and an enrichment or empowerment on the side of Immanence (absolute passivity). And this is the third interpretation we can find in the history of Western thought.

3. *The Positing of the Difference*

The third way of interpreting the distinction between immanence and transcendence (or Transcendence) takes its starting point neither from the side of immanence nor from the side of transcendence (or Transcendence) but from the very act of positing the difference in the first place. But since there is nothing possible or actual that is not either immanent or transcendent or both, there is no third position beyond the difference between Immanence and Absolute Transcendence from which this distinction could be drawn. In particular, there is no neutral space between the marked space of Immanence (or, conversely, Absolute Transcendence) and the unmarked space of Absolute Transcendence (or, conversely, Immanence). No cut of Apelles will allow us to posit ourselves or anyone else on the very dividing line between Immanence and Absolute Transcendence, whether understood as a limit or a boundary. You cannot locate yourself (or anyone else) on the horizon (limit), and you cannot locate yourself (or anyone else) in the betwixt and between (boundary) of strict (i.e., mutually exclusive) and all-comprehensive (i.e., not allowing a neutral position that is neither here nor there) dualities such as creator/creation, sin/faith, new/old, this world/next world, and so on.[56] Therefore, the movement of differentiation or the positing of the difference must itself be located either on the side of Absolute Transcendence or on the side of Immanence.

In the first case it is a movement of Absolute Transcendence (or, rather, the Absolute Transcendent)[57] that posits the difference between Immanence and Absolute Transcendence by re-presenting itself as *Absolute Transcendence in Immanence;* and this has been worked out (in different ways) by Karl Barth[58] and Karl Rahner in their accounts of divine self-transcending in God's self-revelation. For Rahner, God is self-communicating, that is, "God in his own most proper reality makes himself the innermost constitutive element of man."[59] Accordingly, "man is the event of God's absolute self-communication," and "this says at the same time that on the one hand God is present for man in his absolute transcendentality not only as the absolute, always distant, radically remote term and source of his transcendence which man always grasps only asymptotically, but also that he offers himself in his own reality."[60] Thus the decisive act of transcending is not the human self-transcending toward that which is (taken to be) beyond but, on the contrary, the divine self-transcending in which God changes from the unmarked side of Absolute Transcendence to the marked side of Immanence without thereby ceasing to be God. This amounts to nothing less than a radical reversal of the marked and unmarked sides: what used to be the unmarked side now turns out to be the marked side (Absolute Transcendence), and what was taken to be the marked side now proves to be the unmarked side (Immanence). This involves a fundamental inversion of activities: it is not humans who self-transcend to the side of God, but God who self-transcends to the side of his creation. Indeed, it is precisely this unforced self-transcending move to the side of human immanence that shows God to be God by disclosing God to be utter and unrestricted love for the creation that ignores him.

In the second case the movement is situated on the side of Immanence in human transcending, but this can never be more than the positing of a difference between immanence and transcendence in the horizon of Immanence. Transcendence (relative transcendence) here becomes, in Jacques Derrida's terms, a movement of the self-differentiating immanence that in principle remains immanent and can conceive of Absolute Transcendence only in negative terms (negative theology)[61] or in terms of pointing to a gap that might but cannot be filled (a trace of something that never was present).[62] Derrida unfolds his view of transcendence in the context of his criticism of metaphysics. He criticizes metaphysics for its structural "closure," which needs to be interrupted or opened up by deconstruction. However, to overcome metaphysics by transcending it is impossible because there is no "outside" from which one could criticize or deconstruct metaphysics. Since metaphysics is an "excess over the totality, without which no totality would appear,"[63] its very idea depends on a movement of transcendence that cannot be transcended. It is only from within that metaphysics can be deconstructed. However, the transcending movement immanent to metaphysics can never be made present as such, even though it is at work everywhere in metaphysics. One can criticize it from within only by tracing its traces, which mark "the disappearance of any originary presence."[64] This is what Derrida calls *différance,* a "difference still more unthought than the difference between Being and beings," the ontological difference in Heidegger.[65] "Beyond Being and beings, this difference, ceaselessly differing from and deferring (itself), would trace (itself) (by itself)—this *différance* would be the first or last trace if one still could speak, here, of origin and end."[66] Transcendence in the sense of *différance* "'is' neither this nor that, neither sensible nor intelligible, neither inside nor outside, neither positive nor negative, neither superior nor inferior, neither active nor passive, neither present nor absent, not even neutral, not even subject to a dialectic with a third moment, without any possible sublation (Aufhebung). Despite appearances, then, this [*différance*] is neither a concept nor even a name; it does *lend itself* to a series of names, but calls for another syntax, and exceeds even the order and the structure of predicative discourse. It 'is' not and does not say what 'is.' It is written completely otherwise."[67] In short, Absolute Transcendence is neither the utter beyond of Neoplatonist metaphysical transcendence nor the total Other of Levinas's ethical transcendence,[68] but rather the immanent trace of "something missing" that can only obliquely be indicated or referred to by pointing to the gap or absence of that without whose presence immanence could not even be named "immanence" in a meaningful way.

IV. Transcendence as Self-Transcending and Event

The systematic sketch of the various ways of understanding "transcendence," or the distinction between transcendence and immanence, makes it quite clear that we may mean very different things when defining the "Axial Age" in terms of the discovery or emergence of transcendence. There is not just one contrast to be taken into account, and before we compare the different contrasts drawn in different cultures, we must be careful to identify the precise meaning and point of "transcendence" in the cultures we want to compare. The mere fact of first- or second-order "breakthroughs" or the emergence of a capacity for "questioning all human activity and conferring upon it a new meaning"[69] (Jaspers) is not enough to justify the collapsing of all distinctions into a common notion of "transcendence."

On the other hand, the differentiated view of transcendence, which I have sketched, leaves us with basically two alternative perspectives on transcendence.

1. Anthropological Perspectives

The first or *anthropological perspective* understands "transcendence" as the methodological correlate of our transcending, whether in the sense of "ascent" to mystery or in the sense of "lateral transcendence . . . within this world, by transforming it."[70] In either case the paradigmatic phenomenon is *self-transcending,* that is, the moving beyond where and what we are by what we do or what happens to us; the beyond is unspecified and merely indicates the direction in which we transcend or transgress our current position or context; and depending on where and how the self-transcending takes place, we might describe it, for example, as everyday, epistemic, ethical, religious, or some other form of self-transcending. Thus in psychological self-transcending the genesis of the self is understood as a process of internalizing social norms. The self is not an isolated ego but a social being that becomes what it is by and through its interactions with others. To be a social being is a permanent "going beyond itself," a being related to others, a responding to others, and a making others respond to oneself. At no point is the self a fixed or stable entity but always in the process of becoming. To be a self is to be self-transcending, to make—in a multitude of different ways and contexts—the experience of being seized, ruptured, or opened up by something or someone beyond oneself, which may, or may not, be interpreted religiously.[71] The experience of self-transcending is not as such a religious phenomenon, but it can lay the experiential ground for religious life because it cries out for interpretation and is often best interpreted in religious terms. However, to be self-transcending and to be seized by something beyond oneself will never lead beyond the self but only produce another stage, mode, or character of the self. It is an immanent experience (an experience in Immanence) in which the self discovers the possibility, potentiality, and attractiveness of a beyond that discloses the self to be not completely determined by its past history and the actualities of a given situation. As a self-transcending self, the self is not limited to what or how someone is at a given time and in a given situation. There is always more to a self than what it actually is, and this is manifested by its capacity for self-transcending.

This can be understood in at least two ways. On the one hand, self-transcendence can be construed as a discovering, creating, or emerging of a "true self" from its everyday or cultural construction, a liberating creation of an authentic self in contrast to the pre-givens of a particular social and cultural situation. To become a "true self" is to break through the closed circle of a given identity and define what one "truly" is in contrast to it. For just as to be a self is to have the "capacity for self-transcendence," so to become a "true self" (e.g., in the experience of grace) is to have an "unrestricted openness to the intelligible, the true, the good."[72] On the other hand, self-transcendence can also be construed as a critical deconstruction of self-identity, the permanent breaking-open of a closed and consistent identity not in order to replace it by (the construction of) a "true self" but rather by becoming open toward the presence of others and their different values, norms, and ideals.[73] The first type of self-transcending is a creative enhancement of self-identity that aims at establishing a "true self" *(ipse)* in contrast to the social self that appears to others *(idem)*. The second type of self-transcending is permanent overcoming, loss, or surrender of self-identity, a move beyond what one is in order to become accessible to and for others. In religious terms, the first provides the paradigm experience for searching one's "true self" beyond what one actually is (self-enlarging, self-centering, or *ego*-centric self-transcendence),[74] the second is the paradigm experience for seeing one's *ego* as a permanent hindrance of becoming one with true reality (self-surrendering, decentering, or *onto*-centric self-transcendence). In the first sense the goal is the becoming of the self, in the second sense the overcoming of the self.

Common to both types of self-transcending is the concentration on the self, whether as goal or as starting point of the self-transcending movement. In either case the self is seen as being able to move or be moved from one place, mode, or state to another; from a marked space to what was formerly an unmarked space that now becomes (part of) a new marked space, thereby redefining the boundary line between marked and unmarked spaces. What it does *not* allow us to do is to exchange the marked and the unmarked space in a radical manner, because the marked space is wherever we are (the self is) and we can only hypothetically imagine it to be, but not actually perform it, the other way around. In a very important sense, the self of self-transcending never moves beyond the immanent side of the Immanence/Absolute Transcendence distinction which functions as its horizon of transcending.[75]

2. *Theological Perspectives*

This is different in the second or *theological perspective.* Here the transcending movement is not one of the self that moves beyond itself within the horizon of Immanence but rather of the Transcendent which occurs in what thereby becomes "the immanent horizon" (Immanence) and which, in occurring in this way, constitutes the self to which it occurs. It is a truth-event[76] that *occurs as something to someone* in a radical sense: it was unpredictable, it brings out the truth of the situation in which it occurs, and it redefines the self to whom it occurs. That is to say, it is experienced by a self as a break-in of something utterly new, unexpected, and unforeseeable, something that emerges *ex nihilo,* which cannot be accounted for in terms of the given situation; it brings out what is the truth of this situation, if necessary against the common view or against its own self-understanding; and it determines the self in a way that goes beyond anything it could have achieved through self-transcending because it is not merely a modification of the mode of a pre-given self but a constitution of a "new self," the self in a new mode of being. Whereas in self-transcending, to use traditional language, the finite seeks to participate in the infinite;[77] in transcendence occurring as an event the infinite participates in the finite, thereby transforming it into something radically new. The self becomes aware of herself as given, as not of her own making, of being what she could never become by herself: a new self that receives her being through a becoming that she can only describe as pure passivity preceding all her own activity.

This event is *not* an answer to a problem or a making good for a lack or defect that may have provoked or occasioned a self-transcending on the side of the self. It is not the answer to an expectation or hope but "an experience in which we are confronted by a world that contradicts our desires, and by an other who is not an extension of the images we have of him or her."[78] But it is wrong to couch the experience merely in negative terms. On the contrary, what occurs in the event of transcendence is an enrichment or empowering that goes beyond anything the "old self" could have imagined or foreseen, and for this reason is experienced as a completely gratuitous gift and enrichment, a "new creation."

The "new self," therefore, is who or what it is due to this event. What defines it is not its previous history but the occurrence of the event and its fidelity to this event. The new self comes *after* the event and persists in discerning its traces within its situation. It now lives in a situation constituted by the breaking-in of a Transcendence that establishes an irreversible distinction between the immanence of the life of the self and the transcendence that occurred as event. It may symbolize the event in everyday, epistemic, ethical, religious, and other such terms, but the event is always and irreducibly more than anything that can be symbolized or expressed in language. It is different from its symbolizations because it precedes and transcends them in a principal way: it is not a result of acts of symbolizations, rather it is that without which these acts of symbolization would not be possible.

This is how theologies have come to speak of transcendence and, in particular, of Absolute Transcendence. There is no way of reaching the Absolute Transcendence by human self-transcending, because all self-transcending will take place in the horizon of Immanence and not go beyond it. The only way Absolute Transcendence can become accessible in noncontradictory terms is by becoming present as Absolute Transcendence in the present that is constituted by the event of its becoming present.[79] This requires thinking Absolute Transcendence as that which becomes present *as* Absolute Transcendence in the immanence, which it thereby constitutes. This in turn is only possible if Absolute Transcendence is in itself a *Self-Transcending* that establishes the difference between Immanence and Absolute Transcendence precisely by becoming present within the horizon of Immanence as Absolute Transcendence. Absolute Transcendence is not a dimension of Immanence that can be found and addressed in everything that is and becomes in the horizon of Immanence. It is rather that which posits the difference between Immanence/Absolute Transcendence in such a way that it becomes possible, on the one hand, to distinguish between "old" and "new" selves relative to this positing, and on the other, to see the defining feature of

Absolute Transcendence not in its self-possession, difference, and seclusion from Immanence and everything that is and can be in the horizon of Immanence, but rather in its Self-Transcending from the beyond of Absolute Transcendence into the horizon of Immanence without thereby ceasing to be Absolute Transcendence.

3. Divine Self-Transcending

In this sense, the transcendence of Absolute Transcendence is not the completely inaccessible transcendence of the Wholly Other that can only be hinted at in negative terms or in a language of analogy that is dominated by the principle of negative theology that "between the Creator and the creature so great a likeness cannot be noted without the necessity of noting a greater dissimilarity between them."[80] Rather, it is the Self-Transcending of Absolute Transcendence (or, more precisely, of the *Absolute Transcendent*) into the horizons of those who live in Immanence, without Absolute Transcendence thereby ceasing to be Absolute Transcendence.

In Christian terms—and something similar can be said in terms of other religious traditions that define themselves by their fidelity to such a foundational event—God is not the Wholly Other but the one who becomes present to creatures in the horizon of Immanence in Jesus Christ and through the Spirit (i.e., in what those to whom this breaking-in of Absolute Transcendence occurs symbolize as "Jesus Christ," "the Spirit," and "God"). God does not cease to be God in becoming present in this way, but actually defines his divinity in the very act of this divine self-transcending into immanence. By occurring in this contingent way (Jesus' life and death), at this contingent place and time (Roman Judea), and to these contingent people (Jesus' Jewish disciples), the break-in of God's transcendence becomes expressed and symbolized in the imagery of their life and tradition. But it sparked off a semantic revolution that led to a new life and language (Christian faith and theology) and transformed the cultural system of meaning in the Roman Empire and beyond. For Christians, all central questions are now answered by reference to this event. "Who is God?" (i.e., *who* becomes present in this way?) is answered: the one who discloses himself as love in the life and death of Jesus; "What is God?" (i.e., *what* is it that becomes present as God?) is answered: the unbounded love exemplified by Jesus Christ;

The Idea of Transcendence 173

"How is God?" (i.e., *how* does God become present?) is answered: as the event of divine self-transcending that constitutes a "new life" by marking it off from an "old life," and so on.

In short, the transcendence of God is no longer that which makes God wholly other and inaccessible to *human* self-transcending but rather the *divine* Self-Transcending that makes God present as God to humans in the horizon of Immanence before they can even begin to self-transcend. Whereas human beings cannot self-transcend into the horizon of God, God is God precisely by being, in Christian terms, a self-transcending love into the horizon of what is not God. What is a self-transcending activity on God's side is a dislocating passivity on the side of the human self, which thereby becomes divided into an "old self" and a "new self." This distinction between the old self and the new self is in principle inaccessible to the self-transcending self by itself. The difference between "old" and "new" is visible only from the standpoint of the event, not from the standpoint of the self. Its truth and accessibility depend on the self-transcending event of the Absolute Transcendent becoming present in the horizon of Immanence to those who can never break through this horizon into the presence of Absolute Transcendence by their own self-transcending. It is the truth-event of life—the event that brings out the truth of a life *coram deo* that is hidden to itself when merely lived as a life of human self-transcending.

This general pattern has been worked out in a number of different ways in twentieth-century theology, in the Protestant tradition typically by concentrating either on the *That* of divine self-transcending (Paul Tillich), or on its *How* (Barth).

4. Divine Transcending as Breaking-In

Tillich describes the divine self-transcending in phenomenological terms as the breaking-in of eternity into time, the infinite into the finite, the unconditional into the conditioned, or of being itself into being. This breaking-in or rupture can occur at any time, any place, and in any culture. It is the event *(that)* of transcendence that counts, not how the event is symbolized in terms of the symbolic material provided by the situation of the breaking-in. The breaking-in of transcendence into immanence ruptures the structures of immanence and thereby presents or opens up a glimpse on the universal dimension of reality, whereas the way it is re-presented or symbolized is always particular and due to the particularities of the situation or context in which the rupture occurred. What counts in understanding the symbols of a religious tradition are not the particularities of the symbols as such (their particular, historical, cultural, or "immanent" features) but that which they make present or re-present in their distinctive ways (the universal, transhistorical, transcultural, or "transcendent" reality to which they point as their source and origin). Thus the symbols of a religion are important not in themselves but only insofar as they present and point to this event of the rupture of immanence by the breaking-in of transcendence.

This is also true of the symbol of "God." "As the power of being, God transcends every being and also the totality of beings—the world. Being-itself is beyond finitude and infinity; otherwise it would be conditioned by something other than itself, and the real power of being would lie beyond both it and that which conditioned it."[81] Religion, therefore, is not a specific cultural phenomenon alongside others but the permanent and culturally changing reminder of that which grounds all cultural phenomena. No religion is made for eternity. Rather, "a particular religion will be lasting to the degree in which it negates itself as a religion. Thus Christianity will be a bearer of a religious answer as long as it breaks through its own particularity."[82] It is only by negating their own particular symbolic re-presentation of Transcendence that immanent symbols can direct our attention to the transcendent dimension that has manifested itself by rapturing human experience and thereby occasioned its symbolic re-presentation. "This power of unconditional reality in every conditioned actuality is that which is the supporting ground in every thing *(Ding)*, its very root of being, its absolute seriousness, its unfathomable depth, and its holiness."[83] (Absolute) Transcendence is thus described as the self-actualizing unconditional deep structure of conditioned being that can never be exhausted by any re-presentation of it, but which can only become present again and again by and through itself and which thereby occasions its symbolic re-presentation in a multitude of ways in the course of history. Therefore, while there is no question about the *"that"* of Transcendence; its *"what"* is ineffable and inexhaustible. The symbolic re-presentations of the event do not provide a basis for analogical reasoning about Transcendence but only re-present its breaking-in into Immanence. They are backward-looking, not Transcendence-depicting.

Tillich understood this breaking-in of transcendence in a realist sense: the unconditional is the ontological correlate of the conditioned world of phenomena; it cannot be construed or comprehended from within the conditioned but only symbolically gestured at when it breaks into the conditioned; this breaking-in or rupture is what human consciousness perceives as a manifestation of transcendence in immanence. However, "manifestation" can be construed not merely as "manifestation *of something or someone*" but also as "manifestation *to somebody*." By stressing this second aspect of manifestation, Tillich's realist account of rupture can be changed into a phenomenological account that is indifferent to the ontological question. Thus Martin J. De Nys understands religion "as a human response to some manifestation of sacred transcendence, *putative or real*."[84] This amounts to saying that religions spring from what they take to be a manifestation of the transcendent, whether that is the case or not. They are human responses to "the intentional correlate of a consciousness of something supposed to surpass the limits of finite imperfection and to present itself as the final end of human commitment and striving."[85] Since the claim is not that there is something that manifests itself, "transcendence" is here merely a *supposed* transcendence, and the "manifestation of transcendence" not a rupture occasioned by the breaking-in of the unconditional into the conditioned, but rather the retrospective positing of a religion of that to which it believes itself to be a response.

5. Divine Self-Transcending as Self-Revelation

Neither the phenomenological nor Tillich's ontological view of transcendence went far enough for Barth. He construed transcendence not as phenomenological revelation but as divine self-revelation. Revelation must be God's self-revelation or it does not deserve to be called "revelation": "Revelation is *Dei loquentis persona* [God speaking in person],"[86] and unless God's trinitarian self-interpretation as Father, Son, and Spirit is communicating who God is in Godself, it is not God's self-revelation and hence no revelation. The point of self-revelation is that in and through it God "reiterates" for humans in history who, what, and how God is in Godself from all eternity. "In reiteration, that which is reiterated lets itself be known. In God's being for us, God's being for himself makes itself known to us as a being which grounds and makes possible God's being-for-us."[87] In his revelation God reiterates himself for humans in such a way that God can be known as God is in Godself. If it were otherwise, if God's revelation would not be self-revelation in a strict sense, what is called "revelation" would not reveal God but at best something about God who, as God, would remain dark, inaccessible, and ambiguous in himself. In fact, revelation would not reveal God but that God cannot be revealed; and faith would not be faith in God but belief that God is incomprehensible (negative theology) or that there is always more that is incomprehensible about God than what is comprehensible (analogical theology). Only if revelation is divine self-revelation *strictu sensu* can the act of self-revelation as perceived and acknowledged by faith provide a basis for analogical reasoning about God — not in terms of an analogy of being but of an analogy of faith. In revealing himself to humankind in Jesus Christ and through the Spirit, God reiterates himself in history as God is in Godself from all eternity; and since God reveals himself in Christ as redeeming love for his creation, redeeming love is also the essence of the trinitarian life of God. Thus divine self-revelation is not merely the breaking-in of transcendence into the immanence of human life and history but rather the self-presentation and self-communication of God as God to that which is different from God; and since this event "reiterates" for us what God is in Godself, the capacity, power, and potentiality of becoming immanent as God (i.e., a *God for us* or *Immanuel*) is precisely what characterizes God's transcendence and being: God's being is in becoming — in becoming present to us as creative and transforming love.[88]

In short, God is Wholly Other not because God is completely and absolutely beyond all human grasp, but rather because God is eternally self-transcending toward us. The transcendence of God does not signify that God is in principle beyond human comprehensibility, but on the contrary that God has in fact become comprehensible as God to humankind even though the mystery of what this means and involves will never be exhausted. Divine transcendence is the inexhaustible comprehensibility of God rather than God's infinite incomprehensibility. And this comprehensibility is not grounded in the immanent structure of human reason but in the creative self-presentation of God *as God* in human history and to human life. Divine transcendence is God becoming God for humankind by making himself accessible and comprehensible *as God* in human terms. To be accessible as

God under the conditions of immanence is what characterizes God's transcendence.[89] God is the one who becomes present to us, and God is how God becomes present to us: as creative and transforming love.

6. Aspiring and Anaphoric Self-Transcendence

Reference to such a breaking-in of Absolute Transcendence into Immanence is impossible without interpreting or symbolizing it. This symbolization is contingent on the situation in which it occurs, that is, it uses interpretative possibilities and symbolic materials available in that situation. However, the way the breaking-in of Absolute Transcendence is symbolized is not merely an interpretation of the event (descriptive interpretation) but always involves at the same time a corresponding interpretation of those who define or understand themselves in terms of the breaking-in event in question (orienting interpretation). Just as the event is inaccessible without reference to those who understand themselves in the light of this event, so the identity of those who refer to this event depends on the event to which they refer: event and interpreting community mutually determine each other.

This in turn allows us to distinguish two kinds of human self-transcending in Immanence. The first is an aspiring after a beyond that the self can never reach because it can only move within Immanence (aspiring self-transcending). The second is a being opened-up to the presence—in Christian terms—of the self-communicating God in God's Word and Spirit, a human self-transcending into the divine self-transcending of God (anaphoric self-transcending). When God communicates Godself to the creature, the creature cannot *not* react, but rather reacts by either communicating or not communicating with God. Similarly, when God becomes present as God, the creature cannot stay unchanged. Rather, it becomes disclosed and uncovered as a creature that ignores or objects to God's presence (sinner), or it becomes transformed into a creature that looks back on its past as sinner by living a new life through God's grace in the creative presence of God (justified sinner). Human self-transcending in this second sense does not (seek to) break out of its immanence into a transcendent beyond, but rather relates within immanence to God's self-transcending presence as God in this immanence. God is not far away or beyond but rather closer to the creature than it is to itself. God's transcendence, therefore, is not an inaccessible remoteness but rather an unfathomable closeness of God, the creative present of the Transcendent to human life in immanence.

By relating to this creative presence of God, the creature is transformed from a God-ignoring being to a God-adoring creature. It is not the old self that recasts itself in a new way, but rather the new self emerges from God's self-communication, creating a distinction within the addressee between an old self bound to dissolve and a new self that is made a companion of God's immanent self-transcending toward the sinner. This new self perceives itself not as a goal that it has achieved but as a gift that it has received; and the gift is not something given to the self, but rather the very being of the new self is the gift.

V. Transcendence as a Theological Category

1. "Transcendence" as an Interpretative Term

Transcendence in the sense outlined is human self-transcending into the divine self-transcending provoked and enabled by the divine self-transcending toward human persons. Understood in this sense, "transcendence" is neither a descriptive term nor a limit term but rather an interpretative theological category that helps to make sense of human life in the dynamic and creative presence of God.

Methodologically, this is the third use of the term "transcendence" that we must distinguish: in its descriptive use the distinction between *immanence and transcendence* (immanent/transcendent) is read (in a Platonist way) as the difference between two kinds of reality, a *natural* and a *supernatural* reality (natural/supernatural). In its use as a limit term the distinction is used critically to mark the difference between a meaningful use of such terms as "natural," "experience," "value," "person," and so on (immanent) and usages beyond the realm of categorically determined experience where they become meaningless (transcendent). And in its interpretative use they do not describe a specific reality or regulate a particular usage of terms but rather are used to signify a way in which phenomena of this life are reinterpreted in the light of a particular meaning perspective and scheme of orientation.

2. The Structure of Interpretation

Interpretation is a meaning-making procedure in which something (p) is understood or interpreted by someone or something (x) as something (q) to someone (y). The first (p) functions as *interpretandum*, the second (x) as *interpreter*, the third (q) as an *interpretans*. The *interpretans* can only achieve its end of explaining (making sense of) the *interpretandum* if it is composed of terms that are sufficiently clear to the addressee (y)—who could, of course, be also the interpreter (x) herself—in the context of explication, explanation, or interpretation. You cannot explain the dark by the darker or interpret the unclear by something that is even less clear.

Interpretation can concentrate either on interpreting transcendence or on interpreting something as transcendent. In the first case transcendence is explained *as something* (theory of transcendence), in the second case something is explained *as transcendent* (phenomena of transcendence). If "transcendence" functions as the *interpretandum*, the question is what it means and how it is to be understood, and the answer has to explain transcendence *as something*. On the other hand, if it functions as *interpretans*, that is, if something is explained *as transcendence*, its meaning must be sufficiently clear for the purpose of making sense of that to which it is applied, and this is normally the case when the term is defined in the context of a theory with respect to and in contrast to the other terms of that theory. Just as "revelation" is not a name of an event but a theological category to make sense of certain events in a religious tradition, so "transcendence" is used not as a description of a phenomenon but as a philosophical category to make sense of certain (types of) phenomena.

When the distinction *immanent/transcendent* is used to interpret phenomena that are already understood or interpreted in a particular way, its point is to relate those phenomena to other phenomena (immanence) in such a way that it makes explicit the point of reference (transcendence) in terms of which they are integrated in a comprehensive total perspective or scheme (ordering or structuring use) in which everything, the phenomena described *(interpretandum)* as well as those who describe them *(interpreter)*, can be located (localizing use). Thus the term "transcendence" is used not to describe a supernatural reality beyond natural or empirical reality but rather to mark the point of reference or the signifier in light of which all actual and possible phenomena in question are understood, as (for example) "creation," "sin," or "salvation." Used as an interpretative theological category, "transcendence" does not interpret phenomena but rather reinterprets the interpretation of phenomena in a particular theological way: the world is interpreted as creation, living beings as creatures, human persons as images of God, evildoing as sin, forgiveness as redemption, and so on.

When "transcendence" is used as an interpretative theological category in this way, its meaning and point are not determined by that to which it is applied or to which it refers (its referents) but rather by the network of theological terms and concepts to which it belongs. It cannot be used in isolation but only by applying the whole system of theological terms and concepts in the attempt to make sense of human life and experience. Theological systems are meaning-making procedures that help to orient human life in this world by providing a way of ordering human life and experience (scheme of orientation) and a way of locating oneself and others in that scheme of orientation (localizing procedures).

3. The Emergence of Transcendence

However, theological systems differ and the meaning of terms like "God," "creation," "revelation," "sin," "redemption," "eternal life," or "transcendence" is determined in different ways. There is not one theological understanding of "transcendence"; the term is used differently in Roman Catholic theologies and in Protestant theologies, in seventeenth-century dogmatics and in contemporary systematic theologies, in theistic traditions and in pan(en)-theistic or a-theistic conceptions. In each case, however, it cannot be understood in isolation but only as one side of the contrast between immanence and transcendence, and this distinction is determined differently in different theologies. Thus we must not only distinguish between different conceptions of transcendence in different theological systems but also between theological systems that use the categories of transcendence and immanence and those that do not.

It is against this backdrop that we can understand Jaspers' thesis of the emergence of transcendence in the Axial Age. Its point is not the variety of ways the term "transcendence" is used and of what it signifies but the fact that the distinction between immanence and transcendence in one of its many interpretations is used at all. When religious reflection and cultural thinking started to use this orienting distinction, a new way of locating and orienting human life in the world began to emerge. This has not come to an end, as Jaspers feared, in the twentieth century. What has become deeply questionable is a particular interpretation of this distinction: the Platonist view, that beyond the immanence where we live (natural world) there is a transcendence for which we strive but at which we can never arrive (supernatural world). Even though this Platonist tradition with its ontological dualism has deeply influenced theological thinking in the West, the point of the message of the great religions of the West is different. Pace Nietzsche, their message of God is not to be equated with the propagation of a Platonist Absolute Transcendent beyond all human grasp and experience. Christianity in particular has emphasized that God is not beyond our striving but, on the contrary, that God's divinity consists precisely in God transcending the human absence from God by becoming present to humans as God: God is not far away but close, not because God is immanent in everything that is but because nothing that is, is without God, whereas God "is" in no way in which anything else is. God is neither a transcendent (supernatural) nor an immanent (natural) being but rather the creative presence that occurs again and again as the rupturing event that breaks through the boundaries of created being by coming close to us as God. In doing so God opens up possibilities of orienting human life by reference to that which is in every sense beyond what we can control and influence. In anthropological terms, God's self-transcending self-presentation and self-communication to created life constitutes the fundamental passivity that grounds all human life and activity and illumines the contingency of life as a gift. Life is a gift that not only opens up possibilities but also resonates with possibilities that interrupt the course of life and allow us to transcend ourselves by going beyond what we are to what we can be—not because we have the competence to do it but because we have been given the chance and opportunity to become it.[90]

Notes

I thank Marlene Block and the editors of this volume for helpful comments.

1. K. Jaspers, *Vom Ursprung und Ziel der Geschichte* (Munich: Piper, 1988 [1949]; English: *The Origin and Goal of History* (New Haven: Yale University Press, 1953); new edition (London: Routledge, 2010), 4. All subsequent references to Jaspers refer to this edition.

2. Jaspers, *The Origin and Goal*, 219.

3. There clearly is a problem in this view, which Jaspers fails to address. If becoming aware of transcendence is what makes human beings human, "pre-Axial man" is as much an oxymoron as "post-Axial man": both fail to qualify as man on Jaspers' criterion. What he has in mind may be less confusingly stated not as a difference between *human beings* (human animals) and *nonhuman beings* (other animals) but between *inhumane* and *humane* ways of being a human being. That is to say, the decisive distinction in terms of which Jaspers' thesis should be read is not *human/not human* (human animal/nonhuman animal) but *humane/inhumane* (humane human/inhumane human). It is not a thesis about the difference between humans and other creatures in the category of "animal" but a humanist thesis about the difference between humane and inhumane ways of living a human life in the category of "human being."

4. Jaspers, *The Origin and Goal*, 213–228; see K. Jaspers, *Der philosophische Glaube angesichts der Offenbarung* (Munich, 1962).

5. Jaspers, *The Origin and Goal*, 219.

6. Ibid., 259.

7. Ibid., 220.

8. Ibid., 264–265.

9. Ibid., 276.

10. F. Nietzsche, *Twilight of the Idols*, "'Reason' in Philosophy" §6, in Nietzsche, *The Anti-Christ, Ecce Homo, Twilight of the Idols and Other Writings*, ed. A. Ridley and J. Norman (Cambridge, 2005), 170.

11. Nietzsche, *Twilight*, "'Reason' in Philosophy," §3, 168 (emphasis in original).

12. Plato, *The Republic*, Book VII, 514a–520a. See J. N. Findlay, *The Discipline of the Cave* (London and New York, 1966); *The Transcendence of the Cave* (London and New York, 1967).

13. On the use of spatial language and its misreading in light of the homogenization of space in modern science, see W. C. Placher, *The Domestication of Transcendence: How Modern Thinking about God Went Wrong* (Louisville, 1996).

14. See G. B. Vico, *Liber metaphysicus* (Naples, 1710); it is the first and only volume of *De antiquissima Italorum sapientia ex linguae Latinae originibus eruenda libri tres* (Naples, 1710).

15. I use the term "epistemic transcendence" differently from M. Westphal, *Transcendence and Self-Transcendence: On God and the Soul* (Bloomington and Indianapolis, 2004), 93–174, who uses it to refer to discussions of the incomprehensibility of God in Augustine, Pseud-Dionysius, Aquinas, and Barth.

16. See J. P. Sartre, *The Transcendence of the Ego: A Sketch for a Phenomenological Description* (Abingdon, 2004 [1988]); M. Csikszentmihalyi, *The Evolving Self: A Psychology for the Third Millennium* (New York, 1993), 207–251.

17. I. Kant, KrV B131–132 (emphasis in original).

18. Ibid., A366–379. See KrV B276.

19. J. de Gaultier, *Le Bovarysme: La psychologie dans l'oeuvre de Flaubert*, annoté et présenté par Didier Philippot, suivi de neuf études réunies et coordonnées par Per Buvik (Paris, 2007 [1892]. See G. Agamben, *The Time That Remains: A Commentary on the Letter to the Romans* (Stanford, 2005), 37.

20. See B. Forthomme, *Une philosophie de la transcendance: La métaphysique d'Emmanuel Lévinas* (Paris, 1979); É. Feron, *De l'idée de transcendance à la question du langage: L'itinéraire philosophique d'Emmanuel Levinas* (Grenoble, 1992); M. Westphal, *Transcendence and Self-Transcendence: On God and the Soul* (Bloomington and Indianapolis, 2004), 177–226 (on Levinas and Kierkegaard).

21. E. Levinas, *Totality and Infinity: An Essay on Exteriority* (Pittsburgh, 1969), 261ff.

22. R. Horner, "The Betrayal of Transcendence," in R. Schwarz, ed., *Transcendence: Philosophy, Literature, and Theology Approach the Beyond* (New York and London, 2004), 61–79, here 61–62.

23. Levinas, *Totality and Infinity,* 171.

24. E. Levinas, *Time and the Other and Additional Essays,* trans. R. A. Cohen (Pittsburgh, 1987), 75.

25. Ibid., 83.

26. See P. Hayat, *Emmanuel Levinas, Alterity and Transcendence,* trans. M. B. Smith (New York, 1999), xiv.

27. E. Levinas, "Philosophy and Positivity," in Schwarz, ed., *Transcendence,* 31–42, here 41.

28. See C. Pickstock, *After Writing: On the Liturgical Consummation of Philosophy* (Oxford, 1998), 183; M. Rivera, *The Touch of Transcendence: A Postcolonial Theology of God* (Louisville and London, 2007), chap. 1.

29. W. Lowe, "Second Thoughts about Transcendence," in J. D. Caputo, ed., *The Religious* (Malden, 2002), 241–251, here 248.

30. R. Schwarz, "Introduction. Transcendence: Beyond . . . ," in Schwarz, ed., *Transcendence,* vii–xii, here x–xi.

31. For a feminist critique of Levinas' notion of transcendence, see D. Perpich, "From the Caress to the Word: Transcendence and the Feminine in the Philosophy of Emmanuel Levinas," in T. Chanter, ed., *Feminist Interpretations of Emmanuel Levinas* (University Park, 2001); C. Keller, "Rumors of Transcendence:

The Movement, State, and Sex of 'Beyond,'" in J. D. Caputo and M. J. Scanlon, eds., *Transcendence and Beyond: A Postmodern Inquiry* (Bloomington and Indianapolis, 2007).

32. Schwarz, "Introduction," xi.

33. N. Luhmann, "Die Sinnform Religion," *Soziale Systeme* 2 (1996): 3–33, here 20.

34. N. Luhmann, *Ökologische Kommunikation* (Opladen, 1986), 186: "Die Einheit der Differenz (und nicht etwa: die Transzendenz als solche) ist der Code der Religion."

35. N. Luhmann, "Die Ausdifferenzierung der Religion," in Luhmann, *Gesellschaftsstruktur und Semantik: Studien zur Wissenssoziologie der modernen Gesellschaft*, vol. 3 (Frankfurt am Main, 1989), 259–357; *Die Religion der Gesellschaft* (Frankfurt am Main, 2000).

36. Luhmann, "Die Sinnform Religion," 20.

37. Luhmann, "Die Ausdifferenzierung der Religion," 313. Translation by R. Laermans and G. Verschraegen, "'The Late Niklas Luhmann' on Religion: An Overview," *Social Compass* 48 (2001): 7–20, here 18.

38. See N. Luhmann, "Das Erkenntnisprogramm des Konstruktivismus und die unbekannt bleibende Realität," in Luhmann, *Soziologische Aufklärung 5: Konstruktivistische Perspektiven* (Opladen, 1990), 31–58.

39. G. Spencer-Brown, *Laws of Form* (New York, 1979 [1969]).

40. I call a "marked space" the space where we are located in making the distinction and the "unmarked space" everything that is on the other side of the distinction.

41. Nietzsche, *Twilight of the Idols,* 171 (emphasis in original).

42. What sometimes has been called "immanent transcendence" (see Charles Taylor, *A Secular Age* [Cambridge, 2007], 726) is thus reconstructed here as "transcending immanence."

43. This is why the breakthrough of distinguishing between Absolute Transcendence and Immanence is experienced as a *discovery* and not as an invention or a mere emergence that takes place in a particular culture or society.

44. R. G. Collingwood, *An Essay on Metaphysics,* revised edition (Oxford, 1998 [1940]), 47. See R. J. Festin, "Collingwood's Absolute Presuppositions and the Nonpropositionality," *Collingwood and British Idealism Studies* 14 (2008): 65–91.

45. See Taylor, *A Secular Age,* 726.

46. M. Luther, *"Disputatio de homine,"* prop. 35, in G. Ebeling, *Disputatio de Homine: Erster Teil; Text und Traditionshintergrund* (Tübingen, 1977), 23. It is obvious that Nietzsche and Luther use a similar idea in very different ways: in Nietzsche it is a development solely within Immanence that he hopes will lead to the future superman, whereas in Luther it is precisely *not* a move within Immanence that will produce this future form of human life but only the transforming activity of God from the side of the Absolute Transcendence.

47. See the grammatical numbers "dual" (two) and "trial" (three), which refer to two or three items respectively, in contrast to "singular" and "plural," which refer to one or more than one items respectively.

48. Schwartz, "Introduction," xi.

49. I. Kant, *Prolegomena zu einer jeden künftigen Metaphysik, die als Wissenschaft wird auftreten können* §57, AA IV, 352.

50. Kant, *Prolegomena* §57, AA IV, 352.

51. For a discussion of the idea of limit concepts, see H. Schröder, "Zur religionsphilosophischen Bedeutung von Grenzbegriffen: Ein Versuch als Diskussionsgrundlage," www.kaththeol.uni-frankfurt.de/relphil/mitarbeiter/schroedter/Grenzbegriffe.pdf.

52. A. Schütz and T. Luckmann, *The Structures of the Life-World*, vol. 2 (Evanston, 1989), 177–130; T. Luckmann, *The Invisible Religion: The Problem of Religion in Modern Society* (New York, 1967); T. Luckmann, ed., *Die unsichtbare Religion* (Frankfurt am Main, 1991), 164–182; H. Knoblauch, "Die Verflüchtigung der Religion ins Religiöse," in Luckmann, ed., *Die unsichtbare Religion*, 7–41; G. Thomas, *Implizite Religion: Theoriegeschichtliche und theoretische Untersuchungen zum Problem ihrer Identifikation* (Würzburg, 2001).

53. H. Streib and R. W. Hood, "Modeling the Religious Field: Religion, Spirituality, Mysticism and Related World Views," www.uni-bielefeld.de/theologie/CIRRuS-downloads/Streib-Hood_2010_Modeling-the-Religious-Field-CIRRuS-WP9.pdf (p. 2).

54. See E. Wyschogrod, "Intending Transcendence: Desiring God," in *Crossover Queries: Dwelling with Negatives, Embodying Philosophy's Others* (New York, 2006), 13–28, here 25.

55. See U. Goodenough, "Vertical and Horizontal Transcendence," *Zygon* 36 (2001): 21–31; R. W. Hood, P. C. Hill, and B. Spilka, *The Psychology of Religion: An Empirical Approach*, 4th ed. (New York, 2009), 282 and 286; Chr. Bachmann, *Religion und Sexualität: Die Sehnsucht nach Transzendenz* (Stuttgart, Berlin, and Cologne, 1994); A Halsema, "Horizontal Transcendence: Irigaray's Religion after Ontotheology," in H. de Vries, ed., *Religion: Beyond a Concept* (New York, 2008), 813–994; Streib and Hood, "Modeling the Religious Field," 4–6.

56. As ritual theorists remind us, this is exactly where we are in liminal situations. We are, so to speak, neither here nor there, we are betwixt and between, conflating and seeming to interrupt all dualities. This, however, is not a neutral position. It can be disorienting, dangerous, creative, and sometimes destructive. Ritual "experience" will not choose sides (Absolute Transcendence or Immanence), it is the enacted experience of an exception. However, it takes place in Immanence (and not in Absolute Transcendence), and there it is possible only as a symbolic (ritual) enactment of an impossibility—the impossibility of being *here* neither here nor there.

57. "Absolute Transcendence" is the character of the Absolute Transcendent; the Absolute Transcendent is the concrete instantiation of Absolute Transcendence.

58. K. Barth, *Church Dogmatics IV/1–IV, 3* (Edinburgh, 1956–1967). Henceforth cited as "CD."

59. K. Rahner, *Foundations of Christian Faith: An Introduction to the Idea of Christianity,* trans. W. V. Dych (New York, 1987), 116.

60. Rahner, *Foundations,* 119.

61. J. Derrida, *On the Name,* trans. D. Wood, J. P. Leavey Jr., and I. McLeod (Stanford, 1995), 69: "I trust no text that is not in some way contaminated with negative theology, and even among those texts that apparently do not have, want, or believe they have any relation with theology in general."

62. J. Derrida, *Acts of Literature,* ed. D. Attridge (London, 1992), 74. See D. E. Smith, "Deleuze and Derrida, Immanence and Transcendence: Two Directions in Recent French Thought," in P. Patton and J. Protevi, eds., *Between Deleuze and Derrida* (London, 2003), 46–66.

63. J. Derrida, *Dissemination,* trans. B. Johnson (Chicago, 1981), 168.

64. Ibid.

65. J. Derrida, *Margins of Philosophy,* trans. A. Bass (Chicago, 1982), 67.

66. Ibid.

67. J. Derrida, "How to Avoid Speaking: Denials," in *Derrida and Negative Theology,* ed. H. Coward and T. Foshay (Albany, 1992), 74.

68. E. Levinas, *Totality and Infinity,* trans. A. Lingis (Pittsburgh, 1969); *Otherwise than Being or Beyond Essence,* trans. A. Lingis (Dordrecht and Boston, 1978). See F. Ciaramelli, *Transcendance et éthique: Essai sur Lévinas* (Brussels, 1989).

69. Jaspers, *The Origin and Goal,* 9.

70. Lowe, "Second Thoughts," 248.

71. See H. Joas, *Do We Need Religion? On the Experience of Self-Transcendence* (Boulder, 2008), esp. 3–19.

72. B. J. F. Lonergan, "Mission and the Spirit," in *A Third Collection: Papers by Bernhard J. F. Lonergan, S.J.,* ed. Frederick E. Crowe (New York, 1985), 32–33: "Experience of grace ... is experience of man's capacity for self-transcendence, of his unrestricted openness to the intelligible, the true, the good."

73. See H. Joas, *The Creativity of Action* (Chicago, 1996), 148–167; *The Genesis of Values* (Cambridge, 2000).

74. See R. A. Jonas, *Becoming the True Self: Spiritual and Psychological Perspectives for the 21st Century,* www.emptybell.org/articles/Becoming%20the%20True%20Self.pdf.

75. But note the important difference between (what I call) "aspiring self-transcending" and "anaphoric self-transcending" in section IV, 6 below, that is, a self-transcending move within Immanence *tout court* (aspiring self-transcending) and a self-transcending move within Immanence *into* the self-transcending of the Absolute Transcendent into Immanence (anaphoric self-transcending). The latter is always presupposing, and responding to, a prior activity of the Absolute Tran-

scendent that is experienced as pure passivity ("being grasped," "being interrupted") on the side of the human self.

76. See A. Badiou, *Being and Event* (New York, 2007), parts VII and VIII; *The Logic of Worlds: Being and Event II* (New York, 2009). A truth-event is not part of (the knowledge or description of) a situation but breaks into it and thereby brings out its truth by opening up a truth-procedure that unfolds what the situation in question truly is.

77. Lowe, "Second Thoughts," seeks "to disengage the notion of transcendence from that of the infinite" as he finds it in "Plato, Augustine and even Descartes" (242). But this "Cult of the Infinite" cannot be continued in "the air modernity breathes" since "'[t]here is no infinite God put there, just time and space going on and on,' which is to say that time and space go on indefinitely" (244). However, postmodernity's turn to "lateral transcendence" (248) is no viable alternative, as he rightly sees. Therefore he suggests that we should conceive of transcendence as something that "would cease to be the opposite of immanence; for a God of freedom [who] would not be isolated in some lofty place, but would be capable of being immanent precisely *because* of being transcendent" (250). But his reflections end where it could become interesting.

78. P. Moyaert, "On Faith and the Experience of Transcendence: An Existential Reflection on Negative Theology," in I. N. Bulhof and L. ten Kate, eds., *Flight of the Gods: Philosophical Perspectives on Negative Theology* (New York, 2000), 380.

79. See I. U. Dalferth, *Becoming Present: An Inquiry into the Christian Sense of the Presence of God* (Leuven, Paris, and Dudley, 2006).

80. Denzinger, *The Sources of Catholic Dogma,* §432, trans. R. J. Defarrari (St. Louis and London, 1957), 171.

81. P. Tillich, *Systematic Theology,* vol. 1 (London, 1988), 237.

82. P. Tillich, *Christianity and the Encounter of the World Religions* (New York: Columbia University Press, 1963), 97.

83. P. Tillich, "The Conquest of the Concept of Religion in the Philosophy of Religion," in *What Is Religion?,* ed. J. L. Adams (New York, 1969), 140.

84. M. J. De Nys, *Considering Transcendence: Elements of a Philosophical Theology* (Bloomington and Indianapolis, 2009), 14 (my emphasis).

85. Ibid., 10.

86. CD I/1, 304.

87. E. Jüngel, *God's Being Is in Becoming: The Trinitarian Being of God in the Theology of Karl Barth. A Paraphrase,* trans. J. Webster (Edinburgh, 2001), 121.

88. See E. Jüngel, *God as the Mystery of the World: On the Foundation of the Theology of the Crucified One in the Dispute between Theism and Atheism,* part V: *On the Humanity of God,* trans. D. L. Guder (Grand Rapids, 1983), 299–396.

89. It is not enough, therefore, to say as Martin Luther King, Jr., does: "God must be both 'in' and 'beyond' the world. If he is absolutely beyond, then he is not

in; if absolutely in, then not beyond; but remove the absolutely, and he may be both. The doctrines of transcendence and immanence are both half-truths in need of the tension of each other to give the more inclusive truth." ("'A Comparison of the Conceptions of God in the Thinking of Paul Tillich and Henry Nelson Wieman': Abstract of a Dissertation," Boston University Graduate School, 1955, in C. Carson, R. Luker, P. A. Ruessell, and P. Holloran, eds., *The Papers of Martin Luther King, Jr.,* vol. 2: *Rediscovering Precious Values, July 1951–November 1955* [Berkeley: University of California Press, 1994], 517). To argue in this way is to operate with an opposition between transcendence and immanence that is overcome by Barth. God is not marked off from creation by being both transcendent and immanent, but rather God's becoming immanently present as the transcendent God redefines "transcendence" as "God's self-transcending toward us."

90. See I. U. Dalferth, *Umsonst: Eine Erinnerung an die kreative Passivität des Menschen* (Tübingen, 2011).

A Comparative Perspective

8

Religion, the Axial Age, and Secular Modernity in Bellah's Theory of Religious Evolution

JOSÉ CASANOVA

In this essay I propose to bring together into critical reflection Robert Bellah's theory of religious evolution, debates concerning the Axial Age, and the most recent debates concerning our modern "secular age," in order to examine some of the ambiguities, equivocal meanings, and aporetic tensions built into our modern category of "religion."[1] I will proceed in three steps. First, I want to examine some of the difficulties built into any theory of religious evolution that needs to function with some unitary, transhistorical, and transcultural, indeed universally "human" category of "religion" that somehow cuts across pre-Axial, Axial, and modern secular contexts. The difficulties in matching or fitting together the three very different binary classificatory schemes, "sacred-profane," "transcendent-mundane," and "religious-secular" may serve as a telling indication. The pre-Axial sacred, the Axial transcendent, and the modern religious are not necessarily synonymous concepts, much less do they point to some identical conception of reality. In fact, they need to be understood in terms of their corresponding binary opposites—profane, mundane, and secular—which point also to very different structures of meaning and phenomenological conceptions of "worldly" reality.

Secondly, I want to interrogate the meaning of "axiality" within theories of the Axial Age, particularly within Bellah's theory of religious evolution. What is so "Axial" about the Axial Age?[2] How is an epochal theory of Axial emergence in world history congruent with a developmental theory of multiple stages of religious evolution, both pre-Axial and post-Axial? Is the place and role of "religion" in the multiple Axial breakthroughs equivalent? Is "transcendence" necessarily "religious" and are all Axial "theoretic" breakthroughs grounded equally in "religion"?

Finally, I want to briefly examine the relation between theories of the Axial Age and theories of secular modernity, with respect to our modern "religious-secular" system of classification. Is our modern global secular age the teleological unfolding of potentials implicit in the Axial breakthroughs, namely the full crystallization of Axial "theoretic" culture? Or does modernity constitute a post-Axial secular breakthrough of its own? How is the singularity of the development of secular modernity in the Christian West and its globalization through Western colonial expansion and American imperial projects congruent with evolutionary frameworks of human development?

Bellah himself has offered somewhat ambiguous responses to some of these questions, seemingly abandoning or at least significantly revising some of the most modernist, progressive, and teleological evolutionary premises of his two seminal essays of the 1960s, "Religious Evolution" and "Civil Religion in America." In the process he has adopted a much more critical attitude toward one-sided and exaggerated crystallizations of post-Axial theoretic culture and immanentist modern secular trends.[3] The new critical, more reflexively "prophetic," attitude is normatively anchored in a conception of the Axial Age and of human evolution that wants not only to reaffirm Axial transcendence but also to rehabilitate "myth" and "ritual" as constitutive elements of the human condition, and as constitutive "religious" elements of any viable human society and human culture.

Ambiguities in the Category and the Phenomenon of "Religion"

Bellah's theory of religious evolution takes for granted that "religion," both as an evolving sociocultural phenomenon and as an object of study, is historically constituted. As a student of Wilfred Cantwell Smith, Bellah also takes for granted that "in its modern usage, the term 'religion' is only about two hundred years old."[4] The original Latin term, *religio*, is of course more than two thousand years old, but its usage also changed dramatically from Varro's tripartite division of religion into *theologia naturalis, civilis,* and *mythica,* to Augustine's *De vera religione,* which incorporates what Jan Assmann has called "the Mosaic distinction," to the elevation of the "religious" life of the ascetic monk in medieval Christendom as the paradigmatic form of religion.[5] It is well known that most non-Western cultures did not have terms into which the modern Western category of "religion" could be easily translated and had to invent neologisms, such as *shukyo* in Japanese or *zongjiao* in Chinese, to designate what was viewed as a novel foreign phenomenon. Even in ancient Greek there was no single word equivalent to the Latin *religio*. Indeed, as pointed out by Guy Stroumsa, "it is notoriously difficult to define religion in the Greek world."[6] Tellingly, there is also no native word for religion in Byzantine or Slavic Orthodox Christianity, and all Orthodox cultures eventually borrowed the Latin word. But all these examples only prove that religion is indeed historically and culturally constituted and that one must avoid reducing religion or its study to its modern secular, to its Axial Christian, or to its ancient Latin meanings.

But this only sharpens the question of which kind of phenomena are to be designated as "religious" and thus to be included in any theory of religious evolution. In his 1964 essay "Religious Evolution," Bellah defined religion most abstractly as "a set of symbolic forms and acts that relate man to the ultimate conditions of his existence."[7] For Bellah, neither man, who in the broadest sense is and will remain *homo religiosus,* nor the structure of man's ultimate conditions of existence evolve. Leaving aside the ambiguity in the definition of the unit of analysis, which leaves unspecified whether "man" refers to individual humans, to particular societies, or to the human species, the definition presupposes that the ultimate conditions of human existence remain structurally unchanged and that humans and/or human societies cannot but relate somehow to those ultimate conditions. It is the way in which humans and/or societies relate to those ultimate conditions that, according to Bellah, evolves historically. "Neither religious man nor the structure of man's ultimate religious situation evolves then, but rather religion as symbol system."[8] Without assuming that evolution is "inevitable, irreversible, or must follow any single particular course," Bellah claims that one may speak of religious evolution insofar as the pattern of change of the religious symbol system appears to be one from "compact" to more "complex" and "differentiated" religious symbolization.[9]

However, Bellah also recognizes that one could "look at a few of the massive facts of human religious history"[10] in strictly historical terms, as emergent historical phenomena, without necessarily framing these historical changes in terms of a scheme of religious evolution. Following Max Weber's scheme of religious rationalization, Bellah clearly refers to the emergence of the Axial Age and the emergence of modernity as the two crucial or axial turning points in human religious history:

> The first of these facts is the emergence in the first millennium B.C. all across the Old World, at least in centers of high culture, of the phenomenon of religious rejection of the world characterized by an extremely negative evaluation of man and society and the exaltation of another realm of reality as alone true and infinitely valuable. This theme emerges in Greece through a long development into Plato's classic formulation in the *Phaedo* that the body is the tomb or prison of the soul.... A very different formulation is found in Israel, but there too the world is profoundly devalued in the face of the transcendent God.... In India we find perhaps the most radical of all versions of world rejection, culminating in the great image of the Buddha.... In China, Taoist ascetics urged the transvaluation of all the accepted values and withdrawal from human society....
>
> Nor was this a brief or passing phenomenon. For over two thousand years great pulses of world rejection spread over the civilized world.... I want to insist on this fact because I want to contrast it with an equally striking fact, namely the virtual absence of world rejection in primitive religions, in religion prior to the first millennium B.C., and in the modern world.[11]

Although Bellah acknowledges that one could account for "this sequence of presence and absence of world rejection" without ever raising the issue of religious evolution, by simply describing or explaining the transformation from pre-Axial, to Axial, to modern systems of religious symbolization, he chooses to frame these transformations within an evolutionary scheme composed of a series of five stages that he calls "primitive, archaic, historic, early modern, and modern."[12]

Bellah is careful to disclaim that religious evolution needs to imply "religious progress" in an ethical sense, pointing out that "a complex and differentiated religious symbolization is not therefore a better or a truer or a more beautiful one than a compact religious symbolization."[13] Yet following the evolutionary dynamic of the five stages in the 1964 essay, it is hard to avoid the impression that human religious evolution, at least for the time being, finds its teleological culmination in the religious symbol system one finds in the American society of the 1960s. Uniquely striking about Bellah's evolutionary scheme is the fact that he can simultaneously and without evident tension (a) affirm with Mircea Eliade that "primitive man is as fully religious as man at any stage of existence," but, Bellah adds, countering Eliade, not necessarily more religious than man in modern secular society;[14] (b) affirm with Émile Durkheim against Lucien Lévy-Bruhl that the paradigmatic "mythical" and "ritual" compact symbol systems of Australian "primitives," despite the apparent absence of any "religious" differentiation from "the social," should not be viewed as a form of "prereligion" but rather as "the elementary form of religious life," which somehow already contains within itself or "foreshadows" every posterior religious development;[15] (c) affirm with Durkheim that religion is the symbolic self-interpretation of human cultures and the symbolic self-representation of society and that in this respect every society, every collectivity, every social group needs to have some religious dimension, some form of "religious" symbolic self-representation. Following Weber, he can (d) conceptualize the evolutionary dynamics of religious development as a process of religious rationalization that entails increasing demythologization and deritualization culminating in the disenchanted modern secular order; (e) affirm with Weber that the Protestant Reformation was the single paradigmatic expression of "early modern religion" and therefore the privileged carrier of the world-historical process of religious rationalization that culminates in secular modernity; (f) affirm against Weber that this process of radical *Entzauberung der Welt* does not necessarily entail "a collapse of meaning and a failure of moral standards." Instead of interpreting modern religious trends as evidence of "indifference and secularization," Bellah prefers to see in them "the increasing acceptance of the notion that each individual must work out his own ultimate solutions," arguing that "the search for adequate standards of action, which is at the same time a search for personal maturity and social relevance, is in itself the heart of the modern quest for salvation."[16] Bellah can (g) affirm with Durkheim that this radical individualism is an expression of the social sacralization of the individual and constitutes the "religion" of modernity;

and (h) affirm with Talcott Parsons that American society represents a particular form of institutionalization of Christian Protestant values and that therefore the process of modern secularization does not entail so much religious decline as the transformation and relocation of religious symbols and practices into secular forms. By means of such a semantic relocation of the religious symbolization of the "ultimate conditions of existence" the sacred evolves or mutates from the "social collectivity" to divine "transcendence" to the modern secular individual, without apparently losing its religious identity or diminishing its force in the process.

Briefly summarizing the key characteristics of the five stages of religious evolution, one may say that *primitive* religions are oriented to a single cosmos, are concerned with the maintenance of personal, social, and cosmic harmony, pursue mainly worldly goods, and express no need for salvation.[17] Following W. E. H. Stanner, Bellah characterizes primitive religion as a "one possibility thing," which gives practically no leverage from which to change the world. Its very "fluidity and flexibility" is a barrier to radical innovation.[18]

Religious differentiation proper begins with *archaic* religion. Its characteristic feature is "the emergence of true cult with the complex of gods, priests, worship, sacrifice, and in some cases divine or priestly kingship."[19] The myth and ritual complex continues and the basic worldview remains monistic. There is still a single cosmos in which the gods, humans, society, and nature are all interrelated, without clear differentiation of the natural, social, and moral orders.

Historic religions break through the cosmological monism of the previous two stages and proclaim a new, higher, and transcendent realm of universal reality. Despite the significant differences in their symbol systems, all historic religions are "dualistic" and "universalistic." They offer new paths of individual salvation, which make possible for the first time "a clearly structured conception of the self" and the self-conception "of man as such." The religious concern is relocated from the mundane, which now becomes devalued, to a superior transcendent realm. Differentiated religious collectivities and new elites of religious *virtuosi* and *literati* differentiated from the laity emerge for the first time. The single religio-political hierarchy of archaic society also tends to split into two partially autonomous hierarchies. This differentiation and the transcendent standards promoted by the new religious elites bring a new level of tension and a possibility of conflict and change. "Religion" begins to provide "the ideology and social cohesion for many rebellions and reform movements," although it continues to play its traditional function of legitimation and reinforcement of the social order.[20]

The ideal-typical construction of *early modern religion,* unlike the previous general ideal types, which were based on a variety of cases, derives from a single historical development, the Protestant Reformation. Bellah points out that rather than a distinct evolutionary stage, it could be viewed as just "a transitional phase" between "Axial" and "modern" religion. Defining characteristics of early modern religion are "the collapse of the hierarchical structuring of both this and the other world," the relocation of the quest for salvation into worldly "callings," the dissolution of the mediated system of salvation through sacramental rituals and religious *virtuosi,* which gives way to direct relation between the individual and transcendent reality. Bellah reasserts the Weberian thesis of the importance of the Protestant Reformation, especially in its Calvinist wing, for modern developments in economics, science, politics, education, and law. But following Parsons, he stresses that "for the first time pressures to social change in the direction of greater realization of religious values are actually institutionalized as part of the structure of society itself." Supposedly, religious orientations now become mediated through secular institutions "in which religious values have been expressed."[21]

Modern religion represents in Bellah's view a radicalization and the culmination of processes initiated by the Protestant Reformation. It marks the final collapse of the dualism of the historic religions. But it should not be interpreted as a return to "primitive monism." Bellah is not sure whether one can still speak of a *modern religious symbol system* in our post-Kantian and postmetaphysic condition, when the very nature of symbolization is open to increasing reflexive critical analysis and when religion becomes necessarily grounded not only in ethical life but "in the structure of the human situation itself." For Bellah, using a postmodern-sounding discourse *avant la lettre,* an infinitely multiplex world has replaced the simple duplex structure and life "has become an infinite possibility thing." "The symbolization of man's relation to the ultimate conditions of his existence" is "no longer the monopoly of any groups explicitly labeled religious . . . every fixed position has become open to question . . . the fundamental symbolization of modern man and his situation is that of a dynamic multidimensional self capable, within limits, of continual self-transformation and capable, again within limits, of remaking the world, including the very symbolic forms with which he deals with it, even the forms that state the unalterable conditions of his own existence."[22]

One could say that in primitive societies, before the emergence of any religious differentiation, "religion" was diffused throughout the social system. In modern secular societies "religion" becomes once again diffused once its values become institutionalized in secular structures, and individual authenticity and self-expression become its main private "invisible" forms. In between these two beginning and ending stages of religious evolution one finds the world-historical process of religious rationalization so poignantly analyzed by Weber. In this way, religion, while a changing reality, can be affirmed as a permanent social fact that is equally congruous with the pre-Axial sacred, with Axial transcendence, and with the modern secular order. Bellah is well aware that one could offer radically different interpretations of the same evolutionary process either in negative terms as the decline of *homo religiosus,* the Death of God, and postmodern moral relativism, or in positive secularist terms as the triumph of scientific knowledge and reason and the progressive emancipation of humanity from magical rituals, myths, and religion. Ultimately, Bellah understands his own evolutionary scheme not as positivist social science but as an analytically grounded theoretic expression of modern man's effort at self-interpretation and therefore part of the enduring human exercise of religious symbolization.

In the last decades, Bellah has significantly revised his theory of religious evolution, while maintaining that much of the analytical framework of his 1964 essay remains still valid. Without being able in the context of this essay to develop a more systematic analysis, I perceive three major new developments in his revised theory of religious evolution, when compared to the earlier formulation.

Most significantly, as indicated by the title of the book *Religion in Human Evolution,* his theory of religious evolution is now embedded in a much more ambitious and more broadly elaborated theory of the evolution of human consciousness, grounded in significant novel contributions made by developmental cognitive and evolutionary psychology. Most crucially, he has incorporated into his own theory the work of the evolutionary psychologist Merlin Donald, particularly Donald's central thesis of three stages in the evolutionary development of human consciousness and culture: from primate episodic to mimetic, to mythic, and to theoretic.[23] This allows Bellah to reconstruct the crucial role of "religious" ritual and myth in the long process of hominization of the species, culminating in the full linguistification of *homo sapiens*. Religious developments now become embedded within a theory of human cultural evolution, which itself becomes embedded within a theory of human biological evolution.

According to Donald,

> around 100,000 years ago, Mousterian culture emerged, and toolmaking became gradually more refined, until it was revolutionized in the Mesolithic and Neolithic cultures. The correlation with brain size breaks down during this period; cultural change, once it began to accelerate, proceeded without any further change in brain size or, as far as can be determined, brain structure. Whereas change had been agonizingly slow during the period of *Homo erectus,* it now became an increasingly visible characteristic of human society. Ritual, art, myth, and social organizations developed and flourished in rapid succession. A new cognitive factor had obviously been introduced into the equation. The human capacity for continuous innovation and cultural change became our most prominent characteristic.[24]

The second major revision is the reconceptualization of the Axial Age as the passage from narrative mythic to theoretic culture. Axiality, now defined as "instances of the radical reformulation of myth in the light of theoretic criticism," becomes much more central in Bellah's scheme of religious evolution and, paradoxically, attains a new critical normative relevance vis-à-vis the misguided theoretic self-understanding of the modern rationalist Enlightenment project.[25]

Finally, the revaluation of ritual as the embodiment of mimetic culture and of myth as the expression of narrative culture leads Bellah to revise his overreliance on Weber's theory of religious rationalization as demagicization and demythologization and to revise significantly his Protestant modernist evaluation of modern religious trends. Embedding his revised theory of religious evolution within a history of the human species that incorporates "the entire human biosociocultural experience" leads Bellah to "critically reappropriate its mimetic and mythic dimensions in a constant dialectic with the theoretic."[26] "We are," Bellah insists again and again, "embodied, storytelling animals, and it is a 'myth' in the pejorative sense to imagine otherwise."[27]

Those are undoubtedly critically important contributions, but I have the sense that Bellah's reformulation of religious evolution is still overburdened by an overly broad and almost protean or, as Bellah himself recognizes, "pervasive" concept of religion which preserves most of the ambiguities and equivocal meanings already indicated concerning the apparently homologous character of the three different binary systems of classification, sacred-profane, transcendent-mundane, and religious-secular, which in my view correspond to the pre-Axial, Axial, and modern-secular phases.[28] The model has now the additional burden of having to offer some credible criteria in order to be able to distinguish in concrete historical settings, but also transhistorically and transculturally, "religious" ritual from nonreligious one, "religious" myth from nonreligious one, and "religious" Axial theoretic breakthroughs from nonreligious ones, since to define every ritual, every myth, and every theoretic breakthrough *(theoria)* as "religious" would only make the categorical qualifier "religious" analytically meaningless.

Even if one grants some of the basic premises of Bellah's theoretic reconstruction of the processes of human sociocultural evolution, such as "everything starts with religion," "ritual is the key to understanding mimetic culture," and "ritual is the phenomenological basis of all religion," one will still need some criteria for distinguishing between "religious" and "nonreligious" ritual.[29] This will be even more necessary if one holds the view, as Bellah does, following Erving Goffman and Randall Collins, that even now in our secular societies daily life consists in endless "interaction ritual chains."[30] Either one begins with the premise that "once upon a time" all ritual was "religious" and then the task is to develop some kind of interpretation of the process of "desacralization" of ritual through which "sacred" and "profane" or "religious" and "secular" rituals become differentiated. Or, alternatively, one assumes that all societies have made some kind of distinction between ordinary daily profane interaction rituals and extraordinary "sacred rituals" or "ritual culture" proper and then, given a modern "secular" consciousness, one has the double task of explaining in the first place, as Durkheim did, the origins or the social sources of the sacred.

Religion, the Axial Age, and Secular Modernity   201

Having accomplished that, one has then the additional task of developing some kind of theory of the differentiation of spheres of nonreligious ritual culture, such as the arts, science, education, politics, law, and so on, from the core or compact sacred ritual culture of primitive and archaic societies. Concomitantly, one has to explain how a separate and differentiated sphere of "religious" ritual, which also differs somewhat from archaic sacred ritual, becomes constituted. Weber's theory of religious rationalization or disenchantment from magical to ethical religion, as well as his theory of differentiation of the various spheres (economic, political, intellectual-scientific, aesthetic, erotic, and so on), and Habermas's theory of "linguistification of the sacred" constitute two such paradigmatic attempts.[31] While drawing upon both theories critically, Bellah evidently considers some crucial aspects of both theories either insufficient or misguided. One can therefore view Bellah's ambitious project of religious evolution as an attempt to offer a better version of both theories.[32]

In the remaining space I would like to interrogate some of these interrelated issues with respect to Bellah's revised theory of axiality and his critical reevaluation of modernity.

What Is Religiously Axial about the Axial Age?

In *Religion in Human Evolution,* Bellah offers extremely rich, detailed, and illuminating narrative reconstructions of what he considers to be the paradigmatic Axial breakthroughs in the four settings of ancient Israel (Axial Age I), ancient Greece (Axial Age II), China in the first millennium BCE (Axial Age III), and ancient India (Axial Age IV).[33] In this respect, Bellah begins where any comparative-historical sociological study of the Axial Age should begin, that is, with serious historization of each of the cases.[34] The chapters stand as parallel stories that, while following similar related themes, present radically diverse variations in the four different contexts. They are also devoid of the kind of comparative analysis that would try to draw out some of the basic similarities and differences between the cases. In this respect, Bellah's analysis avoids premature analytical theorization that would tend to blend all the cases into versions of the same process. Each story, at least to a reader like me, who can claim no expertise in any of the cases, appears extremely suggestive and compelling and seems to be well grounded in the best scholarly and most up-to-date secondary literature.

Nevertheless, even after granting that each of the stories is basically right and narratively compelling, the theoretic, comparative-analytical task of answering the central question "What is Axial about the Axial Age?" still remains. Bellah, in my view, offers a persuasive answer to the more general and, one could say, more relevant question from the perspective of human cultural evolution, namely "What made the axial age axial?"[35] But the more specific and narrow question, yet the one which is more pertinent from the particular perspective of this essay, namely "What is so Axially 'religious' about the Axial Age?," finds a less satisfactory answer.

Bellah's basic claim is that in all four cases an (evolutionarily) new form of "theoretic" culture was applied to the reformulation of some of the basic cultural premises that had been grounded so far in archaic sacred "ritual" and "myth." Though "mimetic" and "narrative" traditions that had been central in older civilizations continued to be significant, they now became reformulated in the light of the new theoretical understandings. The claim therefore is not that theoretic culture triumphed over and superseded "ritual" and "myth," but rather that a new sphere of theoretic culture emerged and that this led to various reformulations of mimetic and narrative culture. Most significantly, Bellah insists that the four cases are far from homogeneous and the cultural transformations "by no means uniform," so that he seems to accept the notion of "multiple axialities" along with "multiple modernities."[36]

It is at this point that Bellah's ambitious research project on religious evolution encounters Shmuel Eisenstadt's no less ambitious research project on the Axial Age, Axial Age civilizations, and multiple modernities.[37] I will not revisit here the central debates concerning the Axial Age and Axial civilizations and must restrict myself to raising some critical issues concerning the "religious" aspects of the Axial transformations. In any case, Bellah's own reference to "multiple axialities" highlights the need to distinguish, as stressed repeatedly by Johann P. Arnason, between (a) those aspects of the transformations that are "culturally unique," (b) those aspects that are "specifically Axial," and (c) those that appear to be more "universal or evolutionary."[38]

Culturally unique would be those "civilizational" aspects that are specifically "Greek," "Chinese," "Indic," "Judaic," and so on, which therefore must be understood and interpreted within their concrete hermeneutic sociocultural contexts and unique historical trajectories and/or cultural memories, histories which always precede the Axial Age and may have some continuous development well beyond the Axial Age. The entire *problematique* of "Axial civilizations" and "civilizational" analysis and the extent to which one may speak of Axial and non-Axial civilizations is related to those issues.[39]

Specifically "Axial" would be those aspects that are "epochal," that emerge simultaneously by some still not fully clarified "mysterious synchronicity" roughly at the middle of the first millennium BCE at those four particular civilizational settings, but not in others (Egypt, Mesopotamia, or Phoenicia), and that allow us to speak meaningfully of a world-historical "age" (in Karl Jaspers' sense of the term). Axial here, as a "global" epochal category, has to mean something more than simply interesting parallel "types" of transformations one may find happening simultaneously, and apparently unrelatedly, across various civilizations, so that we may speak of typical "Axial" or "classical" ages within each of these civilizations. Axial here has to mean that each of these "ages" is not only "classical" or "Axial" for each of these civilizations but is somehow also of unique significance and relevance for world history and for all of humanity. Obviously, such "significance" or "relevance" is one that emerges only from "the present," that is, from the particular hermeneutic horizon of "our" present global age. For that very reason, it is not possible to separate "evaluations" and "understandings," that is, "the meaning of the Axial Age," from our own "modern" self-understandings.[40]

Finally, "universal" or "evolutionary" aspects would be those aspects of the Axial transformations that are connected with what today we would consider as generally and distinctly "human" characteristics that distinguish *homo sapiens* as an animal species, but that appear to have found various manifest cultural crystallizations first during the Axial Age. One may speak most specifically, following Yehuda Elkana, of "second-order thinking," more broadly, as does Bellah, of "theoretic culture," or most broadly, as does Björn Wittrock, of enhanced "reflexivity," "historicity," and "agentiality."[41] This is the sense in which Assmann talks of "axiality" as a cultural development that should not be circumscribed chronologically to the Axial Age, even if it may have found in this epoch its first full historical manifestation and crystallization.

In fact, Assmann's own work has shown magistrally some of the preliminary and preparatory, one could even say anticipatory, manifestations of axiality (or at least of protoaxiality) in ancient Egypt, a supposedly non-Axial civilization.[42] Similarly, "axiality" or "theoretic culture," as Bellah himself recognizes, may have found further development in later crystallizations, let's say in late antiquity or in the first centuries of the second millennium CE, and "full" institutionalization only in modernity. But once we talk of different epochal crystallizations of "axiality," in various periods of global history, then the unique meaning of the Axial Age for global history and the very category of "axiality" loses some of its symbolic power and significance.

Bellah's evolutionary approach, and his claim that the Axial Age can be best conceptualized as the first historical emergence of phenomena that now, from our present standpoint, can be identified as prototypical manifestations of "theoretic culture," does not need to circumscribe the breakthrough from mythic to theoretic culture within one single historical age or within some kind of synchronous development. The multiple independent emergence of similar yet very diverse phenomena in different civilizational contexts, all indicating some "breakthrough" to theoretic culture, is more central for an evolutionary approach than its synchronicity or simultaneity.

Such an evolutionary approach also does not need to deny the importance of intermediate, preparatory, and anticipatory steps already present in archaic civilizations or the fact that, as Donald has pointed out, Bellah's ideas about a theoretic revolution during the Axial Age simply address "some of the earliest events in the long, painful, bloody (and still unfinished) transition from the governance of Mythic culture to that of Theoretic culture."[43] Thus an evolutionary approach could easily accommodate and stretch chronologically the conditions for the emergence of elements of "axiality" back into the second millennium BCE and forward into modernity, for as Bellah himself indicates, "theoretic culture purged of mythic content did not appear until the scientific revolution of the seventeenth century."[44]

Addressing finally the role of "religion" in the Axial Age's beginning transition to "theoretic culture," one can accept as a starting point the premise suggested by Donald, namely that in the cognitive evolutionary scenario he describes, "one must view religious thinking, and especially the religious innovations of the Axial Age, as the absolute cutting edge of human experience at that time."[45] Yet, in my view, one should distinguish the broader question concerning the role of "religious thinking," whatever this may mean, in the general cognitive evolutionary transition from "mythic" to "theoretic" culture, from the narrower question of "religious evolution" per se. Namely, does the transition to "theoretic culture" necessarily entail the concomitant transition from "archaic" to "Axial" religion, and if so, which would be the specifically "Axial religious innovations" that are characteristic of "Axial" religion? Furthermore, how do we distinguish those "religious innovations" that may be said to be culturally unique for each of the four civilizational settings, from those that are specifically "Axial"? Are all the transformations similarly "religious" in nature and are the outcomes everywhere equally "religious," or is the diversity of those multiple Axial transformations such that some of them appear more "secular" or "mundane" or "this-worldly" in character than others? Bellah acknowledges that in the cases of China and ancient Greece critics have raised valid questions concerning Eisenstadt's emphasis on the distinction between "transcendental" and "mundane" orders as the most fundamental characteristic of "axiality."[46]

Finally, is "religious axiality," like theoretic culture, something that finds its first clear historical manifestations during the Axial Age but only reaches fuller development and institutionalization in late antiquity or even in modernity, so that "early modern" and "modern religions" could be understood as more developed and differentiated forms of "religious axiality," which seems to be Bellah's earlier position? Or does Axial religion truly represent the paradigmatic form of religious axiality, so that all attempts to construct a modern theoretic religion "within the bounds of reason alone" or modern individual "invisible" forms are eventually revealed as misguided attempts that misunderstand the structure of man's ultimate conditions, not only as *homo religiosus* but as a symbolic sociocultural animal? There could be a third alternative, which I will sketch briefly in the final section of my essay, suggesting that our modern secular age creates the social conditions for the synchronous and nonhierarchic, that is, "free and equal" coexistence of all forms of "religion" (pre-Axial, Axial, and post-Axial) and that our modern "religious-secular" binary classification is markedly different from any kind of ontological classification we may define as "Axial" or "pre-Axial."

The distinction between "uniquely civilizational," "specifically Axial," and more "universal normative" assumptions about the kind of religion that we assume is compatible with further developments in theoretic culture is important if we want to avoid the two traps that, as Wittrock has pointed out, are almost inherent to Axial Age theorizing.[47] The first, the ethnocentric trap, would be the tendency to elevate one particular form of religion, which will inevitably be "our" Western form of "Axial religion," either Judeo-Christian or Greek or some combination of the two, into the paradigmatic form of "axiality," so that other non-Western forms appear as somewhat deficient and not fully "Axial." The second trap, the teleological modernist one, would be the tendency to characterize as "Axial" those phenomena that appear to be conducive to our own modernity. As Assmann has so eloquently pointed out, the relevant question appears to be not so much about the "Axial past" per se, "but about the roots of modernity," an impulse that he identifies as the typical mythical question of origins.[48]

There is a relative scholarly consensus concerning the fact that pre-Axial religions, both tribal as well as archaic, can be characterized as manifestations of ontological monism or, in Bellah's new formulation, as "cosmological," "in that supernature, nature, and society were all fused in a single cosmos."[49] There appears to be also some relative consensus that the passage to axiality represents some break in this ontological monism. But there is much less agreement about the kind of dualism, or the kind of multiple and competing ontological visions, that are supposed to be characteristic of the Axial Age. Particularly disputed is the assertion that the new ontological dualism is grounded in every Axial case on a radical gap between a higher "transcendent" order of reality and a devalued order of "mundane" reality. Such analytical characterization appears certainly appropriate for the Israeli path of Axial development, and partially so for the Buddhist challenge to archaic Vedic religion, but much less appropriate for the Greek *philosophical-political* path of development or for the Sinic *universal-inclusive* path.[50]

Even assuming that every Axial path implies some transformation of pre-Axial ontological monism into some kind of new ontological dualist distinction between a higher ultimate and a more derivative order of reality, the question is whether this necessarily implies the emergence of some notion of "transcendence." Moreover, even if one accepts the premise that every Axial path implies some notion of transcendence in the sense that transcendence constitutes the very condition of possibility to gain some reflexive distance from "the world," it does not follow that "transcendence" is always and necessarily "religious" by definition or that the "world" is therefore devalued as "mundane."

Following Durkheim, one may conceptualize "sacred" and "profane" as a general dichotomous classificatory system of reality, characteristic of pre-Axial sociocultural systems, that encompasses within one single, that is, monistic, ontological order various realms which later will be differentiated into different cosmic, earthly, social, and moral orders. All reality, gods and spirits, nature and cosmic forces, humans and other animal species, and the kinship, political, social, and moral orders are integrated into a single order of things precisely according to the dichotomous classificatory system of sacred and profane. The entire system, moreover, is an immanent "this-worldly" one, if one is allowed to use anachronistically another dichotomous category that will only emerge with the Axial breakthroughs, since the very idea of "world," as Rémi Brague has shown, is an Axial one.[51]

Indeed one may postulate that every Axial breakthrough entails some kind of redrawing of the boundaries between sacred and profane, which may be interpreted as a form of semantic relocation of the sacred, which may imply simultaneous processes of desacralization of some aspects of reality and the potential resacralization of other aspects. In the case of ancient Israel, "the Mosaic distinction" entails first a radical exclusive monolatric sacralization of YHWH as the God of the covenant, and eventually in the prophetic age its elevation to the one and only transcendent Holy God, creator of heaven and earth, universal lawgiver, God of history and Lord of all peoples. Such a sacralization of transcendence entails, indeed, an equally radical desacralization of all creatures and of all cosmic and natural forces and, most of all, the demotion of all gods and supernatural beings into "false" idols and evil demonic forces. But in and of itself, all of creation, as God's work, is intrinsically "good" and not profane. Mundane immanent reality, in this respect, is devalued only in relation to God, and it becomes "profane" and "evil" insofar as it refuses to recognize the transcendent sovereignty of God.

Surely the Axial breakthrough in ancient Greece from the Homeric age to the classical age of Athenian democracy entails an equally radical redrawing of the boundaries between sacred and profane, breaking through the archaic ontological monism. But the dynamics of desacralization, the redrawing of the boundaries between various ontological realms and the radical reformulation of myth in the light of theoretical criticism evince significantly different dynamics, dimensions, and directions, which in my view it would be problematic to characterize as "religious" even if the initial dynamics had "sacred" or "divine" dimensions. The very tripartite theological differentiation of archaic divine reality into *mythike* (or the mythical world of the gods), *physike* (or the cosmic order of nature), and *politike* (the conventional *nomoi* of the democratic *polis*) entails certainly a radical desacralization, but its dynamic is not necessarily a "religious" one, and its crystallization is hardly one of a single ontological dualism between "transcendent" *kosmos* and devalued "mundane" reality.[52] Moreover, this desacralization does not lead to "religious" rationalization per se or to any form of resacralization. Indeed, the Greek archaic public religio-political cultic system of worship and sacrifice is somewhat transformed but not radically altered, despite the radical Axial theoretic breakthroughs in other spheres. Only with Plato does one find the combination of radical theoretic deconstruction of mythic culture and the conscious attempt to construct a new myth of radical ontological dualism. But this model of Axial Platonic *theoria*, which occupies such a central role in Bellah's analysis, only emerges after the crisis of Athenian democracy when theoretic breakthroughs of second-order thinking in cosmological, physical, logical, mathematical, ethical, and political ideas had already been accomplished.

One observes therefore two radically different Axial breakthroughs. Both entail processes of desacralization that undermine the archaic monist sacred-profane order. But the dynamics are very different. The Israeli dynamic is "religious" through and through in that, by means of the Mosaic distinction, it invents a new Axial type of "religion." But in fact this new Axial form of "religion" will only find full crystallization in late antiquity with the transformation of Second Temple Judaism into Talmudic Judaism after the destruction of the temple and the end of sacrifice, and the emergence of the two "daughter religions," Christianity and Islam. By contrast, the Greek process of desacralization can hardly be depicted as a process of religious rationalization. Of course, Greek *philosophia* had strong "religious" elements of theoretic divination that entailed the search of spiritual paths of self-realization, at times approximating transcendent "religious" paths "beyond human flourishing."[53] In this respect, it would also be anachronistic to speak of the Greek Axial path as being more "secular," a modern category that has its origins in a radically different Christian theological system than the Greek one. Some of these philosophic paths, Platonic and Stoic, will clearly merge with and enrich more characteristically "religious" Christian paths of otherworldly salvation. But this will happen much later beyond the Axial Age proper.

One could draw similar contrasts between the two radically different Asian Axial paths, the Indic and the Sinic. Buddhism represents a more clearly Axial dynamic of "religious semantic" relocation of the sacred through a radical transvaluation of the Vedic sacro-cosmic-sacrificial ritual order, which much later, beyond the Axial Age proper, was eventually transformed into a different type of Axial "religion" with the institutionalization of Mahayana Buddhism. The various competing Sinic paths of desacralization are less clearly "religious," both in their dynamics and in their outcomes.

Bellah's reliance on Donald's conceptual formulation of "theoretic culture" allows him to reformulate his theory of axiality in such a broad and general way that the central argument is "that the axial breakthrough was essentially the breakthrough of theoretic culture in dialogue with mythic culture as a means for the 'comprehensive modeling of the entire human universe.'"[54] But unless one assumes that every "comprehensive modeling of the entire human universe" is per se "religious," then one should be able to differentiate between those comprehensive worldviews that should be properly called "religious," those that appear to be more humanist ethico-philosophical without apparent reliance on some form of "supraempirical transcendence," and those that appear to be more "protoscientific," thus anticipating modern scientific theoretic culture. In this respect, the relation between these diverse Axial theoretic breakthroughs and later "religious" historical developments, particularly the emergence of the historic "world religions," still remains unclear.

Bellah conjoins Arnaldo Momigliano's notion of "an age of criticism," Elkana's "second-order thinking," Eisenstadt's idea of "transcendence," and Eric Voegelin's concept of "mythospeculation" in an attempt to offer a more precise formulation of the kind of comprehensive modeling he views as characteristically "Axial." What all Axial breakthroughs have in common, according to Bellah, is some kind of "second-order thinking about cosmology, which for societies just emerging from the archaic age meant thinking about the religio-political premises of society itself. It is second-order thinking in this central area of culture, previously filled by myth, that gave rise to the idea of transcendence, so often associated with the axial age."[55]

But Bellah qualifies Elkana's conception of "scientific theorizing" and argues that "because transcendental realms are not subject to disproof the way scientific theories are, they require a new form of narrative, that is, a new form of myth," which, following Voegelin, he calls "mythospeculation." "The transcendental breakthrough," Bellah concludes, "involved a radicalization of mythospeculation, but not an abandonment of it."[56] One needs to ask, however, whether all Axial mythospeculations, in all four Axial cases, ought to be characterized as "religious." One could argue that the most "theoretic" Axial mythospeculations appear to be the least "religious," while the most religious ones appear to be the least "theoretic."[57] Again and again one faces the same terminological difficulty, the moment one tries to use the category of "religion," anachronistically as it were, in order to analyze and compare the diverse Axial cultural transformations. Such a difficulty is inherent in the fact that the very category of "religion" itself emerged out of one of the particular Axial transformations, though eventually it crystallized into the modern Western "religious-secular" system of classification, which has now become globalized.

One can postulate that the Axial breakthroughs certainly prepared the ground and the conditions for the later institutionalization of the "historic" world religions. But that which, following Weber, could be called the dynamics of "religious" rationalization proper were carried by radically new types of distinct religious communities, which offered some form of salvation to the individual qua individual and were in this respect radically different from the "community cults," which had been characteristic of the religio-political archaic order.[58] In fact, as Bellah himself acknowledges, the so-called world religions are "successor faiths" which only emerge after the Axial Age, after all the competing Axial ontological visions failed to establish any long-term institutionalization. Even Talmudic synagogue rabbinic Judaism was a new form of religious community radically different from the religio-political community cult of ancient Israel addressed by the biblical prophets. Under Hellenism, Greek culture underwent a process of archaic resacralization. Confucius was equally unsuccessful in establishing his ethical humanist vision. Confucianism only became established as an official state orthodoxy now linked with the sacro-magical religio-political imperial cult under the Han dynasty.[59] But as Bellah emphasizes, following Donald, it is precisely the evolutionary cognitive advantage of theoretic breakthroughs that they become a form of external memory, which can be reappropriated again and again, as happened repeatedly to all Axial theoretic breakthroughs. In fact, Bellah would argue, they are precisely Axial insofar as they constitute a cultural memory that is still alive today and is the patrimony of all of humanity.

But, as Stroumsa has shown so convincingly, in terms of the dynamics of "religious development" in the strict sense of the term and in terms of world-historical relevance, the truly religious "Axial" transformations happened in late antiquity from the second century CE, with the interlinked coemergence of Talmudic Judaism, Christianity, and Manicheism, to the seventh century, with the later explosive eruption of Islam.[60] This era, Stroumsa asserts, "also has a claim to this title of 'axial age,' an epoch in which the very frameworks of a civilization are transformed in a radical way . . . one may follow from Jesus to Muhammad, the transformation of the very concept of religion. . . . the Christianization of the empire permitted the establishment of a new sort of religion that was unknown in the ancient world."[61]

The new type of religion was based on five interrelated transformations, which were shared by Judaism, Christianity, Manicheism, and many other religious movements of the late Roman Empire, although after the Constantinian establishment of Christian hegemony, those characteristics would appear as paradigmatically "Christian." Stroumsa depicts those five transformations as (a) "a new care of the self," (b) "the rise of the religions of the book," facilitated by the media revolution in the transmission of cultural memory effected by the invention of the codex, (c) "the end of sacrifice" and the radical transformations of mimetic ritual culture associated with such a development, (d) the passage "from civic religion to community religion" with the equally radical cultic transformation from the public open religio-political ceremonies of the outdoor temple to the private closed congregational indoor gathering of the religious community, and (e) the transformation in the model of *paideia* "from wisdom teacher to spiritual master."[62]

But strictly speaking, those were particular historical religious developments that it would not be appropriate to conceptualize in human evolutionary terms. With the institutionalization of Buddhism, another different type of "Axial" religion became institutionalized across Asia, introducing new religious dynamics everywhere, including in China, where it entered a creative interactive relation with Confucianism and Taoism. Eventually this interactive dynamic crystallized in the syncretistic Chinese religious system of "the three teachings" *(sanjiao)*.

Following Stroumsa, one could perhaps attribute "Axial" relevance to the historical religious transformations of late antiquity only in the sense that they formed the basis for the European religious system of medieval Christendom, out of which emerged the modern process of secularization, which in turn culminated in our global secular age. But this is a particular historical development with world-historical consequences, not a universal or evolutionary process of human development.

The Modern "Secular-Religious" System of Classification

The modern "secular-religious" system of classification, which emerged out of the transformation of Western Christianity, has now become globalized, entering in dynamic transformative interaction with all non-Western systems of classification, pre-Axial as well as Axial. All the religio-cultural systems, Christian and non-Christian, Western and non-Western, have been transformed through these global interactive dynamics. As I have stressed throughout my work, one can trace the modern process of secularization, or the crystallization of the modern secular age, by following the semantic transformations in the Latin word *saeculum*.[63]

Originally, the term *saeculum*, as in *per saecula saeculorum*, only meant an indefinite period of time, with a connotation similar to the Greek term *aeon*. But Augustine turned it into a Christian theological category when he used the term to refer to a temporal space between the present and the eschatological *parousia*, the Second Coming of Christ, in which both Christians and pagans could come together to pursue their common interests as a civil community.[64] In this sense, the Augustinian use of "secular" is very similar to the modern meaning of a secular political sphere, that of the constitutional democratic state and of a democratic public sphere, which is supposedly "neutral" with respect to all worldviews, religious as well as nonreligious. Such a theological conception of the secular does not equate it with the "profane," as the other of the "sacred," nor is the secular the other of the "religious." It is precisely a neutral intermediate space, between Christian "sacred" and pagan "profane," which can be shared by all who live in a not religiously homogeneous or in a multicultural society, which by definition will have different and most likely competing conceptions of what is "sacred" and what is "profane."[65]

Eventually, however, with the consolidation of Western medieval Christendom and the hegemonic triumph of the Christian church, the secular became one of the terms of a dyad, religious/secular, which served to structure the entire spatial and temporal reality of medieval Christendom into a binary system of classification separating two worlds, the religious-spiritual-sacred world of salvation and the secular-temporal-profane world. It is from this new theological perspective of medieval Christendom that the modern meaning of "secularization" emerges. This historical process can best be understood as an attempt to bridge, eliminate, or transcend the dualism between the religious and the secular world.

Even in the West, however, this process of secularization follows two different dynamics. One is the dynamic of internal Christian secularization, which aims to spiritualize the temporal and to bring the religious life of perfection out of the monasteries into the secular world. It tends to transcend the dualism by blurring the boundaries between the religious and the secular, by making the religious secular and the secular religious through mutual reciprocal infusion.

The other, almost opposite dynamic of secularization takes the form of laicization. It aims to emancipate all secular spheres from clerical-ecclesiastical control, and in this respect it is marked by a laic-clerical antagonism. Here the boundaries between the religious and the secular are rigidly maintained, but those boundaries are pushed into the margins, aiming to contain, privatize, and marginalize everything religious, while excluding religion from any visible presence in the secular public sphere, now defined as the realm of *laïcité,* freed from religion.

With many variations these are the two main dynamics of secularization which culminate in our secular age. In different ways both paths lead to an overcoming of the medieval Christian dualism through a positive affirmation and revaluation of the *saeculum,* that is, of the secular age and the secular world, imbuing the immanent secular world with a quasi-transcendent meaning as the place for human flourishing.

The function of secularism as a philosophy of history, and thus as ideology, is to turn the particular Western Christian historical process of secularization into a universal teleological process of human development from belief to unbelief, from primitive irrational or metaphysical religion to modern rational postmetaphysical secular consciousness. Even when the particular role of internal Christian developments in the general process of secularization is acknowledged, it is not in order to stress the particular contingent nature of the process, but rather to stress the universal significance of the uniqueness of Christianity as, in Marcel Gauchet's expressive formulation, "the religion to exit from religion."[66]

I would like to propose that this secularist stadial consciousness is a crucial factor in the widespread secularization that has accompanied the modernization of Western European societies. It is, in my view, the presence or absence of this secularist historical stadial consciousness that explains when and where processes of modernization are accompanied by radical secularization. In places where such secularist historical stadial consciousness is absent or less dominant, as in the United States or in most non-Western postcolonial societies, processes of modernization are unlikely to be accompanied by processes of religious decline. On the contrary, they may be accompanied by processes of religious revival.

In fact, the particular Western Christian dynamic of secularization became globalized through the process of Western colonial expansion, entering, however, into dynamic tension with the many different ways in which other civilizations had drawn boundaries between "sacred" and "profane," "transcendent" and "immanent," "religious" and "secular." I would like to reiterate that we should not think of these dyadic pairs of terms as being synonymous. The sacred tends to be immanent in pre-Axial cultures. The transcendent is not necessarily "religious" in some Axial civilizations. The secular is by no means profane in our secular age.

In a certain sense, not only the so-called secular societies of the West but the entire globe is becoming increasingly more secular and "disenchanted" in the sense that the cosmic order is increasingly defined by modern science and technology; the social order is increasingly defined by the interlocking of "democratic" states, market economies, and mediatic public spheres; and the moral order is increasingly defined by the calculations of rights-bearing individual agents, claiming human dignity, liberty, equality, and the pursuit of happiness. Yet comparisons of secular Europe and religious America and the evidence of religious revivals around the world make clear that within the same secular immanent frame one can encounter very diverse religious dynamics. In this respect, the disenchantment of the world does not necessarily entail the disenchantment of consciousness, the decline of religion, or the end of magic. On the contrary, it is compatible with all forms of reenchantment. What characterizes the contemporary global moment is precisely the fact that all forms of human religion, past and present, from the most "primitive" to the most "modern," are available for individual and collective appropriation and tend to coexist increasingly side by side in today's global cities.

We now find ourselves within a global secular/religious system of classification in which the category of religion has to do extra work and serve to articulate and encompass all kinds of different "religious" experiences, individual and collective; all kinds of magical, ritual, and sacramental practices; all kinds of communal, ecclesiastical, and institutional arrangements; and all kinds of processes of sacralization of the social, be it in the form of religious nationalism, secular civil religions, or the global sacralization of human rights. We, as well as Bellah, tend to use the same qualifier, "religious," to characterize all these diverse phenomena in a way that can only be mind-boggling for a "secular" as well as for a "religious" mind-set. Yet despite the futile calls by so many scholars of "religion" to drop the concept altogether because it has become meaningless, there is no point in bemoaning this fact, since the global secular-religious system of classification of reality is here to stay. It has now been adopted by basically every state in the world system. Simultaneously, drawing the proper boundaries between "the religious" and "the secular" has become a source of contestation in every society in the world.[67]

In his most recent work, Bellah has revised his older evolutionary narrative according to which a historic or Axial stage of religious evolution was followed by an early modern and a modern stage. As he acknowledges:

> In my original essay on religious evolution, I made the point that the "stages" were not discrete, that nothing is ever lost. I argued that even aspects of tribal and archaic religion survive among us. What I did not recognize clearly enough is that the axial age remains as determinative for us as ever, that we have not left it behind, that what I called

the early modern and modern were only phases of working out its implications. . . .

Neither the Enlightenment nor any of the great ideological movements of the twentieth century have supplanted the axial heritage; often they have acted it out in parody even as they imagined themselves rejecting it.[68]

In response to Habermas's project of the "linguistification of the sacred," Bellah now writes: "If I am right that not only religious but also ethical and political thought can never be simply theoretic but are always also indelibly mythic and mimetic, then it is not only 'opaque features' and 'bizarre expressions of alien cultures' that we need to understand, but our own modern, partially disguised, mythic and mimetic practice."[69] As to his older rather sanguine analysis of American "civil religion" as the immanent institutionalization of transcendent values, Bellah has also become a "prophetic" harsh "denouncer" of America's delusive self-conception of "immaculate exceptionalism," of being "A City upon a Hill" and the realization of the Kingdom of God on earth. With resigned irony he concludes, "perhaps we are just one more tired example of Augustine's city of man."[70]

Notes

1. In this essay I only want to interrogate some problems in Bellah's usage of the category of religion. I cannot offer here a more systematic analysis of Robert N. Bellah, *Religion in Human Evolution: From the Paleolithic to the Axial Age* (Cambridge, MA: The Belknap Press of Harvard University Press, 2011).

2. Robert N. Bellah, "What Is Axial about the Axial Age?," *European Journal of Sociology* 46 (2005): 69–89.

3. Robert N. Bellah, "Religious Evolution," *American Sociological Review* 29 (1964): 358–374; and "Civil Religion in America," *Daedalus* 96 (1967), no. 1, 1–21. Both essays were reprinted in Robert N. Bellah, *Beyond Belief: Essays on Religion in a Post-Traditional World* (New York: Harper & Row, 1970), 20–50 and 168–189.

4. Robert N. Bellah, "Introduction," in Robert N. Bellah and Steven M. Tipton, eds., *The Robert Bellah Reader* (Durham: Duke University Press, 2006), 6; see also Wilfred Cantwell Smith, *The Meaning and End of Religion* (New York: Macmillan, 1963).

5. Jonathan Z. Smith, "Religion, Religions, Religious," in Mark C. Taylor, ed., *Critical Terms for Religious Studies* (Chicago: University of Chicago Press, 1998), 269–284.

6. Guy G. Stroumsa, "Cultural Memory in Early Christianity: Clement of Alexandria and the History of Religions," in Johann P. Arnason, Shmuel N. Eisenstadt, and Björn Wittrock, eds., *Axial Civilizations and World History* (Leiden: Brill, 2005), 314–315.

7. Bellah, *Beyond Belief*, 21.

8. Ibid.

9. Ibid.

10. Ibid., 22.

11. Ibid., 22–23.

12. Ibid., 24.

13. Ibid., 22.

14. Ibid., 21.

15. Ibid., 21–22.

16. Ibid., 43–44.

17. Bellah will later adopt the less pejorative term "tribal religion."

18. Bellah, *Beyond Belief*, 23 and 29.

19. Ibid., 29 and 31.

20. Ibid., 32–36.

21. Ibid., 36–39.

22. Ibid, 42.

23. See Merlin Donald, *Origins of the Modern Mind: Three Stages in the Evolution of Culture and Cognition* (Cambridge, MA: Harvard University Press, 1991); *A Mind So Rare: The Evolution of Human Consciousness* (New York: Norton, 2001); and "An Evolutionary Approach to Culture: Implications for the Study of the Axial Age," in this volume.

24. Donald, *Origins of the Modern Mind*, 115.

25. Bellah, *The Bellah Reader*, 11.

26. Ibid., 17.

27. Ibid., 11.

28. Bellah's "pervasive" conception of religion is illustrated in his depiction of the folk religion of southern Italian peasants, the official Roman Catholicism, Croce's liberalism, Gramsci's socialism, and Mussolini's fascism as "the five religions of modern Italy." These only enumerate five collective social forms. If one was to add the private individual forms, from the idiosyncratic "cosmos" of Menocchio, the sixteenth-century heretic miller made famous by Carlo Ginzburg, to the many contemporary Italian forms of "Sheilaism," as Bellah and his collaborators depicted the "private faith" of Sheila Larson in *Habits of the Heart*, the number of religions in Italy or in any other society become myriad. See Robert N.

Bellah, "The Five Religions of Modern Italy," in *The Bellah Reader*, 51–80; Robert N. Bellah, Richard Madsen, William M. Sullivan, Ann Swidler, and Steven M. Tipton, *Habits of the Heart* (Berkeley: University of California Press, 1985), 221 and 235; and Carlo Ginzburg, *The Cheese and the Worms: The Cosmos of a Sixteenth-Century Miller* (Baltimore: Johns Hopkins University Press, 1992).

29. One can find such terse formulations, which reflect Bellah's central Durkheimian premises, in "Rethinking Secularism and Religion in the Global Age," a conversation between Mark Juergensmeier and Bellah at the University of California at Berkeley, September 11, 2008, http://blogs.ssrc.org/tif/wp-content/uploads/2009/09/Bellah-Juergensmeyer.pdf.

30. See Robert N. Bellah, "The Ritual Roots of Society and Culture," in Michelle Dillon, ed., *Handbook of the Sociology of Religion* (Cambridge: Cambridge University Press, 2003), 31–44; "Durkheim and Ritual," in *The Bellah Reader*, 150–180; Randall Collins, *Interaction Ritual Chains* (Princeton: Princeton University Press, 2004); and Erving Goffman, *Interaction Ritual: Essays on Face-to-Face Behavior* (Chicago: Aldine, 1967).

31. Weber's theories of rationalization and differentiation appear throughout his work, in his *Collected Essays in the Sociology of Religion* as well as in *Economy and Society*. The most succinct statement of his theory of differentiation appears in the *Zwischenbetrachtung*, translated as "Religious Rejections of the World and Their Directions," in H. H. Gerth and C. Wright Mills, eds., *From Max Weber: Essays in Sociology* (New York: Oxford University Press, 1946), 323–359. Habermas's most systematic formulation of his theory of "linguistification of the sacred" appears in Jürgen Habermas, *The Theory of Communicative Action*, vol. 2: *Lifeworld and System: A Critique of Functionalist Reason* (Boston: Beacon Press, 1987), chap. 5, 1–111.

32. Bellah's critical reviews of both theories appear in "Stories as Arrows: The Religious Response to Modernity," and "Max Weber and World-Denying Love: A Look at the Historical Sociology of Religion," in *The Bellah Reader*, 107–122 and 123–149 respectively.

33. Bellah, *Religion in Human Evolution*.

34. Bellah thus meets Arnason's critical demand to rehistoricize the Axial Age. See Johann P. Arnason, "Rehistoricizing the Axial Age," in this volume.

35. Bellah, "What Is Axial," 77.

36. Ibid., 88.

37. See Shmuel N. Eisenstadt, ed., *The Origins and Diversity of Axial Age Civilizations* (Albany: State University of New York Press, 1986); and Arnason, Eisenstadt, and Wittrock, eds., *Axial Civilizations*.

38. See Arnason's chapter in this volume, p. 337; see also Arnason, "The Axial Age and Its Interpreters: Reopening a Debate," in Arnason, Eisenstadt, and Wittrock, eds., *Axial Civilizations*, 19–49.

39. See Johann P. Arnason, *Civilizations in Dispute: Historical Questions and Theoretical Traditions* (Leiden: Brill, 2003); and "Rehistoricizing the Axial Age." See also Shmuel N. Eisenstadt, "Axial Civilizations and the Axial Age Reconsidered," in Arnason, Eisenstadt, and Wittrock, eds., *Axial Civilizations,* 531–564.

40. On this issue, see Björn Wittrock, "The Meaning of the Axial Age," and Peter Wagner, "Palomar's Questions: The Axial Age Hypothesis, European Modernity and Historical Contingency," in Arnason, Eisenstadt, and Wittrock, eds., *Axial Civilizations,* 51–85 and 87–106 respectively; see also Hans Joas, "The Axial Age as Religious Discourse," in this volume.

41. See Yehuda Elkana, "The Emergence of Second-order Thinking in Classical Greece," in Eisenstadt, ed., *The Origins and Diversity,* 40–64; Bellah, "What Is Axial"; and Wittrock, "The Meaning of the Axial Age."

42. Jan Assmann, *Ma'at. Gerechtigkeit und Unsterblichkeit im alten Ägypten* (Munich: Beck, 1990); *Das kulturelle Gedächtnis* (Munich: Beck, 1992); *Moses the Egyptian: The Memory of Egypt in Western Monotheism* (Cambridge, MA: Harvard University Press, 1997); *Herrschaft und Heil: Politische Theologie in Altägypten, Israel und Europa* (Munich: Hanser, 2000); and "Axial 'Breakthroughs' and Semantic 'Relocations' in Ancient Egypt and Israel," in Arnason, Eisenstadt, and Wittrock, eds., *Axial Civilizations,* 133–156.

43. Donald, "An Evolutionary Approach."

44. Bellah, "Introduction," in *The Bellah Reader,* 11.

45. Donald, "An Evolutionary Approach."

46. See Mark Elvin, "Was There a Transcendental Breakthrough in China?," in Eisenstadt, ed., *Axial Age Civilizations,* 325–359; and Kurt A. Raaflaub, "Polis, 'the Political,' and Political Thought: New Departures in Ancient Greece, c. 800–500 BCE," in Arnason, Eisenstadt, and Wittrock, eds., *Axial Civilizations,* 253–283.

47. Wittrock, "The Meaning of the Axial Age."

48. Jan Assmann, "Cultural Memory and the Myth of the Axial Age," in this volume.

49. Bellah, "What Is Axial," 70.

50. I am using here the typology developed by Wittrock in "The Meaning of the Axial Age," 73–76.

51. Rémi Brague, *The Wisdom of the World: The Human Experience of the Universe in Western Thought* (Chicago: University of Chicago Press, 2003).

52. Brague's insightful comparative analysis of Greek, Jewish, Christian, and Muslim conceptions of the *kosmos* and "world," *physis* and creation, divine law *(nomos)* and the law of God, and so on offers a fruitful model of how to unpack the overly compact and undifferentiated categories of Axial "cosmological transcendent visions" and "mundane reality" in particular civilizational contexts. See Rémi Brague, *The Law of God: The Philosophical History of an Idea* (Chicago: University of Chicago Press, 2007); and *Wisdom of the World.*

53. Charles Taylor, "What Was the Axial Revolution?," in this volume.
54. Bellah, "What Is Axial," 78.
55. Ibid., 81.
56. Ibid.
57. Bellah himself points to this difficulty when he writes: "Formal theoretic developments seem virtually absent in ancient Israel. Compared to the other three cases, Israel approaches theoretic culture only asymptotically, yet it was there, perhaps, that the revolution in mythospeculation was most profound." "What Is Axial," 89.
58. For a critical analysis of this crucial Weberian distinction between undifferentiated "community cult" *(Gemeinschaftskult)* and differentiated "religious community" *(religiöse Gemeinschaft),* see José Casanova, "Welche Religion braucht der Mensch? Theorien religiösen Wandels im globalen Zeitalter der Kontingenz," in Bettina Hollstein, Matthias Jung, and Wolfgang Knöbl, eds., *Handlung und Erfahrung: Das Erbe von Historismus und Pragmatismus und die Zukunft der Sozialtheorie* (Frankfurt am Main: Campus, 2011), 169–189.
59. Tu Wei-ming, "The Structure and Function of the Confucian Intellectual in Ancient China," in Arnason, Eisenstadt, and Wittrock, ed., *Axial Civilizations,* 360–373. Unique about the Chinese case, in comparison to the other Axial Age cases, is the historical continuity between ancient and modern China, notwithstanding the radical modern break that accompanied the abolition of the imperial cult and the disestablishment of Confucianism as state orthodoxy.
60. Guy G. Stroumsa, *The End of Sacrifice: Religious Transformations in Late Antiquity* (Chicago: University of Chicago Press, 2009).
61. Ibid., 6.
62. Ibid.
63. See Charles Taylor, *A Secular Age* (Cambridge, MA: Harvard University Press, 2008). See also José Casanova, *Public Religion in the Modern World* (Chicago: University of Chicago Press, 1994); "A Secular Age: Dawn or Twilight?," in Michael Warner, Craig Calhoun, and Jonathan VanAntwerpen, eds., *Varieties of Secularism in a Secular Age* (Cambridge, MA: Harvard University Press, 2010), 265–281; "The Secular, Secularizations, Secularisms," in Craig Calhoun, Mark Juergensmeier, and Jonathan VanAntwerpen, eds., *Rethinking Secularism* (New York: Oxford University Press, 2011), 54–74.
64. Robert A. Markus, *Christianity and the Secular* (Notre Dame: University of Notre Dame Press, 2006).
65. José Casanova, "Exploring the Postsecular: Three Meanings of 'the Secular' and Their Possible Transcendence," in Craig Calhoun, Eduardo Mendieta, and Jonathan VanAntwerpen, eds., *Habermas and Religion* (Cambridge: Polity Press, forthcoming).
66. Marcel Gauchet, *The Disenchantment of the World: A Political History of Religion* (Princeton: Princeton University Press, 1997).

67. José Casanova, "Westliche christliche Säkularisierung und Globalisierung," in José Casanova, *Europas Angst vor der Religion* (Berlin: Berlin University Press, 2009), 83–119.

68. Robert N. Bellah, "Epilogue. Meaning and Modernity: America and the World," in Richard Madsen, William M. Sullivan, Ann Swidler, and Steven M. Tipton, eds., *Meaning and Modernity: Religion, Polity and Self* (Berkeley: University of California Press, 2002), 273.

69. Bellah, "Introduction," in *The Bellah Reader*, 13.

70. Bellah, "Epilogue," 273.

9

Where Do Axial Commitments Reside?

Problems in Thinking about the African Case

ANN SWIDLER

I am interested in a relatively simple question: Where are Axial commitments located socially, or to put it another way, what does it mean to say that something is an "Axial civilization," especially for latecomers to global modernity in places like Africa, who sometimes receive pieces of the Axial in disconnected chunks? I have been fascinated by Shmuel Eisenstadt's argument in *Japanese Civilization* (1996) that Japan could embrace Axial elements while keeping an archaic core. Despite absorbing many aspects of two great Axial traditions—Buddhist philosophical sophistication and Confucian techniques of governance—Japan remained fundamentally pre-Axial. Japan retained central archaic commitments—the divinity of its imperial system and the unique, particularistic value of "Japaneseness" *(nihonjin)*—despite having assimilated Axial insights into what was understood as fundamentally Japanese. It "contained" Axial cultural elements structurally, incorporating them within robust pre-Axial social forms. For example, according to Eisenstadt, Japanese Buddhist communities, despite their universalistic philosophical orientations, became organized as contained, hierarchical communities, focused on the personal relationship between teacher and disciple, on the model of the Japanese *ie,* or household. So in this case, a "civilization" could remain fundamentally archaic, incorporating many Axial elements while limiting their implications. Conversely (I take this argument from one of Robert Bellah's lectures), when the Hawaiian king Kamehameha III, a descendent of the gods (see Bellah 2011, 197–209), converted to Christianity, Hawaii's archaic religious system collapsed—so one dramatic event at the "center" of an archaic system could transform a civilization.

What, then, does it mean to say that a "civilization" is Axial or pre-Axial? Perhaps with our own commitments to the importance of the political sphere and our belief that public officials should be held to transcendent ethical norms, we define the essence of the "Axial" as the creation (by a core religious community) of a transcendent realm in terms of which "the ruler" can be judged. But is this really the best or only way to think about where Axial understandings reside?

Ambiguities of the African Case

I first want to describe the wide varieties of ways in which Africans and African societies are integrated with—or have integrated into themselves—central elements of the great Axial traditions available in the world today. Here I include not only religious traditions but also other elements of "world society" (Frank and Meyer 2007). Indeed, it would be fair to say that on many fronts Africans have embraced modernity with unparalleled enthusiasm.

Axial Religious Participation

If what it means to be an Axial civilization is that most individuals and communities in Africa have embraced one of the Axial religions, there is no question that Africans have joined the Axial Age. While there is enormous variation in religious belief and practice, Islam and Christianity have attracted large and ever growing numbers of adherents (B. Meyer 2004). In Malawi, where I have worked over the last several years, it is almost unheard of not to be a member of a church or mosque, and many of those we meet are passionately committed to their churches, participating in emotionally vivid, musically intense worship. Especially in the Evangelical and Pentecostal churches, one sees a level of religiosity—a fusion of individual hope and striving, attempts to root out threatening demons and cleanse the community and the self, and a determination that faith and discipline will triumph over obstacles—that makes clear that adherence is genuinely integrated into personal and communal life (B. Meyer 1999, 2004; Marshall 2009; Manglos 2010). Indeed, perhaps the most important and to some degree least explored aspects of African Christianity (Islam may operate somewhat differently in this respect) is that, as it did in the Protestant West, it has introduced the model of a fully voluntarist community, chosen by its members, supported by their contributions, and largely independent of clan or village ties.[1]

World Culture

African communities are also in ever-widening contact with global realities. Examining the response to AIDS in sub-Saharan Africa, one is made vividly aware how broadly universalizing claims about such matters as "human rights," "gender equality," or the right to education (Frye 2012) have become disseminated in Africa.

First, internationally sponsored NGO (nongovernmental organization) and international organizational activity has an enormous presence (Watkins et al. 2012). In Malawi, for example, for most of 2008 and into 2009 UNICEF ran an eye-catching daily banner on the front page of the major newspaper, *The Nation,* proclaiming the right of every child to health and education, and warning against violence against children, sexual abuse, and other ills ("STOP Child Trafficking" with the tagline, "every child has a right to their childhood"; "STOP Sexual Abuse" with "every child has a right to be free from abuse and violence"; "STOP Harmful Cultural Practices" with "every child has a right to good health"; "STOP Early Marriages" with "every girl has a right to complete her education"; "STOP Child Labour" with "every child has a right to go to school"; "STOP Sexual Exploitation" with "every child has the right to be free from sexual exploitation"; "STOP Property Grabbing" with "every orphan has a right to inherit their parents' property"). The same slogans appeared on vivid, cherry-red banners and bumper stickers around the country, strung above town halls, decorating police checkpoints, and on the bumpers of the ubiquitous mini-buses.

At least since the coming of attempts to fight the AIDS epidemic through local community mobilization, and indeed in prior community mobilization for family planning programs, even remote villages often have an entrepreneurial group of young people—perhaps those with Form 4 diplomas (high-school graduates in Malawi's British-style educational system)—who have established a "CBO" (community-based organization). Using globally sanctioned language, they will have written proposals for "training" (which might include "gender sensitization," as well as education in the mysteries of the male and female reproductive tracts, the distinction between HIV and AIDS, and "decision making") and created committees to support those living with AIDS as well as the ever-present (at least in the proposals) "OVCs" (orphans and vulnerable children) and the HBC (home-based care) activities of the group's volunteer members (Swidler and Watkins 2009). The acronyms here (all of which are widely understood by villagers) suggest the facility with which Malawian villagers have appropriated the necessary arcana of globalized social technologies (see Nguyen 2005b, 2010).

Second, as elsewhere in Africa, Malawians also take seriously the universalizing claims of modern science and medicine. As Émile Durkheim noted in the closing pages of *Elementary Forms,* only participation in something like a universal society can ground confidence in the existence of impersonal scientific laws that are somehow "the same" across time and space. While most Malawians still consult traditional healers, and even the educated accept the ever-present danger of witchcraft, they also have a very straightforward confidence in science and modern medical technology. Indeed, one of the difficulties for Malawians in the early days of the AIDS epidemic was accepting that there could be a disease that was, so to speak, a Western-style affliction but that modern medicine could not cure. Medical anthropologists have studied extensively how Africans distinguish the ailments that Western medicine can cure from those that require traditional healing. Some may go to traditional healers (who are less expensive and usually closer by than the local clinic or hospital) and seek regular medical treatment only if traditional remedies fail. In general, however, they treat most illnesses in straightforward scientific materialist ways, seeking an herbal remedy from a healer or an injection or "tablets" from a clinic with the same pragmatic spirit.

Most Africans we have met also show great interest in the scientific or "materialist" explanations of HIV and AIDS. So, for example, if we mention the recent research showing that male circumcision is strongly protective against HIV transmission, the Form 4 graduates who work with us will say, "Yes, I have been very curious. Why is that? What does circumcision do?" These are exactly the questions public health researchers (and our own students in the United States) ask, and the answer that satisfies them—about the vulnerability of the mucosal underside of the foreskin and its rich supply of the very white cells HIV infects—satisfies the Malawians as well. But even uneducated villagers, whose conversations the Malawi Research Group project has captured in a remarkable set of journals recorded by local diarists,[2] often seek quite straightforward, material explanations of biological phenomena. In a journal from 2003, the journalist overhears a bar girl debating with three men whether one is more likely to get AIDS from a circumcised or an uncircumcised man: each uses different empirical evidence. The bar girl says to a client:

> "If you want to have sex with me I have to know first whether you are circumcised or not because I don't use condoms, in so doing, I do go only with those who are circumcised because they don't have AIDS and those who are not circumcised have got AIDS." Manuel's friend got puzzled with that point and he wanted to learn about what she meant with that point. He said to her, "Why do you think so?" She responded, "It is easier for the uncircumcised men to get AIDS because their foreskins wrap the fluids after sexual intercourse and this makes them highly risky of catching AIDS, while the circumcised men don't have the foreskins and in so doing, they remain dry at the tips of the genital organs after sexual contact, thus making them not catch AIDS."
>
> Manuel agreed with the bargirl's point, but Malova disagreed with her and he told her that the circumcised ones are the ones who can easily catch AIDS because their genital tips are always displayed, thus giving them a high chance of catching AIDS, while the uncircumcised do sometimes have sexual contact with their foreskins covering the tip of the genital organ that acts as a barrier to permit the infection to enter into their bodies and that makes it less easy for them to get infected with AIDS.

In another diary, men are discussing the many disadvantages of condoms, and a young man offers a quasi-experimental observation:

> One boy said that he slept with a woman whom people were saying that she had gonorrhoea, but since he had sex with her, he has no sign of gonorrhoea meaning that the condom he used at that time protected him. And he also said that his friend Faston Ngalande slept with the very same woman a week after him and after four (4) days, Faston also had gonorrhoea that is when he started trusting a condom.

Thus empiricism and faith in the universalized discourses of modern medicine and science are joined, even if the details remain open to debate.

Third, Malawians, like others across Africa and in poor countries around the globe, participate in world culture through their passionate faith in education. David Frank and John Meyer (2007) have recently made an extraordinarily interesting argument about what we might think of as the "Axial" implications of the expansion of universities around the world: "The university expands over recent centuries because—as it has from its religious origins—it casts cultural and human materials in universalistic terms" (287).

In parts of Africa I have visited, there is a painful, poignant, almost overwhelmingly powerful thirst for globally legitimated knowledge. This takes the form partly of an obsession with credentials and diplomas. Everyone we meet is longing to better him or herself by completing a two-year degree in accounting, taking a course of study to become a Rural Community Development Officer, or taking a six-week course to become a VCT (Voluntary Counseling and Testing) counselor. But this longing for official knowledge goes far beyond hopes for material betterment. As one of our Malawian interviewers said, when her husband's death ended her hopes of further schooling, "I was going to be something!" Even those who are not trying for more schooling plead with us for books to make their AIDS knowledge official, and others—like the young woman who comes by foot and mini-bus each time she hears we are nearby—simply want the loan of novels or history books to feed their curiosity. It is not just knowledge, but "official knowledge." As Frank and Meyer (2007) note, "the university is positioned to teach both students and society at large the meta-principle that all sorts of particulars can and/or could be understood, and should be understood, as instances of general abstractions" (294). Frank and Meyer further note that the prestige and influence of this officially sanctioned knowledge is directly connected to its claims to transcendent, universalized truth: "The Modern globalized knowledge system increasingly extends into the furthest reaches of daily life, spreading universalized understandings of all aspects of nature and every social institution worldwide" (289).

Social Organization as Personal Dependence

Despite the enormous appeal of universalized understandings and the powerful appeal of connections to that luminous—if distant—sphere of global society, for most Africans, even those in the modern, cosmopolitan sector, life is experienced as dependence on personal relationships (Chabal and Daloz 1999; Swidler and Watkins 2007; Chabal 2009).

Chiefs and Public Goods

As many others have noted, in contexts from the personal to the political, across Africa (and much of the rest of the world; see, e.g., Eisenstadt and Roniger 1984) most social relationships are organized through personal dependence or patron-client ties (Chabal and Daloz 1999). From pervasive corruption in Nigeria (Smith 2006), to political-party affiliations that turn out to be code words for patronage along lines of kinship, clan, and ethnic group (Weinreb 2001; Chabal 2009), across Africa what might seem like aspects of modern economic and political life are often organized structurally through lineage and kinship. What is more, in societies where personhood is defined in large part through the obligations one performs for superiors and the "redistribution" of wealth one performs for inferiors (Collier 2004), even those without pressing kin obligations constitute their personhood relationally by creating ties of unequal interdependence (Swidler and Watkins 2007).

In interviews with those working in AIDS projects around Africa, I have become convinced that chiefship (or in other places the remnants of precolonial and colonial structures like age sets) remains essential to the organization of public, indeed civic, life (see Swidler 2010).[3] Mahmood Mamdani (1996) is certainly right that colonial authorities perverted the fundamental structure of chiefship. The colonial powers both altered and in some respects reinforced (some might say "invented") the powers of chiefs. The ability of people to abandon a bad chief, and the corresponding expectation that chiefs would "consult" with elders and headmen on important decisions, was weakened as colonial authorities made chiefs into tax collectors and legal authorities, backed by force, with power over "customary land" and "native law." Nonetheless, all over Africa, however often people are disappointed by chiefs who take resources and fail to redistribute them, it is through chiefs and similar authorities that collective life can actually be organized.[4] The resilience of African chiefship (Oomen 2005) is evident in a recent Afrobarometer report from nineteen sub-Saharan African countries: Logan (2011, 1) found "startling ... intensity" of support for traditional authority, with "large majorities believing that the institution should still play a significant role in local governance." African publics value "the role traditional authorities continue to play in managing and resolving conflict . . . their leadership qualities and their accessibility to ordinary people," as well as their "essential symbolic role as representatives of community identity, unity, continuity and stability." Indeed, I would hazard that where chiefship has been fatally undermined, as in parts of South Africa, collective capacities for communal action have been undermined as well.

Let me offer a few examples as evidence of how chiefs provide the mechanism for creating public goods.[5] The first, most obvious, point is that in villages various public works are organized by chiefs. If the village paths need to be repaired, the village borehole maintained, or a school building constructed, the chief calls a village meeting and asks the villagers to do the work. Thus cooperation is stimulated by and channeled through chiefs. But the chiefs' role is both more important and more varied than that. It is not just that chiefs organize certain cooperative activities. Even more, the vaunted "generalized reciprocity" of African societies is often organized through them.

I interviewed a young woman who ran an AIDS hospice, attached to a Catholic church, outside Lusaka, Zambia. Among other activities, the hospice provided midday meals and eventually schooling for orphans whose parents had died. The hospice director explained that while the hospice arranged for orphaned children to live with relatives in the ten villages and compounds that constituted their catchment area, relatives were willing to take children in only if the chief told them to. Indeed, she explained, they had to involve the chiefs in everything they did, inviting them to be first to join an AIDS committee or to receive "training" in health practices, or the activity would fail.

Another, very different example comes from a funeral I attended in Botswana in 2003. African funerals are large, expensive, and very important events (see Durham and Klaits 2002; Smith 2004).[6] This funeral, far out in the dry, barren Botswana countryside, drew about 200 mourners for a young man in his forties (a schoolmate of my Motswana friend's fiancé), the unmarried son of a single mother. As the mourners stood in the dusty cemetery singing hymns, and three somewhat bedraggled, dusty pastors from different denominations spoke at the graveside, a small, beat-up white van, off to one side, started up and loudspeakers on its roof suddenly came to life, interrupting the pastors in mid-sentence. My friend whispered that the chief's headman was saying that people were not pressing closely enough around the grave, not providing sufficient comfort to the grieving mother. The ceremony was unceremoniously interrupted twice more when the chief's headman conveyed the chief's wish that people sing the hymns with greater energy and again when he demanded that people stop gossiping and pay full attention to the funeral. Thus it was the chief's responsibility to remind people of their communal obligations and to police, or enforce, those obligations.

In Malawi, the hold of even "bad" chiefs over their people is directly connected to chiefs' authority over funerals (and thus to the all-important relationship to ancestors). When one Malawian acquaintance complained that his chief was corrupt and not respected, we asked why people still were loath to disobey him. Our friend replied, haltingly, as if too appalled to complete the thought, "What if someone in your family died? Or you died..." And then he simply trailed off. It was evident that the chief's cooperation—his presence (or that of one of his counselors), his willingness to give a funeral oration, and more important, his permission to bury a family member in the ancestral burial ground, which the chief controls—was essential. Offending the chief, so that one couldn't have a funeral for one's dead, was unthinkable, and essentially unspeakable.[7]

Chiefs make possible the provision of public goods of all sorts. One village woman, a subsistence farmer like her neighbors, but more fortunate since she had occasional work with our project, was asked by her chief to create a youth group in her village, for which she provided weekly refreshments along with advice about AIDS prevention. Thus it was the chief who made sure she redistributed some of her good fortune. The expectation, indeed, is that the chief will be "self-sacrificing." It is he (or occasionally she) who encourages his village to seek out donor-sponsored funding for a CBO, since these have become a major source of cash infusions for villages largely deprived of access to the cash economy. The chief typically asks a public-spirited villager, somewhat better educated than the rest, to prepare a proposal and organize a group of village volunteers. We learned that a chief will also reward those who have shown selfless devotion to collective life: several of our village informants agreed that the chief might come in person, rather than sending one of his counselors, to give a funeral speech for a "worthy" villager—not a wealthy villager, but one who had worked for the welfare of the whole community. Thus the chief in essence keeps the accounts that reward generalized reciprocity. Another of the village-based interviewers who worked for our project told us proudly how he had helped his village get several grants (from World Vision and other donors) for community benefits ranging from blankets for orphans and those living with AIDS, to cloth sufficient for 200 children to have school uniforms, to plastic water jugs for those living with AIDS to fetch water. He insisted that he and the small number of other volunteers who visit the sick and see to their needs, and in his case coordinate the work of the seven CBOs he has helped to found, receive no benefits from all those donor funds, except the occasional per diem when they go for "training." But he also told us that when his mother died, he went to his uncle, the chief of a nearby village, to ask him for some land. His uncle gave him five hectares—a very large "garden" by Malawi standards—and his own T/A (the Traditional Authority, the top of the chiefly hierarchy in Malawi's "traditional" administrative structure) told the uncle that he was very pleased, since the young man had been such a worthy member of his community. So "what goes around comes around" largely via the chiefs.

In the occasional story in which a chief is run out of his village—in the most recent story we heard, the women (in a matrilineal region) gathered around the chief's hut and shouted humiliating insults until he had to leave—his key failing was that he had behaved selfishly, doing things only when they benefited him, and not when they benefited the village as a whole. Those who recounted the scandal said that if the villagers came to this chief because their paths were overgrown and needed clearing, he might "not show up"; he would say the paths were okay. But if he were invited for training at the District Assembly, for which a per diem and travel allowance would be available, he would be "very punctual." This failure of either the capacity or willingness to be public-regarding, and to produce the public goods on which villagers depend, is the essential failing that could mean disrespect for a chief and ultimately lead to his being deposed.

Finally, the chief's spiritual strength is essential to the health of his community. A chief needs to be "confident," and this confidence makes his village strong enough to resist encroachment by other villages on their lands. He also requires spiritual strength to resist witchcraft and the threat it poses to those under his care. In a fundamental way, villagers are dependent on the cooperation and help of those around them, and this cooperation is tied directly to a person—the person of their chief—in whom spiritual power and personal power are combined.

Personal Dependence and the Danger of Witchcraft

Although witchcraft has been declared illegal throughout most of Africa (in Malawi, officially witchcraft does not exist and witchcraft accusations are a crime), it is a pervasive fact of contemporary life.[8] The belief in witchcraft—at all levels of society—is linked in turn to Africans' direct dependence on personal relationships. One way to think about this is simply to say that in a world in which everything depends on obligations to and from others, but where those obligations have only spiritual and informal, rather than enforceable, legal sanction, it is no wonder that any misfortune must be seen as due to someone's malevolence, even if that other remains hidden. At the same time, fear of witchcraft is also the sanction on those who have resources but fail to redistribute them. As Mark Auslander (1993) notes for Ngoni communities in Zambia, "reciprocity builds up social relationships and ultimately enables social reproduction, as in bridewealth transactions. By contrast, the witch—as the 'excluded other'—who has been denied gifts, commodities or assistance—is held to reciprocate subversively, by endangering the community . . . he or she may be represented as a marginal being excluded from redistributive networks or as an avaricious, secretly wealthy hoarder"(178).

The role of witchcraft beliefs (and actual witchcraft accusations—a terrible danger[9]) is not confined to isolated villagers. Indeed, the continuing role of witchcraft (its "modernity" in Peter Geschiere's [1997] term)—and the continuing social primacy of ties of personal dependence—can be seen in the ways witchcraft accusations follow acts of political betrayal among top African leaders. When Malawi's recently deceased president, Bingu wa Mutharika, was first elected in 2004, he almost immediately declared his independence from the former president, Bakili Muluzi, founding his own breakaway political party. Mutharika (usually called simply "Bingu") faced a scandal in the newspapers because he refused to move into the presidential mansion. The newspapers claimed that he feared the house had been bewitched; Bingu vigorously denied the accusations, while offering a variety of other reasons for refusing to move into the house. The subtext to the scandal, however, was that the former president's people had suggested that Bingu lacked the spiritual strength—as a traitor to his former patron, spiritually in the wrong—to ward off the threat of witchcraft from Muluzi. Bingu's furious denials were not so much denials of backward superstitions and assertions of his modernity or rationality, as declarations that he was more than fortified against any magic Muluzi could muster. In Nigeria (Smith 2006), a similar witchcraft-laden battle erupted when another political leader betrayed his former patron—with open letters published between the two, accusing each other not of corruption, but the former patron accusing the former client of refusing to use government resources to repay the patron who had placed him in power. Witchcraft accusations and terrible panics about children stolen and murdered for witches' rites also erupt where glaring inequalities between rich and poor demand redress (see Smith 2006). How else could the grotesquely wealthy acquire their wealth than by secretly stealing the blood of other people's children? Hence witchcraft accusation can provide a form of political critique, and witchcraft itself can be a sanction against misuse of resources.

Axial Religion and the Social Location of Dependence

Robin Horton, in his classic essay "African Conversion" (1971), developed a brilliant argument to account for the appeal of Axial religions in Africa. Horton argued that both conversion to the world religions, Christianity or Islam, and "internal conversion," in which indigenous African religious systems evolved to emphasize the centrality of a "supreme being," reflected the same social transformation. Africans reworked their faith as they increasingly came into contact with powerful, cosmopolitan forces, so that their fates were determined by forces beyond the local, interpersonal world of the village. As Horton and J. D. Y. Peel (1976) describe it, "economic and political changes... weakened the boundaries which had previously kept the local community more or less insulated from the wider world. They were therefore just the sort of changes which... result in a high level of Christian affiliation" (492). The appeal of the Axial religions is that they offer powerful rituals for gaining access to the forces that now control life: "a person who has found himself thrown into the wider world beyond the bounds of his local community, and who has therefore sought to come to terms directly with the forces underpinning this wider world," engages in a "quest for a more elaborate concept and cult of the Supreme Being" (496).

Horton is certainly right about the individuating and universalizing elements of contemporary African experience that make Axial religions intellectually plausible and experientially resonant. Indeed, he provides a persuasive interpretation of another aspect of African religion—and African attitudes more generally—when he argues that churches like the Aladura churches Peel studied in Nigeria also offer direct linkages to the wider world. As he and Peel (1976) observe:

> whatever the local peculiarities of their origins, [these congregations] are always anxious to see themselves, not as closed, self-contained communities, but as local cells of large, even world-wide organizations, as small parts of the immense body of world Christendom. This is something very obvious to the visiting historian or anthropologist. When he attends a sacrifice to the ancestors in, say, an Ibo village, he is very much aware of being there as an outsider, for they are not *his* ancestors. When, however, he visits an Aladura congregation, he is invited to participate in its religious life as a brother Christian. In this capacity, moreover, he is quite likely to be asked for advice, particularly on the matter of contact with other Christian groups in the world outside. (496, italics in the original)

This is true of African churches I have visited, but also more generally of the Africans who are eager for a business card, for an address, or even a postcard that conveys some image of the wider world the visitor represents.

Horton and Peel (1976) have thoroughly refuted the charge of "intellectualism" leveled at their interpretation of African conversion.[10] Nonetheless, I think there is a fundamental weakness in their model, and thus in the basic interpretation of Africans' embrace of Axial religions as creating an Axial civilization. In a passage I agree with profoundly they say, "Our position is that cosmology, and its related cultic practice, arises as a response to experience. We do maintain that religions must be regarded first and foremost as systems of thought; but experience, not thought, is the object of thought and hence of religion. And as sociologists we are concerned with thought as a response to social experience" (485). But what they miss, at least to some degree, is the "social" in the constitution of social experience.

In Bellah's (1964) original model of religious evolution, the intellectual or cosmological breakthroughs of the historic (Axial) religions were accompanied by profound changes in social and religious organization: toward at least partially autonomous religious organizations, toward a differentiation of worldly and religious authority, and toward new modes of integration of individual personhood (and thus of personal moralities) into collective life. Horton and Peel's model, while it is not "intellectualist," is still at some fundamental level individualist. It focuses on how changes in social and economic organization—in the "scale" of the factors that impinge on people's lives—affect individual experience. What is left out of this way of formulating the issue is the question of how religious ideas and experiences contribute to relocating the sacred, and thus to reformulating the fundamental social codes that *constitute* collective entities. It is at this level, I would argue, that the African case raises fundamental questions about where Axial commitments reside.

Axial Experience without Axial Civilization

In a way that resembles Eisenstadt's (1996) analysis of Japanese civilization, I argue that much of Africans' access to the universalizing elements of global discourses has been incorporated without fundamentally changing their patterns of collective life. Like the Japanese, African social patterns and the cultural codes that govern them have proved extraordinarily resilient. Patrick Chabal (2009), the great authority on Africa, describes the pattern this way:

> One is a person, one belongs, one is part of a community, *in so far* as one is integrated in a complex system of authority, deference and participation, which forms the backbone of the intersecting spheres of identity that matter for life in that given society. The idea that an individual could live utterly detached from any community is not one that finds favour, or is even meaningful in Africa—as is made clear by the pejorative reputation such individuals inevitably acquire. Therefore, the question is not whether to be party to a system of obligations or not but how to manage one's place within such a system. To have no obligations is not to belong; it is not to be fully and socially human. Obligations,

therefore, are not seen—as the Western concept seems to imply—as impositions, claims on one's otherwise better used time and energy, but as a means of sustaining one's place in a network of belonging: that most vital attribute of humanity, sociability and, ultimately, being-in-the-world. (48, italics in the original)

Thus the universalizing elements of NGO discourses are appropriated within an understanding that converts them, both organizationally and cognitively, into ingredients for the formation of patron-client ties. Daniel Jordan Smith (2003), an anthropologist who studies Nigeria, has a wonderful analysis of the "workshop mentality" in family planning programs. Family planning workshops advocate lowered fertility and thus a decreased reliance on accumulating "wealth in people." In practice, however, the workshops allow Nigerians to accumulate precisely the wealth in people that is understood to constitute both personhood and sociality. Those who organize a workshop distribute patronage and accumulate "wealth in people" by choosing who will participate and thus gain access to valuable per diems and travel allowances; participants can use the workshop to reward their own patrons by inviting them as trainers or honored guests.

In an analogous way, as Harri Englund (2003) has argued, Malawian Pentecostal churches frequently split over the distribution of "goods," both spiritual and material, to which their pastors have access by virtue of their connection to foreign church sponsorship, and by virtue of their access to transcendent spiritual powers. Like chiefs, pastors are expected to redistribute spiritual powers and material goods; accusations that a pastor has monopolized those goods can precipitate a church schism. Much as the Japanese assimilated Axial civilizational elements to the cultural framework of the household, many Africans assimilate elements of "universalistic" global modernity within the flexible and robust cultural structure of lineage and chieftaincy, with its hierarchy of sacredness, ties of personal dependence, and redistributive obligations of superiors. Thus the elements of universalizing modernity, such as the discourse of "empowerment" or human rights, are appropriated through and reworked to produce patron-client ties, in which spiritual power and the responsibility for reproducing collective life flow upward in a lineage-like hierarchy (even if such a hierarchy is reinvented by urbanites seeking to define themselves as a community and a political constituency [see Barnes 1986]). This is not simply a matter of political patronage and the persistent routing of political benefits through ethnic loyalties. It goes deeper, to the basic codes through which people can constitute and reconstitute social relationships.

Africans do manifest one fundamental element of the Axial—an enormous longing, a reaching out to grasp "the universal," the global symbols of a higher, transcendent reality (a longing that would be quite unfamiliar, I think, to the Japanese). This "transcendent" reality's presence also, however, suggests the fundamental problem about conceptualizing the social "location" of axialness.

In contrast to Horton's perspective, in my view the worship of a "transcendent being," or in Bellah's (1964) terms a "dualistic" cosmology, is not just a way of mediating individuals' understanding of the world and their need for access to the forces that control it. The creation of Axial civilizations also involved fundamental reorganization of the sacred—in Clifford Geertz's (1968) terms, a new understanding of "the mode in which the divine reaches into the world" (44). Understandings of the sacred are not primarily "about" individual experience, even individual experience of social relationships. Rather, the sacred, as Bellah (1973) suggests in his classic essay on Durkheim's *Elementary Forms,* constitutes and makes accessible (if only as an ineffable possibility) the fundamental organization of collective life. And thus Axial cultural elements acquire their meaning in part from the collective capacities they make possible.[11]

Religious or other ultimate meanings, while they may provide answers to fundamental questions about causality and may promise individuals the possibility of influencing the important powers that impinge on their lives, more importantly provide the basic codes, and encode basic reservoirs of sacredness, that allow the constitution and reconstitution of patterns of collective life. These are the codes through which human communities create, interpret, and regulate authority, preeminence (status), cooperation, and reciprocity—the fundamental processes of social life. Such codes—basic conceptions of obligation or morality but also the imagined shape of the institutional arrangements that create capacities to act as a group—are normally transposed from one familiar realm to another, as when political authority is understood on the model of the relationship between parent and child, or when the relationship between lord and serf provides the template for the practices through which factory labor is organized (Biernacki 1995). Axial elements at the level of individual experience can thus be incorporated within fundamentally pre-Axial forms of social organization.

Africa and Africans have been eager recipients of the increasingly universalized ideologies and forms of social organization being imported wholesale into contemporary societies that are too poor or too unsure of themselves to resist "missionary" intrusions. It is less clear whether, at least in most parts of Africa, there have been new constitutive moments, dramatic collective "events" in William Sewell's (1996) sense, that have been able to reconstitute forms of collective life to match the Axial aspirations of Africa's increasingly universalized global citizens. Indeed, in many ways it is as if Africans were being assimilated directly, at least in their imaginations, into the global institutions of the international community, its international NGOs, churches, courts, and transnational advocacy organizations, bypassing the Axial reconstruction of national or society-wide institutions.[12]

In trying to determine where the Axial is located, I am arguing, we need to look not only at the great traditions that shape individual aspirations and experience, but also at the fundamental "constitutive rules" that define the social location of the sacred power of collective life. Thus we should look not only for the penetration and resonance of Axial traditions but for changes in the rules that constitute forms of individual personhood and collective life. Here the churches, especially the Evangelical and Pentecostal churches, have supported both new forms of community and newly individualized forms of self-discipline, aspiration, and striving. The churches have introduced new, voluntarist forms of group cohesion and obligation at the level of the congregation. But in the wider society, and to some degree penetrating religious congregations as well, the effective forms of obligation and the symbolic resources that underlie them are still modeled on the hierarchical, personalistic ties of lineage, clan, and chieftaincy. Most importantly, capacities for collective action have not really been reconstructed at the societal level. Rulers are not directly held accountable to universalized, transcendent moralities, and capacities for collective action are still very much dependent on the powers of chiefs and other traditional figures to anchor the public-regarding morality that creates collective goods. Whether the attempts of transnational bodies, like the International Criminal Court in the Hague, or the broader attempts to bring war criminals and others to justice under the banner of human rights (Sikkink 2009) can constitute a meaningful form of Axial transcendence for a new global society remains to be seen.

Locating the Axial, finally, raises the question of where authoritative notions of reality are anchored. This question is unresolved in the United States and the rest of the so-called Modern West, as illustrated by the debates between fundamentalists insistent on asserting the literal, scientific reality of biblical truths, and by the many who remain skeptical of the authority of modern science (Whitehead 1974). In contemporary African societies one sees a genuine syncretism with respect to the sources of authoritative understandings of reality, if we mean by this that multiple notions of what is really real can coexist: the one God who created the world, controls its processes, and redeems his children; the universalistic rights of all human beings, anchored in the global claims of World Culture and in the specific slogans and practices of NGOs and other emissaries of the global; and witchcraft and the sacred powers of chiefs and others who anchor the ties of personal dependence on which personhood and collective possibility depend.

In Africa, people increasingly have access to the global, the universalized, the cosmopolitan (blue jeans and the iPod) in just the ways Horton has argued. But there has not been a reconstitution of "society." Rather, there are patches of the Axial in societies where the sacred is fundamentally constituted in archaic ways, even if that archaic pattern can absorb the new patrons who come from abroad, suggesting new projects, altering individuals' fates, requiring propitiation, but without connection to a fundamental social ethics or a realistically accessible set of institutional possibilities.

My final point applies not only to Africa but to societies around the globe. If the social-structural bases of modernity take root—a labor market that grounds the experiential understanding that one is dependent primarily on one's own abilities and efforts rather than on others, and a modern state that anchors and enforces universalized claims to citizenship and individual rights (Soysal 1994; Collier 1997)—we will certainly have a globalized Axial ideology of individual experience, reinforcing and justifying the lived reality of individuals around the world. But without transformation of the basic meanings that govern collective action, and without either the transformation or re-creation of the deepest layers of sacred symbols that constitute new collective capacities, I cannot see how we can have a globalized Axial civilization.

To constitute a globalized Axial civilization, such a culture would have to create symbolic leverage for judging the morality of human conduct and holding rulers accountable; define a transcendent sphere of potential liberation or salvation toward which individuals and communities could strive; construct a narrative of the "radical evil" from which human beings seek to be redeemed; and create the moral basis for a wider community, increasing the capacity of human beings to organize and act in an increasingly interdependent world.

Notes

I am indebted to many people who have helped me think through the issues raised in this essay: Bob Bellah, Dick Madsen, Bill Sullivan, Steve Tipton, Jane Collier, Claude Fischer, Susan Watkins, Arlie Hochschild, Cihan Tugal, Kim Dionne, Adam Ashforth, Tom Hannan, Michelle Poulin, and the many Malawian collaborators and friends who shared their knowledge and experience. Support from the Canadian Institute for Advanced Research is gratefully acknowledged.

1. The creation of a fully voluntarist model of community was, of course, a relatively late development within Protestantism, most fully realized in the Anglo-American tradition where multiple sects competed in the absence of, or in opposition to, a state church. It is perhaps this voluntarist model of how communities can be formed and re-formed that is one of Protestantism's most significant cultural and structural legacies (E. P. Thompson 1963; Walzer 1978; Bellah et al. 1985; Gorski 2005; Fischer 2010; Jepperson and Meyer 2011).

2. A fuller description of the journals can be found in Watkins and Swidler (2009). Papers using material from these diaries suggest their remarkable richness (see, e.g., Kaler 2003, 2004; Swidler and Watkins 2007; Tavory and Swidler 2009). A sampling of the anonymized journals is available at: www.malawi.pop.upenn.edu/Level%203/Malawi/level3_malawi_qualjournals.htm.

3. See Karlström (1996, 1999) and Schaffer (1998) on the fusion of clan and chiefdom with concepts of democracy and civility in Buganda and Senegal, respectively. Both authors report, for example, that civic equality is understood as equal or fair treatment from a superior or chief, who listens to everyone fairly. Karlström (1996, 489) writes: "The concepts of justice *(obwenkanya)* and impartiality *(obutasosola)* were used by informants in explaining both the importance of free speech and their sense of justice. *Obwenkanya* is an abstract noun derived from the verb *kwenkana*, 'to be equal/similar,' and can be loosely translated as 'fairness' or 'equality.' The equation of democracy with *obwenkanya* may seem to indicate something akin to Western egalitarianism. What is im-

plied here, however, is narrower: a situational equality of subjects before a power-holder and decision-maker rather than an ontological equality of persons. Hence the centrality of the implied audience of decision-makers in statements like the following: 'I understand "democracy" to mean *obwenkanya*, like when you give an opinion and it is not ignored but *is also considered and a decision is made taking it into account* (cited by Tidemand, 1995: 127; emphasis added).'"

4. A remarkable work of social history, Landeg White's *Magomero* (1987), shows that Africans were in no way bound by unchanging tradition. Rather, they responded actively and inventively to both threats and opportunities, migrating to new lands, reinventing their genealogies, and sometimes reinventing their family structures and tribal identities as necessity or opportunity dictated. Even in periods of massive disruption, however, chiefdom provided a flexible schema through which people could reestablish community, make claims on others, and recreate capacities for collective action.

5. This line of argument draws on recent work focusing on governance as a crucial aspect of development in poor communities. The study of governance is being embraced by economists, who still think in terms of "transparency" and how to create conditions that maximize things like the flow of information so that well-informed constituents can use their votes effectively. The interesting results, however, are those like Cornell and Kalt's (2000) work on "cultural match" as a predictor of good governance in American Indian tribes and Lily Tsai's (2007) remarkable work on how in contemporary China "accountability" and the provision of local public goods depend on local government officials' participation in traditional cultural groups, such as those that maintain ancestors' graves or perform traditional Chinese dance.

6. *The Daily Times* (Friday, June 27, 2008, p. 1) reported a Malawi government study which found that Malawians spend between 200,000 and 3 million Malawi Kwacha on a funeral—a "fortune" equivalent to $1,400 to $20,000 in a country with GDP per capita of about $300 per year.

7. We have been told that in rare cases failing to "respect" the chief can lead to being "chased" from the village, losing one's land as well as one's community. Denying someone the right to bury a family member would be one form of "chasing" the person away. On the other hand, in addition to reports of chiefs being deposed, in the diaries there is a case of a chief asking people in his village to repair a village road, and the villagers answering that the chief should tell his relatives to repair the road, since they are the only ones who benefit when the chief has something to distribute. Several people also told us that when there is a dispute in a village, or when the person who inherits the chief's position is incompetent or "dull," a section of the village can move a short distance away, retaining their lands but constituting themselves as a new village with a new headman. Such splits are the major way new villages form, either when there is dissatisfaction

or when villages get too large—or, as we learned recently, when new government salaries for chiefs make the multiplication of chiefs (and thus villages) attractive.

8. See Smith (2006) on witchcraft accusations in contemporary Nigeria, Ashforth (1998, 2000, 2005) on South Africa, Abrahams (1994) on contemporary Tanzania, and Englund (1996) on Malawi.

9. See Miguel (2005) on witch killings in contemporary Tanzania.

10. Horton and Peel note that "Horton's approach to religious change in Africa is founded on two premises. First, that where people confront new and puzzling situations, they tend to adapt to them as far as possible in terms of their existing ideas and attitudes, even though they may have to stretch and develop them considerably in the process. Second, that where people assimilate new ideas, they do so because these ideas make sense to them in terms of the notions they already hold" (1976, 482).

11. Bellah (1970) has made the point that sacred symbols make such collective capacities graspable by connecting unconscious emotional energies to collectively accessible symbols.

12. The literature on global and transnational institutions is now vast, but there is little analysis of where their fundamental cultural claims could be worked out institutionally. Vinh-Kim Nguyen (2005a) has articulated the notion of "therapeutic citizenship," in which Africans living with AIDS become direct clients of transnational organizations, and perhaps "citizens" of some global community. John Meyer and his collaborators (J. Meyer et al. 1997; Boli and Thomas 1997) have the boldest description of the creation of a "world polity," but they dismiss the question of the gap between the cultural imaginary that system creates and its institutional embodiments with the simple notion of "decoupling." Many others have written of the varied aspects of an emergent, actual, or failed project of global governance (see, e.g., Keck and Sikkink 1998; Callaghy et al. 2001; Slaughter 2004), but with few exceptions they deal only obliquely with the gaps between the cultural and institutional aspects of a putative "global society" (though see Heydemann and Hammack 2009; Swidler and Watkins 2009; and the quite varied work of critical anthropologists of development, e.g., Mosse and Lewis 2005; Adams and Pigg 2005; Ong and Collier 2005; Ferguson 2006).

References

Abrahams, Ray, ed. 1994. *Witchcraft in Contemporary Tanzania*. Cambridge: African Studies Centre, University of Cambridge.

Adams, Vincanne, and Stacy Leigh Pigg, eds. 2005. *Sex in Development: Science, Sexuality, and Morality in Global Perspective*. Durham: Duke University Press.

Ashforth, Adam. 1998. "Reflections on Spiritual Insecurity in a Modern African City: Soweto." *African Studies Review* 41, no. 3: 39–68.
———. 2000. *Madumo: A Man Bewitched.* Chicago: University of Chicago Press.
———. 2005. *Witchcraft, Violence, and Democracy in South Africa.* Chicago: University of Chicago Press.
Auslander, Mark. 1993. "'Open the Wombs!' The Symbolic Politics of Modern Ngoni Witchfinding." In *Modernity and Its Malcontents,* ed. Jean Comaroff and John C. Comaroff, 167–192. Chicago: University of Chicago Press.
Barnes, Sandra T. 1986. *Patrons and Power: Creating a Political Community in Metropolitan Lagos.* Bloomington: Indiana University Press.
Bellah, Robert N. 1964. "Religious Evolution." *American Sociological Review* 29, no. 3: 358–374.
———. 1970. *Beyond Belief: Essays on Religion in a Post-Traditionalist World.* New York: Harper & Row.
———. 1973. "Introduction." In *Emile Durkheim on Morality and Society,* ed. Robert N. Bellah, ix–lv. Chicago: University of Chicago Press.
———. 2011. *Religion in Human Evolution: From the Paleolithic to the Axial Age.* Cambridge, MA: The Belknap Press of Harvard University Press.
Bellah, Robert N., Richard Madsen, William M. Sullivan, Ann Swidler, and Steven M. Tipton. 1985. *Habits of the Heart: Individualism and Commitment in American Life.* Berkeley: University of California Press.
Biernacki, Richard. 1995. *The Fabrication of Labor: Germany and Britain, 1640–1914.* Berkeley: University of California Press.
Boli, John, and George M. Thomas. 1997. "The World Polity under Construction: A Century of International Non-Governmental Organizing." *American Sociological Review* 62, no. 2: 171–190.
Callaghy, Thomas M., Ronald Kassimir, and Robert Latham, eds. 2001. *Intervention and Transnationalism in Africa: Global-Local Networks of Power.* Cambridge: Cambridge University Press.
Chabal, Patrick. 2009. *Africa: The Politics of Suffering and Smiling.* London: Zed Books.
Chabal, Patrick, and Jean-Pascal Daloz. 1999. *Africa Works: Disorder as Political Instrument.* Bloomington: Indiana University Press.
Collier, Jane Fishburne. 1997. *From Duty to Desire: Remaking Families in a Spanish Village.* Princeton: Princeton University Press.
———. 2004. "A Chief Does Not Rule Land; He Rules People (Luganda Proverb)." In *Law and Empire in the Pacific: Fiji and Hawai'i,* ed. S. E. Merry and D. Brenneis, 35–60. Santa Fe: School of American Research Press.
Cornell, Stephen, and Joseph P. Kalt. 2000. "Where's the Glue? Institutional and Cultural Foundations of American Indian Economic Development." *Journal of Socio-Economics* 29, no. 5: 443–470.

Durham, Deborah, and Fred Klaits. 2002. "Funerals and the Public Space of Sentiment in Botswana." *Journal of Southern African Studies* 28, no. 4: 773–791.

Eisenstadt, Shmuel N. 1996. *Japanese Civilization: A Comparative View.* Chicago: University of Chicago Press.

Eisenstadt, Shmuel N., and Luis Roniger. 1984. *Patrons, Clients, and Friends: Interpersonal Relations and the Structure of Trust in Society.* New York: Cambridge University Press.

Englund, Harri. 1996. "Witchcraft, Modernity and the Person: The Morality of Accumulation in Central Malawi." *Critique of Anthropology* 16: 257–279.

———. 2003. "Christian Independency and Global Membership: Pentecostal Extraversions in Malawi." *Journal of Religion in Africa* 33, no. 1: 83–111.

Ferguson, James. 2006. *Global Shadows: Africa in the Neoliberal World Order.* Durham: Duke University Press.

Fischer, Claude S. 2010. *Made in America: A Social History of American Culture and Character.* Chicago: University of Chicago Press.

Frank, David John, and John W. Meyer. 2007. "University Expansion and the Knowledge Society." *Theory and Society* 36: 287–311.

Frye, Margaret. 2012. "Bright Futures in Malawi's New Dawn: Educational Aspirations as Assertions of Identity." *American Journal of Sociology* 117, no. 6.

Geertz, Clifford. 1968. *Islam Observed: Religious Development in Morocco and Indonesia.* New Haven: Yale University Press.

Geschiere, Peter. 1997. *The Modernity of Witchcraft: Politics and the Occult in Postcolonial Africa.* Charlottesville: University of Virginia Press.

Gorski, Philip S. 2005. "The Little Divergence: The Protestant Reformation and Economic Hegemony in Early Modern Europe." In *The Protestant Ethic Turns 100: Essays on the Centenary of the Weber Thesis,* ed. W. H. Swatos Jr. and L. Kaelber, 165–190. Boulder and London: Paradigm Publishers.

Heydemann, Steven, and David C. Hammack, eds. 2009. *Globalization, Philanthropy, and Civil Society: Projecting Institutional Logics Abroad.* Bloomington: Indiana University Press.

Horton, Robin. 1971. "African Conversion." *Africa: Journal of the International African Institute* 41, no. 2: 85–108.

Horton, Robin, and J. D. Y. Peel. 1976. "Conversion and Confusion: A Rejoinder on Christianity in Eastern Nigeria." *Canadian Journal of African Studies* 10, no. 3: 481–498.

Jepperson, Ronald, and John W. Meyer. 2011. "Multiple Levels of Analysis and the Limitations of Methodological Individualisms." *Sociological Theory* 29: 54–73.

Kaler, Amy. 2003. "'My Girlfriends Could Fill a Yanu-Yanu Bus': Rural Malawian Men's Claims about Their Own Serostatus." *Demographic Research Special Collection* 1, Article 11: 349–372.

———. 2004. "AIDS-Talk in Everyday Life: The Presence of HIV/AIDS in Men's Informal Conversation in Southern Malawi." *Social Science & Medicine* 59: 285–297.

Karlström, Mikael. 1996. "Imagining Democracy: The Political Culture and Democratisation in Buganda." *Africa* 66, no. 4: 485–506.

———. 1999. "Civil Society and Its Presuppositions: Lessons from Uganda." In *Civil Society and the Political Imagination in Africa: Critical Perspectives,* ed. J. L. Comaroff and J. Comaroff, 104–123. Chicago: University of Chicago Press.

Keck, Margaret, and Kathryn Sikkink. 1998. *Activists beyond Borders: Transnational Advocacy Networks in International Politics.* Ithaca: Cornell University Press.

Logan, Carolyn. 2011. "The Roots of Resilience: Exploring Popular Support for African Traditional Authorities." *Afrobarometer Working Paper* 128.

Mamdani, Mahmood. 1996. *Citizen and Subject: Contemporary Africa and the Legacy of Late Colonialism.* Princeton: Princeton University Press.

Manglos, Nicolette D. 2010. "Born Again in Balaka: Pentecostal versus Catholic Narratives of Religious Transformation in Rural Malawi." *Sociology of Religion* 71, no. 4: 409–431.

Marshall, Ruth. 2009. *Political Spiritualities: The Pentecostal Revolution in Nigeria.* Chicago: University of Chicago Press.

Meyer, Birgit. 1999. *Translating the Devil: Religion and Modernity among the Ewe in Ghana.* Trenton and Asmara: Africa World Press.

———. 2004. "Christianity in Africa: From African Independent to Pentecostal-Charismatic Churches." *Annual Review of Anthropology* 33: 447–474.

Meyer, John W., John Boli, George M. Thomas, and Francisco O. Ramirez. 1997. "World Society and the Nation State." *American Journal of Sociology* 103, no. 1: 144–181.

Miguel, Edward. 2005. "Poverty and Witch Killing." *Review of Economic Studies* 72: 1153–1172.

Mosse, David, and David Lewis, eds. 2005. *The Aid Effect: Ethnographies of Development Practice and Neo-Liberal Reform.* London: Pluto Press.

Nguyen, Vinh-Kim. 2005a. "Antiretroviral Globalism, Biopolitics and Therapeutic Citizenship." In *Global Assemblages: Technology, Governmentality, and Ethics as Anthropological Problems,* ed. Aihwa Ong and Stephen J. Collier, 124–144. Malden: Blackwell.

———. 2005b. "Uses and Pleasures: Sexual Modernity, HIV/AIDS, and Confessional Technologies in a West African Metropolis." In *Sex in Development: Science, Sexuality, and Morality in Global Perspective,* ed. Vincanne Adams and Stacy L. Pigg, 245–267. Durham: Duke University Press.

———. 2010. *The Republic of Therapy: Triage and Sovereignty in West Africa's Time of AIDS.* Durham: Duke University Press.

Ong, Aihwa, and Stephen J. Collier, eds. 2005. *Global Assemblages: Technology, Governmentality, and Ethics as Anthropological Problems,* Malden: Blackwell.

Oomen, Barbara. 2005. *Chiefs in South Africa: Law, Power and Culture in the Post-Apartheid Era.* Oxford: James Currey.

Schaffer, Frederic C. 1998. *Democracy in Translation: Understanding Politics in an Unfamiliar Culture.* Ithaca: Cornell University Press.

Sewell, William H., Jr. 1996. "Historical Events as Transformations of Structures: Inventing Revolution at the Bastille." *Theory and Society* 25: 841–881.

Sikkink, Kathryn. 2009. "From State Responsibility to Individual Criminal Accountability: A New Regulatory Model for Core Human Rights Violations." In *The Politics of Global Regulation,* ed. Walter Mattli and Ngaire Woods, 121–150. Princeton: Princeton University Press.

Slaughter, Anne-Marie. 2004. *A New World Order.* Princeton: Princeton University Press.

Smith, Daniel Jordan. 2003. "Patronage, Per Diems and 'The Workshop Mentality': The Practice of Family Planning Programs in Southeastern Nigeria." *World Development* 31, no. 4: 703–715.

———. 2004. "Burials and Belonging in Nigeria: Rural-Urban Relations and Social Inequality in a Contemporary African Ritual." *American Anthropologist* 106, no. 3: 569–579.

———. 2006. *A Culture of Corruption: Everyday Deception and Popular Discontent in Nigeria.* Princeton: Princeton University Press.

Soysal, Yasemin Nuhoglu. 1994. *Limits of Citizenship: Migrants and Postnational Membership in Europe.* Chicago: University of Chicago Press.

Swidler, Ann. 2010. "The Return of the Sacred: What African Chiefs Teach Us about Secularization." *Sociology of Religion* 71, no. 2: 157–171.

Swidler, Ann, and Susan Cotts Watkins. 2007. "Ties of Dependence: AIDS and Transactional Sex in Rural Malawi." *Studies in Family Planning* 38, no. 3: 147–162.

———. 2009. "'Teach a Man to Fish': The Sustainability Doctrine and Its Social Consequences." *World Development* 37, no. 7: 1182–1196.

Tavory, Iddo, and Ann Swidler. 2009. "Condom Semiotics: Meaning and Condom Use in Rural Malawi." *American Sociological Review* 74: 171–189.

Thompson, E. P. 1963. *The Making of the English Working Class.* New York: Random House.

Tidemand, Per. 1995. "The Resistance Councils in Uganda: A Study of Rural Politics and Popular Democracy in Africa." Doctoral diss., Roskilde University.

Tsai, Lily L. 2007. *Accountability without Democracy: Solidary Groups and Public Goods Provision in Rural China.* Cambridge: Cambridge University Press.

Walzer, Michael. 1978. *The Revolution of the Saints.* New York: Atheneum.

Watkins, Susan Cotts, and Ann Swidler. 2009. "Hearsay Ethnography: Conversational Journals as a Method For Studying Culture in Action." *Poetics* 37: 162–184.

Watkins, Susan Cotts, Ann Swidler, and Thomas Hannan. 2012. "Outsourcing Social Transformation: Development NGOs as Organizations." *Annual Review of Sociology* 38.

Weinreb, Alexander A. 2001. "First Politics, Then Culture: Accounting for Ethnic Differences in Demographic Behavior in Kenya." *Population and Development Review* 27: 437–467.

White, Landeg. 1987. *Magomero: Portrait of an African Village.* Cambridge: Cambridge University Press.

Whitehead, Harriet. 1974. "Reasonably Fantastic: Some Perspectives on Scientology, Science Fiction, and Occultism." In *Religious Movements in Contemporary America,* ed. Irving Zaretsky and Mark P. Leone, 547–587. Princeton: Princeton University Press.

10

The Axial Age Theory

A Challenge to Historism or an Explanatory Device of Civilization Analysis? With a Look at the Normative Discourse in Axial Age China

HEINER ROETZ

After the end of the cosmopolitism of the Enlightenment, Occidental uniqueness and superiority have become firm features of the Western self-understanding. Hegel's statement that "the Oriental has to be excluded from the history of philosophy" (1940, 152) and Leopold Ranke's echo that for understanding world history "one cannot start from the peoples of eternal standstill" (1888, viii) are two prominent examples for a conviction that became dominant in the historical disciplines. World philosophy and world history have been Occidental.

There were few serious attempts to overcome this mind-set. One is Karl Jaspers' theory of the "Axial Age," published in 1949 in *Vom Ursprung und Ziel der Geschichte*, which is explicitly directed against Hegel's and Ranke's view of the "Orient." It claims to break through the "self-evident equation of a closed circle of Western culture with world history as such" (Jaspers 1953, 69) and denies the ascendancy of the "Weltgeist" from backward China to enlightened Greece. In its stead, Jaspers proposes the idea of a truly universal world history constituting a "single unity" from different "independent roots."

Jaspers' theory has its antecedents, above all the Enlightenment and its Stoic conviction of a time and space transcending "consensus gentium," which inspired Abraham Hyacinthe Anquetil-Duperron to formulate an early version of the Axial Age idea (Metzler 1991), or Max Scheler's call for a "cosmopolitan world philosophy" after the experiences of World War I (1954, 106). As far as the empirical aspect is concerned, Alfred Weber's notion of a "synchronistic world epoch" has to be mentioned (Weber 1935, 7).[1] However, what makes Jaspers' Axial Age theorem stand out in comparison to forerunners is the systematic importance that he attributes to it for re-orientating Western scholarship and, above all, its strong normative claim under the impression of the German crimes of World War II. Jaspers, unlike most of the scholars who have adopted his theory, does not merely want to explain developments. He wants to draw lessons from the past, and he is convinced that a new approach to history is one of these. There is the "disaster for the West," namely, the "claim to exclusiveness," which has to be warded off by the "language of universal history" (Jaspers 1953, 20).

The possibility of such a language results from what Jaspers regards to be a historical fact: the existence of at least three great and influential "centres of spiritual radiation"—the "Near East" and Greece, China, and India—where around the middle of the last millennium BCE, and from the far perspective of the twentieth century nearly simultaneously, the "step into universality" (1953, 2) was made independently. This step constitutes a fundamental turning point, the "deepcut dividing line in history" (1), by leaving behind hitherto valid orientations and giving birth to "the fundamental categories within which we still think today" (2). "The whole of humanity took a forward leap" (4).

The step in question has a number of facets outlined quite impressionistically rather than with systematic precision in Jaspers' presentation of the epoch in question, which he calls the "Axial Age." He admits that his "thesis" is in need not only of further corroboration but also of "ever greater clarity" (Jaspers 1953, 6). Still, one can roughly distinguish the following main features of the "Axial Age":

Sociologically, the background of all Axial Age developments is a polycentrism of cities and small states, mobility within and between the centers, increasing tension (Jaspers 1953, 5) and "struggle of all against all" (4). For the first time in history, the individual, be it as prophet, hermit, ascetic, or wandering philosopher, becomes an independent social unit; "human beings dared to rely on themselves as individuals" (3) and confront the majority. Correspondingly, the end of the Axial Age is brought about by large empires with their "order of technological and organisational planning" (5) and the final prevalence of the "continued belief of the mass of the people" (3).

On the level of thought, "hitherto unconsciously accepted ideas, customs and conditions were subjected to examination, questioned and liquidated" (Jaspers 1953, 2); the Axial Age is thus characterized by "reflection" rather than "unquestioned grasp of life," "open[ness] to new and boundless possibilities" rather than closedness of mind, man "rais[ing] himself above his own self" (16), "transcendence," the ethicization of religion, the struggle of "*logos* against *mythos*," a new self-understanding of the human being vis-à-vis the world, and the discovery of history (3). In later systematizations, "reflexivity, historicality and agentiality" have been rightly singled out as the most fundamental characteristics of "Axial" consciousness (Wittrock 2005, 67). From a semiotic perspective, they represent the self-reflection of "symbolic culture" made possible by the mastery of writing in a relatively broad intellectual stratum of society.[2]

The "historical fact" (Jaspers 1953, 15) that these developments were not merely local events but happened autochthonously at (at least) three different places in the ancient world reveals exemplarily the basic unity of mankind—there are different modifications of one and the same step. For Jaspers, this is a strong argument against the "claim to exclusive possession of truth" (19) that has in particular marked Western history. The Axial Age works as a bridge to recognize oneself in the other ("daß es sich beim andern auch um das eigene handelt" [Jaspers 1949, 27]), to realize that "profound mutual comprehension" is possible (8). Different cultures become "involved in one another" (8) and are faced with the "challenge to boundless communication" (19). Though *not historically universal,* it is *decisive for universal history* in terms of a common future marked by human solidarity. This is the ethical nucleus of Jaspers' theory. It has consistently been underexposed in most of its later adaptations.

Jaspers borrows the metaphor of the "axis" from Hegel, who has called the appearance of Jesus the "angle around which world history is turning" (Hegel 1939, 408). Hegel understands this crucial historical moment in terms of the self-elevation of "self-consciousness" to "spirit," a step in the "Phänomenologie des Geistes." Jaspers disbelieves that such a turning point can be located in "particular articles of faith," which cannot count as a "common frame of historical self-comprehension for all peoples" (1953, 1). Such a framework must be established on a much broader basis. When Jaspers dates the Axial Age between 800 and 200 BCE, in particular highlighting the time "around 500 B.C." (ibid.), he consciously avoids laying the main accent on Christianity and draws the attention to the founding phase of the classical philosophies. Obviously, he is convinced that in the final analysis an "Axial" function cannot be fulfilled by dogmatic belief systems, but only by the undogmatic "belief of philosophy."

The primarily philosophical rather than religious focus can also make clear the double dimension of the "axis": it is a *turning point* of history and at the same time a *connecting link* between all cultures. This function is rooted above all in the *formal* achievements of the Axial Age on the level of thought rather than in specific contents: in systematic reflection, radical questioning, and "transcendence"—the latter understood not primarily in religious terms but in the more general sense of *detachment* and going beyond existing limits, of "standing back and looking beyond" or recognizing that "another world is possible," as Benjamin Schwartz and Peter Wagner have aptly put it in their reading of the Axial Age theory (Schwartz 1975, 3; Wagner 2005, 97). It is the problematizing, the transcending of one's own reality, that opens the possibility for fully recognizing the other. Even if this potential was not exhausted in the Axial Age itself, turning the eyes back to it will open a *future perspective on a common "goal of history."* Thus to do research on the basis and in the spirit of Jaspers' approach—and he invites this research not only in order to corroborate his thesis, but also to contribute to a normative reorientation of the respective disciplines—would mean developing a specific awareness for formal shifts, for modes of arguments, criteria of justification, detached and second-order reasoning,[3] *and relating these to a universal ethical concern.* "Empirical facts," Jaspers says, are examined "in order to see to what extent they are in accordance with such an idea of unity, or how far they absolutely contradict it" (1953, xv).

Jaspers' theory of the Axial Age thus combines an empirical hypothesis with a two-level normative program: it comprises the rejection of cultural exceptionalism and the promotion of a common future, the "unity of mankind." This has offered a new field for comparative research and has at the same time been a challenge to comparativism, as well as to all historical disciplines and cultural sciences. As Rudolf Schottländer, a Jewish philosopher and classicist who survived the Holocaust hiding in Berlin put it in the first review of Jaspers' book entitled "Die Überwindung des Historismus" ("The overcoming of historism"), "there is a calling for historical reflection in Jaspers' work that couldn't be more urgent. He who after this book buries himself in history is beyond help" (Schottländer 1949, 98). The Axial Age theory, then, demands not only treating non-Western philosophical traditions on eye level, but also seeing the foreign world as a part of one's own world and one's own history as part of the foreign. It demands a hermeneutics based on a dialogical subject-cosubject relationship rather than *only* on the explanatory subject-object perspective (Apel 1994; Roetz 2009b).

However, contrary to Schottländer's expectation, Jaspers' theory has certainly not led to the "overcoming of historism." It has inspired historical research, but it has not shaken the historistic self-understanding of the corresponding disciplines. They have rather singled out the empirical part of the Axial Age idea and neglected or rejected the normative framework that gives meaning to it in the first place. This leads to the curious situation that if one wants to defend Jaspers' theory one has to confront not only its critics but also many of its adherents.

Both critics and adherents are above all to be found in the social sciences. Jaspers' theory had no comparable echo in philosophy, and it didn't have much appeal to the historical disciplines where it has "nearly fallen into oblivion" (Scheit 2000, 49). The foremost scholar who has helped to keep the Axial Age discourse alive is surely Shmuel N. Eisenstadt (ed. 1987, 1992). Nevertheless, the service that the social sciences have done to the Axial Age theory is a mixed blessing.

This might be due to the "typical" sociological view of that which prevails and, above all, materializes in institutions. But this is not Jaspers' outlook. From the beginning, it is his assumption that the Axial Age "ended in failure" (Jaspers 1953, 20). To him, the world-historical meaning of the Axial Age is not dependent on the factual realization of Axial Age ideas. It is grounded in the evidence that human beings independently of each other are able to mentally transcend themselves and their culture under similar circumstances. This is in turn the basis for entering into communication with others. The Axial Age is important as a "symbol" for the possibility of "boundless understanding" (xv). Kant would have called this a *prognostikon* or "sign of history" (1983, A:141–142). For Jaspers, rather than sociologically describable facts, the Axial Age constitutes a "single realm of everlasting spirits" (1953, xv), whereby he calls to mind the old humanist idea of a limitless "colloquium" of the "high minds" of all ages (Brogsitter 1958). "Axial" ideas remain important as a textually fixed repository of "transcending" thinking, even if their effective history has up to now come to nothing.

In the hands of the social sciences, by contrast, Jaspers' *normative* perspective has by and large been replaced by an explanatory and *descriptive* one, the perspective on *mankind* has been replaced by the perspective on a *plurality* of great "civilizations," and the *future* perspective has been replaced by a *retrospective* into the formation of *longue durée* civilizational patterns. This has made the "Axial" approach a variant of comparative civilizational analysis, also in the cultural disciplines. This owes more to Max Weber or the Weber brothers than it owes to Jaspers. It comes as no surprise that Max Weber often has been identified as the true progenitor of the Axial Age theory (e.g., Arnason 2005; Thomassen 2010), although he explicitly formulates a contrastive "idealtypical" rather than an accommodating comparison (Weber 1991, 19). In fact, what Weber offers is a sociologically enriched reformulation of the same Hegelian view of non-Occidental cultures that Jaspers attacks.

The point of my argument is not to question the fruitfulness of a sociological approach to the Axial Age hypothesis, but to recall the normative essence of Jaspers' idea. Still, Jaspers, in his "historical Platonism" (Habermas 1981, 92), links his normative program to an empirical hypothesis and anchors the future goal of history in a historical "origin." His theory, therefore, has to withstand some sort of historical and philological test. And it has been a matter of debate whether it is able to do so.

As to the critique of the Axial Age theory, is has taken two main directions: on the one hand, despite Jaspers' claim to overcome exclusivism, he has been reproached for promoting a new exclusivism himself, namely of Axial against non-Axial cultures; on the other hand, he has been criticized exactly in the name of exclusivism, that is, a reestablished Greek and Judeo-Christian uniqueness.

The first kind of criticism has, for example, been uttered by Aleida Assmann, to the effect that Jaspers' theory is hegemonic, trying to "realize unity at the expense of diversity" (1992, 330–331). Jan Assmann reproaches Jaspers for his "far reaching ignorance of the pre-axial-age world," in particular of Egypt, and his "oversimplified black and white thinking" (1990, 12 and 27). A place has been claimed within an "Axial" theory also for Islam (Arnason et al. 2007, introduction). Critics of "evolutionism" have rejected the whole idea of an epoch threshold in terms of a "breakthrough" as misjudging the efficiency and accomplishments of conventional morality (Rappe 2003).

The exclusion argument is invited by Jaspers' talk of the "three realms" (1953, 8). However, his point is not that *only* three cultures took part in the Axial Age, but, conversely, that is was *not only* the Occident. Occidental antiquity is not the sole witness to the possibility of self-transcendence as a precondition for all-encompassing communication. It would not affect the theory if other "realms" misjudged by Jaspers had to be included in the "Axial Age." It is not of first-rank importance when and where Axial developments in terms of "transcendence" (one could as well speak of the step toward postconventional, detached, decentered, or consciously symbolic thinking) took place, but *that* they took place to a considerable extent.

Still, Jaspers might have chosen an exclusivist indication for "Axial" developments. According to Aleida Assmann, this is the case with the criterion of "reflexivity," which springs from the very "European arrogance" that Jaspers opposes. Her alternative is "historicization and contextualization"— the "same historicization and contextualization that Jaspers was so eager to avoid" (A. Assmann 1992, 38). However, the argument of "historicization and contextualization" itself belongs to the culture of "reflexivity." It is already employed by Axial Age thinkers in order to refute the authority of tradition. In fact, the critique of the criteriology of the Axial Age theory would have to be directed against Axial Age thought itself, because it is here where this criteriology is put into effect for the first time—which in turn has motivated the Axial Age theory. The same applies to the critique of "postconventionalism" in the name of pre-Axial conventional morality. None of these arguments escapes "Axial" reasoning.

As to Islam, to narrow the Axial Age down to a few centuries in the middle of the last millennium BCE seems to be important for Jaspers for two reasons. Firstly, he identifies an early epoch in which a diffusion of ideas between the great civilizational centers is still unlikely, so that one can expect mutually independent developments as an indication of the *inner unity* of humanity. Secondly, Jaspers dates the Axial Age in a way that it does not comprise the founding phase of Christianity, because he is skeptical about the universalizability of religious contents. The inclusion of Islam in the later Axial Age discourse shows the extent to which the content of the original theory has been lost in its reduction to an explanatory device in historico-sociological functionalism: "axis" is no longer the *world historic* moment when the *unity of mankind* becomes imaginable in an exemplary (rather than exclusive) manner, but the *historic* moment of the formation of *different* cultural programs that form basic patterns of long-term developments, the multiplicity of which finally produces culturally distinct "multiple" modernities (Eisenstadt 2001, 332). It is certainly possible to use the concept of "axis"—or, in this case, of a plurality of axes—for the founding phases of the "great traditions," and Jaspers himself calls Christ "the axis of history" for the "consciousness of the West" (1953, 58). But this "Christian axis" is not *the* axis that constitutes *universal* history as a "single overall process" and the "continuity of humanity" (xvi). Jaspers acknowledges that "man's historicity" is always "multiple historicity," but there is no doubt that the "multiple is subject to the imperative of the One" (247). He is not looking for a pseudo-universalism that consists in the generalization of the beliefs of specific systems of self-assertion, but for a true universalism that overcomes the logic of self-assertion itself.

As far as the second kind of criticism, the criticism in the name of exclusivism, is concerned, this was brought forward by Schottländer, who claims, not very consistently with his praise for Jaspers mentioned above, that something happened in Greece "essentially not comparable with seemingly similar steps in China and India, but infinitely superior to them." There are "much deeper" differences, Schottländer stresses, "in the relationship of Greek and Oriental nature" than Jaspers would admit (1949, 97).

In subsequent discussion of the Axial Age theorem, China in particular has become a crucial case to test the empirical soundness of the Axial Age theory. The superiority of Greek thought has above all been defended in relation to the nature of the "breakthrough" from *mythos* to *logos* that according to Jaspers is an essential feature of the epoch as a whole. The Voegelin school has claimed that there was only an "incomplete" breakthrough in China, since, contrary to Greece, it has remained a "cosmological civilization" where the cornerstones of mythical thinking, the "consubstantiality" and "conduration" of the political and cosmological order, have not been consistently called into question (Voegelin 1956, 35 and 39; Weber-Schäfer 1968, 22).[4] Stefan Breuer has given a similar assessment: China has overcome "homology," that is, the assumption of a world of gods conceived in analogy to the human world, and replaced the former by depersonalized concepts like *dao* (Breuer 1994; 1998, 101). But China, according to Breuer, has not broken the "ontological continuum" that fuses everything into a single all-encompassing totality. If there have been deviations from this pattern, they "did not become culturally determinant" (Breuer 1998, 101). The only cultures where both homology and the cosmological continuum were abolished were the ancient Jewish and Greek cultures. For this and other reasons, Breuer suggests dropping the concept of the Axial Age as a temporally fixed epochal threshold brought about by "transcendental [sic] breakthroughs" and rather speaking of "cultural transformations in different directions" (1998, 105). Thus whether "Axial Age" is a meaningful idea in the first place would, among other things, hinge on what is actually offered by the Chinese sources.

With regard to Breuer's critique, Jaspers' hypothesis in fact does not imply that "Axial" developments became "culturally determinant"—this is again rather the standard perspective of the social scientist. It is only from this perspective that one may disregard the disruptions in the "ontological continuum," for example in Xunzi's (c. 310–c. 230 BCE) "separation of the realms of heaven and man" (*Xunzi* 17; Roetz 1984, §21), because they are later overlaid by holistic cosmologies. A major challenge to be dealt with is Breuer's claim that to conceptualize the Axial breakthroughs on the basis of Lawrence Kohlberg's "cognitive developmental theory," as I have done in my own reconstruction of classical Chinese ethics (Roetz 1993a), is misleading, since it encourages one to overlook the fundamental differences between the Chinese and the Western developments. In an elaboration of Jean Piaget's genetic epistemology, Kohlberg has proposed a three-level and six-stage model of the development of moral reasoning in ontogenesis.[5] *Mutatis mutandis* applied to sociogenesis, this model makes visible the genetic structure of moral evolution as based on the growth of human learning as a productive response to challenges. It describes the stages of possible progress, without assuming a strict necessity for it to happen as in nineteenth-century evolutionism.[6] What makes this theory especially promising for reconceptualizing the Axial Age is that Kohlberg shares with Jaspers the universalistic outlook on human culture and likewise works with a stark, empirically testable, and at times normatively laden hypothesis. It is tempting, therefore, to examine the Axial Age phenomenon in the light of developmental psychology, the potential of which for comparative studies is far from exhausted.

In the light of Kohlberg's theory, the entrance into the "Axial Age" would mean the transcending of the "conventional" level of "ethical life" (Hegel's "substantielle Sittlichkeit") in an *adolescent crisis* of society, and the breakthrough toward a "postconventional" perspective from where the "conventional" morality is either rejected or transformed and reestablished on a new level and with new restraints. In the Chinese case, the historical background is the breakdown of the old order in a deep crisis of the ancient society in the middle of the last millennium BCE. It shook the traditional worldview based on the religion of "Heaven" *(tian)* and the code of propriety *(li)* of the Zhou people. There is a very clear notion in Zhou texts that something unprecedented has commenced. They speak of a "chaotic" and "drowning" world that has lost its foundations and is falling apart. The original "undividedness" has been "cut into pieces" (*Laozi* 28), "the great primordial virtue is no longer one" (*Zhuangzi* 11). The main directions of classical Chinese thought are answers to this crisis.

These "Axial" developments and their prehistory can be brought into a Kohlbergian system. A key indication of the transcendence of Kohlberg's "conventional" level of family and state morality can be found in the numerous attacks on culture and custom among the Daoists (similar to Greek Sophism). They are exemplary representations of Kohlberg's Stage 4½, the phase of youthful protest, when conventional mores are typically exposed as artificial. Nature, life, and individual happiness are played off against the despotism of custom by an appeal to the naive rationality of the preconventional stages. The Daoists and their predecessors coin classical topoi for the recourse to preconventional freedom: the unaffected child not yet corrupted by education, the hedonist giving free vent to his inclinations, and the robber (Roetz 1993a, 248–249 and 256–257). The Confucians as well as the Mohists have surpassed this stage in the direction of a quasi-contractual utilitarian Stage 5 and a principled Stage 6 orientation, the latter comprising a nonegoistic fundamental norm, a universality claim, and a principle of autonomy. This is again similar to Greek developments, for example in Protagoras, the Anonymus Iamblichi, Socrates, and the Stoics.[7] In China, among the key elements of these endeavors we find abstract notions of reciprocity (as in Confucius' Golden Rule) and justice (as in the maxim from *Xunzi* 29,

"Follow the Dao and not the ruler, follow justice and not the father"), as well as a notion of the human heart *(xin)* as a sovereign organ of decision.[8]

Such a perspective on Axial Age normative reasoning, of which I can only give a very sketchy impression here, as well as the theoretical model on which it is based, is not without problems. The emphasis of cognitive developmental theory on a principled ethics seems to contradict what has been frequently described as the context sensitivity of Confucian ethics. However, principles and context sensitivity are not necessarily mutually exclusive (Roetz 1996, 351–357), and this wrong alternative is not supported by the late formulations of Kohlberg's theory. Here the highest stage is conceived as a coordination of justice and beneficence, incorporating a concern for interpersonal relations and the well-being of concrete individuals in concrete circumstances, thus transcending the solitariness of the Stage 6 actor in favor of a Stage 7 communicative ethics of responsibility (Habermas 1976, 83–88; Apel 1988, 306–369; Kohlberg 1990). This would also do justice to the fact that Chinese Axial Age thinkers, above all the Confucians, do not necessarily employ "postconventional" thinking in order to dismiss "conventional" duties but in order to reformulate and qualify them.

A methodic problem of the analysis is the loose relationship between chronological and developmentological aspects. For philological reasons it is only partly possible to write a reliable *history* of ideas of Axial Age China. My reconstruction rather assumes the simultaneous presence of a spectrum of positions within an overall discourse in a relatively broad period of time, in "one arena of intellectual articulation" (Hsu 2005, 459). It shows structural and logical relations that cannot always be proven as exactly congruent with historical successions. It has to be admitted, furthermore, that the "reconstructive" method itself (Habermas 1976, 9) is already indebted to the specific perspective on history that is part and parcel of the Axial Age hypothesis. However, it does not necessarily lead to committing intentional fallacies and reading something into the texts—reconstruction is not construction at will. It aims at an equilibrium of philological solidity and normative concern.[9]

A main objection to a Kohlbergian reconstruction of Axial Age thought is that it invites an overinterpretation of the sources. This is the aforementioned objection of Breuer. Without in principle rejecting the application of ontogenetic models to sociogenesis, Breuer argues that, if one follows Kohlberg, one will "read any hints to moral autonomy, mutual respect and reciprocity as indications of postconventional consciousness" and thus of the highest level of moral reasoning, while Piaget has shown them to be possible already on the medium level of "concrete-operational" (logical operations in concrete contexts) rather than "formal-operational" (reflexive, hypothetical, experimental, "second-order") thought (Breuer 1994, 5).[10] This would again open the gap between China and Greece and, according to Breuer, render the Axial Age hypothesis meaningless. His objection is crucial, since what Jaspers calls "transcendence" is marked by structural features and not only by specific contents.

However, the contradiction between a Piagetian and a Kohlbergian outlook on China is relieved when it comes to an analysis of the formal architecture of Chinese normative reasoning. In general, recourse to formal-operational thought is taken for granted only for Greek philosophy (referring to notions like *episteme, techne, organon, logike*) but not for China. This is because of an alleged preference for practical rather than theoretical matters on the Chinese side. But one can admit the primarily practical concern of the Chinese thinkers—as a matter of fact, as Pierre Hadot (1995) has shown, Greek philosophy, too, is not a purely theoretical undertaking—and still recognize the abstract theoretical layer of their thought. This is because in the convulsions of Zhou society, from which Chinese philosophy as a phenomenon of crisis emerges, there were no longer simple and direct answers to practical questions of right and wrong. This is how a contemporary source describes the chaotic situation:

> Numerous are those in the world who explore methods and arts, and all of them think they have something to which nothing can be added. . . . The Dao and the primordial virtue are no longer one, and the world often grasps just one aspect, and is self-complacent upon examining it. . . . Every single man in the world does just what he prefers and *thinks of himself as the model*[11] [compare the Greek notion of *autonomia*]. Alas! The hundred schools proceed and do not return, and will never be reunited. . . . The art of the Dao will be split by the world. (*Zhuangzi* 33, 463–464; my italics)

At a time when "private scholars discuss hither and thither" (*Mengzi* 3b9) and when there is "no longer any measure for right and wrong, and proper and improper change every day,"[12] normative thinking has to be elevated to a new level in order to regain firm ground. This is the background of *formal shifts* typical of Axial Age reasoning. I will now turn to these formal shifts in order to supplement the content analysis given in earlier writings by a discussion of structural features of Zhou philosophy.[13]

In the crisis of Zhou society, above all in its late phase of the "warring states" (fifth to third century BCE), it is no longer possible to talk about morals in a simple *intentio recta,* let alone exclusively performative attitude. In China, like in Greece, *ethics* as a *reflection* of morals comes into existence and is embedded in still more complex considerations. Xunzi's work, together with the Mohist writings, is the best example. Similar to most other thinkers of his time, Xunzi's interest is a practical one: to bring the chaotic world to peace again. But in the debate about normative orientations that actually constitutes the Axial Age, the competing programs have to be justified, defended, and argued for, and there is hardly any writer who has done this in a more systematic manner than Xunzi. For him, at a time when "chaotic rulers of doomed states let themselves bewilder by shamans and priest and believe in oracles" (*Shiji* 74, 2348), any solution for the age presupposes a rational view of nature, and therefore he composes his treatise "On Heaven" *(Tian lun).* Moreover, a realistic assessment of the human being is necessary. Xunzi deals with this in his anthropological chapter "Human nature is bad" *(Xing e).* Both texts break the "ontological continuum" and expound the necessity of human artifice *(wei)* as a cultural achievement neither predisposed in the cosmos nor in the spontaneous natural inclinations *(xing)* of man (Roetz 1984, §21). To appropriate the *dao,* the "right way," is a matter of correct cognition, and this prompts Xunzi's epistemological essay "Dissolving obscurations" *(Jie bi).* Furthermore, since the political and social crisis is reflected in a crisis of language, Xunzi writes his "On the correct use of words" *(Zheng ming).*

The thematic treatise, the appearance of which reflects how much the time is in need of argumentation, is a typical layer of the architecture of the Zhou discourse. It was probably invented by Mo Di (fifth century BCE), and in the Mohist texts we find the most distinct occupation with a new field of formal reasoning: *criteriology. Mozi* 4 states the necessity of having "norms and standards" *(fa yi),* and at the same time denies that the conventional authorities—parents, teachers, and rulers—could serve as such standards, since "only few of them are humane." This throws a light on the connection between content and form of ethical reasoning. Mo Di also explicitly denies that "habits" *(xi)* and "customs" *(su)* can deliver as acceptable norms, because this would logically imply endorsing "inhuman" and "unjust" practices like cannibalism, infanticide, and gerontocide, which are established practices in some cultures.[14] The *Mozi,* moreover, sets up criteria *(biao, fa)* to be fulfilled by any "words" *(yan,* compare the Greek *logos)* that deserve consent: they should have a "foundation" *(ben)* in the works of the sage kings, they should have a "source" *(yuan)* in the sensual perceptions of the majority, and they should be "applicable" *(yong).*[15] The past—in the form of the sage kings—is only one criterion here and has to make room for other criteria located in the *present.* Among the latter criteria we also find consistency *(bu bei)* used in transcendental arguments in the Mohist canon.[16]

Correspondingly, the Mohist canon distinguishes several ways of achieving knowledge: transmission *(chuan)* is supplemented by personal observation *(shen guan)* and explanation *(shuo)* independent of one's position in time or space, "without the location acting as a barrier" (*Mozi* 42, 211). Xunzi, although in many respects a traditionalist, says, "A person who is good in talking about antiquity must have a tally *(jie)* from the present" (*Xunzi* 23, 293). Antiquity is not directly accessible to our knowledge; "it is only by the near that one knows the distant" (*Xunzi* 5, 50–51). The epistemological priority of the "near" over the "distant" corresponds to the priority of "seeing" over "hearing."[17] Han Fei (c. 280–233 BCE), again, stresses that no knowledge based on evidence is possible about the idealized past, adding, "To take something as a given without any proof by examination is stupid, but to base arguments on something that one is unable to confirm is to swindle" (*Hanfeizi* 50, 351). Wang Chong (27–91 CE), a post-Axial Age thinker who continues this line of reasoning, has compared traditionalists to "postmen delivering letters" (*Lunheng* 80, 266).

There is a conspicuous epistemological shift from secondhand knowledge to personal experience, from the "remote" to the "present" and "near," from the indirectly to the directly accessible in Chinese Axial Age texts. It is accompanied by a systematic spectrum of doubt and critique of endorsing the past. We can distinguish at least the following types of arguments: the *logical* argument refers to the paradox that traditionalism appeals to values that originally were not traditional but newly created, as in the statement "What one follows must have been invented by someone," brought forward in the *Mozi* (39, 181; and 46, 262–263) against the maxim "to transmit and not to innovate."[18] This means the logical priority of creativity over preservation. The *historical* argument refers to the futility of tradition in view of the changes of the times, as in the statement from the *Zhuangzi* (14, 227), "Morals and regulations change according to the times. . . . The old is as different from the new as a monkey is different from the Duke of Zhou."[19] The *empirical* argument refers to the heterogeneity, complexity, and even contradictory nature of tradition, as in the rhetorical question from the *Shangjunshu* (1, 2), "The former generations did not follow the same doctrines, so which version of antiquity should we emulate?" The *epistemological* argument refers to the increasing vagueness of transmitted knowledge the farther we go back into the past. Han Fei notes that within a short period of time the Confucians and the Mohists have split into eight and three factions respectively that dispute the original teaching of their founders. How much more futile would it be to achieve accurate knowledge about the remote times of the idealized predynastic rulers, to which both schools refer (*Hanfeizu* 50, 351)? The *ontological* argument refers to the impossibility of transmitting the true, as in the introductory statement of the received *Laozi*, "The Dao that can be spoken about is not the constant Dao" (*Laozi* 1). The *ethical* argument refers to the possible moral questionability of tradition, as in Mo Di's remark mentioned above that he who wants to follow established customs must be ready to practice infanticide and cannibalism, since these are established practices in some cultures. The *invention* argument, added later by Wang Chong, points out the possibility of deliberate manipulation and faking of records from the past, because the "vulgar world esteems the ancient and disparages the present" (*Lunheng* 25, 76; 84, 286).

Normativity comes into tension with history. This shift can even be detected in the still widespread affirmative references to the early "sages" (*shengren*) and kings in late Zhou, above all Confucian, texts. The *shengren* prove to be ideal representations of values that they teach but that genetically do not depend on them and do not presuppose a historical rooting in the first place. They are exemplary embodiments of one and the same human nature inherent in all human beings (*Mengzi* 6a7, 2a2). In the *Xunzi*, the *shengren* of antiquity generate norms, but they are merely particular expressions of human reason, endeavor, and effort within the reach of even the ordinary "man in the street" of today (*Xunzi* 23, 296). Nearly all of the central orientation marks of the different Zhou "schools" no longer share the time paradigm of traditionalistic thinking. In the *Mozi,* we find the abstract criterion of the "good" *(shan),* understood in terms of "utility," regardless of whether old or new.[20] The same applies to the Legalist criterion of practicability *(ke).*[21] The Daoist *dao* is grasped in immediate mystical immersion and explicitly not by transmission. Detachment from the past even holds true for the Confucian school, which upholds the closest ties with tradition. One of the most interesting cases is the Golden Rule, formulated in Confucius' *Analects* (*Lunyu* 15.24) as a general maxim that "consists of one word and can therefore be practiced for all of one's life." The Golden Rule does not draw on a setting of traditional values, virtues, or patterns, but only presupposes the implicit or explicit assumptions of generalizable, and in that sense *timeless,* basic human needs and aspirations, in the form of the self's transfer of its own wishes to the other and taking the other's role. The "transcending" implications of this pattern of thought can be seen from the fact that it also appears in a passage from the "Watch the present" *(Cha jin)* chapter of the *Lüshi chunqiu* (238 BCE), where "knowing others by examining oneself" provides an orientation declaredly set against the unqualified endorsement of past models:

> Why should the ruler not take the standards of the early kings as a model? It is not that the former kings were not wise. It is because they *cannot* be taken as a model. The standards of the former kings have come upon us by passing through the remote ages. Some men have added to them, and some have omitted parts from them. How then could they be taken as a model? But even if nobody would have added or omitted something, they could still not be taken as a model. . . .
>
> The standards of antiquity and of today are different in their language and their statutes. The words of antiquity, therefore, often do not correspond with the expressions of today, and the standards of today often do not accord with the standards of antiquity. . . .
>
> How could the standards of the early kings be taken as a model then? Even if this were possible, it would still not be proper. The stan-

dards of the former kings were somehow required by the times. But the times have not come down to us together with the standards. Thus, even if the standards should have come down to the present, it would still not be proper to take them as a model.

Therefore, we should *abandon the fixed standards* of the early kings and *take as a model how they set up their standards.* But how did the early kings make their standards? That by which they made their standards was *the human being (ren).* But we ourselves are human beings, too. Therefore, *by examining oneself one can know others. By examining the present one can know the past. The past and the present are one, and the others and I are the same.* A scholar who is in possession of the *dao* appreciates knowing the distant by the near, knowing the past by the present, knowing what he has not seen by what he has seen. Therefore, look at the shadow below the hall, and you know the course of sun and moon and the change of yin and yang. Look at the ice in a vase, and you know that it is cold under heaven and fish and turtles will hide. Taste one mouthful of meat, and you know the flavor of the whole cauldron and the seasoning of the whole vessel. (*Lüshi chunqiu* 15.8: 176–177; my italics)

In this passage, which is a theoretical culmination point of classical Chinese critique of tradition, the *Lüshi chunqiu* recommends a shift in category: one should "*abandon the fixed standards* of the early kings and *take as a model how they set up their standards.*" In place of the old models, a new standard is established, which is located in the here and now: the *self* as a generalized human being. The way to set up standards is nothing but self-observation and subsequent generalization—the very way which Confucius calls "the method of humaneness": *neng jin qu pi* ("to be able to take what is near as analogy" [*Lunyu* 6.30]).

The Golden Rule paves the way for the new and likewise nontraditional paradigm that Mengzi, in reply to Daoist naturalism, introduces into Confucian philosophy: the paradigm of innate spontaneity, the *immediate* stimulation of a moral impulse located in the natural disposition *(xing)* of the human being "prior to any learning" (*Mengzi* 7a15), that is, socialization and education. It is later reproached for undermining not only tradition but also political rule (Roetz 1993a, 221–222).

The Chinese Axial Age search for standards no longer rooted in the past but in the present reaches its formal climax in the following passage from the *Mozi*, which is itself the most "formal" Zhou text. It contains a formulation of the *primacy of the better argument* that we cannot surpass even today:

> Humane persons inform each other of the reasons *(li)* why they choose or reject something or why they find something right or wrong. He who cannot bring forward reasons *(gu)* follows the one who brings forward reasons. He who has no knowledge follows the one who has knowledge. He who has no arguments *(ci)* submits to the other, and when he sees something good, he will change his position accordingly. Why then should they [quarrel]? (*Mozi* 39, 182)

I take these arguments together with the underlying and partly explicit structures of Zhou normative reasoning as indications that, even without referring to the "logical" chapters of the *Mozi,* a reading of classical Chinese philosophical texts in terms of concrete-operational (as suggested by Breuer), let alone preoperational thinking, is not plausible. This does not imply that the whole body of texts is on a formal-operational level, but that at least the basics of formal-operational thought must be taken into consideration in order to understand the main positions of the Chinese "Axial Age" discourse.

At the same time, one can admit that neither in content nor in structure was the Axial Age "breakthrough" "complete" in a strict sense. This not only allows us to understand the possibility of regressions behind the standard of developed Axial Age thought in post-Axial times, when the innovatory potential of this thinking was absorbed and monopolized by the novel authoritarian centralistic state. It also allows us to understand the many discrepancies between formal-operational and still-existing concrete-operational and preoperational elements in Axial Age thought itself, which even the *Mozi,* the most "argumentative" Zhou text, is not free of. Mo Di believes, for example, that according to the "source" standard *(yuan)* that he has set up for valid speech, the existence of ghosts and the nonexistence of fate can be proven—ghosts have been sensually perceived by the majority, but fate has not (*Mozi* 31 and 36). Mo Di, furthermore, formulates the principle of the better argument in his polemics against the Confucians. It does not enter his mind that he himself should be bound by this principle when he formulates his own vision of a functioning society as a vertical system of obedience (*Mozi* 11–13). It appears to be a general feature of the Axial Age that the morals proposed for the polity do not necessarily reflect the same level as the elitist thinkers' own consciousness and reasoning standards.

Such reservations do not merely apply to China—in the case of Greece, too, it is not self-evident that we can speak of a "complete breakthrough" in the light of either a Kohlbergian or a Piagetian conceptualization of the Axial Age. It is far from evident that Greek ethicists reached Kohlberg's highest stage.[22] An interesting case is the natural philosophy of Aristotle, which dominated Europe till Kepler and Galileo, and which Piaget has described, in the formulation of Oesterdiekhoff, "as partly right down to the details structurally identical with the third stadium of animistic thinking of ten-year-old children" (Oesterdiekhoff 1997, 83; Piaget 1978; Fetz 1982). To put it another way: Axial Age thinking is not wholly identical with modern thinking. Nevertheless, it contains *anticipations* of modern thought, in the sense that Hegel saw the Greek Sophist movement as an early representation of what he calls the "principle of the modern world"—the "principle of free subjectivity" (Hegel 1938, §§124, 273; 1940, 153). This means that in the final analysis only modernity in terms of this principle, or its "neoclassic" reformulation in terms of intersubjectivity (Habermas 1992, 125 and 156), is the true and full realization of the Axial Age "breakthroughs." The theory of the Axial Age has to be transferred ("aufgehoben") into a theory of modernity.

If this is true, it would have a bearing on the theory of "multiple modernities," currently the most influential elaboration of Jaspers' Axial Age hypothesis. If the Axial Age breakthroughs, as I have tried to show by the Chinese example, essentially comprise a *novel time paradigm*[23] of thought that implicitly or explicitly puts the present, the here and now—the moral impulse, the thought experiment of role taking, self-reflection, the reasoned scrutiny of arguments—in the place of the past as a formal feature of detached thinking, then it would amount to a category mistake to see "Axial" developments primarily as founding phases of a multiplicity of great cultural traditions. It comes as no surprise that in Chinese adaptations of the "multiple modernities" theory all of the constituents of first-order thinking that were transcended in Axial Age philosophy—thinking in terms of "cultural genes" (Hsu 2005, 451), of rootedness, embeddedness, primordiality, or ethnicity (Tu 1998, 2000), of *looking back* to one's "heritage" rather than *looking beyond*—are reenthroned, accompanied by contextualistic, role-moral, ritualistic, aestheticizing, and spiritual readings of Confucianism, in order to bypass the principle of subjectivity of "Western" modernism (see Roetz 2008). If the legacy of the Axial Age lies in the development of "postconventional," "detached," or "second-order" forms of reasoning as an anticipation of modernity (granted that this anticipation is incomplete), being an "Axial Age" culture would first of all be a particular provocation to any kind of cultural self-affirmation. One cannot invoke the Axial Age without living up to its standards, that is, without transcending one's own historical and cultural framework in the direction of a "modern," all-encompassing communicative orientation. The theory of "multiple modernities," which links modernity intrinsically to different cultural programs "rooted" in different "axes," tends to circumvent the main challenge of the Axial Age: that any drawing on the past, on traditions, on "roots" and "origins" is in need of justification by generalizable criteria. If this challenge is accepted, Jaspers' disputed theory of the "age of transcendence" may even itself be "transcended." For Jaspers himself adheres to an ideology of "origin" that is not consistent with Axial Age consciousness. It is only against the Axial Age that one can think with it. The "axis" is wherever there is enlightened thought.

Notes

1. Jaspers also mentions Ernst von Lasaulx and Victor von Strauß among his forerunners.

2. See the contributions of Merlin Donald and Matthias Jung in this volume. For the importance of writing, see also Jan Assmann's article in this volume and Dürnberger 2005 (based on Vilém Flusser's "communicology").

3. The importance of second-order thinking is frequently stressed in the literature on the Axial Age; see for example Bellah 2005, 80.

4. For a critique of this much too undifferentiated assumption with regard to Egypt, see Assmann 1990, passim.

5. Kohlberg's preconventional Level I comprises the stages of punishment and obedience orientation (Stage 1) and of instrumental exchange (Stage 2). The conventional Level II comprises the stages of interpersonal concordance and expectations, above all within the family (Stage 3) and of law and order (Stage 4). The postconventional Level III comprises the stages of utilitarian, relativistic social contract orientation (Stage 5) and of universal ethical principle orientation (Stage 6). See for example Kohlberg 1981, 409–412.

6. In a critique of my approach, Zhang Hao (2000, 4) writes that the application of Kohlberg's theory would make the Axial Age a "natural result" of history. This is a misunderstanding. If one does not want to mystify the emergence of the Axial Age, it can only be the result of an evolution of moral learning. But there is a growing probability rather than necessity that this evolution takes place.

7. For a more detailed Kohlbergian description of the Chinese and Greek developments, see Roetz 1993a, 265–272; and 2000. For Greek postconventional thinking, see Apel 1980. For contractualism in early Chinese thought, above all in the *Xunzi*, see Roetz 2009c.

8. See for these points Roetz 1993a, 119–146, 64–65, and 159–160.

9. See Peter Wagner's felicitous remark on the "double requirement" of Axial Age investigations: "They have to be sustainable in the light of the best available historical evidence, and they have to give answers to the questions we pose to the past from the point of view of the present" (Wagner 2005, 93).

10. Breuer 1994, 5. For the ontogenetic approach to sociogenesis and its problems, see Apel 1980. See also Dux 2000 and Oesterdiekhoff 1992 and 1997.

11. For *fang* in the meaning of "model" or "measure," see *Shijing* 241.6.

12. *Lüshi chunqiu* 18.4, 225 on the situation in the state of Zheng in the sixth century BCE.

13. See for the following Roetz 2005a,b.

14. *Mozi* 25, 115–116: "In ancient times, there was a land named Kaishu east of Yue. Right after birth, the people dismembered the firstborn child and ate it, saying that this was propitious for the younger brothers. When the grandfather died, they loaded the grandmother on their back and abandoned her, saying that they could not live together with the wife of a ghost. The superiors regarded this as the correct order, and the people saw it as a custom. Thus they carried on practicing these things. But how could this, in fact, be the way of humaneness and justice? This means to consider a habit as convenient, and to regard custom as a norm for what is just."

15. *Mozi* 35, 164: "Speech *(yan)* must [comply with] three standards.... There must be something in what it is *founded (ben)*, something which can serve as its *source (yuan)*, and something for which it is *applicable (yong)*. In what should it be founded? It should be founded above in the works of the sage kings of antiquity. What should serve as its source? We should below take as a source and examine what is real *(shi)* in the ears and eyes of the people. For what should it be applicable? When put into practice for administration, one should examine whether it meets the benefit of states and clans, citizens, nobility, and common people. This is meant by the three standards of speech."

16. For example, "To take all statements as contradictory is contradictory. The explanation lies in that statement" (*Mozi* 41, 201, B71); "To refute refutation is contradictory. The explanation lies in not refuting [that one refutes refutation]" (*Mozi* 42, 202, B79); "That learning is useful is explained by those who reject this" (*Mozi*

41, 201–202, B77); "If you think someone does not know that learning is of no use and therefore inform him [of this], this means to let him know that learning is useless. But this is teaching. To think that learning is useless and to teach [this] is contradictory" (*Mozi* 43: 233–234, B77). For this and related topics see Roetz 1993b.

17. "Not to hear something is not as good as hearing it. *To hear something is not as good as seeing it.* To see something is not as good as knowing it. And to know something is not as good as doing it" (*Xunzi* 8, 90; my italics).

18. The phrase is from *Lunyu* 7.1. It was later understood as a traditionalistic maxim.

19. The Duke of Zhou is one of the founders of the Zhou dynasty.

20. *Mozi* 46, 262–263: "Gongmengzi said, 'The gentleman does not innovate, but merely transmits.' Mozi said, 'Not at all. Those who are the most unlike a gentleman neither transmit the good of antiquity nor initiate the good of the present. The next group of people unlike gentlemen [likewise] does not follow the good of antiquity, but if they have something good themselves, they will put it into practice because they want it to emerge from themselves. Now, to transmit but not to innovate is not different from innovating without loving to follow [= without transmitting]. I think that one should transmit the good of antiquity and create the good of today, in order to increase the good all the more.'" It is an interesting parallel that Confucius, too, refers to the "good" *(shan)* as the ultimate value when he rejects the idea of simply taking the opinion of one's fellow citizens as a measure for right conduct: "Zigong asked, 'If everybody in the neighborhood likes a person, how would that be?' The Master said, 'That is not enough.'—'And if everybody in the neighborhood dislikes a person?'—'That is not enough either. It is better if the *good* in the neighborhood like and the bad dislike that person'" (*Lunyu* 13.24).

21. "Those who do not understand politics insist that one must not change old ways and alter long-established regulations. But to change or not to change is something the sage does not listen to. He simply rectifies the government. Whether old ways should not be changed and long-established regulations should not be altered, then, depends on their being *practicable* [for today] or not" (*Hanfeizi* 18, 87; my italics).

22. Socrates (frequently discussed in Kohlberg 1981) would be a candidate, but since he expresses sympathy for the antidemocratic constitution of Sparta (Plato, *Crito* 52e), a stronghold of slavery, his universalism is doubtful.

23. See Roetz 2009a.

References

Apel, Karl-Otto. 1980. "Zur geschichtlichen Entfaltung der ethischen Vernunft in der Philosophie." In *Funkkolleg praktische Philosophie/Ethik, Studienbegleitbrief* 2. Weinheim and Basel: Beltz.

———. 1988. *Diskurs und Verantwortung.* Frankfurt am Main: Suhrkamp.
———. 1994. "Die hermeneutische Dimension von Sozialwissenschaft und ihre normative Grundlage." In *Mythos Wertfreiheit? Neue Beiträge zur Objektivität der Human- und Kulturwissenschaften,* ed. Karl-Otto Apel and Matthias Kettner, 17–47. Frankfurt and New York: Campus.
Arnason, Johann P. 2005. "The Axial Age and Its Interpreters: Reopening a Debate." In *Axial Civilizations and World History,* ed. Johann P. Arnason, Shmuel N. Eisenstadt, and Björn Wittrock, 19–49. Leiden: Brill.
Arnason, Johann P., Shmuel N. Eisenstadt, and Björn Wittrock, eds. 2005. *Axial Civilizations and World History.* Leiden: Brill.
Arnason, Johann P., Armando Salvatore, and Georg Stauth, eds. 2007. *Islam in Process: Historical and Civilizational Perspectives.* Bielefeld: Transcript.
Assmann, Aleida. 1992. "Einheit und Vielfalt in der Geschichte. Jaspers' Begriff der Achsenzeit neu betrachtet." In *Kulturen der Achsenzeit II: Ihre institutionelle und kulturelle Dynamik,* ed. Shmuel N. Eisenstadt. Vol. 3, 330–340. Frankfurt am Main: Suhrkamp.
Assmann, Jan. 1990. *Ma'at: Gerechtigkeit und Unsterblichkeit im Alten Ägypten.* Munich: Beck.
Bellah, Robert. 2005. "What Is Axial about the Axial Age?" *European Journal of Sociology* 46, no. 1: 69–89.
Breuer, Stefan. 1994. "Kulturen der Achsenzeit. Leistungen und Grenzen eines geschichtsphilosophischen Konzepts." *Saeculum* 45, no. 1: 1–33.
———. 1998. *Der Staat: Entstehung, Typen, Organisationsstadien.* Reinbek: Rowohlt.
Brogsitter, Karl Otto. 1958. "Das hohe Geistergespräch. Studien zur Geschichte der humanistischen Vorstellungen von einer zeitlosen Gemeinschaft der großen Geister." Ph.D. diss., University of Bonn.
Dürnberger, Christian. 2005. "Die Achsenzeit—eine Grenzsituation. Karl Jaspers' Achsenzeit interpretiert unter einem kommunikationsgeschichtlichen Horizont." http://sammelpunkt.philo.at:8080/1249/.
Dux, Günter. 2000. *Historisch-genetische Theorie der Kultur.* Weilerswist: Velbrück.
Eisenstadt, Shmuel N. 2001. "The Civilizational Dimension of Modernity: Modernity as Distinct Civilization." *International Sociology* 16, no. 3: 320–340.
Eisenstadt, Shmuel N., ed. 1987. *Kulturen der Achsenzeit: Ihre Ursprünge und ihre Vielfalt.* 2 vols. Frankfurt am Main: Suhrkamp.
———, ed. 1992. *Kulturen der Achsenzeit II: Ihre institutionelle und kulturelle Dynamik.* 3 vols. Frankfurt am Main: Suhrkamp.
Fetz, Reto Luzius. 1982. "Naturdenken beim Kind und bei Aristoteles. Fragen einer genetischen Ontologie." *Tijdschrift voor Filosofie* 44: 473–513.
Habermas, Jürgen. 1976. *Zur Rekonstruktion des historischen Materialismus.* Frankfurt am Main: Suhrkamp.
———. 1981. *Philosophisch-politische Profile.* 3rd ed. Frankfurt am Main: Suhrkamp.

———. 1992. *Texte und Kontexte*. Frankfurt am Main: Suhrkamp.
Hadot, Pierre. 1995. *Philosophy as a Way of Life*. Oxford: Wiley-Blackwell.
Hanfeizi. 1978. Wang Xianshen, *Hanfeizi Jijie, Zhuzi jicheng*. Vol. 5. Hong Kong: Zhonghua.
Hegel, Georg Wilhelm Friedrich. 1938. *Grundlinien der Philosophie des Rechts*. In Hegel, *Sämtliche Werke*, ed. H. Glockner. Vol. 7. Stuttgart-Bad Cannstadt: Frommann.
———. 1939. *Vorlesungen über die Philosophie der Geschichte*. In Hegel, *Sämtliche Werke*, ed. H. Glockner. Vol. 11. Stuttgart-Bad Cannstadt: Frommann.
———. 1940. *Vorlesungen über die Geschichte der Philosophie I*. In Hegel, *Sämtliche Werke*, ed. H. Glockner. Vol. 17. Stuttgart-Bad Cannstadt: Frommann.
Hsu Cho-yun. 2005. "Rethinking the Axial Age—The Case of Chinese Culture." In *Axial Civilizations and World History*, ed. Johann P. Arnason, Shmuel N. Eisenstadt, and Björn Wittrock, 451–467. Leiden: Brill.
Jaspers, Karl. 1949. *Vom Ursprung und Ziel der Geschichte*. Munich: Piper.
———. 1953. *The Origin and Goal of History*, trans. M. Bullock. New Haven: Yale University Press.
Kant, Immanuel. 1983. *Der Streit der Fakultäten*. In *Kants Werke in zehn Bänden*, ed. Wilhelm Weischedel. Vol. 9. Darmstadt: WBG.
Kohlberg, Lawrence. 1981. *The Philosophy of Moral Development* (*Essays on Moral Development*, vol. 1). San Francisco: Harper & Row.
Kohlberg, Lawrence, with Dwight R. Boyd and Charles Levine. 1990. "The Return of Stage 6: Its Principle and Moral Point of View." In *The Moral Domain*, ed. Thomas E. Wren. Cambridge, MA: MIT.
Laozi. 1978. Wang Bi, *Laozi zhu, Zhuzi jicheng*. Vol. 2. Hong Kong: Zhonghua.
Lunheng. 1978. *Zhuzi jicheng*. Vol. 7. Hong Kong: Zhonghua.
Lunyu (Analects). 1972. Harvard-Yenching Institute Sinological Index Series: *A Concordance to the Analects of Confucius*. Reprint. Taipei: Chengwen.
Lüshi chunqiu. 1978. *Zhuzi jicheng*. Vol. 6. Hong Kong: Zhonghua.
Mengzi. 1973. *Concordance to Meng Tzu*. Reprint. Taipei: Chengwen.
Metzler, Dieter. 1991. "A. H. Anquetil-Duperron (1731–1805) und das Konzept der Achsenzeit." In *Achaemenid History 7*, ed. H. Sancisi-Weerdenburg and J. W. Drijvers, 123–133. Leiden: Brill.
Mozi. 1978. Sun Yirang, *Mozi xiangu, Zhuzi jicheng*. Vol. 4. Hong Kong: Zhonghua.
Oesterdiekhoff, Georg W. 1992. *Traditionales Denken und Modernisierung: Jean Piaget und die Theorie der sozialen Evolution*. Mainz: VS.
———. 1997. *Kulturelle Bedingungen kognitiver Entwicklung. Der strukturgenetische Ansatz in der Soziologie*. Frankfurt am Main: Suhrkamp.
Piaget, Jean. 1978. "Die historische Entwicklung und die Psychogenese des Impetus-Begriffs." In *Piaget und die Folgen*, ed. G. Steiner, 64–73. Zurich: Kindler.
Ranke, Leopold v. 1888. *Weltgeschichte*. Vol. 1. 4th ed. Leipzig: Duncker und Humblot.

Rappe, Guido. 2003. *Interkulturelle Ethik*. Vol. 1, *Ethik und Rationalitätsformen im Kulturvergleich: Eine Kritik am Postkonventionalismus*. Bochum: Europäischer Universitätsverlag.
Roetz, Heiner. 1984. *Mensch und Natur im alten China*. Frankfurt am Main: Lang.
———. 1993a. *Confucian Ethics of the Axial Age*. Albany: SUNY Press.
———. 1993b. "Validity in Zhou Thought: On Chad Hansen and the Pragmatic Turn in Sinology." In *Epistemological Issues in Classical Chinese Philosophy*, ed. Hans Lenk and Gregor Paul, 69–112. Albany: SUNY Press.
———. 1996. "Kohlberg and Chinese Moral Philosophy." *World Psychology* 2, nos. 3–4: 335–363.
———. 2000. "Moralischer Fortschritt in Griechenland und China. Ein Vergleich der achsenzeitlichen Entwicklung." In *Politisches Denken Chinas in alter und neuer Zeit*, ed. Oskar Fahr et al., 123–151. Münster: LIT.
———. 2005a. "Normativity and History in Warring States Thought: The Shift towards the Anthropological Paradigm." In *Historical Truth, Historical Criticism, and Ideology: Chinese Historiography and Historical Culture from a New Comparative Perspective*, ed. Helwig Schmidt-Glintzer et al., 79–92. Leiden: Brill.
———. 2005b. "Tradition, Moderne, Traditionskritik. China in der Diskussion." In *Kulturelle und religiöse Traditionen: Beiträge zu einer interdisziplinären Traditionstheorie und Traditionsanalyse*, ed. Torsten Lalbig and Siegfried Wiedenhofer, 124–167. Münster: LIT.
———. 2008. "Confucianism between Tradition and Modernity, Religion and Secularization: Questions to Tu Weiming." *Dao* 7, no. 4: 367–380.
———. 2009a. "Tradition, Universality and the Time Paradigm of Zhou Philosophy." *Journal of Chinese Philosophy* 36, no. 3: 359–375.
———. 2009b. "What It Means to Take Chinese Ethics Seriously." In *Taking Confucian Ethics Seriously*, ed. Yu Kam Por et al., 13–26. Albany: SUNY Press.
———. 2009c. "Xunzi's Vision of Society: Harmony by Justice." In *Governance for Harmony—Linking Visions*, ed. Julia Tao et al., 315–328. New York: Routledge.
Scheit, Hubert. 2000. "Achsenzeit—ein (fast) vergessenes Konzept für eine Wendezeit." In *Zeitenwenden—Wendezeiten: Von der Achsenzeit bis zum Fall der Mauer*, ed. Peter Segl, 37–49. Dettelbach: Röll.
Scheler, Max. 1954. "Der Mensch im Weltalter des Ausgleichs" [1927]. In Max Scheler, *Philosophische Weltanschauung*. Munich: Lehnen.
Schottländer, Rudolf. 1949. "Die Überwindung des Historismus." *Der Monat* 12: 98.
Schwartz, Benjamin. 1975. "The Age of Transcendence." *Daedalus* 104, no. 2: 1–7.
Shangjunshu. 1978. *Zhuzi jicheng*. Vol. 5. Hong Kong: Zhonghua.
Shiji. 1969. Hong Kong: Zhonghua.

Thomassen, Bjørn. 2010. "Anthropology, Multiple Modernities and the Axial Age Debate." *Anthropological Theory* 10, no. 4: 321–342.
Tu Wei-ming. 1998. "A Confucian Perspective on Human Rights." *Harvard International Review* 20, no. 3: 44–49.
———. 2000. "Implications of the Rise of 'Confucian' East Asia." *Daedalus* 129, no. 1 (Multiple Modernities): 195–218.
Voegelin, Eric. 1956. *Order and History.* Vol. 1. Baton Rouge: Louisiana State University Press.
Wagner, Peter. 2005. "Palomar's Questions: The Axial Age Hypothesis, European Modernity and Historical Contingency." In *Axial Civilizations and World History,* ed. Johann P. Arnason, Shmuel N. Eisenstadt, and Björn Wittrock, 87–106. Leiden: Brill.
Weber, Alfred. 1935. *Kulturgeschichte als Kultursoziologie.* Leiden: Sijthoff.
Weber, Max. 1991. *Die Wirtschaftsethik der Weltreligionen: Konfuzianismus und Taoismus.* In Max Weber, *Schriften 1915–1920,* ed. Helwig Schmidt-Glintzer. Tübingen: Mohr.
Weber-Schäfer, Peter. 1968. *Oikumene und Imperium: Studien zur Ziviltheologie des chinesischen Kaiserreichs.* Munich: List.
Wittrock, Björn. 2005. "The Meaning of the Axial Age." In *Axial Civilizations and World History,* ed. Johann P. Arnason, Shmuel N. Eisenstadt, and Björn Wittrock, 51–85. Leiden: Brill.
Xunzi. 1978. Wang Xianqian, *Xunzi jijie, Zhuzi jicheng.* Vol. 2. Hong Kong: Zhonghua.
Zhang Hao. 2000. "Cong shijie wenhuashi kan shuyou shidai" (The Axial Age from the perspective of world cultural history). *Ershiyi shiji* 58: 4–16.
Zhuangzi. 1978. Guo Qingfan, *Zhuangzi jishi, Zhuzi jicheng.* Vol. 3. Hong Kong: Zhonghua.

Destructive Possibilities?

11

The Axial Conundrum between Transcendental Visions and Vicissitudes of Their Institutionalizations

Constructive and Destructive Possibilities

SHMUEL N. EISENSTADT

In this essay I shall examine the tensions and contradictions attendant on the institutionalization of Axial visions. These tensions are, first, the result of problems inherent in the *institutionalization* of Axial visions—for example, the implementation of economic and power structures. Second, these tensions are rooted in the *internal structure* of Axial visions—most notably in the tension between their inclusivist universalist claims and their exclusivist tendency, rendering their institutionalization potentially destructive. These problems point to the continual tension between constructive and destructive elements of social and cultural expansion and evolution.

The crystallization of Axial civilizations constitutes one of the most fascinating developments in the history of mankind, a revolutionary process that has shaped the course of history dramatically. It is not surprising that it constitutes a great challenge to sociological theory as well.

Robert Bellah, in his article "What Is Axial about the Axial Age?," has presented a succinct analysis of the cultural specificity of the Axial breakthrough.[1] The core of this breakthrough, so he argues, has been a change or transformation of basic cultural conceptions—a breakthrough to what he calls the theoretical stage of human thinking, or reflexivity. The distinctiveness of this breakthrough and its impact on world history, however, does not lie solely in the emergence of such conceptions but in the fact that they became the basic, predominant, and indeed hegemonic premises of the cultural programs and institutional formations within a society or civilization. Not all places that witnessed the emergence of such conceptions saw also their transformation into hegemonic cultural premises; even in places where such a transformation took place, it was usually very slow and intermittent—Islam being the only (partial) exception in this regard. It is therefore only when both processes come together that we can speak of an Axial civilization.

This Axial breakthrough occurred in many parts of the world: in ancient Israel, later in Second Commonwealth Judaism and in Christianity, in ancient Greece, (partially) in Zoroastrian Iran, in early imperial China, in Hinduism and Buddhism, and later in Islam. With the exception of Islam, these civilizations crystallized in the first millennium BCE and the first centuries of the Common Era. It was this relative synchronicity that gave rise to the concept of an "Axial Age"—first formulated by Karl Jaspers and imbued with strong, if only implicit, evolutionary notions.[2] Jaspers saw the Axial Age as a distinct, basically universal and irreversible step in the development—or evolution—of human history. However, while the emergence and institutionalization of Axial civilizations heralded revolutionary breakthroughs that developed in parallel or in similar directions in different societies, the concrete constellations within these civilizations differed greatly.

The distinctive characteristics of each Axial civilization lie in the development of a specific combination of cultural orientations and institutional formations that triggered a specific societal dynamic.[3] The core of the Axial "syndrome," to paraphrase Johann Arnason, lies in the combination of two tendencies. The first tendency was the radical distinction between ultimate and derivative reality (or between transcendental and mundane dimensions, to use a more controversial formulation), connected with an increasing orientation toward a reality beyond the given one, with new temporal and spatial conceptions, with a radical problematization of the conceptions and premises of cosmological and social orders, and with growing reflexivity and second-order thinking, with the resultant models of order generating new problems (the task of bridging the gap between the postulated levels of reality is one example).[4] The second tendency was the disembedment of social activities and organizations from relatively closed ascriptive, above all kinship or territorial, units or frameworks; the concomitant development of "free" resources that could be organized or mobilized in different directions gave rise to more complex social systems, creating potential challenges to the hitherto institutional formations.[5] These two tendencies led to the development of specific patterns of social organization and cultural orientation, and ultimately to the crystallization of Axial civilizations. Until the emergence of modernity, they represent probably the most radical pattern of decoupling of various structural and cosmological dimensions of social order.

What was revolutionary about these developments was the fact that the civilizations in question experienced a comprehensive rupture and problematization of order. They responded to this challenge by elaborating new models of order, based on the contrast and the connection between transcendental foundations and mundane life-worlds. The common constitutive features of Axial Age worldviews might be summed up in the following terms: they include a *broadening of horizons,* or an opening up of potentially universal perspectives, in contrast to the particularism of more archaic modes of thought; an *ontological distinction* between higher and lower levels of reality; and a *normative subordination* of the lower level to the higher, with more or less overtly stated implications for human efforts to translate guiding principles into ongoing practices. In other words, the developing Axial visions entailed the concept of a world beyond the immediate boundaries of their respective settings—potentially leading to the constitution of broader institutional frameworks, opening up a range of possible institutional formations, while at the same time making these formations the object of critical reflection and contestation. The common denominator of these formations was their transformation into relatively autonomous spheres of society, regulated according to autonomous criteria.

Part of this process was the attempt to reconstruct the mundane-world human personality and the sociopolitical and economic orders according to the appropriate transcendental vision, to the principles of a higher ontological order formulated in religious, metaphysical, and/or ethical terms—or, in other words, the attempt to implement some aspect of a particular vision in the mundane world. This new attitude toward the development of the mundane world was closely related to concepts of a world beyond the immediate boundaries of a particular society—a world open, as it were, to reconstruction.

An important institutional formation that developed within all Axial civilizations was a new type of societal center or centers constituted as the major embodiment of the transcendental vision of ultimate reality or as the major locus of the charismatic dimension of human existence. In contrast to their non- or pre-Axial counterparts, these new centers attempted to permeate the periphery and restructure it according to the prevailing Axial vision. Axial civilizations also developed a strong tendency to constitute distinct collectivities and institutional arenas as the most appropriate carriers of a particular Axial vision—creating new "civilizational" collectivities, which were often—though not always (as in the case of China)—religious in nature, but in any case distinct from existing "primordial," "ethnic," local, political, or religious collectivities. It is one of the most important features of these broader civilizational frameworks that they were not tied to *one* political or ethnic collectivity. They could encompass many different collectivities, could impinge on existing political, territorial, or kinship collectivities and institutions—challenging them or causing contestations among them over the "cultural" or "ideological" primacy within the broader civilizational framework. Ultimately, this led to continual reconstruction and transformation of the premises and contours of the different collectivities involved.

Such transformations were perhaps most clearly visible in the political realm.[6] The king-god, the embodiment of the cosmic and earthly order, disappeared, and the model of secular ruler appeared, who could still embody sacral attributes, but who was in principle accountable to a higher order or authority, to God and divine law. In other words, there emerged the possibility of calling a ruler to judgment. A dramatic example is the priestly and prophetic pronouncements of ancient Israel, which were transmitted to all monotheistic civilizations. Similar concepts emerged in ancient Greece, in India, and in China—most clearly manifested in the concept of the Mandate of Heaven.

A parallel development was the transformation of family and kinship relations, to some extent also of economic relations. They often emerged as distinct autonomous symbolic and institutional arenas, disembedded from broader ascriptive formations and the criteria and modes of justification governing them.

Another development was the emergence of a new type of reflexivity rooted in "theory," and of new criteria of justification and legitimation of the social and the political order. That entailed the possibility of principled critical examination of these orders and their premises, the awareness that alternative institutional arrangements were possible and could challenge existing institutions—including the possibility of a revolutionary transformation of these institutions.[7]

These new patterns of reflexivity were closely connected with the development of new forms of cultural creativity. On the "intellectual" level, elaborate and highly formalized theological and philosophical discourses flourished, organized in different worlds of knowledge and in manifold disciplines. Within these discourses, the tension between new cultural concepts and the mundane reality was played out—for example between cosmic time and the mundane political realm, between different concepts of *historia sacra* in relation to the flow of mundane time, between sacred and mundane space. New types of collective memory and corresponding narratives developed.[8]

The specific kind of reflexivity, especially second-order thinking, characteristic of Axial visions or programs, produced a number of internal antinomies or tensions. The most important of these tensions concerned, first, the great range of possible transcendental visions and the ways of their implementation; second, the distinction between reason and revelation or faith (or their equivalents in nonmonotheistic Axial civilizations); and third, the *problematique* of whether the full institutionalization of these visions in pristine form is desirable.

One outcome of these modes of reflexivity was the fact that the new societal centers, institutional frameworks, and distinct "civilizational" collectivities were no longer taken for granted; they were no longer perceived as "naturally" given, either by divine prescription or by the power of custom. They could become the object of contestation between different elites and groups.

That such relatively autonomous elites and groups existed was itself a distinctive characteristic of Axial civilizations. They were responsible for the unique dynamics of these civilizations—namely, the possibility of principled, ideological confrontation between hegemonic and challenging groups and elites, of the continual confrontation between orthodoxy and heterodoxy (or sectarian activities), and the potential combination of such confrontations with political struggles over power, with movements of protest, with economic and class conflicts—all of them creating challenges to the existing regimes and their legitimation.

The confrontation between heterodoxy and orthodoxy was by no means limited to matters of ritual, religious observance, or patterns of worship.

What the various "orthodox" and most of the "heterodox" conceptions had in common was the will to reconstruct the mundane world according to their respective Axial visions. They were bound together in their struggle—a struggle through which most elites were transformed, to follow Max Weber's designation of the ancient Israelite prophets, into potential "political demagogues" who often attempted to mobilize wider popular support for the visions they promulgated.

The continual confrontation between hegemonic and secondary elites and between orthodoxy and heterodoxy has been of crucial importance in shaping the concrete institutional formations and dynamics of the various Axial civilizations. It generated the possibility of development within these civilizations, even of revolutionary changes and transformations. It is of special importance in this regard that is was sectarian activities that were among the most important carriers of the broader, often universalistic orientations inherent in Axial cosmological visions. The implications of these developments were summarized by Arnason as follows:

> The cultural mutations of the Axial Age generated a surplus of meaning, open to conflicting interpretations and capable of creative adaptation to new situations. But the long-term consequences can only be understood in light of the interaction between cultural orientations and the dynamics of social power. The new horizons of meaning could serve to justify or transfigure, but also to question and contest existing institutions. They were, in other words, invoked to articulate legitimacy as well as protest. More specific versions of both of these alternatives emerged in conjunction with the social distribution, accumulation and regulation of power. The dynamic of ideological formations led to the crystallization of orthodoxy and heterodoxy, more pronounced and polarizing in some traditions than others. In that sense, the history of ideological politics can be traced back to the Axial Age. But the development of new cultural orientations should not be seen as evidence of a thoroughgoing cultural determinism; rather, it entails the complex interplay of patterns and processes and is conducive to more autonomous action by a broader spectrum of social actors and forces.[9]

With respect to the constitution of different patterns of collective identity, the very distinction between different collectivities generated the possibility that primordial, civil, and sacred themes could be recombined on the local, regional, and central level in ever new ways, and be reconstructed in relation to sacral civilizational themes—including the possibility of continual confrontation between them. No single locus, not even the centers of the most centralized European empires, could effectively monopolize all these themes. Rather, they were represented on different levels of social organization by different collectivities—"ethnic," political, civic, and religious—each with relatively high levels of self-consciousness and different conceptions of time and space.

The tendency within Axial civilizations to constantly reconstitute institutional formations was reinforced by the fact that a new type of intersocietal and intercivilizational world history emerged. All Axial civilizations developed a certain propensity to expansion and combined ideological and religious with political and, to some extent, economic impulses. To be sure, political, cultural, and economic interrelations between different societies—including the development of types of international or "world" systems—existed throughout human history.[10] Concepts of a universal or world kingdom had emerged in many pre-Axial civilizations, for example in the Mongol Empire of Genghis Khan and his descendants.[11] However, it was only with the crystallization of Axial civilizations that a more distinctive ideological mode of expansion developed in which considerations of power and economic interest became closely related to ideological premises and indeed imbued by them.

The zeal for reorganization and transformation of social formations according to particular transcendental visions made the "whole world" at least potentially subject to cultural-political reconstruction. Although often radically divergent in terms of their concrete institutionalization, the political formations within Axial civilizations comprised representations and ideologies of a quasi-global empire. Some civilizations, at specific moments in their history, even managed to build such an empire. This mode of expansion also gave rise to attempts at creating "world histories" encompassing different societies. However, there never existed one homogeneous world history, nor were different types of civilizations similar or convergent in this respect. Rather, a multiplicity of different and mutually impinging world civilizations developed, each attempting to reconstruct the world according to its basic premises either to absorb other civilizations or to consciously segregate itself from them. In any case, the interrelations, contacts, and confrontations between different Axial and between Axial and non-Axial civilizations constituted a fundamental aspect of their dynamics. Such contacts were not only important transmitters of different cultural themes, thus giving rise to different patterns of syncretization of cultural and religious tropes; they could also promote the crystallization of new—both pre-Axial and Axial—civilizations, as was the case with the Ahmenid and Hellenistic empires, with several southeast and east Asian civilizations, and of course with Islam.[12]

It was the potential for change, the attempt, undertaken by different coalitions of elites, political activists, and other social actors, at reconstructing the internal and transsocietal institutional formations, and the close linkage with economic and class conflicts that constitute the core of the revolutionary transformations within Axial civilizations. "Ethnic" group, political, economic, and class conflicts became transformed into ideological ones; conflicts between tribes, political regimes, could become missionary crusades for the transformation of civilizations. All of this generated the possibility of change far beyond existing formations.

Axial Visions and the Crystallization of Institutional Formations

The starting point of an analysis of the institutionalization of Axial visions is naturally the emergence of these visions, the characteristics of their carriers, and the nature of the processes through which these visions were institutionalized.

The most important characteristic of the carriers of Axial visions was their relatively autonomous status as *Kulturträger*—for example the ancient Israelite prophets and priests and later on the Jewish sages, the Greek philosophers and sophists, the various precursors of the Chinese literati, the Hindu Brahmins, the Buddhist "monks" that later became the different Sanghas, and the nuclei of the Ulema among the Islamic tribes and societies.

Such groups developed in all Axial civilizations; they constituted a new social element, a distinct sociocultural mutation, a new type of religious or cultural activist that differed greatly from the ritual, magical, or sacral specialist in pre-Axial civilizations. However, the conditions under which such groups could arise have not yet been adequately addressed or systematically analyzed in the social sciences. There are only indications to be found in the literature—for example the observation, put forward by Bellah, that Axial visionaries tend to emerge especially in secondary centers in relatively volatile international settings, or the more general observation that charismatic tendencies are more likely to arise in periods of social turmoil and disintegration.[13]

Only some of the carriers of Axial visions were successful in the sense that their visions were institutionalized and became influential or even hegemonic in a respective society. In many cases, for example in some Greek city-states, appropriate resources or organizational frameworks for their implementation were not available or could not be mobilized.[14] Even where such visions were implemented, the resulting institutions differed considerably, not only between different Axial civilizations, but also within the framework of the same civilization—be it Jewish, Islamic, Hindu, Buddhist, or Christian. The variety is clearly visible in different institutional choices prevalent in different civilizations: full-fledged empires (such as the Chinese, Byzantine, or Ottoman empires), rather fragile kingdoms or tribal federations (e.g., ancient Israel), combinations of tribal federations and city-states (e.g., ancient Greece), the complex decentralized pattern of the Hindu civilization, or the imperial-feudal configurations of Europe. Moreover, all these institutional formations developed their own distinctive dynamics and were continuously changing, albeit in a different tempo and direction.

The general tendency in which new types of institutional formations developed was prescribed by the particular Axial vision. But this was only a potentiality; the actualization and the nature of the exact modes of institutionalization depended on specific conditions that were not given with the Axial vision itself. In other words, the concretization of these potentialities, the crystallization of new Axial institutional formations, was not given with the mere development of an Axial vision. This helps to explain the great variety of typically Axial institutions. And it suggests that in order to understand the formation and dynamics of Axial civilizations and the nature of their revolutionary impact on world history, we have to focus on the analysis of the processes of their crystallization.

The institutionalization of Axial visions was contingent, first, on the development and mobilization of the necessary resources for their implementation; second, on the availability of organizational frameworks which could facilitate such mobilization; third, on the formation of a coalition between the original carrier of a particular Axial vision and other actors—especially political, economic, and communal activists, potential elites within a given society.

As part of the process of institutionalization, new political, economic, and communal elites emerged. They tended to become disembedded from the major ascriptive frameworks; at the same time, they claimed autonomous access to the new order promulgated by an Axial vision, which resulted in continual contestation about their status in relation to the new order.

These elites were usually recruited and legitimized according to distinct autonomous criteria, promulgated by the elites themselves. They did not think of themselves as only performing specific technical or functional activities—for example as scribes—but indeed as carrying a distinct cultural and social order manifest in the prevailing transcendental vision of this society. They often acquired a countrywide status and claimed an autonomous place within the institutional formations.

But with the successful institutionalization of a particular Axial vision, the carriers of that vision became part of the ruling coalitions, participating in the activities and mechanisms of control and in the regulation of power. Thus the institutionalization of Axial visions often entailed far-reaching transformations of the major social and political elites; they all tended to become more autonomous, claiming a place in the promulgation of the Axial vision, while at the same time challenging the monopoly of the carriers of these visions in the process of their institutionalization. Meanwhile, the growing—if, by comparison with modern societies, still rather limited—autonomy of the major institutional formations led to the parallel development of relatively autonomous media of exchange—power, money, influence, and solidarity—especially as they became attributed to particular societal sectors—which, in turn, exacerbated the problems of regulation and coordination within these societies.[15] With respect to both the extent of autonomy of different elites and the new institutional formations and media of exchange, Axial civilizations could differ markedly.

In India, for example, a very high degree of autonomy among religious elites stands in contrast to a lower degree among political elites. While there was a relatively small degree of differentiation of political roles among the broader strata, European societies developed a much greater degree of autonomy and differentiation among all elites. Similarly, far-reaching differences existed between the different imperial agrarian regimes, as the comparison between the Byzantine and Chinese empires clearly indicates, in the structure of their elites, centers, and their developmental dynamics, despite the fact that they shared rather similar degrees (and relatively high ones for historical societies) of structural and organizational differentiation in the economic and social arenas.

In many Axial societies, the different institutional frameworks—political, economic, cultural, and religious—also acquired a certain degree of autonomy. This is most apparent in the case of empires, but it is also visible in other political formations (for example in patrimonial formations) when compared with non-Axial civilizations. Although, in their basic structural characteristics, many Axial formations are seemingly similar to their counterparts in pre-Axial or non-Axial civilizations, for example the patrimonial societies in southeast Asia, they developed distinct characteristics that set them apart from pre- or non-Axial societies.

The Distinctive Dynamics of Axial Institutional Formations

The variety of institutional patterns and their potential to change was significantly greater in Axial civilizations. Both variety and changeability were the result of multiple factors: a multiplicity of cultural orientations; different ecological and social settings; their volatility; the continuous encounter and contestation between different social, economic, religious, and cultural actors and elites within these settings.

As in other historical cases, any such institutional formation is characterized by different relations between social structure and cosmological vision, manifest in the constitution of institutional boundaries and in different affinities between symbolic orientations and geopolitical conditions and structural formations.

The openness of the relation between "cosmological" visions, ecological settings, and institutional formations is of special importance in the case of what Talcott Parsons called "seedbed societies"—early ancient Greece and ancient Israel being prime illustrations.[16] The characteristic feature of these societies has been a discrepancy between the potential institutional range of their basic visions and the concrete possibilities of their institutionalization—resulting in the fact that many of the institutional potentialities of their visions were in a sense "stored," to be transmitted as components of institutional settings and dynamics of other civilizations.

Each institutional formation is also characterized by different ways of incorporating non- or pre-Axial symbolic and institutional components. Even in new Axial settings, such non-Axial orientations and their carriers still played an important part in the cultural and institutional dynamics of these societies. They created autonomous spaces, which could remain very influential within the new Axial civilization, often persisting (as in the case of Egypt) over a long period of time. They could also (as in the case of Japan) create their own very important niches in an international framework dominated by Axial civilizations.[17]

The distinctive dynamics of each institutional formation were generated by the internal tensions and contradictions that developed in the course of the institutionalization of Axial frameworks, by the tensions and contradictions between these processes and the basic Axial premises of each civilization, and by the ways in which these societies were incorporated into the international framework that was the result of the expansion of particular civilizations. These dynamics intensified the consciousness of the tensions, antinomies, and contradictions inherent in the Axial cultural programs and their institutionalization, which in turn gave rise to the continual reinterpretation of the premises of each Axial civilization. The distinct relations between orthodoxy and heterodoxy and their combination with power structures and economic interests could create—or block—new developmental possibilities, different potentially evolutionary paths. One such development—that of "Western" Christianity—gave rise to the postrevolutionary transformation of the first modernity, which then expanded throughout the world, encountering other Axial civilizations in their respective historical institutional and symbolic settings. These encounters eventually gave rise to multiple modernities.

The fact that the potentialities of the crystallization of Axial symbolic and institutional formations were dependent on broader evolutionary factors attests to the fact that the tendency toward continuous expansion of the range of human activities, the tendency toward a growing complexity of social structures, to the "rationalization" and problematization of symbolic realms[18] and of criteria for the justification of human activities and of social order is, at least potentially, inherent in all human societies. However, historical evidence suggests that such potentialities were not realized in all societies that had seemingly reached the "necessary" evolutionary stage, that the crystallization of concrete institutional patterns is, therefore, not assured or shaped by the mere development or emergence of appropriate symbolic and structural evolutionary tendencies. In other words, the different institutional patterns that crystallized in the Axial civilizations did not develop, as it were, naturally or automatically as manifestations of a distinct stage of evolutionary history. Nor was this process always peaceful. On the contrary, it was usually connected with continual struggles between activists and groups and their respective visions and adaptive strategies. Such contestations constitute an important feature of all Axial civilizations.

Theoretical Implications: Evolutionary Tendencies, Institutional Formations, Agency, and Control

The analysis of the processes of institutionalization within different Axial civilizations has implications for sociological theory and the analysis of world history.

The analysis indicates, first, that the crystallization of any institutional pattern is dependent on social interaction. Second, that it is dependent on mechanisms of control and regulation between major social actors, above all between future elites. Third, the crystallization of institutional and symbolic formations is effected by distinct types of actors, the emergence of which constitutes itself a sociocultural mutation that is not predetermined by broad evolutionary tendencies, even if such tendencies provide the basic framework for such crystallizations. Fourth, historical contingencies play an important role in the process of such crystallization.

The core of the crystallization of any concrete institutional formation is the specification of distinctive boundaries of social interactions. Since the human biological program is, to use Ernst Mayr's expression, an "open program,"[19] such boundaries are not predetermined genetically, but have to be constituted through social interaction. Given this openness and the indeterminacy of the relation between actors' goals and the general conditions of their actions, the crystallization of any concrete pattern of social interaction generates major problems. The most important of these problems were already identified by the founding fathers of sociology: the constitution of trust, regulation of power, and provision of meaning and legitimation of social activities and frameworks.[20] In order to cope with these problems, distinct patterns of interaction between institutional formations—political, economic, or cultural—and between collectivities develop, all of which tend to pursue systemic tendencies of their own. The degree of their autonomy or predominance varies in different societies, depending on the degree of embedment in broader frameworks.

The inherent fragility of the constitution and reproduction of boundaries demands the creation of mechanisms of social integration, regulation, and control. Such regulation is effected by the activities of social actors; the most important actors in this regard are those who structure the division of labor in a society, those who articulate collective political goals, those who specify the borders of different ascriptive social collectivities, and those who articulate the basic cultural visions and models predominant in a particular society.

Such processes of control and regulation entail the transformation of basic symbolic orientations—cosmological visions—into "codes" or schemata. Such codes are akin to what Weber called *Wirtschaftsethik*. This term does not connote specific religious injunctions about the proper behavior in any given sphere, nor is it merely a logical deduction from theological or philosophical principles predominant in a given religion. Rather, it denotes a general mode of "religious" or "ethical" orientation that shapes the major criteria of evaluation and justification of human activities and institutional formations—criteria which then serve as starting points in the regulation of the flow and distribution of resources and media of exchange in a society. Such regulation is supported by organizational means, especially by incentives and sanctions, and exercised in public and semipublic rituals.

The mechanisms and processes of control within a society are hierarchically composed of many intermediate units that are strongly interconnected horizontally, but less strongly vertically. Furthermore, the strength of vertical linkages differs according to their position within the hierarchical order. Lower-level controls manage short-term and local affairs, while higher-level controls provide system-wide decision-making capabilities.[21]

Such mechanisms develop in all societies, but they differ with respect to the degree of complexity: the more complex social and political systems and civilizational frameworks become, the more autonomous and potentially more fragile they tend to be. Axial civilizations provide an excellent illustration of the problems concerning the emergence of complex social systems rooted in evolutionary tendencies. Following the analysis of Herbert Simon, one could say that the modes of institutional formation within Axial civilizations gave rise to potentially fragile modes of control, thus enhancing the possibility of challenge and transformation, which in turn led to multiple new and ever-changing institutional formations.

The preceding analysis indicates that institutional formations, though rooted in evolutionary tendencies and potentialities, cannot be designated as natural manifestations of particular stages in the process of social evolution. Rather, they must be seen as a contingent outcome of a particular historical constellation that allowed for a multitude of possible ways of development. The major dimensions of the social and cultural order within Axial civilizations developed, at least to some extent, independently of one another and often in opposite directions, each pushed, as it were, by its own momentum. Second, this development is exacerbated by the fact that the crystallization of specific patterns of the social always takes place under contingent historical and geopolitical conditions. Third, and most importantly, any such crystallization is effected by distinct types of agency, by entrepreneurial activities that mobilize available resources and develop appropriate patterns of regulation for the flow of these resources.

The emergence of new institutional entrepreneurs and their visions constitutes a distinct mutation which developed in different historical situations and in different parts of the world in seemingly unpredictable ways, producing very different orientations and worldviews (for example, this-worldly and other-worldly orientations) with different institutional implications. The principled openness of any historical situation and of any evolutionary stage of development means that attempts to implement a particular institutional pattern can become subject to continual contestation.

The tendency of human activities to continuously expand their sphere of influence potentially undermines whatever temporary equilibrium may have been attained in any institutional formation with regard to the building of trust, regulation of power, and legitimation of social order. It heightens the awareness that any social order is arbitrary. The history of Axial civilizations and particularly that of modernity (with its Axial roots) attest to the fact that any such extension entails both constructive and destructive potentialities—a fact that has not been given full attention in sociological analyses.[22]

Notes

1. Robert N. Bellah, "What Is Axial about the Axial Age?," *European Journal of Sociology* 46 (2005): 69–89.
2. On the concept of the Axial Age, see Karl Jaspers, *The Origin and Goal of History* (London: Routledge & Kegan Paul / New Haven: Yale University Press, 1953 [1949]); Eric Voegelin, *Order and History*, 5 vols. (Baton Rouge: Louisiana State University Press, 1986–1987); Benjamin I. Schwartz, "The Age of Transcendence," *Daedalus* 104, no. 2 (1975): 1–7; Shmuel N. Eisenstadt, "The Axial Age: The Emergence of Transcendental Visions and the Rise of Clerics," *European Journal of Sociology* 23 (1982): 294–314; see also nn. 3 and 4 below.
3. This analysis is based on Eisenstadt, "The Axial Age"; Eisenstadt, ed., *The Origins and Diversity of Axial Age Civilizations* (Albany: State University of New York Press, 1986); Eisenstadt, ed., *Kulturen der Achsenzeit I: Ihre Ursprünge und ihre Vielfalt* (Frankfurt am Main: Suhrkamp, 1987); Eisenstadt, ed., *Kulturen der Achsenzeit II: Ihre institutionelle und kulturelle Dynamik* (Frankfurt am Main: Suhrkamp, 1992); Johann P. Arnason et al., eds., *Axial Civilizations and World History* (Leiden: Brill, 2005).
4. See Eisenstadt, "Axial Civilizations and the Axial Age Reconsidered," in Arnason et al., eds., *Axial Civilizations*, 531–564, esp. 537–538; Johann P. Arnason, "The Axial Age and Its Interpreters: Reopening a Debate," in Arnason et al., eds., *Axial Civilizations*, 19–49; Eisenstadt, "The Civilizational Dimension in Sociological Analysis," *Thesis Eleven* 62 (2000): 1–21.
5. On the concept of free resources, see Eisenstadt, *The Political Systems of Empires* (New York: Free Press, 1963).
6. Eisenstadt, "Cultural Traditions and Political Dynamics: The Origins and Modes of Ideological Politics," *British Journal of Sociology* 32 (1981): 155–181.
7. See Bellah, "What Is Axial"; Yehuda Elkana, "The Emergence of Second-Order Thinking in Classical Greece," in Eisenstadt, ed., *The Origins and Diversity*, 40–64.
8. Shmuel N. Eisenstadt and Ilana Friedrich Silber, eds., *Cultural Traditions and Worlds of Knowledge: Explorations in the Sociology of Knowledge* (Greenwich: JAI Press, 1988).
9. Arnason, "The Axial Age and Its Interpreters," 2–3.

10. On world systems, see for example André G. Frank and Barry K. Gills, *The World System: Five Hundred Years or Five Thousand?* (London: Routledge, 1993); J. Friedman and Michael J. Rowlands, "Notes towards an Epigenetic Model of the Evolution of Civilizations," in Friedman and Rowlands, eds., *The Evolution of Social Systems* (London: Duckworth, 1977); Immanuel M. Wallerstein, *World-Systems Analysis: An Introduction* (Durham: Duke University Press, 2004).

11. Michal Biran, "The Mongol Transformation: From the Steppe to Eurasian Empire," in Johann P. Arnason and Björn Wittrock, eds., *Eurasian Transformations, Tenth to Thirteenth Centuries: Crystallizations, Divergences, Renaissances* (Leiden: Brill, 2004), 339–363; Biran, *Chinggis Khan* (Oxford: Oneworld, 2007).

12. See the respective chapters in Arnason et al., *Axial Civilizations*.

13. Bellah, "What Is Axial"; see also n. 14 below.

14. Kurt A. Raaflaub, "Polis, 'The Political,' and Political Thought: New Departures in Ancient Greece, c. 800–500 BCE," in Arnason et al., eds., *Axial Civilizations*, 253–283; Eisenstadt, *The Political Systems*.

15. Talcott Parsons, *American Society: A Theory of the Societal Community* (Boulder: Paradigm Publishers, 2007).

16. Talcott Parsons, *The Evolution of Societies* (Englewood Cliffs: Prentice Hall, 1977), 13; see also pp. 99–114 on the "Cultural Legacies for Later Societies: The Hebrew and Greek Concepts of a Moral Order."

17. Eisenstadt, *Japanese Civilization: A Comparative View* (Chicago: University of Chicago Press, 1996).

18. Eisenstadt, *The Great Revolutions and the Civilizations of Modernity* (Leiden: Brill, 2006).

19. Ernst Mayr, *Evolution and the Diversity of Life: Selected Essays* (Cambridge, MA: Belknap Press, 1976).

20. For details, see Eisenstadt, "Action, Resources, Structure, and Meaning," in Eisenstadt, *Power, Trust, and Meaning: Essays in Sociological Theory and Analysis* (Chicago: University of Chicago Press, 1995), 328–389.

21. Herbert A. Simon, "The Architecture of Complexity," *Proceedings of the American Philosophical Society* 106, no. 6 (1962): 467–482; Simon, *Models of Discovery: And Other Topics in the Methods of Science* (Dordrecht: Reidel, 1977), esp. chap. 4 on "Complexity."

22. For attempts in this direction, see for example Edward A. Tiryakian, "War: The Covered Side of Modernity," *International Sociology* 14 (1999): 473–489; Hans Joas, *War and Modernity* (Oxford: Polity Press, 2003); Eisenstadt, "Barbarism and Modernity: The Destructive Components of Modernity," in Eisenstadt, *Comparative Civilizations and Multiple Modernities II* (Leiden: Brill, 2003), 561–571; Eisenstadt, ed., *Max Weber on Charisma and Institution Building: Selected Papers* (Chicago: University of Chicago Press, 1968).

12

Axial Religions and the Problem of Violence

DAVID MARTIN

Pre-Axial religion in archaic societies was replete with sex and violence. Ideally, sex and violence should be treated together, because both are associated with tribal survival as well as with forms of antisocial ecstasy and excess. However, my concern here is solely with violence, because it poses the most acute problems for Axial religion and is a key element in the crucial difference between Us and Them.

Axial religion has many different characteristics. Whereas pre-Axial religion is often bound in with the powers of Nature, its temporal rhythms and cycles, Axial religion either abandons such cycles for timelessness or creates a forward-looking narrative whereby salvation comes in history. Whereas pre-Axial religion accords reverence to inanimate objects as though they were active agents representing "the powers," Axial religion dismisses such reverence as idolatry. Whereas pre-Axial religion is tribal, Axial religion is universalistic. These wide-ranging differences are worked out in a number of ways and in different sectors of human activity, for example the dynamics of power and wealth. These ways are analyzed by Max Weber in two famous essays, "Religious Rejections of the World and Their Direction," and "The Social Psychology of the World Religions," and in what follows I implicitly combine Weber's analysis with Karl Jaspers' understanding of the Axial Age as presented by Robert Bellah.[1] My focus is on that kind of ambivalent rejection of the world represented by Christianity. Christianity accepts the Creation and the social order as in principle good but fallen and in need of redemption. That redemption crucially entails the establishment of a universal reign of peace and the rejection of violence. My argument focuses on the clash between the social logic of human solidarity, which exhibits the mutual entanglement of peace and war, and Christianity's revolutionary attempt to disentangle them. I assume that such disentanglement will only be partially successful, and that Christianity itself will be partially pulled back into the regimen of violence.

Biogenetic versus Cultural Understandings

My approach is rooted in the cultural sciences. Nevertheless, I approach the problem sideways, beginning with the salience of the theme of violence and religion today, because in the popular media, and biogenetic incursions into the media, social-scientific approaches are ignored. Instead we have people who should know better pointing accusingly, and in a simplistic manner, at this or that outcrop of religious violence from the Crusades to September 11, 2001 (and the reaction of George W. Bush), and at the same time offering generalized biogenetic explanations. So I need first to address approaches of this kind before turning directly to the problem of religion and violence in the context of the cultural sciences.

I begin with an obvious philosophical point. If religion and/or violence are indeed part of our genetic program in the form, say, of "memes," apart from a few brave and intellectually superior persons who have the wit to swat a meme before it bites, then moral accusation is beside the point. One might as well complain to the winds and waves about tsunamis.

But that is incidental. There are also important historical and cultural observations to be made. One major version of the biogenetic approach "blames" religion for being an "unconscious" tendency to treat the inanimate as animate, built in to the psychic basement. This is an old theory in modern guise, just as "memes" look like a revised version of William McDougall's psychology of instincts. However, the universal religion of the Axial Age is defined, notwithstanding the richness of imagery in Catholicism and Orthodoxy, by an adamant rejection of the confusion between animate and inanimate as idolatrous. Biogeneticists characteristically talk about "explaining" religion, as though the concept of religion were all of a piece and not an essentially contested category.

Then there is, of course, an enormous variety of evidence illustrating the sheer range of "religious" manifestations. If the biogenetic approach somehow manages to circumvent this, as Pascal Boyer claims, it is still difficult to see how the cultural variations in secularity and secularization can be explained by a biological constant.[2] Whereas Darwin thought that the universality of the idea of God counted in its favor, the cultural variation in the incidence of secularization counts against a universal biogenetic explanation of religion. The Czech Republic, the former German Democratic Republic, and Estonia exhibit the lowest indices of nominal adherence and active religious involvement in Europe, but these indices have nothing to do with a sudden atrophy of the "meme" for religion, or of the tendency to detect agency where there is none, or an inexplicable eradication of the religious virus.

Of course, if you resort to the tactic of labeling all fanaticism as an instance of religion, irrespective of whether it propagates or suppresses what is normally understood by religion, then one could argue that the religious meme of Communism simply replaced that of Christianity. To do that, however, is culpably to ignore the obvious cultural and historical explanation. In the Czech case, to take just one example, that explanation is rooted in the specific history of Czech Lands, and, incidentally, one not applicable to Slovakia, which has a far more positive historical relation to Catholicism, more like that of the Poles than of the Czechs. The myth of Czech nationalism is rooted in the proto-Protestant and incipiently radical Hussite movement of the fifteenth century and not in Counter-Reformation Catholicism, which replaced and literally displaced it after the Czechs were defeated at the Battle of the White Mountain in 1625. Czech liberalism looked back to the Hussites for inspiration, and, given the failure of the Western liberal democracies to succor the Czechs in their hour of need in 1938, there was a considerable volume of support for the Communist takeover a decade later. Catholicism was on the wrong foot, therefore, when it came to defending itself against Communist indoctrination, and extensive secularization was the result. The contrast with Poland has its historical roots in the positive relation of Polish nationalism to Catholicism, not in the reinforced virulence of the religious "meme" east of the Elbe and north of the Tatra Mountains.

The Dubious Light of the French Enlightenment

A historical explanation is also available to help us appreciate the difference between the French Enlightenment and the American one when it comes to understanding the social role of religion. The secularization associated with the French Enlightenment is a specific historical construct occurring in given conditions and it combines a rationalist theory of secularization with a historical proposal for its implementation. It describes and prescribes, as well as elevating itself as the normative Enlightenment above all others. By contrast, the American Enlightenment is a construct that arose in very different sociohistorical conditions, and it treats religion as a source of cohesion, peace, and political liberty.

The essential point here is the historically and socially located character of our theories of religion, and it trails an obvious corollary: we should be very cautious when generalizing about the social role of religion treated as a generic category. It should not be necessary to stress this obvious maxim since it is taken for granted in the social-scientific community. Yet it is necessary here because those promoting biogenetic approaches seem to have thrown scientific caution to the winds. What now follows depends on continuing to observe that scientific caution. That means keeping an open mind about any biogenetic contribution, say, to all the phenomena of social solidarity and conflict, while seeing how much is more plausibly understood in sociohistorical terms. It is, I imagine, on the cards that what makes good sociological sense in terms of solidarity, and its corollary, conflict, has also been selected for in the course of evolution.

Interestingly enough, the contemporary critique of religion attributing to it, and also blaming it for, a supposed peculiar association with violence and oppression, revives the old moral and rationalist position transferred to a biogenetic framework. That comes out in the tendency to treat religious affirmations as positive empirical and logical assertions, and therefore part of the vast corpus of failed science. There seems to be little sense of the nature of religious language as debated philosophically and analyzed in the sciences of religion and in anthropology and sociology.

Moreover, the hostile and rationalist tradition deriving from the French Enlightenment has itself been a major source of violence, arguably far more so than the "religious" (Christian and Deist) tradition of the American Enlightenment. Notoriously the Jacobin variant of the French Revolution is one of the many dramatic and instructive instances of secular ideology reproducing precisely the violence and oppression it identifies as specially associated with religion, and therefore destined to disappear once religion has been adequately suppressed, if necessary with violence. Once again one has to apologize for referring to the history of Marxism in Soviet Russia, Maoist

China, North Korea, Cambodia, and Ethiopia in order to suggest that there may be something more endemic about violence than would be the case if it could be in large measure suppressed simply by repressing religion. Would it were so easy, and would that secularist ideologies were not so fatally prone to think that one great orgy of suppression and violent eradication with respect to one particular type of human institution could at a stroke take us from darkness to light. It is more plausible to suppose that violence has an endemic character, rooted in human association as such, and it is that endemic character the present argument aims to bring out.

Here I refer to the work of S. N. Eisenstadt where he suggests that the Jacobin version of the Enlightenment can be seen as a secular mutation of the sectarian and millenarian strand within Christianity.[3] This suggestion is not to be seen as yet another deployment of the rhetorical tactic which shifts the boundary of what is to count as religion by treating all forms of fanaticism as religious. Rather it shows what is likely to occur when the eschatological judgment of God at the End of History is enacted here and now on earth. During the long centuries of established Christendom, the millenarian and sectarian witness exhibited a dual nature: pacifist and potentially violent, anarchic and totalitarian, immanent and transcendent, all in different combinations. Thus the anarchistic elements that emerged in the Hussite and Puritan revolutions could envisage human beings as immanent gods, and therefore able to renew the earth and human society. At the same time, these have been shadowed, or preceded and succeeded by, pacifist and quietist movements of withdrawal, such as the Mennonites and the Quakers. These wait in patience for the renewal wrought by a transcendent God. He alone is able to bring the earth and everything within it to a primal and/or final perfection. For the most part the sectarian and millenarian strand in Christianity awaited a renewal of the earth to be wrought by the action of God. The Kingdom would come when least expected, like a thief in the night.

However, once the sectarian tradition mutated and took on immanent and secular form, the restraints exercised by the transcendence of God were removed and the violent potential could, under favorable conditions, be released. In Marxism and in anarchism alike, violence could be legitimated and justified precisely because it brought in the kingdom of freedom. You cannot make omelettes without breaking eggs. Thus secular ideology shares with the sectarian strand of Christianity a dual potential, for pacifism and for violence, except that the violent potential is enhanced in the secular variant. By a further paradox, the pacifist revolution, locked in sectarian capsules like the Quakers, slowly seeps out into the social mainstream in any number of reforms, including liberal educational and peace movements. The year 1816 saw the origins of modern peace movements, and can be seen as a benchmark for a partial transition from sectarian pacifism to liberal pacificism and internationalism.

The Entanglement of Violent and Pacific

The dual potential, pacific and violent, found in both religious and secular visions of a better world to come illustrates a fundamental characteristic of human association to be canvassed below, for which one might borrow the natural-scientific term "entanglement." However, it is all too easy for Western liberals to suppose that liberalism is the great exception. Christianity in mainstream and sectarian forms may have a dual nature by reason of entanglement, and anarchism likewise, but liberalism is by definition only benign. Of course, if true liberalism is by definition solely benign the same applies to true Christianity, true anarchism, and true Marxism. But we are dealing with really existing liberalism, and its failure to perform according to its own self-image stems from the dual nature written into the fundamental logic of liberalism. This then is the point at which to illustrate this dual nature before indicating how it inheres in human solidarity as such.

It has always been part of the Marxist critique of liberalism that the pacific and internationalist potential liberals attributed to free trade was in practice only another version of the beneficent invisible hand hiding the aggressive capitalist pursuit of markets. That at least was the argument of the theory of imperialism put forward by J. A. Hobson and by V. I. Lenin.[4] The argument is not without force, in particular in the contemporary world when it comes to the politics of oil and other scarce raw materials. But aggression and violence is also built into the logic of liberalism in a way brought out in a recent book by the philosopher John Gray.[5] It seems that Gray holds two incompatible positions, which are reconcilable if you draw the boundary separating the religious from the secular in a different place. On the one hand, he holds that the Enlightenment itself simply translates the eschatological and deluded historical *telos* of Christianity, so that the horrors of the twentieth century are merely the latest chapters in the history of religion. At the same time, by shifting the boundary of what is to count as religion, he argues that the ideological sources of what is widely seen as religiously inspired violence are not only European but starkly secular, for example the violent anarchist teachings in the Bakuninite tradition that inspired the Baader-Meinhof gang, as well as the technique of suicide bombing invented by the Marxist-inspired Tamil Tigers. What matters most in the context of this discussion, however, is that he includes liberal and enlightened hopes of installing liberal democracy, if necessary by violence, under the head of unreal and deluded hopes.

One such hope is represented by Francis Fukuyama's idea of an end to history once liberal democracy is installed everywhere as in some way the natural destiny of humankind.[6] Under all the apparent variations of a protean and often oppressive human species-being lurks a lovely liberal just waiting for the touch of historical opportunity, if necessary made available by appropriate violence, to emerge into the light. Liberal imperialism has a long history, and it was the two most advanced liberal democracies, France and Britain, who were its most successful practitioners. Notoriously they retained most of the liberal sweetness and light for their own consumption, just as they retained other products of imperialism for their own consumption, but the logic of liberal imperialism is clear enough in its own right. For liberal imperialists, the hand of history may need a violent nudge from time to time to achieve the liberal consummation, nor are there lacking instances where such a position has something to be said for it. Not all violent interventions are unjustified, even though they are usually powered by obvious material interests.

Violence, Nationalism, and Ethnic Cleansing

If our concern is with really existing liberalism rather than the usual self-congratulatory checklist of all the liberal virtues unattended by any correlative costs, then we need also to consider the violence that logically inheres in the ideology of liberal nationalism, and in the right of every ethnic group to self-governance. This is especially revealing because it exposes the potential violence inherent in all forms of human solidarity, not merely the solidarity conferred by religion. The origins of nationalism are much disputed between those who regard it as a product of early modernity and those who trace a consciousness of tribal kind much further back, including an early template provided by the elect status claimed for the Jews in the Hebrew Scriptures. That early template also exhibited a Janus-face, because an initial liberation was followed by the ethnic cleansing of the "people of the land."

In the early modern period, the glory of the nation was focused in the monarch, and the initial expulsions of minorities, in Spain and France for example, were of a religious character. However, the logic of national homogeneity and of the need to secure the dominance of the ethnically central or core group replicated itself in all subsequent forms of nationalism. The same logic applied, whether the nationalism was religious or secular, liberal or otherwise. Whereas in the multiethnic Ottoman and Habsburg empires a Muslim or Catholic core culture was compatible with the continued coexistence of many different groups and ethnicities, once nationalism and ethnic self-governance were conceded, ethnic or ethnoreligious expulsions followed.[7]

America and France are usually regarded as examples of civic rather than ethnic nationalism, but they exemplify the same logic of nationalism. France has a liberal polity, but it released the Jews from the ghetto only on condition that they conceded the supremacy of a French identity over their communal religious identity. In the United States, all identities, whether religious or ethnic, were required to concede supremacy to an American identity, starting with the "native Americans." In the same way, contemporary multiculturalism is everywhere no more than the acceptance of different sub-identities within the overall framework of a majority and dominant identity, British, Dutch, or whatever. Liberal democracy demands no less. Instances of ethnic cleansing initiated by secular regimes are provided by Turkey in 1922 and by the Communist government in Bulgaria. Russian nationalism at the present time is directed against numerous minorities of all kinds. The early stages of liberal nationalism in Britain were marked by stern measures against minority nationalities. The pressure toward uniformity around a core identity, even where that is broadly defined, is based on a logic of attack as the best form of defense, and on some kind of limit to the range of acceptable difference. In World War II, the Japanese minority in the American West was badly treated even though evidence of treasonable activity was minimal. After 1945, vast numbers of Germans were expelled from countries where they had been domiciled for centuries, to create homogeneous national entities. Nations based on a core ethnic identity construct a myth of their historical role, as victim, or bearer of civilization, or whatever. Canada is perhaps the obvious case of a multiethnic national identity, but only at the expense of a mixture of territorial segregation and the fragmentation represented by federalism and local autonomy.

Axial Revolution and Counterrevolution

It does not matter whether we are talking about ideological or political solidarity, or national or religious solidarity, the establishment of a sentiment of unity is achieved at the expense of a potentially divisive relationship with the Other. When the Axial religions attempt to create a sense of the unity of humanity as made in the image of God, they find themselves potentially at war with rival expressions of that unity, or with persistent particularities, as well with the centripetal pull of particular imperial identities priding themselves on being coextensive with civilization, as in China or Rome. In summary, universalism does not do away with boundaries. Rather, the boundary originally marking off the natural group is transferred elsewhere, for example, between rival universalisms. Universalism actually conflicts with the fragmentation represented by contiguous particularisms, and that conflict usually becomes realized because a universalism is normally carried by the interests of an expansive imperial center.

What, then, of the attempt on the part of the universal or quasi-universal Axial religions to overcome the potential of local solidarities for violence against the Other by condemning in its core scriptures the inbuilt aggressive tendency of all forms of human solidarity? For present purposes it is not crucial whether or not these tendencies are fueled to some extent by biological programs rooted in the requirements of survival, notably among males. Axial faith requires a radical devaluation of the logic of defense through preemptive attack, and of the potential for endless and murderous feuding that goes with it. This is where violence is linked to sexuality, since the dynamic of group survival is supported by the biological imperative to create a tribe as numerous as the sands of the seashore. I deliberately use this figure from the Hebrew Scriptures because the announcement of a humanity universally bearing the image of God in the book of Genesis is still attended by a pre-Axial pressure to reproduce. In the same way, the tendency of Axial religion to lay stress on the inward appropriation of the moral law is still attended by the demand for "outward" and automatic ritual performance.

The most dramatic expressions of Axial religion are found in monastic brotherhoods renouncing the imperatives of sex and violence, and the appearance of such brotherhoods can be treated as an index of the radical embrace of Axial principles. A monastic brotherhood stands over against the blood brotherhood of imputed consanguinity and of arms. A monk divorces himself from the "natural" demands of the territorial group and sets up a protected community of peaceful and celibate men in the wilderness and the solitary place. There is perhaps a difference here between the two most obvious instances of the monastic principle in Buddhism and Christianity. Insofar as classical Buddhism lacks a teaching concerning a good Creator responsible for what is in principle a good creation, it initiates a permanent pacific withdrawal without at the same time attempting to realize a good creation here on earth. The same may be true of the kind of radical dualism found in Catharist heresy, where the aim of the last sacrament is not to sanctify this material world but to depart from it into the world of light. In that case, the dual nature of eschatological anticipation, pacific and violent, disappears.

The Revision of Sacrifice

Pre-Axial religion, as Bellah and Charles Taylor point out, often involves violent sacrifice in order to maintain the survival of the group and the fruitfulness of nature.[8] That violent impulse needs to be redirected in a manner compatible with Axial religion. Here we enter the profound mysteries of teachings about salvation through the oblation of the self in a manner absolutely contrary to the imperatives either of blood brotherhoods of arms or of codes of honor. It is in the ethical revision of the practice of sacrifice that the Axial revolution is most evidently realized, since it includes the possibility of a new understanding based on a free-will offering or thanksgiving. In its developed Christian form the gift is fused with a simultaneous self-offering of man to God and God to man in the person of the God-man, Jesus Christ, thereby ushering in the interim consummation of history indicated by the last words from the cross, "It is finished." It is an interim consummation because the End only comes with the arrival of the Kingdom of God beyond history. If this deployment of theological code language seems surprising in a sociological discussion, that is because I do not believe there is a metalanguage into which theology may be translated without a loss of essential character.

One way to approach the revision of the practice of sacrifice can be found in the Christian typological account of Abraham's divinely aborted sacrifice of Isaac. God's intervention deflects the knife onto the scapegoat, seen as a substitute sacrifice, which is in turn deflected onto God in Christ. Christ accepts the burden of sin and carries it away, supremely so when he transcends all the negative reciprocities of violence with unrequited forgiveness. In the language of the New Testament, Christ takes into himself the murderous fracture in human relations represented by Cain, absorbing the wound and the demand of the law that justice be satisfied into his own broken body. Once God in love has taken the brokenness of humanity on himself, humanity is once more made whole: the Father receives the Prodigal and puts on him the robe of grace.

No doubt one can regard the language just used as a theological summary of a narrative myth, but the radical revision of earlier ideas about the hero who physically defends his honor in mortal combat is clear. What was previously putting one's body on the line in obedience to a code of honor has been converted into honoring the law by losing one's life for others and thereby finding it. The religious insight about the efficacy of losing oneself to find oneself is dramatized in the narrative of the Passion and the Resurrection. The procession to the cross enacts self-offering in vulnerability and weakness to the pent-up violence written in human relations, healing the wound by receiving the wound. This is repeated in the pattern of the creed because in Christ the divine descends into the contingency of human existence and frustration that humanity may rise again in him, and with him ascend into an unbroken communion. The interweaving and cross-referencing of motifs to be found in the narrative, and in reflection on the narrative, is astonishingly dense, but the social consequence is quite simple. Particular human blood-brotherhoods united in the guilt of shedding blood (as the conspirators who murdered Caesar were united in dipping their weapons in his blood), give place to a universal brotherhood constituted by the blood donation offered in love, and absorbed into the body as a medicine of immortality.

Once again I turn to Christian typology. The Christian typological revision achieved by superimposing the Passion and Resurrection onto the story of Israel's liberation from oppression through an exodus across the Red Sea to liberty, measures the distance traveled in the moral judgment of violence, and the imperatives of tribalism. As told in the Old Testament, the original story exalts the Lord as a man of war, and as such he periodically licenses his people to ethnically cleanse the "people of the land." But that is not all. Though the Christian understanding stands in opposition to the implications of the Exodus story, it stands in apposition to the eschatological vision of universal peace centered on Jerusalem in Micah and Isaiah, except that the place of the physical Jerusalem is taken by the spiritual "Jerusalem above, the mother of us all." In the same way, the place of the physical temple is taken by the spiritual body of Christ, broken outside Jerusalem but resurrected and present wherever his friends come together.

Military Imagery Taken Over and Reasserted

This account of the Axial transition in Christianity represents the Christian self-understanding as coded in the New Testament, but, of course, things in history turned out rather differently, for reasons to be indicated below. Our object here is to examine the social limits inhibiting the Axial revolution, and even reversing it. Territoriality, the tribe, the biological family, and warfare are not so easily abolished. But as encoded in the New Testament, we have the plenary presence of Axial characteristics, which, however much reversed, are of world historical importance. We have the universality of Genesis united with the prophetic hope of peace and a consummation of the divine purposes, a transvaluation of violence, power, honor, and wealth, and an inward appropriation of the spirit of the law, united with a trustful faith whereby one is accounted righteous by grace in order better to fulfill the works of the law. The metaphors of warfare, honor, and satisfaction are commandeered in the service of the nonviolent "warfare of the cross"; the Son of Man is crowned with glory and honor on account of his humble obedience "even unto death"; and those who are "in him" are armed with "the sword of the spirit" and "the helmet of salvation." Even the metaphors of manly achievement in athletics are taken over and applied to those who run the straight race for the laurel and for the crown of spiritual glory.

That, then, is the coding, and it represents an appropriation of the panoply of warfare and manly heroism so radical that it will be countered by the realities of social life. These will partly reverse the coding, pushing it below the surface in underground and sectarian forms. The injunction to "call no man father" and the claim that we are "all kings and priests," for example, taken together, are so far-reaching in their egalitarian implications that they run counter to the social prerequisites of authority and functional specialization. The "natural" pressure of worldly power and wealth, and indeed everything indicated by the Christian category of "the world," will reappropriate the spiritualized imagery of warfare and status, creating a continuous tension within Christian iconography, evident, for example, in the ideas of the "parfit gentil knight" and the gentleman. A gentleman represents simultaneously a status and a moral disposition.

Creative Tension, Persistent Dichotomies

The Axial revolution in its Christian and indeed its Buddhist forms externalizes the inner tension working away within iconography through monasticism as well as through radical underground movements like the Poor Men of Lyons. There are on the one hand the attainments of the average sensual man or woman, and there are on the other hand the high prizes set before the "athletes of God," and this dichotomy is recognized in the distinction between the City of Man and the peaceable City of God. Earthly temples return in the form of richly appointed basilicas, and sacred territories reappear with holy cities at their center, for example Rome, Santiago, Cologne, and the holy sites of Ethiopia, the Isle of the City in Paris and in Salisbury.[9] In the early Byzantine Empire, the cathedral or principal church replaced the forum and the agora, and the landed elites in conjunction with the bishop replaced the *curiales* of the Roman Empire. It is instructive that when pious ecclesiastics, like St. Theodore of Sykeon, sought to divert resources to the poor in obedience to the Gospel, they found themselves opposed and in danger of being deposed. Once again the power and glory of the city reasserted itself as Christianity became the property of propertied elites. The *saeculum* was, literally, back in force. The pagans in the Byzantine Empire, who continued to make sacrifices, did so in part to make appropriate obeisance to the gods of the city, whereas Christians aspired to be citizens of another city whose builder and maker is God, but they were pulled nevertheless into the aura of the social sacred as the Christian emperor acquired an exalted status as defender and enforcer of their faith.[10]

The Forward Thrust Bent Back

Another manifestation of the return of the irrepressible was bound to occur in the sphere of ritual, where the forward pressure of eschatological hope was bent back into the annual liturgical cycle. These were reconstituted in the mold set by the Easter ceremonies in Jerusalem, no longer mournful and deserted but once again regarded as a holy city. Not only was the *saeculum* back but the social sacred as well, so that the inwardness of faith and trust partly reverted to outward ceremony of the kind that took place in the theaters of the ancient city, for example the tumultuous rites of Diana of the Ephesians. The inner purification and perfecting of the will can only go so far before there is resort once more to materializations and to the tangible signs or icons that the prophetic impulse condemns as idolatry. There are inherent limits, and beyond a certain point purification turns self-destructive in its attempt to escape the material.

That is another way of indicating that Émile Durkheim, in his analysis of the power of the social sacred, and of ritual in sustaining it, was both profoundly right and essentially wrong. There is perpetual recourse to a generalized social sacred, celebrating an idealized vision of the group and uniting the living with the ancestors. But in Christianity, as one of the most radical expressions of the Axial Age, the communion of the Church has to be distinguished from the natural community, its rites of passage from the natural progressions of the life cycle, and its appeal to the foundation in Jesus Christ (and in Abraham, Isaac, and Jacob) from any generalized invocation of the ancestors.

These distinctions become attenuated as the centripetal power of the social sacred and its attendant rituals blunt the countercultural thrust of Christian radicalism. The Christian God is not, any more than the God of the Hebrew Scriptures, a celestial reinforcement and projection of the sacred ruler. Indeed, the reverence due to the Sacred Head of the King of spiritual glory directly contradicted the reverence demanded by the Roman head of state, in an oath known as the *sacramentum*. Nevertheless, the models provided by the Davidic and Solomonic monarchies are always available for redeployment by the monarchs of Christendom. King Edward the Sixth of England even saw himself as another King Josiah in his rediscovery of "the law."[11] Once Christianity becomes established, the Solomonic concept of Wisdom sharply reduces the tensions of eschatological hope in favor of a more quotidian commonsense. Though God and Caesar are assigned different spheres in the Gospels, and the disciples are enjoined not to seek after status in the manner of the gentiles, the day is bound to come when the palace of the Byzantine emperor is part of an architectural complex that includes the Church of the Divine Wisdom. As ever, the spatial proximity of the architecture confirms the *symphonia* of church and state. To take yet another example, in the settled territories of Christendom the sacrament of baptism, originally signifying the transition from death to life, becomes a rite of automatic entry into the tribe. In its social function baptism approximates circumcision. Primitive Christianity experienced major conflict in order to break loose from circumcision and thereby bring in the gentiles as promised in the Magnificat and the last sentences of St. Matthew's Gospel. Yet it returned in another form as infant baptism, and was not seriously challenged until the Radical Reformation restored the voluntary principle of belonging.

Partial Reversions to Tribalism

Nationalism in its contemporary form is a relatively recent development, but insofar as it carries forward the tribal principle and a sense of ethnic belonging, it has deeper and longer historical roots. Sometime between the fifteenth and eighteenth centuries, established Christianity began to mutate into national forms, with all that implied for its relation to power in the state and realpolitik in international relations. In the feudal period, the monastic order of Cluny evolved into a hugely wealthy corporation spread across much of Western Europe, and largely responsible for financing the reconquest of Spain from the Moors. In the post-Reformation period of national states, Protestant and Catholic Christianity alike served to legitimate national monarchies and then popular nationalism. From 1789 on, local circumstances determined whether an elite or a popular nationalism opposed or allied itself to Christianity. In France and Italy, nationalism and the

Church were at odds. All the same one can see in the Italian rallying cry of Risorgimento a national translation of the Christian idea of Resurrection. In Poland and in Serbia, nationalism clothed itself in the idea of messianic people-hood and embraced the concept of a suffering victim. Protestant nations, like the United States and Britain (in particular Ulster), were more likely to think of themselves in Old Testament terms as a New Israel. Their expansion and their survival consequently became sacred causes, so that President McKinley could promote the war with Spain, especially the occupation of the Philippines, as an opportunity for American power to spread the Gospel. In the world wars of the twentieth century the suffering was so great that it translated the death of millions of combatants into the imagery of the saving death of Christ: "Greater love hath no man than this; that he lay down his life for his friends." Once Christianity is nationalized, redemption and sacrifice become collectivized in a manner that echoes the concept of redemption in the Hebrew Scriptures.

Christianity Infiltrating and Infiltrated

All the examples just given serve to show how the inherent constitution of society works against the adoption of the radical revolution represented by Christianity considered as a version of Axial religion. The tension between the Christian revolution and the social sacred might be expressed in terms of a reversion to classical ideas of honor, as in the Renaissance, or in terms of a reversion to the warrior ethos of the peoples of Northern Europe, as in the later stages of German nationalism. The central point is as easily grasped as it is easily ignored: the repertoire of the Christian revolution infiltrates, and is infiltrated by, the characteristics of the kinds of society in which it is incarnated. In feudal society, the warrior ethos is inflected by the ideal of Christian chivalry, and in commercial Amsterdam the embarrassment of riches is inflected by a sense of moral obligation. Most recently, in a mature capitalist society the good news is spun to include health and prosperity, and finds ample justification for that by reverting to a major strand in the teachings of the Hebrew Scriptures.

Once again Bellah is shown to be right in his contention that nothing is finally lost.[12] Almost anything can be recycled as circumstances require, or, as Taylor puts it, can be reconstituted in endlessly variable packages.[13] One might add that the Old Testament provides a major legitimation for the recuperations found throughout Christian history, to be deployed alongside reversions to the classical world and pre-Christian paganism. The Axial revolution is under constant challenge from the past as well as from social realities. Indeed, they reinforce each other, so that some Christian societies strongly resemble Judaic or classical societies. An ancient Roman would not have found Washington in the early years of the American republic unfamiliar. Not for the first time, a republic composed of Christians fused the Virgilian hope of a *novus ordo seclorum* with the Exodus and the Eschaton.

From Outer to Inner

In this recital of recoils from the Axial revolution considered as a revolution too far, I have not followed through one central theme in the Christian repertoire. That is the move from exteriority to inwardness as previewed in the Hebrew Scriptures, deepened by Jesus and St. Paul, revived in medieval devotion (for example, Anselm), and dramatized for the whole of modernity by Luther. The reason for avoiding an extended treatment of this theme, otherwise understood as a move toward private subjectivity, or in Taylor's formulation as the turn to the self, is strategic.[14] One such strategic reason relates to modern concepts of what Taylor has called "human flourishing," because the turn to the self is not only a feature of the Axial revolution, where it remains under some kind of communal restraint, but can be viewed in its extreme manifestations as a feature of a post-Axial world.[15] This turn is not the Catholic recognition of the limits set on heroic virtue by everyday human nature, but humanism as a distinct human ideal.

Humanism etc.

Humanism is one version of this crucial shift to subjectivity, whether expressed in Christian terms or not. Christian love can be expressed as a decent concern for one's neighbor and the proper disciplines of friendship; ascetic rigor can be translated as self-control; holy poverty as being content with a reasonable standard of living; and holiness as personal integrity. As inflected by Christianity, this ideal of human (or humanistic) flourishing will embody the Axial and Christian insight that whosoever seeks his life will lose it and whosoever loses his life will find it. Whether in eighteenth-century Christian Rome or in Boston at the same period, this kind of ideal in Christian dress was an accepted norm. It emerges quite clearly in the moral worlds promoted in the kinds of theater associated with the oratory, and in Baroque oratorio. Indeed, in oratorio the Old Testament is reclothed in humanistic classical dress. It is precisely at this time that the idea of canon as applied to sacred Scripture is extended to include the exalted genealogy of great works of art, so that these are eventually accorded something of the reverence once reserved for sacred Scripture. Moreover, in the Romantic period emerging at the close of the eighteenth century, some of the metaphors and images of the transcendent realm in the church are reused to express a more generic human experience, referred to by Taylor as "transcendence-in-immanence."[16] Examples are to be found in Wordsworth, Novalis, and Friedrich, and in such creative geniuses the Christian reference is retained. In later versions the Christian reference may be discarded with contempt, for example in Swinburne and Nietzsche. Sometimes the boundary becomes blurred, perhaps on account of an oscillation between the religion of art and Catholicism, as in the cases of Wilde and Huysmans, or because the meaning of resurrection and the Holy Spirit acquires a more generic reference, as in Mahler. There is a constant movement back and forth between a Christian reference, often marked by conversions to Catholicism, and the kind of generic and primeval sacred evoked by Wagner, where a pre-Axial fusion of sexual love and death anticipates a possible post-Axial condition.

A rather different marker is provided by the changes in the approach to education associated with Dewey. The objective disciplines embodied in the absorption of the humanistic classics are subverted in favor of whatever serves to locate the authentic self. Thus one has an initial progression from holiness to integrity, which then moves on once more from integrity to something potentially very different: self-realization and authentic being.

The Trail of Popular Protestantism

There is a paradox here worth exploiting, and it is this. The changes just reviewed occurred in the culture of elites, though they moved progressively down the social hierarchy in a sequence from the 1890s to the 1930s and eventually to the 1960s. However, the transition of greater importance for culture in the broader anthropological sense is to be traced in the shift inaugurated by the Reformation away from the tangible, material, and external rituals and icons of devotion to an inward appropriation of trusting faith. In this shift, the reference back to the Old Testament was firmly in line with the Axial revolution because it denied independent reality to idols. Thus references back to the Hebrew Scriptures can be deployed both to mitigate the Axial revolution in order to embrace prosperity, and to reinforce it through the prohibition of idolatry.

The celebration of the created order in the Enlightenment, including a Christian Enlightenment, and the mystical celebration of Nature found in Romanticism, including a Christian Romanticism, mutates under the pressure of a radical turn to the self into environmentalism and into forms of sexuality conceived, not just as forms of natural expression but as a self-expression to be realized "on demand." This is Freud rendered optimistic by being tailored for American consumption: civilization shorn of its repressions and devoid of its discontents. Whereas in Christianity forgiveness coexists with judgment, it now mutates into an indiscriminate compassion that diminishes responsibility and devalues striving. Christianity itself is reformulated in sentimental mode, so that the idea of cost, including the cost of redemption on account of the exactions of sin and evil-doing, ceases to make sense. Once the idea of cost, of limits, of social disciplines, and of the need for striving in order to achieve anything, ceases to make sense, the quotidian frustrations of life come to be experienced as a deprivation of human rights. The figure of the Victim, which in Christianity codes the cost of evil, is now generalized into inevitable grievance against the world. We are all of us victims, but nobody is to blame except an external and inherently oppressive entity called Society.

What has happened can best be focused by the issue of authority, because authority is one of those prerequisites of society that cannot be circumvented, however much it is complained about and rhetorically identified with authoritarianism. Sentimentalized translations of Christianity and of humanism simply cannot cope with the reality principle of politics, which depends on order, discipline, and coordination through structures of authority, and so far as relations between states are concerned, on power and at least the threat of force. Not only are order, discipline, and authority written in to political activity, but they are also necessary for human flourishing, with the result that government lurches between humanistic principles and the demands of popular sentimentality, especially in the spheres of penology, welfare, and education, until reality imposes an inevitable if unacknowledged correction. It is simply not the case that all desirable principles are reconcilable, or that any given principle can be pursued without correlative cost. A costless world is envisaged, and one entirely compatible with a private spirituality. The Pentecostalism now burgeoning throughout the developing world also lacks the sense of cost as that is coded in the narrative of the Passion, but otherwise it knows very well that all gains are costly. In particular, Pentecostalism cannot afford to devalue striving and discipline. Pentecostalism is a kind of Axial religion in its sexual restraint, in its combination of the pacific ideal with eschatological hope, and in its reservations about political power, though these vary with time and place.

Is the Axial Revolution Still Active?

The question now to be asked concerns the extreme extension of the turn to the self inaugurated by the Reformation and the associated potential for an antinomian dismissal of the law. What does a "me" religion mean for Axial religion as represented by Christianity? It means that what was once a creative tension between a hope of a universal brotherhood in pursuit of peace, and the realities of violence, power, wealth, tribe, and family, has now become a blindness induced by sentimentality about the self, to the disciplines of communal living, or the costs necessarily exacted by the exigencies of political action. Such costs have to be presented as "hard choices" to electorates bound to complain whichever choice is made. There is no such thing as a foreign policy without casualties, pursued on a straightforward ethical basis without inconsistency or switching one's allies over time as national interest requires. One cannot simultaneously try to create an educated elite capable of competing internationally and ensure that all shall win and all shall have prizes, or seek a strong and overarching identity while pursuing multiculturalism without limit.

Liberalism demands that religion acts as one of a number of pressure groups translating its viewpoint into the liberal lingua franca. Where more than that is conceded, it is not because a religious viewpoint is accorded independent standing, but because some element in the ideals of the Axial revolution coincides with and overlaps liberal pacificism or concepts of human dignity. The implications of the Catholic tradition of natural law remain problematic in certain areas, for example in gender relations and regarding contraception and abortion, but they can usually be modified to conform to the required liberal consensus. If judgment is a Christian category in a state of mutual interdependence with forgiveness, then there are equivalents to be found in humanistic discourse. In the same way, there are humanistic equivalents of the Christian concept of universal brotherhood.

At one level, religion has a right to be heard in the public forum alongside other views, possibly because it can claim to be a mode of rationality, but more plausibly because it constitutes a body of opinion with interests and values to promote. That at least would be taken for granted in the United States, whatever may be the case in societies influenced by the *laïque* traditions of France. At another level, the insights of Axial religion lie beyond the political realm. For example, the voluntary embrace of celibacy has no salience outside the community of believers. Similarly, the embrace of holy poverty or charity is not a political cause, anymore than nonviolence in all circumstances can be a matter of public policy. The furthest the most faithful of politicians would or could go in implementing the ethic of the Sermon on the Mount is the invocation of the principle of going the extra mile, and for the most part Christian politicians are content to promote charity toward one's neighbor and communal responsibility, and to argue for compassion rather than the war of all against all. Moral stances of this kind are hardly exclusive to Christianity, although some of their authority may historically rest on it.

At the heart of Christianity as an expression, the Axial revolution is the enactment of mutual self-giving between the faithful and God, and shared participation in saving grace and the divine presence. This is eschatological, since this participation anticipates the peace and fullness of joy at the heavenly banquet. The political realm may from time to time claim a false transcendence on its own account, and in its deep structure of hopes and fears it actually carries forward eschatological anticipations, but it is inherently incapable of hosting that banquet. There is, therefore, a boundary between Christianity and politics. The processional banners of Christianity occasionally cross over it to enter the public forum, as they did briefly in 1989, but they can only act as pointers to a different order, and as protests against what are, from an Axial viewpoint, claims to a false transcendence, not as concrete policies. Once they act to promote something else, say the role of the Church as carrier of the national myth, as recently in Greece, they become themselves forms of false transcendence. They represent the Durkheimian social sacred, not the Axial revolution. The Axial revolution may well be a permanent revolution, but the forces of counterrevolution are very resilient, for reasons this essay has attempted to set out.[17]

Notes

1. Hans Gerth and C. Wright Mills, *From Max Weber* (London: Routledge, 1957), 323–359; Robert Bellah, "What Is Axial about the Axial Age?," *Archives Européennes de Sociologie* 46, no. 1 (2005): 69–87.

2. Pascal Boyer, *Explaining Religion: The Human Instincts that Fashion Gods, Spirits and Ancestors* (London: Heinemann, 2001).

3. Shmuel N. Eisenstadt, *Fundamentalism, Sectarianism and Revolution* (Cambridge: Cambridge University Press, 1999).

4. J. A. Hobson, *Imperialism* (London: Allen and Unwin, 1902).

5. John Gray, *Black Mass* (Harmondsworth: Penguin, 2007).

6. Francis Fukuyama, *The End of History and the Last Man* (New York: The Free Press, 1992).

7. Tony Judt discusses how a process of nationalistic ethnic cleansing, begun in the dissolution of multiethnic empires, was resumed when the fall of Communism in 1989–1990 released Eastern European and some Asiatic nationalisms from Soviet control: the ending of vertical oppression released horizontal antagonisms that Communism had sometimes repressed but often manipulated. Tony Judt, *Postwar: A History of Europe since 1945* (Harmondsworth: Penguin, 2005).

8. Bellah, "What Is Axial"; Charles Taylor, *A Secular Age* (Cambridge, MA: The Belknap Press of Harvard University Press, 2007).

9. Martin D. Stringer, *A Sociological History of Christian Worship* (Cambridge: Cambridge University Press, 2005).

10. Mark Whitton, "Ruling the Late Roman and Early Byzantine City," *Past and Present* 129 (November 1990): 3–29; K. W. Hart, "Sacrifice and Pagan Belief in Byzantium," *Past and Present* 128 (August 1990): 7–27.

11. Diarmaid MacCulloch, *Tudor Church Militant* (London: Allen Lane, 1999).

12. Bellah, "What Is Axial."

13. Taylor, *A Secular Age.*

14. Charles Taylor, *Sources of the Self: The Making of the Modern Identity* (Cambridge: Cambridge University Press, 1989).

15. Webb Keane, *Christian Moderns: Freedom and Fetish in the Mission Encounter* (Berkeley: University of California Press, 2007); Adam Seligman, Robert Weller, Michael Puett, and Bennett Simon, *Ritual and Its Consequences: An Essay on the Limits of Sincerity* (New York: Oxford University Press, 2008).

16. Taylor, *A Secular Age*.

17. In the course of this argument I have drawn on several of my own books, in particular: *Pacifism: An Historical and Sociological Study* (London: Routledge, 1965); *The Breaking of the Image* (Oxford: Blackwell, 1980); *Does Christianity Cause War?* (Oxford: Clarendon Press, 1997).

13

Righteous Rebels

When, Where, and Why?

W. G. RUNCIMAN

Whatever disagreements there may be among historians about the provenance, nature, and scope of the intellectual innovations originating in Israel, Greece, Iran, China, and India during Karl Jaspers' "Axial Age," the emergence of critical reflection on the source and use of political power by reference to some transcendental ethical standard marks a major transition in human cultural evolution. How does it come about where and when it does? And what accounts for the different forms that it takes?

The search for an answer to these questions leads far back in the history of the human species. Recent research in paleoanthropology, cognitive archaeology, evolutionary and developmental psychology, and brain science gives strong reason to conclude that long before the advent of written records, human beings were talking to each other in a world of myth, ritual, art, technology, and emotionally charged interpersonal relationships in which past encounters were recalled and discussed and patterns of part-cooperative, part-antagonistic behavior toward others established and sustained. Our human ancestors had inherited from their primate forbears, and shared with their primate cousins, innate mental capacities for beliefs about the workings of the world on the one hand and attitudes toward the things and people in it on the other. But, as Darwin himself had always recognized, for all the similarities between humans and other primates in quarreling, collaborating, befriending, deceiving, imitating, learning from, and showing off to one another, only human beings have the capacity to reflect, as Darwin put it, on whence we come and whither we go, on what is life and death, "and so forth."[1] Thus there are numerous rebellious chimpanzees seeking to reverse the existing rank-order in the troops to which they belong. But no primatologist claims that they share the ideals set out in the United Nations Universal Declaration of Human Rights of 1948. Although field research and laboratory experiments have combined to demonstrate that chimpanzees have mental capacities and cultural traditions of a kind that Darwin's successors were for a long time unwilling to credit them with, critical reflection and moral argument are unique to us, with our larger neocortices and modified vocal tracts and the linguistic skills made possible by them.

We do not know when our distant ancestors first started to hold conversations with one another or what they may have been saying in them during the many tens of millennia before the first epigraphic or literary evidence. But we do know that they began to ask questions about the non- or quasi- or suprahuman agencies acting on the world in which they found themselves. Much information that presupposes a consistent relationship between causes and effects and thereby dictates the performance of everyday behavioral routines can be transmitted from mind to mind without language. But when it comes to exchanging opinions about the weather, the movements of the heavenly bodies, the generation and decay of plants and trees, the habits of birds and beasts, accidents, sickness, and the inescapability of death, language not only makes it possible but steadily expands both its frequency and its coverage. There emerges among other things *Geisterglaube*—the belief that natural objects, animals, and artifacts, as well as persons, are endowed with some form of volition[2] and that, as Marcus Aurelius was to put it, we cannot but believe in the existence of suprahuman agents for the simple reason that we experience their power. By the time that the archaeological record contains the material remains of shrines, altars, idols, talismans, figurines, grave goods, votive offerings, and visual depictions of gods and goddesses, human beings are talking to each other not only about how to interpret the seemingly purposeful actions of beings directly observable in the world but about how the invisible suprahuman agencies seemingly acting on the world might be entreated, propitiated, or manipulated. Is there some way in which their favor can be solicited and their anger appeased? Is there some way of finding out how, given the presumption of their existence, human beings should behave toward them? And with these come the questions of cosmogony and the afterlife. Who or what brought the world into being at all? And is there the possibility of survival or resurrection after death?

Second, we know that our ancestors began to exchange information—gossip, if you prefer—about each other's behavior in ongoing relationships of collaboration and exchange. Who can be trusted, and who can't? Who can be relied on to return a favor—particularly if not someone whose probability of reciprocation will be a function of what "we" now know as Hamilton's Rule? Evidence from cross-cultural ethnography, experimental psychology, and evolutionary game theory all supports the conclusion that behavior perceived as violating an implicit social contract or norm of fairness evokes in all human beings feelings not merely of resentment but of justified resentment. It is true that indignation at misbehavior is equally to be seen among chimpanzees. When Frans de Waal at the Arnhem Zoo observes the punishment meted out to two unruly teenagers who have delayed the group's evening meal, it looks plausible to attribute to the punishers something approximating to "Serve 'em right!" There is also some experimental evidence that primates perceive and resent unequal distribution of food. But it is a big step from there to self-conscious passing of judgment on the offending behavior according to an explicit moral standard. We shall never know who was the first person to express one, or how long ago it was that they did. But at some point, whatever the culturally variable codes of conduct whose violations give rise to accusations of immoral behavior, such accusations begin to be uttered, debated, and on occasion acted on, within human groups.

Third, our ancestors began to exchange information about the traits and behavior of the members of the out-groups with whom they interacted, whether in collaboration or conflict, in the demarcation of territorial boundaries, the exchange of material goods or nubile women, or periodic cultic or ritual observances. As they spread out into increasingly unfamiliar environments, the stereotyping of strangers was an adaptive response to the difficulty of choosing the strategy to follow in relations with persons about whom little was initially known. Mutual differentiation was symbolized by a proliferating range of cultural markers in bodily decoration, clothes, hairstyles, diet, idioms, totems, and taboos that could be interpreted as signals indicative of the behavior to be expected and the likelihood that mutually beneficial relationships could be sustained without excessive risk of treachery and deceit. And with that came discussion of the ways in which their own group's way of life was more deserving of admiration than that of those whom they defined as "other" and stigmatized accordingly.

From then on, all human populations were potential carriers of coherently articulated beliefs and attitudes censorious of the behavior not only of noncooperators and nonconformists but of seekers of power over others. It is notoriously hazardous to read back from the lifestyles of twentieth-century hunter-gatherers to those who lived 100,000 or more years before the present. But the ethnographic evidence for vigilant monitoring of the distribution of food, ridicule or ostracism of would-be self-aggrandizers, punishment of violators of group norms, and formation of coalitions to restrain bullies and braggarts is so extensive and so consistent that the burden of the argument falls on anyone reluctant to agree that the behavior of our remote ancestors is likely to have been similar in these respects. However far short it fell of the formulation of a set of coherent ethical principles, it surely extended to exchanges in which one person conveyed to another not just "Don't go there!" or "Try eating some of this!" or "Look out—the animal is coming this way!" but "That is not the right way to behave around here—okay?"

By this time, whenever it was, human sociology was, so to speak, no longer primate sociology. (I bypass the intriguing but controversial topic of the intellectual and perhaps linguistic capacity of the Neanderthals.) But there was still a long way to go from articulate willingness or refusal to acknowledge a leader whose claim to influence rests on personal attributes (which might include an acknowledged shamanistic or mantic ability to interpret the volitions of suprahuman agents as well as courage in battle, or oratorical skill, or the ability to organize collective activities or tasks) and articulate willingness or refusal to acknowledge the legitimacy of institutions that give rulers power over their subjects underwritten by formal sanctions. Only after the evolution of "society" out of "culture"[3] could self-aggrandizers move into, rather than create, positions of institutional power, whether economic, ideological, or political, and their roles be designated by appropriate words in the vernacular language. It is true that any band of hunters and foragers, or aggregation of members in a voluntary association, or ad hoc group held together by some common purpose can be said to constitute a "society," just as any performance of a ritual or participation in a game can be said to involve playing a "role." But the critical difference is between a world of interpersonal relationships, informal conventions, and habitual behavior patterns, and a world of established institutional modes of production, persuasion, and coercion—of landlords and tenants, priests and parishioners, masters and slaves, and the rest. Only then can the resentment of the more powerful by the less take the form of challenging the system that empowers the incumbents of the superordinate roles to behave as they do. Speculation about suprahuman agencies, denunciation of bad behavior by fellow members of an established community, and stigmatization of persons or groups defined as "other" can now generate explicit repudiation of rulers' claimed entitlement to rule.

Resistance to rulers perceived as misusing their power does not need to be inspired by a vision of an alternative social order. It can be motivated simply by a perceived need for defense, and if possible retaliation, against ill-treatment or a desire for a share in the power which the rulers hold. The secessions of the Roman *plebs* in 494 and 449 BCE were successful attempts to extort concessions from the dominant patricians, not to replace the existing constitution of the Roman state in the name of some higher good. Rulers who are denounced as having forfeited by their impiety the favor of the gods on whom victory and prosperity depend, or deemed to have betrayed an implicit contract with the ruled, or resented as alien intruders can provoke disobedience (or—if the opportunity presents itself—desertion) without any of the ruled being carriers of, in Arnaldo Momigliano's characterization of the Axial Age, "new models of reality, either mystically or prophetically or rationally apprehended," which "are propounded as a criticism of, and alternative to, the prevailing models."[4] In due course, the combination of active opposition to existing rulers with the conviction that a morally superior social order can thereby be brought into being generates the kind of authentically righteous rebellions exemplified by the Jewish uprisings against Rome, the Yellow Turbans in China, the Qarmatians in Iraq, the English Peasants' Revolt of 1381, Müntzer and the Anabaptists, the Scottish Covenanters, Robespierre and the Jacobins, the Taiping, Lenin and the Bolsheviks, the Andalusian anarchists, and Al-Qaeda. But neither a "social bandit"[5] on the one hand nor a preacher in the wilderness prophesying the downfall of the oppressors on the other are at the same time both rebellious and righteous enough to qualify. For that, either the bandit must come to be inspired by the preacher's transcendental moral vision or the preacher must come to be the leader of an organized movement that confronts the rulers and their agents directly.

It seems to be agreed among the authorities on Pharaonic Egypt and the monarchies of Sumerian and Akkadian Mesopotamia that in neither of these were any of the domestic uprisings or foreign invasions by which rulers were periodically faced motivated by a vision of an alternative and morally superior social order. It is not that concepts of both justice and benevolence were not there to be drawn on in the vernacular terminology. The Egyptian *ma'at*, "a term whose meaning goes far beyond legal fairness or factual accuracy" to the point of denoting an all-embracing principle of order governing both the physical universe and human society,[6] imposed on successive kings an obligation to act not only protectively but solicitously toward their subjects. But *ma'at* did not legitimate rebellion against a king who failed to practice it. On the contrary, rebels were "not simply transgressors against *ma'at*; they were accomplices and instruments of superhuman powers of chaos."[7] In Mesopotamia likewise, it is incumbent on the kings to rule justly and benevolently: Hammurabi in his law-code takes explicit pride in doing so. But where they fail to protect and care for their subjects as they should, it is for the gods, not the subjects, to withdraw their support and decree a transfer of power from one to another. Nor, in either case, were the temple priests ever carriers of a rival ethical doctrine and associated political program. The one radical innovation was that of Akhenaten. But his identification of himself with the one true god had nothing to do with a reformation of Egyptian society for the benefit of the ruled, and was in any case immediately reversed by his successor.

Where, as in Egypt and Mesopotamia, rulers are believed either to partake in divinity or to be divinely appointed, the concomitant assumption is that they are the defenders of themselves and their subjects against both their human and their suprahuman enemies. But it can also happen that the forces of evil are seen to be stronger than the forces of good, the enemy triumphant, and the rulers wicked. The idea that the world is a battleground in which beneficent and maleficent quasi-personal suprahuman agencies are engaged in perpetual combat is familiar from many times and places in the historical and ethnographic record. By contrast with the manifestly implausible idea that the world is the creation of a single omnipotent being who is not only wise but good, dualism or polytheism in their various forms are much more obviously consistent with universal human experience. There then arises the question: What is the outcome of the battle between good and evil going to be? It is his answer to it which makes Zoroaster, so far as is known, the first of the many optimistic eschatologists in human history. If

Zoroaster was indeed the first prophetic exponent of a transcendental moral standard which enjoined the members of all classes and categories of men and women to help bring about an impending redemptive transformation of the existing social order, he is the prototype of the whole long tradition of righteous rebellion against rulers perceived as either tacit or open accomplices of the forces of evil which, for the time being, prevail.

The new order that righteous rebels are pledged to bring into being does not necessarily involve the creation of a utopian future. It may equally involve a re-creation of a golden age located somewhere in the past. Or the two can be fused, as when the French revolutionaries harked back to Roman republican virtues and rituals, or the Yellow Turbans harked back to the administrative tradition and system of land distribution of the T'ang. But righteous rebels aim not merely to punish rulers for their misdeeds. Their aspiration is to demolish the institutional structures from which the rulers have derived their power. It may then happen that they have no sooner succeeded than they provoke a new generation of righteous rebels to rise up against them in their turn. But the moral vision by appeal to which authentically righteous rebellion is initially inspired is not merely of the overthrow of a maleficent king but of abolition of the evil institution of kingship; not merely of the defrocking of venal priests but abolition of the corrupt institution of priesthood; not merely of the expropriation of exploitative capitalists but of abolition of the inherently exploitative institution of private property; and so on. Active resistance to the oppressors is legitimated not merely by the oppressiveness of their individual actions, or failures to act, but by the prospect of creating an alternative social order in which such actions, or failures to act, will no longer be possible. The appeal to a transcendental ethic may be bound up with a variety of answers to the question of the origin of evil as such: the Zoroastrian conception of Ahura Mazda as the beneficent creator confronted by Angra Mainyu as the personification of evil is only one among others. But once rulers are seen not merely as impious, or untrustworthy, or alien, but as allies or servants of evil against good, then whatever the explanation given of the existence of evil in the world, the allies or servants of the good are morally in the right if they rise up against them.

Yet that is not by any means what always happens. A comparative sociologist looking across the range of "Axial" societies is likely to be struck more by the differences than by the resemblances between them in this respect. Common to them all is the emergence of critical reflection on the state of not only the natural but the political world. But the advocacy of righteous rebellion, familiar though it becomes in the subsequent course of human history, is only one of several possible inferences to which it may lead. As always in comparative sociology, it is as problematic to explain what doesn't happen as what does. Even if there can be traced a line of intellectual descent from Zoroaster to the Hebrew prophets to the millenarian Christians to Robespierre to Marx and Engels, there are responses other than righteous rebellion open to those who see the all too flagrantly unrighteous all too firmly in possession of worldly power.

One such alternative response is withdrawal from the world altogether. But the hermit living alone on roots and berries and wild honey is a rarity at any place and time. The righteous renouncer is more likely to be either a holy man who, as Louis Dumont puts it in the Indian case, "leaves his social role in order to adopt a role that is both universal and personal" in which he is sustained by alms,[8] or a member of a sectarian or monastic community in which the righteous support themselves in self-quarantined isolation from worldly corruption. Nothing prevents either monks or holy men from intervening on occasion in the affairs of the world, whether cudgel-wielding Circumcellions descending from the deserts of Roman Egypt to attack pagan temples or Buddhist monks actively resisting Chinese Communist rule in Tibet. But that is not the same as casting down the wicked rulers from their seats and replacing them with a new regime staffed by the pure in heart. Renouncers may on occasion inspire, encourage, or assist righteous rebels, but they do so from positions both culturally and socially apart from them.

There is also the middle way between renunciation and rebellion. However much controversy there continues to be among specialists about the reconstruction and interpretation of the teachings of Confucius, there appears to be no disagreement about their distinctiveness, their influence, and their general import. In relation to worldly power, and the failure of its holders to live up to the moral standards to which Confucius held that they ought to subscribe, he preached neither rebellion nor renunciation but reform—that is, the duty of the righteous not merely to expound by precept but to demonstrate by example the right way for both rulers and their subjects to behave. This explicitly involved "reanimation" (in Arthur Waley's translation of *Analects* II.11) of a past in which there had been good kings who behaved as they should and adhered to the traditional rituals by which respect for other persons is both regulated and defined. But it at the same time involved an unambiguous repudiation of the prevailing warrior ethic and associated rituals of hereditary aristocratic elites. For Confucius, righteousness and the conduct in which it finds expression is attainable by anyone who is willing to learn. It follows that the good society will be one whose rulers have absorbed this lesson and surrounded themselves with officials and counselors who have done likewise. But the Confucian ethic disavows rebellion at the same time that it eschews total withdrawal from the world. In Book VIII of the *Analects,* the Master acknowledges that any but the "truly Good" will, if their sufferings are "very great," be likely to rebel. But his disciples are then enjoined neither to enter a state "that pursues dangerous courses" nor to "stay in one where the people have rebelled" (VIII.10 and 13, again following Waley's translation). This is not merely prudential advice. Even though there is no appeal to a suprahuman deity as the source of the transcendental moral standard which the Master is preaching, no reader can doubt that it is indeed a moral standard and one that implies the possibility of an alternative social order. But the truly righteous man will not himself be a rebel, however understandable it may be that an ill-treated subject of a wicked ruler should become one.

Rebellion, renunciation, and reform are not mutually exclusive. Nor need the righteous be precluded by their disapprobation of their rulers from exploring possibilities for negotiation or compromise. Where, in particular, secession is a continuing option, as it is among nomadic pastoralists or in underpopulated regions where cultivable land is readily available elsewhere, the righteous can threaten simply to move out of reach. Many secessions have been no more inspired by a moral vision of an alternative social order than were those of the Roman *plebs,* just as many colonies have been founded not as refuges from evil oppressors but in quest of independent opportunities for exploitation and plunder. But the Pilgrim Fathers who set sail for Plymouth, Massachusetts, in 1620 were "self-conscious separatists who made no bones about their wish to separate completely from corrupt English religion" and set up a self-governing "city upon a hill" by whose example the righteous elsewhere might be inspired.[9] The subsequent fate of the settlement may not have been what the founders had envisaged and worked for. But the self-consciously righteous who despair of reforming their rulers and lack the means to rebel against them are sometimes able to translate their theoretical condemnation of the existing order into action by taking themselves to another place where the righteous, and only the righteous, will hold power.

There still remains, however, the problem posed by those societies where the conditions for the "emergence, conceptualization, and institutionalization of a basic tension between the transcendental and mundane orders," as Shmuel N. Eisenstadt has put it,[10] are present, but these things nonetheless fail to occur. Momigliano remarks of "the China of Confucius and Lao-Tse, the India of Buddha, the Iran of Zoroaster, the Palestine of the Prophets, and the Greece of the philosophers, the tragedians, and the historians" that they all "display literacy, a complex political organization combining central government and local authorities, elaborate town-planning, advanced metal technology and the practice of international diplomacy."[11] But what is to be said about Japan, which Eisenstadt calls "the only non-Axial civilization to have had a continuous, autonomous—and very turbulent—history up to and including modern times"?[12] Or about Rome, which I have cited elsewhere as an exception that proves (or does it?) the rule.[13] No conception of an alternative and morally superior social order ever emerged within Roman culture. The gods were assumed to be supportive of Rome and the expansion of its power provided that they were appropriately honored and propitiated; the conventional code of conduct presupposed the wisdom of ancestral tradition and the need to preserve the virtues of courage, loyalty, and self-discipline; and alien cults and creeds outside the official religion were swiftly and brutally suppressed if they were thought to pose a threat to the Roman state. Misconduct by individual rulers and their agents might be denounced—there can, for example, be no mistaking the authenticity of Cicero's disapproval of a provincial governor who behaved like Verres—but it is symptomatic of the Roman attitude that when, during the period of his retirement from politics, Cicero set himself to write in imitation of Plato's *Republic* and *Laws*, his ideal state turns out to be the Roman state and his ideal laws the laws of Rome. Roman priests were functionaries of the Roman state, not "clerics" in Eisenstadt's sense. For all the lip-service paid to the traditional republican virtues, no contender for power ever did so in the name of constructing, or reconstructing, a world purged of wickedness and injustice. Nor, as pointed out by Mary Beard, John North, and Simon Price, did any Roman ever claim a religious identity separate from identity as a member of a Roman family and a citizen of the Roman state.[14]

But it is Greece that, in the context of the present discussion, is more puzzling still. Its philosophers, tragedians, and historians were all aware of the diversity of forms of government in the world around them and voiced opinions about their respective merits. If, moreover, an Axial breakthrough involves not only theoretical but metatheoretical speculation ("thought about thought"), there can be no doubt whatever that the Greeks achieved one. But it is as true of the Greek *poleis* as it is of Rome that despite frequent usurpations, or attempted usurpations, of power by violence, the rebels weren't righteous and the righteous weren't rebels—Socrates, among the righteous, least of all. There were lawgivers like Solon or Philolaus of Corinth, but they weren't moral reformers: their objective, and that of those who enlisted their services, was the design of constitutional arrangements that would moderate internal strife *(stasis)*. There were scoffers and skeptics, including the original "Cynics," but no renouncers like the Hindu or Christian holy men. The "seers" *(manteis)*, like Teiresias, might warn rulers like Creon of the nemesis awaiting them for their hubris, but Teiresias can no more be equated with Zoroaster or the Hebrew prophets than Antigone, in her defiance of Creon's command, with Rosa Luxemburg. There were no religious wars, no millenarian uprisings, no anarchists, no pacifists, and no armies fighting in the name of good against evil. Why not?

One possible response is to say that the intellectuals whose writings exemplify the breakthrough to critical reflection and theoretical speculation never envisaged the creation of an alternative social order purged of wickedness and injustice as a practical objective. Plato, at the end of Book 9 of *Republic*, has Socrates say that his ideal society exists only "in heaven." Aristotle, in his *Politics*, is concerned above all with the kind of constitution that will have the best prospect of minimizing internal conflict within the *polis*. The "Athenian Stranger" in Plato's *Laws* says that peace is merely a state of undeclared war between rival *poleis*, and Aristotle takes what he calls "neighbortown" *(astygeitones)* wars as to be expected as a matter of course. Neither had ethical qualms about slavery beyond deploring the enslavement of Greeks by other Greeks as opposed to non-Hellenic "barbarians." But these shared assumptions, realistic as no doubt they were, could still have been more actively challenged. Greek religious beliefs offered ample scope for the idea that regimes whose rulers' conduct is offensive to the gods should be replaced by more virtuous ones; Greek moral concepts offered ample scope for the formulation of a political program aimed at realizing a transcendental notion of the good; Greek discussions of the workings of societies other than their own offered ample scope for comparison by reference to a universal criterion of political legitimacy. But there never emerged the righteous rebels (let alone righteous renouncers or righteous reformers) of the kind that public debate about these issues might have been expected to inspire.

Despite the persistent minority of scoffers and skeptics, the capacity of quasi-personal suprahuman agents to intervene in human affairs was taken seriously at all social levels. The *manteis,* as opposed to the *hieropoioi* charged with ensuring that sacrifices were properly conducted, were often castigated by disappointed clients as charlatans, as after the failure of the Athenian invasion of Sicily. But divination and oneiromancy were taken for granted as part of everyday life. There were strict procedural rules governing communication with the gods and the actions to be taken by, or against, anyone guilty of behavior held to be sacrilegious or polluting. A hard-headed professional soldier like Xenophon regularly sought guidance from on high through the performance of animal sacrifices. What is missing is the idea of a god who has laid down the binding moral standard by which the conduct of rulers toward their subjects is to be judged and the regime condemned if it fails to meet it. The "justice of Zeus" had nothing to do with what would much later be called "social justice." Zeus is the punisher *(kolastēs)* of the presumptuous *(tōn agan hyperphronōn),* but not the protector of the humble and weak. The "just deserts" of either an individual or a community are the nemesis following from hubris which has provoked divine jealousy *(phthonos).* Although there were mystery cults offering personal initiation and purification, there was no Weberian "salvation ethic" by which there might have been inspired a social movement whose organizing principle was the mobilization of the righteous against the forces of evil. Tyranny was often hated by its subjects as well as disapproved of by philosophers: Sara Forsdyke has recently drawn attention to the razing to the ground of tyrants' houses and tombs in Corinth after the killing of Cypselus, and in Syracuse after the overthrow of Dionysius II.[15] But their motivation was not that of the English regicides who condemned Charles I to death in 1649 any more than it was that of the religiously inspired assassins, or would-be assassins, of monarchs such as Henri IV of France or Elizabeth of England. The idea of acting as desired, or required, or even compelled against the person's will, by one or another suprahuman agency is thoroughly familiar in Greek culture. But the gods' own motivations are taken to be self-interested in much the same way as those of the mortals in whose lives they intervene. They reward and punish; they take sides; they exact obedience; they on occasion pardon transgressions. But they do not instruct their devotees in the making of a world of peace and goodwill cleansed of evil and relieved of suffering.

The lack of an accepted set of divinely revealed commandments did not in any way inhibit the Greeks from passing judgments on each other's conduct couched in a rich and explicit moral vocabulary. But their conception of good government had to do with maintenance of order, conformity to custom, and enforcement of appropriate penalties, not redress for the humble and powerless who are being denied equality of opportunity as well as condition. Beggars, strangers, and supplicants might receive hospitality from a motive of personal piety, but they were never seen as a public responsibility. For the philosophers, tragedians, and historians alike, the just *(dikaios)* man is the man who pays his debts, keeps his promises, honors the gods, refuses bribes, performs his civic duties, serves in the army when summoned, stands firm in battle, and goes to the help of friends and allies when called on. He is a reciprocal, not an unconditional, altruist. Conversely, the unjust *(adikos)* man is above all *pleonektēs*—he is guilty of wanting more than he should. Aristotle explicitly defines *adikein* as the doing of harm to someone contrary to *nomos,* and *nomos* is much nearer to "good custom" than to a Kantian moral law. The Athenian orators use every rhetorical trick at their command to put their opponents *in* the wrong and to rouse the indignation of the jurors *(andres dikastoi)* against them. But the wrongdoing is conduct alleged to be unpatriotic, or impious, or overweening, or a breach of an undertaking given, or a refusal to meet a recognized obligation. The offences for which holders of public office were systematically held to account were misuse of funds under their control or collusion with a foreign enemy.

The notion of legal equality among citizens *(isonomia)* had nothing to do with universal human rights. In interstate relations, it is symptomatic that when the Spartans momentarily felt, as reported by Thucydides, that they deserved the humiliation they suffered at the hands of the Athenians at Pylos, it was because they had broken the treaty under which they should have agreed to go to arbitration *(es dikas),* with the consequence that the bad behavior *(paranomēma)* was theirs. Rebels against their rulers are righteous rebels only to the extent that they see themselves as having been treated *para nomon*. As Moses Finley pointed out in discussing the ancient historians' treatment of *stasis*, "throughout these accounts legitimacy was never challenged or proclaimed by the rebels, nor was a right of rebellion or even civil disobedience formulated in general terms."[16]

In their attitudes to societies other than their own, the Greeks were as free with explicitly moral judgments as they were in their internal quarrels within their separate *poleis* (or tribal *ethnē*). But recourse to arms, whether against fellow Hellenes or Persia or Macedon (which was both geographically and culturally the borderline case), was dictated by a perceived opportunity or need to gain prestige, or secure independence, or exact revenge, or support an ally, or protect friends and kin, or acquire material resources—as is spelt out in almost exactly these terms by Anaximenes of Lampsacus in his *Rhetoric to Alexander*. When Isocrates argued for a pan-Hellenic campaign against Persia, it was not in order to overthrow an evil regime but to divert the Greeks from fighting one another. For all the eloquence with which Pericles is reported by Thucydides as extolling the virtues of Athens in his Funeral Oration, neither he nor anyone else saw the Peloponnesian War as other than an undisguised struggle for power, whatever differences of view there might be about who was to blame for the rivalry between Athens and Sparta having escalated to the point that it did.

The puzzle accordingly remains. But perhaps the answer is that it is not a puzzle at all. Why should it be assumed that critical reflection and theoretical speculation should lead to the formulation of a transcendental moral standard by which the mighty will be judged and the institutions empowering them found wanting? Why should advances in mathematics and logic on the one hand, and empirical study of the natural and the social worlds on the other, lead to the conclusion that it is the duty of subjects to overturn unrighteous regimes? The political environment in which the Greek philosophers, tragedians, and historians wrote was one in which might was all too visibly right. To recognize this as a matter of observable fact did not imply acceptance of the extreme amoralist position that Plato puts into the mouth of the rhetorician Thrasymachus in *Republic*. There are good reasons why the members of any society should keep promises, return favors, help their friends, and restrain themselves from totally uninhibited exploitation of opportunities for self-aggrandizement, and the Greeks were well aware of them. But in a world of scarce resources, endemic rivalry for prestige, and frequent recourse to violence, the rational strategy is to play to win. This may not be so if there is a life after death: in *Republic,* "Socrates" veers uneasily between claiming that the just who suffer from injustice at the hands of others are rewarded in this life at the end of the day and falling back on the prospect of recompense in the world to come, and Pythagoras and his disciples appear to have believed that the righteous will be reincarnated at a higher level and the unrighteous at a lower one. But to Aristophanes in *The Clouds,* as later to the satirist Lucian in *The Double Indictment,* Socrates was a figure of fun. The role models of the persistently disputatious and (in Jacob Burckhardt's word) "agonistic" citizens of the *poleis* weren't Socrates or Pythagoras but wily Odysseus and man-slaying Achilles. Plato didn't live to witness the career of Alexander of Macedon, but it triumphantly vindicated the observation that he had put into the mouth of Thrasymachus to the effect that successful conquerors are the people who are most admired of all. Nobody suggested that Alexander's motive was to impose a reign of virtue on what came to be called the "Hellenistic" world.

It has long been recognized, as Robert Bellah has pointed out, that "the cultural transformations" of the societies which between them define Jaspers' Axial Age "are by no means uniform."[17] But the culture in which there emerged a tradition of righteous rebellion in its most enduring and persuasive form falls outside Jaspers' period altogether: Islam. Unlike Zoroaster or Confucius or Socrates or Buddha or the Hebrew prophets, the Arabian merchant's son to whom it was revealed early in the sixth century of the Christian era that there is but one true God of whom he is the chosen prophet converted a following which not only challenged by force the power-holders who opposed him but successfully imposed across an increasingly large geographical area the rule of the righteous as defined by adherence to principles laid down by him in the Quran and his posthumously attributed sayings. The consequence was that after his death any Islamic ruler deemed wanting in righteousness was liable to be challenged by rebels seeking to institute government by and for the community of the faithful in accordance with his commands. During the centuries after the proclamation of his message, righteous rebellions against Islamic rulers took many different forms, and the rulers responded in many different ways. Nor did the *ulemate*—the scholars and jurists charged with the interpretation and exposition of the Law—agree with one another on how to reconcile the ideal of rule by a rightly guided spiritual leader with the manifest failings of corrupt and oppressive rulers sustained in power not by their piety but by their control of the means of coercion. Some Islamic intellectuals, including al-Ghazālī, were reformers who, like Confucius, advocated persuasion by precept and example but refused to condone rebellion. Others, like the Sufi masters and their disciples, more nearly resembled some of the monastic and mystical renouncers of Christianity. But the Islamic tradition is unique in the inherent dilemma that it faces about the source and use of power, which derives from the circumstances of its origin. Just as the millenarian tradition gives rise to the idea of permanent revolution as the only means to prevent the initially uncorrupted revolutionaries from abusing their power, so does the Islamic tradition give rise to the idea of a necessary cycle of rebellion and decadence as the only means to prevent the initially uncorrupted rebels from betraying their sacred duty to deploy their power in subservience to a creed that permits no distinction between church and state.

There are, accordingly, more different answers to the questions asked in the opening paragraph of this essay than can be accommodated within a cross-cultural and transsocietal generalization whose applicability throughout the range of cases will not turn out to be an inverse function of its explanatory potential. Jaspers' conception of an Axial Age has a demonstrable rationale in the contrast between societies where a monarch who embodies divine authority holds a monopoly on the means of persuasion as well as coercion, and societies where carriers of alternative visions of a morally superior social order call rulers' legitimacy into question. But the story that he tells in its terms derives from a Hegelian philosophical anthropology rather than from a Weberian comparative sociology within which rebels, renouncers, and reformers are located along a path-dependent sequence of local causal interactions between metaphysical and ethical ideas on the one hand and material and political interests on the other. The two are not mutually exclusive. There is a story to be told in which Zoroaster, Socrates, Confucius, Buddha, and the Hebrew prophets are all protagonists in the long struggle for reflective human self-awareness and the emancipation of critical reason from unexamined traditional attitudes and beliefs. But to accord "Axial" status to those societies where the transition has been achieved leaves it still to be explained whether the achievement is due to homologous cultural descent or convergent cultural evolution, and if the latter, whether there were specific environmental conditions which made it more likely when, or if, there would appear one or more innovative thinkers able to articulate it. It is, to quote Momigliano yet again, remarkable how clearly the personalities of Zoroaster, Buddha, Confucius, the Hebrew prophets, and the Greek philosophers have come down to us: "they are the masters whose thoughts still count today and whose names we remember."[18] But how far may this be due to chance? Once past the initial transition that created the possibility of discussion among the ruled about the prospect of a social order other than the one that has placed their existing rulers in power over them, how can we be sure that there were not other righteous rebels (or renouncers, or reformers) of whom we know nothing because neither the initial carriers of the novel ideas nor their descendants or disciples ever set their ideas down in writing? We must make the most that we can of the sources that we have for the lives and teachings of a set of exceptional individuals who, however much or little influence they had in their lifetimes, have become part of our enduring intellectual legacy. But we must beware of fitting them into a master teleological narrative composed from what is itself a parochial and selective point of view.

Notes

1. Charles Darwin, *The Descent of Man, and Selection in Relation to Sex,* 2nd ed. (London, 1882), 83.
2. Max Weber, *Wirtschaft und Gesellschaft,* 4th ed. (Tübingen, 1956), vol. 1, 246.
3. W. G. Runciman, "From Nature to Culture, from Culture to Society," *Proceedings of the British Academy* 110 (2001): 235–254.

4. Arnaldo Momigliano, *Alien Wisdom: The Limits of Hellenization* (Cambridge, 1975), 9.

5. E. J. Hobsbawm, *Primitive Rebels* (Manchester, 1959), chap. 2.

6. Barry J. Kemp in B. G. Trigger, B. J. Kemp, D. O'Connor, and A. B. Lloyd, *Ancient Egypt: A Social History* (Cambridge, 1983), 74.

7. Norman Cohn, *Cosmos, Chaos and the World to Come: The Ancient Roots of Apocalyptic Faith* (New Haven, 1993), 20.

8. Louis Dumont, *Homo Hierarchicus: The Caste System and Its Implications* (London, 1970), 185.

9. Diarmid MacCulloch, *Reformation: Europe's House Divided 1490–1700* (London, 2003), 185.

10. Shmuel N. Eisenstadt, "The Axial Age: The Emergence of Transcendental Visions and the Rise of Clerics," *Archives Européennes de Sociologie* 23 (1982): 294.

11. Momigliano, *Alien Wisdom*, 8–9.

12. Eisenstadt, *Japanese Civilization: A Comparative View* (Chicago, 1996), 3.

13. W. G. Runciman, "The Exception That Proves the Rule? Rome in the Axial Age," in Eliezer Ben-Rafael and Yitzhak Sternberg, eds., *Comparing Modernities: Pluralism versus Homogenity; Essays in Homage to Schmuel N. Eisenstadt* (Leiden, 2005), 125–140.

14. Mary Beard, John North, and Simon Price, *Religions of Rome* (Cambridge, 1998), vol. 1, 43.

15. Sara Forsdyke, "Street Theatre and Popular Justice in Ancient Greece: Shaming, Stoning, and Starving of Offenders Inside and Outside the Courts," *Past and Present* 201 (2008): 32.

16. M. I. Finley, *Politics in the Ancient World* (Cambridge, 1983), 131.

17. Robert N. Bellah, "What Is Axial about the Axial Age?," *Archives Européennes de Sociologie* 46 (2005): 88.

18. Momigliano, *Alien Wisdom*, 9.

Reevaluations

14

Rehistoricizing the Axial Age

JOHANN P. ARNASON

Since the historicizing argument to be developed below runs counter to stronger trends and more widely shared approaches in the present discussion, it may be useful to begin with a brief indication of the main points at issue. To rehistoricize, or bring history back in, is—most obviously—to make a case for reemphasizing the Axial Age as a historical epoch, with at least approximately definable boundaries, rather than transfiguring its innovations and achievements into an ideal type of "axiality." But it also means to pay more attention to the internal historicity of the epoch: changing constellations as well as diverse lines of development will have to be given their due. A further corollary is that a nuanced historical account of both connections to earlier periods and the transformations that set the Axial Age apart from them is needed. There is no denying that interpreters of the Axial Age—and a fortiori those who preferred to shift the focus toward more abstract categories—have tended to overdraw contrasts with a pre-Axial world. On the other hand, the highly diversified *Wirkungsgeschichte* of traditions taking off from the Axial Age has to be taken into account; the meaning of the sources must be deciphered in light of the whole spectrum of later ramifications. Finally, the proposed historicizing turn would be incomplete without reflection on the premises and problems of historical interpretation as they appear in reconstructions of the Axial Age. All these questions will be touched upon, but no balanced coverage can be attempted within the limits of this essay. The aim is, for the time being, to present a preliminary survey of a problematic that has been unduly simplified by overtheorized accounts of the Axial Age.

Demarcating an Epoch

If we consider the unfolding debate on the Axial Age, there is no reason to disagree with Jan Assmann's suggestion (in this volume) that the interest now seems to focus more on the phenomena themselves than on their chronological location. The question is how far this shift can go. Are the "phenomena themselves" fully separable from the context of a historical epoch? If we subsume the Axial phenomena under general categories, thus converting the phenomenological approach into a typological one, the categories in question—reducible, in one way or another, to heightened levels of reflexivity and agency—can be understood either as recurrent patterns or as cumulative trends. In the former case, we are dealing with a uniform logic that repeats itself at successive moments; the originality of the Axial Age disappears, and with it the points of orientation for comparison with other major cases of sociocultural transformation. We would then need to invent new concepts to recapture the lost ground. In the second case, the Axial Age disappears into an evolutionary vision of history. Here I agree with the point made in Shmuel Eisenstadt's contribution to this volume (although, as will be seen, my reflections on the Axial Age diverge from his argument in fundamental ways): there are evolutionary trends in history, and there is no doubt that some such trends were significantly and conspicuously accelerated during the Axial Age, but above and beyond that, there are the contingent and creative—and therefore divergent—elaborations of possibilities linked to the evolutionary trends. The flowering of such elaborations is what is most noteworthy about the Axial Age. An interpretation that singles out its evolutionary aspects will certainly tell us something, but it will screen out an all-important part of the picture. In both cases, then, the typological perspectives result in one-sided accounts without any clear indication of alternative ways to tackle the neglected themes. If we reverse this trend and set out to rehistoricize the whole problematic, it will no longer be obvious that we need the general category of axiality. The emergence of rational argument, universalistic ethics, theoretical discourse or "second-order thinking" (thinking about thinking) can be described in their own respective terms, without subsuming them under a more abstract structural principle. As for "Axial civilizations," the term can be used to refer to civilizational complexes whose histories can be traced back to comparable origins, but I do not think that it can denote a durable common denominator of civilizational patterns.

The case for rehistoricizing should begin with a reminder of our incomplete knowledge and changing images of the Axial Age. The idea—or, to use a more appropriate German term: the *Denkfigur*—of the Axial Age goes back to eighteenth-century origins, and it resurfaced in various contexts; a comprehensive history of its appearances and reappearances has yet to be written, but it seems clear that it did not develop into a research program until very recently (Karl Jaspers' invitation to grasp the Axial Age as a growing mystery ["als wachsendes Geheimnis vor Augen zu gewinnen"—Jaspers 1949, 39] hardly deserves that label). It was only with Eisenstadt's reformulations in the 1970s and 1980s that systematic inquiry into the comparative history of the Axial Age became possible; the first installment was the one-volume collection published in English in 1986 and the five German volumes published around the same time. This research is still in progress, and in view of that, the typological turn seems decidedly premature, even if we set aside the other arguments against it. Recent scholarship has advanced our understanding of each key case as well as of contrasts and parallels between them. But it has done so in different and uneven ways, and at the same time it has shown how much more work there is to do. During the last twenty or thirty years, our knowledge of archaic and Axial China has made very significant progress due to new evidence as well as new approaches; in the Greek case, these two factors have combined in a different way, but also with noteworthy results. As for other Axial centers, the state of the art is perhaps more controversial, but in general terms, it seems obvious that the research program is still in a phase of growth and ongoing reorientation. We can discuss the relationship between culturally unique, specifically Axial and universal or evolutionary aspects of the transformations in question; but attempts to construct a comprehensive model of "axiality" seem premature.

On these grounds (and for other reasons to be explained later), it seems appropriate to retain the term "Axial Age" as a provisional demarcating label for a historical epoch. It is easily imaginable that historical scholarship might in the end move beyond this terminology. For the time being, however, it remains useful. A historical period cannot be defined without some kind of chronological anchorage. In this case, a long and loosely defined chronology seems preferable; we should, in other words, talk about a long Axial Age, extending roughly from the eighth to the fourth or third century BCE, rather than a short one around 500 BCE. Both alternatives are indicated in Jaspers' *Origin and Goal of History,* but the long chronology is more explicitly proposed at the beginning of the book. The most obvious and elementary feature of the period is a rare flowering of sociocultural creativity. It is one of the basic facts of history that such phases—some longer and some more conspicuous than others—stand out in contrast to less creative ones. In the case of the Axial Age, we can spell out some more specific connotations that will facilitate comparison with other periods. It is not only characterized by an uncommon clustering of cultural innovations, but also by a more sustained activation of innovative capacities; if there is some truth in Arnold Toynbee's conception of "creative minorities" as the representative and pioneering elites of whole civilizations, this would seem to be one of the corroborating cases (the coalitions of these minorities and power elites more directly involved in state- and empire-building seem to be a more variable factor than Eisenstadt's formulations on this subject would suggest). As for the long-term results, the creations of the Axial Age became defining cores of durable and formative traditions, which in turn (although to a varying degree) proved capable of further foundational developments (it seems best to avoid explicit reference to civilizations when defining the Axial Age, but I would of course argue that a civilizational perspective is—ultimately—the best way to make sense of the broader problematic involved in discussions about this period). Moreover, the founding ideas and interpretations of the Axial Age have—also to a varying degree—been recurrent foci of reinterpretations within the framework of the respective traditions; returns to the sources have thus helped to challenge dominant currents and established orthodoxies.

Axiality before and after the Axial Age?

Arguments in favor of the typological turn have often stressed a few salient examples that seem to settle all doubts about Axial turns occurring outside any particular epochal framework. It seems best to quote Assmann's comments on this point (1997, 290–292); he admits "a certain concentration" of the phenomena in question during the period singled out by Jaspers and others, but notes cases of transformations that followed fundamentally similar lines in other chronological settings, and argues that, in the last instance, we are not dealing with a distinctive historical epoch but with a cultural transformation that could occur at different points in time. The main point is the "transition from ritual to textual coherence" (ibid., 291), and neither the use of writing nor the creation of representative texts is a sufficient condition for this. The decisive factor is a culture of interpretation that makes the texts central to cultural memory, and which in turn presupposes supporting institutions and elites. Three breakthroughs before and after the conventionally defined Axial Age stand out: the religious innovation attempted by an Egyptian Pharaoh in the fourteenth century BCE, the emergence of Zoroastrianism in ancient Iran, and the formation of two monotheistic world religions—Christianity and Islam—in and beyond the eastern Roman world during the early centuries of our era. But as I will argue, these examples can be accounted for in a way that does not undermine the rehistoricizing approach.

Ikhnaton's vision of one god was, according to Assmann, "surely the most radical of all monotheistic revolutions" (1997, 291), and the texts that reflect it could have become foundational for a new religious culture; but there was no reinforcing culture of interpretation. Detailed analyses in Assmann's other writings suggest a more nuanced picture. The radicalism of this religious revolution seems to have been of a very specific kind, grounded in a historical context very different from that of the Axial Age. Assmann distinguishes Ikhnaton's revolutionary monotheism from the evolutionary variety that subsequently gained ground within Egyptian religion; the latter grew out of polytheism and avoided a radical break with it (Assmann 1993, 45). But if the revolutionary thrust invites comparison with the later rupture brought about by Jewish monotheism, another feature sets Ikhnaton's monotheism apart from that incomparably more momentous turn: his monotheism is cosmological rather than political, it takes the cosmotheistic aspect of Egyptian religion to extreme lengths at the expense of the polytheistic one, and has no implications of the kind associated with the idea of shifting sovereignty from a sacral ruler to a divine legislator. If there is a revealed side to this monotheism, it is only the "negative revelation" inherent in the "insight that God is only light and time" (1993, 33). As Assmann sees it, the emphasis on the visible world and human belonging to it is more reminiscent of the

Ionian philosophers than of Jewish monotheism, and suggests an even more far-reaching parallel with the French revolutionaries, who tried to engineer enlightenment through the foundation of a new religion. But if such retrospective affinities seem plausible, a closer look at the historical context will highlight their limits. Ikhnaton's monotheistic revolution did not question the institution of sacral kingship. On the contrary: the exclusive position of the ruler seems to have been enhanced by making him the only instance through which "the divine could be addressed as a person" (Assmann 1996, 247). All things considered, then, this episode illustrates the possibilities of religious innovation—and, *sit venia verbo,* enlightenment—within a cultural universe dominated by cosmotheism and an uncontested sacral power center. The Axial Age was to problematize these presuppositions in more fundamental ways.

The problem of Zoroastrianism calls for more detailed comments. In his discussion of the Axial Age, Robert Bellah reviews the question of a Persian contribution and concludes that we have to recognize a significant Persian impact on three of the well-documented cases (Greece, Palestine, and India), while Persia itself remains largely a historical cipher (Bellah 2005). This situation is all the more uncomfortable because of the role played by the Persian connection in earlier interpretations of the Axial Age. As has now been shown, the oldest documented vision of the Axial Age goes back to the eighteenth century: it grew out of Anquetil-Duperron's pioneering work on Zoroastrianism and its surviving heirs (it may be noted that Anquetil-Duperron seems to have built on this basis the most uninhibitedly metaphysical version of axiality ever proposed: "Il se fit alors dans la nature une espèce de révolution qui produisit dans plusieurs parties de la terre des Génies qui devoient donner le ton à l'univers" (quoted by Metzler 1991, 125). For Jaspers, Persia had become much less important, but it was more than a cipher. His references to Zoroastrian dualism do not amount to more than nominal inclusion among Axial breakthroughs, but when he distinguishes three worlds of the Axial Age—the Occident, India, and China—the demarcation of the first one seems to presuppose the Persian Empire. Jaspers uses Max Weber's broad concept of the Occident, without grounding it (as Weber did) in geographical or geo-economic considerations, and decisive encounters with the Persian Empire were—as he notes—the most significant thing that the Greek and the Jewish experience had in common. Apart from that, it is clear that Achaemenid expansion initiated a new phase in relations between the Near East and India, however difficult it may be to illustrate this in detail.

The issue is important enough to merit some further discussion. It boils down to two main points: the dating of Zoroaster's reform and the relationship between Zoroastrianism and the Achaemenid dynasty. On the former point, there is—notoriously—no consensus among scholars in the field. The view that Zoroaster can be dated to the second millennium BCE, perhaps even to the middle of that period, was forcefully defended by Mary Boyce, but it was always contested, and more recently, there has been a pronounced reaction against it—the results were becoming thoroughly implausible. Two of the most eminent authorities, Gherardo Gnoli and Shaul Shaked, have argued for the tenth or the ninth century BCE, which would put Zoroaster a good deal closer to the Axial Age. Shaked defends this view in his contribution to the Florence symposium on Axial civilizations (Shaked 2005); Gnoli linked it to a detailed analysis of the evidence for Zoroaster's homeland. He rejected the idea of Central Asian or Transoxanian origins and located Zoroaster in eastern or southeastern Iran, that is, a region that had gone through a particularly unsettling history. A precocious urbanizing process had been followed by regression and a partial reversion to pastoralism. This kind of background to Zoroaster's reform makes more sense than the picture of a pre-urban environment. But on top of this, there seems to have been a recent shift back to the traditional date (late seventh to sixth century BCE). The case for it was restated by Ilya Gershevitch in the mid-1990s and Gnoli has now come around to it (Gershevitch 1995; Gnoli 2000). In fact, Gnoli speaks explicitly about "restoring him [Zoroaster] to the axial age" (Gnoli 2000, 4) and proposes very precise dates: 618–541 BCE (for an unrepentant statement of the traditionalist view by somebody who never wavered, see Metzler 1991). The vast difference between the world of the Achaemenids and the world of the Gathas remains uncontested, but the question that has at least been reopened is: Exactly what combination of time and space would explain it?

That brings us back to the Achaemenid dynasty and its model of kingship. In my opinion, Gnoli, Shaked, and others have—notwithstanding the very scanty evidence—made a plausible case for the Achaemenids having been some kind of Zoroastrians, although not in a very orthodox or exclusive, and certainly not in a missionary, sense. The author of the most exhaustive account of the Achaemenid Empire seems to be leaning in the same direction when he stresses the special relationship between Ahura Mazda and the Great King, although he cautiously notes that "all these interpretations seem to be built on sand" (Briant 2002, 94). But the Achaemenid model of kingship is a more complex phenomenon: as Gnoli (1983, 62) puts it, it is "a meeting point of many conceptions and cultures." It took shape in the course of the astonishingly rapid rise of the Persian Empire. This was an unprecedented historical achievement, nothing less than a takeover of the whole ecumenic zone of the ancient Near East, not to be equaled until the eruption of Islam more than a millennium later. It is tempting to suggest that this could be the key to Persia's position in the Axial Age: a religious reform that had begun some time before the Achaemenids was partly instrumentalized and partly overshadowed by a multicivilizational version of sacral kingship. And Dieter Metzler's (1977) admittedly speculative conjectures about Zoroastrian involvement in the late sixth-century dynastic crisis do not seem far-fetched: the resistance to a kingship that was drawing closer to ancient Near Eastern patterns may well have sought a stronger Zoroastrian connection than the victorious monarch and his successors were to do.

Finally, a brief comment on Christianity and Islam is in order. The notion of a secondary breakthrough, tentatively used by Eisenstadt in earlier writings, has been abandoned: it cannot do justice to religious transformations that involved much more than reelaborations of Axial visions. From the rehistoricizing viewpoint defended here, it seems appropriate to situate the two monotheistic world religions within a new historical period, posterior to the Axial Age. As already noted by Jaspers, the ascendancy of empires was, for the most part, a post-Axial phenomenon (the Persian Empire appears as a precursor, with an unclear and probably ambiguous relationship to Axial religiosity). It is surely one of the most striking contingent parallels in world history that both the Roman and the Chinese empires took shape as such toward the end of the third century BCE. In both cases, but in very divergent ways, the consolidation of imperial power was accompanied by adaptive uses of Axial legacies. Different constellations emerged in the geopolitical and geocultural space between the eastern- and westernmost Eurasian zones. The Mauryan Empire in India was short-lived, fragmentation followed soon after the fifth-century culmination under Ashoka, and no later attempt resulted in a durable indigenous tradition of imperial rule. In the Near East, the Macedonian takeover of the Persian Empire proved unsustainable, but the outcome was a stalemate: neither the Hellenistic kingdoms nor the half-restored Iranian realm under the Parthians could aspire to imperial power on the Achaemenid scale. The Sasanian state that replaced the Parthians in the third century BCE was a stronger contender, but could not prevail against the expanded Mediterranean empire of the Romans. It was in this new historical environment that the world religions took shape, and their new universalism—more emphatic than Axial precedents—was related to imperial visions, though not always in the same way. It can be argued that Buddhism is more directly linked to Axial beginnings than Christianity or Islam, but the definitive transformation of Buddhism into a missionary world religion seems to have coincided with Ashoka's imperial zenith; the religious innovation survived the political one, and Buddhism (further transformed by the ascendancy of the Mahayana branch) went on to profit from both the crisis and the reconsolidation of the Chinese Empire, as well as from the restructuring of emerging East Asian states along the lines of the Chinese model. By contrast, the imperial vacuum in the Near East was finally overcome by a new religion that became a direct carrier of an imperial vision. It is a measure of the limited impact of the Sasanians that they had neither taken their reactivation of the link to Zoroastrianism to the level of a full-fledged imperial religion, nor continued the brief third-century rapprochement with an aspiring world religion that was to gain adherents in both the East and West but failed to establish itself on an enduring basis. As the outstanding case of an ambitious but ultimately unsuccessful world religion, Manichaeism deserves a more prominent place in comparative studies than it has hitherto been granted.

Parallels and Divergences

All attempts to go beyond this very general characterization of the Axial Age have focused on a configuration of parallels and contrasts. Some consideration has always been given to the contrasts: no account of the Axial Age could ignore the antagonism between Athens and Jerusalem, nor was it ever possible to understand Confucius and Buddha as pursuing the same goals. But there has, from Jaspers to current debates, been a certain shift of emphasis from the parallels to the contrasts and divergences. Notwithstanding

Eisenstadt's focus on "transcendental visions" as the prime defining feature of Axial civilizations, his analyses allow for more pluralism than Jaspers' model of the Axial awakening could do. Constructive critics of Eisenstadt's interpretation have moved further in that direction. And if we think of the Axial problematic as an unfolding research program, it seems best to treat this aspect as an open question: more work on comparative history is needed before we can attempt a more balanced assessment of unity and diversity in the Axial Age. Another open question relates to the parallels as such, and to the underlying unity that has been inferred from them. It is still a matter of debate whether—or more precisely: to what extent—these parallels are contingent or due to identifiable historical connections. At this stage, it seems clear that the most visible connection between Axial centers is an indirect one. The rise and expansion of the Persian Empire decisively affected both Greek and Jewish history, albeit in very different ways; Persian presence in and influence on India clearly marked a new round of interregional contacts, but details are very hard to document. Persian rule in the Near East was the culminating phase of a process that began when eighth-century Assyria embarked on an unprecedented project of world empire; this was the starting-point for the Near Eastern sequence (both real and imaginary) of world empires, and more peripheral parts of the region, including the exceptionally creative "seedbed societies" (Talcott Parsons) of ancient Greece and ancient Israel, were drawn into the process (in earlier discussions, it was occasionally suggested that the Assyrians were on the verge of an "Axial breakthrough," but the evidence does not seem convincing). At the other end of the spectrum, the question of early contacts between India and China is now more vigorously debated than before. Some speculations seem excessive (e.g., claims about Buddhist influence on Daoist thought), but it is probably best to see this controversy as a revision in progress; there was more interaction across the Eurasian macroregion, before and during the Axial Age, than earlier historians tended to think.

To rehistoricize the Axial Age, that is, to bring historiographical and sociological constructs closer to historical experience, is—as the above considerations suggest—to bring more diversity into the evolving accounts of the period. This has so far mainly been done in terms of different paths taken by different civilizations during their Axial phase. But here I will focus on the institutional and interpretive pluralism that may be seen as a precondition for historical differentiation. The divergent paths of traditions or civilizations result from combinations of developments in these different fields. The dominant tendency among interpreters of the Axial Age has been to emphasize the role of explicit cultural (i.e., primarily religious and/or philosophical) elaborations. A more pluralistic view would take into account the immanent logic and ongoing self-reflection of other spheres. Developments in the economic sphere have, on the whole, not figured prominently in the debate. But one somewhat puzzling case should be noted in passing: the question of "money and the early Greek mind"—to quote the title of a recent book (Seaford 2004)—seems to have survived the Marxist answers that for a while gave it a bad name. It can be argued that a monetizing process, much more rapid and pervasive than anything seen in the ancient Near East, was an integral part of the new form of life commonly identified with the *polis;* more controversially, Richard Seaford (2004, 315) maintains that this process "was an important factor in the genesis and form of the first 'philosophy' and of tragedy." This view, not to be confused with the economic reductionism of some earlier accounts, merits a discussion that has hardly begun. More has been said—and more remains to be said—on political transformations. An interpretation of ancient Greek history, developed most eloquently by Christian Meier and Kurt Raaflaub, puts politics (in Meier's terms: "the emergence of the political") at the center of the Axial turn in Greece. Both Meier and Raaflaub have a rather ambivalent attitude toward Axial theorizing, but their arguments are highly relevant to the issue to be discussed here. The primacy of the political manifests itself on several levels. The *polis* represents a new form of political life, more precisely a fundamentally antimonarchic one, with direct and indirect implications affecting the whole social world; it is from the outset conducive to political reflection of a new kind, not to be confused with the more detached political theory that emerges from later crises (Raaflaub has made this distinction very clear); the *polis* also favored the development of philosophical reflection open to broader horizons and engaged in a complex dialogue with other cultural domains. This thesis (one is tempted to call it a model of political axiality) is, especially in Meier's work, linked to a strong defense of Greek uniqueness. There is something to be said for that view (Meier's description of ancient Greece as "das Nadelöhr der Weltgeschichte" does not seem inappropriate), but it has to be handled with care, and when it is linked to the claim that the Greeks—alone among the civilizations of the Axial Age—invented or discovered "das Politische," it oversteps the mark. It would seem more fruitful to use the Greek encounter with the political as a starting point for comparison with other centers of the Axial Age. The most striking example of similarly momentous changes with very different long-term consequences is China during the "Spring and Autumn" and "Warring States" periods. Several trends unfolding from the eighth century BCE onward problematized the political sphere and provoked reflection on its fundamentals as well as strategies for overcoming its crises. The Chinese experienced the multicentrality of the political field through interstate competition on a more massive scale than anywhere else at the time, and through a generalized disruption of hierarchy that brought new contenders for power into the field. Both these processes undermined the previously very close connection between the political and the sacral sphere. On the intellectual level, they led to a systematic elaboration of state-centered rationality, most frequently identified with the current known as Legalism, but to some extent observable in other contexts. But the critical responses were more characteristic of the Chinese Axial Age and more important for the profile of Chinese civilization. A traditionalist but at the same time humanizing countercurrent aimed at a reintegration of the political sphere through a mixture of ritual, cultivation, morality, and wisdom (exactly how these components fitted together in the original Confucian message, and how their interrelations were modified in later Confucian thought, is less relevant to our present concerns). But a shared notion of cosmic order could also be turned into an imaginary space for detachment and liberation from the constraints and dangers of the political domain.

There is thus a prominent political side to the Chinese Axial Age, even if there is no Chinese parallel to the Greek rejection of monarchy. Can we speak of political elements or implications in the other cases? If we follow Assmann's interpretation of ancient Israel (as the present writer is inclined to do), the idea of the divine legislator—the most decisive aspect of the monotheistic turn—represents a very radical devaluation of the political sphere. It emerged in the then most global political context, that is, interimperial competition in the Near East, but it grew into a critique of the domestic monarchic tradition, whose mythologized origins were used to delegitimize a more problematic present. As for India, Louis Dumont and J. C.

Heesterman have insisted on the close but nevertheless competitive relationship between brahmins and kshatriyas; however difficult it may be to reconstruct its early stages and transformations, it seems clear that the outcome was a very distinctive distribution of power and authority, leaving kingship in a particularly exposed position (according to Heesterman [1985, 108], "nowhere is the problematic character of kingship clearer than in the Indian case"; that is another way of saying that the political sphere was problematized, but neither in the Greek nor in the Chinese way).

Excursus I: Schwartz on the Chinese Axial Age

As we have seen, closer examination of the Chinese case suggests ways of thinking about more general issues. A detour through an original and carefully argued but not widely discussed interpretation of the Axial Age may help to take this perspective further. Benjamin Schwartz's work, beginning with his contribution to the 1975 *Daedalus* workshop (to which he seems to have given a more clearly defined direction than any of the other participants), and continuing on a much more massive scale in his history of ancient Chinese thought (Schwartz 1985), represents—so far—the most articulate China-centered perspective on the epoch in question; as such, it becomes especially interesting when set alongside the dominant accounts that have tended to privilege the Greek and Jewish patterns of cultural change (that applies, though not in the same way, to Jaspers and Eisenstadt; it might even be argued that later developments, more precisely the typological turn, shift the Greco-Judaic focus toward a more restrictive Platonic Christian one). Schwartz's Chinese corrective begins with a minimalist description of the Axial opening to transcendence. It is, as he argues, best understood in a broadly existential rather than a definite contextual sense: as a way of "standing back and looking beyond." It would, I think, be more than a play on words to suggest that the Chinese case, with which Schwartz is mainly concerned, can also be understood in inverse order: "standing beyond and looking back." As Schwartz sees it, the most novel aspect of the Confucian turn—the overture to the Chinese age of transcendence—was the emergence of the autonomous thinker, stepping beyond the established social division of labor and thus gaining a vantage point for a new kind of retrospective insight into a whole tradition.

Schwartz's "standing back and looking beyond" acquires a more concrete meaning in the context of his reconstruction of the Chinese "world of thought." Although the work is first and foremost a history of classical Chinese philosophy, it contains comparative reflections that add up to a distinctive vision of the Axial Age, and the most interesting points are made in connection with the Confucian beginnings of classical thought. Schwartz links the attitudes sometimes seen as characteristically Confucian to a general reappraisal of the Axial turn. The starting point is the widely shared view that a this-worldly stance sets Confucius apart from other key figures of the Axial Age; Schwartz objects: "The God of the Bible is transcendental, but what he reveals to Moses is a decidedly this-worldly law; Plato's philosophy may have other-worldly possibilities, but he himself remains devoted in varying degree to his this-worldly mission. Even in India, the Brahmanism of the Upanishads is still deeply committed to the worldly duties of the householder, despite the proliferation of individual ascetics. Only primitive Buddhism seems to call for radical renunciation, for those prepared for the monk's vocation" (Schwartz 1985, 118). Even the Buddhist exception can, on closer examination, be reduced to less radical dimensions. Schwartz refers to the more specific portrayal of Confucius as not just a this-worldly thinker, but a humanistic and pragmatic one, and goes on to argue:

> Again, this pragmatism does not differentiate him notably from great religious figures and wise men of the other contemporary civilizations. While Moses and the prophets may be "god-centered," they are not theologians, and the diverse revelations which they receive all direct their attention back to the concern with the salvation of man. The historic Buddha himself, we are often told in the literature, was a "humanistic" pragmatist whose main and overwhelming concern was with saving humans from the sea of suffering. His "eight-fold path" certainly dwelt above all on the human ethical-spiritual prerequisites for achieving this goal. In one sutra, he is made to dwell at length on a whole series of speculative metaphysical problems which do not "tend to edification" and should be avoided. In the case of Socrates we find, of course, a constant discussion of his "humanistic revolt" against the whole tradition of pre-Socratic natural philosophy and his turn to human concerns—a revolt which he shared with the "Sophists." . . .

If all these figures are, in a sense, pragmatists bent on achieving human ends, it would appear that there really is no such thing as "humanistic pragmatism" in a vacuum and that all pragmatisms tacitly presuppose certain images of the larger frame of things in terms of which pragmatic goals are set and pursued." (118–119)

These encompassing images may be treated as domains of tacit knowledge, but that does not make them less essential to the explicit levels of discourse: "The assertion that Confucius did not discuss the '*tao* of Heaven' does not mean that he had no beliefs about the *tao*" (ibid., 119). Finally, this survey of parallels and affinities leads to a general conclusion: "In all these civilizations the axial age is in fact marked by a kind of transcendental ethical reaction against the total world involvement of the religion of previous centuries, but in most cases this reaction does not necessarily assume an extreme other-worldly form" (ibid., 118).

Schwartz's reflections call for further comments, with particular reference to the assumptions and questions implicit in his statements. The first point to note is that the "total world involvement" mentioned in the last quotation is not an archaic legacy of prehistorical cultures. As Schwartz makes clear elsewhere in the book, he is primarily referring to the dynamics and results of early civilizing processes, and more specifically to the competitive—often mutually destructive—accumulation of wealth and power, as well as to the luxurious lifestyles based on both these kinds of resources. The Axial turns are responses to cultural trends and behavioral patterns seen as endangering or degrading the civilizations within which both kinds of developments—the excesses and the protest—take place; no interpreter of the Axial Age has stressed this connection as strongly as Schwartz did (the focus on China seems to have made it particularly visible, because of the intensive forms of accumulation that emerged in the "Warring States"). Given the close links between religion and social power, the Axial protest had to target inadequate and perverted forms of religious life. And if the response can be described as an "ethical reaction," this term should not be taken to suggest a one-sided emphasis on moral principles or doctrines. The Axial visions are more comprehensive: they have to do with new ways of being in the world. For analysts arguing in light of later differentiations, it is tempting to distinguish between moral, cognitive, and aesthetic aspects. But when it comes to comparing civilizations of the Axial Age, it is more rewarding to focus on the different overall patterns that combine the three dimensions. Although there has never been any doubt about the very prominent place of morality in Confucian teachings, the relative weight of cognitive, moral, and aesthetic moments in the original Confucian vision is uncertain enough to have sparked an unending controversy. At this point, we cannot enter into detailed discussion of the whole Axial spectrum, but let us note in passing that even if Schwartz seems to accept a rather traditional view of Socrates' dissent from the Pre-Socratics, more recent scholarship has moved our understanding of early Greek philosophy closer to the Axial paradigm as summed up in the above quotation: the line of interpretation pioneered by Pierre Hadot has drawn attention to the search for a way of life inherent in philosophical reflection from the beginning.

The rejection of humanly impoverishing or ethically inferior attitudes and relations to the world goes hand in hand with the elaboration of alternative models (the latter may, with varying degrees of justification, be presented as revivals of older traditions). The more radical versions of this reorientation open up "other-worldly possibilities," as Schwartz puts it. His formulations suggest a point that merits further development and discussion: it may not be easy to draw a line between this-worldly and other-worldly trends in Axial thought. The attempt to "look beyond" the boundaries of a given world is fundamental, but whether it results in a clear vision of another world altogether may be a matter of debate for contemporary participants as well as later interpreters. In any case, we should distinguish between Axial beginnings and post-Axial articulations of other-worldliness. The reminder that the prophets were not theologians should be seen in this context. Theology in the strict sense is the joint offspring of metaphysics and monotheism, and thus a combined product of two different traditions that emerged during the Axial Age. In more general terms, the hypothesis implicit in Schwartz's reflections may be summed up as follows: instead of drawing a sharp distinction between this-worldly and other-worldly directions of the Axial turn, we should allow for some initial indeterminacy in this regard, and for the possibility that some civilizations might be more durably attuned to this condition than others; the most emphatic expressions of other-worldly attitudes grew out of developments posterior to the Axial Age, and at least in some prominent cases, they drew on multitraditional sources.

The uncertain range of "other-worldly possibilities" is not unrelated to another point mentioned in the above quotation. The tacitly presupposed "images of the larger frame of things" may be a more significant aspect of the Axial constellations than the most influential accounts have wanted to admit. The problematic of these implicit visions becomes, as Schwartz notes, particularly significant when they serve to back up—broadly speaking—pragmatic projects with a narrower focus. The "assertion" about Confucius, quoted by Schwartz, can in fact be read as more than that. When a disciple says, "The Master's cultural accomplishments—we get to hear them, but the Master's ideas on human nature and the Way of Heaven—we hardly get to hear them" (*Analects* 5.13, trans. Huang 1997), the most plausible interpretation is that more could be done to spell out the tacit knowledge behind an explicit message; later protagonists of Confucian thought did just that, but in ways that brought unsettled questions out into the open and gave rise to alternatives within the tradition. The assumption of a tacit—not ipso facto unimportant or unproblematic—conception of Heaven and its Way runs counter to the idea of an unequivocally "secular" turn, often attributed to Confucius, and it seems even less compatible with the radical indifferentism posited by A. C. Graham ("it is not so much that he [Confucius] is a sceptic as that he does not care whether you are a sceptic or not" [Graham 1989, 15]; but how is this claim to be reconciled with statements to the effect that "Confucius may be seen to fluctuate between a faith that Heaven will protect his mission and despair that Heaven has abandoned him," and that he "struggles to understand 'destiny' [*ming*, literally 'decree' what Heaven has decreed]?" [ibid., 17]) Apart from textual indications, a more general consideration may be adduced. It seems more than unlikely that Confucius' emphatic commitment to the legacy of the Zhou dynasty could have been accompanied by a wholesale devaluation of the relationship to Heaven that was known—or assumed—to have been central to the self-understanding of the Zhou tradition.

To sum up, the Confucian case exemplifies the general question of underlying frameworks that remain implicit in crucial expressions of the Axial turn, and then become focal themes for conflicting interpretations during later phases. The relationship between implicit and explicit visions can vary from one civilizational context to another, and more comparative study of that topic would be instructive. The cases in point include borderline developments, such as Plato's unwritten doctrine. Broad agreement has now been reached on a few basic points (see especially Reale 1997). The unwritten teachings were not of the kind later known as esoteric; they were spelt out for a limited audience under restrictive circumstances; they did not represent a break with the problematic of Plato's dialogues but rather a continuation of the same project in different terms. All this makes them a distinctive and significant offshoot of the Greek Axial Age, and a rewarding topic for the comparative history of philosophy.

Toward a Pluralistic Model

It remains to consider more closely the case for pluralism within the domain of the cultural elaborations mentioned above. It has proved difficult to subsume the whole spectrum of the Axial Age under an idea of transcendence à la Jaspers; critics have also noted problems with Eisenstadt's broader conception of "transcendental visions," as well as with the strict dichotomy of this- and other-worldly versions of them. The phenomenological idea of world articulation and its cultural variations may help to construct a less prejudiced frame of reference. To retain a link to the earlier discussion, the concept of "transcensus" (as distinct from both transcendence and transcendentality) occasionally used by Jan Patočka, may be useful. What Patočka had in mind was the human relationship to the world, and more precisely the mixture of involvement and freedom that characterizes all human cultures, even if the different aspects do not always intertwine in the same way. From this point of view, the historical conceptions and figures of transcendence can be deciphered as interpretive projections of the existential transcensus. One implication to be noted is that there can be no condition of untroubled and quasi-natural absorption in the world: constructions of ontological continuity are always superimposed on underlying tensions between life-world contexts and transcending human capacities. Even when this basic point is accepted (as it is in Eisenstadt's general social theory), it is not clear that the consequences have been given their due, especially not in relation to the contrast between Axial and pre-Axial cultures. Jaspers' notion of "unawakened cultures" is no longer explicitly defended by anybody, but descriptions of a pre-Axial continuity between nature, society, and culture sometimes come uncomfortably close to it. Following Lévi-Strauss and later discussions inspired by his work, even the thought of pre-state and preliterate societies can now be understood as a sustained effort to neutralize basic differences, rather than as marked by a simple inability to grasp them, and constructs of undifferentiated modes of thought are a fortiori implausible when it comes to archaic civilizations. On the other hand, new constructions of ontological continuity, striving to minimize the impact of ruptures and tensions discovered during a phase of intensified reflexivity, can appear in the aftermath of Axial transformations. If we want to distinguish the Axial Age from earlier historical epochs, that cannot be done on the basis of a simple contrast between the presence and absence of differentiation; the question must be posed in terms of changing modes of interplay between differentiating and unifying trends. This phenomenological connection is proposed here as a tentative hypothesis, and the first steps will be enough to show that we will not get much further without closer cooperation of comparative historians and area specialists. To avoid misunderstandings, it should be noted that I am not equating specific attitudes to the world with particular cultural formations. The categories suggested below recur in different contexts; they enter into varying combinations, and the comparison of different Axial patterns can only be developed in terms of such combinations—even if specific orientations are more highly developed in some cases than others. That said, I would—as a first step—propose to distinguish five ways of relating to the world, or directions of world articulation, that are especially important to cultural developments during the Axial Age. This does not necessarily imply that all of them are equally new when compared to trends in archaic civilizations (especially Egypt and Mesopotamia); there is room for variation in that respect, and also in the overall relationship of cultures of the Axial Age to their archaic precursors.

Aspects and Directions of World Articulation

(a) The first aspect to note is explicit *world articulation as such*, the beginning of a "sagesse du monde" (Rémi Brague brought this theme into debates on the Axial Age, but his analysis has not been as widely discussed as it deserves). This explicit conception of the world seems to be the most fundamental Greek achievement (more fundamental than the idea of exclusive theoretical truth), without parallel in the cultures of the ancient Near East.

Several phases may be distinguished. Philosophical reflection begins with the explication of an underlying *Vorverständnis* of the world; it goes on to develop more structured and reasoned models of cosmic order; finally, the notion of cosmic order takes a turn that brings it closer to the vision of another world (how close is still being debated). This is the Platonic moment, but it is neither unequivocal nor irreversible. The ambiguity underlined in Schwartz's comments on Plato, quoted above, also applies to the translation of the doctrine of ideas into positive cosmology: the status and significance of Plato's ventures into this field is as disputed as the meaning of his political projects. And as Brague's (1999, 41–86) discussion stresses, other modes of interpretation—including, in particular, the atomistic school—endured and gave rise to new variants. This point can probably be taken further. It seems likely that the originality of Stoic cosmological conceptions would be more easily acknowledged if the sources had survived in more adequate shape. But in regard to the Greek trajectory as a whole, a further aspect should be underlined. The shift toward explicit world articulation is at the same time a change in conceptions of the divine and the beginning of a dialogue between philosophy and religion that has been noted (see especially Humphreys 2004) but not sufficiently recognized as characteristic of the Greek Axial Age. If rational theology, in a broad sense, is a Greek invention and a prominent thematic focus of Greek thought, this should be a starting point for comparative perspectives. To mention only one case, it can hardly be claimed that rational theology ranks among the inventions of the Chinese Axial Age, but it may be possible to identify another path that bears at least some resemblance to the Greek one. The notion of *dao*, generally seen as the most central but also one of the most elastic ideas of the Chinese tradition, and particularly central to the intellectual movements of the Axial Age, seems to have connected efforts to depersonalize the notion of divinity to evolving conceptions of a cosmic order. Despite growing interest in comparing ancient Greece and ancient China, there has been—to the best of my knowledge—no extensive discussion of these affinities.

(b) Another major shift is perhaps best described as a *recentering* of the world. The logic of recentering is most evident when grasped in opposition to the archaic center par excellence: the institution of sacred kingship, and the most emphatic recentering is the Jewish invention of monotheism. In other cases, recentering can take more pluralistic and/or impersonal forms.

To clarify the differences as well as affinities between different Axial paths, we should distinguish between cosmic and human centers. The institutionalized notion of sacred kingship (or, in broader and less specifically archaic terms, sacral rulership) links these two levels, and when its foundations are problematized, new perspectives emerge on both sides. As otherwise different interpreters of the Greek *polis*—from Jean-Pierre Vernant to Meier—have stressed, the crisis of sovereignty and the new vision of power as situated in the midst of a multipolar political field changed the very idea of center. The *polis* religion that was an integral part of the new form of social life was the outcome of a restructuring process (some historians have speculated about a religious revolution), too elusive for any specific conjectures, but in any case less radical than the political transformation in that it left more space for a supreme and central authority. The personalized idea of divinity was transformed in a more radical way by philosophical reflection, but this did not have an impact comparable to the unfolding political dynamic. Alongside these developments, the imaginary signification of kingship survived in less institutionalized forms, and together with other factors, this created preconditions for the reemergence of sacral rulership in a new context.

A different but comparably complex constellation developed in China during the Axial Age. A particularly intensive phase of state formation unsettled the traditional bonds between rulership and the sacral order (although the ritual frameworks of statehood remained strong). A central current of Chinese thought during this period strove to reestablish the connection between political authority and an inherited vision of order, temporarily disturbed and therefore in need of reflection and instruction. At the same time, alternative notions of order pursued decentering in a way much less amenable to ideological uses by rulers (that is at least a possible interpretation of some "ways of Taoism," to use Schwartz's formulation). In the end, however, an elaborately reconstructed and exceptionally durable version of sacral rulership prevailed and presided over a selective canonization of Axial ideas.

The resurgences of sacral rulership, along different lines in the East and West, are easier to understand if we accept that even its archaic form was never an invariant and unproblematic anchor of order. Recent scholarship on archaic civilizations, especially those of the Near East, has highlighted changes to the conception of kingship over a long period and redefined differences between traditions—for example, those of Egypt and Mesopotamia—in more nuanced terms than before. Moreover, the question of sacred kingship can be linked to the problematic of human being-in-the-world. The sacred (in extreme cases divine, but never wholly and solely) ruler exemplifies the summit but also the limits of human perfection; his status is defined within a broader framework of assumptions about the constraints, possibilities, and orientations inherent in human relations to the world; his authority is embedded in more complex structures of hierarchy. But reflections on sacred kingship and the human condition are also bound to remind us of pre-Axial sources: the epic of Gilgamesh is the oldest recorded elaboration of these themes.

(c) It seems justified to speak of *world negation* as a specific mode. This is the most distinctively Indian contribution to Axial traditions, and an overall interpretation that takes it as a starting point will be discussed in the excursus below. But a few general remarks are in order. "World negation" is, in the given context, a more adequate term than the Weberian "world rejection." The world is envisioned as a place to escape from, rather than a defective order to be reformed or subdued, and there is no reason to regard this attitude as a first step toward the more activist stance that Weber ascribed to the Occidental versions of world rejection. In the Axial Age, a reformist ethos—the aspiration to build, in some sense, a better order—was associated with religious and intellectual orientations of the kind that Weber called world-accepting (that applies to Greek and Chinese visions of a better order, as well as—in a very different way—to the prophetic current in ancient Judaism), rather than with world-negating radicalism. If the latter is preeminently characteristic of the Indian Axial Age, it must be added that its more specific meanings are still very much a matter of debate. The chronological as well as the substantive relationship between Buddhist and proto-Hindu versions of world negation is controversial; the historical relationship between these divergent currents and the rivalry of priests and warriors is not easy to decipher; and some interpretations of early Buddhism suggest that its world-negating ethos was associated with a more inner-worldly ethic adapted to the stronger kingdoms emerging at the time.

(d) There is also, in varying degree across the spectrum of Axial cultures, a shift toward *world extension* (the German term *Welterweiterung* may be suggested in passing). There are two sides to this, a spatial and a temporal one: the discovery and/or imagination of other human forms of life elsewhere, and a growing grasp of "the past as another country"—in other words: some kind of deepening of the "cultural split between antiquity and modernity," to quote Assmann's formulation. Here we have the earliest beginnings of comparative cultural reflection as well as of historiography (Herodotus has come to be regarded as a founding father of the second, but his work is in fact even more relevant to the first). The temporal side raises the question of what Aleida and Jan Assmann call cultural memory. From a phenomenological-hermeneutical point of view, cultural memory appears as one of the world-articulating capacities or dispositions of human societies, and it intertwines with other such capacities in varying ways. Its transformations and potentialities depend on writing as a cultural medium, but when Assmann stresses the distinction between writing systems and writing cultures, and argues against the simplistic "media determinism" defended by some earlier writers on this subject, the other side of that is that a writing culture is always embedded in and codetermined by a broader cultural constellation, and what is being suggested here is that these broader contexts can be deciphered as complexes of relationships to the world.

(e) Finally, it can be argued that the Axial Age saw a shift toward *humanization,* in the sense of a new and enhanced kind of human participation in ordering the world. But care must be taken to avoid absolutizing and overgeneralizing descriptions of this turn. Humanization does not mean the same thing—nor does it lead to the same kind of distinction between a human and a nonhuman world—in Greece and China, the two places where such trends became most significant. The other two key cases seem more ambiguous. There is a humanizing side to the idea of the covenant, but the idea of the divine legislator has the potential for a very radical negation of human autonomy. As for India: can we—as some interpreters have suggested—understand early Buddhism as a humanizing twist to the idea of renouncement? Here I can only signal issues to be explored, and it seems fitting to end on that note. The above suggestions on the phenomenology of world articulation are meant to open up ways of reorienting the debate on the Axial Age, rather than to outline a self-contained model.

Excursus II: Dumont on the Indian Axial Age

As far as I can judge, there has been no India-based approach to the Axial Age that could be compared to Schwartz's work on China (and it is probably true that analysts working with Western models—in the sense of Weber's European-cum–Near Eastern Occident—have, because of the supposedly common focus on transcendence, found it easier to assimilate the Indian experience than the Chinese one). But if we look for adumbrations of a view from India, one obvious choice is Dumont's contribution to the 1975 *Daedalus* discussion. It seems to have gone largely unnoticed by later scholarship, but as I will try to show, it poses problems that will have to be confronted by any interpretation aspiring to comprehensive coverage of Axial transformations.

Before he was drawn into the debate on the Axial Age, Dumont had already developed a comprehensive framework that placed a uniquely strong emphasis on India as the traditional society par excellence, to be contrasted with the very different model of social order that emerged in the modern West. From his point of view, the idea of a broader historical category, encompassing major traditional civilizations and drawing them closer to modernity, was therefore a challenge to basic assumptions. Dumont was quick to dismiss strong claims about parallel developments: "they recede or disintegrate when one tries to grasp them more precisely" (1975, 153). For our purposes it is more important that he went on to sketch an alternative model of contrasts that presupposed a common ground; the Axial Age thus returned as a topic for comparative analysis, but in a shape very different from the mainstream images. For Dumont, the starting point had to be India, and given his Durkheimian presuppositions, it was natural to stress institutional developments and innovations. However, his version of the institutionalist approach did not differ from the otherwise current emphasis on ideas in Axial theorizing, as first impressions might suggest. The institutions in which Dumont was interested—especially the institution of kingship—had a particularly strong interpretive content. They were "meta-institutions," in the sense often used with reference to Émile Durkheim's work, that is, frameworks lending meaning and direction to the formation of more circumscribed institutions. In the case of kingship, and more particularly sacred kingship, the inbuilt idea is a notion (in Cornelius Castoriadis's terms:

an imaginary signification) of sovereignty, which on the one hand lends itself to extension into more or less elaborate patterns of socio-cosmic order, and can on the other hand become a regulating principle for the distribution of social power. In the Indian case, the institution of kingship underwent a particularly momentous process of differentiation. The story begins, as Dumont sees it, with the Indo-Aryan invasion or immigration, and its first formative phase ends with a "proto-Hindu agricultural society with its center in the middle-Ganges region and a distinct polity which is on the verge of developing into a large empire" (1975, 162). With regard to the starting point, Dumont accepts Georges Dumézil's account of an original Indo-European conception of sovereignty, characterized by a strong magico-religious component. The Vedas already reflect an unusually extreme development of this aspect; the historical outcome is a bifurcation of sovereignty, elevating priestly authority above its political counterpart and redefining kingship as "secularized while subordinated" (ibid., 162). The caste order crystallized around this asymmetrically split center. As Dumont's critics have argued, the relationship between kings and priests was more contested, and attempts to readjust the balance in favor of kings more significant than he thought. But here it seems more relevant to note some additional features of his model. The primary distinction between priests and kings (or, in a broader sociological sense, between priests and warriors) is accompanied by the formation of a "peculiar social role outside society proper: the renouncer" (ibid., 163). Although Dumont's genealogy of the renouncer is not always clearly formulated, this is a key aspect of his argument, and some implications should be underlined.

Dumont's image of the renouncer presupposes a specific interpretation of the Indian Axial Age: the decisive change takes place between the Vedas and the Upanishads, and Buddhism appears as nothing more than a variation on proto-Hindu themes, developed by a later generation of renouncers. Other analysts of Axial India have stressed the originality of Buddhism and portrayed it as the most representative product of the epoch; this debate reflects divergent assumptions and is not likely to be settled soon. For Dumont, the figure of the renouncer was invented in the course of the very process that established priesthood as the suprapolitical level of authority. The logic of his argument seems to be that the Brahmin bid for primacy triggered a reflective and imaginative effort transcending the original goal and culminating in a new type of authority that entered into a paradoxical relationship with the priestly one. The renouncer internalized and transfigured sacrifice into ascetic exercises; he could thus be seen as the perfect embodiment of aspirations inherent in the priestly model, but also as the higher instance questioning "priestly representations" (Dumont 1975, 163). What he stood for was "not a revolutionary or reforming, but a relativizing attitude" (ibid.). It is important to note that Dumont describes the existential orientation of the renouncer as "outworldly," rather than other-worldly: the common denominator is an effort to maximize distance from the world, and the other-worldly dimensions thus opened up can be defined in different ways. The emphasis on the "outworldly" stance thus helps to minimize the differences between Hinduism and Buddhism. It is also a key to the dynamics of Indian cultural history. Distance translates into innovative capacities: for Dumont, "the inventions of the renouncers and their sects and the interaction between them and the religion of the man-in-the-world are the vital factors of Indian history, something like the basic 'principle of becoming' of Indian civilization" (ibid., 167).

The Indian Axial Age, as analyzed by Dumont, is characterized by a differentiation between religion and politics. But some qualifications must be added to this description. Dumont uses the concept of differentiation in an emphatically nonevolutionistic sense. It can, in his view, only refer to concrete historical processes, each of which generates its own patterns. In the case at hand we are not dealing with a progressive separation of general principles following their immanent logic; rather, the story begins with the primary institution of kingship, and the changes that it undergoes in a concrete historical setting result in the constitution of separate but interconnected forms of religious and political life. A further crucially important aspect of Dumont's model is the role of the renouncer. On the social level, the separation of priesthood and kingship appears as the most massive and at the same time most meaning-laden expression of a process that draws new boundaries between religious and military elites. But when the cultural context is taken into account, it becomes clear that the binary division is accompanied and modified by a third line of differentiation: the emerging religious culture of renouncement.

With these points in mind we can return to Dumont's India-centered survey of the Axial Age. He first distinguishes a strong and a weak hypothesis. The strong one would claim that the flowering of intellectual life during the Axial Age—a salient and indubitable fact—presupposes a differentiation between religion and politics. According to Dumont, the Chinese experience refutes this thesis: the intellectual achievements of the Chinese Axial Age are beyond doubt, but the unity of religion and politics remained a defining feature of the Chinese imperial order. He then goes on:

> If its case proves intractable, that is, if some unsuspected equivalent to the differentiation cannot be discovered there, then the weaker thesis could be proposed that the previous evolution of kingship—i.e., what happened to the *basileus* in Greece, the relationship between kings and prophets in Israel, the secularization of kingship in India, the permanence of the archetype in China—should have important concomitants regarding the orientation or "dimension" of the intellectual developments in each case. This time, the case of China seems to admit and confirm the thesis by its wholesale and relative "this-worldly" orientation. (Dumont 1975, 166)

We can disregard the speculation about an "equivalent to the differentiation" and adjust the statement about a "previous evolution of kingship"—as even a quick look at Dumont's own reflections on India will show, he is in fact discussing interconnected processes, rather than successive stages. That said, Dumont's overview of the Axial cases is still worth closer examination. It is inadequate, but its very shortcomings are instructive. The "weak thesis" is never formulated in a way that would do justice to available knowledge about the Axial Age. In the first place, it is—as has been seen—more than a little misleading to talk about a Chinese "permanence of the archetype." Sacral rulership was reconstructed after a very eventful phase of several centuries. "[W]hat happened to the *basileus*" is a very cautious reference to radical changes that must be analyzed in more complex terms. In regard to ancient Israel, the most obvious problem with Dumont's description is that the priests are missing. The triangle of kings, priests, and prophets would invite comparison with its Indian counterpart—kings, priests, and renouncers—and closer examination of contrasts and parallels between different roads beyond sacred kingship.

In short, it is not at all clear what the weaker thesis would maintain and how it could be tested. What remains is a useful suggestion: that the debate on the Axial Age would benefit from closer analysis of the diverse and changing relations between religion and politics. Despite a lingering tendency to overemphasize "secularizing" trends in Greece and China during the Axial Age, the religious factors involved in these two very different patterns of political change are now being studied more attentively; Assmann's interpretation of ancient Israel in the context of its Near Eastern environment has thrown new light on the political implications of one of the two most radical religious transformations of the period. The other one is the emergence of Buddhism, and even if doubts can be cast on the details of Dumont's account, his questions seem worth pursuing.

References

Arnason, Johann P., Shmuel N. Eisenstadt, and Björn Wittrock, eds. 2005. *Axial Civilizations and World History*. Leiden: Brill.
Assmann, Jan. 1993. *Monotheismus und Kosmotheismus*. Heidelberg: Winter.
———. 1996. *Ägypten—Eine Sinngeschichte*. Munich: Beck.
———. 1997. *Das kulturelle Gedächtnis: Schrift, Erinnerung und politische Identität in frühen Hochkulturen*. Munich: Beck.
Bellah, Robert. 2005. "What Is Axial about the Axial Age?" *European Journal of Sociology* 46: 69–89.
Brague, Rémi. 1999. *La sagesse du monde. Histoire de l'expérience humaine de l'univers*. Paris: Fayard.
Briant, Pierre. 2002. *From Cyrus to Alexander—A History of the Persian Empire*. Winona Lake: Eisenbrauns.
Dumont, Louis. 1975. "On the Comparative Understanding of Non-modern Civilizations." *Daedalus* 104, no. 2: 153–172.
Eisenstadt, Shmuel N., ed. 1986. *The Origins and Diversity of Axial Age Civilizations*. Albany: State University of New York Press.
———, ed. 1987. *Kulturen der Achsenzeit I: Ihre Ursprünge und ihre Vielfalt*. Part 1: *Griechenland, Israel, Mesopotamien*. Part 2: *Spätantike, Indien, China, Islam*. Frankfurt am Main: Suhrkamp.
———, ed. 1992. *Kulturen der Achsenzeit II: Ihre institutionelle und kulturelle Dynamik*. Part 1: *China, Japan*. Part 2: *Indien*. Part 3: *Buddhismus, Islam, Altägypten, westliche Kultur*. Frankfurt am Main: Suhrkamp.
Gershevitch, Ilya. 1995. "Approaches to Zoroaster's Gathas." *Iran* 33: 1–29.
Gnoli, Gherardo. 1983. *De Zoroastre à Mani*. Paris: Collège de France.
———. 2000. *Zoroaster in History*. New York: Bibliotheca Persica Press.
Graham, Angus C. 1989. *Disputers of the Tao*. La Salle: Open Court.
Heesterman, J. C. 1985. *The Inner Conflict of Tradition: Essays in Indian Ritual, Kingship and Society*. Delhi: Oxford University Press.

Huang, Chichung. 1997. *The Analects of Confucius (Lun Yu)—A Literal Translation with an Introduction and Notes.* Oxford: Oxford University Press.

Humphreys, Sally C. 2004. "Dynamics of the Greek Breakthrough: The Dialogue between Philosophy and Religion." In Humphreys, *The Strangeness of Gods,* 51–76. Oxford: Oxford University Press.

Jaspers, Karl. 1949. *Vom Ursprung und Ziel der Geschichte.* Zurich: Artemis.

Metzler, Dieter. 1977. "Reichsbildung und Geschichtsbild bei den Achämeniden." In *Seminar—Die Entstehung der antiken Klassengesellschaft,* ed. Hans G. Kippenberg, 279–312. Frankfurt am Main: Suhrkamp.

———. 1991. "A. H. Anquetil-Duperron (1731–1805) und das Konzept der Achsenzeit." In *Achaemenid History: Through Travellers' Eyes,* ed. Helen Sancisi-Weerdenburg and J. W. Drivers, 123–133. Leiden: Nederlands Instituut voor het Nabije Oosten.

Reale, Giovanni. 1997. *Toward a New Interpretation of Plato.* Washington, DC: Catholic University of America Press.

Schwartz, Benjamin. 1985. *The World of Thought in Ancient China.* Cambridge, MA: Harvard University Press.

Seaford, Richard. 2004. *Money and the Early Greek Mind: Homer, Philosophy, Tragedy.* Cambridge: Cambridge University Press.

Shaked, Shaul. 2005. "Zoroastrian Origins: Indian and Iranian Connections." In *Axial Civilizations and World History,* ed. Johann P. Arnason, Shmuel N. Eisenstadt, and Björn Wittrock, 183–200, Leiden: Brill.

15

Cultural Memory and the Myth of the Axial Age

JAN ASSMANN

The theory of the Axial Age is the creation of philosophers and sociologists, not of historians and philologists on whose research the theory is based. It is the answer to the question for the roots of modernity. When and where did the modern world begin as we know and inhabit it? The historian investigates the past for the sake of the past. The quest for the roots of modernity, however, is not interested in the past as such but only as the beginning of something held to be characteristic of the present. These are two categorically different approaches that must be carefully kept apart, which does not mean, however, that there could and should not be interaction and cooperation between historians and theorists or, to give the distinction a different turn, between specialists and generalists. On the contrary, I think this interaction indispensable if the theory of the Axial Age should be any more than just a scientific myth.

It is the quest for beginnings that gives the Axial theory or narrative a certain mythical quality; myths tend to construct beginnings, which the historian then feels summoned to deconstruct. In the *Vorspiel* to his Joseph novels, Thomas Mann deals with exactly this tension between the mythical and the historical approach to the past. In the perspective of the historian, the mythical beginnings tend to dissolve and to give way to ever earlier beginnings, and the depth of the "well of the past" proves to be unfathomable. "Tief ist der Brunnen der Vergangenheit. Sollten wir ihn nicht unergründlich nennen?"[1] This opening sentence describes with inimitable precision the misgivings that historians, especially those who, like myself, specialize in "pre-Axial" civilizations, feel with regard to Karl Jaspers' theory of the Axial Age. To them, Jaspers appears as a teller of myths, narrating about beginnings where they see slow developments, continuities, discontinuities, revisions, and recourses.

The myth (and to a large degree also the theory) of the Axial Age is centered on the following principal assumption: there is but One Truth and One Mankind.[2] At a given point in its moral, spiritual, and intellectual evolution, mankind "broke through" to a much clearer apprehension of this Truth. This happened independently at several places at approximately the same time around 500 BCE. In Jaspers' rather tragic view of universal history, these Axial breakthroughs did not really survive their later institutionalizations—at least not undistortedly—when the formative phase of competing small states was followed by the rise of large empires; they remain a goal to be achieved, which gives universal history its normative perspective. If these Axial breakthroughs constitute the roots of modernity, modernity appears as an still unfulfilled project. Mann, in his own ways, adhered to a similar conception. Opposing Oswald Spengler and his theory of eight mutually nontransparent and untranslatable cultural spheres, he propagated the unity of the human spirit ("Die Einheit des Menschengeistes")[3] across cultural boundaries. In his Joseph novels, he not only showed how such a synthesizing view of different cultural traditions could work with regard to ancient Mesopotamia, Egypt, Israel, Greece, Christianity, but devised also a similar normative concept of modernity as a goal still to be achieved.[4] As far as the assumption of the unity of humanity is concerned, Mann agreed with the Axial myth, but—as mentioned above—he would never have subscribed to the idea that all this began only in the first millennium BCE. It is important to recognize the political and ideological context of both Mann's and Jaspers' concept of the unity of the human spirit. In the heydays of nationalism, racism, and other theories of human "pseudo-speciation" (E. H. Erikson)[5] it was necessary to formulate concepts of human intellectual unity and universal Truth—as it is necessary now to remember and to elaborate these concepts in order to overcome the "clash of civilizations" that is now being prophesied by neo-Spenglerian theories. In a normative perspective, the myth of the Axial Age has a clear function of orientation. As a reconstruction of the intellectual and social history of the first millennium BCE, however, it is highly problematic.

In a different way, similar misgivings apply to theories of cultural evolution. Theories of evolution reconstruct history in terms of nature, as a largely unconscious, uncontrolled, and in this respect "blind" accumulative progress.

As far as the history of culture is concerned, however, we are dealing also with processes that involve consciousness, observation, governance, control, reflection, choice, decision, and intervention of various kinds and to various degrees that do not necessarily follow any evolutionary, that is, intrinsic and in this respect "blind" logic. We have to account for losses, intentional breaks, reversions and recourses, rediscoveries, reconstructions. Nobody will deny that there is evolution even in culture. Evolution applies to those areas of culture that lie beyond conscious observation and control, especially processes that run unnoticed and unremembered over a long stretch of time, such as linguistic change or innovations that become an unreflected part of the world in which we are living and that sink below the level of public awareness and discourse to the cultural unconscious. The world we are living in is to a large degree the result of unconscious accumulation. The innovations of former times become the unquestioned and unreflected foundations and presuppositions of later times on which to build in order to find new solutions for new problems. This process, which Pierre Bourdieu called habitualization, may well be described as cultural evolution. It concerns the dark side of collective memory, which lies outside the realm of conscious reflection and communication and which corresponds in many respects to Michel Polanyi's "tacit dimension."[6] However, the paradigm of evolution loses in applicability if the horizon of unconscious accumulation is transcended and we enter the realm of conscious reflection, debate, and decision, the realm where the "Axial" moves take place. Evolution theory works so well with nature because nature knows of no conscious relationship to the past. Nature neither remembers nor forgets its past. Human beings, however, dispose of a form of memory that allows them to orient themselves in time, in memory back to several millennia and in expectation forward to temporal horizons of varying extension. This human capacity of temporal orientation invests the sheer historical process with meaning in various forms and steers it in various directions. For this reason, evolution theory, if applied to the human world, has to be supplemented by a specifically *cultural* theory that accounts for the dynamics of the bright, the conscious side of cultural memory.

The Axial Age is unanimously hailed as an evolutionary achievement, a step forward, a "breakthrough" toward the future, toward modernity. It is certainly not a coincidence that its first discovery happened at that other evolutionary moment in the intellectual history of the West that Reinhart

Koselleck dubbed *Sattelzeit* (literally "saddle time"), the period between 1750 and 1850 when the idea of "progress" began to move to the center of a new paradigm of historical consciousness. The Iranologist Abraham-Hyacinth Anquetil-Duperron (1731–1805) observed as early as 1771 the synchronism between Zoroaster, Confucius, Laotse, Buddha, the prophets in Israel, and the Greek philosophers and spoke of "a great revolution of the human species."[7] For Koselleck, the *Sattelzeit* around 1800 marks the beginning of modernity in much the same way as the Axial Age for Jaspers: the boundary between strangeness and familiarity. Both Jaspers' Axial Age and Koselleck's *Sattelzeit* meant a fundamental restructuring of our orientation in time and our relation to past and future. The paradigm of progress was linked to historicism as a new attitude toward the past, which became important in all its aspects for its own sake, and the Axial "breakthrough" was linked to new forms of relating to the past, of looking backward and cleaving to sanctified, age-old cultural articulations. If it is a breakthrough, this goes in the direction of looking back, of memory, of cultural consciousness and discursive reflection.[8] In a recent paper, Aleida Assmann criticizes what she calls "modernization theory" for its future-orientedness and its all too exclusive concentration on innovations, changes, beginnings, which necessarily leads to a complete blindness as to the cultural achievements of stabilization and of establishing long-term continuity and diachronic identity. In the framework of modernization theory (to which the theory of the Axial Age obviously belongs), tradition and cultural memory appear as factors of mere retardation, regression, and stagnation.[9] In the framework of a theory of cultural memory, the Axial Age complex appears in a different light: as a phenomenon of tradition as much as of innovation. Within this methodological framework, the decisive question is not so much what happened in the Axial Age but how have these events been remembered, represented, and reconstructed in cultural traditions.

As far as the breakthrough to monotheism is concerned, this quintessential Axial event is represented in cultural memory as well as in the Axial Age narrative in terms of revolution rather than evolution. Revolution and evolution are in many respects opposites. It is certainly true that revolutions do not occur without preparatory stages, developments, and movements leading in the direction of what is then achieved by a revolutionary transformation or "breakthrough." Nevertheless, the process leading from state A to state B via a revolutionary intervention could never be adequately described solely in terms of evolution. As stated above, evolution is "blind," whereas revolution implies observation and decision. An evolutionary process follows exclusively intrinsic vectors without exterior intervention and without decision between opposite options. The best example is perhaps the transition from "primary" to "secondary religions" or "polytheism" to "monotheism."[10] Unless we create a specifically cultural (as opposed to biological) meaning of "evolution" that allows for revolution as a means of evolution, this change may never be described in terms of evolution alone. Monotheism is not a more developed state of polytheism. Polytheism does not "lead" to monotheism as its ultimate state of maturity; at most, it leads to a form of inclusive monotheism that views the gods as immanent manifestations of one transcendent supreme deity. Exclusive monotheism, which does not recognize any gods except one, is never the outcome of evolution (as a form of development) but only of revolution (as a form of rejection).[11]

Distance, Disembedment, and Universalism: Features of Axiality

How could such an interaction between theorists and specialists be realized? First of all, it would be important to come to an agreement concerning the characteristic traits or distinctive features of modernity, whose origins we are looking for in the remote past. What were the decisive innovations that brought about the world which we still inhabit? The first candidate, put forward by Jaspers, is something like *general consciousness.* In the Axial Age and in the three spheres of China, India, and the West, Jaspers claims, "man becomes conscious of Being as a whole, of himself and his limitations."[12] This kind of "general consciousness" is the hallmark of philosophy, understood as the art of seeing the world and human existence from a distance, a technique of cognitive disembedding from the symbiotic embeddedness of early man in the cycles of nature, political institutions, and social constellations.

The next two features are cognate to this one and hardly separable from it. The first is *reflexivity,* which Jaspers defines as *second-order thinking,* thinking about thinking. "Consciousness became once more conscious of itself, thinking became its own object" ("Das Bewußtsein machte noch einmal das Bewußtsein bewußt, das Denken richtete sich auf das Denken").[13]

The second is what Shmuel Eisenstadt calls *transcendental visions*. Transcendental visions concern concepts with a claim to absolute, unconditioned Truth, with a capital "T." These visions or conceptualizations presuppose new techniques of "standing back and looking beyond" (Benjamin Schwartz), of self-distanciation from the various conditions under which the traditional truths were believed and transmitted, a distance that could be achieved only by very few and only in the first millennium BCE, which the Sinologist Benjamin Schwartz, for this reason, called "the Age of Transcendence."[14] This is a very convincing characteristic of the intellectual transformations occurring in the first millennium BCE in the East and West, but is it also characteristic of modernity? Are we still living in an "age of transcendence," and if so, in what sense? In another context, modernity is defined by the loss of transcendence in the course of the nineteenth century.[15] More important, however, is the question whether, and in what sense, we can deny the pre-Axial world any notions of transcendence or "transcendental visions." Obviously, only transcendence in the very strong and emphatic sense of "a cosmological chasm between a transcendental and a mundane sphere" (Hans Joas) can qualify as an exclusively "Axial" concept of transcendence. It is precisely this form of "two worlds theory" that is denied, for example, by Nietzsche's concept of modernity. On the other hand, it applies perfectly well to the pre-Axial world. Even the gods of the polytheistic world are "transcendent" in the sense that they belong to "another" world. Transcendence in the sense of other-worldliness is common to all forms of religion and concepts of the sacred. These gods and spirits are, however, not "extra-mundane." Their "other-worldliness" does not prevent them from being immanent in nature. For this reason, Eric Voegelin, Talcott Parsons, Robert Bellah, and others have spoken of "cosmological societies" with regard to pre-Axial civilizations, and I try to capture this concept of cosmic immanence of the divine by preferring the term "cosmotheism" to "polytheism."[16]

Voegelin's main criterion for distinguishing between pre-Axial and Axial civilizations (not his terminology) deserves a discussion in this context. It is *differentiation,* or, in an evolutionary perspective, the transition or turn from "compactness" to "differentiatedness."[17] Axiality, in this perspective, consists primarily in the introduction of new distinctions. My own concept of the "Mosaic distinction" between true and false within the realm of religion and, more generally, between god and world, is in this respect indebted to Voegelin's approach. Conceptual "compactness" goes together with analogical thinking. The human world is symbolically articulated on the model of the cosmos, and vice versa (in Voegelin's terms: "microcosmos" and "macranthropos"), a style of thought that I would call "mutual modeling" and which obviously comes very close to Merlin Donald's concept of "mythic culture." Mutual modeling and the ensuing conceptual compactness are based on the "integration of society in nature" (a concept that Voegelin borrows from the Egyptologist Henri Frankfort). Conceptual compactness results not so much from an inability to differentiate, a mere absence of later achievements, but from a will to connect and to integrate, to establish alliances, equations, and identities. Also in this perspective, the Axial turn appears as a process of distanciation and disembedding, leading to or expressed in conceptual differentiation.

Distanciation or disembedding is also a quintessential trait of another feature, which Jaspers calls critique and which may be defined as a new power of negation. "Hitherto unconsciously accepted ideas, customs and conditions," Jaspers writes, "were subjected to examination, questioned and liquidated."[18] This radical questioning of tradition led, according to Jaspers, to monotheism in the eastern, and to the birth of philosophy in the western part of the Eastern Mediterranean. Arnaldo Momigliano put this feature first and spoke with regard to the Axial Age of the "age of criticism."[19]

It is this power of negation that turns transition into rejection (and evolution into revolution). Unlike Donald and Bellah, who conceive of the various stages of cultural evolution in terms of addition and integration instead of replacement and supersession,[20] Jaspers constructs the transition from A to B in terms of A contra B. The success of *logos* meant the end of *mythos*, the success of monotheism the end of polytheism (or paganism or "cosmotheism"). The critical, antagonistic, or iconoclastic element in monotheism is unmistakable. Both philosophy (since Parmenides and Plato) and religion (since Moses or what this name stands for) imply a strong concept of absolute Truth, which is in fact a great innovation. This new concept of Truth constitutes the borderline separating what Claude Lévi-Strauss called "la pensée sauvage" from logical and scientific thinking, and "primary," culture-specific religions from "secondary" or world religions. I would in fact subscribe to this theory. The appearance of a new concept of absolute and exclusive truth in the Eastern Mediterranean world is a decisive innovation. In the paradigm of cultural memory, however, the former stages are neither only "integrated" in the sense of Donald's and Bellah's evolutionary theory, nor are they totally discarded and overcome in the sense of Jaspers' model of intellectual progress. They are excluded, in Aleida Assmann's terminology, from the "canon" and relegated to the "archive" of cultural memory,[21] from where they might be later recovered, and this rediscovery may then lead to another intellectual revolution such as the Renaissance with its flourishing of cosmotheism, magic, divination, astrology, and other seemingly "pre-Axial" features.

Jaspers describes the direction of this primal turn from *mythos* to *logos* and polytheism to monotheism as *Vergeistigung* (spiritualization), which may be retained as a further feature of axiality. The term comes close to Max Weber's concept of rationalization and disenchantment, and to Sigmund Freud's concept of a progress in *Geistigkeit* (spirituality or intellectuality). The German word *Geist* is a notoriously difficult and untranslatable term. It is best understood in the sense of the Greek *logos,* meaning word, discourse, and reason. *Geist* has an intimate relationship to language. *Vergeistigung* means, therefore, something like *Versprachlichung,* transforming the world into discourse. It is exactly in this sense that Freud interpreted the prohibition of images as a "progress in *Geistigkeit.*"[22] The concept of *Geistigkeit,* which was so important for Freud and Jaspers, gains in significance if seen in the context of the assaults on *Geist* committed by Nazi Germany. Jaspers' theory of the Axial Age with its characteristic traits of "modernity" is not only a self-portrait or a cultural autobiography but also a normative mirror, confronting modern man with an image of how he should be. As far as the Western part of the Axial hemisphere is concerned, the concept of *Geist (ruach, neshamah, pneuma, logos, nous, psyche, animus, spiritus)* plays in fact an enormous and ever-increasing role in the cultural texts of the ancient, especially (neo-)Platonic, Jewish, Christian, and, above all, Gnostic worlds.

Another Axial feature, besides general consciousness, second-order thinking, and critique in the name of a new concept of Truth, is the *rise of great individuals* and the discovery of individuality. The appearance of the "great individuals" such as, from East to West, Confucius, Lao-tse, Meng-tse, Buddha, Zoroaster, the Hebrew prophets and the Greek philosophers, tragedians, and poets is in fact the most striking Axial phenomenon. This is the very core of the Axial myth as it was first designed by Anquetil-Duperron and then taken up and elaborated by Jean Pierre Abel-Rémusat, Ernst von Lasaulx, Victor von Strauss, and many others. The great individuals are the few who effectuated the step back and the look beyond, this great achievement of social and ideological disembedding, this display of negational power and radical questioning. Inseparably linked to the discovery of individuality is the stress on *interiority*, the rise of inner man, *homo interior* (Augustine), *ho endos anthropos* (Paul), a kind of inner transcendence—the turn, in David Riesman's terms, from tradition- to inner-directedness.[23] This turn may also be interpreted as a move of disembedding and distanciation, which appears to be something like a common denominator of all the Axial features enumerated so far.

The most radical form of both social disembedding and interiorization is what Karen Armstrong in her book *The Great Transformation* (which has been published in German under the title *Die Achsenzeit*)[24] calls *kenosis*, a form of radical renunciation, of disembedding oneself from all social and other "worldly" bonds in the search for the absolute.[25] I do not think, however, that we should include *kenosis* within the Axial features. In its radical form, it seems specific to Indian asceticism, lacking the universality characteristic of typical Axial phenomena. In its more general sense of mere altruism, which Armstrong also includes in her notion of *kenosis*, it is, on the contrary, far too unspecific and applies also to non-Axial cultures.[26] This form of renunciation is only a more efficient way of self-embedding into social or communal constellations, not a form of radical disembedding. *Disembedding*, however, deserves to be retained as a decisive and defining factor of axiality. "The surprising feature of the axial religions," writes Charles Taylor, "is that they initiate a break in all three dimensions of embeddedness: social order, cosmos, human good."[27]

A last feature of axiality has such an importance for Jaspers that he puts it in the very title of his book: *history*. History, according to him, is the quintessential feature of axiality. History begins with the Axial Age in its three centers—China, India, Israel/Greece—and everything unrelated to one of these centers stays outside history, as a *Naturvolk* without history. History or historical consciousness functions in Jaspers' theory as a *leitfossil* of axiality. Since the Axial narrative or theory is in itself a prominent manifestation of historical consciousness in the sense of becoming aware and rendering an account of one's own past and origin, it becomes again clear in what sense the Axial narrative is a self-portrait and a cultural autobiography. Historical consciousness, however, is one of the fields where there is most diversity and least convergence among the "Axial" civilizations.[28]

This brief survey has shown that the Axial features have two common denominators. One is a move of distanciation or disembedding, the other the claim for universal validity. To these two general categories, distanciation and universality, has to be added a third one, which, in the context of the Axial narrative, is the most decisive and in my eyes the most problematic one: *synchronicity*. My impression is that time matters too much in the theoretical debates on the Axial Age. There is the danger of being caught in a vicious circle by including time among the features or conditions of axiality. A phenomenon qualifies as "Axial" if it occurred around 500 BCE. It is the temporal argument that gives the Axial process the enigmatic character of an event, a turn, or even a mutation.

Mutation is in fact the way in which Jaspers interpreted the Axial transformation. In the centuries around 500 BCE, "man, as we know him today, came into being," *Homo sapiens axialis,* so to speak. "The whole of humanity took a forward leap."[29] Voegelin will later speak of a "leap in being" with regard to the Axial event.[30] The term "axis" refers to a point—the "Axial moment" as Bellah calls it—that divides the stream of time into "before" and "after" in the manner of the birth of Christ. Jaspers' opposition between the Axial and the pre-Axial worlds appears to me in many respects as a secularized version of the Christian opposition of true religion and paganism or *historia sacra* and *historia profana*. The biblical (both Jewish and Christian) concept of history implies radical changes, sharp discontinuities, a spiritual "mutation," the emergence of a new man. The Axial Age narrative has the structure of such a mnemohistorical construction that dramatizes a tendency, a development, a process of emergence in form of a revolutionary break, and it personifies it in the figure of a great individual.

The most problematic aspect of such a dramatization of change is the alienation or "estrangement" of the past.[31] In the same way as Christian (and, for that matter, also Jewish and Islamic) orthodoxy blinded itself for the truths that may be contained in other religions by constructing and rejecting them as paganism, idolatry, or "ignorance" (*jahiliya,* the Muslim concept of paganism), Jaspers seems to be blind to truly Axial motifs in pre-Axial civilizations.

Little consensus has been achieved as to the agents of change. What could possibly bring about such a general transformation or fuel a process of *longue durée*? Jaspers subscribed to Alfred Weber's theory about the *Reitervölker,* equestrian tribes or peoples, who by means of their new technology of horse-riding and chariot-driving were able to overrun the ancient world.[32] Such migrations, invasions, and conquests did in fact happen, but not in the Axial Age. The most decisive wave occurred in the first half of the second millennium BCE, with a second wave around 1200–1100 BCE. The first gave rise to the Hittite Empire, while the second destroyed it, and it also put an end to the Bronze Age in general. It is, however, more than unclear how these events could be related to intellectual and spiritual breakthroughs of the kind Alfred Weber and Jaspers are reclaiming for the Axial Age. If we look for something similar on the political plane taking place around 500 BCE, we find the establishment of the Persian Empire in the West, the Maurya kingdoms in India, and the period of the warring kingdoms in China.

The interesting fact about the Persian Empire is that it constituted at its time the most extensive move of globalization in human history. This may have promoted the emergence of universalist ideas. By globalization I understand a process of coalescence of various previously isolated zones into one system of interconnections and interdependencies, where everything, that is, all nations, empires, tribes, and states cohere in some way or other by political, economic, or cultural relations. Universalism, on the other hand, refers to the rise of theories, ideas, or beliefs with a claim to universal validity. By universalism, therefore, I understand an intellectual and spiritual phenomenon; by globalism, a political, economic, and civilizational process (implying material rather than spiritual culture).[33] The two typical universalisms of Western antiquity are monotheism, both in its inclusive ("all gods are One") and exclusive, biblical form ("no other gods!") on the one hand, and Greek science and philosophy on the other. Since globalization is a central aspect of modernity, we are in fact dealing here with one of its roots.

Imperialism, however, is not the only form of political globalization. In the ancient world, globalization started much earlier, with the emergence of and the contact between the superpowers of the Late Bronze Age in the second half of the second millennium BCE.³⁴ The transition in cultural and political outlook, orientation, or mentality to this new stage of incipient globalization may most clearly be observed with respect to ancient Egypt. During the Old and Middle Kingdoms, that is, from 3000 until 1500 BCE, the Egyptians quite simply identified their world with the world in general. Egypt is seen as a cosmos, a sphere of order, surrounded by a zone of chaos, inhabited by nomadic tribes whom it is important to ward off but not to conquer and integrate. The symbolic expression of this attitude is the same as in classical China, a great wall "built to fence off the nomads" (Sinuhe, B17).³⁵ Only with the beginning of the New Kingdom around 1500 BCE does the extra-Egyptian world appear as part of God's creation. By then, the Egyptians have learned the lesson that their environment is not only formed by nomadic tribes but by empires much like their own: the Hittite Empire, the empire of Mitanni, the Babylonian and later also the Assyrian empires, the city states of Syria-Palestine, the Minoan and Mycenean states and colonies, and the Nubian state of Kerma that had emerged south of Egypt. Dealing with these states and empires was no longer a matter of exclusion and negation, but of warfare and diplomacy. Egypt had entered the "age of internationalism," a political network that was coextensive with the world as it was known to and conceived of by its members. The change of political and mental orientation was accompanied by a rise of first universalist concepts, above all the idea of a creator who created the whole world in its differentiated variety—including the multiplicity of languages and skin colors—whom the Egyptians identified with the sun. This development culminated in the middle of the thirteenth century BCE, in a veritable religious revolution, the instauration of a purely and exclusively monotheistic religion by King Akhenaten that lasted, however, for only twenty years at most. This Egyptian example provides a paradigm for the connection between globalization and universalism, as well as for the connections between politics and, at least potentially, Axial breakthroughs. We may call this form of globalization "internationalism," which appears as the hallmark of the Late Bronze Age (1500–1100 BCE).

In the form of imperialism, however, globalization seems to be the hallmark of the first millennium BCE. The Assyrians started this politics of unification with the conquests of Tiglat-Pileser III (745–727 BCE), the founder of the Neo-Assyrian Empire, whose successors extended its frontiers as far as Egypt. Forming an alliance with the Medes, the Babylonians under Nabopolassar defeated the Assyrians and founded the Neo-Babylonian Empire, which only ninety years later fell victim to the Persian expansion. The Persian Empire lasted about 300 years, until it was conquered by Alexander the Great. The biblical book of Daniel, composed in the year 165 BCE, gives an account and an interpretation of this sequence of empires in the two visions recorded in chapters 2 and 7. Daniel is an *apocalypsis* prophesying the end of history and the advent of the Kingdom of God after the fall of the fourth empire. In its Christian reception, the fourth empire, which originally referred to Alexander's empire (split up under his successors, the Diadochi), was identified with Rome, and because the end of history was not deemed really desirable, the end of Rome was deferred as far as possible in the form of the "Holy Roman Empire."[36] In this respect, Daniel opens a historical perspective that connects the first millennium BCE with Napoleon, who finally put an end to this construction and aspired to continue this tradition of imperialist globalization by building an ever greater empire. Daniel provided the universalist vision to the globalist project of Hellenistic imperialism. A similar project may have inspired Jaspers after the breakdown of Hitler's global imperialism. It is obvious that the idea of imperialistic globalization emerged in the first millennium BCE and remained a major factor in political thought until modernity. In this respect, we may indeed speak of an "Axial Age." But this is not what Jaspers had in mind, and "globalization" is not his theme.

Literacy as an Agent of Change

As far as the agents of change are concerned, there might indeed exist a relationship between technological and intellectual innovations on the one hand, and political breakdowns and intellectual breakthroughs on the other.[37] In my contribution to the volume *Axial Civilizations and World History*, I tried to shed light on the second aspect with regard to Egypt and Israel.[38] In this contribution, I want to focus on technological and intellectual innovations, dealing, however, not with engineerial technologies of warfare and transportation but with writing as "a technology that restructures thought."[39] I am, therefore, arguing in the field of a semiotics and pragmatics of symbolic forms, which is also treated in the more theoretic contributions to this volume by Merlin Donald and Matthias Jung. As early as 1783, the Jewish philosopher Moses Mendelssohn stated that "the grammatological transformations which occurred in different periods of cultural development had an important impact on the revolutions of human cognition in general and changes in religious concepts in particular."[40] *Homo axialis* is the man, the symbol-user, who by "mutually reinforcing feedback loops between levels of consciousness and different modes of sign-usage" (Matthias Jung) has been formed by the very tools he invented.

Writing as a cultural technique may be looked at under two different aspects: as a technology of creation and a technology of preservation. Nobody will doubt that, without writing, none of the great texts that we are still reading today could have been preserved in such a manner that they could still exert their normative and formative impact, and that writing, therefore, has to be recognized as a *necessary* condition of axiality. Few, however, would subscribe to the idea that writing constitutes also a *sufficient* condition, which would mean that axiality is a causal consequence of writing. I myself would never go so far. There is, however, a third way of conceptualizing the relation between writing and axiality, taking axiality to be not a consequence but an implication of writing, an option opened up by literacy of a certain quality, whose acceptance, exploration, and elaboration, however, depends on historical and cultural circumstances. Until very recently, the invention or reception of writing and the development of literacy have mostly been studied as factors of cultural evolution. In the famous studies of Walter Ong, Jack Goody, Eric Havelock, and others, this has led to a kind of media-determinism, taking for inevitable consequences what at best are potentialities, propensities, and implications that may become real only in interaction with contingent political, social, and cultural factors.[41]

Writing is not the same in every context. We have to distinguish between *systems* and *cultures* of writing (this distinction will be explained later), and within cultures of writing between several stages of literacy. First of all, however, we have to consider writing as a medium not only of communication but also of memory. Under certain conditions, writing restructures thought not only in the direction of invention but also of retention and may eventually lead to a complete restructuring of what we call "cultural memory." Only writing creates the tension between "canon" and "archive" (Aleida Assmann) that accounts for a cultural dynamism typical of "Axial" cultures.[42]

Writing is a technology that makes cultural creations possible that would otherwise never exist, and that preserves cultural creations in memory, making accessible to later recourse what would otherwise be forgotten and have vanished. Writing, in short, is a factor of cultural creativity and cultural memory.

In order to clarify these points, I would like to start with some very general remarks. As human beings we live in a world of symbolic articulation that we ourselves have created. Our world is created through communication. Aristotle's two definitions of man, as *zoon logon echon,* the animal that has language and reason, and as *zoon politikon,* the animal that lives in communities, go together: we possess language as a function of our dependency on, and capacity for, bonding, and we use language and other means of symbolic articulation in order to form social bonds and inhabit the world that we create. This space or world of symbolic articulation borders on the inarticulate that we bear in us as the unconscious and that surrounds our world from without.

It is in this space of symbolic articulation and communication that, 5,000–6,000 years ago, the space of writing emerged at various places on earth, in very different forms and on different scales, and also with different cultural and social consequences. By writing I understand a special kind of symbols that bestow visibility to the invisible, stability to the volatile, and wide dissemination to the locally confined. Language uses sound-symbols that are invisible, volatile, and locally restricted. Therefore, language is the classical case for the application of writing. In everyday language, by writing we understand language made visible. For other domains of the use of symbols for visibilization, fixation, and dissemination such as music and mathematics, we speak of notation and not of writing. At best, musical notation, at least in German, is often called writing. *Notenschrift* is a common term in German.

The human space of symbolic articulation and communication was without doubt always occupied not only by acoustic but also by visible symbols. In this sense, humanity has always used writing alongside language. I am thinking of petroglyphs, cave paintings, pottery marks, knotted cords, and other markers in the space of visual communication and of cultural memory, which Donald calls "exograms."[43] There are various means to visibilize the invisible, stabilize the transient, and disseminate the local. It is, however, obvious that by writing or by the various forms of writing that developed at various places over 5,000 years ago we understand something different, something that must have changed the space of symbolical articulation more or less radically in proportion to its functions and range. Before going into details here and in order to gain a general idea of this connection between writing and change, I refer to the example of musical notation. There are still many traditions of music that are untouched by musical notation and that correspond to what in the domain of language is called orality. They differ mainly in two points from literate musical traditions: in standardization and evolution or innovation. "Oral" musical traditions tend to be less standardized and less innovative. They are more complex in their use of features that cannot be rendered in musical notation and in spontaneous improvisation, and they are less complex and innovative in the lack of polyphony and in a certain formulaic repetitiveness that is characteristic also of "oral literature." The kind of music, however, that develops in the space of writing shows a breathtaking speed and range of evolution. Eighty years lie between Monteverdi's *Poppea* and Handel's *Alcina,* sixty between *Alcina* and Mozart's *Figaro,* and another eighty between *Così fan tutte* and Wagner's *Walküre.* This evolution is a matter both of creativity and of memory. Musical notation enables the composer to create music of unknown complexity and it establishes a memory that excludes unconscious repetition and determines the directions of development by intertextual competition. The Western history of music would not have been possible without the invention of musical notation. This invention brought about a truly Axial turn in that it triggered an evolution of global significance, putting every form of music untouched by it in the position of "folk" or "ethnic" music comparable to the position of oral societies beyond the realm of "history" in Jaspers' sense.

What we may learn from this example of the space of writing is that here a pressure on innovation is prevailing that is alien to the space of orality. There is no more eloquent testimony for this pressure than the *Complaints of Khakheperreseneb,* an ancient Egyptian author writing in the beginning of the second millennium BCE:

Had I but unknown phrases, strange expressions,
new speech that has not yet occurred, free of repetition,
No transmitted proverbs used by the ancestors!
I quench my body of all it contains

> and relieve it from all my words.
> For what has been said, is repetition
> and nothing is said that has not been said.
> One cannot boast with the utterances of the ancestors
> for posterity will find out.
> O that I knew what others ignore
> and what is not repetition![44]

This poignant complaint refers to a problem that only the author has. The public expects from the bard the familiar, but from the author something new. The author has to position himself in a space of intertextual competition. It is through this constant pressure that the space of writing is working on the space of symbolic articulation, modifying but, above all, expanding it. Writing, far from just stabilizing the volatile and visibilizing the invisible, discloses entirely new areas of the inarticulate. Khakheperreseneb's complaint contains many typical Axial motifs such as reflexivity, interiority, individuality: "I quench my body." Tradition made visible through the use of writing assumes an emulatory character. One even thinks of sensing an element of "anxiety of influence" (Harold Bloom) in Khakheperreseneb's complaint. It is, therefore, not enough to state that without writing the great texts would never have been preserved for posterity. Without writing, they would never have been created, because the necessity would not have been felt to go beyond everything already existing in a written tradition. The bard embodies and performs a tradition, an author changes it by adding to it. This is what the Latin word *auctor* (from *augere*, to increase, grow, multiply) means.

These effects, however, did not immediately occur with the invention of writing, nor must we think of these changes in terms of evolution, that is, logical consequence and strict determinism. First of all, we have to distinguish, as has already been suggested, between *systems* and *cultures* of writing. *Writing systems* concern differences such as ideographic, logographic, syllabic, alphabetic scripts, and so on; *writing cultures* concern functions of writing and forms of its social embedding. All the major scripts that are currently in use stem from two sources: the Chinese script and the scripts of the ancient Near East, that is, Egyptian hieroglyphs and Sumerian cuneiform. Already this fact gives us an idea of the interconnectedness of cultural phenomena. India is a latecomer in this context. Its script (Devanagari) is probably a derivative of the Near Eastern alphabets. The invention of writing is indeed an event of Axial range, dividing the world into literate and oral societies. But it was not the invention as such that led to Axial transformations. This was the first step, and I will try to show that it was only the second and above all the third step in the process of literacy that changed the world.

The first step, the invention of writing, led to what I propose to call "sectorial literacy."[45] In this stage, writing is used exclusively in those sectors of cultural activity for whose needs it had been invented. In the case of Mesopotamia, this is economy and administration. In Egypt, too, economy or bookkeeping is the central function besides which, however, writing is also used for political representation, funerary monuments, and cultic recitation. In China, writing seems to have originated in the context of divination. In Minoan and Mycenean Greece, writing (Linear A and B) never transcended the realm of economy (bookkeeping) and vanished with the end of the economic system (the palace-culture) that needed it. In Egypt, Mesopotamia, and China, however, the space of writing soon expanded into other fields of cultural practice.

The turn from "sectorial" to "cultural" literacy occurs when writing penetrates into the central core of culture that we (Aleida Assmann and myself) call "cultural memory." This is a question not of a *system* but of a *culture* of writing. What matters here is not whether we are dealing with an alphabetic (consonantic or vocalized) alphabet or with a syllabic, logographic, or ideographic script, and the theories especially of the Toronto School (Harold Innis, Marshall McLuhan, Eric Havelock, and recently Friedrich Kittler), which put too much stress on the Greek invention of the vocalized alphabet, are in my opinion mistaken on this point. What matters is whether or not writing is used for the composition, transmission, and circulation of "cultural texts." This is the second step toward axiality. It occurred in Mesopotamia toward the end of the third millennium BCE, when the sagas of the Gilgamesh cycle were first collected into a continuous epic, and in Egypt at the beginning of the second millennium BCE, where the first truly literary texts were composed.

"Cultural memory" is that form of collective memory that enables a society to transmit its central patterns of orientation in time, space, and divine and human worlds to future generations and by doing so to continue its identity over the sequence of generations.[46] Cultural memory provides a kind of connective structure in both the social and temporal dimensions. It provides that kind of knowledge that enables an individual to belong, and since human beings need to belong, they serve their drive to belong by acquiring the relevant knowledge, which in German is called *Bildung,* in Greek *paideia,* in Hebrew *musar,* and in Egyptian *sebayt.* We associate with these concepts institutions of reading and writing, bookcases, libraries, schools, universities, and we find it hard to imagine a kind of cultural memory that is not based on writing and literacy.

The contrary, however, is the case. Orality and ritual are the natural media of cultural memory, frequently accompanied with basic methods of notation or prewriting such as the Australian *tchurungas,* the knotted cords *(quipus)* of the Incas, and similar mnemonic devices. For most of the time, these oral mnemotechniques were considered much more efficient than the early forms of writing. This is for many reasons. First, the contents of the cultural memory such as the great myths about the origin of the world, the tribe and its central institutions, the moral norms, and similar cultural texts are, so to speak, "mnemophilic"; they stick in the memory because of their poetic form and substantial relevance. We must not forget that writing was invented to record the non-mnemophilic, the contingent data in economy and administration, which no human memory can keep for a long period of time. Secondly, the various cultural texts (I am using this term like Clifford Geertz, who described the Balinese cockfight as a cultural text) tend to be multimedia productions, involving (besides language) pantomime, music, dance, ritual and may not easily be reduced to that one stratum of symbolic articulation that lends itself to transcription into writing. For this reason, it took the Mesopotamians and Egyptians more than a millennium to take this step. When writing is introduced into this domain, however, there is a high degree of probability that it will lead to drastic transformations.

When writing enters the realm of cultural memory, there seem to be three options: either to transcribe the oral texts and transform them into literature, or to compose entirely new texts whose complexity already requires writing for conceptualization and composition, or, finally, a combination of both. Mesopotamia and Israel seem to belong to the third category, Greece to the first, and Egypt to the second. The Homeric epics present themselves as transcripts of an oral performance, they exhibit their oral character. The same holds for Greek lyrical poetry, drama, and even the Platonic dialogues. This is not to exclude the possibility that Homer used writing for the composition of his epics. I am only stressing the fact that they imitate the form of oral composition and presentation. In Egypt, the situation is different. The earliest literary texts such as the "instructions" of Ptahhotep, Amenemhet I, and (for) Merikare, the complaints of Ipuwer and Khakheperreseneb, the prophecies of Neferti, the tales of the Shipwrecked Sailor, Sinuhe, and the Eloquent Peasant exhibit their genuinely literary character in the richness of vocabulary and grammar and their structural complexity. In Egypt, the use of writing for the work on cultural memory does not lead to the transcription or textualization of oral texts but to the composition of new genuinely written texts, in much the same way as in Western music culture, where the introduction of writing led to the composition of a new kind of music, polyphony. It was only 500 years later, with the New Kingdom and especially in the Ramesside age (1300–1100 BCE), that the use of writing extended to typically oral genres such as folk tales, love songs, harpers' songs, and so on that, however, disappeared again from the space of writing after 1100 BCE.

With the literarization of significant parts of cultural memory and the production of cultural texts that are *conceptually* literate (requiring writing already for composition and addressing a reader), a writing culture changes from sectorial to cultural literacy. Only at this point the techniques of writing and reading affect the connective structure of a society. One of the typical effects of this transformation is the construction of a glorious, heroic, or classical past or "antiquity." The cultural memory becomes two-storied, divided into the new and the old, modernity and antiquity. An important factor in this development is linguistic change. The older texts within the literary tradition, which now become validated as "classics," preserve a linguistic stage that no longer corresponds to the spoken language of the present. At a certain time, this distance between the "classical" and the vernacular idiom grows so wide that the classical language has to be learned specifically; we are dealing with cultural diglossia. This situation is typical of Mesopotamia as early as the third millennium, where Sumerians and Akkadians lived together speaking two completely different languages, and where Sumerian stayed in use for liturgic purposes until the age of Hellenism. With respect to the restricted use of Sumerian in this culture, we may speak of sectorial diglossia, which is a very widespread phenomenon. Cultural diglossia, on the other hand, is reached where and when the other language characterizes the *cultural* texts, those texts that carry the normative and formative knowledge, which constitutes and transmits a cultural identity across the sequence of generations and forms the diachronic backbone or connective structure of a society. This stage of cultural evolution characterizes the Cassite age in Mesopotamia (1550–1150 BCE) and the Ramesside age in Egypt (1300–1100 BCE).

The construction of a classical, heroic, or "golden" age, an "antiquity" as a past to look back at for models of behavior and literary production, means a first step in the direction of canonization. This cultural split into antiquity and modernity seems to me one of the characteristic prerequisites if not elements of axiality. It introduces into a given culture an element of critical distance and reflexivity. Canonization, at this first stage, means the collection of cultural texts of the past to form an obligatory syllabus of cultural knowledge, to be learned by heart and to be referred to as authoritative in critical discussions and situations. An Egyptian wisdom text of the thirteenth century BCE gives a list of eight "classics" of the past, whose models the pupil should follow in his strive for immortality. These authors achieved immortality, not by building pyramids but by writing books that are still read, learned, and quoted because of their ever valid truth and authority:

> Is there anyone among us like Hordjedef?
> Or someone like Imhotep?
> Among our contemporaries, there is none like Neferti
> or Kheti, the greatest of them all.
> I mention to you only the names of Ptahemdjehuti and
>   Khakheperreseneb.
> Is there another Ptahhotep
> or somebody like Kairsu?[47]

A German-Egyptian team discovered some years ago a tomb chapel in Assiut in the northern part of Upper Egypt that was reused during the New Kingdom for what seems to be a chapel of cultural memory. Some learned scribes had covered free spaces on the walls with large sections from classical texts of the Egyptian literary tradition containing two versions of the instruction of *King Amenemhet I,* the *Instruction of Dua-Kheti,* and the *Hymn to the Nile,* all three believed to be works of Kheti, "the greatest of them all," as well as two versions of the *Loyalist Instruction* by Kairsu, the *Teaching of a Man for his Son,* and the *Prophecies of Neferti,*[48] thus six works of the classical tradition whose superior rank and high esteem as cultural texts is also documented by dozens or even hundreds of ostraca, limestone flakes that were used in school. The Egyptian scribe learned the craft by learning by heart the classical texts and by writing them down in appropriate portions using potsherds and limestone flakes as material. Another collection of Egyptian classics of the past can be found on a wall in a tomb at Saqqara dating from the thirteenth century BCE.[49] The two lower registers, the only ones to have survived, list thirteen names apiece, the upper containing names of viziers and high priests of Ptah, the lower those of priests of slightly inferior rank, while the two sections are divided by a horizontal line that contains other names. Of these, four names reappear from the Papyrus Chester Beatty: Kairsu, Imhotep, Khakheperreseneb, and Kheti. The fifth is Ipuwer, the "author" of the *Admonitions of Ipuwer,* whose appearance confirms that lamentations and chaos descriptions (the genre to which belong also the works by Neferti and Khakheperreseneb) were also considered cultural texts of highest rank. Apart from these "authors," the list spans notables from the Old to the New Kingdom. The only name among these classics that is still unknown to us is Ptahemdjehuti. Hordjedef, Neferti, Kheti, Khakheperreseneb, Ptahhotep, Kairsu, and Ipuwer are known by their texts; Imhotep is known by a wealth of data, and his lost instruction is often referred to.

I think that the Egyptian case may be generalized. At a certain stage, every literate culture enters the stage of a split culture, divided into the old and the new, and it is writing in the form of cultural literacy that brings this split about. Since this split is dependent on linguistic change and finds its typical expression in the distinction between classical and vernacular language, and since linguistic change is a largely unconscious and uncontrolled process, we may even speak of evolution. The cultural and social consequences of this split, however, depend on cultural decisions and institutions.

Even the typically Egyptian association of this split with the idea of immortality may, at least to a certain degree, be generalized. In its literate, written form, cultural memory appears as a timeless or at least imperishable space of immortality, which one may enter by creating a book or work of art of everlasting beauty, truth, or significance. This idea of literary or artistic immortality may be considered as a first step in the direction of transcendence or transcendental visions (Eisenstadt). The use of writing for the fulfillment of the desire to transcend one's life span and to live on in the memory of posterity dates back, in Egypt, to the very beginnings of literate culture, but I would classify this use of writing for tomb inscriptions as sectorial literacy. The step toward cultural literacy is achieved when the tomb monument is topped by the literary work, for example in the words of Horace, who said with regard to his book of odes: "exegi monumentum aere perennius / regalique situ pyramidum altius." This motif appears already in the same Egyptian text that contains the canon of classical authors:

> They [the sages of the past] have not created for themselves
>   pyramids of ore
> nor stelae of iron;
> they have not contrived to leave heirs in the form of children,
> to keep their names alive.
> But they created themselves books as heirs
> and teachings that they have written.
> They employed the scroll as lector priest
> and the slate as "loving son."
> Teachings are their pyramids,
> the reed their son,
> the polished stone surface their wife.
> Their tomb chapels are forgotten,
> but their names are recalled on their writings, that they have
>   created,
> as they endure by virtue of their perfection.
> Their creators are remembered in eternity.[50]

We are not yet dealing here with "real" axiality, because this step of canonization is still culture-specific and lacks the global claims typical of Axial movements. But it is a step in the direction of axiality, and it is a step within the space of writing.

Another sphere of cultural memory that is strongly affected by the use of writing is history. The existence of written sources about the past makes it possible to draw the distinction not only between the old and the new, but also between myth and history. The use of written records creates history in the sense of a critical discourse, separating mythical tales about the past from reasoned accounts of documented history. This step seems to be a Greek achievement, but the Greeks themselves attributed it to the Egyptians, opposing their own mythical form of historical consciousness to Egyptian history, which is based on written records. Typical examples of this intercultural comparison are Herodotus' account of the visit of Hecataeus of Miletus with the priests of Amun at Thebes[51] and Plato's account of Solon's visit with the priests at Sais.[52] Both Hecataeus and Solon confront the Egyptian priests with Greek traditions about the past. Hecataeus recites his own genealogy, which leads after fifteen generations to a god as the ancestor of the family, and Solon tells the Greek version of the story of the flood, the myth about Deukalion and Pyrrha. Both are then confronted by the Egyptians with their records. Hecataeus is led into the temple where he is shown 341 statues of high priests, one the son of the other and no god interfering, documenting 11,340 years of purely human history. Solon is shown the Egyptian annals stretching back over more than 9,000 years, where the memory of Athens' glorious past is preserved, for example their victory over Atlantis, which in Greece itself is destroyed and forgotten. All this is, of course, pure fabulation, but it illustrates the principle of critical history with its distinction between myth and history, brought about by the use of writing for chronological bookkeeping, which, in the form of annals and kinglists, belonged to the first and most important applications of writing in Egypt and Mesopotamia. In this sense of documented past and critical verifiability, it is writing that produced history and dispelled mythology. Writing caused history to be where myth was, because it documented conditions in which not gods but human kings reigned and in which humans were responsible for their actions. Writing bestows to historical memory the quality of verifiability and adds a truth value to its accounts about the past that myth, in spite of its truth claims, is lacking.

A third domain of cultural memory where the use of writing leads to dramatic changes is religion. It is here that the second and decisive step toward canonization is achieved, a step of truly global significance, which in my opinion forms the very center of Jaspers' concept of the Axial Age. In the realm of religion, writing appears with the same critical pathos as in the sphere of history, opposing its superior truth to the invalidated truth claims of myth. Here, its claims to superior truth are based on revelation, which it codifies. All world religions—Judaism, Christianity, Islam, Buddhism, Jainism, the religion of the Sikh, Confucianism, Daoism—are founded on a canon of sacred scripture that codifies the will of their founder and the superior truth of his revelation. This step of canonization was invented only twice in the world: with the Hebrew canon and the Buddhist canon. All later canons followed these examples. This second step of canonization changed the world in a truly "Axial" way.

The first step of canonization, which we encountered in Egypt and Mesopotamia, was connected with a cultural split into antiquity and modernity, drawing a distinction within the culture. Canonization here means the selection of the timelessly authoritative and exemplary texts from the plethora of written literature. The second canonization applies a different criterion: the criterion of absolute and universal truth, drawing a distinction that sets one's own culture or religion off against all other religions (including one's own past), which become now excluded as paganism, idolatry, heresy, and error. Some of this pathos of distinction and exclusion seems to me still present in Jaspers' concept of the Axial Age, which in this respect appears as a secularized version of the religious distinction between paganism and true religion. His idea of Axial civilizations puts the pre- and extra-Axial world in a position similar to the Jewish, Christian, and Islamic construction of paganism. This aspect becomes even stronger with Schwartz's definition of the Axial Age as the "age of transcendence" and Eisenstadt's concept of "transcendental visions" as the hallmark of axiality. All this is to a large degree a feat of cultural memory and an effect of writing and canonization. We don't know anything about the transcendental visions of shamans, kings, priests, and seers unless they become not only written down but, above all, are received into a canon of sacred scripture. It is only then that they become part of cultural memory and religious identity.

If primary canonization may be partly explained in terms of evolution dependent, as we have seen, on the truly evolutionary process of linguistic change, secondary canonization is by no means an evolutionary achievement but a matter of conscious revolution, which in individual life could be compared to a conversion. The distinction between evolutionary processes and other forms of change implying conscious interventions and decisions between alternative options seems to me highly important in the study of the Axial Age.

In the West, the Hebrew canon of sacred scripture is complemented by a Greek and Latin canon of classical literature. The cultural memory of the West rests on these two projects of canonization, which were conducted roughly simultaneously—and probably not independently—by specialists in Palestine and Alexandria. The distinctive hallmark of what I call secondary canonization is the rise of exegesis. In the stage of primary canonization, the texts selected as classics exist in a form that the medievalist Paul Zumthor called *mouvance*.[53] The texts were constantly reformulated, amplified, or substituted by other texts in order to accommodate them to the changing conditions of understanding. Their "surface structure" was sacrificed in order to save at least part of their meaning. This is why even written texts tend to exist over a longer stretch of time in many different versions. The continuous growth of the book of Isaiah, first into Deutero- then into Trito-Isaiah, is a typical case of how a cultural text is changing in what the Assyriologist Leo Oppenheim called "the stream of tradition."[54] The *Epic of Gilgamesh* developed in the course of its transmission and redaction from a cycle of sagas into the "twelve-tablets-composition" in which it appears in the Neo-Assyrian library of Assurbanipal at Niniveh. In a similar way, the Egyptian *Book of the Dead* developed from a pool of unconnected spells out of which every individual funerary papyrus picked its own specific selection into a real book with a fixed selection of 167 spells in a fixed order. Written texts, in this "stream of tradition," share to a certain degree the sort of oral texts that are not fixed but subject to much variation over the course of time.

This flexibility or *mouvance* is categorically stopped and excluded by the process of secondary canonization.[55] Secondary canonization means the combination of a sacralization of surface structure typical of sacred texts like hymns, incantations, and ritual spells on the one hand, and the preservation of meaning typical of cultural texts in the state of *mouvance* as the constant adaptation of the text to changing conditions of understanding on the other. Sacred texts are not necessarily cultural texts, since they may be known only to specialists and withheld from public circulation. Sacred texts are verbal enshrinements of the holy. In sacred texts, not a syllable must be changed in order to ensure the "magical" power of the words to "presentify" the divine. In this context, not "understanding" matters but correctness of pronunciation, ritual purity of the speaker, and other requirements concerning proper circumstances of performance. As the case of the Rgveda shows, this principle of non-*mouvance* and verbatim fixation applies to sacred texts independently of their oral or literate form of transmission.[56] Sacred texts, therefore, are exempt from the pressure to adapt to the hermeneutical conditions of a changing world.

In the process of secondary canonization, the principle of sacred fixation is applied to *cultural* texts. On the one hand, they are treated like verbal temples enshrining divine presence, but on the other they require understanding and application in order to exert their formative and normative impulses and demands. The solution to this problem is exegesis. Exegesis or hermeneutics is the successor of *mouvance*. In the *mouvance* stage of literate transmission, the commentary is being worked into the fabric of the text. This method has been shown by Michael Fishbane to be typical of the biblical texts in their formative phase.[57] They are full of glosses, pieces of commentary that later redactors have added to the received text. Only with the closure of the canon is this process stopped, and exegesis has now to take the form of a commentary that stays outside the text itself.[58]

This distinction between text and commentary typical of secondary canonization applies not only to the sacred but also to the classical canon. In this respect, the Alexandrinian *philologoi* seem to have led the way. They introduced into their collection of ancient writings the distinction between *hoi prattómenoi* (literally "those to be treated", that is, the classical texts worthy of exegetical treatment, of a commentary) and the rest.[59] The Latin author Aulus Gellius compared this textual elite to the highest class of Roman taxpayers called "classici." In the Jewish tradition, this split into and relationship between text and commentary typical of secondary canonization finds its earliest expression in the concept of written and oral Torah (*torah she be'al khitav* and *torah she be'al pe*). Here, commentary has to be oral in order not to violate the space of writing, which is exclusively reserved for and occupied by sacred scripture. The oral Torah is a collection of oral debates and commentaries on the written Torah that became itself codified in the Talmudic and Midrashic traditions. It is believed to go back via an unbroken chain of reception *(shalshelet ha-qabbalah)* to Moses himself.

The oral exegesis of a sacred text accompanying its public recitation seems indeed to correspond to Jewish custom dating back to the beginnings of canonization. The book of Nehemiah reports a public reading of the Torah, where Ezra read the text and several of the Levites gave a commentary:

> And Ezra opened the book in the sight of all the people, for he was above all the people, and as he opened it all the people stood. And Ezra blessed the LORD, the great God, and all the people answered, "Amen, Amen," lifting up their hands. And they bowed their heads and worshiped the LORD with their faces to the ground.
>
> Also Jeshua, Bani, Sherebiah, Jamin, Akkub, Shabbethai, Hodiah, Maaseiah, Kelita, Azariah, Jozabad, Hanan, Pelaiah, the Levites, helped the people to understand the Law, while the people remained in their places. They read from the book, from the Law of God, clearly, and they gave the sense, so that the people understood the reading. (Neh. 8:5–8)

Some centuries later, the Jewish historian Flavius Josephus testifies to the same custom, where he confronts Jewish and Greek religion:

> Can any government be more holy than this? or any Religion better adapted to the nature of the Deity? Where, in any place but in this, are the whole People, by the special diligence of the Priests, to whom the care of public instruction is committed, accurately taught the principles of true piety? So that the body-politic seems, as it were, one great Assembly, constantly kept together, for the celebration of some sacred Mysteries. For those things which the Gentiles keep up for a few days only, that is, during those solemnities they call Mysteries and Initiations, we, with vast delight, and a plenitude of knowledge, which admits of no error, fully enjoy, and perpetually contemplate through the whole course of our lives.[60]

It is obvious that Josephus, in this polemical passage, does not do full justice to the Greek organization of cultural memory. He ignores the classical canon, the traditions of scientific discourse, and the various forms of exegesis practiced in the schools of philosophy, medicine, and other branches of knowledge. He focuses only on religion and confronts the Jewish institutions of religious instruction and the Greek mystery cults. Arbitrary and highly selective as this comparison may be, it illustrates a very important distinction: the distinction between ritual and textual continuity.[61]

In spite of their extensive use of writing, Egyptian and other "pagan" religions were still relying on ritual continuity. In the world of ritual continuity, the public has indeed to wait for the next performance in order to get access to the sacred texts of cultural memory. Textual continuity is only achieved when institutions of learning and exegesis are established that keep the ancient texts constantly present and semantically transparent. The transition from ritual to textual continuity means a complete reorganization of cultural memory in the same way that the transition from the ethnically and culturally determined religions of the ancient world to the new type of transcultural and transnational world religions meant a totally new construction of identity. The canon, in a way, functioned as a new transethnical homeland and as a new transcultural instrument of formation and education.

There seems to exist a strong alliance among revelation, transcendence, and secondary canonization. The codification of revelation leads to a expatriation of the holy from the worldly immanence into transcendence and into scripture. The pagan or pre-Axial cult religions presuppose the immanence of the holy in images, trees, mountains, springs, rivers, heavenly bodies, animals, human beings, and stones. All this is denounced as idolatry by the new scripture-based world religions. Scripture requires a total reorientation of religious attention that was formerly directed toward the forms of divine immanence and is now directed toward scripture and its exegesis. Secondary canonization means an exodus both of the holy and of religious attention from the cosmos into scripture. To the extramundane nature of God corresponds the textual character of his revelation. To be sure, these remarks concern only the sacred canon such as the Tanakh, the Christian Bible, and the Qur'an, and not the canon of Greek and Latin classics. The structure of the classical canon is different in that it is open and allows for constant modifications around an unquestionable core, whereas the sacred canon is closed. This distinction between closed and open canons applies, however, only to the West. Eastern, especially Buddhist, canons have a different, less strict structure. Common to all corpora of secondary canonization is the existence of a full-fledged culture of exegesis and the strict distinction between text and commentary.

Seen as an agent of change, we may ask to which aspect of axiality literacy at the stage of secondary canonization makes the most decisive contribution. In my opinion, this is precisely the aspect of axiality that has been shown to function as a common denominator of most of the Axial features discussed above: distanciation and disembedding. Writing is a technology that restructures not only thought but also, under certain cultural circumstances, the whole network of relations between human beings, man and society, man and cosmos, man and god, and god and cosmos. The meaning of distanciation and disembedment as "Axial" moves, however, can only be properly understood if we get a better understanding of what embedment and integration mean.

In the evolutionary framework of the Axial narrative, embeddedness appears as the "not-yet" of the Axial achievement of distanciation and disembedding. What disappears in this perspective is the positive aspect of embedding. Embedding man in a social, political, and conceptual or ideological network of meaning and coherence and embedding the divine in a cosmic network whose meaning and coherence is modeled on the same basic ideas of order, truth, and harmony, should be recognized in its own right as a major civilizational achievement. There is perhaps no society on earth that went so far as the ancient Egyptians in articulating, elaborating, and also institutionalizing their vision of sociocosmic coherence, which they called Ma'at. There is no reason not to call this conceptualization a "transcendental vision." We cannot point to a "great individual" to have first formulated it, since no institutionalization of this first "vision" has been preserved, but the Egyptians themselves would have pointed to Imhotep, the first of their celebrated sages, who worked as a vizier under King Djoser (2750 BCE) and was divinized for his great invention, the art of building in stone, and the erection of the first pyramid, the step pyramid at Saqqara. His often-mentioned "instruction" is lost to us, but the transcendental character of the idea of Ma'at is obvious. Ma'at is what Kant would have called a "regulative idea."

Ma'at, however, works in the opposite direction of distanciation and disembedment. It is the very principle of embedment, of creating connectivity in the social, temporal, and cosmic dimensions, establishing social bonds between humans and temporal connections between yesterday, today, and tomorrow ensuring memory, success, stability, and even immortality. Who lives in and by Ma'at, this is the great Egyptian promise, will not perish but pass through the test of the judgment after death to eternal life in the Elysian fields.[62] However, even this concept implies an element of distanciation, which is self-distanciation, renunciation from an immediate fulfillment of one's drives and impulses. The ideals of self-control, discretion, modesty, altruism, beneficence, openness to the needs of others, pity, compassion, empathy are at the core of the Egyptian concept of virtue. Knowing how to listen well is deemed more important than knowing how to speak well. This form of self-distanciation is the prerequisite for self-integration. It may also be described as a way of standing back and looking beyond: standing back from one's own narrow sphere of interests and looking beyond at the whole or at least a larger horizon of community. It is certainly not a mere coincidence that the hero of Egyptian wisdom was both a vizier and an architect. Knowing how to build a pyramid and knowing how to build a state and a society require comparable qualities. Certainly, this is not the kind of state and society we would very probably like to live in, and "Egyptian man," able to perfectly integrate him/herself into this pyramidal sociopolitical edifice is not man as we know or want him today, at least after the breakdown of the socialist totalitarianism, but even this construction of reality was illumined by transcendental visions, otherwise it would not have persisted for three millennia and more. It was certainly not the "house of slavery" as it is debunked in the Bible.[63] What the Egyptian example may teach us is that even the pre-Axial world is the result of positive achievements and that the Axial breakthrough is not just the result of discoveries of what was unknown before, but also the result of conscious acts of rejection, abolition, rebellion that cannot be accounted for in an evolutionary perspective.

By adopting Christianity, the Egyptians themselves were able to perform a change in the most radical way. From champions of integration they turned into champions of isolation. To the ancient Egyptian mind, nothing could perhaps appear more absurd than total self-disembedding, since social embeddedness was identified with life, virtue, and morality. Seth, the god of evil and brutal violence, is the typical solitary one, and everyone fleeing from social life would be associated with Seth and considered as evil.[64] After converting to Christianity, however, the Egyptians became virtuosos of solitude and went to unprecedented extremes in their search for isolation and renunciation. The Egyptian saint Anthony became the patron of Christian hermits, the Egyptian monasteries with their rules as codified by Pachom and Schenute became the models for Christian monasticism. The Egyptians adopted the Christian idea of the Kingdom of God as a goal of integration and reembedment with the same passion and perfection as previously the kingdom of Pharaoh, who was believed to be a god on earth and the son of the highest god.

To the disembedding of man from society and the world corresponds the disembedding of God from cosmic immanence and a pantheon of co-deities. These two movements of disembedding, that is, monotheism and the birth of individualism, have always been seen in strong connection. The connection becomes only the more obvious if one realizes that it is toward God that the hermit and toward man that God turns. The hermit abandons human society in order to draw nearer to God, and God, one could say, renounces divine companionship in favor of the "covenant" he establishes with his chosen people. In the early stages of biblical monotheism, the texts lay great stress on God's "jealousy" and compare the covenant between God and his people, God and man, to the erotic, sexual, and matrimonial bonds between man (God) and wife or bride (Israel). God can by no means be alone; what he abhors most and what puts him into fits of fury and jealousy is to be abandoned by his people. Man, in turn, leaves society not out of misanthropy but for the love of God. Both forms of solitariness, God's and man's, are not absolute but rest on a new form of partnership. In the frame of this partnership, man grows individualistic and God grows monotheistic.

It is fascinating to see how important a role writing, literacy, and scripture play even in this connection. With monotheism, the case is obvious. No monotheistic religion, in fact no "secondary" (i.e., founded) religion can do without a canon of sacred scripture. The solitude of God is, one could say, scripture-based. Similar statements apply to the solitude of man. Generally speaking, there can be a solitary reader but no solitary listener. Writing and reading create the possibility of communication without interaction. To scripture, however, this concept of interaction-free communication applies in a much more poignant sense. Studying the Torah and learning it by heart is the first and foremost requirement of man in the frame of monotheistic religion. Scripture, that is, the Torah, is the only mediator between the two solitary partners, God and man. *Ger anokhi ba-'aretz* ("I am a stranger on earth") the psalmist says in Psalm 119:19, adding: *al-taster mimméni mitswoteýkha* ("do not conceal thy commandments from me"). We see that also man's solitude, his alienation on earth, is scripture-based. God's commandments, which are codified in the Torah, offer him a home that he is missing "on earth." This home is what Heine called "ein portatives Vaterland" and what Bellah calls "a portable religion."

Conclusion

As a result of these considerations concerning literacy as an agent of change in the structure and organization of cultural memory, I have to confess that I cannot bring myself to really believe in the "Axial Age" as a global turn in universal history occurring *grosso modo* in the middle of the first millennium BCE. On the other hand, I find the concept of axiality (with pre- and post-axiality) a valuable and even indispensable analytic tool in the comparative study of cultures. In my view, the stress on the alleged and in several cases undeniable synchronicity of Axial moves has led to an unnecessary mystification of the historical evidence.[65] These "breakthroughs" occurred in different civilizations at different times and to different degrees under different conditions and with different consequences. The undue fascination with time and simultaneity is the congenital defect of the Axial Age theory, lending it the character of a myth rather than a theory. We should give up the idea of synchronicity and, along with it, the tendency to describe the transition from pre-Axial to Axial to post-Axial stages exclusively in terms of evolution. There is, in my view, no evolutionary logic that leads from pre-Axial to Axial societies. Axiality implies always a revolutionary break, a "vertical" intervention of the spirit into the "horizontal" line of natural and cultural evolution.

As far as the "great individuals" are concerned, their appearance in recorded history stretches over several millennia. Akhenaten, who has every right to be included in this number, lived as early as the fourteenth century BCE, Moses, if he ever lived, must equally belong to the second millennium BCE, to which also Zoroaster is now dated by most scholars, whereas there is no reason why Jesus and Mohammad, who came much later, should be excluded. Had his writings been preserved or his visions been institutionalized, we should even include Imhotep, who lived in the twenty-eighth century BCE. The decisive event is not the terrestrial existence of the great individuals but the canonization of their writings. The real "Axial Age" is not the age of the great individuals such as Akhenaten, Zoroaster, Moses, Homer, Isaiah, Plato, Confucius, Buddha, and so on, who did not wait until 800 BCE to appear and who did not disappear by 200 BCE, but the age of secondary canonization. Canonization, as we have seen, is not an individual but a social and collective process. Canonization is the achievement of a society that decides to invest these texts with the highest values, to hold them in the greatest authority, to make them the basis of its life, or to follow their model in artistic creation. There were presumably always great individuals with "transcendental visions." Decisive is the step to turn these visions into "cultural texts," to select these texts into a canon and to frame the transmission of this canon by institutions of exegesis ensuring its availability, readability, and authority over 3,000 years.

If we insist on a first period of axialization, we could point to the years about 200 BCE to 200 CE when the great canons were established: the Confucian, the Daoist, and the Buddhist canons in the East, and the Avesta, the Hebrew Bible and the canon of Greek "classics" in the West. This is not the time when *Homo sapiens axialis,* "the human being with whom we are still living," came into being, but when the texts were canonized that we are still reading. The Axial Age is nothing else but the formative phase of the textual continuity that is still prevailing in our Western and Eastern civilizations.

If we have to give up the concept of an Axial "age" in the sense of a concrete time period in universal history, this does not mean that we have to give up the adjective "Axial" as well. "Axial," it is true, has strong temporal connotations. The axis around which history is believed to revolve, dividing this history into before and after, is a point or period in time. What we have to give up is the universality of this axis and this history. Different civilizations have different turning points in their history. That these turning points coincide temporally may be due to contact or to structural analogies. By no means, however, should this coincidence be promoted to a major factor in the interpretation of the turning point in question. Having occurred around 500 BCE is not per se a feature of axiality. Neither have we to look for the roots of modernity exclusively in this period. It is our cultural memory that reaches back to Homer and Isaiah, but not the emergence of our modern world.

With regard to the ancient world, we are dealing neither with a mutation nor with a "blind" evolution, but with cultural processes stretching over several millennia, implying various historical factors and agents, and implying even reversibility, backward movements of "de-axialization," as has been rightly stressed by Eisenstadt on various occasions. Instead of an Axial "age," we should speak of axiality and axialization in the sense we speak of globalism and globalization, as a tendency that appears under different conditions in different "ages" of human history. Civilizations with a title to qualify as "Axial" should show significant forms of emancipation from tradition and primary world-embeddedness, and a pronounced tendency to formulate ideas or norms with a claim to universal validity. They should be able to produce a canon of texts enshrining these ideas and norms as well as institutions of learning and exegesis that keep their normative and formative impact alive until today. A given civilization arrives at the stage of axiality if these conditions are fulfilled.

It would be highly desirable to distinguish, within or below the two general categories of distanciation and universality, a certain number of "Axial features" such as reflexivity, individuality, interiority ("inner man"), progress in abstraction and intellectuality, theory, critique of tradition, differentiation, transcendental concepts or visions, and so on, and to arrive at a consensus concerning their definition. It is not necessary that all of them be present in a given civilization at a given epoch. Axiality, in my view, should not be conceived of as a Platonic idea[66] that finds its expression in more or less perfection in the course of history, but rather in terms of "family resemblance" in the sense of Ludwig Wittgenstein. Family resemblance connects a set of items and a set of properties in the way that all items share *some* properties with *some* (not all) other items. Time (occurrence around 500 BCE ± 300) has to be ruled out as a significant property. Literacy in the form of cultural, not sectorial, literacy and perhaps even secondary canonization, together with a culture of exegesis as its necessary complement, are probably to be recognized as indispensable prerequisites for most of the "Axial features."

Another question is how to deal with precursors such as ancient Egypt and ancient Mesopotamia. Generalizing from ancient Egypt, my impression is that we should allow for proto-axiality in the sense of intermediate stages between non-axiality and full axiality in the same way as we distinguish prewriting from both pure orality and literacy proper. Among the proto-Axial features in ancient Egypt, I would include the idea of an individual judgment after death with its concepts of individuality and moral responsibility, a rather strong concept of "inner man" in connection both with the judgment of the dead and the rise of "personal piety," a radical rejection of tradition in the context of King Akhenaten and his religious revolution, and, in the aftermath of this revolution, the development of strong concepts of divine transcendence. With regard to Mesopotamia, we may point to considerable steps toward canonization and a rich tradition of commentaries, to the level of theorizing in the fields of astronomy and mathematics, the astounding depth of certain literary texts (especially the *Epic of Gilgamesh*) and the beginnings of historiography. It should also be possible to discern specific "Axial moments" within the history of these and other civilizations that were obviously not numerous or strong enough to bring about the famous "breakthrough" into something that lasts until this day and has therefore a title to count as a root of modernity. It would also be important to account for this failure. Were there no "transcendental visions" in Mesopotamia and Egypt or were there no means of institutionalizing them?

As historians, we have to be careful not to characterize a civilization exclusively by the absence of features that we classify as "Axial" because they belong to our understanding of modernity, and to reconstruct the way that led from past to present civilizations exclusively in terms of evolution. Antiquity is much more than the mere "not yet" of modernity. Much has doubtlessly been lost along this way and much has been rediscovered that in reemerging from oblivion changed our world no less than real inventions and innovations. This is, however, only the historian's point of view, which is by no means the only one possible with regard to the past. It is equally important to look at the past not only for its own sake but also for the sake of the present and the future in order to get a clearer idea of where we come from and "whither we are tending." The idea of the Axial Age is not so much about "man as we know him" and his/her first appearance in time, but about "man as we want him" and the utopian goal of a universal civilized community.

Notes

1. For this interpretation, see my book *Thomas Mann und Ägypten: Mythos und Monotheismus in den Josephsromanen* (Munich, 2006), 15-36.

2. Aleida Assmann calls this "Zentralperspektive in der Geschichte"; see her "Jaspers' Achsenzeit, oder: Schwierigkeiten mit der Zentralperspektive in der Geschichte," in Dietrich Harth, ed., *Karl Jaspers—Denken zwischen Wissenschaft, Politik und Philosophie* (Stuttgart, 1988), 187-205.

3. Thomas Mann, "Die Einheit des Menschengeistes" [1932], in *Gesammelte Werke* (Frankfurt am Main, 1975), vol. 10, 751-755.

4. For details, see my book *Thomas Mann und Ägypten*.

5. Erik H. Erikson, "The Ontogeny of Ritualization in Man," *Philosophical Transactions of the Royal Society* 251 B (1966): 337-349.

6. See Aleida Assmann, "Zeichen—Sprache—Erinnerung: Voraussetzungen und Strategien kultureller Evolution," in Heinrich Schmidinger and Clemens Sedmak, eds., *Der Mensch—ein animal symbolicum? Sprache—Dialog—Ritual* (Darmstadt, 2007), 27-40, esp. 38-40.

7. Dieter Metzler, *Kleine Schriften zur Geschichte und Religion des Altertums und deren Nachleben* (Münster, 2004), 565ff. and 577ff.

8. See Johann Arnason's inversion of Benjamin Schwartz's characterization of the Axial Age ("standing back and locking beyond") as a way of "standing beyond and looking back" in this volume, p. 349.

9. Aleida Assmann, "The Religious Roots of Cultural Memory," *Norsk Teologisk Tidsskrift* 4 (2008): 270-292. She uses the term in a more general sense than it is used in sociological discourse.

10. The distinction between "primary" and "secondary" religion goes back to Theo Sundermeier, "Religion, Religionen," in K. Müller and Th. Sundermeier, eds., *Lexikon missionstheologischer Grundbegriffe* (Berlin, 1987), 411-423, and *Was ist Religion? Religionswissenschaft im theologischen Kontext* (Gütersloh, 1999). See also Andreas Wagner, ed., *Primäre und sekundäre Religion als Kategorie der Religionsgeschichte des Alten Testaments* (Berlin and New York, 2006). My concept of "primary religion" corresponds to Charles Taylor's concept of "early religion," encompassing Bellah's "primitive" and "archaic" religion, although I agree with Bellah that the distinction between these two forms of religion is important. However, since there is an unbroken continuity between "primitive" or tribal and "archaic" religion (related to states and institutions of priesthood), whereas there is always a revolutionary break between these two and "Axial" or "secondary" religions, the first two types of religion may be taken together. I disagree, however, with Bellah in the assumption that the transition from "archaic" to "Axial" religion might be described in the same terms of evolution as the transition from "primitive" to "archaic."

11. For these questions, see my book *Of God and Gods: Egypt, Israel and the Rise of Monotheism* (Madison, 2008).

12. Jaspers, *The Origin and Goal of History* (New Haven, 1953), 2. See also Johann Arnason, "The Axial Age and Its Interpreters: Reopening a Debate," in Johann Arnason, Shmuel Eisenstadt, and Björn Wittrock, eds., *Axial Civilizations and World History* (Leiden, 2005), 31–32.

13. Jaspers, *Origin*, 2. Yehuda Elkana elaborated on the notion of second-order thinking in his contribution "The Emergence of Second-Order Thinking in Classical Greece" in Shmuel Eisenstadt, ed., *The Origins and Diversity of Axial Age Civilizations* (Albany, 1986), 40–64.

14. Benjamin I. Schwartz, "The Age of Transcendence," *Daedalus* 104, no. 2 (1975): 1–7, here 3. On the concepts of "transcendence" and "transcendental" and Schwartz's contribution, see esp. Johann Arnason's chapter in this volume.

15. See, for example, Charles Taylor, *A Secular Age* (Cambridge, 2007). See also Karl Heinz Bohrer, *Der Abschied: Theorie der Trauer; Baudelaire, Goethe, Nietzsche, Benjamin* (Frankfurt am Main, 1997). Bellah, in his 1964 essay on "Religious Evolution," takes into account this change between the "Axial" form of religion and modernity in distinguishing, after "primitive," "archaic," and "historic religions" (i.e., Axial religions), two more recent steps: "early modern religions" and "modern religion." See "Religious Evolution," *American Sociological Review* 29 (1964): 358–374.

16. Obviously, we have to distinguish between the "other-worldly" and the "extra-mundane." Other-worldliness allows for degrees, extramundaneity has to be defined as a categorical chasm without any intermediate stages.

17. See my introduction to the German translation of Eric Voegelin, *Ordnung und Geschichte*, vol 1: *Die kosmologischen Reiche des Alten Orients—Mesopotamien und Ägypten* (Munich, 2002), 17–23.

18. See Jaspers, *Origin*, 2.

19. Arnaldo Momigliano, *Alien Wisdom: The Limits of Hellenization* (Cambridge, 1975), 8. See Robert Bellah, "What Is Axial about the Axial Age?," *European Journal of Sociology* 46 (2005): 69–89, here 72–73, and Hans Joas's contribution in this volume.

20. See Joas's chapter in this volume, n. 14.

21. Aleida Assmann, "Canon and Archive," in Astrid Erll and Ansgar Nünning, eds., *Cultural Memory Studies: An International and Interdisciplinary Handbook* (Berlin and New York, 2008), 97–107.

22. See Peter Schäfer, *Der Triumph der reinen Geistigkeit: Sigmund Freuds "Der Mann Moses und die monotheistische Religion"* (Berlin, 2002), and my article "Der Fortschritt in der Geistigkeit. Freuds Konstruktion des Judentums," *PSYCHE: Zeitschrift für Psychoanalyse und ihre Anwendungen* 56 (2002): 154–171.

23. David Riesman, *The Lonely Crowd: A Study of the Changing American Character* (New Haven, 1950). Riesman describes the emergence of (American) modernity as the transition from inner- to other-directedness, with reference, of course, not to the Axial Age but to the Industrial Revolution.

24. *The Great Transformation—the Beginning of Our Religious Traditions* (New York, 2006); German translation: *Die Achsenzeit: Vom Ursprung der Weltreligionen* (Berlin, 2006).

25. She takes the term from Philippians 2:7: "he emptied himself taking the form of a bond-servant" (ἀλλὰ ἑαυτὸν ἐκένωσεν μορφὴν δούλου λαβών).

26. For the ancient Egyptian ethics of altruism as self-distanciation, see my book *Ma'at: Gerechtigkeit und Unterblichkeit im Alten Ägypten* (Munich, 1990).

27. Charles Taylor, "The Future of the Religious Past," in Hent de Vries, ed., *Religion: Beyond a Concept* (New York, 2008), 178–244, here 185–186.

28. See, for example, Jörn Rüsen, ed., *Westliches Geschichtsdenken* (Göttingen, 1999).

29. Jaspers, *Origin*, 1 and 4 respectively.

30. Eric Voegelin, *Order and History*, vol. 1: *Israel and Revelation* (Baton Rouge, 1956), passim.

31. Anthony Kemp, *The Estrangement of the Past: A Study in the Origins of Modern Historical Consciousness* (New York and Oxford, 1991).

32. Jaspers, *Origin*, 16–17. Jaspers' indebtedness to Alfred Weber's *Kulturgeschichte als Kultursoziologie* (Leiden, 1935) goes in fact much beyond what he himself acknowledges.

33. This distinction between globalism and universalism corresponds *grosso modo* to Garth Fowden's distinction between "political universalism, which is shorthand for 'political, military, and economic universalism' and cultural universalism, which stands for 'cultural and especially religious universalism,' religions being understood to be a constituent part of the wider concept of culture." See G. Fowden, *Empire and Commonwealth: Consequences of Monotheism in Late Antiquity* (Princeton, 1993), 6–7.

34. Peter Artzi, "Ideas and Practices of International Co-existence in the 3rd mill. BCE," *Bar Ilan Studies in History* 2 (1984): 25–39; Artzi, "The Birth of the Middle East," in *Proceedings of the 5th World Congress of Jewish Studies* (Jerusalem, 1969), 120–124.

35. Miriam Lichtheim, *Ancient Egyptian Literature*, vol. 1: *The Old and Middle Kingdoms* (Berkeley, 1973), 224.

36. See Aleida Assmann, *Zeit und Tradition: Kulturelle Strategien der Dauer* (Cologne and Vienna, 1999); Klaus Koch, *Europa, Rom und der Kaiser vor dem Hintergrund von zwei Jahrtausenden Rezeption des Buches Daniel* (Hamburg, 1997); Mariano Delgado, Klaus Koch, and Edgar Marsch, eds., *Europa, Tausendjähriges Reich und Neue Welt: Zwei Jahrtausende Geschichte und Utopie in der Rezeption des Danielbuches* (Fribourg and Stuttgart, 2003).

37. The relationship between historical breakdown and spiritual breakthrough has already been proposed by Eric Weil in his contribution to the 1975 *Daedalus* volume: "What Is a Breakthrough in History?," 21–36.

38. "Axial 'Breakthroughs' and Semantic 'Relocations' in Ancient Egypt and Israel," in Johann Arnason et al., *Axial Civilizations,* 133–156.

39. Walter J. Ong, "Writing Is a Technology That Restructures Thought," in Gerd Baumann, ed., *The Written Word: Literacy in Transition* (Oxford, 1986), 23–50.

40. "Mich dünkt, die Veränderung, die in den verschiedenen Zeiten der Kultur mit den Schriftzeichen vorgegangen, habe von jeher an den Revolutionen der menschlichen Erkenntnis überhaupt und insbesondere an den mannigfachen Abänderungen ihrer Meinungen und Begriffe in Religionssachen sehr wichtigen Anteil."—Moses Mendelssohn, *Jerusalem oder Über religiöse Macht und Judentum,* in *Schriften über Religion und Aufklärung,* ed. Martina Thom (Berlin, 1989), 422–423.

41. See Aleida and Jan Assmann, "Einleitung: Schrift—Kognition—Evolution. Eric A. Havelock und die Technologie kultureller Kommunikation," in Eric A. Havelock, *Die Schriftrevolution im antiken Griechenland* (Weinheim, 1990), 1–36. On pp. 27–28 we give a bibliography of the works published by Ong, Goody, and Havelock until 1990.

42. On the distinction between "canon" and "archive," see Aleida Assmann, "Memory, Individual and Collective," in Robert E. Goodin and Charles Tilly, eds., *The Oxford Handbook of Contextual Political Analysis* (Oxford, 2006), 210–224.

43. Merlin Donald, *Origins of the Modern Mind: Three Stages in the Evolution of Culture and Cognition* (Cambridge, 1991), 308–315.

44. Schreibtafel BM 5645 rto. 2–7, ed. A. H. Gardiner, *The Admonitions of an Egyptian Sage* (Leipzig, 1909), 97–101; M. Lichtheim, *Ancient Egyptian Literature* I (Berkeley, 1973), 146–147; B. G. Ockinga, "The Burden of Kha^{c}kheperre^{c}sonbu," *JEA* 69 (1983): 88–95.

45. The term corresponds more or less to what Eric Havelock in his *A Preface to Plato* (Cambridge, 1963) calls "craft literacy."

46. See my book *Cultural Memory and Early Civilization: Writing, Remembrance, and Political Imagination* (Cambridge, 2012); see also Aleida Assmann, *Cultural Memory and Western Civilization: Functions, Media, Archives* (Cambridge, 2011).

47. Pap. Chester Beatty IV rto. 2.5–3.11; M. Lichtheim, *Ancient Egyptian Literature,* vol. 2: *The New Kingdom* (Berkeley, 1976), 177.

48. Ursula Verhoeven, "Literarische Graffiti in Grab N13.1 in Assiut/Mittelägypten," in P. Kousoulis, ed., *Tenth International Congress of Egyptologists: Abstract of Papers* (Rhodes, 2008), 262.

49. D. Wildung, *Imhotep und Amenhotep: Gottwerdung im alten Ägypten* (Munich, 1977), 28–29.

50. Pap. Chester Beatty IV rto. 2.5–3.11; D. Wildung, *Imhotep und Amenhotep,* 25–27.

51. Herodotus, *Historiae* II, chap. 143.

52. Plato, *Timaios,* 22b.

53. P. Zumthor, *Introduction à la poesie orale* (Paris, 1983), 245–261; see also Aleida Assmann, "Schriftliche Folklore: Zur Entstehung und Funktion eines Überlieferungstyps," in Aleida and Jan Assmann, C. Hardmeier, eds., *Schrift und Gedächtnis: Beiträge zur Archäologie der literarischen Kommunikation* (Munich, 1983), 175–193.

54. Leo Oppenheim, *Ancient Mesopotamia: Portrait of a Dead Civilization* (Chicago, 1968), 13.

55. See Aleida and Jan Assmann, eds., *Kanon und Zensur* (Munich, 1987).

56. The case of India, where the sacred texts were not written down but memorized by specialists, the Brahmin, seems to contradict this reconstruction, because here, in the context of oral tradition, we also meet with secondary canonization and traditions of exegesis. Here, however, the techniques of memorization have been brought to a degree of perfection that human memory could very well fulfill one of the main functions of writing, which is stabilizing the text. The decision to withhold the sacred texts from writing seems to have been common to several Indo-European religions such as Zoroastrianism and the Celtic Druidism. It is usually explained as an attempt to avoid the mistakes of copyists, but the main motive seems to have been the fear of unwanted dissemination, which is also one of Plato's arguments against writing. Stabilizing the text can be achieved either by writing or by an elaborate mnemotechnique. The latter requires usually a very strict poetic formalization of the text.

57. Michael Fishbane, *Biblical Interpretation in Ancient Israel* (Oxford, 1986).

58. See Jan Assmann and Burghard Gladigow, eds., *Text und Kommentar* (Munich, 1995).

59. See Ernst A. Schmidt, "Historische Typologie der Orientierungsfunktionen von Kanon in der griechischen und römischen Literatur," in Aleida and Jan Assmann, eds., *Kanon und Zensur,* 246–258.

60. Flavius Josephus, *Contra Apionem,* cap. 22, in W. Warburton, *The Divine Legation of Moses* (London, 1738–1741), vol. 1, 192–193.

61. For this distinction, see my book *Das kulturelle Gedächtnis,* 87–103.

62. For these beliefs, see my book *Death and Salvation in Ancient Egypt* (Ithaca, 2005).

63. It is also very important not to mistake the "connectivism" of Ma'at for the collectivism of certain modern ideologies. Collectivism presupposes the existence of ideas of communities such as tribe, people, nation, state, and so on that claim predominance over the individual member. None of these ideas exist in the ancient Egyptian lexicon, unlike, for example, the Hebrew Bible with its emphasis on concepts of community, especially the idea of a "holy people" (*goj qadosh,* Exod. 19:6).

64. See my article "Literatur und Einsamkeit im alten Ägypten," in Aleida and Jan Assmann, eds., *Einsamkeit* (Munich, 2000), 97–112.

65. See also Stefan Breuer, *Der Staat. Entstehung, Typen, Organisationsstadien* (Reinbek, 1998), 101, and "Kulturen der Achsenzeit. Leistungen und Grenzen eines geschichtsphilosophischen Konzepts," *Saeculum* 45, no. 1 (1994): 1–33.

66. Jaspers' "Platonism" has been criticized also by Jürgen Habermas, *Philosophisch-politische Profile,* 3rd ed. (Frankfurt am Main, 1981), 92.

Perspectives on the Future

16

The Axial Invention of Education and Today's Global Knowledge Culture

WILLIAM M. SULLIVAN

Education in its most basic sense is coeval with humanity. In historical societies, as the author of a distinguished study of education in Western antiquity has noted, education can be seen as transmitting "the concentrated epitome of a culture and as such it is inseparable from the form of that culture and perishes with it."[1] In another sense, however, as the conscious effort to form—and reform—human individuals and society to correspond to ideals of imagined but unrealized possibilities, education is one of the great legacies of the Axial turn. The new human possibilities envisioned by the great Axial figures gave rise to formative practices that outlasted the societies in which they first appeared. Moreover, the educational aims and institutions that emerged from Axial movements have in several instances gone on to profoundly shape subsequent human societies, not least our contemporary global era.

In what follows I want to confront one such Axial legacy, Plato's advocacy of a philosophical education to transform individual perspective, with the unintended consequences of one of the most remarkable developments of the past half century, the dramatic worldwide expansion of university education. This educational diffusion represents the propagation of an institutional model derived from European and American developments that can claim an intellectual heritage reaching back to Plato and classical Greece through Latin Christendom. As analyzed by John Meyer and others, the contemporary model of the university can be understood as a great culture-forming agency of modernity, a "secular canopy, drawing cultural matters, people, and nature under a universalized umbrella, and providing religious-like cultural unity."[2]

Today's global knowledge culture centered on the university disseminates cultural norms that everywhere celebrate ideals of individual agency rooted in capacities for grasping experience through abstract, universal concepts. This culture of knowledge understands everyone as potentially rights-bearing individuals capable of entering into political relations and market transactions for mutual benefit. It therefore propagates central features of modernity across older civilizational boundaries. In that sense it carries on the Axial project of universalization.

At the same time, it is both intolerant of nontheoretic forms of knowledge and militant in its advocacy of a strong version of individual agency. This culture trusts wholly in the theoretic in Merlin Donald's and Robert Bellah's sense, while it typically ignores or directly challenges tradition-based understandings of identity and selfhood. In these ways it seems to echo Axial themes associated with the Platonic heritage. However, at the same time its dominant form inculcates as its way of understanding reality a "closed immanent frame," in Charles Taylor's phrase, thereby occluding as a source of meaning the awesome transcendent of the Platonic tradition.

The knowledge culture fostered by the contemporary university is a major feature of the world society prone to what Jürgen Habermas has memorably called crises of legitimation.[3] In the eyes of many, especially outside Europe, Japan, and North America, the workings of the economic and political institutions of today's global society threaten to frustrate and undercut the ethical norms of equality and universality that legitimate this order. Beyond that, the university seems unable to avoid communicating to many a weakening of meaning and sense of alienation even as it expands scientific knowledge and technological capacities. The question I want to address is whether a better understanding of the Axial era and its tensions, such as that proposed by Bellah in his work on religious evolution, could help reshape global educational culture to realign theoretic reason with moral-practical sources of understanding?[4] How might such a reconfigured educational culture sustain the "Axial tension," in S. N. Eisenstadt's phrase, as a creative source for a richer, more ecumenical global culture?

Plato's Complex Legacy: *Paideia* as *Logos* and *Mythos*

Platonic philosophy emerged in Athens of the fourth century BCE as one of several responses to what Bellah calls the perceived "breakdown" of that society's inherited moral order. By emphasizing this cultural breakdown in the face of rapid political expansion, prolonged warfare, and unexpected defeat, Bellah locates the Axial "breakthrough" of Socratic-Platonic philosophy in a situation analogous to the civilizational crises that Karl Jaspers described in his pioneering exposition of the emergence of the Axial figures.[5] Bellah also follows Werner Jaeger in presenting Plato, and his mentor Socrates, as linked to the new cultural movement led by the Sophists. This pioneering cultural movement appeared in response to these tensions, becoming an integral feature of the Hellenic "enlightenment" that would later be so important as a model in the early phases of Western modernity.[6]

The Sophists were itinerant intellectuals who gained livelihood and influence by providing a new kind of training for elite young Greeks, one based not on traditional poetic sources but on a logical analysis of arts of speech and persuasion, the skills of ruling in the contentious Greek cities. Jaeger emphasized that these Sophists were the first to develop a self-conscious art of pedagogy, coining the term *paideia,* or "culture." They embodied this insight in an explicit educational program, the "trivium" familiar to the European Middle Ages: the study of grammar, logic or "dialectic," and rhetoric. Donald has noted that the Sophists' invention of rhetoric was a self-reflective turn within a culture already characterized by argumentative discourse in many areas. For Donald, rhetoric represents the first attempt to separate the forms of the "metalinguistic skills" essential in a mostly oral culture from their traditional content, making possible both a systematic analysis of argumentative discourse and a "systematic curriculum for the training of thought skills and habits."[7]

The invention of rhetoric, at once scientific and pedagogical, was both the product and the basis for the Sophists' remarkable cultural creativity. In effect, they developed a protosocial scientific approach to culture and religion, analyzing traditional practices and beliefs in a consciously critical and reductionistic way. As Plato saw it, the educational and, more broadly, cultural implications of this development were manifest: the subversion of all moral norms through the instrumentalizing of speech in the service of individual advantage. The social consequences seemed equally manifest in the general moral breakdown, and threats of tyranny, endemic in late fifth-century Athenian democracy.

As Bellah presents the situation, Plato saw Socrates as an alternative to such cultural implosion, a figure at once self-consciously critical of aspects of the received culture and yet not nihilistic, committed in both word and deed to a loyalty to norms beyond the purely instrumental and self-regarding. Plato's philosophical writings would become efforts to understand the meaning of Socrates' life and death and, increasingly, essays toward institutionalizing a Socratic perspective as an alternative basis for Greek culture itself. In Plato's hands, this project came to mean a full-scale *paideia* that could compete not only with the traditional *mythos* or narrative imagination of the poets but with the instrumental rationalism of the Sophists as well. That drove Plato to search for ways to find in *logos* an evaluative dimension, to ground the "training of thought skills and habits" within a new sense of the transcendence and objectivity of moral order.

The result, as tentatively articulated and revised in a series of "dialogues," Bellah calls Plato's new "hybrid system." He means a culture that sought guidance in the newly developed capacities of theoretic reason but that was nonetheless deploying all three of Donald's levels of consciousness: mythic and mimetic as well as the theoretic.[8] The dialogues themselves, especially the so-called Middle Dialogues such as the *Republic* (often in antiquity called *On Education*), present the new Platonic arguments within a narrative, indeed dramatic framework, making their interpretation notoriously complex and open-ended. However, it is in these Middle Dialogues that Plato provides the fullest, indeed perhaps *the* paradigmatic articulation of the Axial movement in Greece. Particularly in the *Republic*'s central metaphors or parables, as Bellah calls them, we can see a clear articulation of Taylor's notion of the Axial as "disembedding."[9]

The famous Parable of the Cave seems to set out clearly all three dimensions of Axial disembedding. The "lover of wisdom" who is able to "turn around" and is drawn upward out of the cave in search of the light of reality breaks with the existing social order, now denigrated as a dark place of bondage, with the traditional understanding of the world, suddenly revealed as a realm of shadowy illusion, and even with conventional goals of living, now shown up as guided by no more than futile guesses about the human good. At the climax of the journey, the philosopher experiences a transformative vision of the form of the Good. This encounter with the transcendent source of reality changes the philosopher, who becomes able to imagine a very different kind of self capable of living and shaping another sort of society in accord with transcendent norms of truth and goodness.

Philosophy emerges in the Parable of the Cave as an educational process of expanding the horizon of understanding and aligning oneself with this wider view of the whole of reality instead of the narrow and confused aims of life in the cave. However, the narrative of disembedding is concluded by a reverse journey, a kind of reembedding: the return of the transformed philosopher to the cave for the sake of those still enchained by illusion. So the Axial movement of disembedding is closely followed by a parallel but opposite action by the philosopher, who strives to realign soul and society with this new understanding of reality.

This picture is further developed in the story that in Book VII follows immediately on the Parable of the Cave. Here Plato presents the reader with another kind of narrative: a model curriculum, a developmental *paideia* for shaping the soul of the philosophers who are to rule Socrates' imagined good city. In this narrative, development begins in Donald's *mimetic,* with dance and sports shaping body and sensibilities. To this is added the *mythic* learning of poetry, building on the rhythms established through embodied experience within the linguistic and symbolic realm. Finally, and crucially, the content of these preparatory studies is articulated in *theoretic* form, brought to explicit and critical awareness through a reflective thought process modeled on Greek mathematics and astronomy (*Rep.* 553a–540a).

Plato here provides the historically earliest sketch of the notion that "higher education" should be heavily "theoretic" in nature, focused on developing formal-operational thinking. This higher phase, however, would draw upon but also criticize the concrete-operational thought fostered in the students' earlier induction into literature and culture, the abstract and general building upon and acting back upon the more concrete and particular. So, in Plato's developmental story, philosophy would use mathematics, logic, and rhetorical theory to organize, criticize, and rearticulate literature and the arts. Plato would thereby take up the critical discourse of the Sophists, but in a Socratic moral project. The aim of his educational program would be to instill a reflective reverence and to shape a thoughtful response to the philosopher's encounter with the goodness at the core of reality. As we will see, this is a program strikingly parallel in structure yet different in aim from the modern culture of the university.

In Socrates' telling, after this long and arduous education, the future rulers are then to spend years as apprentices in ruling the good city, learning how in practice to bring unchanging Goodness into the realm of confusion and change. This phase represents what we might call a higher *mimesis,* the conscious modeling of self and activity on the wider reality disclosed by philosophical study. Finally—and the order is different from that in the Parable of the Cave—the development of the philosophers remains incomplete, perhaps not fully authentic, without the experience of encounter with the Good itself, the principle that transcends form yet provides the ground of all structure and the source of all value. Whether Plato considered this critical transformative vision a kind of theoretic reflection or something closer to embodied experience is ambiguous. Famously, in his Seventh Letter, Plato denied that true philosophy can be taught by written concepts, requiring rather that a "spark of understanding and intelligence flashes out and illuminates the subject at issue."[10]

These two central educational narratives from the *Republic* introduce a strong note of "Axial tension" between the conditions of existing life and claims of transcendent reality. The connection between the two movements—the arduous disembedding and the equally demanding efforts to realign oneself with the expanded horizon of reality—is a transformation of understanding that Plato describes in largely mythic terms: enlightenment, seeing, lifting up one's soul, and so forth. This sharpening of insight, however, is followed by the practice of "imitating" what is "seen." The object of such encounters is never described directly. It is said to lie beyond all words and forms. Yet Plato also describes it as the source and ground of being, like the sun in the visible world.

Hans-Georg Gadamer has made the important observation that the philosophical aim at knowing, which starts off the process of seeking reality, necessarily grows out of prior, prereflective involvement in and with the world. Like the "radiance" of a work of art, experiences of truth and goodness can "happen" to us, drawing us into a relationship with a reality that suddenly illuminates but also surpasses us, making demands to which we must respond.[11] Yet finally, the experience calls out for a response: like Plato's philosopher, each person must consciously aim to make an adequate response to Goodness as encountered. Or as Plato describes the psychic dynamic at work throughout the educational narratives of the *Republic*: "Or do you think it possible not to imitate the things to which anyone attaches himself with admiration?" (*Rep.* 500c, Loeb trans.) A return to *mimesis* at a higher level indeed.

Plato's pioneering explorations of these issues bequeathed to posterity a number of ambiguities and unresolved tensions. The whole educational scheme was grounded in a problematic sense of a cosmos in which the transcendent was somehow immanent but never fully embodied. This problem ensured that something of Plato's own Axial tension continued to haunt philosophical education. Even within the Platonic tradition itself, a long argument developed. There were those Platonists who saw the object of the philosophic quest as "flight" from the distorted world of experience to transcendent unity. Others argued that the point was to become "at home" within the wider and deeper context disclosed by appearance of transcendence within the multiplicity.

It was never clear, however, whether Plato's apparent aim to supplant the traditional forms of everyday life with philosophically prescribed *mores,* as depicted in *The Laws* for example, was a practical aim. Furthermore, the issue of how to reshape customs, the proper mix of what Plato had called "persuasion" and "necessity" or coercion remained unresolved as well. It is worth noting, however, that in antiquity the practice of philosophy was always considered a "way of life" that involved practices of self-formation aligned with the metaphysical articulation of a particular philosophical approach. The mythic and mimetic forms of consciousness, therefore, continued to have their place.[12]

When Christianity developed its deep but uneasy symbiosis with Greek philosophy, particularly Platonism, these tensions continued. In the centuries of post-Axial "compromise" in Latin Christendom, as Taylor describes it, intellectual elites tended to adopt a stance of compromise or accommodation with traditional forms of embodiment. This meant that the educational ideals proposed by the Axial movements functioned in rough symbiosis with more particularistic, mythical images and models of human identity and solidarity. The custody of these hybrid cultures was largely the charge of intellectual, usually religious elites who, for both good and ill, became experts in the maintenance, and occasional reworking, of common rituals, myths, and symbols upon which Christendom, like the other post-Axial civilizations, depended.

The slow but decisive disruption of this "compromise" that Taylor calls "Reform" has left in its widening wake the remarkable and historically unprecedented cultural situation we call modernity. By taking an activist stance toward everyday life, the reformers of Latin Christendom set in motion efforts to realize the Axial critique of traditional, or in Bellah's terms, archaic forms of life. One of the most startling results of these efforts has been the diffusion of modern education as an institution for the compulsory reculturation of everyone.

The University as Modern Architectonic Cultural Institution

The kinds of knowledge produced by the university and the personnel it certifies have become central to nearly all aspects of what we understand as progress in the social, economic, and political domains. Indeed, in selecting personnel for occupational roles, educational certification has become virtually the only legitimate form of discrimination. It is as though the utopian proposal of Plato's *Republic* that the rulers of the just city should be chosen on the basis of intellectual and moral merit had been realized—at least as regards the intellectual merit—on a universal scale. (In imperial China, something approaching this idea was institutionalized in the examination system based upon the Confucian classics.) However, the critical certifying role of the university today has not arisen because universities can be shown to do a particularly good job of preparing people for the actual business of carrying on functions in the occupational order, nor because they have necessarily the most egalitarian of selective processes. On the contrary, as David Frank and Meyer argue, there is much evidence that "the university certifies individuals ... without actually preparing them to meet occupational role demands."[13] On a macrolevel across societies, the worldwide expansion of universities since World War II also correlates only weakly with measures of national growth in functional effectiveness in economic, military, or political spheres.[14]

Instead of searching for elusive, and he believes, illusory functional explanations for this expansion, Meyer counters the usual functionalist sociology of education with the argument that the evidence supports a very different hypothesis. "The university," he argues, "is less about training people for jobs in the complex society, and more about establishing the ground rules for this society—the doctrines that local realities and actions can and should be seen in terms of universal principles."[15] The university, in this view, is an institution of culture-formation more than it is a motor of social, economic, or even technological development. Its main function is to induct young people into the use of what Richard Madsen in his contribution to this volume, following Mary Douglas and Basil Bernstein, calls "elaborated speech codes." The "functionality" of the university is in this sense cultural rather than technical.

Meyer characterizes his view as sociological institutionalism. As a theory, it is antireductionistic, postulating institutions as holistic symbolic forms, cultural models made up of constitutive rules that societies use to establish and enforce a particular conception of reality and moral order. That is, institutions both establish what is taken as "real" and also provide individuals and collectivities with legitimation for aspirations and actions in accord with their rule-like norms. The amazing fact about the university-based culture of knowledge, Meyer argues, is that over the past half century it has been able to make its definitions of reality and legitimate purposes prevail against a large variety of more local traditions. In today's world, any state seeking to be seen as modern hastens to establish a university on the cosmopolitan model of the "advanced countries," while it selects its personnel from among those certified by either its own or similar foreign universities. Similarly, for individuals anywhere, university education has become ever more important as the singular route to full participation within the global economic and political order.

It is an important feature of our world that both proponents and critics of today's "globalizing" institutions share this culture in common. Its core is what Meyer and associates call "analytical reason." For members of this culture, knowledge—and therefore reality—share common abstract and universal features. As universities have spread and grown more central to the institutional order everywhere, analytical reason has become established as the only legitimate source and guarantee of knowledge, at least for elites involved in constructing global institutions and relationships. As Meyer puts it: "Universities recast concrete, local, and particular understandings into abstract, global, and universal knowledge."[16] As particular matters are categorized in general terms, what is real is understood as a law-like order of abstract and causal relationships. The model for this is, of course, the natural sciences. However, in an empirical study of university curricula and organizational change around the world over the past century, Frank and Jay Gabler have shown how homogeneous the expansion of such thinking has been as evidenced in changes within university curricula and faculties. They note in particular the growth of the analytical social sciences and the concomitant decline in the traditional humanities disciplines with their concerns for inherited national and religious cultures.[17]

As individuals shaped by the global knowledge culture come to understand it, the world, both natural and social, makes sense as the resultant effects of abstract and universal processes. At the same time, the physical, social, and indeed psychological worlds appear more and more available for use and manipulation. Indeed, the center of the global knowledge culture is occupied by a conception of the individual as actor in a very strong sense. In effect, the global culture of knowledge propagated by the university as an institution "anchors" its claims in "individualized persons" who now claim "sovereignty" over all sorts of realms once controlled by extrahuman forces, increasingly even "over matters of life and death." The basic notion is that self-conscious human initiative can grasp the world and intervene in it for human improvement. This is the context, Meyer asserts, in which notions of promoting human rights and global environmentalism take form.

The premises of the university's sweeping reformation of global culture, however, are rarely fully transparent, even to its most ardent advocates. This is because they are rooted in a kind of mythic structure that sees "progress and justice" as the "natural" goals of human societies. Meyer claims that this "rational myth" is in fact the descendent of medieval Christendom, but in a highly secularized, this-worldly form. Since World War II, American hegemony has facilitated the spread of a highly individualistic, as opposed to more nationalist or corporatist, version of these premises. The result is an emerging world society "founded upon the ultimate rights of human individuals, bound together by common humanity and embedded in a scientized nature and rationalized society."[18] The culture of the university, as Meyer sums it up, is crucial to this myth of "progress and justice." The university "tames and 'scientizes' and universalizes nature; it rationalizes models of society; and it celebrates the extraordinary capabilities for agentic action of the supreme modern individual." This institutionalizing of the culture of analytical reason thereby "creates the cultural conditions enabling the contemporary society."[19]

Meyer places his theory of educational institutions within a narrative of modernity that parallels the accounts of the Axial transformation and its consequences developed by Bellah and Taylor, Eisenstadt and Habermas, among others. Meyer also emphasizes, however, the historically extraordinary optimism embodied in the premises of this culture. It presupposes that both individuals and societies can be "improved" cognitively, technologically, and morally by conscious effort: the primacy of education in modern societies is precisely the embodiment of this optimism about consciously undertaken collective self-improvement.[20] At the same time, Meyer points out, this global educational culture imagines this process as lifting individuals out of less rational, more local and particular understandings of themselves and the world into this modern realm defined by analytical reasoning, universal concepts, and autonomous agency.

Other commentators have noted that the university in its earlier phases was able to rely upon an explicit philosophical Idealism to reveal the idea of a substantive culture immanent in the many forms of analytical thought. Now, whatever cohesion there is can be provided only by common procedures for testing and communicating analytical investigation.[21] It is perhaps an indirect confirmation of Meyer's claim for the mythic status of the underlying dynamic that confidence remains high in the face of institutional imperatives that often seem guided by little substantive purpose or meaning.

Sophism Redivivus? The University and the "Dark Side" of Cosmopolitanism

There is no lack of a literature criticizing these premises. However, it is worth noting the range and persistence of some of these criticisms. For example, in *The Revolt of the Elites* (1995), Christopher Lasch raised concerns about the effects of higher education. He depicts a culture of knowledge that is more Sophistic than Platonic. Higher education's great function is to initiate students into a distinctive "culture of critical discourse" that resembles Meyer's analytical mind and the "elaborated speech codes" of Douglas. This culture values innovation over continuity, flexibility and variety over loyalty, technical intelligence and instrumental finesse over character and moral cultivation, and iconoclasm over reverence. Since this culture is the key to elevation into superior status, possession of the credentials of critical discourse leads those who master it to see themselves as meritorious, problem-solving experts. Lasch points out that such experts tend to see themselves and their lives in strategic terms, often consumed by maneuvering for the better deal in the status competition internal to professional occupations. When embraced naively, Lasch concludes, this apparently sophisticated consciousness becomes the growing soil of nihilism.[22]

Some of the more influential analyses of the "information economy" have raised similar issues. In a succession of studies of the new workforce staffing the advanced sectors of the global economy, former U.S. secretary of labor Robert Reich has called attention to the pivotal position of university-educated workers he calls "symbolic analysts." This is a broad category, as much cultural as economic, that includes researchers, engineers, lawyers, and journalists. Their common identifying feature is that they live by "identifying and solving problems," "doing conceptual puzzles," and playing the role of strategic brokers among various groups and organizations. "The symbolic-analytic mind," Reich summarizes, "is trained to be skeptical, curious, and creative."[23] Their structural position as staff for increasingly global firms and organizations tilts symbolic analysts toward a strategic and instrumental cast of mind.

Reich descries the appearance among the ascendant symbolic analysts of "the darker side of cosmopolitanism." He writes: "Without strong attachments and loyalties extending beyond family and friends, symbolic analysts may never develop the habits and attitudes of social responsibility. They will be world citizens, but without accepting or even acknowledging any of the obligations that citizenship in a polity normally implies."[24] Reich fears that such people will resist any calls for common sacrifice and commitment based on justice and fairness, ideals they may find to be "meaningless abstractions." There are clear echoes of Reich's analysis in the otherwise more enthusiastic portrayals of today's symbolic analysts in David Brook's "bourgeois-bohemian" high achievers and Richard Florida's "creative class."[25]

There may be yet another, paradoxical, problem attendant upon the successful diffusion of the university's culture of analytical reasoning as the lingua franca of our global elites. As we have seen, today's political left and right, both proponents of Neoliberalism and opponents of the World Trade Organization, share a many common assumptions as a result of their schooling. This can and surely does promote global integration, as in the rapid growth in nongovernmental organizations and transnational associations and social movements. Yet Meyer points out that the spread of the culture of analytical discourse can also "serve as a mechanism for greatly enhanced social conflict in a world with so much actual inequality and diversity." Once they come to be seen "in the light of a common universalistic culture and schooled stratification system," inequalities are "increasingly difficult to legitimate," and as Meyer notes, this can make once incidental cultural differences sources of major conflicts over access to and control of societal resources.[26]

The "theoretic" as Bellah and Donald describe it is the horizon of our age. Yet the criticisms just surveyed suggest that the abstract and universalistic features of the current global culture, despite the optimism of their advocates, create problems of legitimacy as they come closer to apparent triumph. Perhaps the ideals of our global culture require a prior, tacit integration into the underlying "rational myth" of "progress and justice" with its attendant attitudes toward change and possibility in order to avoid the alienating consequences that seem all too evident in many parts of the world. Certainly, in a world economy characterized by ever more rapid forms of what Joseph Schumpeter called capitalism's "creative destruction," something like Habermas's colonization of the cultural "life-world" by the "systems" of strategic action seems likely to be an endemic feature of our era.[27]

The final question I want to consider is how to do justice to the claims of modern subjectivity and creativity, themselves legacies of the Axial Age, by developing a culture that can reembed the theoretic within care for the world without losing openness to the transcendent. The culture of the theoretic seems inherently dependent for stability upon its rootedness in narrative and mimetic modes of engaging the world and constituting human selves through social relationships. If this is so, we also need a richer, more comprehensive vision of education for an ecumenical global world. Such a vision of *paideia* for our times has to find ways to integrate rather than suppress both the theoretic and the moral-practical dimensions of consciousness and culture. In what follows I want to suggest such an educational project by building upon the cultural vision of the classic American pragmatist philosophers, especially George Herbert Mead and John Dewey.

Resources for the Renewal of *Paideia* as an Educational Agenda

One of the peculiarities of the global theoretic culture is its belief in its own self-sufficiency as well as the legitimacy of its standing in judgment of various forms of embedded and embodied consciousness. These ideas have long been supported by Enlightenment philosophical epistemology and some versions of moral philosophy. However, if Bellah and Donald are correct, this self-sufficiency is an illusion, and indeed not simply an innocent one. While the theoretic is the most universal and self-aware representational mode available to us as modern humans, in an epigenetic sense it is clear that the development of theoretic consciousness, like learning elaborated speech codes, grows out of and depends upon prior competence in the narrative and mimetic modes. A large body of research in both psychology and sociology supports this conclusion.

Philosophically, the epistemology upon which the self-sufficiency of the theoretic has stood has been challenged by phenomenological thinkers, critiques stemming from the work of the late Wittgenstein, and the American pragmatic tradition. These philosophical currents converge on the notion that explicit, articulate understanding necessarily grows out of and depends upon a prior and more encompassing prereflective sense of things. This "background" or tacit sense of participation within a whole is presupposed by conscious articulation but cannot be encompassed by it without remainder. Human cognition is grounded in social practices, as Taylor emphasizes in his contribution to this volume.

This prereflective grounding of the theoretic in practical engagement provides the inescapable source of linguistic and conceptual meaning. Moreover, since this engagement is unavoidably social, all forms of knowledge, including the theoretic, necessarily presuppose forms of community activity for their functioning and sense. There is no use of the theoretic, even epistemology, that does not tacitly presuppose its own embedding in some linguistic medium and mimetic practices. This philosophical critique has returned engagement with the world to its place as a constitutive feature of all human consciousness. Such a reconnection also opens again the possibility of encounter with transcendence and the question of response to the transcendent that was, as we have seen in the case of Plato, a determining factor in the genesis of Axial movements toward formative education.

Dewey's philosophy provides an instructive example of a systematic working out of the implication of these insights. Dewey's theory of inquiry placed the detached, analytical stance of scientific investigation as a "moment" within the larger process of human experience. Dewey noted how modern natural science has enabled our species to better understand the workings of nature, and in certain areas to control nature in support of human purposes.[28] However, the reason for undertaking the investigation in the first place, as well as its potential meaning, come only from those shared, historically rooted cultural meanings that Dewey sometimes called "experience."

Dewey argued that it was a shared "experience," or cultural ethos, that enables a group of interacting investigators to perceive a situation as "problematic" in the first place, and therefore a stimulus to inquiry. Purposeful human activity, or *praxis* in the Greek sense, is thus the ground and also the goal of analytic thinking. For Dewey, the point of inquiry is to restore, or reconstitute, the flow of meaningful activity in social life. Analytic thinking is successful when it contributes to a fuller, more adequate understanding of the salience of events in light of some aim or purpose. The construction of such aims and purposes is largely the work of narrative and reflection of collective experience rather than a deduction from analytical principles. Human rationality in its full sense is ultimately practical—and therefore social, historical, and narrative—by nature.[29]

With the emergence of theoretic forms of thinking, the analytical phase of inquiry has gradually become codified and institutionalized. However, fixating on the analytical phase of inquiry threatens to short-circuit the crucial relationship between interaction and reflection that Dewey believed constitutes social learning. Dewey's theory of inquiry was his attempt to provide a release from this fixation on analysis at the expense of other dimensions of experience. His theory of inquiry restates and generalizes the central insights of Aristotle's notion of practical reasoning, in effect making theory a special case of practical insight.[30] Dewey set out to map this wider terrain of human rationality in order to circumvent the theoretic trap. What needs more emphasis today than in Dewey's time is the vital necessity of regrounding the university's legitimate concern to foster analytical thinking upon the meaningfulness of lived experience itself. More than ever, today's higher education needs Dewey's insight that intellectual reflection—the transmuting of meaningful experience into general concepts—is not an end in itself, but a potentially helpful guide for engaging more richly and responsibly the terrain of experience.

Dewey also sought to move beyond critique toward the practical reshaping of modern education. Writing in the early twentieth century, his efforts were focused on pre-university schooling, but his approach has two valuable lessons for the global university culture of our time. First, Dewey sought to place education within an explicitly historical, and therefore narrative, context. Second, Dewey sought to make education a conscious form of the kind of normative social experience he called "democracy."

Famously, Dewey thought that learning should be carried out through experience of basic "occupations," in order to locate school learning within what today would be called the "authentic performance" of key social practices. But these occupations were not "jobs" so much as what Dewey termed "points of departure." Deweyan schooling was to be careful induction into the larger narrative of human evolution in which, by taking up an "occupation" in both its concreteness and its imaginative location in this history, all learning could be situated in "the central dramas of humanity, our effort . . . to build civilization in the mutual transformations of earth and humankind."[31] The method of thinking implicit throughout was "inquiry," the movement from "problematic situation" through reflective problem-solving or analysis, to "reconstruction of experience" through redesigned technique or social practice. But this process of remaking and in a sense reenacting human historical development was to be, at the same time, an education for and through democracy. Dewey, like Mead, understood democracy in a wide sense as the goal and means of consciously constructed "conjoint activity."[32] This normative aim, too, was implicit in the method of inquiry used throughout.

Dewey's was perhaps a Romantic and optimistically American vision of education. In that distinctive idiom, however, his program consciously recognized and tried to reconstruct for pedagogical purposes the tension between the theoretic and the narrative and mimetic dimensions of human experience. And it presented these within a "grand narrative" of historical emergence. Dewey was proposing an educational form of "mythistory," to use William McNeill's term, the effort to use critical, analytical insight in the service of the larger goal of providing an account of human affairs that "fits experience better," yet is neither narrowly ethnocentric nor too detached to provide the basis for "coherent public action" within a cosmopolitan world. Discussing the difficult relationship between the critical and the guiding aims of the historians' enterprise, McNeill argues the primacy of aiming at a wide perspective in which "the things that unite human beings would come to the fore . . . a matrix for mutual understanding and more effective public action . . . avoiding the mistaken notion that generalization [in itself] involves error."[33]

The mythistory underlying Dewey's educational program is for many reasons no longer adequate. Yet it clearly was able to play one of the roles of that McNeill singles out for serious, constructive historical narrative: expanding the sympathies of the groups being addressed while yet balancing "ecumenical and parochial" points of view so as to make significant participation in the concerns of human society.[34] But is meaningful education possible without some functional equivalent? Is the "pedagogy" of the world market, including the world labor market, a sufficient basis for the continuing development of the theoretic, analytical culture of knowledge? If not, then we may find earlier orienting models of *paideia* a necessary if not sufficient guide for redeeming the ambiguous promise of global modernity. We will have reason to hope for the truth of Bellah's adage that in human evolution "nothing is ever lost."

Notes

1. Henri Marrou, *A History of Education in Antiquity* (New York: Sheed and Ward, 1956), xviii.

2. David John Frank and John W. Meyer, "Worldwide Expansion and Change in the University," unpublished paper, Stanford University, January 5, 2006, 13. See also Evan Schofer and John W. Meyer, "The Worldwide Expansion of Higher Education in the Twentieth Century," *American Sociological Review* 70 (December 2005): 898–920.

3. Jürgen Habermas, *Legitimation Crisis* (Boston: Beacon Press, 1975).

4. Quotations and references will henceforth be to Robert Bellah, *Religion in Human Evolution: From the Paleolithic to the Axial Age* (Cambridge, MA: The Belknap Press of Harvard University Press, 2011).

5. Karl Jaspers, *The Origin and Goal of History* (New Haven: Yale University Press, 1953).

6. Bellah, *Religious Evolution,* chap. 6, 94ff.

7. Merlin Donald, *Origins of the Modern Mind: Three Stages in the Evolution of Culture and Cognition* (Cambridge, MA: Harvard University Press, 1991), 346.

8. Bellah, *Religious Evolution,* chap. 6, 115.

9. Charles Taylor, *A Secular Age* (Cambridge, MA: Harvard University Press, 2007), 146–158.

10. Plato, *Seventh Letter* (344b) in *Phaedrus and Letters VII and VIII,* trans. Walter Hamilton (London and New York: Penguin Books, 1973), 140.

11. Hans-Georg Gadamer, *Dialogue and Dialectic: Eight Hermeneutical Studies on Plato* (New Haven and London: Yale University Press, 1980), 88–91. See also Gadamer, *Truth and Method,* 2nd ed. (New York: Continuum Press, 1993), 106–169.

12. See Pierre Hadot, *Philosophy as a Way of Life* (Oxford: Blackwell Publishers, 1995), esp. 81–125.

13. Frank and Meyer, "Worldwide Expansion," 10.

14. John W. Meyer, Richard Rubinson, Francisco O. Ramirez, and John Boli-Bennett, "The World Educational Revolution, 1950–1970," *Sociology of Education* 50 (October 1977): 242–258.

15. Frank and Meyer, "Worldwide Expansion," 1.

16. Ibid., 12.

17. David John Frank and Jay Gabler, *Reconstructing the University: Worldwide Shifts in Academia in the 20th Century* (Palo Alto: Stanford University Press, 2006).

18. Frank and Meyer, "Worldwide Expansion," 12.

19. Meyer, "Foreword," in Frank and Gabler, *Reconstructing the University,* x.

20. Meyer et al., "The World Educational Revolution," 255. See also David K. Cohen, "Professions of Human Improvement: Predicaments of Teaching," in Mordechai Nisan and Otto Schremer, eds., *Educational Deliberations* (Jerusalem: Keter Publishers, 2005), 278–294.

21. Bill Readings, *The University in Ruins* (Cambridge, MA: Harvard University Press, 1996), 83.

22. Christopher Lasch, *The Revolt of the Elites* (New York: W. W. Norton, 1995), 34.

23. Robert B. Reich, *The Work of Nations: Preparing Ourselves for 21st Century Capitalism* (New York: Alfred Knopf Publishers, 1991), 230.

24. Ibid., 309.

25. See David Brooks, *Bobos in Paradise: The New Upper Class and How They Got There* (New York: Simon and Schuster, 2000), and Richard Florida, *The Rise of the Creative Class* (New York: Viking Publishers, 2000).

26. Schofer and Meyer, "Worldwide Expansion," 917.

27. See the discussion in Habermas, *The Theory of Communicative Action,* vol. 2: *Lifeworld and System: A Critique of Functionalist Reason* (Boston: Beacon Press, 1987 [1981]).

28. John Dewey, *The Quest for Certainty,* in Dewey, *The Later Works, 1925–1953,* ed. J. A. Boydston (Carbondale: Southern Illinois University Press, 1984), vol. 4.

29. John Dewey, *Logic: The Theory of Inquiry,* in *The Later Works,* vol. 12, 192.

30. I have tried to develop some of the implications of this idea in *A New Agenda for Higher Education: Shaping a Life of the Mind for Practice* (San Francisco: Jossey-Bass Publishers, 2008; with Matthew S. Rosin).

31. David K. Cohen, "Dewey's Problem," *The Elementary School Journal* (John Dewey: The Chicago Years): 98, no. 5 (1998): 427–446, here 433.

32. The importance of the idea of democracy in this wide, Deweyan sense in providing a thematic continuity in Mead's work is developed by Hans Joas in *G. H. Mead: A Contemporary Re-examination of His Thought* (Boston: MIT Press, 1985).

33. William H. McNeill, *Mythistory and Other Essays* (Chicago: University of Chicago Press, 1986), 20–21 and 23.

34. Ibid., 18.

17

The Future of Transcendence

A Sociological Agenda

RICHARD MADSEN

"A total metamorphosis of history has taken place," wrote Karl Jaspers sixty years ago in the immediate aftermath of World War II. "The essential fact is: There is no longer anything outside. The world is closed. The unity of the earth has arrived. New perils and new opportunities are revealed. All the crucial problems have become world problems, the situation a situation of mankind."[1] But it was a spiritually empty unity. There was a universal economic and political interdependence, based on the universal permeation of technologies of dominance, but it did not rest on any common ethical foundation. "[S]omething manifestly quite different from the Axial period is involved. Then the plentitude, now the emptiness."[2]

In the past sixty years, there has been an enormous amount of writing about the unity of the earth—indeed in the past two decades, such discussions, under the rubric of "globalization" have become ubiquitous. But there has been proportionally little systematic reflection on the possible spiritual foundations for global interdependencies of wealth and power. One reason may be that it is so difficult to imagine how this may be done. In this essay I will suggest an agenda for such exploration—or at least review pieces of such an agenda suggested by the writings of Jaspers, Robert Bellah, and Charles Taylor.

Jaspers suggested that a beginning would be to "look back toward our origin. The deep matrix from which we sprang . . . is to become articulate once more. In this process of self-understanding through the knowledge of whence we come the mirror of the great Axial Period of humanity will perhaps, once more, prove one of the essential assurances."[3] But this requires a theoretical depth and historical erudition possessed by few scholars. One of these, however, is Bellah, whose book on religious evolution does indeed undertake to provide a comprehensive self-understanding of our common spiritual situation through the mirror of the Axial period of humanity. Besides demanding theoretical depth and historical erudition, such an effort requires the willingness to undertake great intellectual risks to extract grand unifying visions from the obscurity of history. Having now enjoyed the fruits of Bellah's ordeal, we might now consider an even more perilous undertaking: a prognosis of the future in the light of the past.

The Future in the Mirror of the Past

Jaspers follows his call to deepen our understanding of our present situation through knowledge of our Axial roots with an essay on "The Future"—a call to "look at the present from the viewpoint of the future as well as that of the past. The ideas we have of the future guide the manner in which we look into the past and the present."[4] Prognosis of the future is not only risky because it may be wrong, but because it may be self-fulfilling in harmful ways that preclude more beneficial possibilities. However, in any case, says Jaspers, it cannot be avoided. "All our activity depends upon what we expect from the future, upon the picture we form of chances and certainties. The goals of our activity are set within the area of that which we deem possible."[5]

From his vantage point in 1949, Jaspers described three tendencies in the world, "socialism, world order, and faith."[6] By socialism he meant "the universal tendency of contemporary mankind toward an organization of labor and of participation in the products of labor that will make it possible for all men to be free. To this extent almost everyone is a socialist today."[7] He saw this tendency heading toward two possible outcomes, either a kind of social democracy or the total planning of communism. He saw world unity as possibly taking two forms, "world empire" or "world order." World empire would be based on the coercion of a single great power maintaining itself through the use of force combined with propaganda. World order would achieve unity "without unifying force other than that afforded by common decision in negotiation."[8] By faith, he meant not dogma but "the fulfilling and moving element in the depths of man, in which man is linked, above and beyond himself, with the origin of his being."[9] The alternative to faith was nihilism.

What has been the fate of Jaspers' prognoses? There was indeed a great struggle between communist state socialism and social democracy (practiced even in the United States under the name of the "welfare state"), which ended with the collapse of both communism and social democracy (in the United States at least, where the welfare state has been largely dismantled in the name of a neoliberal free-market fundamentalism). There were attempts to develop a world order through the UN and a declaration of universal human rights, but this was overshadowed through rivalries between the two great superpowers and their client states. After the end of the cold war, the United States has tried to assert itself as the unchallenged hegemonic center of a new world empire, but it now seems to lack sufficient military power to effect this. Moreover, there are no effective international institutions to enforce respect for universal human rights. Finally, although there were impressive movements toward renewal and modernization of Axial faiths—for example in the Catholic Church's Second Vatican Council—these efforts were not sustained. The major current alternative forms for the expression of faith seem to be an archaic "paleo-Durkheimian" submersion of the self into politically organized communities or a "post-Durkheimian" exaltation of the self in an expressive spirituality.[10]

We seem now to be in a liminal period, where the incipient tendencies that Jaspers discerned have now played themselves out, and we are presented with a new phase in history, with a new manifold of possibilities. In the light of a renewed understanding of the Axial Age, what new prognoses might we make for our future?

One difference between our current situation and that faced by Jaspers in 1949 is that the situation at the time of his writing was like a pre- or post-Axial Age, but our situation today is structurally more similar to that of the Axial period. As Jaspers wrote, "the present age is one of real technological and spiritual remolding, not yet of eternal spiritual creations. We may more readily liken ourselves, with our grandiose scientific discoveries and technological inventions, to the epoch of the invention of tools and weapons, of the first use of domestic animals and horses, than with the age of Confucius, Buddha, and Socrates."[11] Elsewhere, Jaspers compares the post–World War II hardening of organizational systems and the consolidations of world empires to the period after the Axial Age, when there were founded the Qin dynasty in China, the Maurya Empire in India, and the Roman Empire.[12] In contrast, our present period is more akin to times like the Warring States in China, when a heretofore stable political and economic order was collapsing and the threat of anarchy impelled a search for new unifying spiritual visions. Under such circumstances, the future of faith, the third of Jaspers' three dimensions of tendencies toward the future, becomes all the more urgently relevant. But it is developments along this line that seem the most confusing and most ambiguous.

Conditions of Axial Creativity

On the one hand, the conditions seem to be ripe for an explosion of spiritual creativity. There is a loosening of older affiliations and anxiety about the meaning of life in a world rife with profoundly destabilizing conflicts. Moreover, new means of communication facilitate the emergence of itinerant intellectuals, like those whose ideas engendered the innovations of the first Axial Age. Finally, modern psychology, philosophy, and cultural studies offer us a more multilayered understanding of human rationality—an understanding more open to possibilities of spiritual innovation than that which has prevailed in post-Enlightenment discourse.

Yet the present global situation seems like that in the early Roman Empire:

> The world was levelled off spiritually into two languages (Greek and Latin), into a shallow ethical system which, because it was without effect on the masses, made room for enjoyment for its own sake and for the desperate sufferings of slaves, of the poor, and of the vanquished.... Where nothing is really believed any more, the most absurd beliefs gain the upper hand. Superstition in manifold guises, doctrines of salvation of the most extraordinary kinds, circles gathered round peripatetic preachers, therapists, poets and prophets, in an endless confusion of vogue, success and oblivion, present a garish picture of narrow fanaticisms, wild adorations, enthusiastic devotion, and also of opportunism, imposture and knavery.[13]

Jaspers says that Christianity brought order to this chaos. Although there is much in our age that is analogous to this period in ancient Rome, however, there is today "nothing corresponding to the Christianity which, at that time, was new and world-transforming."[14] What passes for Christianity today is mostly too trapped in dogmas and creeds to contribute to a new universal world order. Nonetheless, the fundamental insights of Christianity, together with the fundamental insights of the great Axial religious traditions, could provide spiritual resources for a spiritual vision adequate to the challenges of the future.

Although we seem to be living under structural conditions similar to the matrix of creativity found in the Axial Age, and although we are faced with challenges that might only be resolved by a leap to transcendence—by a new Axial Age—it is hard to discern the beginnings of such a leap. Where would we look? What would we look for? How would we recognize the seeds of an emergent world faith even if we saw them? In the remainder of this essay, I suggest a sociological agenda for seeking, recognizing, and guessing the direction of the spiritual movements that could coalesce into a new Axial Age.

I would suggest that we begin the search in contexts where political and social orders have partially but not fully collapsed—where creative energies are freed from previous integuments but where there remain sufficient cultural resources to nourish systematic thinking and teaching. The initial Axial breakthroughs took place on the margins of powerful empires, in small states that had experienced some prosperity but were locked in incessant competition with other states and were insecure and vulnerable.

The work of Bellah goes beyond Jaspers (and Jaspers' mentor Max Weber) by arguing for the complex interplay between the theoretic, critical rationality that we associate with Axial breakthroughs, and the dense, multivocal symbolisms of the mythic and mimetic cultures associated with archaic and primitive religious consciousness. We can (as Bellah indeed has done in some of his previous writings) analyze this interplay in terms of the "grid" and "group" framework developed by another great Durkheimian social scientist, Mary Douglas.

For Douglas, the structure of a society's moral order, the forms of its cosmologies, and the meaningfulness of its rituals all depend on the tightness of its group ties (which, in her shorthand jargon, she calls "group") and the clarity and specificity of its moral norms (which she calls "grid").[15] Societies strong in group are structured into closed corporate groups which are difficult to exit and can put high levels of social pressure on their members. Societies weak in group are assemblages of mobile individuals who can voluntarily choose their associates. Societies strong in grid have clear, coherent, and well-institutionalized systems for classifying roles and statuses, rights and responsibilities. Societies weak in grid are anomic—their institutions are weak and moral standards indistinct.

Societies with different combinations of strong and weak group and grid give rise to different kinds of symbol systems. People socialized under conditions of strong grid and strong group employ a "restricted" symbolic language. We might speculate that conditions of maximally strong grid and group are exclusively associated with the ritual processes of the mimetic consciousness; and that conditions of medium strong grid and group help produce the sacred stories of the mythic consciousness (without giving up on rituals—for as Bellah emphasizes, "nothing is ever lost").

In a context of weak grid and weak group, people use "elaborated" speech codes. These are based on symbols with specific, clearly defined meanings, which each individual can use to communicate his or her unique interests and feelings in the hope of reaching agreement with someone with complementary interests and feelings. It leads to a religion of inner experience rather than external form and to a critical consciousness that frees individuals from authority, even as it allows them to calculate strategically in a complexly organized world. The consequences of extremely weak grid and group would be a Hobbesian world, an anarchic struggle of all against all. A strong grid and weak group might produce a rationalized, bureaucratically structured world, where self-consciously independent individuals seek to express their unique selves and advance their strategic interests through a rigidly fixed, taken-for-granted framework of procedures.[16]

The United States today is a society with a rather weak group life, but it is nonetheless rationalized through strongly enforced, bureaucratically institutionalized "rules of the game." Thus the strong individualism of America, based upon what many Americans would see as their critical-rational, theoretic consciousness, is held in check by a powerful framework of rules and procedures. One sees this in the modern American research university, where the flood of specialized publications is channeled according to strong canons of scientific procedure, and true breakthroughs that would integrate different levels of knowledge are hard to come by.

Closed societies with strong group and grid would not be likely to produce breakthroughs to transcendence. If threatened from outside by an encroaching global system, such societies might produce a rigidly intransigent "fundamentalist" spirituality. But neither would breakthroughs to transcendence come in a society like the United States, for all its wealth and power. America's combination of strong grid and weak group may produce a spiritual life more like the Roman Empire, "circles gathered round peripatetic preachers, therapists, poets and prophets, in an endless confusion of vogue, success and oblivion." Breakthroughs to transcendence might more likely arise in contexts where relatively strong corporate groups were beginning to break down, but still retained much of their coherence; and a grid of moral rules was being called into question, but still provided a foundation on which to build new moral frameworks. It is such a context that might provide a generative dialectic between restricted and elaborated symbol systems, a fruitful interplay between interpenetrating mimetic, mythic, and theoretic consciousness.

Thus a search for tendencies that might lead to new Axial breakthroughs today might best begin at the interstices of the great economic political powers, in societies challenged by neoliberal globalization and made vulnerable by great power rivalries—but which are for now still holding their own in the midst of these challenges.

Examples from Asia

In a recent book, I have described the emergence of new "socially engaged" Buddhist groups in Taiwan, an island that has experienced impressive growth and political development in the past generation, but is extremely vulnerable to military threat from the People's Republic of China, faces intense economic competition from other newly industrializing countries, and is situated at a confluence of Asian and Western popular cultures mediated through new information technologies.[17] In the past generation, roughly coincident with its transition to democracy, it has given rise to Buddhist movements that draw upon core Buddhist understandings about compassion to adapt both Buddhist practices and Confucian ethics to a globalized world.

Let me provide some brief examples of such creativity from my book. Despite their great differences, Taiwanese organizations such as the Buddhist Compassion Relief Society (*Ciji gongde hui*; hereafter referred to as

"Ciji"), Buddha's Light Mountain, and Dharma Drum Mountain follow a broadly similar pattern of creative cultural development.

First of all, they partially demythologize traditional beliefs. That is, instead of taking Buddhist symbols as solid, literal representations of a world beyond the one of ordinary experience, they see the symbols as expressions of a common human life. Some of the members of these Taiwanese organizations describe their beliefs as symbols of traditional moral principles from within their culture.[18] When they say things like this, however, they are not advocating an uncritical acceptance of their inherited culture. As Xingyun, the founder of Buddha's Light Mountain writes:

> Professor John Dewey, the American philosopher, educator, and teacher of Dr. Hu Shih [Hu Shi], once said, "We must reappraise the meaning of value." His remark has had a tremendous impact on my thinking and my method of reappraisal and reorientation when dealing with issues of Buddhism, life, and society . . . I do not unconditionally follow tradition. I do not toy with the idea of emptiness and talk in vain about abstruse things. I do not consciously accept the opinion of the majority. Instead, I constantly review our tradition, observe, and think about the future of Buddhism. I keep on reappraising values as I grow.[19]

Members of Ciji sometimes refer to this process as "adaptation to life" *(shenghuohua)*, adapting the best of their cultural values to the changing conditions of life in modern Taiwan.

In these groups, there is indeed much talk about "cultivating practice" *(xiuxing)*, a term well known from books on Confucian philosophy. The term refers to the process of spiritual development that enables one to understand how to apply basic moral principles in the broadest possible contexts. But this development now is not to be confined to an elite of "great men." With the aid of modern communications and with a democratic spirit that stresses the inherent equality and dignity of all persons, anybody can expand his or her heart. The many multimedia publications of all of the groups aim to facilitate this understanding.

The norms of filial piety, for instance, have to be adapted to a world of high-tech occupations in which, to be successful, children have to learn to think critically for themselves, and may eventually have to move far away from their parents. The religious groups that I have studied all say that one should still hold on to the principle of filial piety under these circumstances, but that one must understand it in a deeper way and exercise it through new methods. To be truly filial, one must not blindly obey one's parents but thoughtfully assimilate the lessons they have taught and carry on their legacy in a cosmopolitan world that they may not be able to comprehend. The collective work of these Buddhist groups is an example of how to do this. They devote themselves to reworking the lessons that Chinese parents typically impart to their children. They encourage followers to help strangers in need as if they were one's own parents. If one is living far away from home, then one can help one's parents by generously caring for someone else's parents—and in the process one can gain confidence that other members of one's religious community will be on hand to take good care of one's own parents. Self-cultivation, then, is not just improvement of one's individual self (using neo-Confucian language, publications of these groups refer to a "small self"—*xiao wo*), but a broadening of vision that generates affiliations to a wider community (a "big self"—*da wo*). Other characteristics are a simplification of ritual and dilution of hierarchy, which gives increasing amounts of initiative to lay devotees.[20]

Sometimes fundamental moral precepts are diluted so as to adapt to the demands of a scientific modernity. But this is done to better enable constructive efforts to transform modernity itself in accord with the moral aspirations of human beings.

Consider, for example, the way Ciji operates its innovative hospitals and medical school. It has adopted a mission to provide the most modern forms of Western medicine, but to carry out this mission it is willing to compromise the basic Buddhist precept forbidding killing of any sentient beings. At the small monastery that is the headquarters of Ciji, both nuns and lay visitors make assiduous efforts not to kill even mosquitoes or ants. But the Ciji hospital and medical schools conduct scientific research that involves killing animals—and Ciji's foundress, Master Zhengyan, permits this if it is "done for a good purpose and if the animals are not made to suffer unnecessarily." At the same time, Ciji seeks creative ways to inject Buddhist values into modern medical practice, to maintain the benefits of scientific medicine while redeeming the practice of healing from its objectifying and alienating tendencies. For example, the Ciji medical school has a distinctive way of conducting its anatomy class. Before students dissect the human cadavers used in the class, they pray for the souls of the deceased. On the walls of the classroom, they post biographies of the cadavers they are working on, and students write essays expressing their gratitude toward the person who donated his or her body. When the bodies are cremated at the conclusion of the class, half the ashes are returned to the deceased's family, and the other half kept in an urn in a chapel next to the anatomy classroom, where students can meditate and give gratitude for the lives of the people who have helped them in their education. The aim is to instill in young doctors a respect for the human persons who will be their patients, and to imbue within them the Ciji commitment to "compassionate care."[21]

Such creative cultural innovation makes various combinations of Buddhism and Confucianism come alive for members of the modern mobile middle classes—white-collar workers, entrepreneurs, professionals who are thoroughly committed to modern scientific worldviews and to work in modern organizations, but who nonetheless feel a need for moral guidance and more comprehensive meanings to put such work into perspective and to help them set life priorities.

One finds analogous innovations in other pressured but still open and coherent societies within Asia. The Dalai Lama has formulated Tibetan Buddhism in such a way as to push it beyond the boundaries of an isolated Himalayan society and, without denying its function as an expression of a particular ethnic identity, he has turned it into a vision of a "middle way" toward universal peace, a vision that (like the Christian variant of prophetic Judaism) might survive the destruction of its territorial temples and national community and, through culturally adaptive diaspora, become a global faith.

Out of the Christian tradition, South Korea meanwhile has produced important innovations with relevance to the whole globe: a vigorous *minjung* (people's) Christian theology, which mixes some of the expansionist passion of evangelical Christianity with the concern for social justice of ecumenical Christianity. Members of such a faith have taken the lead in movements to gain respect and dignity for migrant workers in that relatively closed society.

And in Indonesia, there is the Dian Interfidei organization, founded by the late Dr. Sumartana and based in Yogyakarta. Dian Interfidei has built networks of Muslims, Christians, Hindus, Buddhists, and Confucians. It holds seminars and workshops that introduce participants to the history, theology, and ethics of the various traditions. Each participant is led to emphasize the centrality of their respective faith traditions in building bridges across the bias and distrust that all too often eventuate in violence in Indonesia. All of the organization's programs are aimed at helping participants to listen, to step back and accept difference without any investment in shaping such difference into sameness. Prayer and worship is part of all Interfidei gatherings and always involves multifaith expressions of reverence, including music, prayer, and ritual reflecting several of the religious traditions that constitute Indonesian religious culture. The goal of all this is to create a new kind of religious person, a person Sumartana called a "cross-religious person." Such a religiously endowed person does not abandon one faith tradition for another but becomes an intentional religious citizen of the world.[22]

All such movements arguably take place in contexts of moderately strong grid and group which have been undergoing dynamic change in response to outside political pressure and economic globalization. They share some common characteristics.

First, there is a reinterpretation of tradition. This is not a slavish, "fundamentalist" clinging to a frozen, stereotyped tradition, but an active, creative engagement with tradition from within the wider horizons that the global communications of modernity give us. This involves a struggle to be faithful to the deepest principles of the tradition—in Taiwan, for example, with the principles of filial piety—while shedding parts of that tradition that are no longer compatible with the demands for individual autonomy, personal responsibility, and self-expression that life in dynamic urban societies places upon us.

Second, there is an attempt to communicate this vision through words, images, music, and dance—and practical philanthropic gestures—that link the creative imaginations of cultural entrepreneurs with the expectations of ordinary people embedded in their local cultural communities.

Third, there is active, critical dialogue with other culture creators, even those outside of one's own tradition—Buddhists with Christians, Christians with Muslims, and so forth. Such dialogue best takes place in apolitical venues, so that arguments are won and lost as far as possible on the basis of whose ideas are most convincing, not on who has the most political power.

Identifying Seeds of Transcendence

The examples described above are at least superficially suggestive of preliminary movements to transcendent religious and moral visions. They suggest that we might be looking in the right places. But how could we tell if we were actually observing seeds of transcendence? For initial guidance, we might return to Jaspers.

First of all, he argues, authentic new movements toward transcendence would not take the form of new revelations. "In the lucidity of our world, a prophecy that made its appearance with the claim to a fresh divine revelation would perhaps always give the impression of madness or false prophecy, of superstition, that collapses before the one great, true prophecy which occurred thousands of years ago."[23] Movements toward transcendence would take the form of recovery and readaptation of the roots of the great Axial traditions. But these traditions could not be appropriated as exclusive truths.

> For that the truth of faith lies in the multiplicity of its historical manifestations, in the self-encountering of this multiplicity through ever deeper communication, is an insight and experience of latter centuries which cannot be reversed. This experience cannot be fallacious in its origin....
>
> If it be deemed improbable that a world order will develop without unity of faith, I venture to assert the reverse. The universality of a world order obligatory to all (in contrast to a world empire) is possible *only* when the multiple contents of faith remain free in their historical communication, without the unity of an objective, universally valid doctrinal content. The common element of all faith in relation to world order can only be that everyone desires the ordering of the foundations of existence, in a world community in which he has room to evolve with the peaceful means of the spirit.[24]

At their origins, the great Axial traditions were open-ended. They proclaimed that there was a great universal fountain of Truth that existed beyond all of the particular alliances of this world. The search for this Truth and obedience to its demands was the lever for criticism of exclusive myths and particular communities. But the prophets who initiated the Axial traditions were all, in their own ways, against idolatry—the notion that the ultimate Truth could be definitively captured by symbols or institutions constructed by humans. So the Axial insight impels us to a constant critical search that pushes beyond the symbols that provisionally form the vehicles of its expression. Each of the Axial traditions quickly became mummified. A new Axial Age would break through the mummifications and take up the critical task of seeking a spiritual unity where they left off.

One expression of this is in the writings of Sheng Yen, the Zen master who was the founder of the Dharma Drum Mountain Buddhist organization in Taiwan: "Once on an airplane, I was sitting next to a Christian missionary who was piously reading the Bible and praying. Seeing that I had nothing to do, he gave me a Bible and showed me how to read it. I praised his good intentions and enthusiasm, and agreed with his statement that Christianity is the only religion through which one can attain salvation. He immediately asked me, 'If this is the case, why are you a Buddhist monk? Isn't that a pity?' I said, 'I'm sorry, but for me, Buddhism is most suitable. So I would say that Buddhism is the best religion.' "[25]

Sheng Yen explains this paradoxical position in terms of classical Zen. "Transcending your thoughts . . . is a method that consists of maintaining the attitude of non-involvement with yourself or others. The goal of this method is roughly described as a phrase that translates as, 'Be separate, or free, from the mind, from thoughts, and from consciousness.' To be free from all this is to be in a state of enlightenment. In such freedom of mind it might be said that we see the world."[26]

He supplements this classical Zen analysis, however, with a touch of Durkheim. He distinguishes between a culturally relative "sacred" and the ultimate truth.

> The definition of the "sacred" varies according to time, place, and individual. This is something we must be aware of in a modern, pluralistic, and globalized society. . . . The supreme truth revered by every religion should be absolute and flawless. It is definitely sacred. But once secular elements and outside agendas are incorporated into the interpretation, it becomes a subjective notion and thus generates diversity. For example, the theory of causes and conditions is the utmost sacred in Buddhism. But we do not deny the value of monotheism. While we neither

> identify with nor accept monotheism, we can understand and respect it. We acknowledge that all virtuous religions have room for continuous development and also have the right to proclaim themselves the world's best religion. Likewise, I myself would say that Buddhism is the best religion....
>
> The days of monocultural societies are long gone and will not return again; and fortunately so, otherwise the destiny of humanity would be a very tragic one! Therefore, I would like to make this appeal here for all humanity: humankind must understand that the notion of the *sacred* is interpreted differently in a multicultural pluralistic world, and that we should strive to seek for harmony. Such harmony is not to be found in dogmatic homogenization or elimination of difference. It can only come through a grassroots discovery of commonality within difference, and difference within commonality.[27]

In the Zen Buddhist view, the discovery of commonality within difference comes not from philosophic manipulation of categories but from leaps of consciousness, a passage through the "gateless gate" in which attachment to the self is lost and one faces circumstances and deals with people in clear immediacy. Some such leap of consciousness seems indeed to be the driver of all leaps to transcendence, even though such leaps are inevitably followed by mummification in institutions.

Invoking Ivan Illich's *Corruption of Christianity,* Taylor offers a provocative interpretation of the original Christian insight that, surprisingly, has much in common with the perspective of the Buddhists cited above: the incarnation of God in Jesus pushes us outward, beyond the boundaries of all tribes and nations, beyond all civilizational rules, into direct encounters with other persons based on the unconditional love which God has for us.

> The enfleshment of God extends outward, through such new links as the Samaritan makes with the Jew, into a network, which we call the Church. But this is a network, not a categorical grouping; that is, it is a skein of relations which link particular, unique, enfleshed people to each other, rather than a grouping of people together on the grounds of their sharing some important property (as in modern nations, we are all Canadians, Americans, French people; or universally, we are all

rights-bearers, etc.). It resembles earlier kin networks in this regard....
But it is unlike tribal kinship groups in that it is not confined to the
established "we," that it creates links across boundaries, on the basis of
a mutual fittingness which is not based on kinship but on the kind of
love which God has for us, which is called agape.[28]

This is the kind of Christianity that Jaspers seems to have had in mind when he referred to the new and world-transforming movements that brought order to the spiritual chaos of the Roman Empire.

Inevitably, however, this movement of the Christian spirit ends in the corruption of Christendom, the idolatry of fixed systems of rules and categories, dehumanization and alienation, and violence by Us against Them. But once kindled, the spark of transcendence is never fully lost. It remains buried within the tradition as a heritage of hope.

Authentic movements toward transcendence would then be characterized by new movements within the great Axial traditions toward ecumenical openness. This would be arrived at not through some superficial syncretism but through an intellectual and moral commitment to the deepest roots of a tradition. But how would one distinguish a reactionary, parochial clinging to tradition from a progressive, transcendent springing out of tradition? The only way would be through the fruits of the enterprise.

I have suggested that one might discern the beginnings of such movements within renovations of Buddhist and Confucian traditions within parts of Asia. Within Christian traditions in the West, one might also find such sparks of (all-too-fragile and easily corruptible) movements of transcendence around the world. Examples would perhaps be the Taizé community in France or the Sant'Egidio community in Rome. In the United States in the first half of the twentieth century, the Catholic Worker Movement was inspired by a similar spirit, and out of the evangelical part of the Protestant tradition, the Sojourners seem to be following a similar spiritual path. Other examples might be found in movements like those for "transitional justice," to bring about reconciliation in the wake of conflicts, beginning in South Africa and initially inspired by creative appropriation of Christian traditions, but now being applied in Eastern Europe and Latin America.[29]

Such movements usually occur at the margins of their respective institutionalized religious traditions. They reach across doctrinal religious boundaries to create networks of concern, cross-national and cross-class affiliations of unlikely bedfellows. It is such movements that Jaspers seemed to think were the potential fabric of authentic world community: "He who would like to live in the unclosed and unorganised and unorganisable community of authentic human beings—in what used to be called the invisible Church—does in fact live today as an individual in alliance with individuals scattered over the face of the earth, an alliance that survives every disaster, a dependability that is not fixed by any path or any specific imperative."[30]

Although such movements may contain at least some seeds of a new Axial transcendence, they are not a good object for standard sociological study. They cannot easily be categorized, pinned into a theoretical framework. Sociology is more at home with studying the corruption of the spirit than its emergence. So perhaps we cannot "operationalize" the seeds of global transcendence; sociology in itself cannot tell us when we have encountered them. But by amply theorizing and documenting the boundary development, the alienation and dehumanization that call out for transcendence, and by starting us on a global, comparative search for the contexts in which transcendence might happen, sociology might lead us up to the point where we might actually witness it. Sociology can play the role of "philosophy" in Jaspers' essay on "The Future": "Philosophy leads us along the road to the point at which love acquires its depth in real communication. Then in this love, through the success of communication, the truth that links us together will be disclosed to those who are most remote in the diversity of their historical origin."[31]

Notes

1. Karl Jaspers, *The Origin and Goal of History* (New Haven: Yale University Press, 1953), 127.
2. Ibid., 140.
3. Ibid.
4. Ibid., 141.
5. Ibid., 152.
6. Ibid., 172.
7. Ibid.
8. Ibid., 196.
9. Ibid., 215.

10. Charles Taylor, *A Secular Age* (Cambridge, MA: Harvard University Press, 2007), 455ff and 487ff

11. Jaspers, *Origin,* 140.

12. Ibid., 194.

13. Ibid., 216.

14. Ibid.

15. Mary Douglas, *Natural Symbols: Explorations in Cosmology* (New York: Vintage, 1973), 77–92.

16. Ibid., 19–58.

17. Richard Madsen, *Democracy's Dharma: Religious Renaissance and Political Development in Taiwan* (Berkeley: University of California Press, 2007).

18. Ibid., 5–6.

19. Venerable Master Hsing Yun, *The Philosophy of Being Second* (Hacienda Heights, CA: Hsi Lai University Press, 2000), 76.

20. Madsen, *Democracy's Dharma,* 5–6.

21. Ibid., 40–41.

22. Clare B. Fischer, "Democratic Civility: Interfidei and the Work of Social Harmony in Indonesia," unpublished paper.

23. Jaspers, *Origin,* 226.

24. Ibid., 226–227.

25. Sheng Yen, "Inter-religious Understanding and Cooperation" (concluding address, International Conference on Religious Cooperation, September 20, 2001); see www.chan1.org.

26. Sheng Yen, "Human Consciousness in the Chan Perspective," *Chan News Letter* 84 (March 1991).

27. Sheng Yen, "The Sacred in a Pluralistic World: Seeking Common Ground while Preserving Differences" (speech, World Economic Forum, New York, February 1, 2002); see www.chan1.org. Quotes from Sheng Yen are included in Madsen, *Democracy's Dharma,* 96–98.

28. Taylor, *Secular Age,* 739.

29. See Daniel Philpott, ed., *The Politics of Past Evil: Religion, Reconciliation, and the Dilemmas of Transitional Justice* (Notre Dame, IN: University of Notre Dame Press, 2006).

30. Jaspers, *Origin,* 228.

31. Ibid.

18

The Heritage of the Axial Age

Resource or Burden?

ROBERT N. BELLAH

In this volume the contributors are focusing on the Axial Age and my chapter will do likewise. However, my work on the Axial Age comes out of a larger project concerning religion in human evolution from the Paleolithic to the Axial Age.[1] I will therefore begin with a word about evolution itself as a concept. I assume that none of the contributors to this volume has a problem with the theory of biological evolution, even though we may have some different ways of interpreting it. Problems arise when we speak of social and cultural evolution: Is that even a valid idea and, if we think it is, what do we mean by it? Here I will briefly state my position insofar as it is fundamental to my whole project, before turning to a consideration of the Axial Age and its consequences.

Although I will want to qualify it, my conception of social and cultural evolution is basically neo-Darwinian, with variation and selection operating not with genes but with cultural traits and institutional structures. For example, no tribal society, and so no tribal religion, anywhere in the world today can survive without some kind of state protection. That says nothing about the value of tribal societies or their religions, only that they cannot compete against state societies and today must be protected by them. This does not at all mean that state societies are better than tribal societies. Left alone, tribal societies might have survived for millions of years, whereas state societies seem to have a strong tendency toward mutual extinction. I believe that progress, even ethical progress, is an important issue. However, an evolutionary increase in complexity, and, in the short term, viability, tells us nothing about the ethical quality of the apparently more viable society, or about its long-term fate. There have been and surely will be again cases in which increased complexity and apparent viability turn out to be an evolutionary dead end, leading to extinction.

I can certainly understand the anxiety that speaking of social evolution would reduce culture and society to biology, an anxiety not unwarranted in a world where sociobiology and the selfish gene have become popular ideas. As a defense against that kind of reductionism, there has been an effort to distinguish evolution and history: evolution occurs in nature, history occurs in culture. This distinction is, I think, a somewhat modified version of the old distinction between *Naturwissenschaft* and *Geisteswissenschaft*. And, as in this older distinction, there is the sense that evolution involves determinism, whereas history involves freedom, or at least a degree of contingency that is incompatible with deterministic natural science.

I believe this whole distinction is misplaced: evolution is historical; history is evolutionary. Evolutionary biologists have come to recognize that they often deal with contingent events—global warming or cooling, for example—that have major consequences for the survival or extinction of species. They also realize that species play an active part in their own future, having an impact on their own environment. Both biologists and historical sociologists recognize path dependence. Species and societies are enormously flexible, but once they go down a certain path, some alternatives become difficult or impossible. This can be seen as a historical fact with evolutionary consequences. We do not have to choose: evolution and history are two mutually compatible ways of looking at long-term development in nature and in culture.

The most complete discussion of the several ways of thinking about social evolution that I know of is an early essay of Jürgen Habermas, "Toward a Reconstruction of Historical Materialism." Habermas, while accepting the validity of neoevolutionist approaches in their own terms, still finds them in need of supplementation. He believes, if I understand him rightly, that we human beings are involved in our own evolution and cannot escape making judgments that are evaluative as well as cognitive. The evolution of complexity is one standard of evolutionary development, but, Habermas writes, "Social scientific neoevolutionism is usually satisfied with the directional criterion of increasing steering (or adaptive) capacity. . . . [However] even in natural evolution the degree of complexity is not a sufficient condition for placing a species in the evolutionary rank order; for increasing complexity in physical organization or mode of life often proves to be an evolutionary dead end."[2] Habermas argues that in the very use of linguistic communication we have built-in standards that are not only cognitive but normative, and that lead us to view human evolution not only in scientific but in moral-practical terms, that is, in terms of increasing capacities for social learning. He concludes his essay by saying, "The development of productive forces, in conjunction with the maturity of the forms of social integration, means progress of learning ability in both dimensions: progress in objectivating knowledge and in moral-practical insight."[3]

Habermas argues that in studying social evolution we will inevitably be governed not only by cognitive standards but by normative ones, though I am sure he would not want to confound the two levels. Even if we can speak of normatively lower and higher levels of social learning capacity, we can never assume that there is anything inevitable about attaining the higher levels. If we are going to talk about levels at all, as I am prepared to do, we must expect to find regress as well as progress and face the possibility that the human project may end in complete failure.[4]

This brief discussion of the idea of social evolution provides a prelude to my real subject: whether the heritage of the Axial Age is a resource or a burden in our current human crisis. I remember that Louis Dumont long ago pointed out that intellectuals specialize in crises and can always find one to talk about. True though that may be, I have lived long enough to experience a sea change with respect to popular sentiments about the human future. William Sullivan, in our collective book *The Good Society,* wrote about the 1939 New York World's Fair and about the General Motors exhibition, "Futurama," that had over five million visitors and set the tone for the Fair. Futurama was a celebration of the technological advance, material abundance, and rewarding leisure that the future was assumed to hold, if not for the world, at least for the United States. It was about fleshing out the progress that most Americans took for granted and making it come alive. I was twelve years old in 1939 and visited the San Francisco World's Fair, which rivaled New York's in celebrating the brave new world that was expected. That 1939 was on the verge of World War II, which saw the worst horrors in human history up to that time, was an irony lost on the millions of visitors to these two fairs.

Yet in the immediate years after the war, when I was an undergraduate and then a graduate student in the Department of Social Relations at Harvard, I experienced an extraordinary euphoria about how good things were going to be. We had fought the good war. Though the Cold War was already underway, we assumed that "modernization" was the wave of the future, that what was then called "the developing world" would soon become more or less the same as "the advanced world," and that convergent development would even gradually minimize the differences between the Soviet Union and the West.

It took the sixties to puncture that dream and, one might say, it has been all downhill ever since. Cultural pessimism *(Kulturpessimismus)* goes back a long way—Max Weber was not immune to it—but until relatively recently it remained a property of one section of the intellectual elite. What has become ever clearer to me in recent years is that the old dream of progress in popular culture is being replaced by visions of disaster, ecological catastrophe in particular. If, as I believe, we human beings are at least to some extent in charge of our own evolution, we are in a situation of high demand. The social learning capacity that might enable us to deal with our current challenges does not seem very adequate at the moment.[5]

If I am right, there is today a feeling of crisis that is first of all ecological, but also social and cultural, having to do with global inequality and instability that is deeper and more widespread than has been the case for a long time. It is in this context, then, that I want to inquire whether the Axial heritage can help us or hinder us in our current crisis. Here I would like to return to Habermas's previously cited essay, "Toward a Reconstruction of Historical Materialism," as a point of departure. In speaking of the transition from tribal societies organized by kinship to the emergence of the early state, he writes:

> Social integration accomplished via kinship relations . . . belongs, from a developmental-logical point of view, to a lower stage than social integration accomplished via relations of domination. . . . Despite this progress, the exploitation and oppression *necessarily* practiced in political class societies has to be considered retrogressive in comparison with the less significant social inequalities *permitted* by the kinship system. Because of this, class societies are structurally unable to satisfy the need for legitimation that they themselves generate.[6]

It is true that the early state and its accompanying class system emerge in what I have called archaic societies well before the Axial Age and generate a degree of popular unhappiness that can be discerned in the texts we have from such societies, but the legitimation crisis of which Habermas speaks arises with particular acuteness in the Axial Age, when mechanisms of social domination increase significantly relative to archaic societies and when coherent protest for the first time becomes possible. It would surely be far too simple to interpret the Axial transitions as forms of class struggle, but that they all involved social criticism and harsh judgments on existing social and political conditions cannot be denied.

In answer to the question of where this criticism was coming from there has been a tendency to speak of intellectuals, though what that term means in the first millennium BCE is not obvious. Scribal and priestly classes come to mind, but we can assume that most of them were too tied in to the existing power systems to be very critical. Even though the kind of state that existed then tried and in some important ways succeeded in overriding kinship relations, various kinds of particularistic and ascriptive associations were widespread. It is not easy to imagine the social space for criticism in such societies. It is in this context that we have to consider the role of the renouncer, to take a term most often used for ancient India.

There are renouncers already in late Vedic India; perhaps the first of whom we have an account is Yajnyavalkya, who appears in the Brhadaranyaka Upanishad. What the renouncer renounces is the role of the householder and all of the social and political entanglements that go with it. Buddhism provides a radical form of the renouncer, whose initial act is to "leave home," and to be permanently homeless. If the renouncer is "nowhere," he, and sometimes she, can look at established society from the outside, so to speak. It is not hard to see the Hebrew prophets as, in a sense, renouncers, though I have also called them denouncers. They too stood outside the centers of power, attempting to follow the commandments of God, whatever the consequences. Even in opposition, they were more oriented to power than were Buddhist monastics, to be sure, but, as we will see, the Buddhist monks also had a radical critique of worldly power. It is easy to see the Daoists who appear in Warring States China as renouncers, and they too have a critique of power, though perhaps more satirical than ethical. But there is a sense in which the Confucians, especially the greatest ones who never held office or held only lowly ones briefly, and were in principle opposed to serving an unethical lord, were renouncers, criticizing power from the outside. And finally

I will argue that Socrates and Plato were, in different ways, also renouncers, who were in but not of the city and also criticized it from the outside, so to speak.[7]

For all the differences in what can in most cases only loosely be called renouncers in the several Axial cultures, the one thing they shared was that they were teachers, and founders of schools or orders, thus more or less, and often less, securely institutionalizing a tradition of criticism. Ultimately their power was exercised through the extent to which they influenced or even controlled elite education, as, to some degree paradoxically, many of them ultimately did.[8] And inevitably their survival depended on what they charged for their services or what they were freely given. By pointing out the significance of renouncers we in a sense return to our original question. How did renouncers garner the support that allowed them to survive in their outsider position? It seems apparent that some degree of unease about the state of the world must have been relatively widespread, even among the elite, to provide the support without which renouncers would simply have faded away into the wilderness.

If Habermas is right about the legitimation crisis of the Axial Age state brought on by the dissonance between the developmental-logical advance and the moral-practical regression, as I think he is, I would like to illustrate the response to this legitimation crisis by referring to the utopian projections of a good society that the various kinds of renouncers offered in criticism of the existing order. These utopian projections took quite different forms in the four cases, but each one of them was harshly critical of existing social-political conditions.

In ancient Israel the prophets sharply criticized the behavior of foreign states, but also conditions within the kingdoms of Israel and Judah. According to Amos, the rich and the rulers "trample the head of the poor into the dust of the earth, and turn aside the way of the afflicted" (Amos 2:6–7). In contrast, the prophets look forward to the Day of the Lord when judgment will come to the earth and justice will "roll down like the waters, and righteousness like an ever-flowing stream" (Amos 5:24). The prophets admonish rulers and people alike to change their ways, but look forward to a divine intervention that will finally put things right.

In ancient China Mencius, for example, but many Confucians before and after him, bemoaned the sad state of society, the corruption of the rulers and the oppression of the peasantry, and offered an alternative form of government: rule by moral example, by conformity with the *li,* the normative order, and not by punishment. The Confucian hope for an ethical ruler who would follow Confucian injunctions did not involve any idea of divine intervention, except a vague notion that Heaven would eventually punish behavior that was too outrageous, but it was in its own way as utopian as was the prophetic hope of ancient Israel.

Plato, in the *Gorgias* and in the first book of the *Republic,* is a critic of a politics in which the strong could inflict harm on the weak with impunity: for him, despotism was always the worst form of government. In the *Republic* and the *Laws* he depicted a good society in contrast to the one he criticized, but which he knew was a "city in words," or a "city in heaven," and not one likely to be realized on this earth.

The Hindu epic, the Ramayana, can be seen as a critique of existing society, offering a different ideal of kingship. The early Buddhist canon describes an ideal society so different from existing reality as to be perhaps the most radical utopia of all, the most drastic criticism of society as it is.

In each Axial case, what I am calling social criticism is combined with religious criticism and the form and content of the Axial symbolization take shape in the process of criticism. I will take the Greek case as exemplary because our term "theory," which I, following Merlin Donald, take as diagnostic of the Axial transition, first appeared there. I argued in my chapter on ancient Greece that it was Plato who completed the Axial transition: it is therefore not surprising that it was Plato who took the traditional term for ritual *theoria* and transmuted it into philosophical *theoria,* which, as I will attempt to show, is not the same as what we mean by theory, but is its lineal predecessor, and we can also see the beginning of the transition to what we mean by the term in Aristotle, Plato's pupil.

My discussion of theory in Plato would not be possible except for the remarkable book by Andrea Nightingale, *Spectacles of Truth in Classical Greek Philosophy:* Theoria *in Its Cultural Context,* from which I will draw extensively. Nightingale describes *theoria* before Plato as "a venerable cultural practice characterized by a journey abroad for the sake of witnessing an event or spectacle." It took several forms, but the one which Plato took as the analogy for philosophical *theoria,* most extensively in the Parable of the Cave in Books V–VII of the *Republic,* was the civic form where the *theoros* (viewer, spectator) was sent as an official representative of his city to view a religious festival in another city and then return to give a full report to his fellow citizens. Nightingale notes that by its very nature *theoria* in this sense was "international," Panhellenic, and that Athens itself attracted many *theoroi* from other cities to view its great festivals, the Panathenaia and the City Dionysia.[9] She notes that Plato himself begins and ends the *Republic* with examples of traditional *theoria*. The dialogue begins with Socrates going to the Piraeus, the port of Athens, to attend the festival of the Thracian goddess, Bendis, suggesting that the festival was more "international" than the short distance to the Piraeus might indicate, especially in view of Socrates' remark that the Thracian procession was as fine as the Athenian one, expressing a Panhellenic viewpoint. And the *Republic* ends with the Myth of Er, which turns out to be a most remarkable *theoria*, since Er, who had been killed in battle and was about to be cremated, awoke and told his fellow countrymen about a journey he had made to the land of the dead and the festival he had attended there.[10]

Nightingale notes that in *Republic* Books V–VII Plato for the first time has Socrates give an account of what he meant by "philosophy," a term which confused his interlocutors, who only knew it in its previous sense of broad intellectual cultivation, but which is now to be understood in the context of a new meaning of *theoria* as the "quintessential activity of the true philosopher."[11] The traditional *theoros* was a lover of spectacles, particularly of religious rituals and festivals, while the philosophical *theoros* "loves the spectacle of truth."[12] Plato puts great emphasis on vision, on seeing the truth more than hearing it; it is also a special kind of seeing, seeing with "the eye of the soul." It is this kind of seeing that requires a protracted philosophical education to prepare for, but it ends with the "*theoria* [the "seeing"] of all time and being" (Rep. 486d).

Thinking of this kind of vision from an Indian or Chinese perspective, one might imagine that the way to attain it would be through some form of meditation, probably involving breath control. Although Socrates is portrayed twice in the *Symposium* as in some kind of trance, it is not meditation that Plato finds to be the way to philosophical vision. The education that ends with "seeing reality," or "seeing Being," begins with number and calculation, which "enables the mind to 'view' the great and the small in themselves, abstracted from their concrete manifestations."[13] Geometry and astronomy follow, each of which involves "seeing" higher truths. What Plato meant by astronomy is not so much stargazing as "the mathematical principles that govern the motions of the heavenly bodies," which one "sees" when "gazing with the mind and not the eyes." Finally comes "dialectic," which Socrates never plainly defines but uses metaphors to describe, speaking of the "journey of dialectic" toward the contemplation of "true being."[14] What is involved is not "implanting vision in the soul," but turning the vision in a new direction, "away from the world of becoming and toward true being" (521d).[15]

At the critical moment, then, Plato turns to narrative, what Nightingale calls the Analogy of the Cave, but which is not simply an allegory that can be translated into propositional language, but a kind of myth that reveals truth on its own terms, and that I would rather call the Parable of the Cave. The Buddha too uses stories, often referred to as "similes" in the secondary literature, to make a point, as in the famous Parable of the Blind Men and the Elephant. It seems that at the very point when thought was moving from myth to theory, narrative still had to function as the midwife.

I cannot here give an account of the beauty and complexity of the Parable of the Cave, but only allude to those aspects of it that relate to my argument. It begins with a person who is "at home," though home in the *Republic* is more apt to be the *polis,* the city, than the *oikos,* the household. Home, however, turns out to be a dark cave that is in fact a prison where one is in bonds so that one is forced to look at shadows on the wall cast by people (ideologists?) behind one's back projecting images by holding various objects in front of fires. Still, those shadowy images are what one is used to, so that in a situation where one is freed from one's bonds and, in Plato's words, "compelled to suddenly stand up and to turn [one's] head and to walk and turn upward toward the light" (515c), one will be confused, in a state of *aporia,* that is, profound uncertainty, the opposite of *poria,* certainty. One will have entered, in Nightingale's words, "a sort of existential and epistemic no-man's-land," being able no longer to recognize the old familiar shadows nor yet to see anything in the blinding light above, so that one would be tempted to flee from the whole journey and return to the old familiar prison.[16]

Yet the would-be philosopher does not flee back, and even gets used in some degree to the condition of uncertainty, *aporia,* which Nightingale describes as "(among other things) a state of homelessness." She goes on to describe the new state as basically similar to the renouncer position in other cultures:

> In addition to the state of *aporia,* the philosopher's departure from home leads to a permanent state of *atopia* [no place, nowhere]. For the person who has detached himself from society and gone on the journey of philosophic *theoria* will never be fully "at home" in the world. *Theoria* uproots the soul, sending it to a metaphysical region where it can never truly dwell and from which it will inevitably have to return. As a *theoros,* the Platonic philosopher must journey to "see" truth (in various degrees of fullness) and bring his vision back to the human world.[17]

In a good city he will be given civic office and expected to serve, even though he would rather spend his time in contemplation, yet even in office he is still a kind of foreigner in his own city. But if he returns to a bad city, his report of what he has seen will be mocked as foolish and nonsensical: he will be abused, he may even be killed. Nightingale sums up: "When he returns to the human world, then, he is *atopos,* not fully at home: he has become a stranger to his own kind."[18]

We still need to understand what philosophical *theoria* itself is; the ritual *theoros* sees the festival; what does the philosophic *theoros* see? Here we need to discount the caricature of classical theory, which assumes that the philosopher is a disengaged spectator, viewing at a distance what is an object different from himself as a subject, a kind of premature Descartes. Plato does not help us understand what the philosopher sees, that is, the "forms," *eide,* and in particular the "form of the good," *agathon,* which seems to be truth and reality itself, because he stays in the myth to talk about them. In the myth, Plato compares the form of the good to the source of all light, something like the sun to the eye of the soul. But if we gazed at the sun very long with our physical eye, we would go blind, whereas the soul who gazes at the form of the good sees all things as they really are.

Nightingale shows us that the forms are not abstractions, but are, to the eye of the soul, ontological presences, "beings" or "substances." Further, the vision of the forms is not disengaged, but involves participation, for part of ourselves, our *nous,* inadequately translated as "rational soul," is akin to the forms. The vision is genuinely interactive: as Nightingale puts it, the vision is "granted to us as a gift."[19] Furthermore, it is anything but cool and detached: it is affective and emotional, it brings intense pleasure and happiness, it is erotic, even sexual. The soul, says Plato, "draws near to and has intercourse with (makes love to) reality." (490b) Furthermore, the experience of the vision is utterly transformative; one becomes a different person as a result.[20] One could speak of the soul as "enlightened," but if, as in translating *nirvana* or *moksha,* one wanted to avoid eighteenth-century terminology, one could speak of the soul as "awakened," or even "released," for has the transformed soul not been released from the prison of the cave in order to participate in the really real?

Plato then goes on to describe the good city to which the fortunate philosophic *theoros* returns. To discuss that in detail would take us too far afield, but I want to allude to a couple of aspects of the good city. The good city, as we noted, is ruled by the philosophically liberated, even though they would rather be doing something else. Why then do they take on political responsibility? Nightingale interestingly discusses this issue:

> *If* there is an ideal city—and it is by no means clear that Plato believed in its possibility—then it can and must be ruled by philosophers. In this case alone, the philosopher must live a double life (as it were): he will practice philosophy and serve as a ruler. To qualify for this position, an individual must possess theoretical wisdom and practical virtue; in addition, he or she must not want to rule or lead a political life (347c–d, 521a–b, 540b). A person who does want to rule is, by definition, not a true philosopher and thus disqualified from ruling. The philosopher in the ideal city, however, will agree to rule, in spite of his disinclination to do so. Since he is a "just" person responding to a "just command," the philosopher is "willing" to return and rule the city (520d–e).[21]

This is all the more odd since, as Nightingale notes, the philosopher remains a foreigner in his own city, a "non-mercenary mercenary" who is supported but not paid, can own nothing, and can never touch gold or silver. Many scholars have been puzzled by this situation, but Nightingale, drawing on the work of Christopher Gill, points out that because they are "'just men obeying just commands,' they are eager to pay back their city for the education and rearing that has been granted them."[22] And remember that it had been the obligation of the ritual *theoros* to return and give an account of what he had seen to his fellow citizens.

The rulers, or as they are often called, the "guardians," are an ascetic lot, and have been compared to a monastic order. Not only are they committed to a life of poverty (they live on what the city gives them, not on anything of their own, and can be considered in a way to be beggars), but their sexual life is so regulated that, though they have children, they have no family life, no personal household: the children are raised in common. They embody the virtue of wisdom, but they preside over a city that is characterized by the virtues of justice and moderation, and, not insignificantly, where there are no slaves. A democracy the ideal city is not, and I'm sure we wouldn't want to live in it, and perhaps even Plato would have had his doubts.

In Books VIII and IX of the *Republic* Plato describes a steady decline from a mythical first regime that is a version of his ideal city, a decline that begins because some of the guardians go astray, desiring personal enrichment, even though that involves, for the first time, the enslavement of fellow citizens. This produces timocracy, the rule of honor, with Sparta as an actual example. But unchecked desires lead to a further downward spiral, first to oligarchy and then democracy. While Plato's argument compels him to say that democracy is the worst regime short of tyranny, he also says it is the freest of regimes, and the freedom of democracy is what makes it the only regime where philosophy is possible. Within the multicolored variety of democratic ways of life, the philosophical life can be pursued, at least until the democratic lack of self-control leads to tyranny, the worst of all possible regimes. Outside the rigid logic of decline, it would seem that Plato has more sympathy with democracy than he admits. In any case, in the only great dialogue in which someone else takes the part of Socrates, the *Laws*, the central character is an Athenian philosopher, not a Spartan, that is, someone from what in the scheme of decline should have been a better city than Athens. But then, there were no philosophers in Sparta, and besides, no Spartan could ever have talked as much as the Athenian in the *Laws*.

Compared to the cities of his day, Plato was holding up an ideal. It has often been called an aristocratic ideal, but aristocrats on the whole favored oligarchy, which Plato despised, and Nightingale argues that Plato used aristocratic ideals against the aristocrats, who were not "real" aristocrats in his eyes, just as the Buddha criticized the Brahmins for not being "real" Brahmins.

Which takes us to the Buddhist case, where religious reform and political criticism also went hand in hand. I have been presenting a more Buddhist Plato than usual before turning to the Buddha himself. There are some interesting parallels between them: recent revisions of the dates of the Buddha bring him into the fourth century BCE, and make them possible contemporaries. One striking parallel is the degree to which each one threw out his respective inherited tradition and attempted to replace it with an entirely new one. Plato composed a huge corpus intended to replace the entire poetic, dramatic, and wisdom traditions that preceded him. Fortunately, he did not succeed in eliminating his forbears, but start a new tradition he did, as the famous quip of Alfred North Whitehead that all of Western philosophy is nothing but footnotes to Plato indicates. The Buddha similarly threw out the entire Vedic tradition, from the Rig Veda to the Upanishads, and in its place left us with a collection of sermons and dialogues, the Buddhist canon, that is several times bigger than Plato's complete works. We can be relatively sure that all that is attributed to the Buddha is not his, that successive generations added to the tradition in his name. It is not improbable that the Platonic corpus is similarly layered. But here we are interested in the degree to which both men succeeded in starting something quite new.

Of course, the Buddha, like Plato, owed a great deal to his predecessors, is inconceivable without them. But, as Richard Gombrich has pointed out, those who see Buddhism simply as a later school of Brahmanism and those who see it as a totally new conception are equally mistaken: Buddhism is a reformulation of Brahmanism so radical that it began a new and enormously influential tradition, even though it did not survive in India. Both men could be seen as in some ways visionaries; both also as great rationalists, adept in argument, superb in dialogue; and both were before all else teachers and, though we often fail to see this side of Plato because of the quite artificial distinction we make between philosophy and religion, or that we project back into premodern times, both were teachers of salvation.

The Buddhist version of the Parable of the Cave is in an important sense the whole elaborate story of the Buddha's life as the tradition handed it down. Just as the philosopher had to leave his *oikos* and his *polis,* so the Buddha had to leave his *oikos* and his *polis,* or rather his kingdom, the rule of which should have come to him. But, seeing sickness, old age, and death, the Buddha wanted to leave that cave and spent years of suffering and deprivation trying to do so. In the end, however, he found a middle way between the sensual indulgence of the world and the harsh austerities of the renouncers who preceded him, a way in which serene meditation could lead him to the truth and the release which he sought.

It was during his meditation under the Bodhi tree that he famously attained his vision of the truth and his release from this world of *samsara.* Sometime later when he was considering what to do next he almost concluded that there was no use in trying to teach what he had learned to a world filled with lust and hate. But just then he was approached by a Brahman, not the Upanishadic absolute, but one of the many high gods whose ultimacy but not whose existence Buddhism always doubted, who implored him to return to the world after all:

> Let the Sorrowless One survey this human breed,
> Engulfed in sorrow, overcome by birth and old age.
> Arise, victorious hero, caravan leader,
> Debtless one, and wander in the world.
> Let the blessed One teach the Dhamma,
> There will be those who will understand.

And so the Buddha undertook, out of compassion for all sentient beings, forty-five years of itinerant preaching to make sure that the truth he had seen would not be lost to the world.[23]

That followers of the Buddha, like those of Plato, knew a lot about the legitimation crisis of Axial Age society is evident in many texts, but we can, following Steven Collins, take a particularly vivid example from one of the Jataka stories (stories of the Buddha's previous lives, among the most widely known genres of the Buddhist canon), long and fascinating, that I will all too briefly summarize.[24] "Once upon a time there was a king of Benares who ruled justly *(dhammena).* He had sixteen thousand women, but did not obtain a son or daughter from any of them."[25] Indra, the king of the gods, took pity on him and sent the future Buddha to be born as a son to his chief queen. The child was named Temiya, and his father was delighted with him.

When he was a month old, he was dressed up and brought to his father, who was so pleased with him that he held him in his lap as he held court. Just then four criminals were brought in and the king sentenced one of them to be imprisoned, two to be lashed or struck with swords, and one to be impaled on a stake. Temiya was extremely upset and worried that his father would go to hell for his terrible deeds. The next day Temiya remembered his previous births, including that in the past he had been king of this very city and that, as a result of his actions, he subsequently spent eighty thousand years in an especially terrible hell, where he had been cooked on hot metal in excruciating pain the whole time. He determined that this would not happen again, so he pretended to be lame, deaf, and dumb so that he could not succeed to the kingship.

Since he was beautiful and had a perfectly formed body, people found it hard to believe in his defects, but because he was a future Buddha, he was able to resist all temptations to give himself away, whether with loud noises, terrifying snakes, or beautiful girls. When he was sixteen, the soothsayers told the king that he would bring bad luck to the royal house and should be killed. His mother begged him to save himself by showing that he was without defect but, knowing his fate if he succeeded to the kingship, he refused. Temiya was sent in his chariot to the charnel-ground where he was to be killed, but the gods saw to it that the charioteer took him to the forest instead. At that point Temiya revealed his true self, showing himself strong and fit. His charioteer offered to take him back to the city so he could claim his succession to the throne, but Temiya explained to him the dreadful fate in hell that awaited him if he did so and declared his intention to become an ascetic instead. At that point, "the chariot-driver, seeing that Temiya had cast kingship aside 'as if it were a dead body,' wanted to become an ascetic also."[26] Temiya ordered him instead to return to the city and tell his parents what had happened.

When Temiya's parents received the news, they rushed to the forest where he was, and overwhelmed with his new self, proceeded to renounce the world themselves. Soon the whole city had come out to the forest and everyone became a renouncer. They left gold and jewels in the streets of the city as of no more use. Soon a neighboring king, hearing what had happened, decided to annex Benares and scoop up the gold and jewels, but once in the city, he felt an overwhelming impulse to find the ascetic prince and his parents. Upon finding them, he, too, and his subjects following him, became renouncers. Another king followed his example. Soon it was clear that Temiya was, after all, a *cakravartin,* a universal ruler, though his rule was renunciation.

Collins sums up by saying, "It is difficult to imagine a more explicit condemnation of kingship: despite the narrative voice's assertion in the first sentence that Temiya's father ruled justly, or 'in accordance with what is right' *(dhammena).*"[27] Collins points out that *dhamma* is used in two senses, worldly *dhamma* and *buddhadhamma,* and that it is the former that the kingdom embodied and the latter that it drastically violated. Temiya's father's kingdom represented what Peter Brown, the great historian of late classical antiquity, described as "the more predictable, but no less overbearing 'gentle violence' of a stable social order."[28] In a class society, even if those who serve and are never served are not beaten or hungry, as in fact they often are, they are always at the whim of those they serve; they have no control over their own lives. If it is unlikely that Plato ever imagined that his ideal city could be realized, it is very clear that in this Buddhist story Temiya's universal empire of renunciation could never be realized on this earth: it would involve not only the absence of violence; it would involve the absence of sex. Nonetheless, as with all the great Axial utopias, it stands as a measure of just how short life in this world falls compared to what it ought to be.

The great utopias served for the renouncers as stark contrasts to the actual world and their vision of that other world could be called "theory" in Plato's sense. But the very distance they felt from the world to which they returned made possible another kind of "theory," another kind of seeing, that is, a distant, critical view of the actual world in which they lived. The renouncer sees the world with new eyes: as Plato says of the ones who have returned to the cave, they see the shadows for what they are, not naively as do those who have never left. One could say that the ideological illusion is gone. One gazes at a distance, objectively, so to speak.

Once disengaged vision becomes possible, then theory can take another turn: it can abandon any moral stance at all and look simply at what will be useful, what can make the powerful and exploitative even more so. One thinks of the Legalists in China and of Kautilya's *Arthashastra* in India. Although the Hebrew prophets saw and condemned the self-serving manipulations of the rich and powerful, we can find in the Bible no example of someone arguing for such behavior in principle. Except possibly for some of the Sophists, whose surviving writings are fragmentary, we have nothing quite like Han Fei or Kautilya in Greece. Or do we?

Aristotle was not an amoralist; he was one of the greatest moral theorists who ever lived. Yet in Aristotle we can see the possibility of a split between knowledge and ethics that will, when it is fully recognized, have enormous consequences in later history. Pierre Hadot argues that Plato's school, for all its concern for mathematics and dialectic, had an essentially political aim: philosophers in principle should be rulers. Aristotle's school, however, is specifically for philosophers, those who do not participate actively in the life of the city, in a way a school for renouncers.[29] But in distinguishing the philosophical life from the political life so clearly, Aristotle threatens the link between wisdom *(sophia)* and moral judgment *(phronesis)*, in which he still clearly believed. Most of his surviving texts were notes for lectures within the school and express aspects of the philosophical life, though the *Ethics* and the *Politics* were intended for a larger audience of active citizens. The link between the two realms is not direct but appears in the fact that both are oriented to good forms of life, one toward knowledge for its own sake, the other for the creation of a good city.

Although the highest form of *theoria* is contemplation of the divine and through it the philosopher, however briefly and partially, actually participates in the divine, *theoria* includes the search for knowledge of all things, including the transient ones. Hadot, however, argues that Aristotle's massive research project is not quite what it seems to modern minds:

> It is thus indisputable that for Aristotle the life of the mind consists, to a large degree, in observing, doing research, and reflecting on one's observations. Yet this activity is carried out in a certain spirit, which we might go so far as to describe as an almost religious passion for reality in all its aspects, be they humble or sublime, for we find traces of the divine in all things.[30]

He goes on to quote a passage in which Aristotle says, "In all natural things there is something wonderful."[31] It is as though *theoria* in its highest form is close to what the developmental psychologist Alison Gopnik calls "lantern consciousness," the apprehension of reality as a whole, but in its lesser forms it becomes various kinds of "spotlight consciousness," focusing on each aspect of reality, however humble, in an effort to understand it and what causes it.[32]

So one possible split apparent in Aristotle is that between his metaphysics, where he describes the ultimate source of all knowledge, and the many particular fields of inquiry that he had so much to do with founding. But the second possible split is between *theoria,* contemplation, in all its various levels, as the best life for human beings, and the life of the city, of politics and ethics. *Theoria,* in his words, is useless. It is a good internal to itself, but it has no consequences for the world.

But perhaps we miss Aristotle's point if we ask what the theoretical life is good for. Being the best kind of life, and good in itself, then the question is what kind of person and what kind of society could make this life possible. The *Ethics* and *Politics,* then, describe the conditions under which the theoretical life could be pursued. But unlike Plato's *Republic,* Aristotle's *Politics* is no utopia but an empirical and analytical description of actual Greek society, containing ethical judgments between better and worse, but objective, distant, as an analysis of the second best kind of life, one that has its final value in making possible the first kind of life. Aristotle was the founder of sociology, which Émile Durkheim recognized when he assigned the *Politics* as the basic textbook for his students when he first began to teach at the University of Bordeaux. What I am suggesting is that the distinctions between two kinds of *theoria,* pure contemplation and various fields of inquiry, and two kinds of ethical life, the intellectual and the practical, made possible, once the unity of Aristotle's thought was broken, separate developments that could lead to autonomous sciences and utilitarian ethics in the long run.

Aristotle was really a stranger in his own city, if Athens was his own city: he was not a citizen. He had to set up his school, the Lyceum, in a public building because, as an alien, he could not own land in Athens and so could not buy land for his school. And when things turned grim, he, unlike Socrates, had no compunction about getting out in time. He was a teacher, one of the greatest who ever lived, but one of his (not very apt) pupils was Alexander, the greatest conqueror of the ancient world. Aristotle on the whole used the word *theoria* in Plato's sense, but he also used it from time to time for "investigation," or "inquiry," that is, for the study of all things in the world, natural and cultural, to see how they worked and what they are for.

My point is that the Axial Age gave us "theory" in two senses, and neither of them has been unproblematic ever since. The great utopian visions have motivated some of the noblest achievements of mankind; they have also motivated some of the worst actions of human beings. Theory in the sense of disengaged knowing, inquiry for the sake of understanding, with or without moral evaluation, has brought its own kind of astounding achievements but it has also given humans the power to destroy their environment and themselves. Both kinds of *theoria* have criticized but also justified the class society that first came into conscious view in the Axial Age. They have provided the intellectual tools for efforts to reform and efforts to repress. It is a great heritage. I doubt that any of us would rather live in a tribal society than in one whose beginnings lie in the Axial Age; I know I would not. Yet it is a heritage of explosive potentialities for good and for evil. It has given us the great tool of criticism. How will we use it?

Notes

Portions of this chapter first appeared as the concluding chapter to my *Religion in Human Evolution: From the Paleolithic to the Axial Age* (Cambridge, MA: The Belknap Press of Harvard University Press, 2011).

1. See Robert N. Bellah, *Religion in Human Evolution: From the Paleolithic to the Axial Age* (Cambridge, MA: The Belknap Press of Harvard University Press, 2011).
2. Jürgen Habermas, "Toward a Reconstruction of Historical Materialism," in *Communication and the Evolution of Society* (Boston: Beacon, 1979 [1976]), 130–177, here 174.
3. Ibid., 177.
4. Eli Sagan believes there is an inherent drive toward higher levels of morality, though such a drive may suffer blockage and regression. In chapter 4 of my book on the evolution of religion I speak of a biological drive toward domination on the one hand and toward nurturance on the other. Human culture has greatly elaborated these drives but has not eliminated them. We must face the reality that these remain two of our deepest motives. For Sagan's views see his *Freud, Women, and Morality* (New York: Basic Books, 1988), 222ff.
5. For a penetrating analysis of just where many of our problems lie in this respect see Jürgen Habermas, "The Postnational Constellation and the Future of Democracy," in *The Postnational Constellation: Political Essays* (Cambridge, MA: MIT Press, 2002 [1998]), 58–112.
6. Habermas, "Toward a Reconstruction," 163 (emphasis in original).

7. Perhaps it would be best to call only Plato a renouncer. Andrea Nightingale argues with Simon Goldhill, who called Socrates a "performer in exile" because he did not display his wisdom in the assembly or other political gatherings (except on one important occasion). She holds that in his exchanges with his fellow citizens he remained intimately tied to the city. See Andrea Nightingale, *Spectacles of Truth in Classical Greek Philosophy: Theoria in Its Cultural Context* (Cambridge: Cambridge University Press, 2004), 73, n. 2. Can we call Socrates a "dissident," who, like Václav Havel, criticized his city but refused to leave it at whatever cost? Fortunately for Havel, he only had to serve four years in prison.

8. Of course, as in many legitimation struggles, what began as a tradition of criticism could become a tradition of legitimation.

9. Nightingale, *Spectacles*, 40–41.

10. Ibid., 74–77.

11. Ibid., 78.

12. Ibid., 98.

13. Ibid., 80.

14. Ibid., 81.

15. Ibid., 80.

16. Ibid., 105–106.

17. Ibid., 106.

18. Ibid., 106–107.

19. Ibid., 111.

20. Ibid., 110–116.

21. Ibid., 134 (emphasis in original).

22. Ibid., 135.

23. On the Buddha's visions in his "meditative trance" on the night of his "Awakening," see Gananath Obeyesekere, *Imagining Karma: Ethical Transformation in Amerindian, Buddhist, and Greek Rebirth* (Berkeley: University of California Press, 2002), 158. For the words of the Brahman see *Ariyapariyesana Sutta* 19–21, in Bhikkhu Bodhi, trans., *The Middle Length Discourses of the Buddha: A Translation of the Majjhima Nikaya* (Boston: Wisdom, 1995), 261.

24. This is the well-known "Birth Story of the Dumb Cripple" (*Mugapakkha Jataka*, Ja 6.1ff., 158) as recounted and partly translated in Steven Collins, *Nirvana and Other Buddhist Felicities: Utopias of the Pali Imaginaire* (Cambridge: Cambridge University Press, 1998), 425–433. For a complete translation see "The Story of Temiya, the Dumb Cripple," in *The Jatakas: Birth Stories of the Bodhisatta*, trans. Sarah Shaw (New Delhi: Penguin, 2006), 179–221.

25. Collins, *Nirvana*, 426.

26. Ibid., 430.

27. Ibid., 233–234.

28. Ibid., 417. The quote is from Peter Brown, *Authority and the Sacred: Aspects of the Christianisation of the Roman World* (Cambridge: Cambridge University

Press, 1995), 53. It is worth noting that the "gentle violence" of which Brown speaks was inflicted by an empire that had become "Christian," just as "Buddhist" empires would do the same.

29. Pierre Hadot, *What Is Ancient Philosophy?* (Cambridge, MA: Harvard University Press, 2002 [1995]), 78. My discussion of Aristotle draws heavily from Hadot's chapter on Aristotle in this book, pp. 77–90.

30. Hadot, *What Is Ancient Philosophy?*, 82.

31. Aristotle, *De partibus animalium* I and *De generatione animalium I*, trans. David M. Balme (Oxford: Clarendon Press, 1972), p. 18, 645a.

32. Alison Gopnik, *The Philosophical Baby: What Children's Minds Tell Us about Truth, Love, and the Meaning of Life* (New York: Farrar, Straus and Giroux, 2009), 129.

Bibliography

Works on the Axial Age

Primary Sources (in chronological order)

Anquetil-Duperron, Abraham Hyacinthe. 1771. *Zend-Avesta: Ouvrage de Zoroastre; Contenant les idées théologiques, physiques et morales de ce législateur.* 2 vols. Paris: Tilliard.

Fabre d'Olivet, Antoine. 1822. *De l'état social de l'homme ou vues philosophiques sur l'histoire du genre humain.* Précédées d'une dissertation introductive sur les motifs et l'objet de cet ouvrage. Paris: Brière.

Hess, Moses. 1837. *Die heilige Geschichte der Menschheit: Von einem Jünger Spinoza's.* Stuttgart: Hallberger'sche Verlagshandlung, 1837. English: *The Holy History of Mankind and Other Writings,* trans. and ed. Shlomo Avineri. Cambridge: Cambridge University Press, 2004.

Sigwart, Heinrich Christoph Wilhelm. 1844. *Geschichte der Philosophie vom allgemeinen wissenschaftlichen und geschichtlichen Standpunkt.* Vol. 1. Stuttgart: Cotta'scher Verlag.

Röth, Eduard. 1846. *Die ägyptische und die zoroastrische Glaubenslehre als die ältesten Quellen unserer spekulativen Ideen.* Mannheim: Bassermann.

Gfrörer, August Friedrich. 1855. *Urgeschichte des menschlichen Geschlechts.* Schaffhausen: Hurter.

Lasaulx, Ernst von. 1856. *Neuer Versuch einer alten auf die Wahrheit der Thatsachen gegründeten Philosophie der Geschichte.* Munich: Literarisch-Artistische Anstalt der J. G. Cotta'schen Buchhandlung. New ed.: *Neuer Versuch einer alten, auf die Wahrheit der Tatsachen gegründeten Philosophie der Geschichte,* ed. Eugen Thurnher. Munich: Oldenbourg, 1952.

Burckhardt, Jakob. 1868–1873. *Weltgeschichtliche Betrachtungen.* Berlin: Spemann, 1905.

Strauss, Victor von. 1870. *Laò-tsè's Taò tĕ kīng.* Leipzig: Fleischer.

Stuart-Glennie, John Stuart. 1873. *The Modern Revolution: Introductory Historical Analysis; In the Morningland. Or: The Law of the Origin and Transformation of Christianity.* Vol. 1: *The New Philosophy of History* and *The Origin of the Doctrines of Christianity.* London: Longmans, Green & Co.[1]

Brodbeck, Adolf. 1893. *Zoroaster: Ein Beitrag zur vergleichenden Geschichte der Religionen und philosophischen Systeme des Morgen- und Abendlandes.* Leipzig: Friedrich.
Davids, T. W. Rhys. 1903. *Buddhist India.* London: T. F. Unwin.[2]
Wirth, Albrecht. 1913. *Der Gang der Weltgeschichte.* Gotha: Perthes.
Simmel, Georg. 1918. *Lebensanschauung: Vier metaphysische Kapitel.* Munich: Duncker & Humblot. English: *The View of Life: Four Metaphysical Essays with Journal Aphorisms.* Chicago: University of Chicago Press, 2010.
Rachel, Hugo. 1920. *Geschichte der Völker und Kulturen von Urbeginn bis heute.* Berlin: Parey.
Weber, Max. 1920–1921. *Gesammelte Aufsätze zur Religionssoziologie.* Vol. 1: *Die protestantische Ethik und der Geist des Kapitalismus; Die protestantischen Sekten und der Geist des Kapitalismus; Die Wirtschaftsethik der Weltreligionen—*part I: *Konfuzianismus und Taoismus.* Vol. 2: *Die Wirtschaftsethik der Weltreligionen—*part II: *Hinduismus und Buddhismus.* Vol. 3: *Die Wirtschaftsethik der Weltreligionen—*part III: *Das antike Judentum.* Tübingen: J. C. B. Mohr.

———. 1921–1922. *Wirtschaft und Gesellschaft* (Grundriß der Sozialökonomik, III. Abteilung). Tübingen: J. C. B. Mohr.
Bury, J. B., S. A. Cook, and F. E. Adcock, eds. 1925. *The Cambridge Ancient History.* Vol. 3: *The Assyrian Empire.* Cambridge: Cambridge University Press.[3]
Hanslick, Erwin, Emerich Kohn, Ernst Georg Klauber, and C. F. Lehmann-Haupt. 1925. *Einleitung und Geschichte des alten Orients.* Gotha: Perthes.
Menghin, Oswald. 1931. *Weltgeschichte der Steinzeit.* Vienna: Schroll.
Weber, Alfred. 1935. *Kulturgeschichte als Kultursoziologie.* Leiden: Sijthoff.
Cook, Stanley A. 1936. *The Old Testament: A Reinterpretation.* Cambridge: Heffer.[4]
Teggart, Frederick J. 1939. *Rome and China: A Study of Correlations in Historical Event.* Berkeley: University of California Press.[5]
Weber, Alfred. 1943. *Das Tragische und die Geschichte.* Hamburg: Goverts.
Jaspers, Karl. 1946. *Vom europäischen Geist.* Vortrag, gehalten bei den Rencontres Internationales de Genève, September 1946. Munich: Piper. Reprinted in Jaspers, *Rechenschaft und Ausblick: Reden und Aufsätze,* 233–264. Munich: Piper, 1951. English: *The European Spirit.* London: S. C .M. Press, 1948.
Weber, Alfred. 1946. *Abschied von der bisherigen Geschichte: Überwindung des Nihilismus?* Hamburg: Claaßen und Goverts.
Altheim, Franz. 1947–1948. *Weltgeschichte Asiens im griechischen Zeitalter.* 2 vols. Halle: Niemeyer.
Freyer, Hans. 1948. *Weltgeschichte Europas.* 2 vols. Wiesbaden: Dieterich.
Jaspers, Karl. 1948. "The Axial Age of Human History," *Commentary* 6: 430–435. Reprinted in *Identity and Anxiety: Survival of the Person in Mass Society,* ed. Maurice R. Stein, Arthur J. Vidich, and David Manning White, 597–605. New York: Free Press, 1960.

———. 1949. *Vom Ursprung und Ziel der Geschichte.* Zurich: Artemis / Munich: Piper. English: *The Origin and Goal of History,* trans. Michael Bullock. London: Routledge & Kegan Paul / New Haven: Yale University Press, 1953.

———. 1950. *Einführung in die Philosophie: Zwölf Radiovorträge.* Zurich: Artemis. English: *Way to Wisdom: An Introduction to Philosophy,* trans. Ralph Manheim. New Haven: Yale University Press, 1951.

———. 1950. *Vernunft und Widervernunft in unserer Zeit.* Munich: Piper.

Needham, Joseph. 1954. *Science and Civilisation in China.* 7 vols. Cambridge: Cambridge University Press.[6]

Voegelin, Eric. 1956–1987. *Order and History.* Vol. 1: *Israel and Revelation.* Vol. 2: *The World of the Polis.* Vol. 3: *Plato and Aristotle.* Vol. 4: *The Ecumenic Age.* Vol. 5: *In Search of Order.* Baton Rouge: Louisiana State University Press.[7]

Jaspers, Karl. 1957. "Antwort." In *Karl Jaspers,* ed. Paul Arthur Schilpp, 750–852. Stuttgart: Kohlhammer. English: "Reply to My Critics." In *The Philosophy of Karl Jaspers,* ed. Paul Arthur Schilpp, 749–869. New York: Tudor Publishing Company, 1957.

———. 1957. *Die großen Philosophen.* Vol. 1: *Die maßgebenden Menschen: Die fortzeugenden Gründer des Philosophierens. Aus dem Ursprung denkende Metaphysiker.* Munich: Piper.

Voegelin, Eric. 1963. "What Is History?" In *The Collected Works of Eric Voegelin,* ed. Thomas A. Hollweck and Paul Caringella. Vol. 28, 1–51. Baton Rouge: Louisiana State University Press, 1990.

———. 1964. "Ewiges Sein in der Zeit." In *Zeit und Geschichte. Dankesgabe an Rudolf Bultmann zum 80. Geburtstag,* ed. Erich Dinkler, 591–614. Tübingen: Mohr Siebeck.

———. 1966. *Anamnesis: Zur Theorie der Geschichte und Politik.* Munich: Piper.

———. 1989. *Auto-biographical Reflections,* ed. Ellis Sandoz. Baton Rouge: Louisiana State University Press.

Secondary Literature

Encyclopedia Entries

Anon. 1992. "Axial Age." In *Chambers Dictionary of Beliefs and Religions,* ed. Rosemary Goring, 49. Edinburgh: Chambers.

———. 1997. "Axial Age." In *The Oxford Dictionary of World Religions,* ed. John Bowker, 116. Oxford: Oxford University Press.

Arnason, Johann P. 2001. "Civilizational Analysis, History of." In *International Encyclopedia of the Social and Behavioral Sciences,* ed. Neil J. Smelser and Paul B. Baltes. Vol. 3, 1909–1915. Oxford: Elsevier.

Baudler, Georg. 1994. "Frieden/Krieg." In *Wörterbuch der Religionssoziologie,* ed. Siegfried Rudolf Dunde, 83–91. Gütersloh: Gütersloher Verlagshaus.

Bellah, Robert N. 2001. "Religion: Evolution and Development." In *International Encyclopedia of the Social & Behavioral Sciences*, ed. Neil J. Smelser and Paul B. Baltes. Vol. 19, 13062–13066. Oxford: Elsevier.

Boon, James A. 2005. "Anthropology, Ethnology and Religion." In *Encyclopedia of Religion*, ed. Lindsay Jones. 2nd ed. Vol. 1, 378–388. Detroit: Macmillan Reference USA.

Eisenstadt, Shmuel N. 2001. "Civilizations." In *International Encyclopedia of the Social & Behavioral Sciences*, ed. Neil J. Smelser and Paul B. Baltes. Vol. 3, 1915–1921. Oxford: Elsevier.

———. 2005. "Religious Diversity." In *Encyclopedia of Religion*, ed. Lindsay Jones. 2nd ed. Vol. 11, 7725–7731. Detroit: Macmillan Reference USA.

———. 2007. "Civilizations." In *The Blackwell Encyclopedia of Sociology*, ed. George Ritzer. Vol. 2, 519–529. Malden: Blackwell.

Freyer, Hans. 1965. "Geschichtsphilosophie." In *Handwörterbuch der Sozialwissenschaften*, ed. Erwin v. Beckerath et al. Vol. 4, 403–408. Stuttgart: Fischer/ Tübingen: J. C. B. Mohr/Göttingen: Vandenhoeck & Ruprecht.

Iwersen, Julia. 2005. "Virgin Goddess." In *Encyclopedia of Religion*, ed. Lindsay Jones. 2nd ed. Vol. 14, 9601–9606. Detroit: Macmillan Reference USA.

Lanczkowski, Günter. 1984. "Geschichte—Geschichtsschreibung—Geschichtsphilosophie. I. Religionsgeschichtlich." In *Theologische Realenzyklopädie*, ed. Gerhard Krause and Gerhard Müller. Vol. 12, 565–569. Berlin: de Gruyter.

Lohff, W. 1971. "Achsenzeit." In *Historisches Wörterbuch der Philosophie*, ed. Joachim Ritter. Vol. 1, 74–75. Basel: Schwabe.

Neumann, Johannes. 1994. "Recht." In *Wörterbuch der Religionssoziologie*, ed. Siegfried Rudolf Dunde, 249–259. Gütersloh: Gütersloher Verlagshaus.

Pieper, Annemarie. 1996. "Jaspers, Karl." In *Lexikon für Theologie und Kirche*, ed. Walter Kasper et al. 3rd ed. Vol. 5, 758–760. Freiburg im Breisgau: Herder.

Salaquarda, Jörg. 1987. "Jaspers, Karl (1883–1969)." In *Theologische Realenzyklopädie*, ed. Gerhard Müller. Vol. 16, 539–545. Berlin: de Gruyter.

Szakolczai, Arpad. 2006. "Historical Sociology." In *Encyclopedia of Social Theory*, ed. Austin Harrington, Barbara L. Marshall, and Hans-Peter Müller, 249–251. London: Routledge.

Woschitz, Karl. 1998. "Achsenzeit." In *Religion in Geschichte und Gegenwart*, ed. Hans Dieter Betz et al. 4th ed. Vol. 1, 98. Tübingen: Mohr Siebeck. English: "Axial Age." In *Religion Past & Present: Encyclopedia of Theology and Religion*, ed. Hans Dieter Betz et al. Vol. 1, 531. Leiden: Brill, 2007.

Monographs and Articles

Abitbol, Michel, Naomi Chazan, and Shmuel N. Eisenstadt. 1987. "Cultural Premises, Political Structures and Dynamics." *International Political Science Review* 8: 291–306.

———. 1988. "State Formation in Africa: Conclusions." In Michel Abitbol, Naomi Chazan, and Shmuel N. Eisenstadt, eds., *The Early State in African Perspective: Culture, Power and Division of Labor,* 168–200. Leiden: Brill.

Adams, Suzi. 2005. "Interpreting Creation: Castoriadis and the Birth of Autonomy." *Thesis Eleven* 83: 25–41.

Adas, Michael. 1998. "Bringing Ideas and Agency Back In: Representation and the Comparative Approach to World History." In Richard H. Elphick, Philip Pomper, and Richard T. Vann, eds., *World History: Ideologies, Structures and Identities,* 81–104. Oxford: Blackwell.

Alexander, Jeffrey C. 1992. "The Fragility of Progress: An Interpretation of the Turn toward Meaning in Eisenstadt's Later Work." *Acta Sociologica* 35: 85–94.

———. 2001. "The Long and Winding Road: Civil Repair of Intimate Injustice." *Sociological Theory* 19: 371–400.

———. 2005. "The Dark Side of Modernity: Tension Relief, Splitting and Grace." In Eliezer Ben-Rafael and Yitzhak Sternberg, eds., *Comparing Modernities: Pluralism versus Homogenity; Essays in Homage to Shmuel N. Eisenstadt,* 171–179. Leiden: Brill.

———. 2006. *The Civil Sphere.* Oxford: Oxford University Press.

———. 2007. "The Meaningful Construction of Inequality and the Struggles against It: A 'Strong Program' Approach to How Social Boundaries Change." *Cultural Sociology* 1: 23–30.

Alitto, Guy. 1992. "Orthodoxie in der chinesischen Kultur." In Shmuel N. Eisenstadt, ed., *Kulturen der Achsenzeit II: Ihre institutionelle und kulturelle Dynamik.* Part 1: *China, Japan,* 126–174. Frankfurt am Main: Suhrkamp.

Allardt, Erik. 2005. "Europe's Multiple Modernity." In Eliezer Ben-Rafael and Yitzhak Sternberg, eds., *Comparing Modernities: Pluralism versus Homogenity; Essays in Homage to Shmuel N. Eisenstadt,* 483–499. Leiden: Brill.

Althaus, Horst. 2007. *"Heiden," "Juden," "Christen": Positionen und Kontroversen von Hobbes bis Carl Schmitt.* Würzburg: Königshausen & Neumann.

Altheim, Franz. 1952. "Zarathustra." *Neue Rundschau* 63: 165–190.

Amore, Roy C., and Julia Ching. 2002. "The Buddhist Tradition." In Willard G. Oxtoby, ed., *World Religions: Eastern Traditions.* 2nd ed., 199–315. Toronto: Oxford University Press.

Anderle, Othmar F., ed. 1964. *The Problems of Civilizations.* Report of the First Synopsis Conference of the S.I.E.C.C. / International Society for the Comparative Study of Civilizations, Salzburg, October 8–15, 1961. The Hague: Mouton.

Andriolo, Karin R. 1981. "Myth and History: A General Model and Its Application to the Bible." *American Anthropologist* 83: 261–284.

Angenendt, Arnold. 1997. *Geschichte der Religiosität im Mittelalter.* Darmstadt: Wissenschaftliche Buchgesellschaft.

———. 1997. "Religion zwischen Mündlichkeit und Schriftlichkeit: Der Prozeß des Mittelalters." In Clemens M. Kasper and Klaus Schreiner, eds., *Viva vox und ratio scripta: Mündliche und schriftliche Kommunikationsformen im Mönchtum des Mittelalters*, 37–50. Münster: LIT.

———. 2005. "Welt- und Personverständnis in christlicher Auffassung: Grenzen und Entgrenzungen." In Justin Stagl and Wolfgang Reinhard, eds., *Grenzen des Menschseins: Probleme einer Definition des Menschlichen*, 293–321. Vienna: Böhlau.

Arden, John Boghosian. 1998. *Science, Theology and Consciousness: The Search for Unity*. Westport: Praeger.

Arendt, Hannah. 1957. "Karl Jaspers—Citizen of the World." In Paul Arthur Schilpp, ed., *The Philosophy of Karl Jaspers*, 539–549. New York: Tudor Publishing Company.

Arévaldo de León, Bernardo. 1988. "De-Axialization/Re-Axialization: The Case of Brazilian Millennialism." *International Journal of Comparative Sociology* 29: 44–61.

Arjomand, Saïd Amir. 1989. "History, Structure and Revolution in the Shi'ite Tradition in Contemporary Iran." *International Political Science Review* 10 (The Historical Framework of Revolutions): 111–119.

———. 1993. "Millennial Beliefs, Hierocratic Authority and Revolution in Shi'ite Iran." In Saïd Amir Arjomand, ed., *The Political Dimensions of Religion*, 219–239. Albany: State University of New York Press.

———. 1993. "Religion and the Diversity of Normative Orders." In Saïd Amir Arjomand, ed., *The Political Dimensions of Religion*, 43–68. Albany: State University of New York Press.

———. 2004. "Social Theory and the Changing World: Mass Democracy, Development, Modernization and Globalization." *International Sociology* 19: 321–353.

———. 2005. "Political Culture in the Islamicate Civilization." In Eliezer Ben-Rafael and Yitzhak Sternberg, eds., *Comparing Modernities: Pluralism versus Homogenity; Essays in Homage to Shmuel N. Eisenstadt*, 309–325. Leiden: Brill.

———. 2006. "Comparing the Development of the Political Arena in Three Axial Civilizations." *Erwägen, Wissen, Ethik* 17: 17–18.

———. 2006. "Islam and the Path to Modernity: Institutions of Higher Learning and Secular and Political Culture." In Johann P. Arnason, Armando Salvatore, and Georg Stauth, eds., *Islam in Process: Historical and Civilizational Perspectives*, 241–257. Bielefeld: Transcript.

———. 2006. "Revolution in Early Islam: The Rise of Islam as a Constitutive Revolution." In Johann P. Arnason, Armando Salvatore, and Georg Stauth, eds., *Islam in Process: Historical and Civilizational Perspectives*, 125–157. Bielefeld: Transcript.

———. 2011. "Axial Civilizations, Multiple Modernities, and Islam." *Journal of Classical Sociology* 11, no. 3: 327–335.
Armstrong, Karen. 1993. *A History of God: From Abraham to the Present; The 4,000-Year Quest for God*. London: Heinemann.
———. 2002. *Islam: A Short History*. New York: Modern Library.
———. 2005. *A Short History of Myth*. Edinburgh: Canongate.
———. 2006. *The Great Transformation: The Beginning of Our Religious Traditions*. New York: Knopf.
Arnason, Johann P. 1993. "Comparing Japan and the West: Prolegomena to a Research Programme." In Lars Gule and Oddvar Storebø, eds., *Development and Modernity: Perspectives on Western Theories of Modernisation*, 167–195. Bergen: Ariadne.
———. 1994. "The Human Condition and the Modern Predicament." In John Burnheim, ed., *The Social Philosophy of Agnes Heller*, 57–77. Amsterdam: Rodopi.
———. 1997. *Social Theory and Japanese Experience: The Dual Civilization*. London: Kegan Paul.
———. 1999. "East Asian Approaches: Region, History and Civilization." *Thesis Eleven* 57: 97–112. Reprinted in Johann P. Arnason, *The Peripheral Centre: Essays on Japanese History and Civilization*, 24–40. Melbourne: Trans Pacific Press.
———. 2000. "Introduction." *Thesis Eleven* 62: iii–v.
———. 2001. "Autonomy and Axiality: Comparative Perspectives on the Greek Breakthrough." In Johann P. Arnason and Peter Murphy, eds., *Agon, Logos, Polis: The Greek Achievement and Its Aftermath*, 155–206. Stuttgart: Steiner.
———. 2002. "Introduction: The Peripheral Centre and Its Transformations." In Johann P. Arnason, *The Peripheral Centre: Essays on Japanese History and Civilization*, 1–23. Melbourne: Trans Pacific Press.
———. 2002. "Multiple Modernities and Civilizational Contexts: Reflections on the Japanese Experience." In Johann P. Arnason, *The Peripheral Centre: Essays on Japanese History and Civilization*, 132–157. Melbourne: Trans Pacific Press.
———. 2003. *Civilizations in Dispute: Historical Questions and Theoretical Traditions*. Leiden: Brill.
———. 2003. "East and West: From Invidious Dichotomy to Incomplete Deconstruction." In Gerard Delanty and Engin F. Isin, eds., *Handbook of Historical Sociology*, 220–234. London: Sage Publications.
———. 2004. "Introduction." *Thesis Eleven* 76: 5–8.
———. 2004. "Parallels and Divergences: Perspectives on the Early Second Millennium." In Johann P. Arnason and Björn Wittrock, eds., *Eurasian Transformations, Tenth to Thirteenth Centuries: Crystallizations, Divergences, Renaissances*, 13–40. Leiden: Brill.

———. 2005. "The Axial Age and Its Interpreters: Reopening a Debate." In Johann P. Arnason, Shmuel N. Eisenstadt, and Björn Wittrock, eds., *Axial Civilizations and World History*, 19–49. Leiden: Brill.

———. 2005. "The Axial Conundrum: Between Historical Sociology and the Philosophy of History." In Eliezer Ben-Rafael and Yitzhak Sternberg, eds., *Comparing Modernities: Pluralism versus Homogenity; Essays in Homage to Shmuel N. Eisenstadt*, 57–81. Leiden: Brill.

———. 2006. "Civilizational Analysis, Social Theory and Comparative History." In *Handbook of Contemporary European Social Theory*, ed. Gerard Delanty, 230–241. London: Routledge.

———. 2006. "Civilizations in History." *European Journal of Social Theory* 9: 288–299.

———. 2006. "The Emergence of Islam as a Case of Cultural Crystallization: Historical and Comparative Reflections." In Johann P. Arnason, Armando Salvatore, and Georg Stauth, eds., *Islam in Process: Historical and Civilizational Perspectives*, 95–122. Bielefeld: Transcript.

———. 2006. "Marshall Hodgson's Civilizational Analysis of Islam: Theoretical and Comparative Perspectives." In Johann P. Arnason, Armando Salvatore, and Georg Stauth, eds., *Islam in Process: Historical and Civilizational Perspectives*, 23–47. Bielefeld: Transcript.

———. 2007. "The Idea of Negative Platonism: Jan Patočka's Critique and Recovery of Metaphysics." *Thesis Eleven* 90: 6–26.

———. 2010. "The Cultural Turn and the Civilizational Approach." *European Journal of Social Theory* 13: 67–82.

———. 2010. "Domains and Perspectives of Civilizational Analysis." *European Journal of Social Theory* 13: 5–13.

———. 2011. "Negative Platonism: Between the History of Philosophy and the Philosophy of History." In Erika Abrams and Ivan Chvatík, eds., *Jan Patočka and the Heritage of Phenomenology*, 215–227. Dordrecht: Springer.

Arnason, Johann P., Shmuel N. Eisenstadt, and Björn Wittrock, eds. 2005. *Axial Civilizations and World History*. Leiden: Brill.

———. 2005. "General Introduction." In Johann P. Arnason, Shmuel N. Eisenstadt, and Björn Wittrock, eds., *Axial Civilizations and World History*, 1–12. Leiden: Brill.

———. 2005. "Introduction: Archaic Backgrounds and Axial Breakthroughs." In Johann P. Arnason, Shmuel N. Eisenstadt, and Björn Wittrock, eds., *Axial Civilizations and World History*, 125–132. Leiden: Brill.

———. 2005. "Introduction: Extending the Axial Model to South and East Asia." In Johann P. Arnason, Shmuel N. Eisenstadt, and Björn Wittrock, eds., *Axial Civilizations and World History*, 361–367. Leiden: Brill.

———. 2005. "Introduction: History, Theory and Interpretation." In Johann P. Arnason, Shmuel N. Eisenstadt, and Björn Wittrock, eds., *Axial Civilizations and World History*, 15–18. Leiden: Brill.

———. 2005. "Introduction: Late Antiquity as a Sequel and Counterpoint to the Axial Age." In Johann P. Arnason, Shmuel N. Eisenstadt, and Björn Wittrock, eds., *Axial Civilizations and World History*, 287–293. Leiden: Brill.
Arnason, Johann P., and Peter Murphy. 2001. "Introduction." In Johann P. Arnason and Peter Murphy, eds., *Agon, Logos, Polis: The Greek Achievement and Its Aftermath*, 7–14. Stuttgart: Steiner.
Arnason, Johann P., Armando Salvatore, and Georg Stauth. 2006. "Introduction." In Johann P. Arnason, Armando Salvatore, and Georg Stauth, eds., *Islam in Process: Historical and Civilizational Perspectives*, 8–19. Bielefeld: Transcript.
Arnason, Johann P., and Björn Wittrock. 2004. "Introduction." In Johann P. Arnason and Björn Wittrock, eds., *Eurasian Transformations, Tenth to Thirteenth Centuries: Crystallizations, Divergences, Renaissances*, 1–10. Leiden: Brill.
Assmann, Aleida. 1989. "Jaspers' Achsenzeit, oder Schwierigkeiten mit der Zentralperspektive in der Geschichte." In Dietrich Harth, ed., *Karl Jaspers: Denken zwischen Wissenschaft, Politik und Philosophie*, 187–205. Stuttgart: Metzler.
———. 1992. "Einheit und Vielfalt in der Geschichte: Jaspers' Begriff der Achsenzeit neu betrachtet." In Shmuel N. Eisenstadt, ed., *Kulturen der Achsenzeit II: Ihre institutionelle und kulturelle Dynamik*. Part 3: *Buddhismus, Islam, Altägypten, westliche Kultur*, 330–340. Frankfurt am Main: Suhrkamp.
———. 2001. "Herder zwischen Nationalkulturen und Menschheitsgedächtnis." *Saeculum* 52, no. 1: 41–54.
Assmann, Jan. 1990. *Ma'at: Gerechtigkeit und Unsterblichkeit im Alten Ägypten*. Munich: C. H. Beck.
———. 1991. "Der Einbruch der Geschichte: Wandlungen des Welt- und Gottesbegriffs in der 18. Dynastie." In Jan Assmann, *Stein und Zeit: Mensch und Gesellschaft im alten Ägypten*, 288–302. Munich: Fink.
———. 1992. "Große Texte ohne eine Große Tradition: Ägypten als eine vorachsenzeitliche Kultur." In Shmuel N. Eisenstadt, ed., *Kulturen der Achsenzeit II: Ihre institutionelle und kulturelle Dynamik*. Part 3: *Buddhismus, Islam, Altägypten, westliche Kultur*, 245–280. Frankfurt am Main: Suhrkamp.
———. 1992. *Das kulturelle Gedächtnis: Schrift, Erinnerung und politische Identität in frühen Hochkulturen*. Munich: C. H. Beck.
———. 1994. "Zur Verschriftung rechtlicher und sozialer Normen im Alten Ägypten." In Hans-Joachim Gehrke, ed., *Rechtskodifizierung und soziale Normen im interkulturellen Vergleich*, 61–86. Tübingen: Narr.
———. 2000. *Herrschaft und Heil: Politische Theologie in Altägypten, Israel und Europa*. Munich: Hanser.
———. 2000. *Religion und kulturelles Gedächtnis: Zehn Studien*. Munich: C. H. Beck.
———. 2003. *Die Mosaische Unterscheidung oder der Preis des Monotheismus*. Munich: Hanser.
———. 2005. "Axial 'Breakthroughs' and Semantic 'Relocations' in Ancient Egypt and Israel." In Johann P. Arnason, Shmuel N. Eisenstadt, and Björn Wittrock, eds., *Axial Civilizations and World History*, 133–156. Leiden: Brill.

———. 2005. "'Axial' Breakthroughs and Semantic 'Relocations' in Ancient Egypt and Israel." In Bernhard Giesen and Daniel Šuber, eds., *Religion and Politics: Cultural Perspectives*, 39–53. Leiden: Brill.

———. 2005. "Monotheism and Its Political Consequences." In Bernhard Giesen and Daniel Šuber, eds., *Religion and Politics: Cultural Perspectives*, 141–159. Leiden: Brill.

———. 2006. "Gottesbilder—Menschenbilder: Anthropologische Konsequenzen des Monotheismus." In Reinhard Gregor Kratz and Hermann Spieckermann, eds., *Götterbilder—Gottesbilder—Weltbilder: Polytheismus und Monotheismus in der Welt der Antike*. Vol. 2: *Griechenland und Rom, Judentum, Christentum und Islam*, 313–329. Tübingen: Mohr Siebeck.

———. 2006. *Thomas Mann und Ägypten: Mythos und Monotheismus in den Josephsromanen*. Munich: C. H. Beck.

———. 2008. *Of God and Gods: Egypt, Israel, and the Rise of Monotheism*. Madison: University of Wisconsin Press.

Assmann, Jan, and Guy G. Stroumsa. 1999. "Introduction." In Jan Assmann and Guy G. Stroumsa, eds., *Transformations of the Inner Self in Ancient Religions*, 1–6. Leiden: Brill.

Avnon, Dan. 1998. *Martin Buber: The Hidden Dialogue*. Lanham: Rowman & Littlefield.

Bachmann, Thorsten. 2002. *Existentieller Mythos—mythische Existenz: Rekonstruktionen—Kritik und Transformation des Mythos bei Karl Jaspers*. Essen: Die Blaue Eule.

Baeck, Louis. 1994. *The Mediterranean Tradition in Economic Thought*. London: Routledge.

Baines, John, and Norman Yoffee. 2000. "Order, Legitimacy and Wealth: Setting the Terms." In Janet E. Richards and Mary Van Buren, eds., *Order, Legitimacy and Wealth in Ancient States*, 13–20. Cambridge: Cambridge University Press.

Balthasar, Hans Urs von. 1963. *Das Ganze im Fragment: Aspekte der Geschichtstheologie*. Einsiedeln: Benziger.

Barbour, Ian G. 1998. *Religion and Science: Historical and Contemporary Issues*. London: S.C.M. Press. Rev. and expanded ed. of *Religion in an Age of Science*. San Francisco: Harper & Row, 1990.

Barnes, Michael H. 1992. "Primitive Religious Thought and the Evolution of Religion." *Religion* 22: 21–46.

———. 1997. "Rationality in Religion." *Religion* 27: 375–390.

———. 2000. *Stages of Thought: The Co-Evolution of Religious Thought and Science*. New York: Oxford University Press.

———. 2003. *In the Presence of Mystery: An Introduction to the Story of Human Religiousness*. Rev. ed. Mystic: Twenty-Third Publications.

Barrow, Ian J. 2000. "Agency in the New World History." In Neil L. Waters, ed., *Beyond the Area Studies Wars: Toward a New International Studies*, 190–212. Middlebury: Middlebury College Press.

Barth, Heinrich. 1950. "Karl Jaspers über Glaube und Geschichte." *Theologische Zeitschrift* 6: 434–460. Reprinted in Hans Saner, ed., *Karl Jaspers in der Diskussion*, 274–296. Munich: Piper, 1973.

Bary, William Theodore de. 1992. "Neokonfuzianismus als 'sekundärer Durchbruch.'" In Shmuel N. Eisenstadt, ed., *Kulturen der Achsenzeit II: Ihre institutionelle und kulturelle Dynamik*. Part 1: *China, Japan*, 175–198. Frankfurt am Main: Suhrkamp.

Bauer, Wolfgang. 1965. "China: Verwirklichungen einer Utopie." In Golo Mann, Alfred Heuß, and August Nitschke, eds., *Propyläen Weltgeschichte*, Vol. 11: *Summa Historica*, 129–196. Berlin, Frankfurt am Main, and Vienna: Propyläen Verlag.

Bechert, Heinz. 1992. "Orthodoxie und Legitimation im Kontext des Früh- und des Thēravāda-Buddhismus." In Shmuel N. Eisenstadt, ed., *Kulturen der Achsenzeit II: Ihre institutionelle und kulturelle Dynamik*. Part 3: *Buddhismus, Islam, Altägypten, westliche Kultur*, 18–36. Frankfurt am Main: Suhrkamp.

Bellah, Robert N. 1964. "Religious Evolution." *American Sociological Review* 29: 358–374.

———. 1999. "Max Weber and World-Denying Love: A Look at the Historical Sociology of Religion." *Journal of the American Academy of Religion* 67: 277–304. Reprinted in Robert N. Bellah and Steven M. Tipton, eds., *The Robert Bellah Reader*, 123–149. Durham: Duke University Press, 2006.

———. 2002. "Epilogue: Meaning and Modernity. America and the World." In Richard Madsen, William M. Sullivan, Ann Swidler, and Steven M. Tipton, eds., *Meaning and Modernity: Religion, Polity and Self*, 255–276. Berkeley: University of California Press.

———. 2005. "Durkheim and Ritual." In *The Cambridge Companion to Durkheim*, ed. Jeffrey C. Alexander and Philip Smith, 183–210. New York: Cambridge University Press. Reprinted in Robert N. Bellah and Steven M. Tipton, eds., *The Robert Bellah Reader*, 150–180. Durham: Duke University Press, 2006.

———. 2005. "What Is Axial about the Axial Age?" *European Journal of Sociology* 46: 69–89.

———. 2010. "Confronting Modernity: Maruyama Masao, Jürgen Habermas, and Charles Taylor." In Michael Warner, Jonathan VanAntwerpen, and Craig Calhoun, eds., *Varieties of Secularism in a Secular Age*, 32–53. Cambridge, MA: Harvard University Press.

———. 2011. *Religion in Human Evolution: From the Paleolithic to the Axial Age*. Cambridge, MA: The Belknap Press of Harvard University Press.

Bellers, Jürgen, and Markus Porsche-Ludwig. 2010. *Achsenzeiten—Mythos und Zukunft der Geschichte: Ein ideen- und geistesgeschichtlicher Überblick von Aristoteles bis Heidegger*. Berlin: LIT.

Bendle, Mervyn F. 2003. "Militant Religion and the Crisis of Modernity: A New Paradigm." In David O. Moberg and Ralph L. Piedmont, eds., *Research in the Social Scientific Study of Religion*. Vol. 14, 229–252. Leiden: Brill.

Ben-Dor Benite, Zvi. 2011. "Religions and World History." In *The Oxford Handbook of World History*, ed. Jerry H. Bentley, 210–228. Oxford: Oxford University Press.

Ben-Rafael, Eliezer, and Yitzhak Sternberg. 2005. "Introduction: Civilization, Pluralism and Uniformity." In Eliezer Ben-Rafael and Yitzhak Sternberg, eds., *Comparing Modernities: Pluralism versus Homogenity; Essays in Homage to Shmuel N. Eisenstadt*, 1–27. Leiden: Brill.

Bentley, Jerry H. 1993. *Old World Encounters: Cross-Cultural Contacts and Exchanges in Pre-Modern Times*. New York: Oxford University Press.

———. 1998. "Hemispheric Integration, 500–1500 C.E." *Journal of World History* 9: 237–254.

Berger, Peter, and Stanley Pullberg. 1965. "Reification and the Sociological Critique of Consciousness." *History and Theory* 4: 196–211.

Berkey, Jonathan P. 2003. *The Formation of Islam: Religion and Society in the Near East, 600–1800*. Cambridge: Cambridge University Press.

Berkhof, Hendrik. 1962. *Der Sinn der Geschichte—Christus*. Göttingen: Vandenhoeck & Ruprecht.

Berman, Morris. 2000. *Wandering God: A Study in Nomadic Spirituality*. Albany: State University of New York Press.

Bernhardt, Reinhold. 2002. "Die Pluralistische Religionstheologie: Relativitätsschock für den christlichen Glauben?" In Wolfram Weiße, ed., *Wahrheit und Dialog: Theologische Grundlagen und Impulse gegenwärtiger Religionspädagogik*, 19–34. Münster: Waxmann.

Berthrong, John H. 1994. *All under Heaven: Transforming Paradigms in Confucian-Christian Dialogue*. Albany: State University of New York Press.

———. 1998. "Confucian Piety and the Religious Dimension of Japanese Confucianism." *Philosophy East and West* 48: 46–79.

———. 1998. *Transformations of the Confucian Way*. Boulder: Westview Press.

———. 2004. "Love, Lust and Sex: A Christian Perspective." *Buddhist-Christian Studies* 24: 3–22.

Beyme, Klaus von. 2002. *Politische Theorien im Zeitalter der Ideologien, 1789–1945*. Wiesbaden: Westdeutscher Verlag.

———. 2009. *Geschichte der politischen Theorien in Deutschland, 1300–2000*. Wiesbaden: Verlag für Sozialwissenschaften.

Bhambra, Gurminder K. 2006. "From Civilisational Analysis to Connected Histories and Cosmopolitanisms: A Response to Professor Eisenstadt's 'Culture and Power.'" *Erwägen, Wissen, Ethik* 17: 20–22.

Bielefeldt, Heiner. 1994. *Kampf und Entscheidung: Politischer Existentialismus bei Carl Schmitt, Helmuth Plessner und Karl Jaspers*. Würzburg: Königshausen & Neumann.

Black, Antony. 2008. "The 'Axial Period': What Was It and What Does It Signify?" *Review of Politics* 70: 23–39.

Blanton, Richard E., and Lane Fargher. 2008. *Collective Action in the Formation of Pre-modern States.* New York: Springer.
Blenkinsopp, Joseph. 1996. *A History of Prophecy in Israel.* Rev. ed. Louisville: Westminster John Knox Press.
Bloom, Irene. 1996. "Confucian Perspectives on the Individual and the Collectivity." In Irene Bloom, J. Paul Martin, and Wayne L. Proudfoot, eds., *Religious Diversity and Human Rights,* 114–151. New York: Columbia University Press.
———. 1997. "The Analects of Confucius, Then and Now." In Ainslie T. Embree and Carol Gluck, eds., *Asia in Western and World History: A Guide for Teaching,* 295–308. Armonk: Sharpe.
———. 1998. "Fundamental Intuitions and Consensus Statements: Mencian Confucianism and Human Rights." In Wm. Theodore de Bary and Tu Wei-ming, eds., *Confucianism and Human Rights,* 94–116. New York: Columbia University Press.
Böhm, Winfried. 2004. *Geschichte der Pädagogik: Von Platon bis zur Gegenwart.* Munich: C. H. Beck.
Bonacker, Thorsten. 2007. "Der Kampf der Interpretationen: Zur Konflikthaftigkeit der politischen Moderne." In Thorsten Bonacker and Andreas Reckwitz, eds., *Kulturen der Moderne: Soziologische Perspektiven der Gegenwart,* 199–218. Frankfurt and New York: Campus.
Bondarenko, Dmitri M., and Andrey V. Korotayev. 2003. "'Early State' in Cross-Cultural Perspective: A Statistical Reanalysis of Henri J. M. Claessen's Database." *Cross-Cultural Research* 37: 105–132.
Borgolte, Michael. 2005. "Wie Europa seine Vielfalt fand: Über die mittelalterlichen Wurzeln für die Pluralität der Werte." In Hans Joas and Klaus Wiegandt, eds., *Die kulturellen Werte Europas,* 117–163. Frankfurt am Main: Fischer. English: "How Europe Became Diverse: On the Medieval Roots of the Plurality of Values." In Hans Joas and Klaus Wiegandt, eds., *The Cultural Values of Europe,* 77–114. Liverpool: Liverpool University Press, 2008.
———. 2007. "Die Geburt Europas aus dem Geist der Achsenzeit." In Moritz Csáky and Johannes Feichtinger, eds., *Europa—geeint durch Werte? Die europäische Wertedebatte auf dem Prüfstand der Geschichte,* 45–60. Bielefeld: Transcript.
Bosley, Richard N. 2003. "Jaspers on Lao Tzu, Nāgārjuna and Dialectic." In Joseph W. Koterski and Raymond J. Langley, eds., *Karl Jaspers on Philosophy of History and History of Philosophy,* 56–63. Amherst: Humanity Books.
Bouquet, Alan C. 1958. *The Christian Faith and Non-Christian Religions.* Welwyn: Nisbet.
———. (1941) 1961. *Comparative Religion: A Short Outline.* Rev. ed. London: Cassell.
———. 1968. *Religious Experience: Its Nature, Types and Validity.* Rev. ed. Cambridge: Heffer.

Bowersock, Glen W. 1986. "Architects of Competing Transcendental Visions in Late Antiquity." In Shmuel N. Eisenstadt, ed., *The Origins and Diversity of Axial Age Civilizations*, 280–287. Albany: State University of New York Press.
———. 1986. "From Emperor to Bishop: The Self-Conscious Transformation of Political Power in the Fourth Century A.D." *Classical Philology* 81: 298–307.
Braach, Regina. 2003. *Eric Voegelins politische Anthropologie*. Würzburg: Königshausen & Neumann.
Brague, Rémi. 1999. *La sagesse du monde: Histoire de l'expérience humaine de l'univers*. Paris: Fayard. English: *The Wisdom of the World: The Human Experience of the Universe in Western Thought*. Chicago: University of Chicago Press, 2003.
Breuer, Stefan. 1994. "Kulturen der Achsenzeit: Leistung und Grenzen eines geschichtsphilosophischen Konzepts." *Saeculum* 45: 1–33.
———. 1998. *Der Staat: Entstehung, Typen, Organisationsstadien*. Reinbek: Rowohlt.
Brimnes, Niels. 2002. "Globalization and Indian Civilization: Questionable Continuities." In Mehdi Mozaffari, ed., *Globalization and Civilizations*, 242–263. London: Routledge.
Brown, Peter. 1975. "Society and the Supernatural: A Medieval Change." *Daedalus* 104, no. 2 (Wisdom, Revelation and Doubt: Perspectives on the First Millennium B.C.): 133–151.
Browne, Craig. 2009. "Democracy, Religion and Revolution." *Thesis Eleven* 99: 27–47.
Brüning, Walther. 1961. *Geschichtsphilosophie der Gegenwart*. Stuttgart: Klett.
Brunner, August. 1961. *Geschichtlichkeit*. Bern: Francke.
Brunner-Traut, Emma. 1990. *Frühformen des Erkennens am Beispiel Altägyptens*. Darmstadt: Wissenschaftliche Buchgesellschaft.
Bultmann, Rudolf. 1957. *History and Eschatology*. Edinburgh: University Press.
Burke, Edmund, III. 1979. "Islamic History as World History: Marshall Hodgson, 'The Venture of Islam.'" *International Journal of Middle East Studies* 10: 241–264. Reprinted in Marshall G. S. Hodgson, *Rethinking World History: Essays on Europe, Islam and World History*, ed. Edmund Burke III, 301–328. Cambridge: Cambridge University Press, 1993.
Burn, Andrew Robert. 1956. "The Comparative Study of Civilizations: Toynbee's Study of History." *History* 41: 1–15.
———. 1960. *The Lyric Age of Greece*. London: Edward Arnold.
Buss, Andreas E. 2003. *The Russian-Orthodox Tradition and Modernity*. Leiden: Brill.
Buss, Martin J. 2006. "The Place of Israelite Prophecy in Human History." In Brad E. Kelle and Megan Bishop Moore, eds., *Israel's Prophets and Israel's Past: Essays on the Relationship of Prophetic Texts and Israelite History in Honor of John H. Hayes*, 325–341. New York: T & T Clark.
Cajani, Luigi. 2011. "Periodization." In *The Oxford Handbook of World History*, ed. Jerry H. Bentley, 54–71. Oxford: Oxford University Press.

Calne, Donald Brian. 1999. *Within Reason: Rationality and Human Behavior.* New York: Pantheon Books.

The Cambridge History of Ancient China: From the Origins of Civilization to 221 B.C., ed. Michael Loewe and Edward L. Shaughnessy. Cambridge: Cambridge University Press, 1999.

Camic, Charles, and Hans Joas. 2004. "The Dialogical Turn." In Charles Camic and Hans Joas, eds., *The Dialogical Turn: New Roles for Sociology in the Postdisciplinary Age,* 1–19. Lanham: Rowman & Littlefield.

Cao, Deborah. 2004. *Chinese Law: A Language Perspective.* Aldershot: Ashgate.

Carr, Godfrey Robert. 1983. *Karl Jaspers as an Intellectual Critic: The Political Dimension of His Thought.* Frankfurt am Main: Lang.

Carrasco, David. 1980. "Quetzalcoatl's Revenge: Primordium and Application in Aztec Religion." *History of Religions* 19: 296–320.

Casanova, José. 1992. "Private and Public Religions." *Social Research* 59: 17–57.

———. 1994. *Public Religions in the Modern World.* Chicago: University of Chicago Press.

———. 2007. "Rethinking Secularization: A Global Comparative Perspective." In Peter Beyer and Lori G. Beaman, eds., *Religion, Globalization and Culture,* 101–120. Leiden: Brill.

Cesana, Andreas. 1984. "Werdende Existenz: Zur Geschichtsphilosophie von Karl Jaspers." *Philosophisches Jahrbuch* 91: 341–357.

———. 2003. "Jaspers' Projekt 'Weltphilosophie': Paradigma interkultureller Kommunikation?" In Leonard H. Ehrlich and Richard Wisser, eds., *Karl Jaspers' Philosophy: Rooted in the Present, Paradigm for the Future / Karl Jaspers' Philosophie: Gegenwärtigkeit und Zukunft,* 223–232. Würzburg: Königshausen & Neumann.

———. 2006. "Historismus und Existenzphilosophie, Kulturalismus und Weltphilosophie: Zur Vernunftphilosophie von Karl Jaspers." In Konstantin Broese, Andreas Hütig, Oliver Immel, and Renate Reschke, eds., *Vernunft der Aufklärung—Aufklärung der Vernunft,* 293–302. Berlin: Akademie Verlag.

Cheddadi, Abdesselam. 2004. *Les Arabes et l'appropriation de l'histoire.* Arles: Sindbad.

Ching, Julia, and Willard G. Oxtoby. 1997. "Religions and World Views in Asian and World History." In Ainslie T. Embree and Carol Gluck, eds., *Asia in Western and World History: A Guide for Teaching,* 309–315. Armonk: Sharpe.

Cho, Joanne Miyang. 1999. "The German Debate over Civilization: Troeltsch's Europeanism and Jaspers's Cosmopolitanism." *History of European Ideas* 25: 305–319.

Chun Jin-sung. 2000. *Das Bild der Moderne in der Nachkriegszeit: Die westdeutsche "Strukturgeschichte" im Spannungsfeld von Modernitätskritik und wissenschaftlicher Innovation, 1948–1962.* Munich: Oldenbourg.

Clark, Mark W. 2002. "A Prophet without Honour: Karl Jaspers in Germany, 1945–48." *Journal of Contemporary History* 37: 197–222.

———. 2006. *Beyond Catastrophe: German Intellectuals and Cultural Renewal after World War II, 1945–1955*. Lanham: Lexington Books.

Coates, Willson H., and Hayden V. White. 1970. *The Ordeal of Liberal Humanism: An Intellectual History of Western Europe*. Vol. 2: *Since the French Revolution*. New York: McGraw-Hill.

Cobb, John B. 1967. *The Structure of Christian Existence*. Philadelphia: Westminster Press.

———. 1982. *Beyond Dialogue: Toward a Mutual Transformation of Christianity and Buddhism*. Philadelphia: Fortress Press.

Cohen, Erik. 1987. "Thailand, Burma and Laos: An Outline of the Comparative Social Dynamics of Three Theravada Buddhist Societies in the Modern Era." In Shmuel N. Eisenstadt, ed., *Pattern of Modernity*. Vol. 2: *Beyond the West*, 192–216. New York: New York University Press, 1987.

———. 1988. "Radical Secularization and the Destructuration of the Universe of Knowledge in Late Modernity." In Shmuel N. Eisenstadt and Ilana Friedrich Silber, eds., *Cultural Traditions and Worlds of Knowledge: Explorations in the Sociology of Knowledge*, 203–224. Greenwich: JAI Press.

———. 1991. "Christianity and Buddhism in Thailand: The 'Battle of the Axes' and the 'Contest of Power.'" *Social Compass* 38: 115–140.

———. 1992. "Siam und der Westen: Das Problem der Thai-Modernisierung." In Shmuel N. Eisenstadt, ed., *Kulturen der Achsenzeit II: Ihre institutionelle und kulturelle Dynamik*. Part 3: *Buddhismus, Islam, Altägypten, westliche Kultur*, 75–100. Frankfurt am Main: Suhrkamp.

Cold, Eberhard. 1955. "Allgemeine Religionsgeschichte als Universalgeschichte: Eine wissenschaftstheoretische Skizze." *Numen* 2: 217–227.

Cook, Michael. 1986. "The Emergence of Islamic Civilisation." In Shmuel N. Eisenstadt, ed., *The Origins and Diversity of Axial Age Civilizations*, 476–483. Albany: State University of New York Press.

Corrington, Robert S. 2003. "Jaspers and the Axial Transfiguration of History." In Joseph W. Koterski and Raymond J. Langley, eds., *Karl Jaspers on Philosophy of History and History of Philosophy*, 295–302. Amherst: Humanity Books.

Costello, Paul. 1993. *World Historians and Their Goals: Twentieth-Century Answers to Modernism*. DeKalb: Northern Illinois University Press.

Cousins, Ewert H. 1999. "The Convergence of Cultures and Religions in Light of the Evolution of Consciousness." *Zygon* 34: 209–219.

Cowgill, George L. 1988. "Onward and Upward with Collapse." In George L. Cowgill and Norman Yoffee, eds., *The Collapse of Ancient States and Civilizations*, 244–276. Tucson: University of Arizona Press.

Crahay, Franz. 1965. "Conceptual Take-Off Conditions for a Bantu Philosophy." *Diogenes* 13: 55–78.

Cummings, Robert C. 2007. "The Role of Concepts of God in Crosscultural Comparative Theology." In Norbert Hintersteiner, ed., *Naming and Thinking God in Europe Today: Theology in Global Dialogue*, 513–530. Amsterdam: Rodopi.

Delanty, Gerard. 2003. "The Making of a Post-Western Europe: A Civilizational Analysis." *Thesis Eleven* 72: 8–25.

———. 2005. "Cultural Translations and European Modernity." In Eliezer Ben-Rafael and Yitzhak Sternberg, eds., *Comparing Modernities: Pluralism versus Homogenity; Essays in Homage to Shmuel N. Eisenstadt*, 442–460. Leiden: Brill.

———. 2006. "The Exhaustion of the Axial Age? Remarks on Eisenstadt's Civilizational Theory of Modernity." *Erwägen, Wissen, Ethik* 17: 26–28.

———. 2009. *The Cosmopolitan Imagination: The Renewal of Critical Social Theory*. Cambridge: Cambridge University Press.

Demandt, Alexander. 1978. *Metaphern für Geschichte: Sprachbilder und Gleichnisse im historisch-politischen Denken*. Munich: C. H. Beck.

Deutschmann, Christoph. 2000. "Japan from the Viewpoint of Civilization Theory: Arnason's Contribution." *Thesis Eleven* 61: 99–105.

Dietrich, Richard. 1964. "Karl Jaspers als Geschichtsdenker." In Richard Dietrich, ed., *Historische Theorie und Geschichtsforschung der Gegenwart*, 75–98. Berlin: de Gruyter.

Dietrich, Wolfgang. 2008. *Variationen über die vielen Frieden*. Vol. 1: *Deutungen*. Wiesbaden: Verlag für Sozialwissenschaften.

Dillon, Matthew. 2000. "Dialogues with Death: The Last Days of Socrates and the Buddha." *Philosophy East and West* 50: 525–558.

Dirks, Nicholas B. 1992. "Rituelles Königtum und Kultur: Die politische Dynamik kulturellen Wandels in der mittelalterlichen Geschichte Südindiens." In Schmuel N. Eisenstadt, ed., *Kulturen der Achsenzeit II: Ihre institutionelle und kulturelle Dynamik*. Part 2: *Indien*, 38–79. Frankfurt am Main: Suhrkamp.

Dittmer, Jörg. 1999. "Jaspers' 'Achsenzeit' und das interkulturelle Gespräch: Überlegungen zur Relevanz eines revidierten Theorems." In Dieter Becker, ed., *Globaler Kampf der Kulturen? Analysen und Orientierungen*, 191–214. Stuttgart: Kohlhammer.

Duara, Prasenjit. 2010. "The Historical Roots and Character of Secularism in China." In Zheng Yongnian, ed., *China and International Relations: The Chinese View and the Contribution of Wang Gungwu*, 58–72. London: Routledge.

Dumont, Louis. 1975. "On the Comparative Understanding of Non-Modern Civilizations." *Daedalus* 104, no. 2 (Wisdom, Revelation and Doubt: Perspectives on the First Millennium B.C.): 153–172.

Durfee, Harold A. 1964. "Karl Jaspers' Christology." *Journal of Religion* 44: 133–148.

Dux, Günter. 2010. "The Genesis of Philosophy in the History of Mind: A Cross-Cultural Comparison between Classical Greece and China." In Hans Ulrich Vogel and Günter Dux, eds., *Concepts of Nature: A Chinese-European Cross-Cultural Perspective*, 102–135. Leiden: Brill.

Ecker, Hans-Peter. 1993. *Die Legende: Kulturanthropologische Annäherung an eine literarische Gattung*. Stuttgart: Metzler.

Eckstein, Jerome. 2002. *On Meanings of Life: Their Nature and Origin.* Albany: State University of New York Press.

Eglauer, Martina. 2001. *Wissenschaft als Chance: Das Wissenschaftsverständnis des chinesischen Philosophen Hu Shi (1891–1962) unter dem Einfluss von John Deweys (1859–1952) Pragmatismus.* Stuttgart: Steiner.

Ehrlich, Leonard H. 2003. "Jaspers and the Philosophy of History." In Joseph W. Koterski and Raymond J. Langley, eds., *Karl Jaspers on Philosophy of History and History of Philosophy,* 267–278. Amherst: Humanity Books.

Eickelman, Dale F., and Armando Salvatore. 2002. "The Public Sphere and Muslim Identities." *European Journal of Sociology* 43: 92–115.

Einsiedel, Wolfgang von. 1968. "Die Weltliteratur und ihre Provinzen." *Merkur* 22: 85–100.

Eisenstadt, Shmuel N. 1978. *Revolution and the Transformation of Societies: A Comparative Study of Civilizations.* New York: Free Press.

———. 1980. "Comparative Analysis of State Formation in Historical Contexts." *International Social Science Journal* 32: 624–654.

———. 1981. "Cultural Traditions and Political Dynamics: The Origins and Modes of Ideological Politics." *British Journal of Sociology* 32: 155–181. Reprinted in Shmuel N. Eisenstadt, *Comparative Civilizations and Multiple Modernities I,* 219–247. Leiden: Brill, 2003.

———. 1981. "Max Webers antikes Judentum und der Charakter der jüdischen Zivilisation." In Wolfgang Schluchter, ed., *Max Webers Studie über das antike Judentum: Interpretation und Kritik,* 134–184. Frankfurt am Main: Suhrkamp. English: "The Format of Jewish History: Some Reflections on Weber's Ancient Judaism." *Modern Judaism* 1 (1981): 54–73, 217–234. Reprinted in Shmuel N. Eisenstadt, *Explorations in Jewish Historical Experience: The Civilizational Dimension,* 3–44. Leiden: Brill, 2004.

———. 1982. "The Axial Age: The Emergence of Transcendental Visions and the Rise of Clerics." *European Journal of Sociology* 23: 294–314. Reprinted in Shmuel N. Eisenstadt, *Comparative Civilizations and Multiple Modernities I,* 197–217. Leiden: Brill, 2003.

———. 1982. "Heterodoxies, Sectarianism and Dynamics of Civilizations." *Diogenes* 120: 1–21.

———. 1983. "Innerweltliche Transzendenz und die Strukturierung der Welt: Max Webers Studie über China und die Gestalt der chinesischen Zivilisation." In Wolfgang Schluchter, ed., *Max Webers Studie über Konfuzianismus und Taoismus: Interpretation und Kritik,* 363–411. Frankfurt am Main: Suhrkamp. English: "This Worldly Transcendentalism and the Structuring of the World: Weber's 'Religion of China' and the Format of Chinese History and Civilization." *Journal of Developing Societies* 1 (1985): 168–186. Reprinted in Andreas E. Busse, ed., *Max Weber in Asian Studies,* 46–64. Leiden: Brill, 1985. And in Shmuel N. Eisenstadt, *Comparative Civilizations and Multiple Modernities I,* 281–303. Leiden: Brill, 2003.

———. 1983. "Transcendental Visions, Other Worldliness and Its Transformations: Some More Comments on L. Dumont." *Religion* 13: 1–17.

———. 1984. "Dissent, Heterodoxy and Civilizational Dynamics: Some Analytical and Comparative Indications." In Shmuel N. Eisenstadt, Reuven Kahane, and David Shulman, eds., *Orthodoxy, Heterodoxy and Dissent in India*, 1–9. Berlin: Mouton.

———. 1984. "Heterodoxies and Dynamics of Civilizations." *Proceedings of the American Philosophical Society* 128: 104–113.

———. 1984. "Die Paradoxie von Zivilisationen mit außerweltlichen Orientierungen: Überlegungen zu Max Webers Studie über Hinduismus und Buddhismus." In Wolfgang Schluchter, ed., *Max Webers Studie über Hinduismus und Buddhismus: Interpretation und Kritik*, 333–360. Frankfurt am Main: Suhrkamp.

———. 1985. "Comparative Liminality: Liminality and Dynamics of Civilization." *Religion* 15: 315–338. Reprinted in Shmuel N. Eisenstadt, *Comparative Civilizations and Multiple Modernities I*, 165–192. Leiden: Brill, 2003.

———. 1986. "Culture and Social Structure Revisited." *International Sociology* 1: 297–320. Reprinted in Shmuel N. Eisenstadt, *Power, Trust and Meaning: Essays in Sociological Theory and Analysis*, 280–305. Chicago: University of Chicago Press.

———. 1986. "Introduction: The Axial Age Breakthrough in Ancient Greece." In Shmuel N. Eisenstadt, ed., *The Origins and Diversity of Axial Age Civilizations*, 29–39. Albany: State University of New York Press.

———. 1986. "Introduction: The Axial Age Breakthrough in Ancient Israel." In Shmuel N. Eisenstadt, ed., *The Origins and Diversity of Axial Age Civilizations*, 127–134. Albany: State University of New York Press.

———. 1986. "Introduction: The Axial Age Breakthrough in China and India." In Shmuel N. Eisenstadt, ed., *The Origins and Diversity of Axial Age Civilizations*, 291–305. Albany: State University of New York Press.

———. 1986. "Introduction: The Axial Age Breakthroughs—Their Characteristics and Origins." In Shmuel N. Eisenstadt, ed., *The Origins and Diversity of Axial Age Civilizations*, 1–25. Albany: State University of New York Press.

———. 1986. "Introduction: The Secondary Breakthrough in Ancient Israelite Civilization—The Second Commonwealth and Christianity." In Shmuel N. Eisenstadt, ed., *The Origins and Diversity of Axial Age Civilizations*, 227–240. Albany: State University of New York Press.

———. 1987. "Caste and the Construction of Other-Worldly Civilizations." In Paul Hockings, ed., *Dimensions of Social Life: Essays in Honor of David G. Mandelbaum*, 681–698. Berlin: de Gruyter.

———. 1987. "Civilizational Formations, Ecological Frameworks and Political Dynamics." In Shmuel N. Eisenstadt, *European Civilization in a Comparative Perspective: A Study in the Relations between Culture and Social Structure*, 15–45. Oslo: Norwegian University Press.

———. 1987. "European Tradition and the Crisis of European Liberalism." In Shmuel N. Eisenstadt, *European Civilization in a Comparative Perspective: A Study in the Relations between Culture and Social Structure*, 95–107. Oslo: Norwegian University Press.

———. 1987. "Introduction." In Shmuel N. Eisenstadt, *European Civilization in a Comparative Perspective: A Study in the Relations between Culture and Social Structure*, 1–14. Oslo: Norwegian University Press.

———. 1987. "Introduction: Historical Traditions, Modernization and Development." In Shmuel N. Eisenstadt, ed., *Patterns of Modernity*. Vol. 1: *The West*, 1–11. New York: New York University Press.

———. 1987. "The Kemalist Revolution in Comparative Perspective." In Shmuel N. Eisenstadt, *European Civilization in a Comparative Perspective: A Study in the Relations between Culture and Social Structure*, 135–152. Oslo: Norwegian University Press.

———. 1987. "Webers Analyse des Islams und die Gestalt der islamischen Zivilisation." In Wolfgang Schluchter, ed., *Max Webers Sicht des Islams: Interpretation und Kritik*, 342–359. Frankfurt am Main: Suhrkamp.

———. 1988. "Beyond Collapse." In George L. Cowgill and Norman Yoffee, eds., *The Collapse of Ancient States and Civilizations*, 236–243. Tucson: University of Arizona Press.

———. 1988. "Explorations in the Sociology of Knowledge: The Soteriological Axis in the Construction of Domains of Knowledge." In Shmuel N. Eisenstadt and Ilana Friedrich Silber, eds., *Cultural Traditions and Worlds of Knowledge: Explorations in the Sociology of Knowledge*, 1–71. Greenwich: JAI Press.

———. 1988. "Max Webers Überlegungen zum westlichen Christentum." In Wolfgang Schluchter, ed., *Max Webers Sicht des okzidentalen Christentums: Interpretation und Kritik*, 554–580. Frankfurt am Main: Suhrkamp. English: "Max Weber on Western Christianity and the Weberian Approach to Civilizational Dynamics." *Canadian Journal of Sociology* 14 (1989): 203–223.

———. 1988. "Transcendental Vision, Center Formation and the Role of Intellectuals." In Liah Greenfeld and Michel Martin, eds., *Center, Ideas and Institutions*, 96–109. Chicago: University of Chicago Press. Reprinted in Shmuel N. Eisenstadt, *Comparative Civilizations and Multiple Modernities I*, 249–264. Leiden: Brill.

———. 1988. "Utopias and Dynamics of Civilizations: Some Concluding Comparative Observations." *International Journal of Comparative Sociology* 29: 139–149. Reprinted in Adam Seligman, ed., *Order and Transcendence: The Role of Utopias and the Dynamics of Civilizations*, 139–149. Leiden: Brill, 1989. And in Shmuel N. Eisenstadt, *Comparative Civilizations and Multiple Modernities I*, 265–277. Leiden: Brill, 2003.

———. 1989. "Cultural Premises and the Limits of Convergence in Modern Societies: An Examination of Some Aspects of Japanese Society." *Diogenes* 147: 125–147.

———. 1989. "Structure and History: Introductory Observations." *International Political Science Review* 10 (The Historical Framework of Revolutions): 99–110.

———. 1990. "Cultural Tradition, Historical Experience and Social Change: The Limits of Convergence." In Grethe B. Peterson, ed., *The Tanner Lectures on Human Values.* Vol. 11, 441–505. Salt Lake City: University of Utah Press.

———. 1990. "Functional Analysis in Anthropology and Sociology: An Interpretative Essay." *Annual Review of Anthropology* 19: 243–260.

———. 1990. "Modes of Structural Differentiation, Elite Structure and Cultural Visions." In Jeffrey C. Alexander and Paul Colomy, eds., *Differentiation Theory and Social Change: Comparative and Historical Perspectives,* 19–51. New York: Columbia University Press.

———. 1990. "Origins of the West: The Origins of the West in Recent Macrosociological Theory. The Protestant Ethic Reconsidered." *Cultural Dynamics* 3: 119–153. Reprinted in Shmuel N. Eisenstadt, *Comparative Civilizations and Multiple Modernities II,* 577–611. Leiden: Brill, 2003.

———. 1990. "The Paradox of the Construction of Other-Worldly Civilizations: Some Observations on the Characteristics and Dynamics of Hindu and Buddhist Civilizations." In Yogendra K. Malik, ed., *Boeings and Bullock-Carts: Studies in Change and Continuity in Indian Civilization; Essays in Honor of K. Ishwaran.* Vol. 1: *India—Culture and Society,* 21–56. Delhi: Chanakya Publications.

———. 1991. "The Dispute about the Birthdate of the Buddha from a Comparative Civilizational Perspective." In Heinz Bechert, ed., *The Dating of the Historical Buddha/Die Datierung des historischen Buddha.* Vol. 1, 503–505. Göttingen: Vandenhoeck & Ruprecht.

———. 1991. "The Expansion of Religions: Some Comparative Observations on Different Modes." *Comparative Social Research* 13: 45–73.

———. 1992. "Die chinesische Geschichtserfahrung." In Shmuel N. Eisenstadt, ed., *Kulturen der Achsenzeit II: Ihre institutionelle und kulturelle Dynamik.* Part 1: *China, Japan,* 11–24. Frankfurt am Main: Suhrkamp.

———. 1992. "Frameworks of the Great Revolutions: Culture, Social Structure, History and Human Agency." *International Social Science Journal* 133: 386–401. Reprinted in Shmuel N. Eisenstadt, *Comparative Civilizations and Multiple Modernities II,* 613–639. Leiden: Brill, 2003.

———. 1992. "Die Geschichtserfahrung des Islam." In Shmuel N. Eisenstadt, ed., *Kulturen der Achsenzeit II: Ihre institutionelle und kulturelle Dynamik.* Part 3: *Buddhismus, Islam, Altägypten, westliche Kultur,* 153–160. Frankfurt am Main: Suhrkamp.

———. 1992. "Die indische (hinduistische) Geschichtserfahrung." In Shmuel N. Eisenstadt, ed., *Kulturen der Achsenzeit II: Ihre institutionelle und kulturelle Dynamik.* Part 2: *Indien,* 9–16. Frankfurt am Main: Suhrkamp.

———. 1992. "Die japanische Geschichtserfahrung." In Shmuel N. Eisenstadt, ed., *Kulturen der Achsenzeit II: Ihre institutionelle und kulturelle Dynamik*. Part 1: *China, Japan*, 235–241. Frankfurt am Main: Suhrkamp.

———. 1992. *Jewish Civilization: The Jewish Historical Experience in a Comparative Perspective*. Albany: State University of New York Press.

———. 1992. "The Order-Maintaining and Order-Transforming Dimensions of Culture." In Richard Münch and Neil J. Smelser, eds., *Theory of Culture*, 64–87. Berkeley: University of California Press. Reprinted in Shmuel N. Eisenstadt, *Power, Trust, and Meaning: Essays in Sociological Theory and Analysis*, 306–327. Chicago: University of Chicago Press, 1995.

———. 1992. "A Reappraisal of Theories of Social Change and Modernization." In Hans Haferkamp and Neil J. Smelser, eds., *Social Change and Modernity*, 412–429. Berkeley: University of California Press.

———. 1992. "Die (thēravāda-)buddhistische Geschichtserfahrung." In Shmuel N. Eisenstadt, ed., *Kulturen der Achsenzeit II: Ihre institutionelle und kulturelle Dynamik*. Part 3: *Buddhismus, Islam, Altägypten, westliche Kultur*, 9–17. Frankfurt am Main: Suhrkamp. English: "A Short Comparative Excurse on the (Theravada) Buddhist Civilizational Format and Historical Experience." In Shmuel N. Eisenstadt, *Comparative Civilizations and Multiple Modernities I*, 319–327. Leiden: Brill, 2003.

———. 1993. "Introduction: Some Reflections on Sociological Theory and of an Illusion Free Sociology." In Klaus Plake and Wolfgang K. Schulz, eds., *Entillusionierung als Programm: Beiträge zur Soziologie von Shmuel N. Eisenstadt*, 7–23. Weinheim: Deutscher Studien Verlag.

———. 1993. "Religion and the Civilizational Dimensions of Politics." In Saïd Amir Arjomand, ed., *The Political Dimensions of Religion*, 13–41. Albany: State University of New York Press.

———. 1994. "Japan: Non-Axial Modernity and the Multiplicity of Cultural and Institutional Programmes of Modernity." In Josef Kreiner, ed., *Japan in Global Context: Papers Presented on the Occasion of the Fifth Anniversary of the German Institute for Japanese Studies*, 63–95. Tokyo: Iudicium.

———. 1995. "Action, Resources, Structure and Meaning." In Shmuel N. Eisenstadt, *Power, Trust, and Meaning: Essays in Sociological Theory and Analysis*, 328–389. Chicago: University of Chicago Press.

———. 1995. "Introduction: Social Structure, Culture, Agency and Change." In Shmuel N. Eisenstadt, *Power, Trust, and Meaning: Essays in Sociological Theory and Analysis*, 1–40. Chicago: University of Chicago Press.

———. 1996. "The Jacobin Component of Fundamentalist Movements." *Contention* 5: 155–170. Reprinted in Shmuel N. Eisenstadt, *Comparative Civilizations and Multiple Modernities II*, 937–951. Leiden: Brill, 2003.

———. 1996. *Japanese Civilization: A Comparative View*. Chicago: University of Chicago Press.

―――. 1996. "Some Observations on the Transformation of Confucianism (and Buddhism) in Japan." In Tu Wei-ming, ed., *Confucian Traditions in East Asian Modernity*, 175–185. Cambridge, MA: Harvard University Press. Reprinted in Shmuel N. Eisenstadt, *Comparative Civilizations and Multiple Modernities I*, 305–318. Leiden: Brill, 2003.

―――. 1998. *Die Antinomien der Moderne: Die jakobinischen Grundzüge der Moderne und des Fundamentalismus: Heterodoxien, Utopismus und Jakobinismus in der Konstitution fundamentalistischer Bewegungen*. Frankfurt am Main: Suhrkamp.

―――. 1998. "Comparative Studies and Sociological Theory: Autobiographical Notes." *American Sociologist* 29, no. 1: 38–58. Reprinted as "Introduction: Comparative Studies and Sociological Theory. From Comparative Studies to Civilizational Analysis. Autobiographical Notes." In Shmuel N. Eisenstadt, *Comparative Civilizations and Multiple Modernities I*, 1–28. Leiden: Brill, 2003.

―――. 1998. "The Construction of Collective Identities in Latin America: Beyond the European Nation State Model." In Luis Roniger and Mario Sznajder, eds., *Constructing Collective Identities and Shaping Public Spheres: Latin American Paths*, 245–263. Brighton: Sussex Academic Press.

―――. 1998. "The Construction of Collective Identities: Some Analytical and Comparative Indications." *European Journal of Social Theory* 1: 229–254.

―――. 1998. "Modernity and the Construction of Collective Identities." *International Journal of Comparative Sociology* 39: 138–158.

―――. 1998. "The Paradox of Democratic Regimes: Fragility and Transformability." *Sociological Theory* 16: 211–238.

―――. 1998. "Sectarianism and the Dynamics of Islamic Civilization." In Georg Stauth, ed., *Islam—Motor or Challenge of Modernity*, 15–33. Hamburg: LIT.

―――. 1998. "Social Division of Labor, Construction of Centers and Institutional Dynamics." In Gerhard Preyer, ed., *Strukturelle Evolution und das Weltsystem: Theorien, Sozialstruktur und evolutionäre Entwicklungen*, 29–46. Frankfurt am Main: Suhrkamp. Reprinted as "Social Division of Labor, Construction of Centers and Institutional Dynamics: A Reassessment of the Structural-Evolutionary Perspective." In Shmuel N. Eisenstadt, *Comparative Civilizations and Multiple Modernities I*, 57–74. Leiden: Brill, 2003.

―――. 1998. "World Histories and the Construction of Collective Identities." In Richard H. Elphick, Philip Pomper, and Richard T. Vann, eds., *World History: Ideologies, Structures and Identities*, 105–125. Oxford: Blackwell.

―――. 1999. "Die Dimensionen komparativer Analyse und die Erforschung sozialer Dynamik: Von der vergleichenden Politikwissenschaft zum Zivilisationsvergleich." In Hartmut Kaelble and Jürgen Schriewer, eds., *Diskurse und Entwicklungspfade: Der Gesellschaftsvergleich in den Geschichts- und Sozialwissenschaften*, 3–28. Frankfurt and New York: Campus.

———. 1999. *Fundamentalism, Sectarianism and Revolution: The Jacobin Dimension of Modernity.* Cambridge: Cambridge University Press.

———. 1999. *Paradoxes of Democracy: Fragility, Continuity, and Change.* Baltimore: Johns Hopkins University Press.

———. 2000. "The Civilizational Dimension in Sociological Analysis." *Thesis Eleven* 62: 1–21. Reprinted in Shmuel N. Eisenstadt, *Comparative Civilizations and Multiple Modernities I,* 33–56. Leiden: Brill, 2003.

———. 2000. "Fundamentalist Movements in the Framework of Multiple Modernities." In Almut Höfert and Armando Salvatore, eds., *Between Europe and Islam: Shaping Modernity in a Transcultural Space,* 175–196. Brussels: PIE Lang.

———. 2000. "Multiple Modernities." *Daedalus* 129, no. 1: 1–29. Reprinted in Shmuel N. Eisenstadt, ed., *Multiple Modernities,* 1–29. New Brunswick, NJ: Transaction Publishers, 2002. And in Shmuel N. Eisenstadt, *Comparative Civilizations and Multiple Modernities II,* 535–560. Leiden: Brill, 2003.

———. 2000. "The Reconstruction of Religious Arenas in the Framework of 'Multiple Modernities.'" *Millennium: Journal of International Studies* 29: 591–611. Reprinted in Shmuel N. Eisenstadt, *Comparative Civilizations and Multiple Modernities II,* 953–979. Leiden: Brill, 2003.

———. 2000. *Die Vielfalt der Moderne.* Weilerswist: Velbrück Wissenschaft.

———. 2001. "Axial Age Sectarianism and the Antinomies of Modernity." In Glenn Hughes, Stephen A. McKnight, and Geoffrey L. Price, eds., *Politics, Order and History: Essays on the Work of Eric Voegelin,* 233–258. Sheffield: Sheffield Academic Press.

———. 2001. "The Civilizational Dimension of Modernity: Modernity as a Distinct Civilization." *International Sociology* 16: 320–340. Reprinted in Shmuel N. Eisenstadt, *Comparative Civilizations and Multiple Modernities II,* 493–518. Leiden: Brill, 2003. And in Saïd Amir Arjomand and Edward A. Tiryakian, eds., *Rethinking Civilizational Analysis,* 48–66. London: Sage Publications, 2004.

———. 2001. "Vertrauen, kollektive Identität und Demokratie." In Martin Hartmann and Claus Offe, eds., *Vertrauen: Die Grundlage des sozialen Zusammenhalts,* 333–363. Frankfurt am Main: Campus.

———. 2001. "The Vision of Modern and Contemporary Society." In Eliezer Ben-Rafael and Yitzhak Sternberg, eds., *Identity, Culture and Globalization,* 25–47. Leiden: Brill.

———. 2002. "Barbarism and Modernity: The Destructive Components of Modernity—The Perennial Challenge." In Ernest Krausz and Gitta Tulea, eds., *Starting the Twenty-First Century,* 225–35. New Brunswick: Transaction Publishers. Reprinted as "Barbarism and Modernity: The Destructive Components of Modernity." In Shmuel N. Eisenstadt, *Comparative Civilizations and Multiple Modernities II,* 561–571. Leiden: Brill, 2003.

———. 2002. "The Civilization of the Americas: The Crystallization of Distinct Modernities." *Comparative Sociology* 1: 43–61. Reprinted as "The First Multiple Modernities: The Civilizations of the Americas." In Shmuel N. Eisenstadt, *Comparative Civilizations and Multiple Modernities II*, 701–722. Leiden: Brill, 2003.

———. 2002. "Concluding Remarks: Public Sphere, Civil Society and Political Dynamics in Islamic Societies." In Shmuel N. Eisenstadt, Miriam Hoexter, and Nehemia Levtzion, eds., *The Public Sphere in Muslim Societies*, 139–161. Albany: State University of New York Press.

———. 2002. "The Construction of Collective Identities and the Continual Reconstruction of Primordiality." In Siniša Malešević and Mark Haugaard, eds., *Making Sense of Collectivity: Ethnicity, Nationalism and Globalisation*, 33–87. London: Pluto Press. Reprinted as "The Construction of Collective Identities and the Continual Reconstruction of Primordiality and Sacrality: Some Analytical and Comparative Indications." In Shmuel N. Eisenstadt, *Comparative Civilizations and Multiple Modernities I*, 75–134. Leiden: Brill, 2003.

———. 2002. "The First Multiple Modernities: Collective Identities, Public Spheres and Political Order in the Americas." In Luis Roniger and Carlos H. Waisman, eds., *Globality and Multiple Modernities: Comparative North American and Latin American Perspectives*, 7–28. Brighton: Sussex Academic Press.

———. 2002. "Mirror-Image Modernities: Contrasting Religious Premises of Japanese and U.S. Modernity." In Richard Madsen, William M. Sullivan, Ann Swidler, and Steven M. Tipton, eds., *Meaning and Modernity: Religion, Polity, and Self*, 56–77. Berkeley: University of California Press. Reprinted in Shmuel N. Eisenstadt, *Comparative Civilizations and Multiple Modernities II*, 723–757. Leiden: Brill, 2003.

———. 2002. "Some Observations on Multiple Modernities." In Shmuel N. Eisenstadt, Dominic Sachsenmaier, and Jens Riedel, eds., *Reflections on Multiple Modernities: European, Chinese and Other Interpretations*, 27–41. Leiden: Brill.

———. 2003. "Center Formation and Protest Movements in Europe and the United States: A Comparative Perspective." In Shmuel N. Eisenstadt, *Comparative Civilizations and Multiple Modernities II*, 831–848. Leiden: Brill.

———. 2003. "Civil Society, Public Sphere, the Myth of Oriental Despotism and Political Dynamics in Islamic Societies." In Shmuel N. Eisenstadt, *Comparative Civilizations and Multiple Modernities I*, 399–433. Leiden: Brill.

———. 2003. "Construction of Trust, Collective Identity and the Fragility and Continuity of Democratic Regimes." In Shmuel N. Eisenstadt, *Comparative Civilizations and Multiple Modernities II*, 877–908. Leiden: Brill.

———. 2003. "The Crystallization of Christian Civilization in Europe." In Shmuel N. Eisenstadt, *Comparative Civilizations and Multiple Modernities I*, 345–358. Leiden: Brill, 2003.

———. 2003. "Die institutionellen Ordnungen der Moderne: Die Vielfalt der Moderne aus einer weberianischen Perspektive." In Gert Albert, Agathe Bienfait, Steffen Sigmund, and Claus Wendt, eds., *Das Weber-Paradigma: Studien zur Weiterentwicklung von Max Webers Forschungsprogramm*, 328–351. Tübingen: Mohr Siebeck.

———. 2003. "Israeli Politics and the Jewish Political Tradition: Principled Political Anarchism and the Rule of the Court." In Shmuel N. Eisenstadt, *Comparative Civilizations and Multiple Modernities II*, 759–780. Leiden: Brill. Reprinted in Shmuel N. Eisenstadt, *Explorations in Jewish Historical Experience: The Civilizational Dimension*, 216–237. Leiden: Brill, 2004.

———. 2003. "Japan and the Multiplicity of Cultural Programmes of Modernity." In Shmuel N. Eisenstadt, *Comparative Civilizations and Multiple Modernities I*, 435–455. Leiden: Brill, 2003.

———. 2003. "The Jewish Historical Experience in the Framework of Comparative Universal History." In Shmuel N. Eisenstadt, *Comparative Civilizations and Multiple Modernities I*, 359–398. Leiden: Brill. Reprinted in Shmuel N. Eisenstadt, *Explorations in Jewish Historical Experience: The Civilizational Dimension*, 45–84. Leiden: Brill, 2004.

———. 2003. "The Moral Dimension and Tensions of Modernity." In Grażyna Skąpska and Annamaria Orla-Bukowska, eds., *The Moral Fabric in Contemporary Societies*, 203–217. Leiden: Brill.

———. 2003. "The Puzzle of Indian Democracy." In Shmuel N. Eisenstadt, *Comparative Civilizations and Multiple Modernities II*, 781–829. Leiden: Brill.

———. 2003. "The Sectarian Origin of Modernity." In Shmuel N. Eisenstadt, *Comparative Civilizations and Multiple Modernities II*, 641–671. Leiden: Brill.

———. 2003. "Some Comparative Indications about the Dynamics of Historical Axial and Non-Axial Civilizations." In Shmuel N. Eisenstadt, *Comparative Civilizations and Multiple Modernities I*, 457–488. Leiden: Brill.

———. 2003. "Some Observations on Problems of Trust in Modern Societies: Construction of Trust, Collective Identity and the Fragility and Continuity of Democratic Regimes." In Grażyna Skąpska and Annamaria Orla-Bukowska, eds., *The Moral Fabric in Contemporary Societies*, 67–81. Leiden: Brill.

———. 2004. "Did Zionism Bring the Jews Back to History?" In Shmuel N. Eisenstadt, *Explorations in Jewish Historical Experience: The Civilizational Dimension*, 105–121. Leiden: Brill.

———. 2004. "Interdisciplinary Reflections on the Civilizational Dimensions of Modernity." In Charles Camic and Hans Joas, eds., *The Dialogical Turn: New Roles for Sociology in the Postdisciplinary Age*, 275–295. Lanham: Rowman & Littlefield.

———. 2004. "Preface." In Shmuel N. Eisenstadt, *Explorations in Jewish Historical Experience: The Civilizational Dimension*, ix–xiv. Leiden: Brill.

———. 2004. "Social Evolution and Modernity: Some Observations on Parsons's Comparative and Evolutionary Analysis. Parsons's Analysis from the Perspective of Multiple Modernities." *American Sociologist* 35, no. 4: 5–24.

———. 2005. "Die Achsenzeit in der Weltgeschichte." In Hans Joas and Klaus Wiegandt, eds., *Die kulturellen Werte Europas*, 40–68. Frankfurt am Main: Fischer. English: "The Axial Age in World History." In Hans Joas and Klaus Wiegandt, eds., *The Cultural Values of Europe*, 22–42. Liverpool: Liverpool University Press, 2008.

———. 2005. "Axial Civilizations and the Axial Age Reconsidered." In Johann P. Arnason, Shmuel N. Eisenstadt, and Björn Wittrock, eds., *Axial Civilizations and World History*, 531–564. Leiden: Brill.

———. 2005. "Collective Identity and the Constructive and Deconstructive Forces of Modernity." In Eliezer Ben-Rafael and Yitzhak Sternberg, eds., *Comparing Modernities: Pluralism versus Homogenity; Essays in Homage to Shmuel N. Eisenstadt*, 635–653. Leiden: Brill.

———. 2005. "Fundamentalism, Phenomenology and Comparative Dimensions." In R. Scott Appleby and Martin E. Marty, eds., *Fundamentalism Comprehended*, 259–276. Chicago: University of Chicago Press.

———. 2005. "The Jewish Historical Experience: Heterodox Tendencies and Political Dynamics in a De-Territorialized Axial Civilization." In Johann P. Arnason, Shmuel N. Eisenstadt, and Björn Wittrock, eds., *Axial Civilizations and World History*, 225–251. Leiden: Brill.

———. 2005. "Modernity in Socio-Historical Perspective." In Eliezer Ben-Rafael and Yitzhak Sternberg, eds., *Comparing Modernities: Pluralism versus Homogenity; Essays in Homage to Shmuel N. Eisenstadt*, 31–56. Leiden: Brill.

———. 2005. "The Religious Origins of Modern Radical Movements." In Bernhard Giesen and Daniel Šuber, eds., *Religion and Politics: Cultural Perspectives*, 161–192. Leiden: Brill.

———. 2005. "The Transformations of the Religious Dimension in the Constitution of Contemporary Modernities." In Bernhard Giesen and Daniel Šuber, eds., *Religion and Politics: Cultural Perspectives*, 17–37. Leiden: Brill.

———. 2006. "Culture and Power: A Comparative Civilizational Analysis." *Erwägen, Wissen, Ethik* 17: 3–16.

———. 2006. "Multiple Modernen im Zeitalter der Globalisierung." In Thomas Schwinn, ed., *Die Vielfalt und Einheit der Moderne: Kultur- und strukturvergleichende Analysen*, 37–62. Wiesbaden: Verlag für Sozialwissenschaften.

———. 2006. "Public Spheres and Political Dynamics in Historical and Modern Muslim Societies." In Johann P. Arnason, Armando Salvatore, and Georg Stauth, eds., *Islam in Process: Historical and Civilizational Perspectives*, 306–318. Bielefeld: Transcript.

———. 2006. "Reply." *Erwägen, Wissen, Ethik* 17: 80–91.

———. 2006. *The Great Revolutions and the Civilizations of Modernity.* Leiden: Brill.

———. 2007. "Multiple Modernities: Analyserahmen und Problemstellung." In Thorsten Bonacker and Andreas Reckwitz, eds., *Kulturen der Moderne: Soziologische Perspektiven der Gegenwart,* 19–45. Frankfurt and New York: Campus.

———. 2007. "The Resurgence of Religious Movements in Processes of Globalization—Beyond the End of History or the Clash of Civilizations." In Matthias Koenig and Paul de Guchteneire, eds., *Democracy and Human Rights in Multicultural Societies,* 239–250. Aldershot: Ashgate.

———. 2008. "Axial Visions and Axial Civilizations: The Transformations of World Histories between Evolutionary Tendencies and Institutional Formations." In Peter Hedström and Björn Wittrock, eds., *Frontiers of Sociology,* 113–146. Leiden: Brill.

———. 2009. "Cultural Programmes, the Construction of Collective Identities and the Continual Reconstruction of Primordiality." In Gerhard Preyer, ed., *Neuer Mensch und kollektive Identität in der Kommunikationsgesellschaft,* 135–184. Wiesbaden: Verlag für Sozialwissenschaften.

Eisenstadt, Shmuel N., ed. 1986. *The Origins and Diversity of Axial Age Civilizations.* Albany: State University of New York Press.

———, ed. 1987. *Kulturen der Achsenzeit I: Ihre Ursprünge und ihre Vielfalt.* Part 1: *Griechenland, Israel, Mesopotamien.* Part 2: *Spätantike, Indien, China, Islam.* Frankfurt am Main: Suhrkamp.

———, ed. 1992. *Kulturen der Achsenzeit II: Ihre institutionelle und kulturelle Dynamik.* Part 1: *China, Japan.* Part 2: *Indien.* Part 3: *Buddhismus, Islam, Altägypten, westliche Kultur.* Frankfurt am Main: Suhrkamp.

Eisenstadt, Shmuel N., and Bernhard Giesen. 1995. "The Construction of Collective Identity." *European Journal of Sociology* 36: 72–102.

Eisenstadt, Shmuel N., and Harriet Hartman. 1992. "Cultural Traditions, Conceptions of Sovereignty and State Formations in India and Europe: A Comparative View." In A. W. van den Hoek, Dirk H. A. Kolff, and M. S. Oort, eds., *Ritual, State and History in South Asia: Essays in Honour of J. C. Heesterman,* 493–506. Leiden: Brill. Reprinted in Shmuel N. Eisenstadt, *Comparative Civilizations and Multiple Modernities I,* 329–344. Leiden: Brill, 2003.

———. 1997. "Historical Experience, Cultural Traditions, State Formation and Political Dynamics in India and Europe." In Martin Doornbos and Sudipta Kaviraj, eds., *Dynamics of State Formation: India and Europe Compared,* 27–55. New Delhi: Sage Publications.

Eisenstadt, Shmuel N., and Wolfgang Schluchter. 1998. "Introduction: Paths to Early Modernities—A Comparative View." *Daedalus* 127, no. 3: 1–18. Reprinted in Shmuel N. Eisenstadt, Wolfgang Schluchter, and Björn Wittrock, eds., *Public Spheres and Collective Identities,* 1–18. New Brunswick: Transaction Publishers, 2001.

Eisenstadt, Shmuel N., and Arie Shachar. 1987. *Society, Culture and Urbanization.* Newbury Park: Sage Publications.

Elkana, Yehuda. 1986. "The Emergence of Second-Order Thinking in Classical Greece." In Shmuel N. Eisenstadt, ed., *The Origins and Diversity of Axial Age Civilizations,* 40–64. Albany: State University of New York Press.

Ellwood, Robert S. 1973. "Shinto and the Discovery of History of Japan." *Journal of the American Academy of Religion* 41: 493–505.

———. 1986. *Theosophy: A Modern Expression of the Wisdom of the Ages.* Wheaton: Quest Books.

———. 2003. *Cycles of Faith: The Development of the World's Religions.* Walnut Creek: AltaMira Press.

———. 2010. *Tales of Lights and Shadows: Mythology of the Afterlife.* London: Continuum.

Elvin, Mark. 1986. "Was There a Transcendental Breakthrough in China?" In Shmuel N. Eisenstadt, ed., *The Origins and Diversity of Axial Age Civilizations,* 325–359. Albany: State University of New York Press. Reprinted in Mark Elvin, *Another History: Essays on China from a European Perspective,* 261–301. Broadway, Australia: Wild Peony, 1996.

———. 1990. "The Collapse of Scriptural Confucianism." *Papers on Far Eastern History* 41: 45–76. Reprinted in Mark Elvin, *Another History: Essays on China from a European Perspective,* 352–389. Broadway, Australia: Wild Peony, 1996.

Ess, Josef van. 2006. "Islam and the Axial Age." In Johann P. Arnason, Armando Salvatore, and Georg Stauth, eds., *Islam in Process: Historical and Civilizational Perspectives,* 220–237. Bielefeld: Transcript.

Fahrenbach, Helmut. 1989. "Zeitanalyse, Politik und Philosophie der Vernunft im Werk von Karl Jaspers." In Dietrich Harth, ed., *Karl Jaspers: Denken zwischen Wissenschaft, Politik und Philosophie,* 139–185. Stuttgart: Metzler.

Fairfield, Paul. 2001. *Death and Life.* New York: Algora.

Fawcett, Thomas. 1970. *The Symbolic Language of Religion: An Introductory Study.* London: S. C. M. Press.

Ferwerda, Rein. 1986. "The Meaning of the Word σῶμα (Body) in the Axial Age: An Interpretation of Plato's Cratylus 400c." In Shmuel N. Eisenstadt, ed., *The Origins and Diversity of Axial Age Civilizations,* 111–124. Albany: State University of New York Press.

Fett, Othmar Franz. 2000. *Der undenkbare Dritte: Vorsokratische Anfänge des eurogenen Naturverhältnisses.* Tübingen: Edition Diskord.

Feuerstein, Georg. 1998. *The Yoga Tradition: Its History, Literature, Philosophy and Practice.* Prescott: Hohm Press.

Fikentscher, Wolfgang. 1975–1977. *Methoden des Rechts in vergleichender Darstellung.* Vol. 1: *Frühe und religiöse Rechte—Romanischer Rechtskreis.* Vol. 4: *Dogmatischer Teil.* Tübingen: J. C. B. Mohr.

———. 1995. *Modes of Thought: A Study in the Anthropology of Law and Religion.* Tübingen: Mohr Siebeck.

———. 2006. "Power Controlling Societal Order, Economy, Religion and the Modes of Thought." *Erwägen, Wissen, Ethik* 17: 31–34.

Fischer, David Hackett. 1980. "Climate and History—Priorities for Research." *Journal of Interdisciplinary History* 10 (History and Climate: Interdisciplinary Explorations): 821–830.

Fischer, Shlomo. 1988. "Jewish Salvation Visions, Utopias and Attitudes towards the Halacha." *International Journal of Comparative Sociology* 29: 62–75.

Fishbane, Michael. 1990. "From Scribalism to Rabbinism: Perspectives on the Emergence of Classical Judaism." In John G. Gammie and Leo G. Perdue, eds., *The Sage in Israel and the Ancient Near East*, 439–456. Winona Lake: Eisenbrauns.

Folkers, Karl-Heinz. 1968. *Die Demokratie als Gesellschaftssystem: Vom Sinn und Ziel der Geschichte; Soziologische Theorie der Evolution.* Berlin: Duncker & Humblot.

Frank, Andre Gunder. 1993. "Bronze Age World System Cycles." *Current Anthropology* 34: 383–429.

Frank, Andre Gunder, and Barry K. Gills. 1993. "World System Cycles, Crises and Hegemonic Shifts, 1700 BC to 17 AD." In Andre Gunder Frank and Barry K. Gills, eds., *The World System: Five Hundred Years or Five Thousand?*, 143–199. London: Routledge, 1993.

Franke, Herbert. 1992. "Die unterschiedlichen Formen der Eingliederung von Barbaren im Lauf der chinesischen Geschichte." In Shmuel N. Eisenstadt, ed., *Kulturen der Achsenzeit II: Ihre institutionelle und kulturelle Dynamik.* Part 1: *China, Japan*, 25–70. Frankfurt am Main: Suhrkamp.

Franke, Leo. 1972. "Die Achsenzeit als Wendung zur Idee: K. Jaspers und G. Simmel." *Zeitschrift für philosophische Forschung* 26: 83–102.

Friese, Joachim. 1967. *Die säkularisierte Welt: Triumph oder Tragödie der christlichen Geistesgeschichte.* Frankfurt am Main: Schulte-Blumke.

Frohock, Fred M. 2002. "Words and Things: Religious and Political Domains." *Journal of Religion* 82: 365–392.

Fuchs, Franz Josef. 1984. *Seinsverhältnis: Karl Jaspers' Existenzphilosophie.* Vol. 1: *Existenz und Kommunikation: Die kommunikative Vermittlung des Existenz-Transzendenz-Verhältnisses in der Philosophie von Karl Jaspers.* Frankfurt am Main: Lang.

Gabriel, Leo. 1968. *Existenzphilosophie: Kierkegaard, Heidegger, Jaspers, Sartre. Dialog der Positionen.* Rev. ed. Vienna: Herold.

Gabrielsen, Vincent. 1997. *The Naval Aristocracy of Hellenistic Rhodes.* Aarhus: Aarhus University Press.

Gaidenko, Piama. 1991. "Die Achsenzeit und das Problem des philosophischen Glaubens bei Karl Jaspers." In Kurt Salamun, ed., *Karl Jaspers: Zur Aktualität seines Denkens*, 86–94. Munich: Piper.

Gangadean, Ashok K. 1997. "Dialogical Awakening in the Global Evolution of Cultures." In Steven Chase, ed., *Doors of Understanding: Conversations in Global Spirituality in Honor of Ewert Cousins*, 335–356. Quincy: Franciscan Press.

Garelli, Paul. 1975. "The Changing Facets of Conservative Mesopotamian Thought." *Daedalus* 104, no. 2 (Wisdom, Revelation and Doubt: Perspectives on the First Millennium B.C.): 47–56.

Gauchet, Marcel. 1985. *Le désenchantement du monde*. Paris: Editions Gallimard. English: *The Disenchantment of the World: A Political History of Religion*. Princeton: Princeton University Press, 1997.

Gebhardt, Jürgen. 2008. "Political Thought in an Intercivilizational Perspective: A Critical Reflection." *Review of Politics* 70: 5–22.

Gebhardt, Jürgen, and Wolfgang Leidhold. 1990. "Eric Voegelin." In Karl Ballestrem and Henning Ottmann, eds., *Politische Philosophie des 20. Jahrhunderts*, 123–145. Munich: Oldenbourg.

Gellner, David N. 1997. "Does Symbolism 'Construct an Urban Mesocosm'? Robert Levy's Mesocosm and the Question of Value Consensus in Bhaktapur." *International Journal of Hindu Studies* 1: 541–564. Reprinted in David N. Gellner, *The Anthropology of Buddhism and Hinduism: Weberian Themes*, 293–315. New Delhi: Oxford University Press, 2001.

Gellner, Ernest. 1988. *Plough, Sword and Book: The Structure of Human History*. London: Collins Harvill.

———. 1992. "Die Besonderheit des muslimischen Staates." In Shmuel N. Eisenstadt, ed., *Kulturen der Achsenzeit II: Ihre institutionelle und kulturelle Dynamik*. Part 3: *Buddhismus, Islam, Altägypten, westliche Kultur*, 189–209. Frankfurt am Main: Suhrkamp.

———. 1992. *Postmodernism, Reason and Religion*. London: Routledge.

Gier, Nicholas F. 1995. "Hindu Titanism." *Philosophy East and West* 45: 73–96.

Giesen, Bernhard. 1991. "Code, Process and Situation in Cultural Selection." *Cultural Dynamics* 4: 172–185.

———. 2002. "Constitutional Practice or Community of Memory? Some Remarks on the Collective Identity of Europe." In Shmuel N. Eisenstadt, Dominic Sachsenmaier, and Jens Riedel, eds., *Reflections on Multiple Modernities: European, Chinese and Other Interpretations*, 193–213. Leiden: Brill.

———. 2005. "Collective Identity and the Representation of Liminality." In Eliezer Ben-Rafael and Yitzhak Sternberg, eds., *Comparing Modernities: Pluralism versus Homogenity; Essays in Homage to Shmuel N. Eisenstadt*, 245–258. Leiden: Brill.

———. 2005. "Performing Transcendence in Politics: Sovereignty, Deviance and the Void of Meaning." *Sociological Theory* 23: 275–285.

———. 2005. "Tales of Transcendence: Imagining the Sacred in Politics." In Bernhard Giesen and Daniel Šuber, eds., *Religion and Politics: Cultural Perspectives*, 93–137. Leiden: Brill.

Gillette, P. Roger. 2002. "A Religion for an Age of Science." *Zygon* 37: 461–472.
Gluck, Carol. 1997. "Asia in World History." In Ainslie T. Embree and Carol Gluck, eds., *Asia in Western and World History: A Guide for Teaching*, 199–216. Armonk: Sharpe.
Gnoli, Gherardo. 2000. *Zoroaster in History*. New York: Bibliotheca Persica Press.
Gnuse, Robert. 1997. *No Other Gods: Emergent Monotheism in Israel*. Sheffield: Sheffield Academic Press.
———. 2007. "Breakthrough or Tyranny: Monotheism's Contested Implications." *Horizons* 34, no. 1: 78–95.
Goedert, Georges. 1998. "Die universalgeschichtliche Einheitsidee bei Karl Jaspers." *Jahrbuch der Österreichischen Karl-Jaspers-Gesellschaft* 11: 9–27.
Goldstone, Jack A. 1998. "The Problem of the 'Early Modern' World." *Journal of the Economic and Social History of the Orient* 41: 249–284.
Goodwin Raheja, Gloria. 1988. "India: Caste, Kingship and Dominance Reconsidered." *Annual Review of Anthropology* 17: 497–522.
Gorski, Eugene F. 2008. *Theology of Religions: A Sourcebook for Interreligious Study*. New York: Paulist Press.
Gorski, Philip S. 2005. "The Return of the Repressed: Religion and the Political Unconscious of Historical Sociology." In Julia Adams, Elisabeth S. Clemens, and Ann Shola Orloff, eds., *Remaking Modernity: Politics, History and Sociology*, 161–189. Durham: Duke University Press.
Grabau, Richard F. 1967. "Karl Jaspers: Communication through Transcendence." In George A. Schrader, ed., *Existential Philosophers: Kierkegaard to Merleau-Ponty*, 109–160. New York: McGraw-Hill.
Graham, Angus Charles. 1989. *Disputers of the Tao: Philosophical Argument in Ancient China*. La Salle: Open Court.
Green, William A. 1995. "Periodizing World History." *History and Theory* 34 (World Historians and Their Critics): 99–111. Reprinted in Richard H. Elphick, Philip Pomper, and Richard T. Vann, eds., *World History: Ideologies, Structures and Identities*, 53–65. Oxford: Blackwell, 1998.
Grenz, Stanley J., and Ed. L. Miller. 1998. "Global Theology: John Hick." In Stanley J. Grenz and Ed. L. Miller, *Fortress Introduction to Comtemporary Theologies*, 177–199. Minneapolis: Fortress Press.
Grosby, Steven. 1996. "The Category of the Primordial in the Study of Early Christianity and Second-Century Judaism." *History of Religions* 36: 140–163.
———. 2002. *Biblical Ideas of Nationality: Ancient and Modern*. Winona Lake: Eisenbrauns.
Grottanelli, Cristiano. 1982. "The King's Grace and the Helpless Woman: A Comparative Study of the Stories of Ruth, Charila, Sītā." *History of Religions* 22: 1–24.
Grün, Udo. 1993. "Zugänge zur Soziologie: Die Buber-Rezeption von Shmuel N. Eisenstadt." In Klaus Plake and Wolfgang K. Schulz, eds., *Entillusionierung*

als Programm: Beiträge zur Soziologie von Shmuel N. Eisenstadt, 39–51. Weinheim: Deutscher Studien Verlag.

Haarmann, Harald. 1998. *Religion und Autorität: Der Weg des Gottes ohne Konkurrenz*. Hildesheim: Olms.

Habermas, Jürgen. 1958. "Jaspers und die Gestalten der Wahrheit: Geschichtsphilosophische Betrachtung zu einer Geschichte der Philosophie. Zum 75. Geburtstag von Karl Jaspers." *Frankfurter Allgemeine Zeitung*, February 22, 1958. Reprinted as "Die Gestalten der Wahrheit." In Jürgen Habermas, *Philosophisch-politische Profile*, 99–109. Frankfurt am Main: Suhrkamp, 1971. And in Hans Saner, ed., *Karl Jaspers in der Diskussion*, 309–316. Munich: Piper, 1973. And in Jürgen Habermas, *Philosophisch-politische Profile*. Rev. ed., 87–96. Frankfurt am Main: Suhrkamp, 1984.

———. 1976. "Geschichte und Evolution." *Geschichte und Gesellschaft: Zeitschrift für Historische Sozialwissenschaft* 2: 310–357. Reprinted in Jürgen Habermas, *Zur Rekonstruktion des Historischen Materialismus*, 200–259. Frankfurt am Main: Suhrkamp, 1976.

———. 1992. "Die Einheit der Vernunft in der Vielfalt ihrer Stimmen." In Jürgen Habermas, *Nachmetaphysisches Denken: Philosophische Aufsätze*, 153–185. Frankfurt am Main: Suhrkamp. English: "The Unity of Reason in the Diversity of Its Voices." In James Schmidt, ed., *What Is Enlightenment? Eighteenth-Century Answers and Twentieth-Century Questions*, 399–425. Berkeley: University of California Press, 1996.

———. 1999. "Ein Gespräch über Gott und die Welt." *Jahrbuch für Politische Theologie* 3: 190–211. Reprinted in Jürgen Habermas, *Zeit der Übergänge* (Kleine Politische Schriften IX), 173–196. Frankfurt am Main: Suhrkamp, 2001. English: "A Conversation about God and the World." In Ciaran Cronin and Max Pensky, eds., *Time of Transition*, 149–169. Cambridge: Polity Press, 2006.

———. 2010. "Ein neues Interesse der Philosophie an der Religion? Zur philosophischen Bewandtnis von postsäkularem Bewusstsein und multikultureller Weltgesellschaft." *Deutsche Zeitschrift für Philosophie* 58, no. 1: 3–16.

Halbfass, Wilhelm. 1981. *Indien und Europa: Perspektiven ihrer geistigen Begegnung*. Basel: Schwabe. English: *India and Europe: An Essay in Understanding*. Albany: State University of New York Press, 1988.

———. 1992. "Mensch und Selbst im traditionellen indischen Denken." In Shmuel N. Eisenstadt, ed., *Kulturen der Achsenzeit II: Ihre institutionelle und kulturelle Dynamik*. Part 2: *Indien*, 129–152. Frankfurt am Main: Suhrkamp.

Hall, David L., and Roger T. Ames. 1995. *Anticipating China: Thinking through the Narratives of Chinese and Western Culture*. Albany: State University of New York Press.

Hall, John A. 1985. "Religion and the Rise of Capitalism." *European Journal of Sociology* 26: 193–223.

Hallberg, Peter, and Björn Wittrock. 2006. "From *koinonìa politikè* to *societas civilis*: Birth, Disappearance and First Renaissance of the Concept." In Peter Wagner, ed., *The Languages of Civil Society*, 28–51. New York: Berghahn Books.

Hampel, Franz. 1975. "Neuere deutsche Geschichtsdenker in kritischer Sicht." In Franz Hampel, *Geschichte als kritische Wissenschaft*, ed. Ingomar Weiler, 73–110. Darmstadt: Wissenschaftliche Buchgesellschaft.

Handelman, Don. 1987. "Myths of Murugan: Asymmetry and Hierarchy in a South Indian Puranic Cosmology." *History of Religions* 27: 133–170.

Hansen, Chad. 2001. "Metaphysical and Moral Transcendence in Chinese Thought." In Bo Mou, ed., *Two Roads to Wisdom? Chinese and Analytic Philosophical Traditions*, 197–228. Chicago: Open Court.

Hao Chang. 1990. "Some Reflections on the Problems of the Axial-Age Breakthrough in Relation to Classical Confucianism." In Paul A. Cohen and Merle Goldman, eds., *Ideas across Cultures: Essays on Chinese Thought in Honor of Benjamin I. Schwartz*, 17–31. Cambridge, MA: Harvard University Press.

Hara Kazuko. 2003. "Philosophischer Glaube bei Karl Jaspers und die Zukunft der Religionen." In Leonard H. Ehrlich and Richard Wisser, eds., *Karl Jaspers' Philosophy: Rooted in the Present, Paradigm for the Future / Karl Jaspers' Philosophie: Gegenwärtigkeit und Zukunft*, 159–164. Würzburg: Königshausen & Neumann.

Harbsmeier, Christoph. 2005. "The Axial Millennium in China: A Brief Survey." In Johann P. Arnason, Shmuel N. Eisenstadt, and Björn Wittrock, eds., *Axial Civilizations and World History*, 469–507. Leiden: Brill.

Harrington, Austin. 2004. "Ernst Troeltsch's Concept of Europe." *European Journal of Social Theory* 7: 479–498.

———. 2006. "Social Theory and Theology." In Gerard Delanty, ed., *Handbook of Contemporary European Social Theory*, 37–47. London: Routledge.

———. 2007. "Habermas and the 'Post-Secular Society.'" *European Journal of Social Theory* 10: 543–560.

———. 2008. "A Sociology of the Demonic? Alfred Weber's Conception of 'Immanent Transcendence.'" *Journal of Classical Sociology* 8: 89–108.

Harth, Dietrich, ed. 1989. *Karl Jaspers: Denken zwischen Wissenschaft, Politik und Philosophie*. Stuttgart: Metzler.

Harth, Dietrich. 2006. "Einige Einwände gegen eine auf den Vergleich religiöser Weltbilder reduzierte Kulturkomparatistik." *Erwägen, Wissen, Ethik* 17: 43–46.

Hartman, Harriet. 1988. "Can a Hindu Utopia Be a Moslem Utopia? Examples from 12th Century India and Beyond." *International Journal of Comparative Sociology* 29: 111–125. Reprinted in Adam Seligman, ed., *Order and Transcendence: The Role of Utopias and the Dynamics of Civilizations*, 111–125. Leiden: Brill, 1989.

Haught, John F. 1990. *What Is Religion? An Introduction*. New York: Paulist Press.
Hay, Eldon. 1988. "God, Creativity and the World: A Process Typology of Religions?" *Studies in Religion* 17, no. 2: 131–142.
Heesterman, Jan C. 1979. "Power and Authority in Indian Tradition." In R. J. Moore, ed., *Tradition and Politics in South Asia*, 60–85. New Delhi: Vikas Publishing House. An expanded version appeared as "Power, Priesthood and Authority" in Jan C. Heesterman, *The Inner Conflict of Tradition: Essays in Indian Ritual, Kingship and Society*, 141–157. Chicago: University of Chicago Press, 1985.
———. 1984. "Kaste und Karma: Max Webers Analyse der indischen Sozialstruktur." In Wolfgang Schluchter, ed., *Max Webers Studie über Hinduismus und Buddhismus: Interpretation und Kritik*, 72–86. Frankfurt am Main: Suhrkamp. English: "Caste and Karma: Max Weber's Analysis of Caste." In Jan C. Heesterman, *The Inner Conflict of Tradition: Essays in Indian Ritual, Kingship and Society*, 194–202. Chicago: University of Chicago Press, 1985.
———. 1985. "Introduction." In Jan C. Heesterman, *The Inner Conflict of Tradition: Essays in Indian Ritual, Kingship and Society*, 3–9. Chicago: University of Chicago Press.
———. 1986. "Ritual, Revelation and Axial Age." In Shmuel N. Eisenstadt, ed., *The Origins and Diversity of Axial Age Civilizations*, 393–406. Albany: State University of New York Press. Reprinted in Jan C. Heesterman, *The Inner Conflict of Tradition: Essays in Indian Ritual, Kingship and Society*, 95–107. Chicago: University of Chicago Press, 1985.
———. 1992. "Die gebrochene Ordnung: Indiens 'nachachsenzeitliche' Erfahrung." In Shmuel N. Eisenstadt, ed., *Kulturen der Achsenzeit II: Ihre institutionelle und kulturelle Dynamik*. Part 2: *Indien*, 80–101. Frankfurt am Main: Suhrkamp.
———. 1992. "Ein geteiltes Haus: Die hinduistisch-muslimische Beziehung." In Shmuel N. Eisenstadt, ed., *Kulturen der Achsenzeit II: Ihre institutionelle und kulturelle Dynamik*. Part 2: *Indien*, 275–293. Frankfurt am Main: Suhrkamp.
———. 1993. *The Broken World of Sacrifice: An Essay in Ancient Indian Ritual*. Chicago: University of Chicago Press.
———. 1995. "Warrior, Peasant and Brahmin." *Modern Asian Studies* 29: 637–654.
Heit, Helmut. 2004. "Die Griechen, die Barbaren und Wir: Kontinuität und griechischer Ursprung in westlichen Identitätsdiskursen." In Iris Därmann, Steffi Hobuß, and Ulrich Lölke, eds., *Konversionen: Fremderfahrungen in ethnologischer und interkultureller Perspektive*, 211–230. Amsterdam: Rodopi.
———. 2007. *Der Ursprungsmythos der Vernunft: Zur philosophiehistorischen Genealogie des griechischen Wunders*. Würzburg: Königshausen & Neumann.
Helman, Sarit. 1988. "The Javanese Conception of Order and Its Relationship to Millenarian Motifs and Imagery." *International Journal of Comparative Sociology* 29: 126–138.

Hennig, John. 1957. "Karl Jaspers' Attitude towards History." In Paul Arthur Schilpp, ed., *The Philosophy of Karl Jaspers*, 565–591. New York: Tudor Publishing Company.
Herders kleine Weltgeschichte: Der Weg der Menschheit, ed. Thomas Urban. 3rd ed. Freiburg im Breisgau: Herder, 1959.
Hersch, Jeanne. 1953. "The Recent Work of Karl Jaspers." *Diogenes* 1: 138–143.
Hick, John. 1989. *An Interpretation of Religion: Human Responses to the Transcendent.* New Haven and London: Yale University Press.
———. 1999. *The Fifth Dimension: An Exploration of the Spiritual Realm.* Oxford: Oneworld.
———. 2006. "Exclusivism versus Pluralism in Religion: A Response to Kevin Meeker." *Religious Studies* 42: 207–212.
Hinchman, Lewis P., and Sandra K. Hinchman. 1991. "Existentialism Politicized: Arendt's Debt to Jaspers." *Review of Politics* 53: 435–468.
Hodgson, Marshall G. S. 1963. "The Interrelations of Societies in History." *Comparative Studies in Society and History* 5: 227–250. Reprinted in Marshall G. S. Hodgson, *Rethinking World History: Essays on Europe, Islam and World History*, ed. Edmund Burke III, 3–28. Cambridge: Cambridge University Press, 1993.
———. 1970. "The Role of Islam in World History." *International Journal of Middle East Studies* 1: 99–123. Reprinted in Marshall G. S. Hodgson, *Rethinking World History: Essays on Europe, Islam and World History*, ed. Edmund Burke III, 97–125. Cambridge: Cambridge University Press, 1993.
———. 1974. *The Venture of Islam: Conscience and History in a World Civilization.* Vol. 1: *The Classical Age of Islam.* Vol. 2: *The Expansion of Islam in the Middle Periods.* Vol. 3: *The Gunpowder Empires and Modern Times.* Chicago: University of Chicago Press.
Holzinger, Markus. 2007. *Kontingenz in der Gegenwartsgesellschaft: Dimensionen eines Leitbegriffs moderner Sozialtheorie.* Bielefeld: Transcript.
Homer-Dixon, Thomas. 2008. *The Upside of Down: Catastrophe, Creativity and the Renewal of Civilization.* Washington, DC: Island Press.
Hösle, Vittorio. 2009. "Eine metaphysische Geschichte des Atheismus." *Deutsche Zeitschrift für Philosophie* 57, no. 2: 319–327.
Hsu Cho-yun. 1986. "Historical Conditions of the Emergence and Crystallization of the Confucian System." In Shmuel N. Eisenstadt, ed., *The Origins and Diversity of Axial Age Civilizations*, 306–324. Albany: State University of New York Press.
———. 1992. "Die chinesische Reaktion auf Eroberung: Die verschiedenen Methoden zur Rekonstruktion der konfuzianischen Staatsordnung." In Shmuel N. Eisenstadt, ed., *Kulturen der Achsenzeit II: Ihre institutionelle und kulturelle Dynamik.* Part 1: *China, Japan*, 71–90. Frankfurt am Main: Suhrkamp.

———. 1997. "The Origins of Civilization in China." In Ainslie T. Embree and Carol Gluck, eds., *Asia in Western and World History: A Guide for Teaching*, 251–256. Armonk: Sharpe.

———. 2005. "Rethinking the Axial Age: The Case of Chinese Culture." In Johann P. Arnason, Shmuel N. Eisenstadt, and Björn Wittrock, eds., *Axial Civilizations and World History*, 451–467. Leiden: Brill.

Hsu Cho-yun and Katheryn M. Linduff. 1988. *Western Chou Civilization*. New Haven: Yale University Press.

Huang Xiao-ming. 2002. "What Is 'Chinese' about Chinese Civilization: Culture, Institutions and Globalization?" In Mehdi Mozaffari, ed., *Globalization and Civilizations*, 218–241. London: Routledge.

Hübsch, Stefan. 2004. "Elemente und Ursprünge von Jaspers' Geschichtsverständnis." In Bernd Weidmann, ed., *Existenz in Kommunikation: Zur philosophischen Ethik von Karl Jaspers*, 79–95. Würzburg: Königshausen & Neumann.

Humphreys, Sally C. 1975. "'Transcendence' and Intellectual Roles: The Ancient Greek Case." *Daedalus* 104, no. 2 (Wisdom, Revelation and Doubt: Perspectives on the First Millennium B.C.): 91–118.

———. 1986. "Dynamics of the Greek Breakthrough: The Dialogue between Philosophy and Religion." In Shmuel N. Eisenstadt, ed., *The Origins and Diversity of Axial Age Civilizations*, 92–110. Albany: State University of New York Press. Reprinted in Sally C. Humphreys, *The Strangeness of Gods: Historical Perspectives on the Interpretation of Athenian Religion*, 51–75. Oxford: Oxford University Press, 2004.

Idel, Moshe. 2002. *Absorbing Perfections: Kabbalah and Interpretation*. New Haven: Yale University Press.

Inada, Kenneth K. 1988. "The Range of Buddhist Ontology." *Philosophy East and West* 38: 261–280.

Inglis, David. 2010. "Civilizations or Globalization(s)? Intellectual Rapprochements and Historical World-Visions." *European Journal of Social Theory* 13: 135–152.

Ione, Amy. 1995. *Nature Exposed to Our Method of Questioning*. Berkeley: Diatrope Press.

Ishida Takeshi. 1992. "Die Orthodoxie des japanischen Reichs." In Shmuel N. Eisenstadt, ed., *Kulturen der Achsenzeit II: Ihre institutionelle und kulturelle Dynamik*. Part 1: *China, Japan*, 279–292. Frankfurt am Main: Suhrkamp.

Jacobsen, Bjarne. 2001. "Hiatus Irrationalis: Der Bruch zwischen Sein und Sollen." In Hans G. Kippenberg and Martin Riesebrodt, eds., *Max Webers "Religionssystematik,"* 31–50. Tübingen: Mohr Siebeck.

Jansen, Marius B. 1992. "Die japanische Erfahrung des Wandels." In Shmuel N. Eisenstadt, ed., *Kulturen der Achsenzeit II: Ihre institutionelle und kulturelle Dynamik*. Part 1: *China, Japan*, 242–262. Frankfurt am Main: Suhrkamp.

Joas, Hans. 2009. "Die säkulare Option: Ihr Aufstieg und ihre Folgen." *Deutsche Zeitschrift für Philosophie* 57, no. 2: 293–300.
Joas, Hans, and Wolfgang Knöbl. 2004. *Sozialtheorie: Zwanzig einführende Vorlesungen*. Frankfurt am Main: Suhrkamp. English: *Social Theory: Twenty Introductory Lectures*. Cambridge: Cambridge University Press, 2009.
Joffe, Alexander H. 2002. "The Rise of Secondary States in the Iron Age Levant." *Journal of the Economic and Social History of the Orient* 45 (Excavating the Relations between Archaeology and History in the Study of Pre-Modern Asia): 425–467.
Johnson, Jean Elliott. 1994. "Patterns and Comparisons in the Human Drama." *History Teacher* 27: 433–447.
Junge, Friedrich. 2003. *Die Lehre Ptahhoteps und die Tugenden der ägyptischen Welt*. Göttingen: Vandenhoeck & Ruprecht.
Kaegi, Werner. 1977. *Jacob Burckhardt: Eine Biographie*. Vol. 6.1: *Weltgeschichte—Mittelalter—Kunstgeschichte. Die letzten Jahre, 1886–1897*. Basel: Schwabe & Co.
Kamlah, Wilhelm. 1951. *Christentum und Geschichtlichkeit: Untersuchungen zur Entstehung des Christentums und zu Augustins "Bürgerschaft Gottes."* Stuttgart: Kohlhammer.
Kang, David C. 2010. "Civilization and State Formation in the Shadow of China." In Peter J. Katzenstein, ed., *Civilizations in World Politics: Plural and Pluralist Perspectives*, 91–113. London: Routledge.
Katzenstein, Peter J. 2011. "Civilizational States, Secularisms, and Religions." In Craig Calhoun, Mark Juergensmeyer, and Jonathan VanAntwerpen, eds., *Rethinking Secularism*, 145–165. Oxford: Oxford University Press.
Kaufmann, Fritz. 1957. "Karl Jaspers and a Philosophy of Communication." In Paul Arthur Schilpp, ed., *The Philosophy of Karl Jaspers*, 210–295. New York: Tudor Publishing Company.
Kaufmann, Walter. 1957. "Jaspers' Relation to Nietzsche." In Paul Arthur Schilpp, ed., *The Philosophy of Karl Jaspers*, 407–436. New York: Tudor Publishing Company.
Kennedy, Philip. 2006. *A Modern Introduction to Theology: New Questions for Old Beliefs*. London: I. B. Tauris.
Kesting, Hanno. 1959. *Geschichtsphilosophie und Weltbürgerkrieg: Deutungen der Geschichte von der Französischen Revolution bis zum Ost-West-Konflikt*. Heidelberg: Winter.
Keulman, Kenneth. 1983. "The Tension of Consciousness: The Pneumatic Differentiation." In John Kirby and William M. Thompson, eds., *Voegelin and the Theologian: Ten Studies in Interpretation*, 61–103. New York: Mellen Press.
Khazanov, Anatoly M. 1993. "Muhammad and Jenghiz Khan Compared: The Religious Factor in World Empire Building." *Comparative Studies in Society and History* 35: 461–479.

Khoury, Raif Georges. 2006. "Story, Wisdom and Spirituality: Yemen as the Hub between the Persian, Arabic and Biblical Traditions." In Johann P. Arnason, Armando Salvatore, and Georg Stauth, eds., *Islam in Process: Historical and Civilizational Perspectives*, 190–219. Bielefeld: Transcript.

Kim Sanjun. 2002. "The Genealogy of Confucian *Moralpolitik* and Its Implications for Modern Civil Society." In Charles K. Armstrong, ed., *Korean Society: Civil Society, Democracy and the State*, 57–91. London: Routledge.

Kimmerling, Baruch. 2007. "The Exhaustion of the Primary Zionist Program: S. N. Eisenstadt between Dynamic Conservativism and Critical Perspectives." *European Journal of Sociology* 48: 149–172.

King, Barbara J. 2007. *Evolving God: A Provocative View of the Origins of Religion*. New York: Doubleday.

Kippenberg, Hans G. 1986. "The Role of Christianity in the Depolitization of the Roman Empire." In Shmuel N. Eisenstadt, ed., *The Origins and Diversity of Axial Age Civilizations*, 261–279. Albany: State University of New York Press.

———. 1991. *Die vorderasiatischen Erlösungsreligionen in ihrem Zusammenhang mit der antiken Stadtherrschaft*. Heidelberger Max-Weber-Vorlesungen. Frankfurt am Main: Suhrkamp.

Kirkbright, Suzanne. 2004. *Karl Jaspers: A Biography—Navigations in Truth*. New Haven: Yale University Press.

Klein, Aloys. 1973. *Glaube und Mythos: Eine kritische, religionsphilosophisch-theologische Untersuchung des Mythos-Begriffs bei Karl Jaspers*. Munich: Schöningh.

Klenk, G. Friedrich. 1953. "Die Achse der Weltgeschichte." *Stimmen der Zeit* 151: 241–250.

Kliever, Lonnie D. 1986. "Confessions of Unbelief: In Quest of the Vital Lie." *Journal for the Scientific Study of Religion* 25: 102–115.

Knöbl, Wolfgang. 2001. *Spielräume der Modernisierung: Das Ende der Eindeutigkeit*. Weilerswist: Velbrück Wissenschaft.

———. 2006. "Verwerfungen in der klassischen Moderne: Der US-amerikanische Süden als Problemfall in der Debatte um die 'Multiple Modernities.'" In Thomas Schwinn, ed., *Die Vielfalt und Einheit der Moderne: Kultur- und strukturvergleichende Analysen*, 71–100. Wiesbaden: Verlag für Sozialwissenschaften. English: "Of Contingencies and Breaks: The American South as an Anomaly in the Debate on Multiple Modernities." *European Journal of Sociology* 47 (2006): 125–157.

———. 2007. *Die Kontingenz der Moderne: Wege in Europa, Asien und Amerika*. Frankfurt and New York: Campus.

———. 2010. "Path Dependency and Civilizational Analysis: Methodological Challenges and Theoretical Tasks." *European Journal of Social Theory* 13: 83–97.

———. 2011. "Contingency and Modernity in the Thought of J. P. Arnason." *European Journal of Social Theory* 14: 9–22.

Knohl, Israel. 2005. "Axial Transformations within Ancient Israelite Priesthood." In Johann P. Arnason, Shmuel N. Eisenstadt, and Björn Wittrock, eds., *Axial Civilizations and World History*, 201-224. Leiden: Brill.

———. 2005. "Shmuel Noah Eisenstadt." In Dirk Kaesler, ed., *Aktuelle Theorien der Soziologie: Von Shmuel N. Eisenstadt bis zur Postmoderne*, 41-63. Munich: C. H. Beck.

Koenig, Matthias. 2005. *Menschenrechte*. Frankfurt: Campus.

———. 2006. "Herrschaft als Thema historischer Religionssoziologie." *Erwägen, Wissen, Ethik* 17: 50-51.

———. 2006. "Shmuel Noah Eisenstadt: Kulturtheoretische Zivilisationsanalyse." In Stephan Moebius and Dirk Quadflieg, eds., *Kultur: Theorien der Gegenwart*, 571-579. Wiesbaden: Verlag für Sozialwissenschaften.

———. 2007. "Kulturelle Konstruktionen und institutionelle Varianten der Moderne in der Weltgesellschaft." In Thorsten Bonacker and Andreas Reckwitz, eds., *Kulturen der Moderne: Soziologische Perspektiven der Gegenwart*, 71-96. Frankfurt: Campus.

———. 2008. "Kampf der Götter: Religiöse Pluralität und gesellschaftliche Integration." In Christine Langenfeld and Irene Schneider, eds., *Recht und Religion in Europa: Zeitgenössische Konflikte und historische Perspektiven*, 102-118. Göttingen: Universitätsverlag Göttingen.

Kohaut, Erwin, and Walter Weiss. 2004. *Universum und Bewußtsein: Philosophisch-physikalische Gedanken zur Welt*. Vienna: Edition Va Bene.

Köhler, Oskar. 1950. "Das Bild der Menschheitsgeschichte bei Karl Jaspers." *Saeculum* 1: 477-486.

———. 1951. "Idealismus und Geschichtlichkeit: Über Neuerscheinungen aus dem Gebiete der Geschichtsphilosophie." *Saeculum* 2: 122-151.

———. 1955. "Was ist 'Welt' in der Geschichte?" *Saeculum* 6: 1-9.

———. 1958. "Versuch, Kategorien der Weltgeschichte zu bestimmen." *Saeculum* 9: 446-457.

Koselleck, Reinhart. 1986. "Jaspers, die Geschichte und das Überpolitische." In Jeanne Hersch, Milič Lochmann, and Reiner Wiehl, eds., *Karl Jaspers: Philosoph, Arzt, politischer Denker; Symposium zum 100; Geburtstag in Basel und Heidelberg*, 291-302. Munich: Piper.

Kössler, Reinhart. 2006. "Eisenstadt, Weber and the Ambiguity of Modernity." *Erwägen, Wissen, Ethik* 17: 51-54.

Krejčí, Jaroslav. 1990. *The Civilizations of Asia and the Middle East: Before the European Challenge*. Basingstoke: Macmillan.

———. 2004. *The Paths of Civilization: Understanding the Currents of History*. Basingstoke: Macmillan.

Krins, Holger. 2000. "Die politischen Entscheidungsträger in Athen und China: Ein Vergleich der achsenzeitlichen Entwicklung." In Oskar Fahr, Wolfgang Ommerborn, and Konrad Wegmann, eds., *Politisches Denken Chinas in alter und neuer Zeit*, 152-183. Münster: LIT.

Krüger, Hans-Peter. 2009. *Philosophische Anthropologie als Lebenspolitik: Deutsch-jüdische und pragmatistische Moderne-Kritik*. Berlin: Akademie Verlag.

Kuhn, Helmut. 1954. "Nichts—Sein—Gott." In Joachim Moras and Hans Paeschke, eds., *Deutscher Geist zwischen Gestern und Morgen: Bilanz der kulturellen Entwicklung seit 1945*, 211–247. Stuttgart: Deutsche Verlags-Anstalt.

Kulke, Hermann. 1982. "Gibt es ein indisches Mittelalter? Versuch einer eurasiatischen Geschichtsbetrachtung." *Saeculum* 33: 221–239.

——. 1986. "The Historical Background of India's Axial Age." In Shmuel N. Eisenstadt, ed., *The Origins and Diversity of Axial Age Civilizations*, 374–392. Albany: State University of New York Press.

——. 1991. "Some Considerations on the Significance of Buddha's Date for the History of North India." In Heinz Bechert, ed., *The Dating of the Historical Buddha / Die Datierung des historischen Buddha*. Vol. 1, 100–107. Göttingen: Vandenhoeck & Ruprecht.

——. 1992. "Ausgrenzung, Rezeption und kulturelles Selbstbewußtsein: Formen indischer Reaktion auf fremde Eroberungen in der frühen Geschichte." In Shmuel N. Eisenstadt, ed., *Kulturen der Achsenzeit II: Ihre institutionelle und kulturelle Dynamik*. Part 2: *Indien*, 17–37. Frankfurt am Main: Suhrkamp.

Kull, Anne. 2007. "Speaking of God in the New World Order." In Norbert Hintersteiner, ed., *Naming and Thinking God in Europe Today: Theology in Global Dialogue*, 51–68. Amsterdam: Rodopi.

Kurth, James. 2010. "The United States as a Civilizational Leader." In Peter J. Katzenstein, ed., *Civilizations in World Politics: Plural and Pluralist Perspectives*, 41–65. London: Routledge.

Kwong, Luke S. K. 2001. "The Rise of the Linear Perspective on History and Time in Late Qing China c. 1860–1911." *Past and Present* 173: 157–190.

Lambert, Yves. 1999. "Religion in Modernity as a New Axial Age: Secularization or New Religious Forms?" *Sociology of Religion* 60: 303–333. Reprinted in William H. Swatos Jr. and Daniel V. A. Olson, eds., *The Secularization Debate*, 95–125. Lanham: Rowman & Littlefield, 2000.

——. 2003. "New Christianity, Indifference and Diffused Spirituality." In Hugh McLeod and Werner Ustorf, eds., *The Decline of Christendom in Western Europe, 1750–2000*, 63–78. Cambridge: Cambridge University Press.

Lanczkowski, Günter. 1960. *Altägyptischer Prophetismus*. Wiesbaden: Harrassowitz.

Landon, John C. 1999. *World History and the Eonic Effect: Civilization, Darwinism, and Theories of Evolution*. Philadelphia: Xlibris.

Lang, Bernhard. 2001. "Prophet, Priester, Virtuose." In Hans G. Kippenberg and Martin Riesebrodt, eds., *Max Webers "Religionssystematik,"* 167–191. Tübingen: Mohr Siebeck.

Lapidus, Ira M. 1992. "Islamisches Sektierertum und das Rekonstruktions- und Umgestaltungspotential der islamischen Kultur." In Shmuel N. Eisenstadt, ed., *Kulturen der Achsenzeit II: Ihre institutionelle und kulturelle Dynamik*.

Part 3: *Buddhismus, Islam, Altägypten, westliche Kultur,* 161–188. Frankfurt am Main: Suhrkamp.

———. 1996. "State and Religion in Islamic Societies." *Past and Present* 151: 3–27.

Lauer, Robert H. 1971. "The Scientific Legitimation of Fallacy: Neutralizing Social Change Theory." *American Sociological Review* 36: 881–889.

Lawrence, Bruce B. 2010. "Islam in Afro-Eurasia: A Bridge Civilization." In Peter J. Katzenstein, ed., *Civilizations in World Politics: Plural and Pluralist Perspectives,* 157–176. London: Routledge.

Lazarus-Yafeh, Hava. 1992. "Die islamische Reaktion auf den Rationalismus." In Shmuel N. Eisenstadt, ed., *Kulturen der Achsenzeit II: Ihre institutionelle und kulturelle Dynamik.* Part 3: *Buddhismus, Islam, Altägypten, westliche Kultur,* 210–225. Frankfurt am Main: Suhrkamp.

Lee Eun-jeung. 2003. *"Anti-Europa": Die Geschichte der Rezeption des Konfuzianismus und der konfuzianischen Gesellschaft seit der frühen Aufklärung; Eine ideengeschichtliche Untersuchung unter besonderer Berücksichtigung der deutschen Entwicklung.* Münster: LIT.

Lerro, Bruce. 2000. *From Earth Spirits to Sky Gods: The Socioecological Origins of Monotheism, Individualism, and Hyperabstract Reasoning from the Stone Age to the Axial Iron Age.* Lanham: Lexington Books.

Levine, Donald N. 2004. "Note on the Concept of an Axial Turning in Human History." In Saïd Amir Arjomand and Edward A. Tiryakian, eds., *Rethinking Civilizational Analysis,* 67–70. London: Sage Publications.

———. 2005. "Civilizational Resources for Dialogic Engagement?" In Eliezer Ben-Rafael and Yitzhak Sternberg, eds., *Comparing Modernities: Pluralism versus Homogenity; Essays in Homage to Shmuel N. Eisenstadt,* 501–512. Leiden: Brill.

Levtzion, Nehemia. 1992. "Islamisierungsmuster: Die Begegnung des Islam mit 'Achsenzeitreligionen.'" In Shmuel N. Eisenstadt, ed., *Kulturen der Achsenzeit II: Ihre institutionelle und kulturelle Dynamik.* Part 3: *Buddhismus, Islam, Altägypten, westliche Kultur,* 226–241. Frankfurt am Main: Suhrkamp.

———. 2005. "A Scholarly Portrait: Multiple Openings for Sociological Discourse." In Eliezer Ben-Rafael and Yitzhak Sternberg, eds., *Comparing Modernities: Pluralism versus Homogenity; Essays in Homage to Shmuel N. Eisenstadt,* 662–670. Leiden: Brill.

Levy, David J. 2005. "'The Religion of Light': On Mani and Manichaeism." In Johann P. Arnason, Shmuel N. Eisenstadt, and Björn Wittrock, eds., *Axial Civilizations and World History,* 319–336. Leiden: Brill.

Levy, Robert I. 1990. *Mesocosm: Hinduism and the Organization of a Traditional Newar City in Nepal.* Berkeley: University of California Press.

Lewis, Bernard. 1995. *The Middle East: A Brief History of the Last 2,000 Years.* New York: Scribner.

Ley, Michael. 2005. *Zivilisationspolitik: Zur Theorie einer Weltökumene.* Würzburg: Königshausen & Neumann.

Li Chen-yang. 2008. "The Ideal of Harmony in Ancient Chinese and Greek Philosophy." *Dao* 7: 81–98.
Li You-sheng. 2005. *A New Interpretation of Chinese Taoist Philosophy: An Anthropological/Psychological View.* London: Taoist Recovery Centre.
Liebsch, Burkhard. 2004. "Gastlichkeit als Anspruch? Kulturkritische Überlegungen im Ausgang von Jaspers, Arendt, Levinas und Derrida." In Christof Mandry, ed., *Kultur, Pluralität und Ethik: Perspektiven in Sozialwissenschaften und Ethik,* 89–136. Münster: LIT.
Linares, Filadelfo. 1988. *Beiträge zur Staats- und Geschichtsphilosophie.* Hildesheim: Olms.
Lindenfeld, David. 2005. "Indigenous Encounters with Christian Missionaries in China and West Africa, 1800–1920: A Comparative Study." *Journal of World History* 16: 327–369.
Lipson, Leslie. 1993. *The Ethical Crises of Civilization: Moral Meltdown or Advance?* Newbury Park: Sage Publications.
Liu Shu-hsien. 2003. *Essentials of Contemporary Neo-Confucian Philosophy.* Westport: Praeger.
Liu Yameng. 1996. "Three Issues in the Argumentative Conception of Early Chinese Discourse." *Philosophy East and West* 46: 33–58.
———. 1996. "To Capture the Essence of Chinese Rhetoric: An Anatomy of a Paradigm in Comparative Rhetoric." *Rhetoric Review* 14: 318–335.
Liverani, Mario. 2005. *Israel's History and the History of Israel.* London: Equinox.
Lloyd, G. E. R. 2002. *The Ambitions of Curiosity: Understanding the World in Ancient Greece and China.* Cambridge: Cambridge University Press.
Long, Charles H. 2004. "A Postcolonial Meaning of Religion: Some Reflections from the Indigenous World." In Jacob K. Olupona, ed., *Beyond Primitivism: Indigenous Religious Traditions and Modernity,* 89–98. New York: Routledge.
Loy, David R. 1996. "'... While the Scholar in His Wisdom Bows Down to the Truth': Asia, the West and the Dynamic of Truth." *Cultural Dynamics* 8: 147–160.
———. 1998. "On Eisenstadt's Japanese Civilization." *Cultural Dynamics* 10: 84–90.
Machinist, Peter B. 1986. "On Self-Consciousness in Mesopotamia." In Shmuel N. Eisenstadt, ed., *The Origins and Diversity of Axial Age Civilizations,* 183–202. Albany: State University of New York Press.
Mackey, James P. 2000. *The Critique of Theological Reason.* Cambridge: Cambridge University Press.
MacQueen, Graeme. 1981. "The Conflict between External and Internal Mastery: An Analysis of the Khantivādi and Jātaka." *History of Religions* 20: 242–252.
Magee, John Benjamin. 1967. *Religion and Modern Man: A Study of the Religious Meaning of Being Human.* New York: Harper & Row.
Mahmood, Saba. 2010. "Can Secularism Be Other-wise." In Michael Warner, Jonathan VanAntwerpen, and Craig Calhoun, eds., *Varieties of Secularism in a Secular Age,* 282–299. Cambridge, MA: Harvard University Press.

Mainz, Klaus. 2002. *Zeit: Von der Urzeit zur Computerzeit*. Munich: C. H. Beck.
Majid, Anouar. 2007. *A Call for Heresy: Why Dissent Is Vital to Islam and America*. Minneapolis: University of Minnesota Press.
Mall, Ram Adhar. 1995. *Philosophie im Vergleich der Kulturen: Interkulturelle Philosophie—eine neue Orientierung*. Darmstadt: Wissenschaftliche Buchgesellschaft.
Mall, Ram Adhar, and Heinz Hülsmann. 1989. *Die drei Geburtsorte der Philosophie: China, Indien, Europa*. Bonn: Bouvier.
Manasse, Ernst Moritz. 1957. "Jaspers' Relation to Max Weber." In Paul Arthur Schilpp, ed., *The Philosophy of Karl Jaspers*, 369–391. New York: Tudor Publishing Company.
Mandalios, John. 2003. "Civilizational Complexes and Processes: Elias, Nelson and Eisenstadt." In Gerard Delanty and Engin F. Isin, eds., *Handbook of Historical Sociology*, 65–79. London: Sage Publications.
Mann, Golo. 1957. "Freedom and the Social Sciences in Jaspers' Thought." In Paul Arthur Schilpp, ed., *The Philosophy of Karl Jaspers*, 551–564. New York: Tudor Publishing Company.
Mann, Ulrich. 1962. *Vorspiel des Heils: Die Uroffenbarung in Hellas*. Stuttgart: Klett.
———. 1970. *Das Christentum als absolute Religion*. Darmstadt: Wissenschaftliche Buchgesellschaft.
———. 1970. *Theogonische Tage: Die Entwicklungsphasen des Gottesbewußtseins in der altorientalischen und biblischen Religion*. Stuttgart: Klett.
Marangudakis, Manussos. 2006. "The Social Sources and Environmental Consequences of Axial Thinking: Mesopotamia, China and Greece in Comparative Perspective." *European Journal of Sociology* 47: 59–91.
Markham, Ian. 2004. "Christianity and Other Religions." In Gareth Jones, ed., *The Blackwell Companion to Modern Theology*, 405–417. Oxford: Blackwell.
Martin, David. 2008. "The Religious and the Political." In Eileen Barker, ed., *The Centrality of Religion in Social Life: Essays in Honour of James A. Beckford*, 161–174. Aldershot: Ashgate.
———. 2011. *The Future of Christianity: Reflections on Violence and Democracy, Religion and Secularisation*. Farnham: Ashgate.
Martin, Thomas. 1982. "Griechisches Mittelalter? Versuch einer Problemskizze." In Herbert Ludat and Rainer Christoph Schwinges, eds., *Politik, Gesellschaft, Geschichtsschreibung. Gießener Festgabe für František Graus zum 60. Geburtstag*, 1–38. Cologne: Böhlau.
Martindale, Don. 1962. *Social Life and Cultural Change*. Princeton: Van Nostrand.
———. 1987. "The Sociology of Intellectual Creativity." In Raj P. Mohan, ed., *The Mythmakers: Intellectuals and the Intelligentsia in Perspective*, 1–19. Westport: Greenwood Press.

Masur, Gerhard. 1962. "Distinctive Traits of Western Civilization—Through the Eyes of Western Historians." *American Historical Review* 67: 591–608.

Matsuo Hōsaku. 1987. *The Logic of Unity: The Discovery of Zero and Emptiness in Prajñāpāramitā Thought.* Albany: State University of New York Press.

Mayer, John D., Stephanie C. Lin, and Maria Korogodsky. 2011. "Exploring the Universality of Personality Judgments: Evidence from the Great Transformation (1000 BCE–200 BCE)." *Review of General Psychology* 15, no. 1: 65–76.

Mayes, A. D. H. 1993. "On Describing the Purpose of Deuteronomy." *Journal for the Study of the Old Testament* 18, no. 58: 13–33.

Mbogu, Nicholas Ibeawuchi. 2008. *Christology and Religious Pluralism: A Review of John Hick's Theocentric Model of Christology and the Emergence of African Inculturation Christologies.* Münster: LIT.

McDonald, Kevin. 2006. *Global Movements: Action and Culture.* Malden: Blackwell.

McGaughey, William. 2000. *Five Epochs of Civilization: World History as Emerging in Five Civilizations.* Minneapolis: Thistlerose Publications.

McLennan, Gregor. 2000. "Sociology's Eurocentrism and the 'Rise of the West' Revisited." *European Journal of Social Theory* 3: 275–291.

Meier, Christian. 1980. "Einführung." In Christian Meier, *Die Entstehung des Politischen bei den Griechen,* 12–24. Frankfurt am Main: Suhrkamp.

———. 1982. "Die Griechen—die politische Revolution der Weltgeschichte." *Saeculum* 33: 133–147.

———. 1986. "The Emergence of an Autonomous Intelligence among the Greeks." In Shmuel N. Eisenstadt, ed., *The Origins and Diversity of Axial Age Civilizations,* 65–91. Albany: State University of New York Press.

———. 2001. "Das 'europäische Wunder': Die Frage nach seinen Voraussetzungen." *Merkur* 55: 399–411.

———. 2001. "The Greeks: The Political Revolution in World History." In Johann P. Arnason and Peter Murphy, eds., *Agon, Logos, Polis: The Greek Achievement and Its Aftermath,* 56–71. Stuttgart: Steiner.

———. 2005. "Die griechisch-römische Tradition." In Hans Joas and Klaus Wiegandt, eds., *Die kulturellen Werte Europas,* 93–116. Frankfurt am Main: Fischer. English: "The Greco-Roman Tradition." In Hans Joas and Klaus Wiegandt, eds., *The Cultural Values of Europe,* 59–76. Liverpool: Liverpool University Press, 2008.

Merlio, Gilbert. 1989. "Karl Jaspers als Anti-Spengler." In Dietrich Harth, ed., *Karl Jaspers: Denken zwischen Wissenschaft, Politik und Philosophie,* 65–86. Stuttgart: Metzler.

Metzger, Thomas A. 1990. "Continuities between Modern and Premodern China: Some Neglected Methodological and Substantive Issues." In Paul A. Cohen and Merle Goldman, eds., *Ideas across Cultures: Essays on Chinese Thought in Honor of Benjamin I. Schwartz*, 263–292. Cambridge, MA: Harvard University Press.

Metzler, Dieter. 1991. "A. H. Anquetil-Duperron (1731–1805) und das Konzept der Achsenzeit." *Achaemenid History* 7: 123–133.

Meyer, Enno. 1962. *Juden und Judenfeinde in der christlichen Welt*. Cologne: Melzer.

Meyer, John W., and Ronald L. Jepperson. 2000. "The 'Actors' of Modern Society: The Cultural Construction of Social Agency." *Sociological Theory* 18: 100–120.

Michalowski, Piotr. 2005. "Mesopotamian Vistas on Axial Transformations." In Johann P. Arnason, Shmuel N. Eisenstadt, and Björn Wittrock, eds., *Axial Civilizations and World History*, 157–181. Leiden: Brill.

Miliopoulos, Lazaros. 2007. *Atlantische Zivilisation und transatlantisches Verhältnis: Politische Idee und Wirklichkeit*. Wiesbaden: Verlag für Sozialwissenschaften.

Miller, James. 2003. *Daoism: A Short Introduction*. Oxford: Oneworld.

Minkenberg, Michael. 2003. "Staat und Kirche in westlichen Demokratien." In Michael Minkenberg and Ulrich Willems, eds., *Politik und Religion*, 115–138. Wiesbaden: Westdeutscher Verlag.

———. 2004. "Heilige Versteinerung? Das Verhältnis von Religion und Demokratie an der Jahrtausendwende." In Birgit Schwelling, ed., *Politikwissenschaft als Kulturwissenschaft: Theorien, Methoden, Problemstellungen*, 277–307. Wiesbaden: Verlag für Sozialwissenschaften.

Mirgeler, Albert. 1954. "Geschichte aus der Distanz." In Joachim Moras and Hans Paeschke, eds., *Deutscher Geist zwischen Gestern und Morgen: Bilanz der kulturellen Entwicklung seit 1945*, 298–314. Stuttgart: Deutsche Verlags-Anstalt.

Modelski, George. 2000. "World System Evolution." In Robert A. Denemark, Jonathan Friedman, Barry K. Gills, and George Modelski, eds., *World System History: The Social Science of Long-Term Change*, 24–53. London: Routledge.

Momigliano, Arnaldo. 1975. *Alien Wisdom: The Limits of Hellenization*. Cambridge: Cambridge University Press.

———. 1975. "The Fault of the Greeks." *Daedalus* 104, no. 2 (Wisdom, Revelation and Doubt: Perspectives on the First Millennium B.C.): 9–19. Reprinted in Arnaldo Momigliano, *Essays in Ancient and Modern Historiography*, 9–23. Oxford: Blackwell, 1977.

Mommsen, Wolfgang. 1992. "Geschichte und Geschichten: Über die Möglichkeiten und Grenzen der Universalgeschichtsschreibung." *Saeculum* 43: 124–135.

Moore, R. I. 2004. "The Transformation of Europe as a Eurasian Phenomenon." In Johann P. Arnason and Björn Wittrock, eds., *Eurasian Transformations, Tenth to Thirteenth Centuries: Crystallizations, Divergences, Renaissances*, 77–98. Leiden: Brill.

Morrow, William. 2006: "The Affirmation of Divine Righteousness in Early Penitential Prayers: A Sign of Judaism's Entry into the Axial Age." In Mark J. Boda, Daniel K. Falk, and Rodney A. Werline, eds., *Seeking the Favor of God.* Vol. 1: *The Origins of Penitential Prayer in Second Temple Judaism,* 101–117. Atlanta: Society of Biblical Literature.

Mueller, Gert H. 1990. "Max Weber and the Religions of Asia." In William H. Swatos Jr., ed., *Time, Place and Circumstance: Neo-Weberian Studies in Comparative Religious History,* 17–27. New York: Greenwood Press.

Muesse, Mark W. 2011. *The Hindu Traditions: A Concise Introduction.* Minneapolis: Fortress Press.

Mühlmann, W. E. 1954. "Ethnologie und Geschichte." *Studium Generale* 7: 165–177.

Mumford, Lewis. 1956. "A Study of History." *Diogenes* 4: 11–28.

———. 1956. *The Transformations of Man.* New York: Harper & Brothers Publishers.

Murakami Yasusuke. 1987. "Modernization in Terms of Integration: The Case of Japan." In Shmuel N. Eisenstadt, ed., *Patterns of Modernity.* Vol. 2: *Beyond the West,* 65–88. New York: New York University Press.

Murphy, Peter. 1993. "Romantic Modernism and the Greek Polis." *Thesis Eleven* 34: 42–66.

Nafissi, Mohammad. 2005: "Reformation, Islam and Democracy: Evolutionary and Antievolutionary Reform in Abrahamic Religions." *Comparative Studies of South Asia, Africa and the Middle East* 25: 407–437.

Nakamura Hajime. 1975. *Parallel Developments: A Comparative History of Ideas,* ed. Ronald Burr. Tokyo and New York: Kodansha.

Narr, Karl J. 1965. "Ursprung und Frühkulturen." In *Saeculum Weltgeschichte.* Vol. 1: *Ursprung und Frühkulturen: Primäre Zentren der Hochkultur; Weltgeschichtliche Berührungszonen,* ed. Herbert Franke et al., 21–235. Freiburg: Herder.

Nasr, Seyyed Hossein. 2002. *The Heart of Islam: Enduring Values for Humanity.* San Francisco: HarperSanFrancisco.

Nelson, Benjamin. 1986. "Einleitung." In Benjamin Nelson, *Der Ursprung der Moderne: Vergleichende Studien zum Zivilisationsprozeß,* i–xvi. Frankfurt am Main: Suhrkamp. English: "On the Origins of Modernity: The Author's Point of View." In Benjamin Nelson, *On the Roads to Modernity: Conscience, Science and Civilizations,* ed. Toby E. Huff, 3–14. Totowa: Rowman & Littlefield, 1981.

Neville, Robert C. 1989. "Value, Courage and Leadership." *Review of Metaphysics* 43: 3–26.

———. 1991. "On the Buddha's Answer to the Silence of God." *Philosophy East and West* 41: 557–570.

———. 1996. *The Truth of Broken Symbols.* Albany: State University of New York Press.

———. 2002. *Religion in Late Modernity*. Albany: State University of New York Press.

———. 2006. *On the Scope and Truth of Theology: Theology as Symbolic Engagement*. New York: T & T Clark.

———. 2009. *Realism in Religion: A Pragmatist's Perspective*. Albany: State University of New York Press.

Niedenzu, Heinz-Jürgen. 2006. "Macht und Kultur: Das Modell der Zivilisationsdynamik von Shmuel N. Eisenstadt." *Erwägen, Wissen, Ethik* 17: 54–56.

Nielsen, Donald A. 2001. "Rationalization, Transformations of Consciousness and Intercivilizational Encounters: Reflections on Benjamin Nelson's Sociology of Civilizations." *International Sociology* 16: 406–420. Reprinted in Saïd Amir Arjomand and Edward A. Tiryakian, eds., *Rethinking Civilizational Analysis*, 119–131. London: Sage Publications, 2004.

Nikiprowetzky, Valentin. 1975. "Ethical Monotheism." *Daedalus* 104, no. 2 (Wisdom, Revelation and Doubt: Perspectives on the First Millennium B.C.): 69–89.

Noetzel, Thomas. 1999. *Authentizität als politisches Problem: Ein Beitrag zur Theoriegeschichte der Legitimation politischer Ordnung*. Berlin: Akademie Verlag.

Obeyesekere, Gananath. 1992. "Buddhismus: Die Begegnung einer Achsenzeitreligion mit dem Modernismus." In Shmuel N. Eisenstadt, ed., *Kulturen der Achsenzeit II: Ihre institutionelle und kulturelle Dynamik*. Part 3: *Buddhismus, Islam, Altägypten, westliche Kultur*, 101–150. Frankfurt am Main: Suhrkamp.

———. 2002. *Imagining Karma: Ethical Transformation in Amerindian, Buddhist and Greek Rebirth*. Berkeley: University of California Press.

O'Donovan, Leo J., SJ. 1971. "Evolution under the Sign of the Cross." *Theological Studies* 32: 602–626.

O'Hear, Anthony. 1992. "The real or the Real? Chardin or Rothko?" In Michael McGhee, ed., *Philosophy, Religion and the Spiritual Life*, 47–58. Cambridge: Cambridge University Press. Reprinted in Paul J. Griffiths and Charles Taliaferro, eds., *Philosophy of Religion: An Anthology*, 523–529. Malden: Blackwell.

Oliver, Harold H. 2003. "Jaspers on Jesus of Nazareth." In Joseph W. Koterski and Raymond J. Langley, eds., *Karl Jaspers on Philosophy of History and History of Philosophy*, 99–111. Amherst: Humanity Books.

Olson, Alan M. 1993. "Hegel and Jaspers on the Comparative Philosophy of Religion." In Leonard H. Ehrlich and Richard Wisser, eds., *Karl Jaspers: Philosopher among Philosophers / Karl Jaspers: Philosoph unter Philosophen*, 41–56. Amsterdam: Rodopi / Würzburg: Königshausen & Neumann.

Opitz, Peter J. 1968. "Einleitung." In Peter J. Opitz, ed., *Chinesisches Altertum und konfuzianische Klassik: Politisches Denken in China von der Chou-Zeit bis zum Han-Reich*, 7–15. Munich: List.

———. 2000. *Der Weg des Himmels: Zum Geist und zur Gestalt des politischen Denkens im klassischen China*. Munich: Fink.

Oppenheim, A. Leo. 1975. "The Position of the Intellectual in Mesopotamian Society." *Daedalus* 104, no. 2 (Wisdom, Revelation and Doubt: Perspectives on the First Millennium B.C.): 37–46.
Orihara Hiroshi. 1999. "Emile Durkheim und Max Weber." In Wolfgang J. Mommsen and Wolfgang Schwentker, eds., *Max Weber und das moderne Japan*, 335–438. Göttingen: Vandenhoeck & Ruprecht.
Örnek, Yusuf. 1988. "Politik und Freiheit." In Leonard H. Ehrlich and Richard Wisser, eds., *Karl Jaspers Today: Philosophy at the Threshold of the Future*, 257–273. Washington, DC: University Press of America.
Osterhammel, Jürgen. 2001. *Geschichtswissenschaft jenseits des Nationalstaats: Studien zu Beziehungsgeschichte und Zivilisationsvergleich.* Göttingen: Vandenhoeck & Ruprecht.
Ostrovsky, Max. 2007. *Y: The Hyperbola of the World Order.* Lanham: University Press of America.
Ott, Heinrich. 1953. "Neuere Publikationen zum Problem von Geschichte und Geschichtlichkeit." *Theologische Rundschau* 21: 63–96.
Ownby, David. 1999. "Chinese Millenarian Traditions: The Formative Age." *American Historical Review* 104: 1513–1530.
Pacho, Julián. 2010. "The Universe as Cosmos: On the Ontology of the Greek World-Image." In Hans Ulrich Vogel and Günter Dux, eds., *Concepts of Nature: A Chinese-European Cross-Cultural Perspective,* 136–160. Leiden: Brill.
Paek Seung-kyun. 1975. "Geschichte und Geschichtlichkeit: Eine Untersuchung zum Geschichtsdenken in der Philosophie von Karl Jaspers." Ph.D. diss., University of Tübingen.
Pajin, Dushan. 1987. "The Legitimacy of the Term 'Philosophy' in an Asian Context: The Beginnings of Indian Philosophy." *Journal of Indian Philosophy* 15: 349–362.
Panikkar, Raimon. 1989. *The Silence of God: The Answer of the Buddha.* Maryknoll: Orbis Books.
Papadopoullos, Theodore. 1975. "Anthropological Criteria for a Notion of Progress." *Diogenes* 23: 32–56.
Parkes, Henry Bamford. 1960. *Gods and Men: The Origins of Western Culture.* London: Routledge & Kegan Paul.
Patterson, Robert L. 1971. "The Future of Religion." *International Journal for Philosophy of Religion* 2: 65–77.
Paul, Lothar. 1978. *Gesetze der Geschichte: Geschichtslogische Rekonstruktionen zur Ortsbestimmung der Gegenwart.* Weinheim: Beltz.
Peach, Filiz. 2006. "Phenomenology, History and Historicity in Karl Jaspers' Philosophy." In Anna-Teresa Tymieniecka, ed., *Logos of Phenomenology and Phenomenology of the Logos,* Book III: *Logos of History—Logos of Life: Historicity, Time, Nature, Communication, Consciousness, Alterity, Culture,* 45–64. Dordrecht: Springer.

Peiser, Benny Josef. 1993. *Das Dunkle Zeitalter Olympias: Kritische Untersuchung der historischen, archäologischen und naturgeschichtlichen Probleme der griechischen Achsenzeit am Beispiel der antiken Olympischen Spiele*. Frankfurt am Main: Lang.

Pepper, George B. 1991. "Die Relevanz von Jaspers' Achsenzeit für interkulturelle Studien." In Kurt Salamun, ed., *Karl Jaspers: Zur Aktualität seines Denkens*, 70–85. Munich: Piper.

Peukert, Helmut. 2004. "Erziehungswissenschaft—Religionswissenschaft—Theologie—Religionspädagogik: Eine spannungsgeladene Konstellation unter den Herausforderungen einer geschichtlich neuartigen Situation." In Engelbert Groß, ed., *Erziehungswissenschaft, Religion und Religionspädagogik*, 51–91. Münster: LIT.

Pfluger, Carl. 1995. "Progress, Irony and Human Sacrifice." *Hudson Review* 48: 67–92.

Phillips, Andrew. 2011. *War, Religion and Empire: The Transformation of International Orders*. Cambridge: Cambridge University Press.

Pitz, Ernst. 2001. "Nachwort: Über eine Möglichkeit, vergleichend europäische Geschichte zu schreiben." In Ernst Pitz, *Die griechisch-römische Ökumene und die drei Kulturen des Mittelalters: Geschichte des mediterranen Weltteils zwischen Atlantik und Indischem Ozean 270–812*, 521–544. Berlin: Akademie Verlag.

Plaks, Andrew. 2002. "Means and Means: A Comparative Reading of Aristotle's Ethics and the Zhongyong." In Steven Shankman and Stephen W. Durrant, eds., *Early China / Ancient Greece: Thinking through Comparisons*, 187–206. Albany: State University of New York Press.

Plaut, W. Gunther. 1963. "The Emergence of Neo-Biblical Man." *Religious Education* 58: 160–165.

Plott, John C. 1963. *Global History of Philosophy*. Vol. 1: *The Axial Age*. Delhi: Motilal Banarsidass.

Pocock, J. G. A. 1997. "Enthusiasm—The Antiself of Enlightenment." *Huntington Library Quarterly* 60 (Enthusiasm and Enlightenment in Europe, 1650–1850): 7–28.

———. 2005. *Barbarism and Religion*. Vol. 4: *Barbarians, Savages and Empires*. Cambridge: Cambridge University Press.

Pollock, Sheldon. 2004. "The Transformation of Culture-Power in Indo-Europe, 1000–1300." In Johann P. Arnason and Björn Wittrock, eds., *Eurasian Transformations, Tenth to Thirteenth Centuries: Crystallizations, Divergences, Renaissances*, 247–278. Leiden: Brill.

———. 2005. "Axialism and Empire." In Johann P. Arnason, Shmuel N. Eisenstadt, and Björn Wittrock, eds., *Axial Civilizations and World History*, 397–450. Leiden: Brill.

———. 2006. *The Language of the Gods in the World of Men: Sanskrit, Culture and Power in Premodern India*. Berkeley: University of California Press.

Pot, Johan Hendrik Jacob van der. 1999. *Sinndeutung und Periodisierung der Geschichte: Eine systematische Übersicht der Theorien und Auffassungen.* Leiden: Brill.

Preyer, Gerhard. 1998. "Einleitung." In Gerhard Preyer, ed., *Strukturelle Evolution und das Weltsystem: Theorien, Sozialstruktur und evolutionäre Entwicklungen*, 9–26. Frankfurt am Main: Suhrkamp.

———. 2011. *Zur Aktualität von Shmuel N. Eisenstadt: Einleitung in sein Werk.* Wiesbaden: Verlag für Sozialwissenschaften.

Puett, Michael J. 2002. *To Become a God: Cosmology, Sacrifice and Self-Divinization in Early China.* Cambridge, MA: Harvard University Asia Center.

Pyysiäinen, Ilkka. 1999. "Holy Book—A Treasury of the Incomprehensible: The Invention of Writing and Religious Cognition." *Numen* 46: 269–290.

Raaflaub, Kurt A. 2005. "Polis, 'The Political,' and Political Thought: New Departures in Ancient Greece, c. 800–500 BCE." In Johann P. Arnason, Shmuel N. Eisenstadt, and Björn Wittrock, eds., *Axial Civilizations and World History*, 253–283. Leiden: Brill.

———. 2011. "From City-State to Empire: Rome in Comparative Perspective." In Johann P. Arnason and Kurt A. Raaflaub, eds., *The Roman Empire in Context: Historical and Comparative Perspectives*, 39–66. Malden: Wiley-Blackwell.

Rahimi, Babak. 2004. "Between Chieftaincy and Knighthood: A Comparative Study of Ottoman and Safavid Origins." *Thesis Eleven* 76: 85–102.

———. 2006. "The Middle Period: Islamic Axiality in the Age of Afro-Eurasian Transcultural Hybridity." In Johann P. Arnason, Armando Salvatore, and Georg Stauth, eds., *Islam in Process: Historical and Civilizational Perspectives*, 48–67. Bielefeld: Transcript.

Ramanujan, A. K. 1989. "Where Mirrors Are Windows: Toward an Anthology of Reflections." *History of Religions* 28: 187–216.

Raubitschek, Antony E. 1950. "Toynbee and the Classics." *The Classical Weekly* 43, no. 7: 99–104.

Ray, Himanshu Prabha. 2006. "The Axial Age in Asia: Archaeology of Buddhism 500 B.C.–A.D. 500." In Miriam T. Stark, ed., *Archaeology of Asia*, 303–323. Malden: Blackwell.

Redner, Harry. 2001. *Ethical Life: The Past and Present of Ethical Cultures.* Lanham: Rowman & Littlefield.

Reisch, George A. 1991. "Chaos, History and Narrative." *History and Theory* 30: 1–20.

Retsö, Jan. 2005. "Arabia and the Heritage of the Axial Age." In Johann P. Arnason, Shmuel N. Eisenstadt, and Björn Wittrock, eds., *Axial Civilizations and World History*, 337–358. Leiden: Brill.

Riesebrodt, Martin. 2001. "Ethische und exemplarische Prophetie." In Hans G. Kippenberg and Martin Riesebrodt, eds., *Max Webers "Religionssystematik,"* 193–208. Tübingen: Mohr Siebeck.

Rigali, Norbert. 1968. *Die Selbstkonstitution der Geschichte im Denken von Karl Jaspers.* Meisenheim am Glan: Hain.

———. 1970. "A New Axis: Karl Jaspers' Philosophy of History." *International Philosophical Quarterly* 10: 441–457.

Robbins, Joel. 2003. "What Is a Christian? Notes toward an Anthropology of Christianity." *Religion* 33: 191–199.

———. 2009. "Is the *Trans-* in *Transnational* the *Trans-* in *Transcendent?*" In Thomas J. Csordas, ed., *Transnational Transcendence: Essays on Religion and Globalization,* 55–71. Berkeley: University of California Press.

Röd, Wolfgang, Heinrich Schmidinger, and Rainer Thurnher. 2002. *Die Philosophie des ausgehenden 19. und des 20. Jahrhunderts III: Lebensphilosophie und Existenzphilosophie.* Munich: C. H. Beck.

Roetz, Heiner. 1992. *Die chinesische Ethik der Achsenzeit: Eine Rekonstruktion unter dem Aspekt des Durchbruchs zu postkonventionellem Denken.* Frankfurt am Main: Suhrkamp. English: *Confucian Ethics of the Axial Age: A Reconstruction under the Aspect of the Breakthrough toward Postconventional Thinking.* Albany: State University of New York Press, 1993.

———. 2000. "Moralischer Fortschritt in Griechenland und China: Ein Vergleich der achsenzeitlichen Entwicklung." In Oskar Fahr, Wolfgang Ommerborn, and Konrad Wegmann, eds., *Politisches Denken Chinas in alter und neuer Zeit,* 123–151. Münster: LIT.

———. 2006. *Konfuzius.* Rev. ed. Munich: C. H. Beck.

———. 2008. "Confucianism between Tradition and Modernity, Religion and Secularization: Questions to Tu Weiming." *Dao* 7: 367–380.

———. 2010. "On Nature and Culture in Zhou China." In Hans Ulrich Vogel and Günter Dux, eds., *Concepts of Nature: A Chinese-European Cross-Cultural Perspective,* 198–220. Leiden: Brill.

Rosa, Susan, and Dale Van Kley. 1998. "Religion and the Historical Discipline: A Reply to Mack Holt and Henry Heller." *French Historical Studies* 21: 611–629.

Rothacker, Erich. 1950. "Karl Jaspers' Geschichtsphilosophie." *Deutsche Vierteljahrsschrift für Literaturwissenschaft und Geistesgeschichte* 24: 402–404.

Rothermund, Dietmar. 1994. *Geschichte als Prozeß und Aussage: Eine Einführung in Theorien des historischen Wandels und der Geschichtsschreibung.* Munich: Oldenbourg.

Rothert, Hans-Joachim. 1963. *Gewißheit und Vergewisserung als theologisches Problem: Eine systematisch-theologische Untersuchung.* Göttingen: Vandenhoeck & Ruprecht.

Rowlands, Michael. 1998. "Conceptualising the European Bronze and Early Iron Age." In Kristian Kristiansen and Michael Rowlands, *Social Transformations in Archaeology: Global and Local Perspectives,* 49–69. London: Routledge.

Rue, Loyal D. 2000. *Everybody's Story: Wising Up to the Epic of Evolution.* Albany: State University of New York Press.

Rüegg, Walter. 1992. "Humanistische Elitenbildung im antiken Rom und in der europäischen Renaissance." In Shmuel N. Eisenstadt, ed., *Kulturen der Achsenzeit II: Ihre institutionelle und kulturelle Dynamik.* Part 3: *Buddhismus, Islam, Altägypten, westliche Kultur,* 358–384. Frankfurt am Main: Suhrkamp.

Runciman, W. G. 2005. "The Exception That Proves the Rule? Rome in the Axial Age." In Eliezer Ben-Rafael and Yitzhak Sternberg, eds., *Comparing Modernities: Pluralism versus Homogenity; Essays in Homage to Shmuel N. Eisenstadt,* 125–140. Leiden: Brill.

Rundell, John, and Stephen Mennell. 1998. "Introduction: Civilization, Culture and the Human Self-Image." In Stephen Mennell and John Rundell, eds., *Classical Readings in Culture and Civilization,* 1–36. London: Routledge.

Rupp, A. 1970. "Gedanken zu einer religionsgeschichtlichen Anthropologie." *Numen* 17: 60–82.

Rüsen, Jörn. 1989. *Lebendige Geschichte: Grundzüge einer Historik III: Formen und Funktionen des historischen Wissens.* Göttingen: Vandenhoeck & Ruprecht.

Saburō Ichii. 1974. "On Tradition and Innovation." *Japan Quarterly* 21: 273–283.

Salamun, Kurt. 1985. *Karl Jaspers.* Munich: C. H. Beck.

———. 1996. "The Concept of Liberality in Jaspers's Philosophy and the Idea of the University." In Gregory J. Walters, ed., *The Tasks of Truth: Essays on Karl Jaspers's Idea of the University,* 39–53. Frankfurt am Main: Lang.

Salamun, Kurt, and Gregory J. Walters, eds. 2008. *Karl Jaspers's Philosophy: Expositions and Interpretations.* Amherst: Humanity Books.

Saler, Benson. 1993. *Conceptualizing Religion: Immanent Anthropologists, Transcendent Natives and Unbounded Categories.* Leiden: Brill.

Salkever, Stephen G., and Michael Nylan. 1994. "Comparative Political Philosophy and Liberal Education: 'Looking for Friends in History.'" *Political Science and Politics* 27: 238–247.

Salvatore, Armando. 1998. "Staging Virtue: The Disembodiment of Self-Correctness and the Making of Islam as Public Norm." In Georg Stauth, ed., *Islam—Motor or Challenge of Modernity,* 87–120. Hamburg: LIT.

———. 2006. "Beyond the Power of Power? The Public Sphere in Islamic Societies in Comparative Perspective." *Erwägen, Wissen, Ethik* 17: 66–68.

———. 2006. "Reflexivity, Praxis and 'Spirituality': Western Islam and Beyond." In Johann P. Arnason, Armando Salvatore, and Georg Stauth, eds., *Islam in Process: Historical and Civilizational Perspectives,* 279–305. Bielefeld: Transcript.

Salvatore, Armando, and Schirin Amir-Moazami. 2002. "Religiöse Diskurstraditionen: Zur Transformation des Islam in kolonialen, postkolonialen und

europäischen Öffentlichkeiten." *Berliner Journal für Soziologie* 12, no. 3: 309–330.
Sanderson, Stephen K. 2000. "World Systems and Social Change in Agrarian Societies, 3000 BC to AD 1500." In Robert A. Denemark, Jonathan Friedman, Barry K. Gills, and George Modelski, eds., *World System History: The Social Science of Long-Term Change*, 185–197. London: Routledge.
———. 2008. "Adaptation, Evolution and Religion." *Religion* 38: 141–156.
Sandywell, Barry. 1996. *The Beginnings of European Theorizing: Reflexivity in the Archaic Age*. London: Routledge.
Saner, Hans. 1970. *Karl Jaspers in Selbstzeugnissen und Bilddokumenten*. Reinbek: Rowohlt.
———. 1988. "Jaspers' Idee einer kommenden Weltphilosophie." In Leonard H. Ehrlich and Richard Wisser, eds., *Karl Jaspers Today: Philosophy at the Threshold of the Future*, 75–92. Washington, DC: University Press of America.
Sarin, Indu. 2009. *The Global Vision*. Bern: Lang.
Saussy, Haun. 2001. *Great Walls of Discourse and Other Adventures in Cultural China*. Cambridge, MA: Harvard University Asia Center.
Schachermeyr, Fritz. 1960. *Griechische Geschichte: Mit besonderer Berücksichtigung der geistesgeschichtlichen und kulturmorphologischen Zusammenhänge*. Stuttgart: Kohlhammer.
Scharfstein, Ben-Ami. 1998. *A Comparative History of World Philosophy: From the Upanishads to Kant*. Albany: State University of New York Press.
Scheit, Herbert. 2000. "'Achsenzeit': Ein (fast) vergessenes Modell für eine Wendezeit." In Peter Segl, ed., *Zeitenwenden—Wendezeiten: Von der Achsenzeit bis zum Fall der Mauer*, 37–49. Dettelbach: Röll.
Scheliha, Arnulf von. 2004. *Der Islam im Kontext der christlichen Religion*. Münster: Waxmann.
Schelkshorn, Hans. 2004. "Dialogische Vernunft und die Grundlagen interkultureller Ethik: Thesen zu einer Revision der Diskursethik." In Niels Gottschalk-Mazouz, ed., *Perspektiven der Diskursethik*, 203–235. Würzburg: Königshausen & Neumann.
Schemeil, Yves. 2000. "Democracy before Democracy?" *International Political Science Review* 21: 99–120.
Scherer, Georg. 2000. "Die Idee der Achsenzeit und die europäische Philosophie." In Justus Cobet, Carl Friedrich Gethmann, and Dieter Lau, eds., *Europa: Die Gegenwärtigkeit der antiken Überlieferung*, 33–46. Aachen: Shaker.
Schiffrin, Harold Z. 1992. "Kriegsherrentum in der chinesischen Geschichtserfahrung." In Shmuel N. Eisenstadt, ed., *Kulturen der Achsenzeit II: Ihre institutionelle und kulturelle Dynamik. Part 1: China, Japan*, 108–125. Frankfurt am Main: Suhrkamp.
Schluchter, Wolfgang. 1981. "Altisraelitische religiöse Ethik und okzidentaler Rationalismus." In Wolfgang Schluchter, ed., *Max Webers Studie über das*

antike Judentum: Interpretation und Kritik, 11–77. Frankfurt am Main: Suhrkamp.

———. 1988. *Religion und Lebensführung.* Vol. 1: *Studien zu Max Webers Kultur- und Werttheorie.* Frankfurt am Main: Suhrkamp.

———. 1996. *Paradoxes of Modernity: Culture and Conduct in the Theory of Max Weber.* Stanford: Stanford University Press.

———. 2005. "Kampf der Kulturen?" In Wolfgang Schluchter, ed., *Fundamentalismus, Terrorismus, Krieg,* 25–43. Weilerswist: Velbrück Wissenschaft. Reprinted in Wolfgang Schluchter, *Handlung, Ordnung und Kultur: Studien zu einem Forschungsprogramm im Anschluss an Max Weber,* 159–172. Tübingen: Mohr Siebeck, 2005.

———. 2005. "Rationalität—das Spezifikum Europas?" In Hans Joas and Klaus Wiegandt, eds., *Die kulturellen Werte Europas,* 237–264. Frankfurt am Main: Fischer. Reprinted in Wolfgang Schluchter, *Handlung, Ordnung und Kultur: Studien zu einem Forschungsprogramm im Anschluss an Max Weber,* 139–158. Tübingen: Mohr Siebeck, 2005. English: "Rationality—A Specifically European Characteristic?" In Hans Joas and Klaus Wiegandt, eds., *The Cultural Values of Europe,* 166–186. Liverpool: Liverpool University Press, 2008.

Schmidt, Volker H. 2006. "Multiple Modernities or Varieties of Modernity?" *Current Sociology* 54: 77–97.

Schmidt-Glintzer, Helwig. 1997. *China: Vielvölkerreich und Einheitsstaat: Von den Anfängen bis heute.* Munich: C. H. Beck.

———. 2003. "Die Stellung des Menschen zur Natur in China." In Karl-Heinz Pohl and Dorothea Wippermann, eds., *Brücke zwischen Kulturen: Festschrift für Chiao Wei zum 75. Geburtstag,* 309–320. Münster: LIT.

Schmitt, Rüdiger. 2004. *Magie im Alten Testament.* Münster: Ugarit-Verlag.

Schulin, Ernst. 1974. "Einleitung." In Ernst Schulin, ed., *Universalgeschichte,* 11–56. Cologne: Kiepenheuer & Witsch.

Schulze, Reinhard. 2010. "Die Dritte Unterscheidung: Islam, Religion und Säkularität." In Walter Dietrich and Wolfgang Lienemann, eds., *Religionen—Wahrheitsansprüche—Konflikte: Theologische Perspektiven.* Zurich: Theologischer Verlag Zürich.

Schüßler, Werner. 1995. *Jaspers zur Einführung.* Hamburg: Junius.

———. 1999. *"Was uns unbedingt angeht": Studien zur Theologie und Philosophie Paul Tillichs.* Münster: LIT.

Schwaiger, Axel. 2001. *Christliche Geschichtsdeutung in der Moderne: Eine Untersuchung zum Geschichtsdenken von Juan Donoso Cortés, Ernst von Lasaulx und Vladimir Solov'ev in der Zusammenschau christlicher Historiographieentwicklung.* Berlin: Duncker & Humblot.

Schwartz, Benjamin I. 1975. "The Age of Transcendence." *Daedalus* 104, no. 2 (Wisdom, Revelation and Doubt: Perspectives on the First Millennium B.C.): 1–7.

———. 1975. "Transcendence in Ancient China." *Daedalus* 104, no. 2 (Wisdom, Revelation and Doubt: Perspectives on the First Millennium B.C.): 57–68.

———. 1985. *The World of Thought in Ancient China*. Cambridge, MA: Harvard University Press.

Schwarz, Theodor. 1973. *Sein, Mensch und Gesellschaft im Existentialismus: Mit zwei Arbeiten über Schopenhauer und Nietzsche*. Frankfurt am Main: Verlag Marxistische Blätter.

Schwinn, Thomas. 2003. "Kulturvergleich in der globalisierten Moderne." In Gert Albert, Agathe Bienfait, Steffen Sigmund, and Claus Wendt, eds., *Das Weber-Paradigma: Studien zur Weiterentwicklung von Max Webers Forschungsprogramm*, 301–327. Tübingen: Mohr Siebeck.

Seele, Katrin. 2006. *"Das bist Du!": Das "Selbst" (ātman) und das "Andere" in der Philosophie der frühen Upaniṣaden und bei Buddha*. Würzburg: Königshausen & Neumann.

Segl, Peter. 2000. "Zeitenwenden—Wendezeiten: Eine Einführung." In Peter Segl, ed., *Zeitenwenden—Wendezeiten: Von der Achsenzeit bis zum Fall der Mauer*, 1–35. Dettelbach: Röll.

Seligman, Adam B. 1988. "The Comparative Study of Utopias." *International Journal of Comparative Sociology* 29: 1–12. Reprinted in Adam Seligman, ed., *Order and Transcendence: The Role of Utopias and the Dynamics of Civilizations*, 1–12. Leiden: Brill.

———. 2000. *Modernity's Wager: Authority, the Self, and Transcendence*. Princeton: Princeton University Press.

Shaked, Shaul. 2005. "Zoroastrian Origins: Indian and Iranian Connections." In Johann P. Arnason, Shmuel N. Eisenstadt, and Björn Wittrock, eds., *Axial Civilizations and World History*, 183–200. Leiden: Brill.

Sharot, Stephen. 2001. *A Comparative Sociology of World Religions: Virtuosos, Priests, and Popular Religion*. New York: New York University Press.

Sheehan, Jonathan. 2010. "When Was Disenchantment? History and the Secular Age." In Michael Warner, Jonathan VanAntwerpen, and Craig Calhoun, eds., *Varieties of Secularism in a Secular Age*, 217–242. Cambridge, MA: Harvard University Press.

Sheridan, Daniel P. 1986. "Discerning Difference: A Taxonomy of Culture, Spirituality and Religion." *Journal of Religion* 66: 37–45.

Shichor, Yitzhak. 1992. "Konfuzianismus in einem Land: Einige Betrachtungen zur universalistischen und partikularistischen Kollektividentität in China." In Shmuel N. Eisenstadt, ed., *Kulturen der Achsenzeit II: Ihre institutionelle und kulturelle Dynamik*. Part 1: *China, Japan*, 91–107. Frankfurt am Main: Suhrkamp.

Shillony, Ben-Ami. 1992. "Das Fehlen fremder Besatzung als zentraler Faktor für die Ausgestaltung der japanischen Kultur." In Shmuel N. Eisenstadt, ed.,

Kulturen der Achsenzeit II: Ihre institutionelle und kulturelle Dynamik. Part 1: *China, Japan,* 263–278. Frankfurt am Main: Suhrkamp.
Shils, Edward. 1986. "Some Observations on the Place of Intellectuals in Max Weber's Sociology, with Special Reference to Hinduism." In Shmuel N. Eisenstadt, ed., *The Origins and Diversity of Axial Age Civilizations,* 427–452. Albany: State University of New York Press.
Shlain, Leonard. 1998. *The Alphabet versus the Goddess: The Conflict between Word and Image.* New York: Viking.
Shulman, David. 1986. "Aśvatthāman and Bṛhannaḍā: Brahmin and Kingly Paradigms in the Sanskrit Epic." In Shmuel N. Eisenstadt, ed., *The Origins and Diversity of Axial Age Civilizations,* 407–426. Albany: State University of New York Press.
———. 1986. "Terror of Symbols and Symbols of Terror: Notes on the Myth of Śiva as Sthāṇu." *History of Religions* 26: 101–124.
———. 1992. "Die Dynamik der Sektenbildung im mittelalterlichen Südindien." In Shmuel N. Eisenstadt, ed., *Kulturen der Achsenzeit II: Ihre institutionelle und kulturelle Dynamik.* Part 2: *Indien,* 102–128. Frankfurt am Main: Suhrkamp.
———. 1992. "Vom Zeichen zum Symbol im frühen Śaiva-Mythos." In Shmuel N. Eisenstadt, ed., *Kulturen der Achsenzeit II: Ihre institutionelle und kulturelle Dynamik.* Part 2: *Indien,* 189–222. Frankfurt am Main: Suhrkamp.
———. 2005. "Axial Grammar." In Johann P. Arnason, Shmuel N. Eisenstadt, and Björn Wittrock, eds., *Axial Civilizations and World History,* 369–395. Leiden: Brill.
Silber, Ilana Friedrich. 1985. "'Opting Out' in Theravada Buddhism and Medieval Christianity: A Comparative Study of Monasticism as Alternative Structure." *Religion* 15: 251–277.
———. 1988. "Soteriology and Knowledge: Some Issues in the Cultural Structuration of Symbolic Domains." In Shmuel N. Eisenstadt and Ilana Friedrich Silber, eds., *Cultural Traditions and Worlds of Knowledge: Explorations in the Sociology of Knowledge,* 225–238. Greenwich: JAI Press.
———. 1995. *Virtuosity, Charisma and Social Order: A Comparative Sociological Study of Monasticism in Theravada Buddhism and Medieval Catholicism.* Cambridge: Cambridge University Press.
———. 2011. "Deciphering Transcendence and the Open Code of Modernity: S. N. Eisenstadt's Comparative Hermeneutics of Civilizations." *Journal of Classical Sociology* 11, no. 3: 269–280.
Simon, Gabriel. 1965. *Die Achse der Weltgeschichte nach Karl Jaspers.* Rome: Libreria Editrice dell'Università Gregoriana.
Singer, Gerwulf. 2004. "Chancen für persönliche Autonomie: Ideengeschichtliche Überlegungen zu Max Webers Begriff der innerweltlichen Askese." In Horst

Pöttker and Thomas Meyer, eds., *Kritische Empirie: Lebenschancen in den Sozialwissenschaften. Festschrift für Rainer Geißler,* 309–330. Wiesbaden: Verlag für Sozialwissenschaften.

Sivers, Peter von. 2000. "Zur Achsenzeit im Mittleren Osten (600–500 v. Chr.)." In Wolfgang Leidhold, ed., *Politik und Politeia: Formen und Probleme politischer Ordnung. Festgabe für Jürgen Gebhardt zum 65. Geburtstag,* 159–173. Würzburg: Königshausen & Neumann.

———. 2005. "No Time to Rest: Hurtling from One Modernity to the Next." In Gabriele von Sivers and Ulrich Diehl, eds., *Wege zur politischen Philosophie. Festschrift für Martin Sattler,* 135–153. Würzburg: Königshausen & Neumann.

Smith, Mark S. 2001. *The Origins of Biblical Monotheism: Israel's Polytheistic Background and the Ugaritic Texts.* New York: Oxford University Press.

———. 2002. "Ugaritic Studies and Israelite Religion: A Retrospective View." *Near Eastern Archaeology* 65: 17–29.

Smith, Steven G. 2005. *Appeal and Attitude: Prospects for Ultimate Meaning.* Bloomington: Indiana University Press.

Smith, Suzanne. 2011. "Partial Transcendence, Religious Pluralism, and the Question of Love." *Harvard Theological Review* 104: 1–32.

Snell, Daniel C. 1997. *Life in the Ancient Near East, 3100–332 B.C.E.* New Haven: Yale University Press.

Söder, Hans Peter. 2007. "From Universal History to Globalism: What Are and for What Purposes Do We Study European Ideas?" *History of European Ideas* 33: 72–86.

Sommer, Michael. 2001. "Der Untergang des hethitischen Reiches: Anatolien und der östliche Mittelmeerraum um 1200 v. Chr." *Saeculum* 52, no. 2: 157–176.

Spinner, Helmut F. 1978. *Popper und die Politik: Rekonstruktion und Kritik der Sozial-, Polit- und Geschichtsphilosophie des kritischen Rationalismus.* Berlin: Dietz.

Spohn, Willfried. 2001. "Eisenstadt on Civilizations and Multiple Modernity." *European Journal of Social Theory* 4: 499–508.

———. 2003. "Multiple Modernity, Nationalism and Religion: A Global Perspective." *Current Sociology* 51: 265–286. Reprinted in Ulrike Schuerkens, ed., *Global Forces and Local Life-Worlds: Social Transformations,* 67–87. London: Sage Publications.

———. 2006. "Globale, multiple und verwobene Modernen: Perspektiven der historisch-vergleichenden Soziologie." In Thomas Schwinn, ed., *Die Vielfalt und Einheit der Moderne: Kultur- und strukturvergleichende Analysen,* 101–128. Wiesbaden: Verlag für Sozialwissenschaften.

———. 2010. "Political Sociology: Between Civilizations and Modernities: A Multiple Modernities Perspective." *European Journal of Social Theory* 13: 49–66.

———. 2011. "An Appraisal of Shmuel Noah Eisenstadt's Global Historical Sociology." *Journal of Classical Sociology* 11, no. 3: 281-301.
———. 2011. "World History, Civilizational Analysis and Historical Sociology: Interpretations of Non-Western Civilizations in the Work of Johann Arnason." *European Journal of Social Theory* 14: 23-39.
Staal, Frits. 1965. "Euclid and Pāṇini." *Philosophy East and West* 15: 99-116.
———. 1995. "The Sanskrit of Science." *Journal of Indian Philosophy* 23: 73-127.
Stackhouse, Max L., and Stephen E. Healey. 1996. "Religion and Human Rights: A Theological Apologetic." In John Witte Jr. and Johan D. van der Vyver, eds., *Religious Human Rights in Global Perspective: Religious Perspectives*, 485-516. The Hague: Nijhoff Publishers.
Stark, Miriam T. 2006. "Contextualizing an Archaeology of Asia." In Miriam T. Stark, ed., *Archaeology of Asia*, 3-13. Malden: Blackwell.
Stark, Rodney. 2007. *Discovering God: The Origins of the Great Religions and the Evolution of Belief*. New York: HarperOne.
Stauth, Georg. 1998. "Geschichte, Modernität, Fundamentalismus: Eisenstadts zivilisationstheoretischer Ansatz zum vergleichenden Studium moderner fundamentalistischer Bewegungen." In Shmuel N. Eisenstadt, *Die Antinomien der Moderne: Die jakobinischen Grundzüge der Moderne und des Fundamentalismus; Heterodoxien, Utopismus und Jakobinismus in der Konstitution fundamentalistischer Bewegungen*, 131-152. Frankfurt am Main: Suhrkamp.
———. 1998. "Introduction." In Georg Stauth, ed., *Islam—Motor or Challenge of Modernity*, 5-13. Hamburg: LIT.
———. 2006. "'Abdallah b. Salam: Egypt, Late Antiquity and Islamic Sainthood." In Johann P. Arnason, Armando Salvatore, and Georg Stauth, eds., *Islam in Process: Historical and Civilizational Perspectives*, 158-189. Bielefeld: Transcript.
———. 2010. *Herausforderung Ägypten: Religion und Authentizität in der globalen Moderne*. Bielefeld: Transcript.
Stavrianos, Leften Stavros. 1997. *Lifelines from Our Past: A New World History*. Rev. ed. Armonk: M. E. Sharpe.
Stenger, Georg. 1998. "Structures of World-Oriented Encounter: The World Concept and the Intercultural Basic Situation." *Topoi* 17: 37-47.
Stephens, Lester D. 1974. *Probing the Past: A Guide to the Study and Teaching of History*. Boston: Allyn & Bacon.
Stikker, Allerd. 1990. "Evolution and Ecology." *Futures* 22: 167-180.
Stone, Lawrence. 1992. "Der Wandel der Werte in England 1660 bis 1770: Säkularismus, Rationalismus und Individualismus." In Shmuel N. Eisenstadt, ed., *Kulturen der Achsenzeit II: Ihre institutionelle und kulturelle Dynamik*. Part 3: *Buddhismus, Islam, Altägypten, westliche Kultur*, 341-357. Frankfurt am Main: Suhrkamp.

Stone, Michael E. 1985. "Three Transformations in Judaism—Scripture, History and Redemption." *Numen* 32: 218–235.

———. 1986. "Eschatology, Remythologization and Cosmic Aporia." In Shmuel N. Eisenstadt, ed., *The Origins and Diversity of Axial Age Civilizations*, 241–251. Albany: State University of New York Press.

———. 2011. *Ancient Judaism: New Visions and Views*. Grand Rapids: Eerdmans.

Strathern, Alan. 2007. "Transcendentalist Intransigence: Why Rulers Rejected Monotheism in Early Modern Southeast Asia and Beyond." *Comparative Studies in Society and History* 49, no. 2: 358–383.

Strickrodt, Georg. 1979. *Zeitalterprägung und Standortbestimmung des personalen und des politischen Bewußtseins*. Wiesbaden: Steiner.

Stroumsa, Gedaliahu G. 1986. "Old Wine and New Bottles: On Patristic Soteriology and Rabbinic Judaism." In Shmuel N. Eisenstadt, ed., *The Origins and Diversity of Axial Age Civilizations*, 252–260. Albany: State University of New York Press.

———. 1990. "Caro salutis cardo: Shaping the Person in Early Christian Thought." *History of Religions* 30: 25–50.

———. 2005. "Cultural Memory in Early Christianity: Clement of Alexandria and the History of Religions." In Johann P. Arnason, Shmuel N. Eisenstadt, and Björn Wittrock, eds., *Axial Civilizations and World History*, 295–317. Leiden: Brill.

Super, John C., and Briane K. Turley. 2006. *Religion in World History: The Persistence of Imperial Communion*. New York: Routledge.

Swabey, Marie C. 1958. "Toynbee and the Limits of Religious Tolerance." *Journal of Philosophy* 55: 1029–1042.

Swearer, Donald K. 1994. "Fundamentalistic Movements in Theravada Buddhism." In Martin E. Marty and R. Scott Appleby, eds., *Fundamentalisms Observed*, 628–690. Chicago: University of Chicago Press.

Swidler, Leonard. 1997. "The Age of Global Dialogue." In Steven Chase, ed., *Doors of Understanding: Conversations in Global Spirituality in Honor of Ewert Cousins*, 1–25. Quincy: Franciscan Press.

Szakolczai, Arpad. 2000. *Reflexive Historical Sociology*. London: Routledge.

———. 2001. "Civilization and Its Sources." *International Sociology* 16: 369–386. Reprinted in Saïd Amir Arjomand and Edward A. Tiryakian, eds., *Rethinking Civilizational Analysis*, 87–102. London: Sage Publications, 2004.

———. 2003. *The Genesis of Modernity*. London: Routledge.

———. 2005. "Between Tradition and Christianity: The Axial Age in the Perspective of Béla Hamvas." In Johann P. Arnason, Shmuel N. Eisenstadt, and Björn Wittrock, eds., *Axial Civilizations and World History*, 107–121. Leiden: Brill.

———. 2005. "Moving beyond the Sophists: Intellectuals in East Central Europe and the Return of Transcendence." *European Journal of Social Theory* 8: 417–433.

———. 2006. "Global Ages, Ecumenic Empires and Prophetic Religions." In Johann P. Arnason, Armando Salvatore, and Georg Stauth, eds., *Islam in Process: Historical and Civilizational Perspectives,* 258–278. Bielefeld: Transcript.

———. 2006. "Identity Formation in World Religions: A Comparative Analysis of Christianity and Islam." In Johann P. Arnason, Armando Salvatore, and Georg Stauth, eds., *Islam in Process: Historical and Civilizational Perspectives,* 68–94. Bielefeld: Transcript.

———. 2006. "World-Rejections and World-Conquests: The Spiralling Dynamics of War and Peace." In Tilo Schabert and Matthias Riedl, eds., *Die Menschen im Krieg, im Frieden mit der Natur / Humans at War, at Peace with Nature,* 147–164. Würzburg: Königshausen & Neumann.

———. 2007. "Image-Magic in *A Midsummer Night's Dream*: Power and Modernity from Weber to Shakespeare." *History of the Human Sciences* 20: 1–26.

———. 2007. "In Pursuit of the 'Good European' Identity: From Nietzsche's Dionysos to Minoan Crete." *Theory, Culture & Society* 24: 47–76.

Szakolczai, Arpad, and Laszlo Füstös. 1998. "Value Systems in Axial Moments: A Comparative Analysis of 24 European Countries." *European Sociological Review* 14: 211–229.

Tadmor, Hayim. 1986. "Monarchy and the Elite in Assyria and Babylonia: The Question of Royal Accountability." In Shmuel N. Eisenstadt, ed., *The Origins and Diversity of Axial Age Civilizations,* 203–224. Albany: State University of New York Press.

Tambiah, Stanley J. 1986. "The Reflexive and Institutional Achievements of Early Buddhism." In Shmuel N. Eisenstadt, ed., *The Origins and Diversity of Axial Age Civilizations,* 453–471. Albany: State University of New York Press.

Tarnas, Richard. 2006. *Cosmos and Psyche: Intimations of a New World View.* New York: Viking.

Taylor, Charles. 2004. "The Great Disembedding." In Charles Taylor, *Modern Social Imaginaries,* 49–67. Durham: Duke University Press.

———. 2004. "Notes on the Sources of Violence: Perennial and Modern." In James L. Heft, ed., *Beyond Violence: Religious Sources of Social Transformation in Judaism, Christianity, Islam,* 15–42. New York: Fordham University Press. Reprinted in Charles Taylor, *Dilemmas and Connections: Selected Essays,* 188–213. Cambridge, MA: Harvard University Press, 2010.

———. 2004. "Die Religion und die Identitätskämpfe der Moderne." In Ludwig Ammann and Nilüfer Göle, eds., *Islam in Sicht: Der Auftritt von Muslimen im öffentlichen Raum,* 342–378. Bielefeld: Transcript.

———. 2007. *A Secular Age.* Cambridge, MA: The Belknap Press of Harvard University Press.

———. 2008. "The Future of the Religious Past." In Hent de Vries, ed., *Religion: Beyond a Concept,* 178–244. New York: Fordham University Press. Reprinted in Charles Taylor, *Dilemmas and Connections: Selected Essays*, 214–286. Cambridge, MA: Harvard University Press, 2010.

———. 2010. "What Was the Axial Revolution?" In Charles Taylor, *Dilemmas and Connections: Selected Essays*, 367–379. Cambridge, MA: Harvard University Press.

———. 2011. "Western Secularity." In Craig Calhoun, Mark Juergensmeyer, and Jonathan VanAntwerpen, eds., *Rethinking Secularism*, 31–53. Oxford: Oxford University Press.

Taylor, Romeyn. 1989. "Chinese Hierarchy in Comparative Perspective." *Journal of Asian Studies* 48: 490–511.

Teoharova, Genoveva. 2005. *Karl Jaspers' Philosophie auf dem Weg zur Weltphilosophie*. Würzburg: Königshausen & Neumann.

Thapar, Romila. 1975. "Ethics, Religion and Social Protest in the First Millennium B.C. in Northern India." *Daedalus* 104, no. 2 (Wisdom, Revelation and Doubt: Perspectives on the First Millennium B.C.): 119–132. Reprinted in Romila Thapar, *Ancient Indian Social History: Some Interpretations*, 40–62. New Delhi: Orient Longman, 1978.

———. 1994. "Sacrifice, Surplus and the Soul." *History of Religions* 33: 305–324.

Thomassen, Bjørn. 2010. "Anthropology, Multiple Modernities and the Axial Age Debate." *Anthropological Theory* 10, no. 4: 321–342.

Thompson, William Irwin. 2004. *Self and Society: Studies in the Evolution of Consciousness*. Exeter: Imprint Academic.

Thompson, William M. 1976. "The Risen Christ, Transcultural Consciousness and the Encounter of the World Religions." *Theological Studies* 37: 381–409.

Thurman, Robert A. F. 1983. "Beyond Buddhism and Christianity." *Buddhist-Christian Studies* 3: 21–35.

———. 1996. "Human Rights and Human Responsibilities: Buddhist Views on Individualism and Altruism." In Irene Bloom, J. Paul Martin, and Wayne L. Proudfoot, eds., *Religious Diversity and Human Rights*, 87–113. New York: Columbia University Press.

Timmermann, Johannes. 1958. "Auf dem Wege zum Geschichtsbild." In Günter Stachel and Paul Ascher, eds., *Weltall, Weltbild, Weltanschauung: Ein Bildungsbuch*, 295–351. Würzburg: Echter.

Tinker, Hugh. 1969. "Continuity and Change in Asian Societies." *Modern Asian Studies* 3: 97–116.

Tiryakian, Edward A. 1992. "From Modernization to Globalization." *Journal for the Scientific Study of Religion* 31: 304–310.

———. 1996. "Three Metacultures of Modernity: Christian, Gnostic, Chthonic." *Theory, Culture & Society* 13: 99–118.

———. 2001. "Introduction: The Civilization of Modernity and the Modernity of Civilizations." *International Sociology* 16: 277–292. Reprinted as "Civilizational Analysis: Renovating the Sociological Tradition." In Saïd Amir Arjo-

mand and Edward A. Tiryakian, eds., *Rethinking Civilizational Analysis,* 30–47. London: Sage Publications, 2004.
———. 2005. "Comparative Analysis of the Civilization of Modernity: 1203 and 2003." In Eliezer Ben-Rafael and Yitzhak Sternberg, eds., *Comparing Modernities: Pluralism versus Homogenity; Essays in Homage to Shmuel N. Eisenstadt,* 287–308. Leiden: Brill.
———. 2011. "A Sociological Odyssey: The Comparative Voyage of S. N. Eisenstadt." *Journal of Classical Sociology* 11, no. 3: 241–250.
Tomberg, Friedrich. 2003. *Habermas und der Marxismus: Zur Aktualität einer Rekonstruktion des historischen Materialismus.* Würzburg: Königshausen & Neumann.
Tong Shijun. 2000. *The Dialectics of Modernization: Habermas and the Chinese Discourse of Modernization.* Sydney: Wild Peony.
Toynbee, Arnold J. 1954. *A Study of History.* Vol. 7. London: Oxford University Press.
———. 1962. "Die höheren Religionen." In *Propyläen Weltgeschichte,* ed. Golo Mann, Alfred Heuß, and August Nitschke. Vol. 2, 621–637. Berlin: Propyläen Verlag.
Trigger, Bruce G. 2003. *Understanding Early Civilizations: A Comparative Study.* Cambridge: Cambridge University Press.
Truxillo, Charles A. 2008. *Periods of World History: A Latin American Perspective.* Fremont: Jain Publishing.
Tu Wei-ming. 1985. "The Way, Learning and Politics in Classical Confucian Humanism." *Occasional Papers* 2, Institute of East Asian Philosophies, Singapore. Reprinted in Tu Wei-ming, *Way, Learning, and Politics: Essays on the Confucian Intellectual,* 1–12. Albany: State University of New York Press, 1993.
———. 1986. "The Structure and Function of the Confucian Intellectual in Ancient China." In Shmuel N. Eisenstadt, ed., *The Origins and Diversity of Axial Age Civilizations,* 360–373. Albany: State University of New York Press. Reprinted in Tu Wei-ming, *Way, Learning, and Politics: Essays on the Confucian Intellectual,* 13–28. Albany: State University of New York Press, 1993.
———. 1988. "A Confucian Perspective on the Rise of Industrial East Asia." *Bulletin of the American Academy of Arts and Sciences* 42: 32–50.
———. 1989. "The Sung Confucian Idea of Education: A Background Understanding." In Wm. Theodore de Bary and John W. Chaffee, eds., *Neo-Confucian Education: The Formative Stage,* 139–150. Berkeley: University of California Press.
———. 1997. "Crisis and Creativity: A Confucian Response to the Second Axial Age." In Steven Chase, ed., *Doors of Understanding: Conversations in Global Spirituality in Honor of Ewert Cousins,* 399–417. Quincy: Franciscan Press.

———. 2000. "Implications of the Rise of 'Confucian' East Asia." *Daedalus* 129, no. 1: 195–218. Reprinted in Shmuel N. Eisenstadt, ed., *Multiple Modernities*, 195–218. New Brunswick: Transaction Publishers, 2002.

———. 2001. "The Ecological Turn in New Confucian Humanism: Implications for China and the World." *Daedalus* 130, no. 4: 243–264.

———. 2005. "Intellectuals in a World Made of Knowledge." *Canadian Journal of Sociology* 30: 219–226.

Tucker, Carlton H. 1994. "From the Axial Age to the New Age: Religion as a Dynamic of World History." *The History Teacher* 27: 449–464.

Turchin, Peter. 2009. "A Theory for Formation of Large Empires." *Journal of Global History* 4: 191–217.

Turner, Bryan S. 2001. "On the Concept of Axial Space: Orientalism and the Originary." *Journal of Social Archaeology* 1, no. 1: 62–74.

———. 2006. "Body." *Theory, Culture & Society* 23: 223–229.

Tyrell, Hartmann. 2011. "Religion und Politik: Max Weber und Émile Durkheim." In Agathe Bienfait, ed., *Religionen verstehen: Zur Aktualität von Max Webers Religionssoziologie*, 41–91. Wiesbaden: Verlag für Sozialwissenschaften.

Uffenheimer, Benjamin. 1986. "Myth and Reality in Ancient Israel." In Shmuel N. Eisenstadt, ed., *The Origins and Diversity of Axial Age Civilizations*, 135–168. Albany: State University of New York Press.

Ungern-Sternberg, Jürgen von. 1998. "Innovation in Early Greece: The Political Sphere." In Peter Bernholz et al., eds., *Political Competition, Innovation and Growth: A Historical Analysis*, 85–107. Berlin: Springer.

Vacano, Otto Wilhelm von. 1952. *Im Zeichen der Sphinx: Griechenland im VII. Jahrhundert. Ende und Beginn eines Zeitalters*. Stuttgart: Kohlhammer.

Vernant, Jean-Pierre. 1979. "Religion grecque, religions antiques." In *Religions, histoires, raisons*, 5–34. Paris: Maspero. English: "Inaugural Address at the Collège de france, 5th December 1975." *Social Science Information* 16 (1977): 5–24. Reprinted in Jean-Pierre Vernant, *Mortals and Immortals: Collected Essays*, 269–289. Princeton: Princeton University Press, 1991.

Vester, Heinz-Günter. 1995. *Geschichte und Gesellschaft: Ansätze historisch-komparativer Soziologie*. Berlin: Quintessenz-Verlag.

Vigil, José M. 2008. *Theology of Religious Pluralism*. Münster: LIT.

Vogelsang, Kai. 2007. *Geschichte als Problem: Entstehung, Formen und Funktionen von Geschichtsschreibung im Alten China*. Wiesbaden: Harrassowitz.

Vogt, Joseph. 1966. "Einleitung." In *Saeculum Weltgeschichte*. Vol. 2: *Neue Hochkulturen in Asien: Die ersten Hochreligionen; Die griechisch-römische Welt*, ed. Herbert Franke et al., 1–20. Freiburg: Herder.

Wagner, Peter. 2005. "Palomar's Question: The Axial Age Hypothesis, European Modernity and Historical Contingency." In Johann P. Arnason, Shmuel N. Eisenstadt, and Björn Wittrock, eds., *Axial Civilizations and World History*, 87–106. Leiden: Brill.

———. 2005. "The Political Form of Europe, Europe as a Political Form." *Thesis Eleven* 80: 47–73.
———. 2008. *Modernity as Experience and Interpretation: A New Sociology of Modernity.* Cambridge: Polity.
———. 2010. "Europe—What Unity? Reflections between Political Philosophy and Historical Sociology." In Johann P. Arnason and Natalie J. Doyle, eds., *Domains and Divisions of European History,* 21–39. Liverpool: Liverpool University Press.
Wakeman, Frederic, Jr. 2005. "The Ming-Qing Transition: Seventeenth-Century Crisis or Axial Breakthrough?" In Johann P. Arnason, Shmuel N. Eisenstadt, and Björn Wittrock, eds., *Axial Civilizations and World History,* 509–528. Leiden: Brill.
Wald, Salomon, 2008. "Chinese Jews in European Thought." In Peter Kupfer, ed., *Youtai—Presence and Perception of Jews and Judaism in China,* 217–272. Frankfurt am Main: Lang.
Walters, Gregory J. 1988. "Karl Jaspers on the Role of 'Conversion' in the Nuclear Age." *Journal of the American Academy of Religion* 56: 229–256.
Walther, Manfred. 2005. "Stategien der politischen Neutralisierung des Gewaltpotenzials monotheistischer Offenbarungsreligionen." In Mathias Hildebrandt and Manfred Brocker, eds., *Unfriedliche Religionen? Das politische Gewalt- und Konfliktpotenzial von Religionen,* 95–117. Wiesbaden: Verlag für Sozialwissenschaften.
Wang, Aihe. 2000. *Cosmology and Political Culture in Early China.* Cambridge: Cambridge University Press.
Warth, Hermann. 1974. *Epoche und Repräsentation: Zum Verfall mythologischer und philosophischer Erfahrungen im Oikumenismus Alexanders des Großen.* Frankfurt am Main: Akademische Verlagsgesellschaft.
Weiers, Michael. 2009. *Geschichte Chinas: Grundzüge einer politischen Landesgeschichte.* Stuttgart: Kohlhammer.
Weil, Eric. 1975. "What Is a Breakthrough in History?" *Daedalus* 104, no. 2 (Wisdom, Revelation and Doubt: Perspectives on the First Millennium B.C.): 21–36.
Weinfeld, Moshe. 1986. "The Protest against Imperialism in Ancient Israelite Prophecy." In Shmuel N. Eisenstadt, ed., *The Origins and Diversity of Axial Age Civilizations,* 169–182. Albany: State University of New York Press.
Weller, Paul. 2005. *Time for a Change: Reconfiguring Religion, State and Society.* London: T & T Clark International.
Wenskus, Reinhard. 1991. "Mittel- und Nordeuropa um die Zeit des Buddha: Der religiöse Umbruch im barbarischen Europa in der frühen Eisenzeit." In Heinz Bechert, ed., *The Dating of the Historical Buddha / Die Datierung des historischen Buddha.* Vol. 1, 506–522. Göttingen: Vandenhoeck & Ruprecht.
Whimster, Sam. 2007. *Understanding Weber.* London: Routledge.

Wiebe, Donald. 1991. *The Irony of Theology and the Nature of Religious Thought.* Montreal: McGill-Queen's University Press.

Wiedenhofer, Siegfried. 2007. "Thinking God between Fundamentalism and Liberalism." In Norbert Hintersteiner, ed., *Naming and Thinking God in Europe Today: Theology in Global Dialogue,* 203–210. Amsterdam: Rodopi.

Wiersing, Erhard. 2007. *Geschichte des historischen Denkens: Zugleich eine Einführung in die Theorie der Geschichte.* Paderborn: Schöningh.

Willey, Gordon R. 1976. "Mesoamerican Civilization and the Idea of Transcendence." *Antiquity* 50: 205–215.

Wimbush, Vincent L. 1993. "The Ascetic Impulse in Early Christianity: Methodological Challenges and Opportunities." In Elizabeth A. Livingstone, ed., *Papers Presented at the Eleventh International Conference on Patristic Studies Held in Oxford 1991,* 462–478. Leuven: Peeters.

Wiser, James L. 1974. "Michael Polanyi: Personal Knowledge and the Promise of Autonomy." *Political Theory* 2: 77–87.

Wisser, Richard. 1995. "Projekt und Vision einer 'Weltgeschichte der Philosophie' und 'Weltphilosophie' als Folgen der 'Grundverfassung' von Karl Jaspers." In Richard Wisser, *Karl Jaspers: Philosophie in der Bewährung; Vorträge und Aufsätze,* 123–135. Würzburg: Königshausen & Neumann. Reprinted in Leonard H. Ehrlich and Richard Wisser, eds., *Philosophy on the Way to "World Philosophy" / Philosophie auf dem Weg zur "Weltphilosophie,"* 61–70. Amsterdam: Rodopi / Würzburg: Königshausen & Neumann, 1998.

Wittrock, Björn. 1998. "Early Modernities: Varieties and Transitions." *Daedalus* 127, no. 3: 19–40. Reprinted in Shmuel N. Eisenstadt, Wolfgang Schluchter, and Björn Wittrock, eds., *Public Spheres and Collective Identities,* 10–40. New Brunswick: Transaction Publishers.

———. 2000. "Modernity—One, None or Many? European Origins and Modernity as a Global Condition." *Daedalus* 129, no. 1: 31–60. Reprinted in Shmuel N. Eisenstadt, ed., *Multiple Modernities,* 31–60. New Brunswick: Transaction Publishers, 2002.

———. 2001. "Rethinking Modernity." In Eliezer Ben-Rafael and Yitzhak Sternberg, eds., *Identity, Culture and Globalization,* 49–73. Leiden: Brill.

———. 2001. "Social Theory and Global History: The Three Cultural Crystallizations." *Thesis Eleven* 65: 27–50.

———. 2003. "The Cultural Constitution of Modernity." In Grażyna Skąpska and Annamaria Orla-Bukowska, eds., *The Moral Fabric in Contemporary Societies,* 219–240. Leiden: Brill.

———. 2003. "Cultural Crystallization and Conceptual Change: Modernity, Axiality and Meaning in History." In Jussi Kurunmäki and Kari Palonen, eds., *Zeit, Geschichte und Politik / Time, History and Politics: Zum achtzigsten Geburtstag von Reinhart Koselleck,* 105–134. Jyväskylä: Jyväskylä University Printing House.

———. 2004. "Cultural Crystallizations and World History: The Age of Ecumenical Renaissances." In Johann P. Arnason and Björn Wittrock, eds., *Eurasian Transformations, Tenth to Thirteenth Centuries: Crystallizations, Divergences, Renaissances,* 41–73. Leiden: Brill.

———. 2005. "Cultural Crystallization and Civilization Change: Axiality and Modernity." In Eliezer Ben-Rafael and Yitzhak Sternberg, eds., *Comparing Modernities: Pluralism versus Homogenity; Essays in Homage to Shmuel N. Eisenstadt,* 83–123. Leiden: Brill.

———. 2005. "The Meaning of the Axial Age." In Johann P. Arnason, Shmuel N. Eisenstadt, and Björn Wittrock, eds., *Axial Civilizations and World History,* 51–85. Leiden: Brill.

———. 2008. "History and Sociology: Transmutations of Historical Reasoning in the Social Sciences." In Peter Hedström and Björn Wittrock, eds., *Frontiers of Sociology,* 77–112. Leiden: Brill.

Witzel, Michael. 2003. "Vedas and Upaniṣads." In Gavin Flood, ed., *The Blackwell Companion to Hinduism,* 68–98. Oxford: Blackwell.

Wolf, Eric R. 1967. "Unterstanding Civilizations: A Review Article." *Comparative Studies in Society and History* 9: 446–465.

Wright, J. Edward. 2000. *The Early History of Heaven.* New York: Oxford University Press.

Wulff, Karl. 2006. *Naturwissenschaften im Kulturvergleich: Europa—Islam—China.* Frankfurt am Main: Deutsch.

Yoffee, Norman. 1998. "The Economics of Ritual at Late Old Babylonian Kish." *Journal of the Economic and Social History of the Orient* 41: 312–343.

———. 2005. *Myths of the Archaic State: Evolution of the Earliest Cities, States and Civilizations.* Cambridge: Cambridge University Press.

Yonker, Nicholas J. 1978. *God, Man, and the Planetary Age: Preface for a Theistic Humanism.* Corvallis: Oregon State University Press.

Yoshizawa Denzaburo. 1988. "The Reception of Jaspers in Japan." In Leonard H. Ehrlich and Richard Wisser, eds., *Karl Jaspers Today: Philosophy at the Threshold of the Future,* 395–400. Washington, DC: University Press of America.

Young-Bruehl, Elisabeth. 1981. *Freedom and Karl Jaspers's Philosophy.* New Haven: Yale University Press.

———. 1989. "Cosmopolitan History." In Elisabeth Young-Bruehl, *Mind and the Body Politic,* 65–81. New York: Routledge.

Yu Haiqing. 2009. *Media and Cultural Transformation in China.* London: Routledge.

Zagzebski, Linda Trinkaus. 2007. *Philosophy of Religion: An Historical Introduction.* Malden: Blackwell.

Zaleski, Carol, and Philip Zaleski. 2005. *Prayer: A History.* Boston: Houghton Mifflin.

Zamulinski, Brian. 2003. "Religion and the Pursuit of Truth." *Religious Studies* 39: 43–60.

Zhi Chen. 2004. "From Exclusive Xia to Inclusive Zhu-Xia: The Conceptualisation of Chinese Identity in Early China." *Journal of the Royal Asiatic Society* 14: 185–205.

Zürcher, Erik. 1992. "Buddhismus in China: Die Grenzen der Innovation." In Shmuel N. Eisenstadt, ed., *Kulturen der Achsenzeit II: Ihre institutionelle und kulturelle Dynamik*. Part 1: *China, Japan*, 199–232. Frankfurt am Main: Suhrkamp.

Notes

1. "Anything like complete proof of a Revolution of such a mental character as we should deduce from our Ultimate Law, having actually occurred in the Sixth Century B.C. cannot of course here be given. For our main purpose here is but to state some of the larger deductions from this Law, and we can refer, in but the most summary manner, to the facts by which we believe that these deductions will be found verified. This being understood, I would now proceed summarily to state ... some of those more important synchronous events of the Sixth Century B.C., which appear to me to imply a new mental development, constituting, in fact, such a Revolution, as we have above deduced from our Ultimate Law.... Note, then, first, as illustrative of the *Intellectual Revolution* of this Century, three great general facts. Throughout the civilised world, in Japan, China, India, Persia, Judaea, Greece, and Egypt, we find a new intellectual activity in collecting, editing, and for the first time writing down in alphabetic characters the Literature of the preceding centuries. It is only in this century that a Profane, as distinguished from a Sacred Literature arises; only from this time forth that, speaking generally, we have independent and nameable individual authors; and only now that, in the speculations of Thales, philosophical, as distinguished from religious Speculation, begins.... But far more extraordinary still will this Century be found as an Era of Religious Revolution. Independent investigators of the history of Japan, of China, of India, of Persia, of Assyria, of Judaea, of Greece, and of Egypt have found that the Religion of each of them underwent a great moral change or transformation in the same Sixth Century B.C. In Japan, there then arose the religion of Sinto; in China, that of Confucius; in India, that of Buddha. If the Polytheisms of Assyria, of Greece, and of Egypt did not, like that of India, give birth in this century to a distinctly new religion, to this century we trace a profound disorganisation of them, and change in their spirit. And the Aryan and Semitic Monotheisms of Persia and of Judaea ... came now, at Babylon, into contact, and, in the new enthusiasm of the Messiahism of the one, and the World-conquest of the other,

exercised the most profoundly revolutionary effects on the creeds and institutions of Mankind...."

2. "Then suddenly, and almost simultaneously, and almost certainly independently, there is evidence, about the sixth century B.C. in each of these widely separated centres of civilisation, of a leap forward in speculative thought, of an new birth in ethics, of a religion of conscience threatening to take the place of the old religion of custom and magic."

3. "The age of the exile and the reconstruction of Israel was one of unrest; there was a widespread religious awakening. To China with Lao-tse and Confucius, to India with the Buddha, Gautama, and with Mahavira, the founder of Jainism, to Persia with Zoroaster (probably), and to the Greek world with its mystic cults, we must add the movement lying behind Isaiah xl–lv" (p. 489, 3rd reprint 1954).

4. [As part of the "Chronological Summary"] "*c.* 581 Age of Jeremiah, Ezekiel ... and later, the age of the Deutero-Isaiah.... Note the dates—Zoroaster, *c.* 600 ...; Confucius, 551–478, and his older contemporary Laò-tse; Buddha, *c.* 560–480, and his older contemporary Mahavira, the founder of Jainism. Solon (*c.* 638–538). The Ionian school of philosophers, followed by the Italian school (Pythagoras)" (p. 230).

5. "It may possibly be thought at this point that the study of history cannot well be organized with reference solely to the incidence of barbarian attacks on a vanished empire.... It must be stated, therefore, that classes of events are in number practically unlimited, and are by no means restricted to the outbreak of wars.

"As an example of a wholly different type, I may point to the great religious movements associated with the names of Zoroaster in Persia, Lao-tzŭ" and Confucius in China, Mahavira (founder of Jainism) and Gautama Buddha in India, the prophets Ezekiel and Second Isaiah, Thales in Ionia, and Pythagoras in southern Italy. All these great personages belong to the sixth century B.C., and their appearance certainly constitutes a class of events. Yet, though the correspondence of these events has frequently been observed, no serious effort has ever been made, so far as I have been able to discover, to treat the appearance of these great teachers—within a brief compass of time—as a problem which called for systematic investigation" (p. xi).

6. "The close coincidence in date between the appearance of many of the great ethical and religious leaders has often been remarked upon: Confucius, *c.*—550; Gautama (Buddhism), *c.*—560; Zoroaster (if a historical personage), *c.*—600; Mahāvīra (Jainism), *c.*—560, and so on" (vol. 1, p. 99).

7. References (page numbers refer to *Collected Works of Voegelin*): no direct references in vol. 1 (indirect reference on p. 44, according to other sources also the chapter on *The Prophets*, pp. 481ff.); vol. 2: 86–87, 90; vol. 4: 47–51, 276, 380–385.

Contributors

JOHANN P. ARNASON is Emeritus Professor of Sociology at La Trobe University, Melbourne, and Visiting Professor at the Faculty of Human Studies, Charles University, Prague. He has published *Civilizations in Dispute* (Brill, 2003) and *Axial Civilizations and World History* (edited, with Shmuel N. Eisenstadt and Björn Wittrock; Brill, 2005). His main research interests are in historical sociology, with particular emphasis on the comparative analysis of civilizations.

JAN ASSMANN is Professor Emeritus of Egyptology at Heidelberg University and Honorary Professor of Cultural and Religious Studies at the University of Constance. He has published on ancient Egyptian religion, literature, and history, the afterlife of Egypt in Western thought (*Moses the Egyptian:* Harvard University Press, 1997), and the origins of monotheism (*Of God and Gods:* Madison University Press, 2008).

ROBERT N. BELLAH is Elliot Professor of Sociology Emeritus at the University of California, Berkeley. He is the author of *Religion in Human Evolution* (The Belknap Press of Harvard University Press, 2011), coauthor of *Habits of the Heart* (University of California Press, 1985), and a winner of the National Humanities Medal.

JOSÉ CASANOVA is Professor of Sociology at Georgetown University and heads the Berkley Center's Program on Globalization, Religions and the Secular. He is the author of *Public Religions in the Modern World* (University of Chicago Press, 1994).

INGOLF U. DALFERTH is Danforth Professor of Philosophy of Religion at Claremont Graduate University, California, and also Director of the Institute of Hermeneutics and Philosophy of Religion at the University of Zurich, Switzerland. He is the author of, among other works, *Umsonst: Eine Erinnerung an die kreative Passivität des Menschen* (Mohr Siebeck, 2011), *Radikale Theologie* (EVA Leipzig, 2010), *Malum: Theologische Hermeneutik des Bösen* (Mohr Siebeck, 2008), *Becoming Present: An Inquiry into the Christian Sense of the Presence of God* (Leuven, 2006), and *Die Wirklichkeit des Möglichen: Hermeneutische Religionsphilosophie* (Mohr Siebeck, 2003).

MERLIN DONALD is Emeritus Professor of Psychology and Education at Queen's University, Ontario, Canada, and Honorary Professor at Aarhus University, Denmark. He is the author of *Origins of the Modern Mind: Three Stages in the Evolution of Culture and Cognition* (Harvard University Press, 1991) and *A Mind So Rare: The Evolution of Human Consciousness* (W. W. Norton, 2001).

SHMUEL N. EISENSTADT (1923–2010) was born in Warsaw and received his Ph.D. in Jerusalem in 1947. He was Professor Emeritus at the Hebrew University of Jerusalem and Senior Research Fellow at the Jerusalem Van Leer Institute. He was a member of many academies and recipient of several honorary doctoral degrees. His main publications include *The Political Systems of Empires* (1963), *The Origins and Diversity of Axial Age Civilizations* (edited, 1986), *Axial Civilizations and World History* (edited, with Johann Arnason and Björn Wittrock, 2005), and *Comparative Civilizations and Multiple Modernities* (2 vols. of collected essays, 2003).

HANS JOAS is Professor of Sociology and Social Thought at the University of Chicago. He is also Permanent Fellow of the School of History at the Freiburg Institute for Advanced Studies based at the Albert Ludwig University of Freiburg, Germany. Among his book publications in English are *The Creativity of Action* (University of Chicago Press, 1996), *The Genesis of Values* (University of Chicago Press, 2000), *War and Modernity* (Polity Press, 2003), *Do We Need Religion?* (Paradigm Publishers, 2008), *Social Theory* (Cambridge University Press, 2009; with Wolfgang Knöbl), and *War in Social Thought* (Princeton University Press, 2012; with Wolfgang Knöbl).

MATTHIAS JUNG is Professor of Philosophy at the University of Koblenz, Germany. He is the author of *Der bewusste Ausdruck* (Berlin: de Gruyter, 2009), *Erfahrung und Religion* (Freiburg: Alber, 1999), and other books. His main interests are moral philosophy, philosophy of religion, and philosophical anthropology.

RICHARD MADSEN is Distinguished Professor of Sociology at the University of California, San Diego. He is a coauthor with Robert Bellah, Steven Tipton, Ann Swidler, and William Sullivan of *Habits of the Heart* and *The Good Society*. He has also authored or coauthored five books on Chinese societies, the latest of which is *Democracy's Dharma: Religious Renaissance and Political Development in Taiwan.*

Contributors

DAVID MARTIN is Emeritus Professor of Sociology at the London School of Economics. His main interests are in global Pentecostalism, religion and secularization, religion and violence, theology and sociology, and religion and music, especially the Baroque.

GANANATH OBEYESEKERE is Emeritus Professor of Anthropology at Princeton University. He has published several books on religion, psychoanalysis and anthropology, voyages of discovery, and the ethnography of Sri Lanka.

HEINER ROETZ is Professor of Chinese Philosophy and History at Ruhr University, Bochum. His main interests are classical Chinese philosophy and its relation to modernity. He is the author of *Mensch und Natur im alten China* (Frankfurt am Main, 1984), *Confucian Ethics of the Axial Age* (Albany, 1993), and *Confucius* (Munich, 2006).

W. G. RUNCIMAN is a Fellow of Trinity College, Cambridge University. He is the author of *A Treatise on Social Theory* (Vol. 1, 1983; Vol. 2, 1989, Vol. 3, 1997) and *The Theory of Cultural and Social Selection* (2009).

WILLIAM M. SULLIVAN is a senior scholar at the Center of Inquiry in the Liberal Arts at Wabash College. Formerly senior scholar at the Carnegie Foundation for the Advancement of Teaching, he is the author of *Work and Integrity: The Crisis and Promise of Professionalism* (2005) and coauthor of *Habits of the Heart* (1985).

ANN SWIDLER is Professor of Sociology at the University of California, Berkeley. She is the author of *Talk of Love* (University of Chicago Press, 2001) and coauthor of *Habits of the Heart* (University of California Press, 1985) and *Inequality by Design* (Princeton University Press, 1996). Her current research is on cultural and institutional responses to the AIDS epidemic in sub-Saharan Africa.

CHARLES TAYLOR is Professor Emeritus of Philosophy at McGill University. He is the author of *A Secular Age* (Harvard University Press, 2007) and other books.

BJÖRN WITTROCK is University Professor at Uppsala University and Principal of the Swedish Collegium for Advanced Study, Uppsala. He is the editor of *Frontiers of Sociology* (2009, with Peter Hedström), *Axial Civilizations and World History* (2004, with Johann Arnason and Shmuel N. Eisenstadt), and *The Rise of the Social Sciences and the Formation of Modernity: Conceptual Change in Context, 1750–1850* (1998, with Johan Heilbron and Lars Magnusson).

Index

Abel-Rémusat, Jean Pierre, 374
Acton, John Emmerich Dalberg, Lord, 13–14
Akhenaten (Amenhotep IV), 322, 341–342, 377, 398–399, 401
Alexander of Macedon, 331, 378, 464
Amenemhet I, 385, 387
Amos, 1, 452
Anaximenes of Lampsacus, 330
Anquetil-Duperron, Abraham-Hyacinthe, 11, 25nn8,9, 248, 342, 369, 374
Anselm of Canterbury, 310
Anthony the Great, 397
Apelles of Kos, 165
Aristophanes, 331
Aristotle, 1, 106, 149, 266, 327, 329, 380, 425, 453, 463–464, 467n29
Armstrong, Karen, 374
Arnason, Johann, 4, 12, 26n14, 202, 218n34, 278, 282, 402n8
Arndt, Johann, 99
Ashoka, 116, 344–345
Assmann, Aleida, 253–254, 359, 369, 373, 379, 383, 402n2
Assmann, Jan, 4, 30, 93, 114, 124n12, 192, 203, 206, 253, 338, 340–342, 348, 359, 364
Assurbanipal, 391
Augustine, 10, 27n29, 162, 183n15, 187n77, 192, 212, 216, 374
Aulus Gellius, 392
Auslander, Mark, 232

Baader, Franz von, 13
Barth, Karl, 166, 173, 175, 183n15, 188n89

Beard, Mary, 327
Bellah, Robert N., 2–3, 6, 24, 26nn13,15, 31, 44, 45n8, 48, 68, 70, 73, 79, 80–83, 85–87, 89, 91, 93, 96, 107–108, 110, 124nn11,14, 139, 141, 191–206, 208–211, 215–216, 217nn17,28, 218nn29,32,34, 220n57, 222, 235, 237, 242n11, 277, 285, 294, 303, 309, 331, 342, 371–373, 375, 398, 402n10, 403n15, 412–414, 418, 421, 423–424, 427, 430–431, 434–435
Berlin, Isaiah, 39
Bernstein, Basil, 419
Blake, William, 135–136, 138
Blavatsky, Helena, 135, 138
Bloom, Harold, 382
Bonjour, Casimir, 130
Bourdieu, Pierre, 368
Bousset, Wilhelm, 10, 17, 27n23
Boyce, Mary, 343
Boyer, Pascal, 296
Brague, Rémi, 207, 219n52, 355–356
Brandom, Robert, 81–82, 84, 86, 88, 96
Breuer, Stefan, 255–256, 258–259, 265
Brook, David, 422
Brown, Peter, 107, 462, 466n28
Brown, Spencer, 154
Buddha. See Siddhārtha Gautama Buddha
Burckhardt, Jacob, 13, 331
Bush, George W., 295

Caesar, Gaius Julius, 304
Casanova, José, 5, 107
Cassirer, Ernst, 4, 81, 83
Castoriadis, Cornelius, 360–361
Catherine of Siena, 138
Chabal, Patrick, 235

Charles I of England, 329
Cicero, Marcus Tullius, 326
Collingwood, Robin G., 156
Collins, Randall, 200
Collins, Steven, 460, 462
Confucius, 1, 15, 34–35, 108, 115, 210, 257, 263–264, 269n20, 324–326, 331–333, 345, 348–353, 369, 373, 399, 432, 536n1, 537nn3,4,5,7
Cornell, Stephen, 241n5
Croce, Benedetto, 217n28
Cypselus, 329

Dalai Lama (Tenzin Gyatso), 439
Dalferth, Ingolf, 5
Darnton, Robert, 107
Darwin, Charles, 67, 296, 317–318
Davids, Thomas W. Rhys, 11
De Nys, Martin J., 175
De Waal, Frans, 319
Deacon, Terrence W., 57, 81–83, 87, 90, 97–98
Dennett, Daniel, 80–81
Derrida, Jacques, 166–167, 186n61
Descartes, René, 144n12, 150–151, 162, 187n77, 456
Dewey, John, 83, 311, 423, 425–427, 429n32, 437
Dilthey, Wilhelm, 90
Dionysius II of Syracuse, 329
Djoser, 395
Döllinger, Ignaz von, 16
Donald, Merlin, 3–4, 78, 80–86, 89–90, 97, 110, 198–199, 204, 209–210, 372–373, 379–380, 412–415, 423–424, 453
Douglas, Mary, 419, 421, 434
Dumézil, Georges, 361
Dumont, Louis, 38, 41, 46n16, 107, 324, 348, 360–364, 449
Durkheim, Émile, 140, 195, 200, 207, 218n29, 225, 237, 307, 315, 360, 442, 464

Eckhart, Meister, 132, 143, 147
Edward VI of England, 308
Eisenstadt, Shmuel N., 5, 11–12, 24, 45n10, 46n12, 107–108, 112, 120–121, 139, 202, 205, 209, 222, 228, 235, 252, 255, 298, 326, 338–340, 344, 346, 349, 354, 371, 388, 390, 400, 412, 421

Eliade, Mircea, 195
Eliot, T. S., 143
Elizabeth I of England, 329
Elkana, Yehuda, 106, 203, 209–210, 403n13
Engels, Friedrich, 324
Englund, Harri, 236
Ezekiel, 537nn4,5

Finley, Moses, 330
Fishbane, Michael, 392
Florida, Richard, 422
Forsdyke, Sara, 328–329
Forst, Rainer, 94–95
Fowden, Garth, 404n33
Frank, David J., 227, 418, 420
Frankfort, Henri, 372
Frege, Gottlob, 138
Freud, Sigmund, 130, 312, 373
Friedrich, Caspar David, 311
Frye, Northrop, 47
Fukuyama, Francis, 300

Gabler, Jay, 420
Gadamer, Hans-Georg, 416
Galileo Galilei, 266
Gallagher, Shaun, 82, 91
Gauchet, Marcel, 214
Gaultier, Jules de, 151
Geertz, Clifford, 237, 384
Genghis Khan, 283
Gershevitch, Ilya, 343
Geschiere, Peter, 232
Gfrörer, August Friedrich, 25n8
Ghazālī, al, 332
Gill, Christopher, 457
Ginzburg, Carlo, 217n28
Gluck, Christoph Willibald, 16
Gnoli, Gherardo, 343–344
Goethe, Johann Wolfgang von, 16
Goffman, Erving, 200
Goldhill, Simon, 466n7
Gombrich, Richard, 459
Goody, Jack, 379
Gopnik, Alison, 463–464
Görres, Joseph, 13, 16, 26n16
Graham, Angus C., 353
Gramsci, Antonio, 217n28
Gray, John, 299
Grotius, Hugo, 43

Habermas, Jürgen, 23, 26n15, 88, 107, 120, 201, 216, 218n31, 407n66, 412, 421, 423, 448–452
Hadot, Pierre, 259, 352, 463
Hamann, Johann Georg, 16
Hamilton, William D., 319
Hammurabi, 322
Han Fei, 261–262, 463
Handel, George Frideric, 381
Hausmann, Sebastian, 135
Havel, Vaclav, 466n7
Havelock, Eric, 379, 383, 405n45
Hebb, Donald O., 47
Hecataeus of Miletus, 389
Heesterman, Jan C., 348–349
Hegel, Georg Wilhelm Friedrich, 10, 102–103, 120, 124n11, 248, 250, 253, 257, 266, 332
Heidegger, Martin, 24n1, 167
Helling, Victor, 135
Henri IV of France, 329
Herder, Johann Gottfried, 90
Herodotus, 359, 389
Hildebrand of Fossombrone, 41
Hitler, Adolf, 378
Hobbes, Thomas, 435
Hobson, John A., 299
Homer, 384–385, 399–400
Horace (Quintus Horatius Flaccus), 388
Hordjedef, 386–387
Horton, Robin, 233–235, 237, 239, 242n10
Hu Shih, 437
Humboldt, Wilhelm von, 81, 90
Huysmans, Joris-Karl, 311

Iamblichus, 257
Ikhnaton. *See* Akhenaten
Imhotep, 386–387, 395, 399
Innis, Harold, 383
Ipuwer, 385, 387
Isaiah, 1, 305, 391, 399–400, 537nn3,4,5
Isocrates, 330

Jaeger, Werner, 413
Jaspers, Karl, 1, 5–6, 9–11, 13, 16–17, 21–24, 26n15, 34, 45n10, 77, 79, 102–108, 110, 113, 120–121, 124n11, 139, 146–147, 153, 158, 168, 180–181, 182n3, 203, 248–256, 259, 266–267, 278, 294, 317, 331–332, 339–340, 342, 344–346, 349, 354, 366–367, 369–370, 372–376, 378, 381, 390, 404n32, 407n66, 413, 430–434, 441, 444–445
Jellinek, Georg, 24
Jeremiah, 1, 537n4
Jesus of Nazareth, 10, 16, 102, 172, 211, 250, 303, 307, 310, 375, 398, 443
Joas, Hans, 1, 6, 93, 107, 125n23, 371, 429n32
John of the Cross, 132
Josephus, Flavius, 393–394
Judt, Tony, 315n7
Julian of Norwich, 131
Jung, Matthias, 4, 379

Kairsu, 386–387
Kalt, Joseph P., 241n5
Kamehameha III of Hawaii, 222
Kant, Immanuel, 16, 144n12, 151, 158–159, 162, 197, 252, 329, 395
Kapferer, Bruce, 40
Karlström, Mikael, 240n3
Kautilya (Chanakya), 462–463
Kepler, Johannes, 266
Khakheperreseneb, 381–382, 385–387
Kheti, 386–387
King, Martin Luther, Jr., 187n89
Kittler, Friedrich, 383
Kohlberg, Lawrence, 256–259, 266, 267n5, 268n6
Kosambi, Dharmananda D., 139–140
Koselleck, Reinhart, 368–369

Lanzky, Paul, 135
Lao Tse, 11, 25n6, 326, 369, 373, 537nn3,4,5
Larson, Sheila, 217n28
Lasaulx, Catherine von, 26n16
Lasaulx, Ernst von, 11, 13–17, 23, 25n8, 26n16, 267n1, 374
Lasch, Christopher, 421–422
Lenin, Vladimir Ilyich, 299, 321
Levinas, Emmanuel, 152–153, 162, 167
Levine, Donald N., 10
Lévi-Strauss, Claude, 83, 354–355, 372
Lévy-Bruhl, Lucien, 195
Lipsius, Justus, 43
Lowe, Walter, 187n77
Lucian of Samosata, 331
Luckmann, Thomas, 161
Luhmann, Niklas, 153, 157

Luther, Martin, 99, 157, 184n46, 310
Luxemburg, Rosa, 327

Madsen, Richard, 6, 419
Mahavira, 139, 537nn3,4,5,7
Mahler, Gustav, 311
Mamdani, Mahmood, 228
Mann, Thomas, 366–367
Marcus Aurelius, 318
Martin, David, 5
Marvell, Andrew, 137
Marx, Karl, 324
Mayr, Ernst, 289
McDougall, William, 295
McKinley, William, 309
McLuhan, Marshall, 383
McNeill, William, 426–427
Mead, George Herbert, 423, 426, 429n32
Meier, Christian, 347, 357
Meinecke, Friedrich, 102
Mencius (Meng Tzu), 108, 115, 264, 269n20, 373, 452
Mendelssohn, Moses, 379, 405n40
Menocchio (Domenico Scandella), 217n28
Merikare, 385
Metzler, Dieter, 344
Meyer, Eduard, 17
Meyer, John W., 227, 242n12, 411, 418–421, 423
Micah, 305
Michelangelo di Lodovico Buonarroti Simoni, 25n2
Mill, John Stuart, 34
Momigliano, Arnaldo, 11, 209, 321, 326, 333, 372
Montesquieu, Charles-Louis de Secondat, 11
Monteverdi, Claudio, 381
Montez, Lola (Elizabeth Rosanna Gilbert), 14
Moses, 16, 91, 92–93, 96, 350, 372, 393, 398–399
Mozart, Wolfgang Amadeus, 16, 381
Mozi, 115, 260–262, 265, 269n20
Muhammad, 211, 331–332, 398
Muluzi, Bakili, 232–233
Müntzer, Thomas, 321
Mussolini, Benito, 217n28
Mutharika, Bingu wa, 232–233

Nabopolassar, 378
Nagarjuna, 135

Napoleon Bonaparte, 378
Neferti, 385–387
Nelson, Katherine, 62–63
Nguyen, Vinh-Kim, 242n12
Nicholas of Cusa, 147
Nietzsche, Friedrich, 132, 135–138, 144n12, 147–148, 154, 157, 181, 184n46, 311, 371
Nightingale, Andrea, 453–458, 466n7
North, John, 327
Novalis (Friedrich von Hardenberg), 311
Numa Pompilius, 15

Oakley, Francis, 34
Obeyesekere, Gananath, 4–5
Oesterdiekhoff, Georg W., 266
Olcott, Henry Steele, 132
Ong, Walter, 379
Oppenheim, Leo, 391
Otto, Eckart, 21
Otto of Greece, 13

Pachom, 397
Parmenides, 143, 372
Parsons, Talcott, 196–197, 288, 346, 371
Patočka, Jan, 354
Paul of Tarsus, 310, 374
Peel, J. D. Y., 233–235, 242n10
Peirce, Charles Sanders, 57, 83, 90
Pemalingpa, 131
Pericles, 330
Philolaus of Corinth, 327
Piaget, Jean, 256, 259, 266
Plato, 1, 35, 37, 39, 132, 143, 147–148, 187n77, 194, 208, 326–327, 331, 350, 354, 356, 372, 385, 389, 399, 406n56, 411–418, 424, 452–460, 462–464, 466n7
Plessner, Helmuth, 81
Polanyi, Michel, 368
Pollock, Sheldon, 117
Price, Simon, 327
Protagoras, 257
Pseudo-Dionysius the Areopagite, 183n15
Ptahemdjehuti, 386–387
Ptahhotep, 385–387
Pythagoras, 331, 537nn4,5

Raaflaub, Kurt, 347
Rahner, Karl, 166

Ranke, Leopold von, 248
Reich, Robert, 422
Ricoeur, Paul, 79
Riesman, David, 374, 403n23
Robespierre, Maximilien de, 321, 324
Roetz, Heiner, 4–5
Röth, Eduard, 25n8
Runciman, W. G., 5
Russell, Bertrand, 138

Sagan, Eli, 465n4
Sakuludayin, 134
Savage-Rumbaugh, Emily Sue, 56
Schaller, Susan, 63
Scheler, Max, 248–249
Schenute, 397
Schirnhofer, Resa von, 136
Schlette, Magnus, 101n37
Schluchter, Wolfgang, 107
Schopenhauer, Arthur, 144n12
Schottländer, Rudolf, 251–252, 255
Schumpeter, Joseph, 423
Schütz, Alfred, 161
Schwartz, Benjamin, 11, 26n13, 107, 251, 349–353, 356–357, 360, 371, 390, 402n8
Seaford, Richard, 347
Sellars, Wilfrid, 81
Sewell, William, 238
Seydlitz, Reinhardt von, 136
Shaked, Shaul, 343
Sheng Yen, 442
Siddhārtha Gautama Buddha, 1, 15–16, 30–31, 34, 41, 108, 126–137, 139–140, 142–143, 194, 326, 331, 333, 345, 350, 369, 373, 399, 432, 437, 455, 459–461, 536n1, 537nn3,4,5,7
Siebeck, Hermann, 11
Simmel, Georg, 9–10, 24n1, 25n2
Simon, Herbert A., 291
Smith, Daniel Jordan, 236
Smith, Joseph, 135
Smith, Wilfred Cantwell, 192
Socrates, 16, 30, 34, 132, 257, 269n22, 327, 331, 333, 350, 352, 413–415, 432, 452, 454–455, 458, 464, 466n7
Solon, 327, 389, 537n4
Spener, Philipp Jakob, 100
Spengler, Oswald, 15, 367
Stanner, W. E. H., 36, 196

Strauss, Victor von, 11, 25n6, 267n1, 374
Stroumsa, Guy, 193, 211–212
Sullivan, William, 5, 449
Sumartana, Thomas, 439–440
Sundermeier, Theo, 402n10
Swidler, Ann, 5
Swinburne, Algernon Charles, 311

Tambiah, Stanley J., 46n16
Taylor, Charles, 4, 28, 41, 61, 97–99, 107, 156–157, 303, 309–311, 374, 402n10, 412, 414, 417–418, 421, 424, 430, 443
Teresa of Avila, 138
Thales of Miletus, 536n1, 537n5
Theodore of Sykeon, 306
Thomas Aquinas, 183n15
Thrasymachus, 331
Thucydides, 330
Tiglat-Pileser III, 377
Tillich, Paul, 173, 175
Tomasello, Michael, 62
Toynbee, Arnold, 340
Trevarthen, Colwyn, 62
Troeltsch, Ernst, 10, 16, 21, 23–24, 28n34
Tsai, Lily, 241n5
Turner, Victor, 41

Varro, Marcus Terentius, 192
Vernant, Jean-Pierre, 357
Verres, Gaius, 326
Vico, Giovanni Battista, 150
Virgil (Publius Vergilius Maro), 310
Voegelin, Eric, 13, 107, 209–210, 255, 371–372, 375

Wagner, Peter, 251, 268n9
Wagner, Richard, 311, 381
Waley, Arthur, 325
Walzer, Michael, 93
Wang Chong, 261–262
Weber, Alfred, 10, 13, 102–103, 107, 249, 253, 376, 404n32
Weber, Max, 10, 13, 17–21, 23, 27n34, 28n41, 29n47, 37–38, 103, 107, 124n11, 141, 194–195, 197–199, 201, 210, 218n31, 220n58, 253, 282, 290, 294, 328, 332, 342, 358, 360, 373, 434, 450
Weil, Eric, 107, 404n37
Westphal, Merold, 183n15
White, Landeg, 241n4

Whitehead, Alfred North, 459
Wilde, Oscar, 311
Wittgenstein, Ludwig, 87, 135–138, 400, 424
Wittrock, Björn, 4, 12, 46n10, 203, 205–206, 219n50
Wordsworth, William, 311

Xenophanes, 78
Xenophon, 328

Xingyun (Hsing Yun), 437
Xunzi (Hsün Tzu), 256, 260–261

Zhang Hao, 268n6
Zhengyan (Cheng Yen), 438
Zigong, 269n20
Zoroaster, 11, 15–16, 25n9, 322–324, 326–327, 331, 333, 342–343, 369, 373, 398–399, 537nn3,4,5,7
Zumthor, Paul, 391